IFIP Advances in Information and Communication Technology 808

IFIP Advances in Information and Communication Technology

The IFIP AICT series publishes state-of-the-art results in the sciences and technologies of information and communication. The scope of the series includes: foundations of computer science; software theory and practice; education; computer applications in technology; communication systems; systems modeling and optimization; information systems; ICT and society; computer systems technology; security and protection in information processing systems; artificial intelligence; and human-computer interaction.

Edited volumes and proceedings of refereed international conferences in computer science and interdisciplinary fields are featured. These results often precede journal publication and represent the most current research.

The principal aim of the IFIP AICT series is to encourage education and the dissemination and exchange of information about all aspects of computing.

More information about this series at https://link.springer.com/bookseries/6102

Giuditta Pezzotta · Paolo Gaiardelli ·
Chiara Cimini · Roberto Sala · David Romero ·
Jannicke Baalsrud-Hauge
Editors

Advances in Production Management Systems

Shaping the Future of Industry Through Sustainable, Data-Driven, and Human-Centric Production Systems

45th IFIP WG 5.7 International Conference, APMS 2026
Bergamo, Italy, September 13–17, 2026
Proceedings, Part II

Springer

Editors
Giuditta Pezzotta
University of Bergamo
Bergamo, Italy

Chiara Cimini
University of Bergamo
Bergamo, Italy

David Romero
Tecnológico de Monterrey
Mexico City, Mexico

Paolo Gaiardelli
University of Bergamo
Bergamo, Italy

Roberto Sala
University of Bergamo
Bergamo, Italy

Jannicke Baalsrud-Hauge
KTH Royal Institute of Technology
Stockholm, Sweden

ISSN 1868-4238 ISSN 1868-422X (electronic)
IFIP Advances in Information and Communication Technology
ISBN 978-3-032-38593-2 ISBN 978-3-032-38594-9 (eBook)
https://doi.org/10.1007/978-3-032-38594-9

This Springer imprint is published by the registered company Springer Nature Switzerland AG
The registered company address is: Gewerbestrasse 11, 6330 Cham, Switzerland

Preface

The 45th IFIP WG 5.7 International Conference on "Advances in Production Management Systems" (APMS 2026), the flagship annual event of the IFIP Working Group (WG) 5.7 on Advances in Production Management Systems, was held in Bergamo, Italy, from 13 to 17 September 2026, under the theme "Shaping the Future of Industry through Sustainable, Data-Driven, and Human-Centric Production Systems". The APMS conference has long provided an international forum for scholars, practitioners, and policy-oriented experts concerned with the design, engineering, management, and continuous improvement of production systems. As the annual meeting of the IFIP WG5.7 community, APMS 2026 marked another important milestone in the development of a scientific network that, since its establishment, has grown into a broad and active international community, today comprising 138 full and candidate members and 37 honorary members.

The choice of Bergamo as the host city provided a particularly meaningful setting for APMS 2026. Located in one of Europe's most dynamic manufacturing regions, Bergamo combines a distinctive historical and cultural heritage with a strong industrial and technological environment. This context offered an appropriate background for reflecting on the future of production management systems at a time when manufacturing, service, and logistics organisations are being asked to reconcile competitiveness, sustainability, resilience, technological innovation, and human well-being. In this sense, APMS 2026 continued the tradition of the conference as a meeting point between scientific advancement and the practical challenges faced by industry and society. It also reaffirmed the importance of conferences such as APMS as spaces for dialogue, intellectual exchange, and mutual learning between academia and industry, as well as within the academic community itself. At a time when digital technologies increasingly mediate many forms of interaction, the opportunity to meet, discuss, challenge assumptions, and compare different ideas and visions remains essential for the advancement of research and for the development of shared directions for the future of production management systems.

The theme of APMS 2026 addressed three closely interrelated dimensions of contemporary production systems. First, sustainability is no longer a peripheral concern but a central requirement for the design, engineering, and management of industrial systems, supply networks, products, services, and business models. Second, data-driven decision-making is increasingly shaping the way organisations plan, control, monitor, and improve operations across complex value chains. Third, human-centricity has become a defining principle for the development of next-generation production systems, particularly in the context of Industry 5.0, where digital and artificial intelligence technologies are expected to assist, augment, and collaborate with people rather than automate their work.

APMS 2026 brought together leading international experts from academia and industry to explore how sustainability, data, and human factors are reshaping the future of production. The conference focused on innovations that enable sustainable manufacturing, data-driven decision-making, and the integration of human and artificial intelligence in next-generation production systems. Key themes included smart and autonomous factories, resilient and sustainable supply chains, human-centric AI applications, new approaches to data governance, and collaborative forms of industrial innovation. These topics reflect the growing need for production management research that is scientifically rigorous, technologically informed, and attentive to the social and environmental responsibilities of industrial transformation. Through its regular and special sessions, APMS provides a setting in which emerging research results can be critically discussed, connected to industrial needs, and enriched by the plurality of perspectives represented in the IFIP WG5.7 community.

The papers included in this seven-volume proceedings set address a broad spectrum of research questions, methods, and application domains within production management systems. Overall, 269 full papers were accepted for inclusion in the proceedings out of 320 submissions. The contributions reflect the multidisciplinary scope of APMS and are organized into seven topical sections: Sustainable, Circular and Responsible Production Systems; Collaborative Manufacturing, Service Systems and Lifecycle Management; Resilient, Sustainable and Digital Supply Networks; Smart Manufacturing, Digital Twins and Industrial Intelligence; Data-Driven and AI-Enabled Production Management; Human-Centered Production Systems, Work and Skills; and Production Management Theory, Education and Research Methods.

The review process followed a double-blind procedure and involved 320 reviewers from 44 countries, who collectively performed more than 1,500 reviews across the first and second review rounds. This rigorous process supported the selection of high-quality contributions and provided authors with the opportunity to revise and strengthen their papers before final acceptance. Submissions received three reviews each on average.

The special sessions further demonstrated the breadth and vitality of the APMS community. They covered, among other topics, eco-efficient and circular industrial systems, lean-green production systems, smart manufacturing ontologies and data interoperability, human-centric lifecycle management of products and assets, smart manufacturing for circularity and resilience, servitisation for sustainable manufacturing, smart and sustainable supply chains, digital transformation in production and management, jobs and skills for sustainable and resilient industrial systems, human-centric and data-driven AI, industrialisation of digital twins, interactive and explainable AI for production planning and scheduling, cyber-physical systems for sustainability, digital product passports, sustainable battery value chains, value-chain resilience, agentic AI in operations and supply chain networks, trust in digital technologies, and organisational transformation towards Industry 5.0. The contributions provide a comprehensive view of how production management research is responding to the combined challenges of the green transition, digital transformation, and the renewed centrality of human work.

The international program committee, the reviewers, and the special session organisers supported the review process. Their work was essential in ensuring the scientific quality, relevance, and coherence of the papers selected for publication. We are grateful to all authors for submitting their research to APMS 2026 and for contributing to a rich scientific dialogue across disciplines, sectors, and countries. Their contributions confirm the continuing importance of APMS as a forum for advancing knowledge in production management systems and for connecting theoretical developments with emerging industrial needs.

We also wish to acknowledge the contribution of the conference co-chairs, the program co-chairs, the organising committee, the doctoral workshop co-chairs, the advisory committee, the program committee and the wider IFIP WG5.7 community. Their commitment made it possible to develop a program that reflects both the consolidated strengths of the APMS tradition and the new directions in which the field is moving. We are equally grateful to all those who contributed to creating the conditions for an open and constructive exchange among researchers, practitioners, and institutions, recognising that such exchange is one of the foundations on which high-quality and impactful research communities are built.

We hope that these APMS 2026 proceedings will serve as a valuable reference for researchers, practitioners, educators, and decision-makers working on the future of production management systems. By bringing together contributions on sustainable, data-driven, and human-centric production, APMS 2026 aimed to support the development of industrial systems that are not only more efficient and technologically advanced but also more responsible, resilient, inclusive, human-centered, and capable of addressing the complex challenges of the years ahead.

September 2026

Giuditta Pezzotta
Paolo Gaiardelli
Chiara Cimini
Roberto Sala
David Romero
Jannicke Baalsrud-Hauge

Organization

Conference Co-chairs

Giuditta Pezzotta	University of Bergamo, Italy
Paolo Gaiardelli	University of Bergamo, Italy
David Romero	Tecnológico de Monterrey, Mexico

Honorary Chair

Sergio Cavalieri	University of Bergamo, Italy

Program Co-chairs

Chiara Cimini	University of Bergamo, Italy
Fabiana Pirola	University of Bergamo, Italy
Roberto Pinto	University of Bergamo, Italy
Roberto Sala	University of Bergamo, Italy
Jannicke Baalsrud-Hauge	KTH Royal Institute of Technology, Sweden

Organizing Committee Chairs and Vice-Chairs

Veronica Arioli	University of Bergamo, Italy
Chiara Cimini	University of Bergamo, Italy
Beatrice Colombo	University of Bergamo, Italy
Mattia Galimberti	University of Bergamo, Italy
Roberto Sala	University of Bergamo, Italy
Alexandra Lagorio	University of Bergamo, Italy

Doctoral Workshop Co-chairs

Alexandra Lagorio	University of Bergamo, Italy
Claudia Piffari	University of Bergamo, Italy
Matteo Zanchi	University of Bergamo, Italy
Jannicke Baalsrud-Hauge	KTH Royal Institute of Technology, Sweden

David Romero	Tecnológico de Monterrey, Mexico

Advisory Committee

Farhad Ameri	Arizona State University, USA
Sang Do Noh	Sungkyunkwan University, South Korea
Irene Roda	Politecnico di Milano, Italy
Gregor von Cieminski	ZF Friedrichshafen AG, Germany
Hajime Mizuyama	Aoyama Gakuin University, Japan
Eiji Morinaga	Osaka Metropolitan University, Japan
Tomomi Nonaka	Waseda University, Tokyo
Shota Suginouchi	Osaka Metropolitan University, Japan
Ralph Riedel	Westsächsische Hochschule Zwickau, Germany
Matthias Thürer	TU Chemnitz, Germany
Anita Romsdal	Norwegian University of Science and Technology, Norway

Program Committee

Federica Acerbi	Politecnico di Milano, Italy
Kwaku Adu-Amankwa	University of Strathclyde, UK
Oheneba Aggrey	University of Twente, Netherlands
Rajeev Agrawal	Malaviya National Institute of Technology Jaipur, India
Shaikh Shehab Ahamed	Khulna University of Engineering & Technology, Bangladesh
Feryaal Ahmed	Western University, Canada
Waqas Ahmed	Husqvarna Group, Sweden
Md Ali Akram	Norwegian University of Science and Technology, Norway
Alexander Albers	ETH Zurich, Switzerland
Erlend Alfnes	Norwegian University of Science and Technology, Norway
Volodymyr Alieksieiev	Hamburg University of Technology, Germany
Zeynab Allahkarami	Chalmers University of Technology, Sweden
Farhad Ameri	Arizona State University, USA
Matthew Anderson	Blekinge Institute of Technology, Sweden
Yevheniia Andriichenko	Campus 02 UAS, Austria
Elena Andrushchenko	Technical University of Berlin, Germany
Eiji Arai	Osaka University, Japan

Simone Arena	Università di Cagliari, Italy
Veronica Arioli	University of Bergamo, Italy
Rebeca Arista	Airbus, France
Joel Ärlebrandt	Linköping University, Sweden
Susanna Aromaa	VTT Technical Research Centre of Finland Ltd., Finland
Thant Zin Aung	Maastricht University, Netherlands
Néstor Fabián Ayala	Federal University of Rio Grande do Sul, Brazil
Samaneh Azarakhsh	Politecnico di Milano, Italy
Jannicke Baalsrud-Hauge	KTH Royal Institute of Technology, Sweden
Vitalina Babenko	Kharkiv National University of Radio Electronics, Ukraine
Jenny Bäckstrand	Jönköping University, Sweden
Jiwon Baek	Seoul National University, South Korea
Bahador Bahramimianrood	University of New South Wales, Australia
Ottar Bakås	SINTEF, Norway
Juliane Balder	TU Berlin, Germany
Romeo Bandinelli	University of Florence, Italy
Giacomo Barbieri	University of Twente, Netherlands
Natalie Basedow	Hochschule Aalen, Germany
Frederique Biennier	INSA Lyon, France
Alessia Bilancia	Rotterdam Business School, Netherlands
Erik Billing	University of Skövde, Sweden
Max-Heiner Birk	Furtwangen University, Germany
Seyoum Eshetu Birkie	KTH Royal Institute of Technology, Sweden
Umit S. Bititci	Heriot-Watt University, UK
Vlad Bocanet	Technical University of Cluj-Napoca, Romania
Jon Bokrantz	Chalmers University of Technology, Sweden
Alessia Boscarato	Politecnico di Milano, Italy
Enrico Botticella	Politecnico di Torino, Italy
Wassim Bouazza	Nantes Université, France
Kaouther Boulaouinat	LGI, CentraleSupélec, France
Abdelaziz Bouras	Qatar University, Qatar
Mattia Braggio	Università degli Studi di Cagliari, Italy
Jim Browne	University of Galway, Ireland
James Browne	CIM Research Unit University College, Ireland
Jessica Bruch	Mälardalen University, Sweden
Ilaria Bucci	University of Florence, Italy
Kay Burow	BIBA, Germany
Ricardo Caballero	BIBA - Bremer Institut für Produktion und Logistik GmbH, Germany
Anna Corinna Cagliano	Politecnico di Torino, Italy

Qingwei Cai	University of Trento, Italy
Matteo Cais	University of Udine, Italy
Miguel Calvache	Delft University of Technology, Colombia
Luis Camarinha-Matos	NOVA University Lisbon, Portugal
Violetta Giada Cannas	LIUC – Carlo Cattaneo University, Italy
Luca Cannava	Politecnico di Milano, Italy
Alessandra Cantini	Politecnico di Milano, Italy
Huizhong Cao	Chalmers University of Technology, Sweden
Silvia Cardini	University of Brescia, Italy
Luca Carminati	University of Bergamo, Italy
Alessandra Valeria Castruccio Castracani	University of Catania, Italy
Ayoub Chakroun	University of Technology of Troyes, France
Perawit Charoenwut	National Institute of Standards and Technology, USA
Ana Carolina Chaves	INESC TEC, Portugal
Jin Chen	Southern University of Science and Technology, China
Siyuan Chen	Chalmers University of Technology, Sweden
Stephen Childe	University of Plymouth, UK
Franco Chiriacò	Politecnico di Milano, Italy
Koteshwar Chirumalla	Mälardalen University, Sweden
Alessandra Chisari	Politecnico di Milano, Italy
Hyunbo Cho	POSTECH, South Korea
Won Seok Choi	Seoul National University, South Korea
Byoung-Kyu Choi	Korea Advanced Institute of Science & Technology, South Korea
Chiara Cimini	University of Bergamo, Italy
Paola Cocca	Università degli Studi di Brescia, Italy
Claudia Colicchia	Politecnico di Milano, Italy
Beatrice Colombo	University of Bergamo, Italy
Paula Ferreira Da Cruz Correia	Universidade Paulista, Brazil
Ana Correia Simões	INESC TEC, Portugal
Federica Costa	Politecnico di Milano, Italy
Vincenzo Cutrona	University of Applied Sciences and Arts of Southern Switzerland, Switzerland
Marcin Czubaszek	Bialystok University of Technology, Poland
Catherine Da Cunha	École Centrale de Nantes, France
Fabio Daniele	University of Applied Sciences and Arts of Southern Switzerland, Switzerland
Marco Dautaj	Politecnico di Milano, Italy
Flavia De Cassan	University of Florence, Italy

Chiara Forgione	University of Modena and Reggio Emilia, Italy
Chiara Franciosi	Université de Lorraine, France
Tobias Franz	University of Applied Sciences Zwickau, Germany
Enzo Morosini Frazzon	Federal University of Santa Catarina, Brazil
Mike Freitag	Fraunhofer IAO, Germany
Jan Frick	University of Stavanger, Norway
Susumu Fujii	Kobe University, Japan
Paolo Gaiardelli	University of Bergamo, Italy
Nilakshi Galahitiyawe	Herriot Watt University, UK
Mattia Galimberti	University of Bergamo, Italy
Mosè Gallo	University of Naples Federico II, Italy
Margaretha Gansterer	University of Klagenfurt, Austria
Anna Geliev	Institute for Business Cybernetics, e. V., Germany
Harris Gerzic	FH CAMPUS 02, Austria
Lorenzo Ghedini	Politecnico di Milano, Italy
Antonio Giallanza	University of Messina, Italy
Mattia Gianassi	Università di Pisa, Italy
Bartlomiej Gladysz	Politechnika Warszawska, Poland
Elisa Gonzalez Santacruz	Chalmers University of Technology, Sweden
Vicente González-Prida	University of Seville, Spain
Jon Gosling	Cardiff University, UK
Anupama Govindaraj	Mälardalen University, Sweden
Akshay Goyal	Mälardalen University, Sweden
Bernard Grabot	National Engineering School of Tarbes, France
Robert W. Grubbström	Linköping Institute of Technology, Sweden
Linyi Guo	University of Manchester, UK
Gideon Halevi	Hal Tech LTDhi, Israel
Roland Hall	Fraunhofer Institute for Manufacturing Engineering and Automation IPA, Germany
Bernd Hamacher	Bremer Institut für Produktion und Logistik GmbH (BIBA) and University of Bremen, Germany
Irina-Emily Hansen	Norwegian University of Science and Technology, Norway
Synnøve Sunne Hasslan	University of South-Eastern Norway, Norway
Djerdj Horvat	Fraunhofer Institute for Systems and Innovation Research ISI, Germany
Po-Chien Huang	Pennsylvania State University, USA
Shizhen Huang	Southern University of Science and Technology, China
Hans-Henrik Hvolby	University College of Northern Denmark, Denmark

Guven Gurkan Inan	Heriot Watt University, UK
Ichiro Inoue	Kyoto Sangyo University, Japan
Vito Introna	Tor Vergata University of Rome, Italy
Christopher Irgens	University of Strathclyde, UK
Harinder Jagdev	University of Galway, Ireland
Sandra Jakšić	Chalmers University of Technology, Sweden
Hyun Woo Jeon	Kyung Hee University, South Korea
Yongkuk Jeong	KTH Royal Institute of Technology, Sweden
Berndt Jesenko	CAMPUS 02, UaS, Austria
Johannes Jordan	Otto von Guericke University Magdeburg, Germany
Hong-Bae Jun	Hongik University, South Korea
Kefa Kafuluma	Linköping University, Sweden
Toshiya Kaihara	Osaka Institute of Technology, Japan
Matthias Kalverkamp	RheinMain University of Applied Sciences, Germany
Niloofar Katiraee	Free University of Bozen-Bolzano, Italy
Muztoba Khan	Carroll University, USA
Janne Kilpua	Aalto University, Finland
Tomiya Kimura	Fukuoka Institute of Technology, Japan
Dimitris Kiritsis	EPFL, Switzerland
Jan-Felix Klein	KTH Royal Institute of Technology, Sweden
Christian Kober	ETH Zürich, Switzerland
Sri Kolla	University of Twente, Netherlands
Aziz Kemal Konyalioglu	Istanbul Technical University, Turkey
Sepideh Kordestani	Jönköping University, Sweden
Kolitha Kottagaha	University of Groningen, Netherlands
Steve Morel Kountchou Ghomsi	Robert Bosch Electronik GmbH & University of Twente, Germany
Gerald Kremer	Technische Universität Berlin, Germany
Boonserm Kulvatunyou	NIST, USA
Takeshi Kurata	AIST, Japan
Martin Kurdve	RISE AB, Sweden
Cinzia La Mattina	University of Trento, Italy
Alexandra Lagorio	University of Bergamo, Italy
Angelos Ioannis Lagos	Athens University of Economics and Business, Greece
Oscar Larsson	Chalmers tekniska högskola AB, Sweden
Nicolas Leberruyer	Mälardalen University, Sweden
Jan-Peter Lechner	FGL, Germany
Ga Hyun Lee	Kyung Hee University, South Korea

Jürgen Lenz	Technical University of Applied Sciences Augsburg, Germany
Rosanna Leone	University of Palermo, Italy
Leonardo Leoni	eCampus University, Italy
Ming K. Lim	University of Glasgow, UK
Xiaoshan Liu	Fachhochschule der Wirtschaft Campus 02, Austria
Sandi Ljubic	University of Rijeka, Croatia
Hermann Lödding	TU Hamburg, Germany
Malin Löfving	Jönköping University, Sweden
Marco Macchi	Politecnico di Milano, Italy
Antonio Maffei	KTH Royal Institute of Technology, Sweden
Mohammed Malaibari	University of New South Wales, Australia
Diego Mallada Conte	Universidad de Navarra, Spain
Francesco Mancusi	University of Basilicata, Italy
Giulio Mangano	Politecnico di Torino, Italy
Stefano Marazzini	LIUC University, Italy
Mariavittoria Marinucci	Università degli studi di Bergamo, Italy
Ugljesa Marjanovic	University of Novi Sad, Serbia
Julia Christina Markert	Helmut Schmidt University, Germany
Melissa Marques-McEwan	Heriot-Watt University, UK
Davide Matteri	University of Applied Sciences and Arts of Southern Switzerland, Italy
Sandra Mattsson	RISE Research Institutes of Sweden AB, Sweden
Nenad Medić	University of Novi Sad, Serbia
Khaled Medini	Mines Saint-Étienne, LIMOS UMR 6158, France
Jorn Mehnen	Strathclyde University, UK
Joao Gilberto Mendes Dos Reis	University of Campinas, Brazil
Antonella Meneghetti	University of Udine, Italy
Kai Mertins	Knowledge Raven Management GmbH, Germany
Nour El Houda Mezni	INSA Lyon, France
Kaoru Mitsuhashi	Teikyo University, Japan
Hajime Mizuyama	Aoyama Gakuin University, Japan
Florian Möhle	Hamburg University of Technology, Germany
Ilkyeong Moon	Seoul National University, South Korea
Eiji Morinaga	Osaka Metropolitan University, Japan
Christopher Mundt	Hamburg University of Technology, Germany
Mircea Muntean	Technical University of Cluj-Napoca, Romania
Ayah Mustafa	Norwegian University of Science and Technology, Norway
Nithin Nagendra	Mälardalen University, Sweden
Mohamed Naim	Cardiff University, UK

Lukas Rauh	Fraunhofer Institute for Manufacturing Engineering and Automation IPA, Germany
Jonas Reinhold	Leibniz University Hannover, Germany
Eivind Reke	SINTEF Industry, Norway
Iracyanne Retto Uhlmann	Federal University of Amazonas, Brazil
Christian Ricky	Tokyo City University, Japan
Ralph Riedel	Westsächsische Hochschule Zwickau, Germany
Jonas Rieder Rieder	Eagle Creative, Netherlands
Irene Roda	Politecnico di Milano, Italy
Asbjörn Rolstadås	Norwegian University of Science and Technology, Norway
Giovanni Romagnoli	University of Parma, Italy
David Romero	Tecnológico de Monterrey, Mexico
Anita Romsdal	Norwegian University of Science and Technology, Norway
Christoph Roser	Karlsruhe University of Applied Sciences, Germany
Nataliia Roskladka	Politecnico di Milano, Italy
Martin Rudberg	Linköping University, Sweden
Tamas Ruppert	University of Pannonia, Hungary
Thomas E Ruppli	University of Basel, Switzerland
Giacomo Russo	University of Pisa, Italy
Roberto Sala	University of Bergamo, Italy
Carlos Salamanca	Universidad Surcolombiana, Colombia
Omkar Salunkhe	Chalmers University of Technology, Sweden
Adrian Sanchez De Ocana	Alfa Laval and Mälardalen University, Sweden
Annalisa Santolamazza	Tor Vergata University of Rome, Italy
Adriana Saraceni	Maastricht University, Netherlands
Arkopaul Sarkar	National Institute of Standards and Technology, USA
Claudio Sassanelli	Politecnico di Bari, Italy
Mizuho Sato	Tokyo University of Agriculture, Japan
Paul Schönsleben	ETH Zürich, Switzerland
Kjersti Øverbø Schulte	SINTEF Industry, Norway
Jonah Schulz	Leuphana University Lüneburg, Germany
Fabio Sgarbossa	Norwegian University of Science and Technology, Norway
Rosalina Silva	INESC TEC - Institute for Systems and Computer Engineering, Technology and Science, Portugal
Anders Skoogh	Chalmers University of Technology, Sweden
Riitta Smeds	Aalto University, Finland

Safet Softic	CAMPUS 02 University of Applied Sciences, Austria
Selver Softic	CAMPUS 02 University of Applied Sciences, Austria
Linda Helen Sperre	SINTEF Industry, Norway
Iulian Stanasel	University of Oradea, Romania
Julian Stang	Technical University of Munich, Germany
Kenn Steger-Jensen	Aalborg Universitet, Denmark
Volker Stich	Aachen University of Technology, Germany
Jo Wessel Strandhagen	SINTEF, Norway
Jan Ola Strandhagen	Norwegian University of Science and Technology, Norway
Stanislaw Strzelczak	Warsaw University of Technology, Poland
Shota Suginouchi	Osaka Metropolitan University, Japan
Anne Grethe Syversen	Norwegian University of Science and Technology, Norway
Nick Szirbik	University of Groningen, Netherlands
Elena Tappia	Politecnico di Milano, Italy
Yannick Taschbach	RWTH Aachen University, Germany
Ahmed Alaa Eddine Tebboune	Sonelgaz, Algeria
Sergio Terzi	Politecnico di Milano, Italy
Ibrahim Teymurlu	Eindhoven University of Technology, Netherlands
Alix Thecle	École Nationale Superieure d'Arts et Métiers, France
Lennard Thielager	Technical University of Hamburg, Germany
Klaus Thoben	BIBA - Bremer Institut für Produktion und Logistik, Germany
Maria Kollberg Thomassen	SINTEF, Norway
Peter Thorvald	University of Skövde, Sweden
Matthias Thürer	TU Chemnitz, Germany
Kai-Wen Tien	National Yang Ming Chiao Tung University, Taiwan
Greta Tjaden	TRUMPF SE + Co. KG, Germany
Fabiana Tornese	University of Salento, Italy
Natalia Trapani	University of Catania, Italy
Mario Tucci	Università di Firenze, Italy
Vittoria Tudisco	Politecnico di Milano, Italy
Ebru Turanoglu Bekar	Chalmers University of Technology, Sweden
Ioan Turcin	CAMPUS 02 University of Applied Sciences, Austria
Shigeki Umeda	Musashi University, Japan
Bruno Vallespir	University of Bordeaux, France
Margarida Vasconcelos	University of South-Eastern Norway, Norway

Agostino Villa	Politecnico di Torino, Italy
Cristian Vizitiu	Institute of Space Science-INFLPR Subsidiary, Romania
Gregor Von Cieminski	ZF Friedrichshafen AG, Germany
Shaun West	Hochschule Luzern/Luzern University of Applied Science and Art, Switzerland
Hans-Hermann Wiendahl	University Stuttgart, Germany
Stefan Alexander Wiesner	BIBA - Bremer Institut für Produktion und Logistik GmbH, Germany
Joakim Wikner	Jönköping University, Sweden
Magnus Wiktorsson	KTH Royal Institute of Technology, Sweden
Emma Bødker Worup	Aalborg University, Denmark
Thor Wuest	University of South Carolina, USA
Zhichao Yang	University of Twente, Netherlands
Heechang Yoon	Seoul National University, South Korea
Hiroyuki Yoshikawa	University of Tokyo, Japan
Joseph Zammit	University of Malta, Malta
Francesco Zammori	Università di Parma, Italy
Matteo Zanchi	Università degli studi di Bergamo, Italy
Giovanni Zenezini	Politecnico di Torino, Italy
Xiaochen Zheng	Southern University of Science and Technology, China
Anne Zouggar	Université de Bordeaux, France
Gert Zülch	University of Karlsruhe, Germany

Contents

Collaborative Manufacturing, Service Systems and Lifecycle Management

Sustainable, Circular and Responsible Production Systems

Simulation of Circular Product Management Based on a Blockchain Platform

Sogo Hirata(✉), Yuto Izumida, and Shinichi Fukushige

Department of Business Design and Management, Waseda University, Tokyo 169-8555, Japan
hiratas@akane.waseda.jp

Abstract. Circular product management plays a crucial role in establishing circular production systems based on the stock of artefacts distributed in society. The cyber-physical lifecycle system (CPLS) is a digital platform that supports decision-making through material flow analysis for circular product management based on product lifecycle models. This paper proposes a matching function between suppliers and demanders of end-of-use products that is implemented in a blockchain-based CPLS. In a case study focusing on the circular business of refurbished industrial motors, a CPLS prototype was created, and conditions for successful transactions were identified through economic experiments. Subsequently, a lifecycle simulation was performed using the experimental data as input, which demonstrated the effectiveness of the circular management approach based on demand–supply matching within a CPLS.

Keywords: Lifecycle management · Cyber-physical system · Lifecycle simulation · Blockchain · Circular production

1 Introduction

The global population growth and economic expansion have intensified environmental challenges, such as the increased demand for resources, energy, and food. Consequently, linear models based on mass production, mass consumption, and mass disposal have become unsustainable for the global economy. Within this context, society must transition toward circular production systems that enhance added value while effectively utilizing the stock of artefacts [1].

To achieve high-value-added circularity in the manufacturing industry, advanced digital infrastructures that share information among stakeholders regarding the state of products during production, distribution, use, and disposal, as well as their circulation pathways, are required. The cyber-physical lifecycle system (CPLS) is a conceptual framework that constructs a product lifecycle model as a digital twin in cyberspace. Based on real data acquired from the physical space, the digital twin of a product lifecycle enables analysis and decision-making for circular management [2].

While existing research has extensively explored blockchain for traceability and procurement in supply chains, its application to the dynamic management of artefact

Published by Springer Nature Switzerland AG 2027
G. Pezzotta et al. (Eds.): APMS 2026, IFIP AICT 808, pp. 3–15, 2027.
https://doi.org/10.1007/978-3-032-38594-9_1

stocks—specifically, facilitating early matching between product owners and refurbishers based on real-time usage data—remains underexplored. To address this gap, this study formulates the following research question: How does an early supply-demand matching mechanism on a blockchain-based CPLS improve the economic and environmental performance of circular product management? To answer this question, this paper proposes a blockchain-based matching system that visualizes the status of end-of-use products and connects stakeholders. The primary contribution of this research lies not only in integrating CPLS, blockchain, and lifecycle simulation (LCS) into a single framework, but also in quantitatively demonstrating the effectiveness of "early matching." Through an economic experiment and subsequent LCS evaluation using industrial motors as a case study, we clarify the appropriate timing and transaction prices, proving that treating in-use products as tradable stocks significantly enhances both profitability and environmental efficiency compared to conventional post-use collection models.

2 Related Works

A cyber-physical system (CPS) is a system that collects data on an object from the physical space, analyzes the digital twin of the physical object in cyberspace, and applies the insights from the analysis to solve problems in the real world. As key technologies within Industrie 4.0, CPSs are utilized to revitalize industries and solve societal challenges [3].

Lifecycle simulation (LCS) is a method for simulating the material flow of a given number of products and their components as they undergo lifecycle processes over a specific period. The product lifecycle is evaluated from both economic and environmental perspectives [4].

Blockchain is a digital technology that links datasets in block units and records a series of transactions in a distributed manner within the same system. It achieves high availability and data integrity by using digital signatures and hash pointers to detect tampering within the data structure and ensure that numerous nodes distributed across the network maintain the data [5]. Digital platforms that share resource information and connect supply and demand are essential technologies for realizing a circular economy [6]. Accordingly, blockchain-based platforms have been actively researched globally. For instance, Xia et al. designed an information-sharing framework integrating blockchain technology and the Digital Product Passport (DPP) to address the lack of traceability and uncertainty in reverse supply chains [7]. Centobelli et al. proposed a framework for designing a circular blockchain platform that includes recycling processes [8]. Additionally, commercialized examples of such platforms already exist, including BLUE Plastics [9] and the Aura Blockchain Consortium [10]. Furthermore, in Europe, blockchain is being considered as the underlying technology for circulating information within the Digital Product Passport (DPP) [11], with initial applications to lithium-ion batteries scheduled to begin in 2027 [12]. However, discussions on its application to high-value-added circularity—such as reuse, remanufacturing, repair, rental, and sharing—have only just begun, and research on specific methodological approaches remains scarce. By focusing on the application of the DPP to high-value-added circularity ahead of broader European implementation, this study develops a blockchain-based system designed with a view toward future integration with the DPP.

Additionally, blockchain technology has increasingly been applied to supply chain and circular management recently. Blockchain can effectively support supply chain decision-making, transaction coordination, and planning problems by providing transparent information sharing and process monitoring [13]. Moreover, blockchain significantly enhances traceability, smart contract-based automation, and sustainability tracking within complex supply chains [14]. Regarding specific circular economy applications, Liu et al. proposed an industrial blockchain framework for product lifecycle management to automate shipment management of parts and recycling processes through smart contracts [15]. Rolinck et al. proposed a blockchain-based data management system to comprehensively perform lifecycle assessment in aircraft maintenance and repair and similar processes [16]. Chen et al. applied blockchain to a transaction system for efficiently matching supply and demand within supply chains [17].

While existing research has extensively explored blockchain for procurement, transaction coordination, and traceability in supply chains, its specific application to the dynamic management of artefact stocks—particularly integrating LCS to facilitate early matching between product owners and refurbishers—remains underexplored. Therefore, rather than proposing an entirely new methodological paradigm, this study is positioned as a use-case-oriented proof of concept. Using the refurbishment of industrial motors as a specific case study, this study aims to demonstrate how integrating established technologies—specifically blockchain-based information sharing and LCS—within a CPLS can support circular product management in practice.

3 Proposed System

3.1 Outline of the Method

The CPLS developed in this research is a digital platform that reflects information obtained from the product lifecycle in physical space into a lifecycle model in cyberspace. The performance of LCS within cyberspace enables the material flow of the product and its components to be analyzed to support circular management. The LCS model serves as a digital twin of the product lifecycle, visualizing the overall material flow within resource circulation and supporting optimal decision-making for each stakeholders involved in the management process. A schematic of the CPLS is shown in Fig. 1.

3.2 Matching System Between Suppliers and Demanders for Circular Management

The proposed CPLS based on blockchain introduces a matching system for product owners and refurbishers. This system consists of a blockchain platform, a cloud database, and an Application Programming Interface(API) platform. Each stakeholder executes operations on the blockchain platform through API requests. Specifically, suppliers register information about the products they own, whereas demanders register information about the products they wish to purchase. Product information includes the product type, frequency of use, duration of use, and desired price. The system matches supply and demand information, and when a transaction is concluded, products and money are exchanged in the real world. Additionally, data and transaction records registered on the blockchain are stored in a cloud database, and stakeholders refer to this information to make decisions. Figure 2 shows the configuration diagram of the matching system.

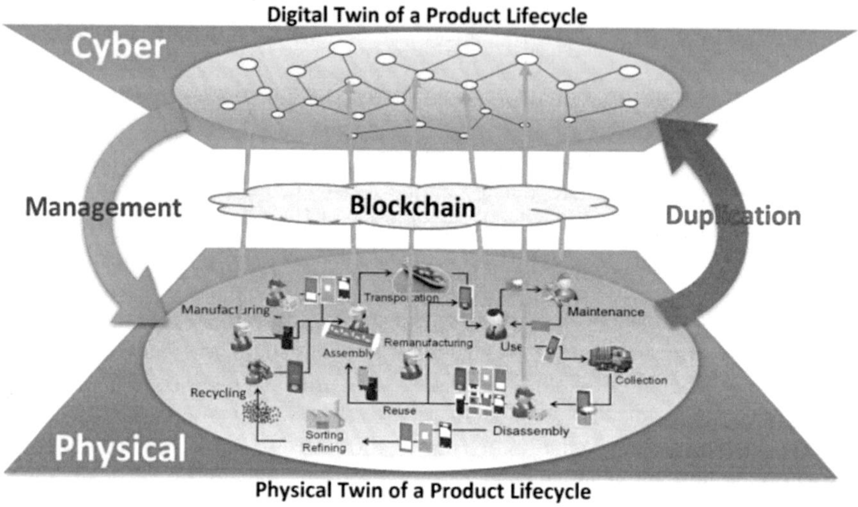

Fig. 1. Concept of the CPLS based on blockchain technology

The product lifecycle model consists of various processes, such as material procurement, component manufacturing, product assembly, transportation, sales, use, recovery, reuse, and recycling. For efficient circular product management, product information should be monitored at each stage of the lifecycle. This requires tracking both the processes and the transfer of ownership. However, conventional data management systems based on central servers cannot fully capture the status of the entire lifecycle. Within the CPLS, information can be collected from each stakeholder through blockchain, with accessibility controlled according to stakeholders role for resource circulation.

3.3 Steps for Constructing the CPLS

The construction steps of the proposed system are outlined as follows.

1. Create an LCS model for the target product lifecycle. Define the states of the product and components within the system boundary.
2. Connect the blockchain platform to the LCS model. Build a mechanism to collect data from the real world using the blockchain system interface and adjust the simulation model so that it serves as a digital twin of the target product lifecycle.
3. Build a matching system for product suppliers and demanders on the blockchain platform. Based on matching results, execute the LCS and provide feedback for decision-making in circular management.

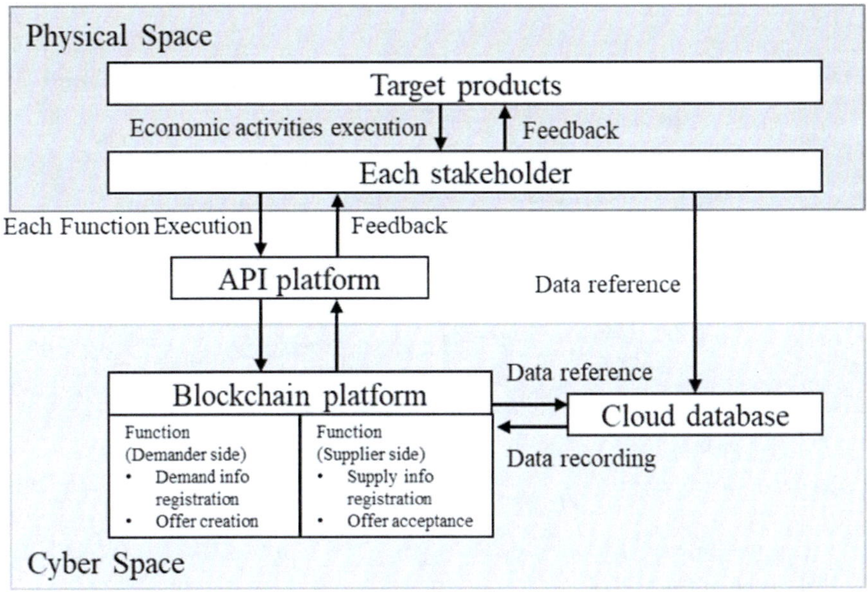

Fig. 2. Configuration diagram of the matching system in the CPLS prototype

4 Case Study

We conducted an economic experiment using the developed CPLS prototype. The data obtained from the experimental results were used to perform simulations to evaluate the effectiveness of circular management.

This experiment assumed a refurbishment business for products equipped with industrial motors. Figure 3 shows the assumed lifecycle model. In this scenario, compressors and vacuum pumps were selected as the target products. Industrial motors are delivered to compressor and vacuum pump manufacturers upon order and incorporated into their products. They are then shipped to the market and sold to users. Users are categorised into three groups based on usage frequency: heavy, medium, and light users, with respective probabilities of 50%, 30%, and 20%. Without a matching system, products are only collected when users cease using them, and end-of-life products are sent for material recycling. However, with a matching system, products matched between an owner and a refurbisher are sold to the refurbisher at that point and refurbished. Refurbished products are then delivered back to the market and reach users in the same condition as new products. In this study, the maximum number of motor refurbishments is set to one. If a refurbished product is collected, it is entirely recycled for materials.

The experiment aimed to clarify the timing and prices of transactions when introducing the matching system into the business. By incorporating the data from the experiment into simulations, we verified the economic and environmental effectiveness of the proposed system.

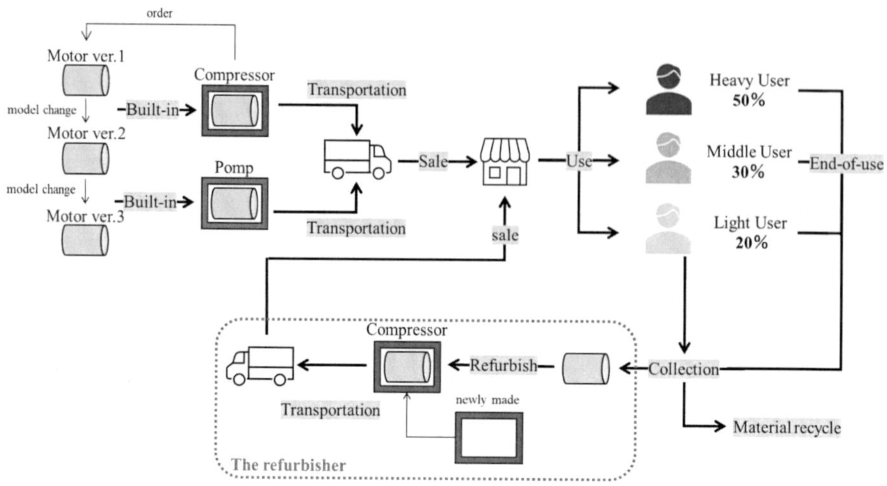

Fig. 3. Lifecycle flow model

4.1 Prototype of the CPLS

Product lifecycle models were created using the simulation tool AnyLogic. The lifecycle process flow is shown in Fig. 3. The blockchain platform Oracle Cloud Infrastructure and its database were used for information collection from physical space.

4.2 Economic Experiment

This experiment clarified the timing of sales from product owners to refurbishers and the prices of the end-of-use products. Multiple participants in the experiment played a game using the proposed system. The experiment was designed as a virtual profit-maximization game without real financial incentives, played by a fixed group of four participants. The players were assigned as either product owners (suppliers) or refurbishers (demanders), and they made decisions on product sales and purchases while seeking to maximize their individual profits.

The participants were divided into one supplier and three demanders. The game proceeded in a turn-based manner, with each turn representing 12 months. The experiment was conducted according to the following constraints: The supplier has three products simultaneously. The supplier also decides whether to sell products in response to offers from demanders. Demanders can view product information registered by suppliers through the system and submit purchase price offers at any time. These offers are not disclosed to other demanders. As a prerequisite for the experiment, the supplier is provided with information on the "sales price of the new product," "future revenue generated by the product," and "sales price during material recycling." Based on this information, the supplier decides whether to accept the offer and sell the product. When a match is established, the refurbishers acquire the product. Products for which no match is established are sold to material recyclers when they reach the end of their life. The supplier aims to maximize profit through purchasing, using, and selling products. The demanders aim to maximize profit through purchasing end-of-use products and selling refurbished products.

Figure 4 illustrates the matching procedure using the proposed system. First, suppliers purchase products and generate ongoing revenue by using them. They then register and update information about the products they are using on the blockchain platform. Meanwhile, demanders search for product information registered on the blockchain platform and create offers if they find a product they want. The transaction is executed when the supplier reviews and approves the offer. Subsequently, the supplier purchases a new product to use again, while the demander refurbishes the purchased product and sells it to generate revenue.

The experiments in this study were conducted under three scenarios. Table 1 shows the settings for each scenario. The frequency of product use by suppliers differs for each scenario, and the product lifespan was set accordingly. Furthermore, based on the product lifespan, the "future revenue generated by the product", "sales price of refurbished products," and "sale proceeds from material recycling" were set. After the experiments under three different scenarios, the allocation of suppliers and demanders was changed, and the game was repeated multiple times until every participant had experienced the role of the supplier, ensuring robust behavioral data.

Table 2 shows the average product sales cycle and average sales price resulting from the experiment. These values were calculated as the arithmetic mean of all successfully matched transactions across all repeated rounds for each scenario.

Table 2 shows the average product sales cycle and average sales price when each player sought to maximize their own profit.

Using the lifecycle flow model shown in the Fig. 3, we ran the LCS under two patterns: with and without matching. The detailed process flow for products was created based on data obtained from the experiments, with matching occurring at similar intervals, followed by sale and refurbishment. The simulation calculated economic and environmental performance. We employed two metrics: product owner and refurbisher profits, and refurbishment rate and environmental efficiency. Where R denotes the refurbishment rate and E denotes the environmental efficiency, these are expressed as shown in Eqs. (1) and (2).

$$R = \frac{N_{Refurbished}}{N_{Released}} \tag{1}$$

$$E = \frac{D}{LCCO_2} \tag{2}$$

where $N_{Refurbished}$ represents the number of refurbished products, $N_{Released}$ represents the number of products released by suppliers, and D represents the average product usage duration. $LCCO_2$ indicates the amount of carbon dioxide emitted by the product throughout its lifecycle. It is calculated in the LCS model as the sum of emissions from new product manufacturing, transportation, collection, refurbishment, and the material recycling process. However, material recycling credits, which account for the avoided emissions from substituting virgin materials through recycling, are not evaluated in this assessment.

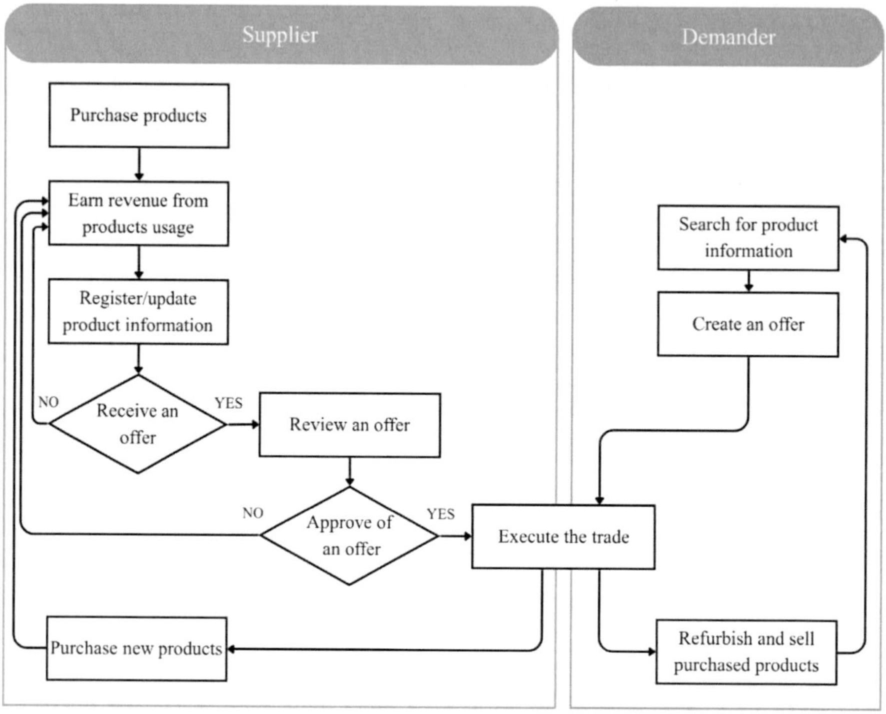

Fig. 4. Procedure for matching using the proposed system

The supplier's profit $P_{supplier}$ and demander's profit $P_{demander}$ are shown in Eqs. (3) and (4), respectively. U represents the total revenue generated by products. Additionally, A_{sales} indicates the sum of the product's sales values, and $A_{purchase}$ represents the sum of the product's purchase values. Suppliers purchase new and refurbished products while selling used products, whereas demanders buy used products and resell them as refurbished products. Additionally, Eq. (5) indicates the transaction price ratio T. V_{new} represents the price when new, whereas V_{used} represents the sale price when transferred from the supplier to the demander. This value indicates the price at which the used product is traded relative to its new price, serving as an indicator of how much sooner the sale occurs.

$$P_{supplier} = U + A_{sales} - A_{purchase} \tag{3}$$

$$P_{demander} = A_{sales} - A_{purchase} \tag{4}$$

$$T = \frac{V_{used}}{V_{new}} \tag{5}$$

Figure 5 compares total profits with and without utilizing the proposed system. When the matching system was used, the total supplier profit increased by approximately 3.40 times, and the total demander profit increased by approximately 1.47 times.

Table 1. Product lifespans by scenario

	Short-lifespan Scenario	Medium-lifespan Scenario	Long-lifespan Scenario
Sales Price of New Product [yen]	20,000		
Product Lifespan [month]	36	84	144
Future Revenue Generated by Product [yen]	$-1{,}667t + 60{,}000$	$-1{,}282t + 108{,}000$	$-1{,}000t + 144{,}000$
Sales Price of Refurbished Product [yen]	$-33.3t + 16{,}000$	$-33.3t + 16{,}000$	$-31.2t + 16{,}000$
Sales Price during Material Recycling [yen]	4,800	3,600	3,000

Table 2. Average sales cycle and average sales price

Scenarios	Average Sales Cycle [month]	Average Sales Price [yen]
Short-term Lifespan	27.96	9,333
Medium-term Lifespan	31.38	12,615
Long-term Lifespan	64.00	11,333

Table 3. Comparison of average usage period, average number of uses, and environmental efficiency

Matching System	Average Usage Duration [month]	Average Number of Uses	Environmental Efficiency
Not Used	58.88	1.24	0.105
Used	74.48	1.64	0.129

Figure 6 shows the refurbishment rate and transaction price ratio of recovered products with and without the proposed system. When the matching system was used, the refurbishment rate improved by approximately 2.61 times, and the transaction price ratio improved by approximately 1.15 times.

Table 3 compares product lifespans, usage intensity, and environmental efficiency with and without utilizing the proposed system. The system extended the average product lifespan and increased the average usage intensity. Consequently, environmental efficiency, which is the ratio of value generated by the product to its environmental impact, also improved.

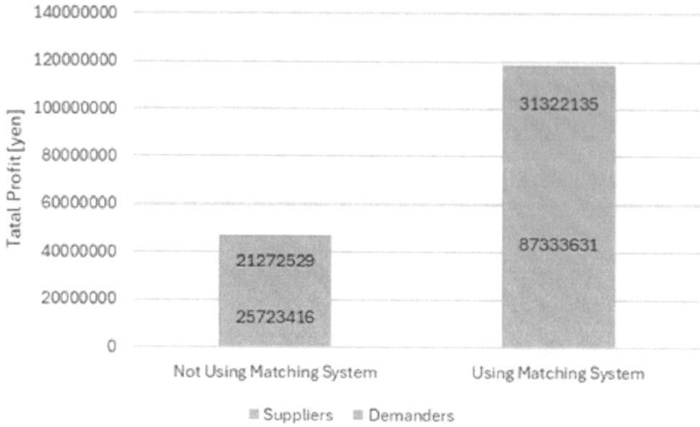

Fig. 5. Comparison of total profits

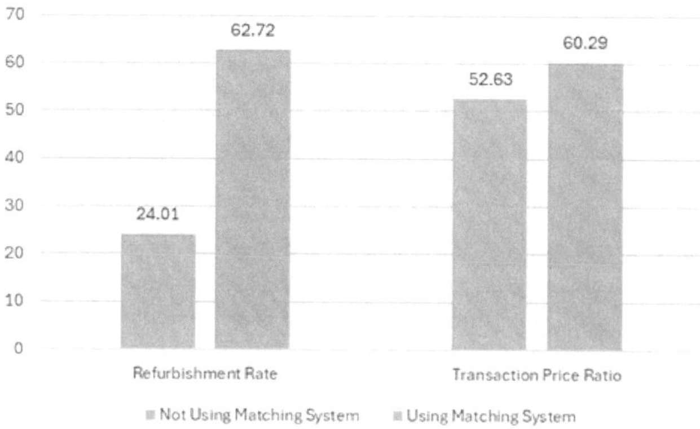

Fig. 6. Comparison of refurbishment rate and transaction price ratio

5 Discussion

In the economic experiment, the business game demonstrated the essential matching function of the blockchain-based CPLS, which includes registering product information, creating offers, and approving offers. Specifically, suppliers input information about products they own, such as usage frequency and duration, into the system. Demanders then create offers by setting conditions, enabling matching between suppliers and demanders. If the supplier approves, a transaction occurs. This approach treats products in use as components of the stock of artefacts, thereby establishing a foundation for transactions at appropriate timing.

The experimental results revealed that products were sold earlier than their physical lifetime, particularly in the medium- and long-lifespan scenarios. Two factors were considered to contribute to this: the first was insufficient decision-making criteria for suppliers. Suppliers were provided only limited information. These factors caused the product owners to accept buyers' offers without being able to determine an appropriate selling price. Second, the costs and time involved in refurbishment were not considered.

Consequently, buyers could be certain of a profit by purchasing below the refurbished resale price, leading them to early offers to secure products ahead of competitors.

Regarding the economic aspect, as shown in Fig. 5, it was found that both suppliers and demanders achieved higher total profits when utilizing the proposed system. Tables 4 and 5 show the breakdowns of total profits for suppliers and demanders, respectively. For suppliers, the introduction of the matching system significantly increased the number of sales transactions. Although this also increased the number of product purchases, the total profit increased. This profit increase occurred as selling products early for refurbishment, before their physical lifespan was exhausted, resulted in a higher selling price per unit. For demanders, the introduction of the matching system increased the number of products purchased, leading to increases in both the purchase value of products and the sales value of refurbished products. Since the sales value of refurbished products exceeded the purchase value of products, the total profit increased as the number of products purchased increased. Specifically, the ability to purchase products earlier increased the cycles of buying, refurbishing, and reselling products, indicating that the profit improvement was primarily driven by an increase in transaction opportunities.

The proposed system enabled the transactions of products in use before they reached the end of their life. Therefore, opportunities increased for products to circulate under conditions suitable for refurbishment. Consequently, as shown in Fig. 6, the matching system improved both the refurbishment rate and the transaction price ratio. The refurbishment rate improved as enabling transactions during the usage phase allowed products to be collected before failure or before reaching end-of-life, at which point they would otherwise be diverted to material recycling. Furthermore, the transaction price ratio improved as earlier sale timings resulted in products being traded while their residual value remained significantly higher. Accordingly, the average usage period and average usage intensity of products also improved, as shown in Table 3. Therefore, extending the usage period increases the value generated by the product, thereby improving environmental efficiency.

Table 4. Breakdown of suppliers' total profit

Matching System	Not Used	Used
Total Purchase Amount [yen]	458,195,484	436,655,580
Total Product Revenue [yen]	440,803,945	424,131,766
Total Sales Amount [yen]	43,114,955	99,857,445
Total Profit [yen]	25,723,416	87,333,631

Table 5. Breakdown of demanders' total profit

Matching System	Not Used	Used
Total Purchase Amount [yen]	43,114,955	99,857,445
Total Sales Amount [yen]	64,387,484	131,179,580

(continued)

Table 5. (*continued*)

Matching System	Not Used	Used
Total Profit [yen]	21,272,529	31,322,135

6 Conclusion

We have proposed a CPLS that supports the circular management of industrial products based on a blockchain platform. The function of matching product suppliers and demanders visualises the stock of artefacts in society and improves the circularity of resources. An economic experiment using the developed system revealed the optimal timing and price of transactions. Subsequently, an LCS incorporating experimental results demonstrated that treating products in use as stocks and trading them through blockchain technology can enhance the efficiency of circular resource management.

A key future challenge is establishing an information management framework for the proposed system. The CPLS is designed on the premise that participants can access information registered by other users. Therefore, defining the scope of registrable information and access conditions is crucial for implementation.

Disclosure of Interests. The authors have no competing interests to declare that are relevant to the content of this article.

References

1. Imai, M., Fukushige, S.: Simulation-based management method for circular manufacturing using response surfaces. Procedia CIRP. **122**, 390–394 (2024)
2. Izumida, Y., Hada, C., Fukushige, S.: Simulation of a cyber-physical lifecycle system based on a blockchain platform. TESConf2024. (2024)
3. Vogt, A., Müller, R.K., Kampa, T., Stark, R., Großmann, D.: Concept and architecture for information exchange between digital twins of the product (CPS) and the production system (CPPS). Procedia CIRP. **104**, 1292–1297 (2021)
4. Umeda, Y., Nonomura, A., Tomiyama, T.: Study on life-cycle design for the post mass production paradigm. AIEDAM. **14**(2), 149–161 (2000)
5. Hanafizadeh, P., Alipour, M.: Taxonomy of theories for blockchain applications in business and management. Digit. Bus. **4**(2), 100080 (2024)
6. Petrik, D., Hiller, S., Morar, D.: Digital platforms for circular economy: empirical development of a taxonomy and archetypes. Electron. Markets. **35**, 60 (2025)
7. Xia, H., Li, J., Li, Q.J., Milisavljevic-Syed, J., Salonitis, K.: Integrating blockchain with digital product passports for managing reverse supply chain. Transp. Res. Part E Logist. Transp. Rev. **202**, 104336 (2025)
8. Centobelli, P., Cerchione, R., Vecchio, P.D., Oropallo, E., Secundo, G.: Blockchain technology for bridging trust, traceability and transparency in circular supply chain. Inf. Manag. **59**(7), 103508 (2022)
9. BLUE Plastics: https://www.3r-suishinkyogikai.jp/data/event/R04_3rce-005.pdf

10. Aura Blockchain Consortium: https://auraconsortium.com
11. da Silva, E.R., Lohmer, J., Rohla, M., Angelis, J.: Unleashing the circular economy in the electric vehicle battery supply chain: a case study on data sharing and blockchain potential. Resour. Conserv. Recycl. **193**, 106969 (2023)
12. Centre for European Policy Studies: Implementing the EU Digital Battery Passport. European Circular Economy Stakeholder Platform (2024) https://www.ceps.eu/ceps-publications/implementing-the-eu-digital-battery-passport/
13. Risso, L.A., Ganga, G.M.D., Godinho Filho, M., de Santa-Eulalia, L.A., Chikhi, T., Mosconi, E.: Present and future perspectives of blockchain in supply chain management: a review of reviews and research agenda. Comput. Ind. Eng. **179**, 109195 (2023)
14. Kumar, N., Kumar, K., Aeron, A., Verre, F.: Blockchain technology in supply chain management: innovations, applications, and challenges. Telemat. Inform. Rep. **18**, 100204 (2025)
15. Liu, X.L., Wang, W.M., Guo, H., Barenji, A.V., Li, Z., Huang, G.Q.: Industrial blockchain based framework for product lifecycle management in industry 4.0. Robot. Comput. Integr. Manuf. **63**, 101897 (2020)
16. Rolinck, M. et al.: A concept for blockchain-based LCA and its application in the context of aircraft MRO. Procedia CIRP. **98**, 394–399 (2021)
17. Chen, H., Ye, Y.: Blockchain-based supply and demand system for matching transactions. In: Proceedings Sixth International Conference on Computer Information Science and Application Technology, vol. 12800, (2023)

A Multi-Layered and Conceptual Framework for the Digital Product Service System Passport

Luca Carminati(✉), Veronica Arioli, Roberto Sala, Fabiana Pirola, and Giuditta Pezzotta

Dipartimento di Ingegneria Gestionale dell'Informazione e della Produzione, University of Bergamo, Viale Marconi, 5-20044, Dalmine (BG), Italy
{luca.carminati,veronica.arioli,roberto.sala,fabiana.pirola, giuditta.pezzotta}@unibg.it

Abstract. The transition toward Product-Service Systems (PSS) requires continuous and seamless data exchange across the value chain. However, fragmented data silos and stakeholder reluctance often hinder this process. While the emerging Digital Product Passport (DPP) offers a structured approach to data sharing, current literature predominantly views it as a static regulatory compliance tool, lacking a cohesive framework to support dynamic PSS provision. To address this gap, this study proposes a comprehensive and multi-layered framework for the Digital Product Service System Passport (DPSSP). Grounded in Design Research Methodology (DRM), the framework was developed by synthesizing current academic literature and EU-funded projects and subsequently validated through cross-sectoral expert focus groups spanning the machinery, manufacturing, and textile industries. The proposed framework shifts the passport's paradigm from compliance to a dynamic PSS enabler. Specifically, this paper details the Conceptual Layer of the DPSSP, mapping the interactions among lifecycle phases, a criticality-driven hierarchical data structure (product vs. component levels), multi-level decision-making processes, acquisition and analysis technologies and multi-actor ecosystem. The findings demonstrate that the DPSSP can act as a strategic facilitator for servitization, providing practitioners with a modular blueprint to improve PSS business models.

Keywords: Digital Product Passport (DPP) · Product-Service Systems (PSS) · Digital Product Service System Passport (DPSSP) · Circular Economy · Conceptual Framework

1 Introduction

In the last decade, the manufacturing paradigm has increasingly shifted from traditional product sales toward the provision of integrated solutions, a transition widely known as servitization [1]. At the core of this shift are Product-Service Systems (PSSs), whether product-, use-, or result-oriented, which require continuous and seamless data

Published by Springer Nature Switzerland AG 2027
G. Pezzotta et al. (Eds.): APMS 2026, IFIP AICT 808, pp. 16–30, 2027.
https://doi.org/10.1007/978-3-032-38594-9_2

exchange to be effectively delivered [2]. However, critical information is typically distributed across a wide network of stakeholders who are often reluctant to share their data [3, 4]. Traditional PSS implementations frequently lack interoperable and standardized systems, hindering dynamic data exchange [5]. Gathering data from various actors is further complicated by the use of isolated databases with heterogeneous structures and operational logics [6].

In this context, the Digital Product Passport (DPP), formally established by Regulation (EU) 2024/1781, emerges as a promising solution to enhance data sharing among stakeholders [7]. Functioning as a structured digital dataset tied to a specific product, the DPP provides customized, secure and role-based access, differentiating who can read and/or write specific data [8, 9].

Despite the DPP's potential as an enabler and facilitator for PSSs (framed as the Digital Product-Service System Passport, or DPSSP [8]), the literature remains sparse on this intersection [8]. Furthermore, even within the broader DPP literature, there is a distinct lack of conceptual frameworks guiding its design and implementation. Current research has investigated isolated components of the DPP ecosystem (such as ontologies [10–12], system architectures [13–16], integration with advanced technologies like IoT and Artificial Intelligence/Machine Learning [17–19] and data requirements [8, 20–23]), but fails to address the interactions among these elements within a cohesive framework.

To address this gap, this paper proposes a multi-layered and conceptual framework for the DPSSP. This framework integrates the diverse aspects currently discussed in scientific literature, defining their roles and mutual interactions. Consequently, this study is guided by the following Research Question (RQ): "How can a DPSSP framework be designed to enable collaborative and value-oriented data exchange to improve PSS effectiveness?".

This paper is then structured as follows: Sect. 2 outlines the methodology applied to construct the multi-layered and conceptual framework. Section 3 presents the proposed DPSSP framework, followed by an in-depth discussion of it in Sect. 4. Finally, Sect. 5 concludes the paper, summarizing the theoretical and managerial contributions, acknowledging research limitations, and suggesting avenues for future research.

2 Methodology

To develop and validate the conceptual framework, this study adopted a multi-step and iterative approach grounded in the principles of Design Research Methodology (DRM) [24]. This methodology, which is also widely recognized as a robust approach within the PSS context [25], is particularly suitable for developing conceptual frameworks that address practical problems while contributing to theoretical knowledge [24]. Following the DRM framework, the research process was iteratively structured into four main stages (illustrated in Fig. 1):

Phase 1: Research Clarification (RC) The initial stage aimed to define the research goals and clarify the problem. Given the lack of existing literature specifically addressing the DPSSP, a twofold exploratory approach was adopted, focusing on the broader concept of the DPP. First, a targeted Literature Review (LR) was conducted on the Scopus database using keywords including "Digital Product Passport", "DPP", "Product Passport", and "Material Passport". To ensure the relevance and quality of the sources, the search

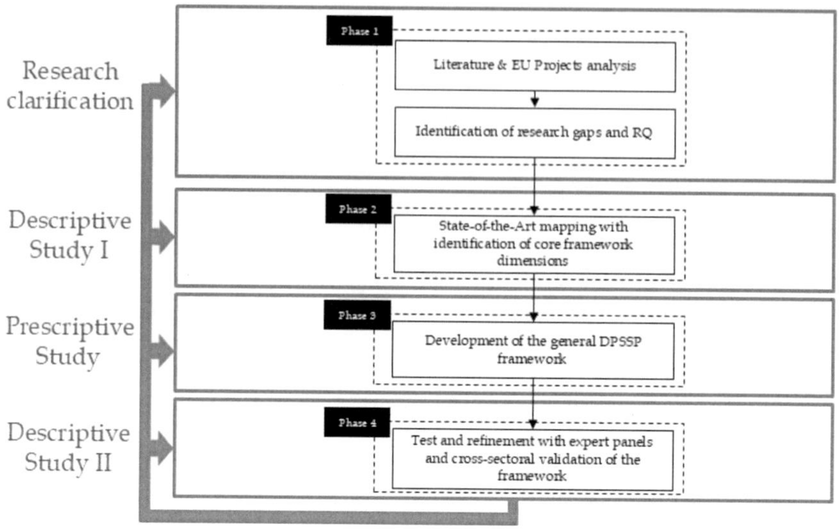

Fig. 1. DRM framework followed

was limited to peer-reviewed journal articles and conference proceedings published in English with no time limits. Second, parallel to the LR, an analysis of ongoing and recently concluded European-funded projects was performed. This focus was preferred over general grey literature as EU-funded research represents the primary vehicle for testing and implementing the DPP initiative, involving high-level consortia that bridge the gap between policy-making and industrial practice. This parallel investigation (LR – EU funded projects) was crucial to capture the latest industrial and applied research trends on the DPP and identify existing gaps.

Phase 2: Descriptive Study I (DS-I) Building upon the RC, this stage focused on gaining a clear understanding of the context. The initially identified documents underwent a rigorous three-step screening process: first by title, second by abstract evaluation, and subsequently by full-text reading. This filtering process resulted in a final core set of 35 highly relevant papers. Simultaneously, the objectives, use cases, and preliminary deliverables of the selected EU projects (5) were examined. Through a systematic analysis of both the academic literature and the applied project outputs, the current state-of-the-art was mapped to identify the key variables at play. This led to the identification of the core framework dimensions, namely technologies, actors, infrastructure, ontologies, data, KPIs, lifecycle phases, decision-making processes, and the DPSSP environment, providing essential insights into their mutual interactions.

Phase 3: Prescriptive Study (PS) In this stage, the synthesis of the theoretical assumptions and context analysis was performed to develop the multi-layered and conceptual framework. The implicit criterion for selecting the framework's core elements was their thematic relevance and recurrence within the analyzed scientific literature and EU projects. Recurrent critical dimensions (i.e., stakeholders, data acquisition technologies, lifecycle phases, KPIs, etc.) consistently emerged as fundamental concepts for the

DPSSP. These elements were logically connected to form the preliminary structure of the conceptual framework, which was then iteratively refined and adapted during the validation focus groups in Phase 4. In this way, an initial draft of the multi-layered and conceptual framework for the DPSSP was synthesized and conceptualized.

Phase 4: Descriptive Study (DS-II) The final stage aimed to evaluate the applicability and usefulness of the developed framework. To achieve that, the framework underwent a rigorous and iterative validation process. The validation was structured around six focus group sessions involving a heterogeneous panel of experts (from ten to twelve, depending on the session). This panel was specifically composed of R&D partners and academic researchers specializing in DPP architectural infrastructure, Artificial Intelligence, Digital Twins and Simulation, Sustainability, LCA/LCC, Ontologies and semantics, and PSSs, alongside industrial stakeholders. Each session followed a structured format, beginning with a presentation of the framework's current version, followed by an open moderated discussion. Participants were invited to identify potential criticalities and suggest refinements, with a specific focus on the framework's cross-sectoral applicability. The inclusion of R&D partners was crucial to evaluate the technical feasibility of the DPSSP framework, while the industrial partners from the manufacturing, machinery, and textile sectors provided insights into operational viability. Through these sessions, specific criticalities regarding data flows and support technologies were identified, leading to the iterative refinement of the model. Crucially, this collaborative process ensured that the proposed DPSSP framework possesses both theoretical soundness and robust practical relevance, confirming its modular structure and adaptability to various application contexts.

While the conceptual framework may appear highly generalized, this abstraction is an intentional design choice. As the validation phase demonstrated, a rigid and specific structure would fail to accommodate the diverse needs and lifecycle complexities across different industries. Instead, its modular and cross-sectoral nature allows practitioners to operationalize only the dimensions relevant to their specific industrial context, ensuring broad applicability.

3 The Proposed DPSSP Framework

Based on the gaps and requirements identified during the literature and EU project analysis (Phase 1 - RC and 2 – DS-I of the methodology), it became evident that deploying a DPSSP requires more than a technological infrastructure. In fact, drawing from the results of RC and DS-I phases and specifically on the gaps identified in Carminati et al. (2025) [8], the current DPP implementation landscape appears fragmented, being characterized by: (i) a lack of standardized architectures and component-level hierarchies; (ii) a weak integration between DPP data and PSS business logic; and (iii) a lack of a shared and robust implementation framework. For this reason, to effectively support PSSs, the proposed DPSSP is conceptualized (in the PS phase) as a multi-layered framework that separates the IT backbone from the theoretical logic and the practical application. This structure ensures a holistic alignment between technical requirements, theoretical foundations, and implementation procedures, answering respectively the questions of how it is built, how its core logic integrates with the variables of an industrial system, and how it is practically designed, deployed and used. Specifically, the multi-layered framework is articulated into three interconnected layers (Fig. 2).

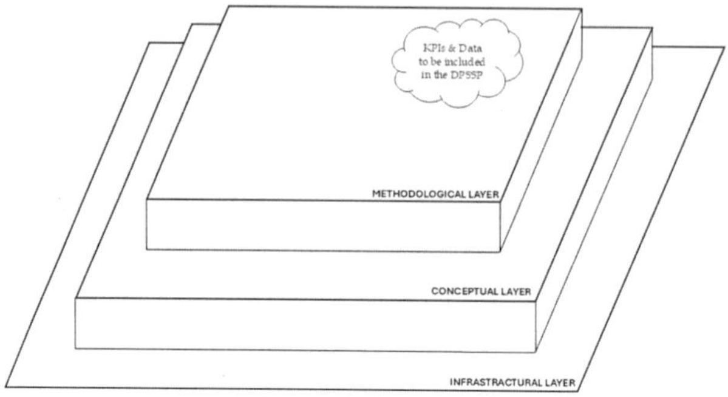

Fig. 2. DPSSP multi-layered framework

The first is the Infrastructural Layer [13–16, 26, 27], which addresses technical implementation by defining the architecture, alongside decentralized digital ecosystems [15, 16, 26, 28], trust-enabling technologies like blockchain [15, 16, 29–32] and other support technologies such as Internet of Things, Artificial Intelligence, Digital Twins and Machine Learning for data collection and updating [17–19, 33]. These elements are necessary for secure, standardized, and interoperable data exchange across the network. Previous research has already addressed the definition of a technical architecture capable of supporting the DPSSP [34]; therefore, an in-depth analysis of this layer is beyond the scope of this study.

Building upon this technical base is the Conceptual Layer, which serves as the theoretical core of the framework. It defines the fundamental system components, bridging Product Lifecycle Management (PLM) and PSS provision by delineating the logic of data flows [17, 35–37], actor roles [38–40], and technological interactions [14, 41–43].

Finally, the Methodological Layer outlines the step-by-step procedural pathway for the practical design, deployment, and use of the DPSSP. Crucially, as illustrated by the data cloud in Fig. 2, this layer dictates the specific key performance indicators (KPIs) and the exact data to be included in the passport [8, 20–23, 44–46], encompassing scenario identification, service specification, technological selection, ontologies selection and data acquisition strategies.

While the infrastructural and methodological layers are vital for practical deployment, this paper primarily focuses on detailing the Conceptual Layer (Fig. 3). This layer represents the direct synthesis of the DS-I, mapping the core dimensions extracted from the literature analysis onto a unified logical structure.

Specifically, the literature and EU project analysis highlighted distinct critical dimensions that a DPSSP must embed: lifecycle data integration, an organized data hierarchy, specific enabling technologies, multi-level decision-making logic, and a multi-actor ecosystem. The following paragraphs detail how each of these literature-derived dimensions has been operationalized within the conceptual model.

The conceptual foundation of the DPSSP is deeply grounded in the product and service lifecycle, acting as a dynamic digital enabler. As emerged from the literature analysis, standard DPPs are often limited to tracking static compliance data. To address this gap, the proposed framework is intentionally designed to be "dynamic." It is considered "dynamic" because, unlike traditional static databases that merely archive "as-built" data, the DPSSP continuously evolves by capturing real-time operational feedback and service events during the PL. The DPSSP aggregates data comprehensively from the Beginning of Life (BOL) through the Middle of Life (MOL) to the End of Life (EOL) [47]. During the BOL phase, the passport is initialized with design and manufacturing data, including product identifiers and Bill of Materials (BoM), alongside service-specific parameters like Service Level Agreements (SLAs) and return channel definitions.

To manage this data complexity, the DPSSP environment is structured around a hierarchical architecture. At the system level, the Product DPSSP is conceptualized as the synergistic integration of the standard DPP, which embeds the physical asset's structural and material data, and a complementary, service-oriented "PSS Passport", which tracks service provisions, performance, and usage contracts. Furthermore, this architecture extends downwards to the component level. Establishing distinct, linked DPSSPs for critical sub-components is essential for granular traceability. This component-level hierarchy becomes particularly valuable during the MOL and EOL phases to track maintenance history, part replacements, and component-specific degradation over time, thereby facilitating targeted maintenance, remanufacturing or recycling strategies.

The continuous flow of data across these hierarchical levels is facilitated by a comprehensive technological ecosystem, which can be conceptually divided into data acquisition and data elaboration technologies. First, data acquisition technologies serve as the critical bridge between the physical and digital realms. Technologies such as the Internet of Things (IoT), smart sensors, AI and Enterprise Resource Planning (ERP) software are deployed to continuously gather data regarding product and user interactions or to estimate them in case they are not available. As the product enters the MOL phase, the DPSSP is continuously enriched with this operational data, such as working hours, component health status, and maintenance interventions.

Beyond serving as a comprehensive data repository, the DPSSP acts as a critical enabler for value creation and decision-making within the entire PSS ecosystem. Data elaboration technologies (such as AI and simulation models) process this input to help in decision-making. By computing operational, economic, social, and environmental KPIs [48–51], the data contained in the DPSSP, and the analysis that can be done on that leveraging the technologies mentioned before, support decision-making across three distinct but interconnected time horizons. At the operational level, the DPSSP facilitates short-term and routine optimizations. This includes adjusting product usage based on real-time energy consumption or triggering preventive or predictive maintenance interventions driven by continuous component health and usage monitoring. Moving to the tactical level, the medium-term insights generated by the DPSSP drive iterative improvements in product and service design. This allows manufacturers to adapt their offerings based on field data or identify specific components suitable for a second lifecycle in new manufacturing cycles. Finally, at the strategic level, long-term decisions shape the

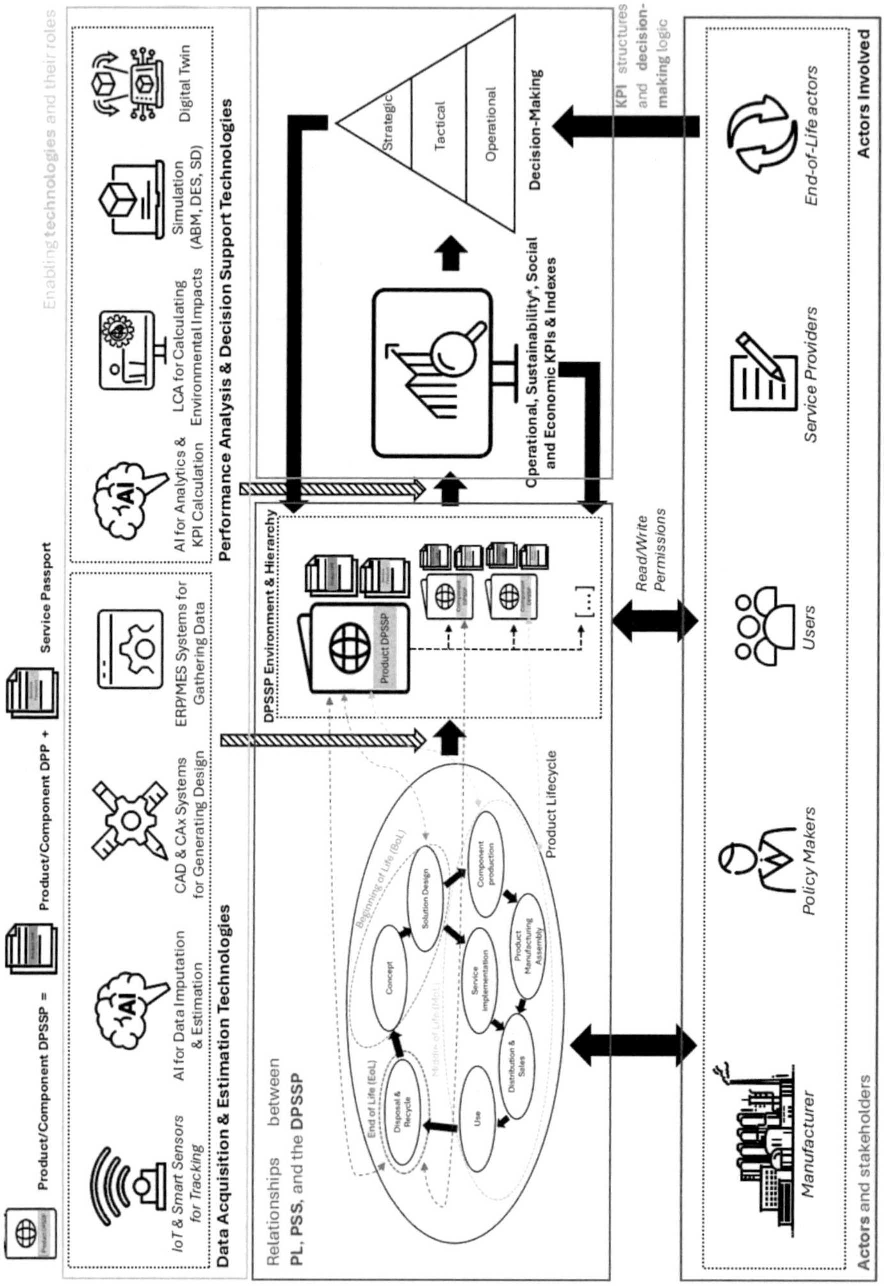

Fig. 3. Conceptual layer of the DPSSP Framework

business model of the company. For example, the data from the DPSSP could enable the assessment of innovative PSS value propositions and support the establishment of new strategic partnerships for service delivery. The output indices could be continuously fed back into the passport to ensure alignment with long-term sustainability and business goals.

Finally, the successful operationalization of the DPSSP inherently relies on a complex ecosystem of actors. As illustrated in Fig. 3, the multi-actor ecosystem involves specific stakeholder categories, each interacting with the DPSSP through tailored read/write permissions. For instance, Manufacturers (e.g., OEMs, component producers, suppliers) hold write permissions during the BOL phase to input baseline design and BoM data. Service Providers (e.g., technology partners, maintainers and repairers, refurbishers, revampers, logistics providers) require read access to this baseline data and write permissions to continuously log maintenance interventions and updates during the MOL. Users (e.g., owners and customers) primarily access the DPSSP with read-only permissions for operational monitoring and usage optimization. At the end of the lifecycle, End-of-Life actors (e.g., recyclers, remanufacturers, and waste management operators) read material compositions to optimize dismantling and write back recycling outcomes. Finally, Policy Makers (e.g., regulators and standardization bodies) may be granted aggregated read-only access to verify regulatory compliance and monitor circularity indices. This strict, role-based governance of read/write permissions ensures data security while maintaining seamless interoperability. However, this collaboration must be rigorously governed both technologically, with the DPSSP, and semantically [10–12, 52]. Semantically, this alignment is achieved through the development and adoption of shared domain ontologies. Ontologies provide a standardized vocabulary that maps and harmonizes heterogeneous data formats across the ecosystem. This ensures that a specific data point (e.g., "component wear" or "service intervention") is unambiguously interpreted by all networked actors, thereby overcoming data silos and enabling true interoperability and trust.

4 Discussion

As demonstrated by the framework presented in Sect. 3, the potential of the DPSSP extends far beyond mere compliance with emerging regulatory mandates. Rather than acting as a static repository of "as-built" characteristics, it serves as a dynamic enabler for value creation within PSS ecosystems. The DPSSP actively addresses the data exchange bottlenecks highlighted in existing PSSs literature [5]. Specifically, by structurally linking the physical asset's baseline data with service-oriented parameters (such as usage contracts, real-time performance metrics, and maintenance history), the framework provides the continuous feedback loop that is intrinsically required by PSS strategies. The DPSSP provides a structured, secure, and efficient means for communication across the value chain. Furthermore, stakeholders' reluctance to share sensitive operational data can be mitigated by the infrastructural security mechanisms and the data logic inherent to the DPSSP. These mechanisms guarantee tailored and role-based access rights, ensuring that different stakeholders only view or modify data pertinent to their specific role in the product-service lifecycle. Finally, semantic alignment through shared ontologies ensures clear and effective communication among diverse actors who occupy different positions in the value chain and may have varying perspectives on the same data point.

This guarantees that all parties unambiguously interpret the data, thereby significantly improving coordination and fostering ecosystem trust [53].

A defining structural feature of the conceptual framework is the hierarchical organization of the DPSSPs, which provides the necessary granularity to differentiate and optimize complex PSS offerings. For instance, in an advanced predictive maintenance scenario, knowing the overall status of a machine is insufficient; tracking the precise condition and degradation of individual sub-components is crucial. However, establishing and maintaining a hierarchical architecture of component-level DPSSPs introduces significant data management costs, complexity, and time overhead. Therefore, the logic behind creating a component-level DPSSP must be carefully evaluated through a rigorous cost-benefit analysis. A "criticality-driven" approach is recommended: standalone, linked DPSSPs should be designed and created exclusively for high-value and critical parts (e.g., a motor in a washing machine, or a battery module in an electric vehicle). For low-value or non-critical components, tracking at the parent-product level remains the most economically viable and sustainable choice.

This calibrated granularity, in turn, directly enhances the multi-level decision-making process (operational, tactical, and strategic). The paradigm shift of the DPSSP is that it does not merely support short-term and isolated interventions on a single asset. By securely accumulating lifecycle data, it acts as a longitudinal facilitator. Crucially, advanced data analytics and AI models enable practitioners to move beyond analyzing a single passport; they can aggregate and compare data from multiple DPSSPs belonging to the same product family or operating fleet. For example, while operational decisions focus on real-time alerts, at a tactical level, AI can cross-reference anomaly reports across hundreds of DPSSPs to identify a systemic and premature pattern in a specific operating environment, prompting targeted engineering PSS redesigns. Strategically, this aggregated "fleet-wide" data analysis allows management to confidently transition from basic maintenance contracts to highly complex and result-oriented PSSs (e.g., guaranteeing a specific production output), as the financial risks of the business model are mitigated by the empirical data gathered from the DPSSP network.

However, this transition also exposes a critical challenge: integrating information regarding intangible service aspects into a passport structure primarily conceived for physical products. While physical components can be easily tracked through BoM and sensor data, services are inherently difficult to quantify and standardize. To effectively manage this complexity, the proposed framework suggests anchoring the service to the physical product/process via standardized service event logs within the DPSSP. The log records all service interventions performed throughout the lifecycle of the product, including maintenance activities, repairs, upgrades, retrofits, and software updates, either automatically acquired by the product or manually registered by the service provider. This enables a traceable history of service actions linked to the physical asset. Moreover, each logged service intervention must be strictly correlated with their measurable impact on the physical asset. For instance, a software update (reported within the passport) should be connected conceptually to a subsequent and verified increase in energy efficiency or a reduction in machine downtime. By translating service activities into physical observations, the DPSSP can comprehensively enable and improve the PSS offering.

Finally, the rigorous validation conducted with experts from diverse industrial fields (machinery, manufacturing, and textiles) in the DS-II phase was instrumental in ensuring the framework's generalizability. Confronting the model with disparate industrial realities demonstrated that the framework is highly modular and adaptable, rather than a rigid structure. Across the different contexts analyzed, the primary differentiation of interest in this paper emerges within the Conceptual Layer, which must adapt to varying product complexities and lifecycle requirements.

For example, in the machinery sector, the Conceptual Layer is primarily used to deeply map product-component hierarchies. This level of data granularity is essential for tracking high-value subcomponents and enabling advanced PSS models, such as predictive maintenance. It also involves defining technologies, such as IoT devices and machine-mounted sensors, for continuous and automated data acquisition to support these advanced PSS business models. Similarly, in the manufacturing sector, the Conceptual Layer focuses on defining technologies to gather real-time data and on the product-component DPSSP hierarchy. However, its use places major emphasis on collecting comprehensive product information and usage data during the Use phase, so stakeholders can leverage operational insights to proactively optimize EoL strategies, such as remanufacturing or component recovery.

In contrast, in the textile sector, automated data acquisition during the Use phase is rarely feasible due to the lack of embedded IoT sensors in garments. Instead, crucial data, often qualitative, is gathered manually at the moment of take-back, helping to select the optimal end-of-life routing (e.g., resale, recycling, or downcycling). The proposed framework seamlessly accommodates this variability: the data acquisition technological block represented in the framework acts as a mediator between the product lifecycle and the DPSSP, allowing for manual or alternative data entry methods where automated data acquisition technologies are absent. Similarly, the product-component DPSSP hierarchy, while crucial for machinery and manufacturing, may be entirely irrelevant in textiles, given the negligible return on investment in tracking a low-cost component like a button. The framework does not impose a single logic but maintains its modularity, allowing practitioners to activate only the dimensions relevant to their specific context.

The successful deployment of a DPSSP relies on viewing it not merely as an IT deployment, but as an organizational transformation. The conceptual framework highlights that technological infrastructure, lifecycle data management and business logic are inextricably linked to the diverse actors involved. Therefore, practitioners must leverage the Methodological Layer to carefully calibrate the Conceptual Layer's dimensions to their specific reality, balancing data granularity with management costs, and technological integration with the actual digital maturity of their specific plants and value chain.

5 Conclusion

This study addressed the critical need for seamless data exchange mechanisms within Product-Service Systems (PSS) by proposing a comprehensive multi-layered and conceptual framework for the DPSSP. Grounded in DRM, the research synthesized existing literature and current EU projects to move beyond the fragmented state of current

DPP research. By conceptualizing a multi-layered framework, this paper answers the research question, demonstrating how a DPSSP can be structured to foster collaborative data exchange and actively improve PSS effectiveness across the entire product/service lifecycle.

From a theoretical standpoint, this study significantly advances literature at the intersection of PSSs and DPPs. While existing research predominantly views the DPP through the lens of End-of-Life regulatory compliance, this paper conceptually positions the DPSSP as a dynamic enabler for PSS. Furthermore, it introduces a holistic perspective that bridges isolated technological studies by explicitly mapping the interactions between lifecycle phases, hierarchical data structures (product vs. component levels), enabling technologies and multi-actor ecosystem.

For industrial practitioners, the proposed DPSSP framework serves as a strategic blueprint for navigating the transition from product sales to integrated solutions. The framework emphasizes that implementing a DPSSP is an organizational transformation rather than a mere IT upgrade. Managerially, the introduction of a "criticality-driven" approach provides a practical logic for balancing the costs of data management with the benefits of granular tracking. Additionally, by highlighting how the DPSSP enables multi-level decision-making, from real-time operational alerts to tactical redesigns and strategic business model innovations, the framework provides managers with a clear pathway to leverage lifecycle data for tangible competitive advantage and risk mitigation in PSS contracts.

Despite its robust methodological foundation, this study has certain limitations. First, while the conceptual framework was rigorously validated through focus groups with experts from diverse sectors (machinery, manufacturing, and textiles), this validation remains qualitative. The framework has not yet been subjected to a full-scale and longitudinal quantitative implementation in a live industrial environment. Second, while the paper explicitly focused on the Conceptual Layer to establish the theoretical core of the DPSSP, the intricate technical complexities of the Infrastructural Layer and the detailed, step-by-step KPI definitions of the Methodological Layer were consciously kept outside the primary scope of this discussion. Finally, while the study proposed a "criticality" logic for component-level tracking, it lacks an empirical method for assessing the criticality of such components.

These limitations prepare the way for promising future research. The next step is to deeply investigate the Methodological Layer, potentially developing standardized sets of PSS-specific KPIs and tailored DPSSP ontologies for different industrial sectors. Future studies are needed to establish criteria for determining the discretion of designing DPSSP for some product components rather than others. Finally, further research should analyze the empirical deployment of the framework through real-world pilot case studies, which would enable quantitative measurements of the DPSSP's impact on PSS performance.

Acknowledgments. The research described has been carried out as part of the PSS-Pass Project, which has received funding from the European Union's Horizon Europe Research and Innovation Programme under grant agreement No. 101177594.

Disclosure of Interests. The authors have no competing interests to declare.

References

1. Arioli, V. et al.: Digital servitization business typologies in the manufacturing sector. Int. J. Ind. Eng. Manag. **16**, 1–23 (2025). https://doi.org/10.24867/IJIEM-378
2. Rapaccini, M., Adrodegari, F.: Conceptualizing customer value in data-driven services and smart PSS. Comput. Ind. **137**, 103607 (2022)
3. Carminati, L., Pirola, F., Lagorio, A., Cimini, C., Jurczuk, A., Boucher, X.: Skills, technical and organizational support needed for collaborative networks 5.0. In: Camarinha-Matos, L.M., Ortiz, A., Boucher, X., Barthe-Delanoë, A.-M. (eds.) Navigating Unpredictability: Collaborative Networks in Non-linear Worlds, pp. 380–396. Cham, Springer Nature Switzerland (2024)
4. Rönnberg Sjödin, D., Parida, V., Wincent, J.: Value co-creation process of integrated product-services: effect of role ambiguities and relational coping strategies. Ind. Mark. Manage. **56**, 108–119 (2016). https://doi.org/10.1016/j.indmarman.2016.03.013
5. Acerbi, F., Sassanelli, C., Terzi, S., Taisch, M.: A systematic literature review on data and information required for circular manufacturing strategies adoption. Sustainability. **13**, 2047 (2021). https://doi.org/10.3390/su13042047
6. Chavez, R., Yu, W., Jacobs, M.A., Feng, M.: Data-driven supply chains, manufacturing capability and customer satisfaction. Prod. Plan. Control. **28**, 906–918 (2017)
7. European Parliament: Regulation (EU) 2024/1781: a framework for the setting of ecodesign requirements for sustainable products
8. Carminati, L., Arioli, V., Sala, R., Pirola, F., Pezzotta, G.: Towards effective implementation of digital product passports: stakeholders involved and data requirements. In: Mizuyama, H., Morinaga, E., Nonaka, T., Kaihara, T., Von Cieminski, G., Romero, D. (eds.) Advances in Production Management Systems. Cyber-Physical-Human Production Systems: Human-AI Collaboration and beyond, pp. 537–553. Springer Nature, Switzerland, Cham (2026)
9. Plociennik, C. et al.: Towards a digital lifecycle passport for the circular economy. In: Procedia CIRP, vol. 105, pp. 122–127 (2022)
10. Jansen, M. et al.: Designing an ontology network for digital product passports. In: Meroño Peñuela, A., Corcho, O., Groth, P., Simperl, E., Tamma, V., Nuzzolese, A.G., Poveda-Villalón, M., Sabou, M., Presutti, V., Celino, I., Revenko, A., Raad, J., Sartini, B., Lisena, P. (eds.) The Semantic Web: ESWC 2024 Satellite Events, pp. 220–237. Springer Nature Switzerland, Cham (2025)
11. Pourjafarian, M. et al.: An ODP-based ontology for the digital product passport. Procedia CIRP. **135**, 930–935 (2025). https://doi.org/10.1016/j.procir.2024.12.125
12. Gianvincenzi, M., Marconi, M., Mosconi, E.M., Pennino, D., Tola, F.: Digital product passports: a framework for developing adaptable and compliant data models. In: Di Stefano, P., Gherardini, F., Nigrelli, V., Rizzi, C., Sequenzia, G., Tumino, D. (eds.) Design Tools and Methods in Industrial Engineering IV, pp. 182–189. Springer Nature Switzerland, Cham (2025)
13. Belova A, Gallina V, Revenko A, Ahmeti A: Digital Product Passport: Initial System Architecture with Knowledge Graphs and Data Spaces
14. Pourjafarian, M. et al.: A multi-stakeholder digital product passport based on the asset administration Shell. In: 2023 IEEE 28th International Conference on Emerging Technologies and Factory Automation (ETFA), pp. 1–8. IEEE, Sinaia, Romania (2023)
15. Kim, J., Lee, S., Kim, H.: Blockchain-based digital product passport for the circular economy. In: 2024 International Conference on Platform Technology and Service (PlatCon), pp. 188–191. Jeju, Korea, Republic of, IEEE (2024)

16. Greiner, M., Seidenfad, K., Langewisch, C., Hofmann, A., Lechner, U.: The digital product passport: enabling interoperable information flows through blockchain consortia for sustainability. In: Phillipson, F., Eichler, G., Erfurth, C., Fahrnberger, G. (eds.) Innovations for Community Services, pp. 377–396. Springer Nature Switzerland, Cham (2024)
17. Telfort, T.E., Valilai, O.F.: A framework for sustainable textile waste management using digital product passports and artificial intelligence. Procedia CIRP. **134**, 909–914 (2025)
18. Wan, P.K.F., Jiang, S.: Enabling a dynamic information flow in digital product passports during product use phase: a literature review and proposed framework. Sustainable Prod. Consumption. **54**, 362–374 (2025). https://doi.org/10.1016/j.spc.2025.01.014
19. Deepshikha, K.A.: IOT for digital product passport system in India. In: Fong, S., Dey, N., Joshi, A. (eds.) ICT Analysis and Applications, pp. 181–190. Springer Nature Singapore, Singapore (2025)
20. Gieß, A., Möller, F.: Exploring the value ecosystem of digital product passports. J. Ind. Ecol. **29**, 561–573 (2025). https://doi.org/10.1111/jiec.13621
21. Jensen, S.F., Kristensen, J.H., Adamsen, S., Christensen, A., Waehrens, B.V.: Digital product passports for a circular economy: data needs for product life cycle decision-making. Sustainable Prod. Consumption. **37**, 242–255 (2023). https://doi.org/10.1016/j.spc.2023.02.021
22. Stiksma, F., Van Sinderen, M., Moreira, J.L.R.: Value assessment of consumer electronics with digital product passports: a case study of lifetime extension assessment of disposed washing machines. In: Borbinha, J., Prince Sales, T., Da Silva, M.M., Proper, H.A., Schnellmann, M. (eds.) Enterprise Design, Operations, and Computing, pp. 81–98. Springer Nature Switzerland, Cham (2025)
23. Popowicz, M., Pohlmann, A., Schöggl, J., Baumgartner, R.J.: Digital product passports as information providers for consumers—the case of digital battery passports. Bus Strategy Environ. **34**, 7700–7722 (2025). https://doi.org/10.1002/bse.4346
24. Blessing, L.T.M., Chakrabarti, A.: DRM, a Design Research Methodology. Springer, London, London (2009)
25. Pezzotta, G. et al.: The product service system lean design methodology (PSSLDM): integrating product and service components along the whole PSS lifecycle. J. Manuf. Technol. Manag. **29**, 1270–1295 (2018). https://doi.org/10.1108/JMTM-06-2017-0132
26. Miron, R., Hulea, M.: Digital product passport implementation based on Hyperledger fabric technology. In: Machado, J., Soares, F., Trojanowska, J., Ivanov, V., Antosz, K., Cagáňová, D., Manupati, V.K., Pereira, A. (eds.) Innovations in Industrial Engineering III, pp. 51–62. Springer Nature Switzerland, Cham (2024)
27. Wiesner, M., Moreira, J., Guizzardi, R., Scholz, P.: A reference architecture for digital product passports at batch level to support manufacturing supply chains. In: Araújo, J., De La Vara, J.L., Santos, M.Y., Assar, S. (eds.) Research Challenges in Information Science, pp. 307–323. Springer Nature Switzerland, Cham (2024)
28. Morellini, L., Ferrando, A., Cabri, G., Garuti, M.: Design and implementation of a software system for digital product passport. In: 2025 33rd International Conference on Enabling Technologies: Infrastructure for Collaborative Enterprises (WETICE), pp. 1–6. IEEE, Catania, Italy (2025)
29. Canciani, A., Felicioli, C., Severino, F., Tortola, D.: Enhancing supply chain transparency through blockchain product passports. In: 2024 IEEE International Conference on Pervasive Computing and Communications Workshops and Other Affiliated Events (PerCom Workshops), pp. 751–756. IEEE, Biarritz, France (2024)
30. Nowacki, S., Sisik, G.M., Angelopoulos, C.M.: Digital product passports: use cases framework and technical architecture using DLT and smart contracts. In: 2023 19th International Conference on Distributed Computing in Smart Systems and the Internet of Things (DCOSS-IoT), pp. 373–380. IEEE, Pafos, Cyprus (2023)

31. Keles, C., Cruz Rios, F., Hoque, S.: Digital technologies and circular economy in the construction sector: a review of lifecycle applications, integrations, potential, and limitations. Buildings. **15**, 553 (2025). https://doi.org/10.3390/buildings15040553
32. Paolucci, A., Gianvincenzi, M., Marconi, M., Favi, C., Pennino, D.: Development of a decentralized digital product passport for enhanced lifecycle Management of Electrical and Electronic Equipment. Procedia CIRP. **135**, 356–361 (2025). https://doi.org/10.1016/j.procir.2024.12.030
33. Melo, V., De La Prieta, F., Leitao, P.: Relationship of digital product passport and digital twin in industry 4.0 context. In: Borangiu, T., Trentesaux, D., Leitão, P., Legat, C. (eds.) Service Oriented, Holonic and Multi-Agent Manufacturing Systems for Industry of the Future, pp. 187–200. Cham, Springer Nature Switzerland (2025)
34. Maló, P. et al.: From static records to smart passports: evolving digital product passports toward product-service system integration. In: 2025 21st International Conference on Distributed Computing in Smart Systems and the Internet of Things (DCOSS-IoT), pp. 1087–1094. IEEE, Lucca, Italy (2025)
35. Glišić, M., Møller, C., Veluri, B., Ramanujan, D.: Digital process passport: a conceptual model for information collection and sharing in sustainable manufacturing. Procedia CIRP. **130**, 1077–1083 (2024). https://doi.org/10.1016/j.procir.2024.10.209
36. Çetin, S.: Towards a Circular Building Industry through Digitalisation. Exploring how Digital Technologies Can Help Narrow, Slow, Close, and Regenerate the Loops in Social Housing Practice. BK Books, Delft (2023)
37. Pohlmann, A., Popowicz, M., Schöggl, J.-P., Bachler, J., Keler, J., Baumgartner, R.J.: Conceptualization of a digital product passport to enable circular and sustainable automotive value chains – the combustion engine use case. Procedia CIRP. **122**, 169–174 (2024). https://doi.org/10.1016/j.procir.2024.01.025
38. Kim, J., Moon, J., Do, Y., Kim, H., Jeong, J.: Research on a SaaS (software as a service)-based digital product passport system model for the EV battery industry value chain. WSEAS Trans. Bus. Econ. **20**, 2466–2475 (2023). https://doi.org/10.37394/23207.2023.20.211
39. CIRPASS-2: Digital Product Passports Enabling At-Scale and Real-Life Circular Economy Use Cases in electronics, textiles, tires and construction value chains (2024)
40. CIRPASS: Collaborative Initiative for a Standards-based Digital Product Passport for Stakeholder-Specific Sharing of Product Data for a Circular Economy (2022)
41. Hermann, Y., Patlakis, C., Hörger, M., May, M.C., Lanza, G.: Digital product passport enabled production control in the context of circular economy. Procedia CIRP. **132**, 221–226 (2025). https://doi.org/10.1016/j.procir.2025.01.037
42. Panza, L., Bruno, G., Lombardi, F.: A collaborative architecture to support circular economy through digital material passports and internet of materials. IFAC-Pap. **55**, 1491–1496 (2022). https://doi.org/10.1016/j.ifacol.2022.09.601
43. Voulgaridis, K., Lagkas, T., Angelopoulos, C.M., Boulogeorgos, A.-A.A., Argyriou, V., Sarigiannidis, P.: Digital product passports as enablers of digital circular economy: a framework based on technological perspective. Telecommun. Syst. **85**, 699–715 (2024)
44. DaCapo: D2.3 Data sharing protocols and DPP conceptualisation (2024)
45. CircThread: Building the Digital Thread for Circular Economy Product, Resource & Service Management (2021)
46. GEAR-UP: Green Engineering, Analysis, & Reskilling for Unbounded Production (101178484). (2024)
47. Timms, P.D., King, M.R.N.: Complexity in the delivery of product passports: a system of systems approach to passport lifecycles. In: 2023 18th Annual System of Systems Engineering Conference (SoSe), pp. 1–8. IEEE, Lille, France (2023)

48. King, M.R.N., Timms, P.D., Mountney, S.: A proposed universal definition of a digital product passport ecosystem (DPPE): worldviews, discrete capabilities, stakeholder requirements and concerns. J. Clean. Prod. **384**, 135538 (2023)
49. Gleich, K., Behrendt, S., Hörger, M., Benfer, M., Lanza, G.: An asset administration Shell-based digital product passport as a Gaia-X service. Procedia CIRP. **127**, 224–229 (2024). https://doi.org/10.1016/j.procir.2024.07.039
50. Alves, L. et al.: A traceability platform for monitoring environmental and social sustainability in the textile and clothing value chain: towards a digital passport for textiles and clothing. Sustainability. **16**, 82 (2023). https://doi.org/10.3390/su16010082
51. Lopes, C., Barata, J.: Digital product passport: a review and research agenda. Procedia Comput Sci. **246**, 981–990 (2024). https://doi.org/10.1016/j.procs.2024.09.517
52. Ajdinović, S., Maisch, N., Dzubba, M., Lechler, A., Riedel, O.: Defining scalable data models for operational data integration in manufacturing processes within the digital product passport framework through OPC UA and asset administration Shell. In: Wang, Y.-C., Chan, S.H., Wang, Z.-H. (eds.) Flexible Automation and Intelligent Manufacturing: Manufacturing Innovation and Preparedness for the Changing World Order, pp. 117–124. Springer Nature Switzerland, Cham (2024)
53. Langley, D.J., Rosca, E., Angelopoulos, M., Kamminga, O., Hooijer, C.: Orchestrating a smart circular economy: guiding principles for digital product passports. J. Bus. Res. **169**, 114259 (2023). https://doi.org/10.1016/j.jbusres.2023.114259

DT-Based Simulation Framework Based on Digital Product Service System Passport

Luigi Manca[1(✉)], Tommaso G. Cesati[1], Giorgio Battiato[1], Marta Calderaro[1], Mattia G. Marzano[1], Angelo Marguglio[1], Luca Carminati[2], Veronica Arioli[2], and Fabiana Pirola[2]

[1] Engineering Ingegneria Informatica S.p.A., P.le dell' Agricoltura 24, 00144 Rome, IT, Italy
{Luigi.Manca,TommasoGiovanni.Cesati,Marta.Calderaro, MattiaGiuseppe.Marzano,Angelo.Marguglio}@eng.it

[2] University of Bergamo, Viale Marconi 5, 24040, Dalmine, IT, Italy
{luca.carminati,veronica.arioli,fabiana.pirola}@unibg.it

Abstract. The transition toward Product-Service Systems (PSS) and smart PSS offers integrated, sustainable value propositions but faces challenges in systematic data integration across heterogeneous stakeholder ecosystems. While the Digital Product Passport and its evolution into Digital Product-Service Systems Passport (DPSSP) aims to consolidate lifecycle, regulatory, and circularity data, within a unified framework, operationalizing this intelligence lacks standardized modeling approaches capable of capturing the dynamic nature of PSS. Furthermore, despite the recognized potential of Digital Twins (DTs) and simulation techniques to support data-driven decisions, their methodological application in PSS remains fragmented. To address these gaps, this study proposes a novel DT-based simulation framework that integrates Multi-Agent Simulation (MAS), DPSSP data structures, and Asset Administration Shell (AAS) interoperability. By systematically integrating product-service data along the entire lifecycle—integrated through the DPSSP—and capturing complex stakeholder interactions, this unified DT-based simulation framework enables decision making throughout the entire PSS lifecycle, from design and operation to maintenance and end of life. The framework provides a risk-free environment for scenario exploration, allowing stakeholders to evaluate the implications of functional and non-functional changes.

Keywords: Simulation Framework · Multi Agent Model · Decision Making · smart Product-Service Systems · Digital Product Passport.

1 Introduction

The increasing diffusion of Product-Service Systems (PSS) reflects a structural shift in manufacturing toward integrated value propositions capable of addressing evolving customer requirements and sustainability challenges [1–3]. The emergence of smart PSS, enabled by pervasive digital technologies, has expanded opportunities for leveraging product-use data, although their systematic integration into decision-making remains

Published by Springer Nature Switzerland AG 2027
G. Pezzotta et al. (Eds.): APMS 2026, IFIP AICT 808, pp. 31–45, 2027.
https://doi.org/10.1007/978-3-032-38594-9_3

limited due to fragmented infrastructures and heterogeneous stakeholder ecosystems [4–6]. In parallel, the Digital Product Passport (DPP) and its evolution into the Digital Product-Service System Passport (DPSSP) have been introduced as comprehensive mechanisms to consolidate lifecycle information, regulatory compliance requirements, circularity indicators, and service-related data within a unified framework [7–9]. Despite these developments, the operationalization of DPSSP-enabled intelligence is hindered by the absence of standardized modelling approaches able to represent the dynamic and multi-stakeholder nature of PSS ecosystems, particularly when circularity and environmental performance are considered [10–12].

Digital Twins (DTs), simulation and modelling techniques are increasingly recognized as key enablers of data-driven decision support across the product-service lifecycle, yet consensus on their methodological formulation and application in PSS remains partial and fragmented within the literature [13–16]. Against this backdrop, this research addresses four central questions: (i) how product- and service-related data part of the DPSSP can be systematically integrated into a simulation engine [9, 10]; (ii) how DT-based simulation can enhance lifecycle intelligence and sustainability assessments [11, 13]; (iii) how Multi-Agent Simulation (MAS) can formally capture PSS behaviours and stakeholder interactions [11, 15, 17]; and (iv) how a unified modelling framework can support decision-making at strategic, tactical, and operational levels [10, 18]. To this end, the paper proposes a DT-based simulation framework that integrates MAS, DPSSP data structures, and Asset Administration Shell (AAS)-based interoperability to enable rigorous evaluation of PSS configurations, maintenance strategies, supply chain impacts, and circular business opportunities throughout the entire lifecycle [2, 6, 9].

This paper is structured as follows: Sect. 2 explains the literature background and foundations for this study; Sect. 3 presents the DT-based simulation framework in its main conceptual elements; Sect. 4 operationalizes the framework, showing its implementation; and, finally, Sect. 5 concludes the work.

2 Background and Foundations

2.1 Product-Service Systems

Over the last two decades, a growing number of manufacturing companies have incorporated services into their product offerings as a response to the increasingly sophisticated customers' requests in terms of products' characteristics and functionalities, resulting in business models of integrated bundles of products and services defined as Product-Service Systems (PSS) [1]. With the rise of digital technologies, the possibility to retrieve a large amount of data from connected sources has become a key source of value creation in the context of service provision. Nevertheless, PSS that are built on data retrieved from connected products, are nowadays called smart PSS [4]. PSS and smart PSS are characterized by: (i) physical products, the tangible part, (ii) services, the often intangible part, designed together with the products, (iii) physical and digital infrastructure, and (iv) supporting network of multiple stakeholders in the supply chain which create a large network of collaborating teams and a dynamic working environment of actors.

This complex system is able to create value managing the entire lifecycle of products, generating competitive advantage for providers, lowering customer costs, reducing the environmental impacts, and favoring social integration [2, 3, 13]. However, not always this is true, therefore company developing PSSs must undertake supported decision-making processes at strategical, tactical and operational levels, that can enhance the achievement of such objectives [10].

2.2 Digital Product Passport Enhanced by Product-Service Systems Data

Despite the established nature of smart PSS literature, the potential of services in a PSS as source of (digitalized) product-use data remains largely untapped. Consequently, PSSs still require the integration of advanced digital systems to optimize processes as well as data collection and analysis, leaving significant room for further improvement [5]. This limitation can be explained by the lack of reliable infrastructure capable of supporting and connecting the complex networks that characterize PSS models [6].

To address this gap, recent studies have explored the concept of Digital Product Passport in combination with PSS, leading to the definition of the Digital Product Service System Passport (DPSSP) [7, 8]. The DPSSP can be understood as an integrated framework that enables companies to leverage DPP data to improve existing PSS models or develop new ones [8]. Beyond supporting DPP regulatory compliance, the DPSSP also promotes innovative and service-oriented solutions capable of meeting both customer demands and sustainability objectives [8]. Indeed, as lifecycle intelligence becomes increasingly central to product innovation, it is relevant to explore how design tools and simulation platforms can feed forward and backward into the DPSSP [7], augmenting business models and raising opportunities from and to an effective and efficient use of the DPSSP.

2.3 Augmenting Business Models Innovation Through Simulation

Simulation and Digital twins (DTs) play a critical role in supporting PSS, and potentially DPSSP adoption and optimization, by granting a solid support for innovative business models centered on services spanning from PSS model design to PSS management, up to the end of their lifecycle across a vast array of applications [9, 11, 12, 14–17]. Multiple literature papers and simulation use cases have been applied to model various, specific, scattered systems and problems – at both strategic, tactical and operational level – regarding services in manufacturing, sustainability, logistics and supply chain management environments.

Indeed, simulation refers to the process of creating and executing a computational model that emulates a real system's behaviour over time to analyse performance and test alternative strategies [4], without necessarily relying on linearity relationship of inputs and outputs. Each agent or entity type (i.e. PSS manufacturer, PSS consumers, PSS maintainer) is characterized by a specific and simplified behavior. Therefore, through a simulation model, it is possible to replicate complex situations, test hypotheses and analyze how a system responds to different inputs, variables or conditions without having to test it in the real system. Each input set constitutes a scenario that can be compared with others. It can be eventually integrated with optimization solvers, machine learning or evolving to create DTs.

A Digital Twin is defined as a dynamic, data-driven digital representation of a physical asset, process, or system that mirrors its state and behaviour in near real time, enabling continuous monitoring, prediction, and decision support across its lifecycle [4]. They provide the foundation for tracking performance, assessing environmental impacts, and exploring alternative service configurations in a PSS context.

Due to divergent authors' interpretation, there is a lack of common baseline in holistic simulation application and modeling for PSS. Limited contributions and little advancements were achieved in creating and formulating a standardized simulation framework for PSS models. This can be explained by the lack of established knowledge and consensus, particularly regarding the service conceptualization and its modeling [18].

This study proposes a DT-based simulation framework to support PSS decision-making, thankful to the integration of DPSSP data as comprehensive digital ledger documenting every phase of a product's lifecycle – collecting data sources on the use of products and services, operational performances, environmental footprint, LCA analysis, and any relevant information for the purposes.

3 Modeling Product-Service Systems

3.1 Model Foundation

The proposed DT-based Simulation Framework, complemented common techniques and tools for modelling standardized and interoperable DTs for PSS lifecycle analysis, focuses on interconnected simulation capabilities across different stages of the value chain. To manage the inherent complexity of PSS, the framework is based on Multi-Agent Simulation (MAS), investigating the following advantages on PSS modeling:

(a) More realistic representation of the dynamic behaviour of PSS;
(b) Enhanced modelling of interactions between stakeholders and subsystems;
(c) Exploration of the effects of different designs of PSS, management and impact performances;
(d) Support for decision-making that considers the full PSS lifecycle and its implications for Carbon Footprint indices.

A central assumption is that DTs can enhance circularity by enabling continuous monitoring, simulation, and optimization of products and services across their lifecycle [4]. However, realizing such circular feedback loops requires interoperable infrastructures capable of linking product-level data (as in DPPs) with service-level intelligence, which remains only partially demonstrated in industrial practice. The Asset Administration Shell (AAS) is considered the most promising foundation for structuring DPP information in a standardized and machine-readable form [7].

According to [7], Industrie 4.0 standardized AAS specifications (IEC 63278) is used to structure DPSSP information – a clearly defined format, including semantic identification of each information element – enabling users to access product information across the entire value chain (cross-domain/cross-sector) quickly and easily based on their needs, enhancing the connection of the DPSSP to different machines and expose its data to simulation engines. Recent work suggests using DTs as a solution for keeping the KPIs up to date and build upon this approach by using the AAS as a standard for DTs as well as circularity KPIs derived from standards and norms, but these methods are still in their infancy and need validation in dynamic multi-stakeholder environments such as servitized ecosystems.

In this context, integrating service-related indicators, Carbon Footprint and lifecycle intelligence enable predictive, sustainability-oriented decision-making throughout the product-service lifecycle. Indeed, the proposed framework enables lifecycle intelligence by combining DTs, Simulation, and the AAS under a unified architecture, so to enable data sharing among DTs and DPSSPs.

To precisely contextualize the Digital Twin, this framework is formulated as a DT-ready simulation model designed to operate as a synchronized architecture when operationalized. Rather than relying on continuous telemetric data streaming—an approach that is impractical for long-term product–service system lifecycle management—the framework introduces a near real-time, event-driven data integration layer. Within this paradigm, physical assets transmit structured data packets exclusively upon the occurrence of specific operational events, such as maintenance interventions, state transitions, or deviations in usage intensity. The AAS serves as the interoperable event broker: upon event detection, the corresponding sub-model captures the observed variation, standardizes the data payload, and dynamically updates the DPSSP ledger.

As illustrated in Fig. 1, this process ensures the continuous alignment of baseline state parameters, including asset reliability metrics and carbon footprint indicators. These updated parameters are subsequently ingested by the Multi-Agent Simulation engine, which autonomously reinitializes system conditions and executes prospective scenario forecasting.

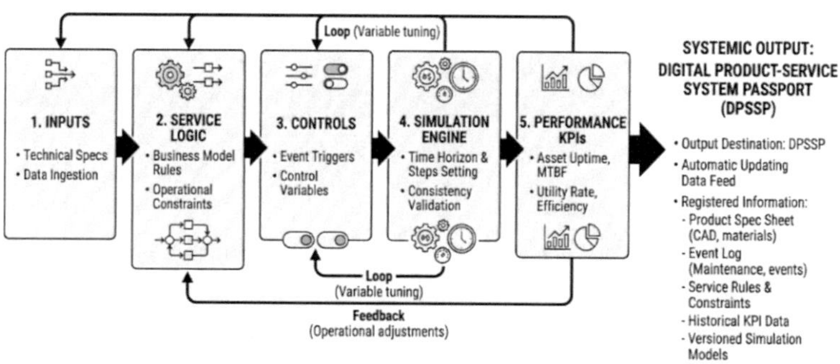

Fig. 1. DT–based simulation framework and DPSSP integration flow

Within this architecture, lifecycle intelligence is achieved through the operational interplay of DT, AAS, DPSSP, and MAS. DT acts as the real-time boundary, continuously capturing asset operational states and dynamically updating reliability parameters (e.g., MTTF) based on actual usage intensity. These live state variations are systematically structured via AAS specifications (IEC 63278), providing the semantic interoperability required to seamlessly update the DPSSP. The DPSSP serves as the comprehensive, standardized lifecycle ledger that materializes this data-driven history. Finally, the MAS engine ingests these historical and state parameters from the DPSSP to project future scenarios.

3.2 PSS & DPSSP Agents

Multi-Agent Simulation (MAS), as implemented in AnyLogic, provides a flexible and scalable paradigm for representing complex systems composed of interacting entities. In this approach, a model is structured around agent classes, which define the properties, behaviors, and interaction logic of different system components. Each agent is instantiated as an autonomous entity capable of evolving over time and interacting with other agents and the surrounding environment. Figure 2 presents DT–based simulation framework, its agents, interaction logics, and continuous data update integrated into the DPSSP.

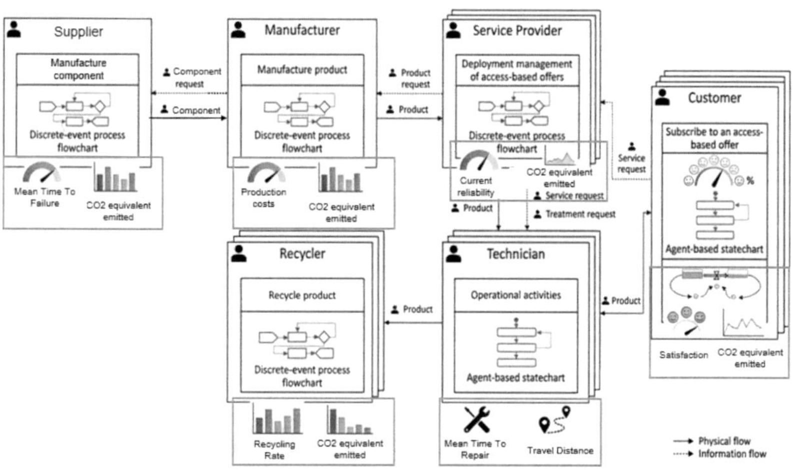

Fig. 2. DT–based simulation framework agents, adapted from [11]

In the proposed framework, agents are used to represent the heterogeneous elements of the PSS, enriched with data from the DPSSP. Each agent encapsulates economic, environmental, and behavioral attributes, enabling a detailed and dynamic representation of system-level phenomena during simulation execution.

To ensure clarity and modularity, agents are organized into two main categories:

Organizational agents represent stationary system actors, such as manufacturers, service providers, and customers. These agents represent the decision and aggregation nodes characterizing the PSS ecosystem. These agents are geographically located within the GIS-based simulation environment and act as hubs where key lifecycle activities occur. Each organizational agent is associated with a fixed position on the GIS map; it can host and manage one or more product agents; and it collects and aggregates lifecycle data from the products interacting with it.

In particular, these agents are responsible for tracking and computing:

- Economic indicators, including production costs, transportation costs, repair costs, and total lifecycle costs;
- Environmental indicators, such as CO_2 emissions associated with production, transportation, repair, and their cumulative impact.

By aggregating these data, organizational agents contribute to the generation and continuous update of the DPSSP data, enabling traceability and lifecycle assessment at system level.

Operational agents represent dynamic entities that actively evolve within the simulation environment, enabling the evolution or even execution of processes and PSS lifecycles over time. These include product agents, vehicles, and workers, each characterized by specific behaviors and roles. Among them, the *product agent* plays a central role in simulation. It represents the core entity whose lifecycle is tracked and analyzed across different stages of the PSS. Each product agent evolves through a defined lifecycle, interacting with multiple organizational agents and generating data that feed the DPSSP. Operational agents are characterized by:

- Mobility within the GIS environment;
- State-dependent behaviors and lifecycle transitions;
- The execution of specific functions (e.g., transportation by vehicles, operations performed by workers).

During the simulation, operational agents continuously generate and update a wide range of data, including cost-related information; environmental impacts (e.g., CO_2 emissions); time-related metrics (e.g., processing and transportation times); current operational state.

By simulating autonomous interactions among organizational and operational agents, MAS bridges the gap between static passport records and dynamic operational forecasting, enabling risk-free strategic and tactical decision-making regarding maintenance costs and Carbon Footprint impacts. Moreover, the integration of agent-level data with the DPSSP ensures that each lifecycle event contributes to a comprehensive and continuously evolving digital representation of the Product-Service System.

3.3 Simulation Scenarios

To ensure that the research approach used supports the entire PSS lifecycle, different decision-making processes, and the different actors across the value chain, a set of simulation scenarios has been proposed to cover impact estimation, end-of-life decision making, supply chain impact, usage monitoring and maintenance approaches evaluation.

All the proposed simulation scenarios, as described in Table 2, apply a multi-agent simulation approach, where strategy monitoring and decision-making processes at operational, tactical and strategical levels are enabled by interaction among the stakeholders involved in the value chain.

Furthermore, key elements derived from the research assumptions—reflecting the primary simulation objectives—have been systematically embedded within the scenarios. These include: (i) the environmental impact of alternative supply chain configurations at both local and global scales; (ii) the adoption of eco-friendly practices;

(iii) the emergence of novel product behaviours; and (iv) the redesign of Product–Service Systems (PSS) across the entire lifecycle. These dimensions are coherently integrated while ensuring alignment with data-sharing mechanisms enabled by the Digital Product–Service System Passport (DPSSP) (Table 1).

Table 1. Simulation scenarios description in terms of involved actors and simulation purposes

Simulation Scenario	As a (Role)	I want to	So that
PSS Impact Estimation	PSS Manufacturer	be able to estimate the impact of new and existing PSS based on different usage scenarios and business models	I can optimize the product design and business model to minimize environmental impact
End of Life Decision Making	PSS Manufacturer, Service provider	be able to virtually test multiple End of Life options (e.g. recycle, refurbish, reuse) and define their flows	I can better support circular economy decisions and improve the spare parts management
Supply Chain Impact	Supplier	be able to estimate the impact of new and existing PSS designed by the service provider on my supply chain	I can adapt the logistic and production operations to the new PSS product
PSS Usage Monitoring	Customer	be able to monitor and forecast my energy and material consumptions	I can adjust my habits to reduce energy bills and carbon footprint
Maintenance Approaches Evaluation	Service provider, PSS manufacturer	be able to test impacts of different maintenance flows (remote, on site, self) and approaches (i.e. predictive)	I can set business targets and estimate CF and costs savings

4 Implementing the Model

Due to space limitations, it is not possible to provide a comprehensive description of all the implemented simulation scenarios. Therefore, this section focuses on the scenario related to PSS Impact Estimation, which represents a key aspect for supporting decision-making within the proposed framework.

4.1 Model's Main Elements

The simulation model is initialized at time zero by instantiating all *organizational agents* (e.g., manufacturers, service providers, customers) and any *operational agent* already present at the beginning of the simulation. This initial configuration defines the structural backbone of the PSS within the GIS-enabled environment.

The model evolves over discrete time steps, where each simulated year introduces a new set of *product agents*, representing market demand. The number of products generated annually is defined as an input parameter, enabling the simulation of different demand scenarios and production strategies.

Upon creation, each product agent is assigned a set of attributes that define its lifecycle behavior, including:

- The *associated service type*, determined statistically based on input distributions;
- The *target customer*, also assigned probabilistically;
- The *pricing model*, currently defined as either pay-per-use or one-off.

The model also incorporates *service contract management*, which governs the interaction between products and customers. Each product is associated with a service contract characterized by:

- A predefined duration (input parameter);
- A specific cost structure for the customer.

According to Table 2, each agent is directly connected to an agent attribute derived from the DPSSP.

Table 2. Agent attributes derived from DPSSP data structure

Agent Type	Agent Economic Attributes	Agent Environmental Attributes
Manufacturer/Service Provider	• Production Cost • Transportation Cost • Repair Cost	• Production CO_2 emissions • Transportation CO_2 emissions • Repair CO_2 emissions
Product	• Production Cost • Transportation Cost • Repair Cost • Life time • MTTF and MTTR	• Production CO_2 emissions • Transportation CO_2 emissions • Repair CO_2 emissions • Product usage CO_2 emissions
Maintener	• Repair Cost	Repair CO_2 emissions

From a structural perspective, each product agent embeds a list of *subcomponents*, whose data are derived from the product's DPSSP, and which play a key role in determining maintenance dynamics throughout the lifecycle. Each component is characterized by reliability parameters, namely *Mean Time To Failure (MTTF)* and *Mean Time To Repair (MTTR)*. The MTTF is dynamically influenced by the component's usage intensity, defined as an input parameter; therefore, the MTTF can be continuously updated within the component's DPSSP to assess its current reliability. In the current scenario, both MTTF and MTTR are provided as input parameters to the simulation and are retrieved from the DPSSP data structure. Conversely, in the maintenance approaches evaluation scenario, which will be implemented in future work, the MTTR will be calculated directly within the simulation environment by modelling and simulating the maintenance intervention and product repair times.

The lifecycle of a product agent is modeled as a sequence of states (Fig. 3), including production, distribution, operation, maintenance, and contract-related phases. Initially, newly created products are located within the corresponding manufacturer agent. They are subsequently transferred, if applicable, to service providers and then to end customers. These transitions occur within the GIS environment and contribute to the continuous update of both *product-level* and *organizational-level* indicators, including costs and CO_2 emissions.

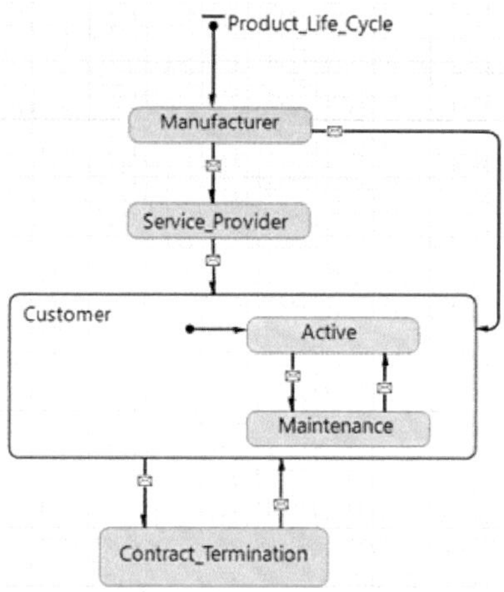

Fig. 3. Product lifecycle

4.2 Key Functionalities

The model implements a set of core functionalities aimed at capturing the dynamic, economic, and environmental behavior of the PSS enriched by DPSSP data.

A key functionality is the lifecycle tracking of product agents, which continuously updates:

- Economic indicators (e.g., production, transportation, maintenance, and service costs);
- Environmental indicators (e.g., CO_2 emissions associated with each lifecycle phase);
- Operational metrics (e.g., time in state, current status).

During the middle-of-life phase, when the product is actively operated by the customer, periodic updates are performed to capture usage-related costs and associated emissions. This approach enables a more accurate representation of operational impacts over time. The aforementioned indicators may be incorporated into the DPSSP to enhance product transparency and support compliance requirements or, alternatively, shared with stakeholders across the value chain. While not mandatory, this functionality represents a valuable capability enabled by the DPSSP.

Another core functionality is the maintenance management mechanism, driven by component-level reliability parameters. While the product is in operation, the model identifies the component with the minimum MTTF and schedules a failure event accordingly. Once the failure occurs, the product transitions to a maintenance state, where it remains for a duration equal to the corresponding MTTR. After maintenance completion, all relevant product parameters are updated, and the product returns to an operational state.

At the end of the service contract period, the product enters an unsubscribed state, where a probabilistic decision is made between:

- Contract renewal, potentially with a different service configuration;
- Service termination.

In the case of renewal, the product re-enters the active state, and its lifecycle continues with updated parameters. Conversely, if the service is terminated, the product is no longer tracked within the simulation, even if it remains physically operational, as it is no longer associated with an active service contract.

Overall, these functionalities enable the model to simulate complex PSS dynamics, supporting the evaluation of different business models, service strategies, and lifecycle configurations, while ensuring continuous data updates that can be integrated into the DPSSP to facilitate collaboration among stakeholders and/or to ensure transparency for customers.

5 Discussion

The proposed DT-based simulation framework has been designed to ensure a high degree of adaptiveness, scalability, and replicability, which are key requirements for its applicability across different PSS contexts and industrial domains. In particular, these characteristics are further strengthened by the integration with the DPSSP, which provides a structured and lifecycle-oriented data backbone for the framework.

From an adaptiveness perspective, the model is highly configurable through input parameters that govern both structural and behavioral aspects. These include demand profiles (e.g., number of products introduced per year), service configurations, pricing models, component reliability parameters (MTTF and MTTR), and contract conditions. This parameterization enables the model to adapt to different business scenarios, market conditions, and product typologies without requiring structural modifications. Thanks to the DPSSP integration, such configurations can be directly linked to standardized product- and service-related data, ensuring consistency and traceability across lifecycle phases. Moreover, the agent-based architecture allows the easy extension of agent behaviors and the introduction of new service logics or lifecycle states, making it suitable for exploring multiple PSS decision-making processes, including maintenance optimization, usage monitoring, supply-chain analysis, and end-of-life decision-making.

Regarding scalability, the use of an agent-based approach allows the model to handle increasing levels of complexity in terms of both the number of agents and the richness of interactions. A comparison with prior simulation-based approaches for PSS, such as the work of Rondini et al. (2017) [12], further highlights the contribution of the proposed framework. While Rondini et al. (2017) [12] focused on evaluating the effectiveness of hybrid simulation models—combining discrete event and agent-based paradigms—to capture the dynamic and behavioural complexity of PSS provision processes, the present work extends this perspective by embedding simulation within a DT–based architecture, and integrating the whole framework with the DPSSP as principal backbone of the framework. In particular, whereas Rondini et al. (2017) [12] primarily addressed the representation of customer behaviour, resource management, and process performance within a simulation environment, the proposed framework integrates simulation with structured lifecycle data as part of the DPSSP and thankful to AAS. This enables continuous data exchange and supports a more comprehensive lifecycle-oriented analysis, including economic and environmental indicators.

Moreover, the adoption of a Digital Twin paradigm allows the transition from isolated simulation models toward an interoperable and potentially real-time decision-support system, where simulation results can be dynamically updated and contextualized using data from the physical system. As a result, the proposed approach can be interpreted as an evolution of simulation-based PSS modelling toward data-driven and interoperable Digital Twin ecosystems.

Indeed, the framework can simulate large populations of product agents over extended time horizons, while maintaining a clear separation between organizational and operational entities. This modular structure supports the incremental addition of new agents (e.g., additional manufacturers, service providers, or logistics entities) and functionalities without affecting the overall model consistency. Furthermore, the integration with a GIS environment enables the model to scale geographically, supporting analyses at different spatial resolutions.

Finally, replicability is ensured through the formalization of the model structure and the use of standardized data inputs. The clear definition of agent classes, lifecycle logic, and interaction mechanisms allows the framework to be reproduced and applied to different case studies with limited effort. By relying on configurable input datasets, rather than hard-coded assumptions, the model can be easily transferred to other industrial sectors or adapted to different PSS configurations. In this context, DPSSP plays a key role by providing a common and reusable reference for lifecycle, operational, and sustainability data, facilitating the replication of the framework across different domains while preserving data interoperability.

6 Conclusions

This study positions the convergence of DPP, servitization, DTs, AAS, and data sharing paradigms as a foundational enabler for advancing data-driven and circular manufacturing systems. By proposing a unified DT-based simulation framework, the research demonstrates how structured lifecycle data—integrated through the DPSSP—can enhance decision making throughout the entire PSS lifecycle, from design and operation to maintenance and end of life. The framework provides a risk-free environment for scenario exploration, allowing stakeholders to evaluate the implications of functional and non-functional changes across operational, tactical, and strategic levels.

Through its interoperable architecture, grounded in AAS principles, it enables scalable orchestration of DTs and simulations across distributed infrastructures, thereby supporting transparency, sustainability assessment, and the redesign of PSS models based on predictive insights and simulated scenarios. Furthermore, the proposed approach lays the groundwork for next generation DPSSP implementations capable of fostering circularity, reducing environmental impacts, and strengthening service-driven business models, while offering a robust methodological and technological foundation for future research and industrial adoption.

While the proposed framework is demonstrated through the specific "PSS Impact Estimation" simulation scenario, this application should be interpreted as an illustrative instantiation. The selected use case effectively showcases the capabilities of the DT–based simulation framework and its integration with the DPSSP. At the same time, the model has been deliberately generalised to support seamless adaptation across a wide range of PSS contexts and different scenarios, without requiring substantial structural modifications. This highlights its intrinsic flexibility, positioning it as a replicable solution for multiple domains and use cases. While certain aspects—such as stakeholder behaviour, service contracts, and decision-making logic—are represented through simplified or parametric assumptions, this modelling strategy enhances the portability of the framework and facilitates its deployment in heterogeneous environments. Consequently, even though complex real-world dynamics (e.g., human decision processes, regulatory constraints, and market conditions) are not exhaustively captured, the framework provides a robust and extensible foundation that can be progressively refined and specialised according to the needs of specific PSS scenarios.

Future developments will primarily focus on extending and consolidating the framework along two main directions. First, additional simulation scenarios will be implemented and validated, allowing a more comprehensive assessment of the framework's applicability across different lifecycle phases and PSS decision-making contexts.

It will furtherly investigate the extension of operational agents, as for example by integrating recyclers and remanufacturers in the already presented *PSS impact estimation* and, specifically, in the *End-of-Life Decision Making* one thus enabling the evaluation of circularity-oriented strategies supported by DPSSP lifecycle data. Furthermore, *PSS Usage Monitoring* and *Maintenance Approaches Evaluation* scenarios will be investigated by introducing real-time data integration, enabling a tighter integration between the simulated environment and the physical counterpart, and allowing model inputs and outputs to be directly compared with, or calibrated against, the behavior of the real system. Finally, the framework will also be extended toward *Supply Chain Impact* assessment scenario to evaluate the economic and environmental impacts across all stakeholders within the PSS ecosystem. Such a closed-loop interaction is expected to enhance the reliability of the simulation results and to support more effective real-time and data-driven decision-making across the PSS lifecycle.

Lastly, the model will be progressively refined in terms of functional coverage, scalability, and behavioral realism, enabling a closer approximation of real-world PSS dynamics, thankful to the demonstration in different application scenarios. This includes the enhancement of agent interaction logics, lifecycle representations, and service execution flows, while preserving the DPSSP as the central source of structured lifecycle information.

Acknowledgments. The research described has been carried out as part of the PSS-Pass Project, which has received funding from the European Union's Horizon Europe Research and Innovation Programme under grant agreement No. 101177594.

Disclosure of Interests. The authors have no competing interests to declare that are relevant to the content of this article.

References

1. Mont, O.K.: Clarifying the concept of product-service system. J. Clean. Prod. **10**, 237–245 (2002). https://doi.org/10.1016/S0959-6526(01)00039-7
2. Baines, T.S. et al.: State-of-the-art in product-service systems. Proc. Inst. Mech. Eng. Part B J. Eng. Manuf. **221**, 1543–1552 (2007). https://doi.org/10.1243/09544054JEM858
3. Tukker, A.: Eight types of product-service system: eight ways to sustainability? Experiences from SusProNet. Bus. Strategy Environ. **13**, 246–260 (2004). https://doi.org/10.1002/bse.414
4. Pirola, F., Boucher, X., Wiesner, S., Pezzotta, G.: Digital technologies in product-service systems: a literature review and a research agenda. Comput. Ind. **123** (2020). https://doi.org/10.1016/j.compind.2020.103301
5. Mourtzis, D., Angelopoulos, J.: Challenges and opportunities for the design and development of intelligent, sustainable and resilient personalized product-service systems towards industry 5.0. In: Pezzotta, G., Sala, R., Boucher, X., Bertoni, M., Pirola, F. (eds.) Data-Driven Decision Making for Product Service Systems, pp. 27–62. Springer International Publishing, Cham (2024). https://doi.org/10.1007/978-3-031-60082-1_2
6. Acerbi, F., Sassanelli, C., Terzi, S., Taisch, M.: A systematic literature review on data and information required for circular manufacturing strategies adoption. Sustainability. **13**, 2047 (2021). https://doi.org/10.3390/su13042047
7. Maló, P. et al.: From static records to smart passports: evolving digital product passports toward product-service system integration. In: 2025 21st International Conference on Distributed Computing in Smart Systems and the Internet of Things (DCOSS-IoT), pp. 1087–1094 (2025). https://doi.org/10.1109/DCOSS-IoT65416.2025.00163
8. Carminati, L., Arioli, V., Sala, R., Pirola, F., Pezzotta, G.: Towards effective implementation of digital product passports: stakeholders involved and data requirements. In: Mizuyama, H., Morinaga, E., Nonaka, T., Kaihara, T., von Cieminski, G., Romero, D. (eds.) Advances in Production Management Systems. Cyber-Physical-Human Production Systems: Human-AI Collaboration and beyond, pp. 537–553. Springer Nature, Cham (2025)
9. Monteiro, J., Barata, J., Gentilini, S.: A digital twin-based digital product passport. Procedia Comput. Sci. **246**, 4123–4132 (2024)
10. Arioli, V., Sala, R., Pirola, F., Pezzotta, G.: Requirements definition for the economic, environmental and social sustainability assessment of product-service systems: state-of-the-art. Comput. Ind. Eng. **208** (2025)
11. Roci, M. et al.: Towards circular manufacturing systems implementation: a complex adaptive systems perspective using modelling and simulation as a quantitative analysis tool. Sustainable Prod. Consumption. **31**, 97–112 (2022). https://doi.org/10.1016/j.spc.2022.01.033

12. Rondini, A., Tornese, F., Gnoni, M.G., Pezzotta, G., Pinto, R.: Hybrid simulation modelling as a supporting tool for sustainable product service systems: a critical analysis. Int. J. Prod. Res. **55**, 6932–6945 (2017). https://doi.org/10.1080/00207543.2017.1330569
13. Lee, S., Geum, Y., Lee, H., Park, Y.: Dynamic and multidimensional measurement of product-service system (PSS) sustainability: a triple bottom line (TBL)-based system dynamics approach. J. Clean. Prod. **32**, 173–182 (2012). https://doi.org/10.1016/j.jclepro.2012.03.032
14. Fani, V., Pirola, F., Bindi, B., Bandinelli, R., Pezzotta, G.: Design product-service systems by using a hybrid approach: the fashion renting business model. Sustain. Switz. **14** (2022). https://doi.org/10.3390/su14095207
15. Koide, R., Yamamoto, H., Nansai, K., Murakami, S.: Agent-based model for assessment of multiple circular economy strategies: quantifying product-service diffusion, circularity, and sustainability. Resour. Conserv. Recycl. **199**, 107216 (2023). https://doi.org/10.1016/j.resconrec.2023.107216
16. Dobaj, J., Riel, A., Macher, G., Egretzberger, M.: A method for deriving technical requirements of digital twins as industrial product-service system enablers. In: Yilmaz, M., Clarke, P., Messnarz, R., Wöran, B. (eds.) Systems, Software and Services Process Improvement, pp. 378–392. Springer International Publishing, Cham (2022). https://doi.org/10.1007/978-3-031-15559-8_27
17. Alix, T., Zacharewicz, G.: Product-service systems modelling and simulation as a strategic diagnosis tool. In: Emmanouilidis, C., Taisch, M., Kiritsis, D. (eds.) Advances in Production Management Systems. Competitive Manufacturing for Innovative Products and Services, pp. 361–368. Springer, Berlin, Heidelberg (2013). https://doi.org/10.1007/978-3-642-40361-3_46
18. Coba, C.M., Boucher, X., Medini, K., Gonzalez-Feliu, J.: Simulation-based approach to apply uncertainty evaluation framework, for PSS economic models. Procedia CIRP. **83**, 50–56 (2019). https://doi.org/10.1016/j.procir.2019.02.138

A Model-Based Testing Framework for Digital Battery Passport Lifecycle Systems

Elena Andrushchenko(✉), Dogan Efe, and Roland Jochem

Technical University of Berlin, Pascalstr. 8-9, 10587 Berlin, Germany
e.andrushchenko@tu-berlin.de

Abstract. From February 2027 onward, the Digital Battery Passport (DBP), required under EU Battery Regulation 2023/1542, must operate as a distributed compliance-critical system whose correctness is determined by regulatory obligations rather than by implementation logic alone. The published standard EN 18222 defines a REST-based lifecycle API for registration, update, deletion, and archiving, while EN 18239 specifies an access control concept that separates openly available public data from controlled data restricted to authenticated and authorized actors. Verifying that a DBP implementation enforces this two-level access model, performs deletion correctly across five interacting system components, and preserves a legally compliant audit trail cannot be achieved through isolated testing of single API functions. This paper presents a four-layer Model-Based Testing (MBT) framework derived from the JTC-24 standards. The DBP lifecycle is represented as an Extended Finite State Machine (EFSM) comprising seven states and nineteen transitions. On this basis, test purposes are derived systematically using transition coverage, guard inversion, and boundary value analysis, resulting in forty-two test cases spanning nine API operations and seven failure classes. Abstract test cases are specified in accordance with ETSI ES 201 873 (TTCN-3), while authentication-related testing is aligned with the ETSI EN 319 and TS 119 standards. Remaining normative uncertainties are captured as assumption points, allowing the framework to remain adaptable as the specifications evolve. The framework is pre-operational, since test purposes can be developed before a complete DBP implementation is available.

Keywords: Digital Battery Passport · Model-Based · ETSI TTCN-3 · Extended Finite State Machine · Distributed Systems Testing · Regulatory Compliance

1 Introduction

From 18 February 2027, electric vehicle batteries, industrial batteries above 2 kWh, and other regulated battery categories placed on the European Union market must be accompanied by a Digital Battery Passport (DBP) [1]. The DBP is intended to provide structured digital information on battery identification, sustainability, performance, and lifecycle-related data. As the battery-specific implementation of the broader Digital Product Passport (DPP) concept, it is not merely an information repository, but a distributed compliance-critical system whose behaviour is defined by regulatory and standardization requirements.

Published by Springer Nature Switzerland AG 2027
G. Pezzotta et al. (Eds.): APMS 2026, IFIP AICT 808, pp. 46–60, 2027.
https://doi.org/10.1007/978-3-032-38594-9_4

The emerging European standardization landscape makes DBP lifecycle management a compliance-critical testing problem. Registration, creation, update, archiving, and deletion are not merely isolated implementation functions, but interdependent operations whose correctness depends on access rights, persistence, registry coordination, backup synchronization, and auditability [2–4]. A conforming implementation must therefore be assessed across lifecycle states, actors, and system components rather than through isolated API responses alone.

This complexity becomes especially visible in update and deletion processes. An update may require the previous DBP version to be archived, while deletion must remove the active version from public visibility without compromising archived records required for regulatory access. At the same time, the DBP ecosystem is still evolving, and several lifecycle, access-control, and archiving parameters remain insufficiently specified for deterministic testing. Conformance testing must therefore address both defined requirements and areas of normative uncertainty.

Conventional unit and integration testing are insufficient for this purpose. They can verify isolated functions or pairwise interactions, but they do not provide systematic evidence that the complete lifecycle choreography conforms to the normative specification. In the DBP context, the test oracle is not derived from implementation logic alone, but from legal and technical requirements distributed across several standards. This creates the need for a traceable, model-based testing approach that connects regulatory clauses to lifecycle states, transitions, guards, and test purposes.

Model-Based Testing (MBT) offers a suitable foundation for this task. In MBT, expected system behaviour is represented through a formal model, from which test cases can be derived systematically [5, 6]. For DBP lifecycle systems, an Extended Finite State Machine (EFSM) is particularly appropriate because the correctness of API operations depends on lifecycle state, actor permissions, credential validity, payload conditions, and interactions with external components. However, the application of MBT to DBP lifecycle conformance testing under evolving regulatory and standardization conditions has not yet been sufficiently addressed.

Therefore, this paper addresses the following research question:

How can a model-based testing framework be designed to support pre-operational conformance testing of Digital Battery Passport lifecycle systems under evolving regulatory and standardization requirements?

To answer this question, the paper develops a four-layer MBT framework derived from JTC-24 standards and related regulatory requirements. The contribution is fourfold. First, it provides an EFSM-based lifecycle model for DBP systems. Second, it defines a systematic procedure for deriving test purposes using transition coverage, guard inversion, and boundary value analysis. Third, it integrates ETSI testing concepts into a four-layer framework architecture. Fourth, it introduces assumption points to document unresolved regulatory parameters and link them to affected model elements and test purposes.

The proposed framework supports early-stage DBP testing by translating regulatory requirements into testable conditions before the complete infrastructure is available. Since it has not yet been validated with a real DBP system, future work should evaluate it using prototype or operational implementations.

2 Related Work

2.1 Model-Based Testing for Regulatory Compliance

Model-based testing (MBT) derives test cases from formal models of expected system behaviour. This is particularly relevant for compliance-driven systems, where expected behaviour is defined not only by implementation requirements but also by external regulations and standards. The theoretical foundation for conformance testing is provided by the ioco relation, while finite state machines and extended finite state machines are commonly used for systems whose behaviour depends on states, inputs, outputs, and transition conditions [5–7].

Prior work has applied MBT in regulated domains such as avionics, automotive software, railway control, and GDPR compliance [8–11]. These studies show that regulatory and standardisation requirements can be transformed into formal models and testable specifications. However, they do not address Digital Product Passport systems, where lifecycle management, REST-based interfaces, access control, archiving, registry interaction, and evolving requirements must be tested together.

2.2 State-Based Testing of REST APIs

REST API testing increasingly considers state-dependent behaviour, since many API operations are valid only after previous operations have established the required system state. Existing approaches use finite state machines, UML protocol state machines, property graphs, or OpenAPI-derived dependency models to represent valid and invalid operation sequences [12–17]. This is relevant for DBP lifecycle testing because registration, creation, update, deletion, and deregistration are not independent API calls, but state-dependent lifecycle transitions.

Most existing REST API testing approaches derive such dependencies from technical artefacts such as OpenAPI specifications or observed API behaviour. In the DBP context, however, the relevant constraints originate primarily from regulatory and standardisation documents. The test oracle must therefore be derived from normative requirements rather than from implementation-level API descriptions alone.

2.3 TTCN-3 and Conformance Testing in Distributed Systems

TTCN-3 is a standardised language for specifying and executing conformance tests. Although it was originally developed for telecommunications, it has also been applied in domains such as automotive systems, railway control, vehicle-to-grid communication, IoT protocols, and security testing [9, 10, 18–24]. These applications show that TTCN-3 is suitable for abstract test specification, platform-specific adapters, and verdict assignment.

This is relevant for DBP systems because conformance testing must cover distributed interactions between the Economic Operator's (EO) DBP server, Backup Service Provider (BSP), authentication services, audit mechanisms, and the EU Registry. Nevertheless, existing TTCN-3 applications do not address the specific combination of DBP lifecycle regulation, two-tier data access, archiving obligations, deletion choreography, and evolving DPP standards.

2.4 Specification Uncertainty and Digital Passport Research

A further challenge is that the DPP standardization environment is still evolving. Several testing-relevant parameters remain underspecified, which means that open assumptions must be represented explicitly rather than ignored. Research on uncertain and underspecified requirements shows that such open parameters can be represented explicitly rather than ignored [25–27]. This provides a theoretical basis for the assumption point mechanism used in this paper.

Digital Product Passport research has mainly focused on requirements, technical architectures, implementation concepts, data structures, and value ecosystems [28–34]. Related reviews also show that regulatory compliance and testing remain underdeveloped topics in this field [35, 36].

Existing research therefore provides important foundations, but these strands have not yet been integrated for pre-operational DBP lifecycle conformance testing. MBT offers formal test derivation, REST API testing provides methods for state-dependent operation sequences, TTCN-3 supports standardized conformance test specification, and uncertainty research enables the explicit representation of incomplete requirements. This gap is addressed by the framework proposed in this paper.

3 Methodological Approach and Normative Basis

3.1 Methodological Approach

This study follows a document-based framework development approach. Its objective is not to evaluate existing DBP implementation, but to derive a pre-operational conformance testing framework from regulatory and standardization requirements.

The methodological process consisted of five steps. First, the relevant sources were selected, including the EU Battery Regulation [1], the Ecodesign for Sustainable Products Regulation [37], the JTC-24 standards on lifecycle APIs, access control, storage and archiving, communication protocols, and identifiers [2–4, 38, 39], as well as ETSI conformance testing standards [18, 40–43]. Second, requirements were extracted if they influenced externally observable system behaviour, including lifecycle operations, permitted and prohibited states, actor roles, access conditions, authentication levels, data visibility rules, archiving obligations, synchronization requirements, registry notifications, and audit obligations.

Third, the extracted requirements were translated into an EFSM by representing lifecycle phases as states, API operations as input events, HTTP responses and state changes as outputs, and access, payload, synchronization, and audit requirements as guards and actions. Fourth, test purposes were derived using transition coverage, guard inversion, and boundary value analysis. Fifth, unresolved or underspecified requirements were documented as assumption points whenever a standard defined required behaviour in principle but did not yet specify a parameter needed for deterministic testing. Each assumption point was linked to the affected EFSM transition and test purpose.

3.2 Normative Basis of the DBP Testing Challenge

The proposed framework is derived from the European standardization landscape for Digital Product Passports. EN 18222 defines the REST-based lifecycle and registry API operations that form the input alphabet of the EFSM [3]. EN 18239 specifies access rights management, authentication requirements, role-based access, and audit logging [2]. EN 18221 defines requirements for storage, archiving, and persistence, including the obligation to preserve archived versions [4]. EN 18216 and EN 18219 provide supporting requirements for communication protocols and unique identifiers [38, 39].

In the proposed framework, these documents serve as the normative basis for deriving the EFSM, test purposes, and assumption points. Lifecycle and registry operations are translated into input events, access and state conditions into guards, and requirements related to archiving, synchronization, registry notification, and auditability into actions and postconditions. This translation makes it possible to use the regulatory and standardization requirements as a structured test oracle for DBP lifecycle conformance testing.

3.3 The Two-Tier Data Access Model and Its Testing Implications

The DBP access model distinguishes between a public and a controlled data tier. Public data must be accessible without authentication, whereas controlled data may only be disclosed to authenticated and authorized actors with a verified role. This distinction creates a central conformance-testing challenge: the system must provide open access to legally public information while preventing unauthorized disclosure of controlled data.

The two-tier model is used as a testing abstraction and does not imply identical access conditions for all controlled data. Within the controlled tier, access rights may differ by actor group, role, assurance level, and intended purpose, for example for market surveillance authorities, notified bodies, the Commission, repairers, remanufacturers, second-life operators, recyclers, or other actors with a legitimate interest [1, 37]. Controlled-access testing must therefore verify not only authentication, but also whether the requested data elements are justified for the specific actor and use case.

For testing, public access tests verify that unauthenticated requests return the required public fields while excluding controlled data. Controlled access tests verify credential validity, role scope, assurance level, and field-level permissions, including negative cases such as missing credentials, insufficient assurance levels, invalid roles, or access outside the permitted scope. Both successful and rejected controlled-access attempts must be auditable.

These requirements are represented in the EFSM as guards, postconditions, and observable outputs. Authentication, authorization, role scope, and field-level permissions define guard conditions, while data disclosure, rejection, and audit logging are treated as observable outputs. The resulting test purposes therefore cover unauthenticated public access, authorized controlled access, role-scope violations, and field-level permission boundaries. Figure 1 summarizes the two-tier access model and its conformance testing scope.

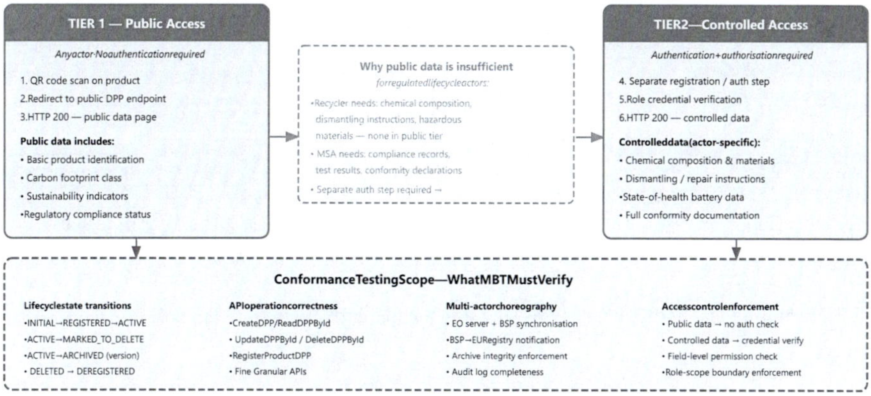

Fig. 1. DPP two-tier data access model and conformance testing scope

4 Extended Finite State Machine Based Lifecycle Model

This section translates the normative lifecycle requirements identified in Sect. 3 into an EFSM-based lifecycle model. The model defines the states, transitions, guards, and actions that later serve as the basis for test purpose derivation.

4.1 Model Structure

The DBP lifecycle is modelled as an EFSM $M = (S, \Sigma I, \Sigma O, T, V, s_0, F)$. The set S contains the seven lifecycle states INITIAL, REGISTERED, ACTIVE, ARCHIVED, MARKED_TO_DELETE, DELETED, and DEREGISTERED. The input alphabet ΣI consists of API method invocations defined in EN 18222, while the output alphabet ΣO includes HTTP status codes, returned data, state updates, and audit outcomes. The transition relation T defines how the DBP moves from one lifecycle state to another when a specific input is received and the corresponding guard conditions are satisfied. The variable set V captures compliance-relevant information, including actor credentials, role permissions, payload validity, synchronization status, registry notification status, and audit log status.

The initial state s_0 is INITIAL, representing a DBP before registration. The final state set F contains DEREGISTERED, representing a passport whose active lifecycle has been completed and for which the registry has been notified. Figure 2 illustrates the principal lifecycle transitions of the EFSM. The complete model contains nineteen transitions, including additional read, access-control, archive-access, invalid-state, synchronizations, registry-notification, and audit-related transitions used for test purpose derivation.

The EFSM is not intended to reproduce a legally prescribed lifecycle sequence one-to-one. Instead, it represents a conformance-testing abstraction that translates lifecycle API behaviour, access-control requirements, archiving and persistence obligations, registry interaction, and auditability requirements into a testable state model.

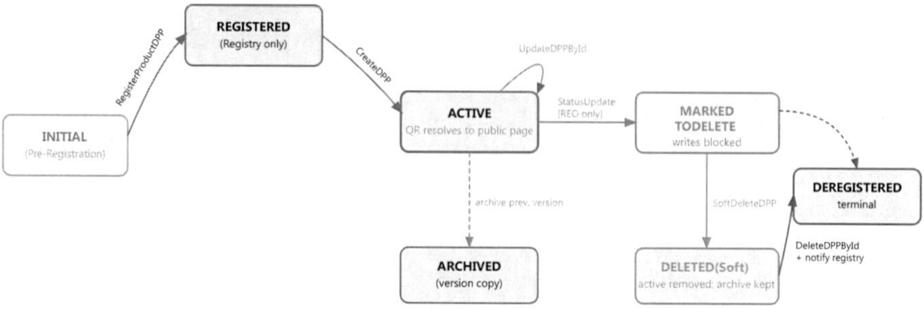

Fig. 2. Simplified DBP lifecycle EFSM showing the main lifecycle states and principal transitions

4.2 Lifecycle Logic

The EFSM represents the DBP as a regulated lifecycle object rather than as a set of independent API endpoints. A passport moves from INITIAL to REGISTERED after successful registry registration and then to ACTIVE after creation of the operational DBP record. In the ACTIVE state, read operations, authorized updates, and fine-granular lifecycle operations are permitted according to the applicable access rights. Each valid update creates an archived version of the previous record, while the current version remains active.

Deletion is represented as a multi-step conformance-testing abstraction rather than a legally prescribed technical sequence. A passport first enters the state MARKED_TO_DELETE, where deletion has been initiated and further write operations are blocked. The state DELETED represents the removal of the active DBP record from public availability, while archived versions remain accessible to authorized actors where required. The lifecycle reaches DEREGISTERED only after the relevant synchronization and registry notification conditions have been fulfilled. This abstraction enables deletion-related conformance risks to be tested systematically, including not only individual API calls but also the required order of lifecycle transitions and the preservation of compliance-relevant evidence, while remaining adaptable to future standards on deletion, deregistration, or recycling-related semantics.

The EFSM also captures invalid behaviour through guards. For example, an update is rejected if the passport is already marked for deletion, controlled data access is rejected if the actor lacks the required role or assurance level, and deletion cannot be completed if the required synchronization or registry notification condition is not satisfied. These guards later serve as the basis for negative test purposes derived through guard inversion.

4.3 Assumption Points

Some lifecycle conditions cannot yet be translated into deterministic test oracles because the underlying standards are still evolving. These uncertainties are documented as assumption points and linked to the affected transitions and test purposes. Table 1 presents selected assumption points that are relevant for the proposed lifecycle model.

Table 1. Selected assumption points for underspecified DBP lifecycle conditions

Assumption point	Underspecified condition and working assumption	Impact on testing
AP-RET-01	Retention period for archived versions	Defines archive accessibility tests after simulated time expiry
AP-SLA-01	BSP synchronization window	Defines timing conditions for deletion and synchronization failure tests
AP-FLD-01	Field-level permissions for controlled data	Defines access-control and role-scope boundary tests
AP-ARC-01	Archival granularity for frequent updates	Defines future scalability, retention, and environmental-impact tests
AP-DEL-01	Deletion and deregistration semantics	Defines test conditions for active-record removal, archive preservation, registry deregistration, and final passport cessation
AP-REG-01	Registry notification timing	Defines deregistration and notification-related test conditions

The assumption points allow test purposes to be derived before all regulatory details are finalized. When a delegated act or final standard clarifies an open parameter, only the affected transition and related test purposes need to be revised.

5 Four-Layer MBT Framework Architecture

The proposed approach structures the transformation of regulatory and standardization requirements into conformance-oriented test artefacts. As summarized in Table 2, the framework consists of four layers: normative specification, abstract system modelling, abstract test design, and executable test specification. The layer separation allows changes in evolving DBP standards to be localized. For example, a clarified access rule affects the actor-permission logic and related test purposes, while a revised synchronization requirement affects the corresponding transition guard and executable test condition.

The framework differs from conventional unit or integration testing because it does not focus on isolated API functions or pairwise component interactions. Instead, it evaluates whether lifecycle behaviour conforms to the normative specification across states, actors, components, and audit obligations. This is necessary for DBP systems because compliance depends on the combined execution of lifecycle APIs, access-control rules, archiving, backup synchronization, registry notification, and audit logging.

The framework is aligned with established ETSI conformance testing concepts. TTCN-3 provides the target notation for abstract and executable test specification [18], while ETSI ETR 141 supports test purpose derivation and verdict assignment [40]. In this framework, PASS indicates behaviour consistent with the normative requirement,

FAIL indicates observable non-conformance, and INCONCLUSIVE is used where the current specification does not yet provide a deterministic test oracle.

Table 2. Four-layer MBT framework for DBP lifecycle conformance testing

Layer	Function	Main output
Layer 1: Normative specification	Defines the regulatory and standardization requirements used as the test oracle	Compliance-relevant requirements
Layer 2: Abstract modelling	Translates requirements into lifecycle states, transitions, guards, actions, actor permissions, and assumption points	EFSM-based lifecycle model
Layer 3: Test purpose derivation	Applies transition coverage, guard inversion, and boundary value analysis to the EFSM	Abstract test purposes with verdict logic
Layer 4: Executable test specification	Transforms abstract test purposes into executable test artefacts	HTTP/JSON scripts, TTCN-3 modules, adapters, and mocks

Authentication-related tests for controlled DBP access are aligned with ETSI trust service and identity-proofing standards [41–43]. Since Tier 2 access depends on credential verification, assurance levels, and relying-party obligations, these requirements are represented as guards, postconditions, and verdict criteria attached to controlled-access, write, update, and delete transitions.

This architecture supports pre-operational DBP conformance testing. Test purposes can be derived before all infrastructure components are available, while mocks can represent external services such as the Backup Service Provider, authentication service, or EU Registry.

6 Test Purpose Derivation

This section operationalizes Layer 3 of the proposed framework by deriving abstract test purposes from the EFSM introduced in Sect. 4. The objective is to transform lifecycle states, transitions, guards, and assumption points into testable conformance conditions. Each test purpose is linked to an EFSM element and to the corresponding normative requirement or assumption point. This ensures traceability between regulatory expectations, model behaviour, and later executable test artefacts.

6.1 Derivation Criteria

Three criteria are used to derive test purposes from the DBP lifecycle EFSM. Transition coverage (TC) is used to derive positive test purposes for valid lifecycle transitions. Each

EFSM transition gives rise to at least one test purpose that verifies whether the transition is executed correctly when all required guards are satisfied. This forms the basic level of coverage needed to demonstrate lifecycle conformance.

Table 3. Representative excerpt from the DBP test purpose catalogue. (+) = positive test; (−) = negative/guard-inversion test

ID / API Method	Test Purpose and Precondition	Expected Outcome / Verdict
TP-01 RegisterProductDPP (+)	A correctly authenticated responsible EO (REO) can register a new DPP with valid identifiers. Precondition: REO holds valid credential; product ID is unique in registry.	HTTP 200 + registry ID; REGISTERED state confirmed; audit entry created → PASS
TP-02 RegisterProductDPP (−)	An unauthenticated actor cannot register a DPP. Precondition: No credential presented.	HTTP 401; no registry entry created; AUTH_FAIL logged → PASS
TP-05 UpdateDPPById (+)	Write-authorized actor can partially update an ACTIVE passport. Precondition: Actor holds write-scoped credential; DPP ACTIVE; payload valid.	HTTP 200 + updated DPP; previous version archived; EORI and timestamp in audit log → PASS
TP-06 UpdateDPPById (−)	Update of MARKED_TO_DELETE passport is blocked. Precondition: DPP status MARKED_TO_DELETE; actor otherwise authorized.	HTTP 409 PRECONDITION_VIOLATED; state unchanged; violation logged → PASS
TP-07 DeleteDPPById (+)	Full soft-deletion choreography executes correctly. Precondition: REO authenticated; MARKED_TO_DELETE; BSP reachable; registry available.	EO: HTTP 200; QR → HTTP 410; BSP confirms within SLA; registry: DEREGISTERED; complete audit trail → PASS
TP-09 ReadDPPById (+)	Unauthenticated request returns only public data tier. Precondition: No credential; DPP ACTIVE.	HTTP 200; only public data elements returned; no controlled data exposed → PASS

Guard inversion (GI) is used to derive negative test purposes. For every guard attached to a transition, a corresponding test purpose is created in which the guard is deliberately violated. This includes missing authentication, invalid credentials, insufficient role permissions, violated lifecycle preconditions, synchronization failure, data integrity failure, or missing audit evidence. Guard inversion is therefore used to verify that non-conforming behaviour is rejected correctly.

Boundary value analysis (BVA) is applied where transition behaviour depends on data-related or timing-related constraints. This includes payload schema validity, identifier formats, timing assumptions, retention assumptions, and field-level access boundaries. Boundary value analysis supports the derivation of test purposes close to the limits of valid and invalid behaviour.

When applied to the nineteen transitions of the DBP EFSM and their associated guard conditions, these three derivation criteria result in forty-two test cases. The number is obtained by deriving one positive test purpose for each valid transition and adding negative or boundary-oriented test purposes only where access, state, synchronization, audit, or data-related guards are defined.

6.2 Test Purpose Catalogue

Table 3 presents a representative excerpt from the test purpose catalogue. The selected test purposes illustrate how the derivation criteria are applied to registration, update, deletion, and two-tier access-control scenarios. The full catalogue comprises forty-two test cases derived from the nineteen EFSM transitions.

The excerpt covers both valid lifecycle progression and guard-inversion cases. It also shows how access-control tests distinguish between public visibility, controlled access, and role-scope violations.

7 Coverage Analysis

Figure 3 summarizes the test scope derived from the EFSM and the three derivation criteria. The matrix maps the main DBP lifecycle API operations to seven failure classes and distinguishes between mandatory, planned, and non-applicable tests.

The coverage distribution shows that operations involving state changes, access rights, payload validation, synchronization, or audit obligations require broader testing than public read operations. DeleteDPPById has the highest concentration of mandatory tests because deletion affects the active DBP record, archived versions, BSP synchronization, EU Registry notification, and audit evidence. A partial deletion may therefore cause regulatory non-conformance.

Audit gap tests are mandatory for all compliance-relevant operations because lifecycle changes, access decisions, failed authorization attempts, and registry interactions must remain traceable. Overall, the matrix follows a risk-oriented coverage logic: testing intensity increases with the regulatory relevance of the operation and the potential compliance impact of failure.

8 Discussion

The framework shows how conformance testing for DBP lifecycle systems can be approached before all infrastructure components are operational. Expected DBP behaviour is not defined by a single software specification, but by several regulatory and standardization documents. Treating these documents as the test oracle improves traceability between legal requirements, lifecycle behaviour, and test purposes.

API Operation	Auth Failure	Precond. Violation	Concurrent Conflict	BSP Sync Failure	Registry Gap	Data Integrity	Audit Gap
RegisterProductDPP Registry API	■	✓	✓	—	■	✓	■
CreateDPP Lifecycle API	■	✓	✓	■	—	■	■
ReadDPPById Lifecycle API	■	✓	—	—	—	■	■
ReadDPPByProductId Lifecycle API	■	✓	—	—	—	■	■
ReadDPPVersionByIdAndDate Lifecycle API	■	✓	—	✓	—	■	■
ReadDataElement Fine Granular API	■	■	—	—	—	■	■
UpdateDPPById Lifecycle API	■	■	■	■	—	■	■
UpdateDataElement Fine Granular API	■	■	✓	■	—	■	■
DeleteDPPById Lifecycle API	■	■	✓	■	■	■	■

■ **Mandatory** — required by a specific normative clause; test must exist for regulatory compliance

✓ **Planned** — structurally possible failure; recommended for comprehensive coverage

— **Not applicable** — failure class is structurally impossible for this operation

Fig. 3. Test coverage matrix

For model-based testing, the main implication is that regulatory requirements can be represented not only as high-level compliance goals, but also as concrete model elements. Lifecycle states define valid DBP progression, guards represent access, payload, synchronization, and state preconditions, and actions capture compliance-relevant effects such as archiving, registry notification, and audit logging. This supports more systematic derivation of positive and negative conformance tests.

For practice, the framework can support DBP service providers, testing bodies, regulators, and standardization bodies. Service providers can use the model to identify lifecycle and access-control requirements during system design. Testing bodies can use the derived test purposes for structured conformance assessment. Regulators and standardization bodies can use assumption points to identify unclear requirements that still prevent deterministic testing.

The assumption point mechanism also marks a limitation. Several test oracles still depend on the assumption points defined in Sect. 4.3. Until these parameters are clarified, some tests can only rely on provisional assumptions.

The framework has not yet been validated with an implemented DBP system. Future work should therefore translate the abstract test purposes into executable TTCN-3 and HTTP/JSON test artefacts and evaluate them using prototype or reference DBP systems. This would allow the practical feasibility of the EFSM, test purposes, and verdict logic to be assessed under realistic conditions. Future research should also refine archival logic for high-frequency dynamic DBP data by comparing full-version, delta-based, periodic, and event-based strategies in terms of scalability, storage effort, environmental impact, and conformance-testing implications.

9 Conclusion

Digital Battery Passport systems require conformance testing across lifecycle states, access rules, archiving, deletion, synchronization, registry notification, and auditability. Since these requirements are defined by regulatory and standardization documents, isolated unit or integration tests are not sufficient to assess lifecycle conformance.

This paper presented a four-layer model-based testing framework for DBP lifecycle systems. The framework formalizes the lifecycle as an EFSM and derives test purposes using transition coverage, guard inversion, and boundary value analysis. It also uses assumption points to document unresolved parameters in the current standardization landscape.

The framework remains conceptual and pre-operational. It has not yet been validated with an implemented DBP system. Future work should therefore focus on executable test implementation, empirical validation with prototype or reference systems, refinement of assumption points, and suitable archiving strategies for dynamic DBP data.

Acknowledgments. The project BatteryPass-Ready (01 April 2025–31 March 2027) is funded by the German Federal Ministry for Economic Affairs and Energy (BMWE) under grant agreement No. 16BZF363C.

Disclosure of Interests The authors have no competing interests to declare that are relevant to the content of this article.

References

1. Regulation (EU): 2023/1542 of the European Parliament and of the Council of 12 July 2023 concerning batteries and waste batteries, amending Directive 2008/98/EC and Regulation (EU) 2019/1020 and repealing Directive 2006/66/EC (2023)
2. EN 18239:2026: Digital Product Passport – Access rights management, information system security, and business confidentiality: English version EN 18239:2026 (2026)
3. EN 18222:2026: Digital Product Passport – Application Programming Interfaces (APIs) for the product passport lifecycle management and searchability: English version EN 18222:2026 (2026)
4. EN 18221:2026: Digital product passport - Data storage, archiving, and data persistence: English version EN 18221:2026 (2026)
5. Utting, M., Legeard, B.: Practical model-based testing: a tools approach. Elsevier. Amsterdam. https://doi.org/10.1016/B978-0-12-372501-1.X5000-5
6. Utting, M., Pretschner, A., Legeard, B.: A taxonomy of model-based testing approaches. Softw. Test. Verif. Reliab. **22**, 297–312 (2012). https://doi.org/10.1002/stvr.456
7. Tretmans, J.: Model based testing with labelled transition systems. In: Formal Methods and Testing, vol. 4949, pp. 1–38 (2008). https://doi.org/10.1007/978-3-540-78917-8_1
8. Elqortobi, M., El-Khouly, W., Rahj, A., et al.: Model-based verification and testing methodology for safety-critical airborne systems. In: New Trends in Model and Data Engineering, vol. 929, pp. 63–74. Springer (2018). https://doi.org/10.1007/978-3-030-02852-7_6
9. Ameur-Boulifa, R., Cavalli, A., Maag, S.: From formal test objectives to TTCN-3 for verifying ETCS complex software control systems. In: ICSOFT 2019, pp. 156–178. Springer (2020). https://doi.org/10.1007/978-3-030-52991-8_8

10. Gilberg, A., Kunkel, B., Ribault, A., et al.: Conformance testing for the AUTOSAR standard. In: Embedded Real Time Software & Systems, pp. 1–9
11. Torre, D., Soltana, G., Sabetzadeh, M., et al.: Using models to enable compliance checking against the GDPR: an experience report. In: 2019 ACM/IEEE Models, pp. 1–11 (2019). https://doi.org/10.1109/MODELS.2019.00-20
12. Golmohammadi, A., Zhang, M., Arcuri, A.: Testing RESTful APIs: a survey. ACM Trans. Softw. Eng. Methodol. **33**, 1–41 (2024). https://doi.org/10.1145/3617175
13. Fertig, T., Braun, P.: Model-driven testing of RESTful APIs. In: Proc. WWW'15, pp. 1497–1502. ACM, New York (2015). https://doi.org/10.1145/2740908.2743045
14. Pinheiro, P.V.P., Endo, A.T., Da Simão, A.S.: Model-based testing of RESTful web services using UML protocol state machines. In: The 7th Brazilian Workshop on Systematic and Automated Software Testing (SAST), pp. 1–10 (2013)
15. Liu, Y., Li, Y., Deng, G., et al.: Morest. In: Proc. ISCE, pp. 1406–1417. ACM, New York (2022). https://doi.org/10.1145/3510003.3510133
16. Atlidakis, V., Godefroid, P., Polishchuk, M.: RESTler: Stateful REST API Fuzzing. In: IEEE/ACM ICSE, pp. 748–758. IEEE (2019). https://doi.org/10.1109/ICSE.2019.00083
17. Karlsson, S., Causevic, A., Sundmark, D.: QuickREST: property-based test generation of OpenAPI-described RESTful APIs. ICST. **2020**, 131–141 (2020). https://doi.org/10.1109/ICST46399.2020.00023
18. European Telecommunications Standards Institute: Methods for Testing and Specification (MTS); The Testing and Test Control Notation version 3; Part 1: TTCN-3 Core Language(201 873-1) (2024)
19. Łukasik, Z., Nowakowski, W.: ETSI ES 201 873-1 application of TTCN-3 for testing of railway interlocking systems. In: Mikulski, J. (ed.) Transport Systems Telematics, vol. 104, pp. 447–454. Springer, Berlin Heidelberg (2010). https://doi.org/10.1007/978-3-642-16472-9_49
20. Gröning, S., Lewandowski, C., Schmutzler, J., et al.: Interoperability testing based on TTCN-3 for V2G communication interfaces. In: 2012 ICCVE, pp. 298–303. IEEE (2012). https://doi.org/10.1109/ICCVE.2012.67
21. Shin, M., Kim, H., Kim, H., et al.: Building an interoperability test system for electric vehicle chargers based on ISO/IEC 15118 and IEC 61850 standards. Appl. Sci. **6**, 165 (2016). https://doi.org/10.3390/app6060165
22. Eclipse Foundation: Eclipse IoT-Testware (2020). https://projects.eclipse.org/projects/technology.iottestware
23. Krichen, M., Alroobaea, R.: A new model-based framework for testing security of IoT Systems in Smart Cities using attack trees and Price timed automata. In: Proceedings of the 14th International Conference on Evaluation of Novel Approaches to Software Engineering, pp. 570–577. SCITEPRESS - Science and Technology Publications (2019). https://doi.org/10.5220/0007830605700577
24. Grabowski, J., Schieferdecker, I., Ulrich, A.: History, status, and recent trends of the testing and test control notation version 3 (TTCN-3). Int. J. Softw. Tools Technol. Transfer. **16**, 215–225 (2014). https://doi.org/10.1007/s10009-014-0302-9
25. Zhang, M., Ali, S., Yue, T., et al.: Uncertainty-wise cyber-physical system test modeling. Softw. Syst. Model. **18**, 1379–1418 (2019). https://doi.org/10.1007/s10270-017-0609-6
26. Whittle, J., Sawyer, P., Bencomo, N., et al.: RELAX: a language to address uncertainty in self-adaptive systems requirement. Requirements Eng. **15**, 177–196 (2010). https://doi.org/10.1007/s00766-010-0101-0
27. van der Bijl, M., Rensink, A., Tretmans, J.: Compositional testing with ioco. In: Goos, G., Hartmanis, J., van Leeuwen, J., et al. (eds.) Formal Approaches to Software Testing, vol. 2931, pp. 86–100. Springer, Berlin Heidelberg (2004). https://doi.org/10.1007/978-3-030-52991-8

28. Jansen, M., Meisen, T., Plociennik, C., et al.: Stop Guessing in the Dark: Identified Requirements for Digital Product Passport Systems. https://doi.org/10.3390/systems11030123
29. Plociennik, C., Pourjafarian, M., Nazeri, A., et al.: Towards a digital lifecycle passport for the circular economy. Procedia CIRP. **105**, 122–127 (2022). https://doi.org/10.1016/j.procir.2022.02.021
30. Battery Pass Consortium: Battery Passport Technical Guidance: Technical guidance for implementing a battery passport (2024). https://thebatterypass.eu/resources/
31. BatteryPass-Ready: Advancing battery passport readiness by delivering a test environment (2025). https://www.circular-economy-initiative.de/batterypassready_en
32. Catena-X Automotive Network: CX-0143 v3.0.0 — Use Case Circular Economy: Digital Product Passport Standard (2024). https://catenax-ev.github.io/docs/Jupiter/standards/CX-0143
33. Wiesner, M., Moreira, J., Guizzardi, R., et al.: A reference architecture for digital product passports at batch level to support manufacturing supply chains. In: RCIS 2024, Guimarães, Portugal, May 14–17, 2024, Proceedings, Part I, pp. 307–323. Springer, Cham (2024). https://doi.org/10.1007/978-3-031-59465-6_19
34. Gieß, A., Möller, F.: Exploring the value ecosystem of digital product passports. J. Ind. Ecol. **29**, 561–573 (2025). https://doi.org/10.1111/jiec.13621
35. Kosenkov, O., Elahidoost, P., Gorschek, T., et al.: Systematic Mapping Study on Requirements Engineering for Regulatory Compliance of Software Systems (2024).
36. Zhang, Z., Gu, J., Li, R., et al.: Bridging digital and green transitions: a literature review of digital product passport systems. Renew. Sust. Energ. Rev. **228**, 116600 (2026). https://doi.org/10.1016/j.rser.2025.116600
37. Regulation (EU) 2024/1781 of the European Parliament and of the Council of 13 June 2024 establishing a framework for the setting of ecodesign requirements for sustainable products, amending Directive (EU) 2020/1828 and Regulation (EU) 2023/1542 and repealing Directive 2009/125/EC
38. EN 18216: 2026 Digital product passport – Data exchange protocols: English version EN 18216:2026 (2026)
39. EN 18219: 2026 Digital product passport – Unique identifiers: English version EN 18219:2026 (2026)
40. European Telecommunications Standards Institute: ETSI ETR 141: Methods for Testing and Specification (MTS): Protocol and Profile Conformance Testing Specifications (1994). https://www.etsi.org/deliver/etsi_etr/100_199/141/01_60/etr_141e01p.pdf
41. European Telecommunications Standards Institute: Electronic Signatures and Trust Infrastructures (ESI): Trust service provider standards. https://portal.etsi.org/TBSiteMap/ESI/ESIActivities.aspx
42. European Telecommunications Standards Institute: ETSI TS 119 461 V2.1.1: Electronic Signatures and Trust Infrastructures (ESI); Policy and security requirements for trust service components providing identity proofing of trust service subjects (2025)
43. European Telecommunications Standards Institute: ETSI TS 119 475 V1.1.1: Electronic Signatures and Trust Infrastructures (ESI); Relying party attributes supporting EUDI Wallet user's authorization decisions (2025)

Access Rights Management and Digital Identity for Digital Product Passports

Dogan Efe(✉), Elena Andrushchenko, and Roland Jochem

Technical University of Berlin, Pascalstr. 8-9, 10587 Berlin, Germany
dogan.efe@tu-berlin.de

Abstract. The Digital Product Passport (DPP), established by the Ecodesign for Sustainable Products Regulation (ESPR, EU 2024/1781), is a regulated multi-actor digital infrastructure in which economic operators, market surveillance authorities, recyclers, repairers, and consumers each require access to different subsets of product data under different conditions. Managing these access rights correctly constitutes a legal compliance requirement, a governance challenge, and a systems engineering problem simultaneously. This paper makes four integrated contributions. First, a cross-regulation taxonomy is developed that classifies DPP data along three axes: data sensitivity tier, lifecycle mutability, and entitlement source. Second, the three generations of EU digital identity regulation eIDAS (2014), eIDAS 2.0 (2024), and the European Business Wallet (EBW) systematically analysed against the seven core DPP identity requirements, showing that eIDAS meets none, eIDAS 2.0 meets some, and the EBW is near-complete. Third, an updated hybrid authentication architecture is proposed that integrates three pathways: OAuth 2.0/OpenID Connect for operator-delegated business actors, the EU Digital Identity Wallet (eIDAS 2.0) for individual authority and base-role actors, and the EBW for organisational and automated flows. Fourth, the taxonomy and architecture are evaluated against the battery passport the first mandatory DPP under EU law confirming full coverage and alignment with EN 18239 and the JTC 24 standard family. The EBW's credential ecosystem gap and the unspecified presentation protocol layer (OID4VP, W3C VC 2.0) are identified as the critical near-term implementation risks for systems that must be operational before the February 2027 battery passport mandate.

Keywords: Digital Product Passport · Access Rights Management · eIDAS 2.0 · European Business Wallet · Digital Identity

1 Introduction

The Ecodesign for Sustainable Products Regulation (ESPR, Regulation (EU) 2024/1781), which entered into force in July 2024, establishes the Digital Product Passport (DPP) as a mandatory instrument for an expanding range of product categories. A DPP is a structured, machine-readable digital record that accompanies a product throughout its lifecycle and makes product-specific information accessible to a defined

Published by Springer Nature Switzerland AG 2027
G. Pezzotta et al. (Eds.): APMS 2026, IFIP AICT 808, pp. 61–75, 2027.
https://doi.org/10.1007/978-3-032-38594-9_5

set of actors through a data carrier and supporting digital infrastructure. It is not merely a technical data repository, but a regulated information ecosystem in which disclosure obligations, confidentiality requirements, update responsibilities, and access rights are distributed across multiple independent actors.

This multi-actor structure creates two closely interrelated challenges: access rights management and digital identity. The access rights challenge concerns how read and write permissions can be structured across heterogeneous actor groups, including economic operators, market surveillance authorities, customs authorities, recyclers, repairers, and consumers. These actors require access to different subsets of DPP data under different legal, technical, and lifecycle-related conditions. At the same time, DPP data is not homogeneous. Some information must be publicly accessible without authentication, whereas other data elements are commercially sensitive, legally restricted, or dynamically updated during repair, reuse, refurbishment, recycling, or ownership transfer.

The digital identity challenge concerns how the actors requesting access can be reliably authenticated and how their legal roles, organisational affiliations, mandates, and entitlements can be verified. This challenge is particularly relevant because the European digital identity landscape is currently evolving. The original eIDAS Regulation, the revised eIDAS 2.0 framework, and the emerging European Business Wallet each provide different capabilities for identity verification, attribute attestation, organisational identity, delegation, and automated business-to-business or business-to-government interactions. However, it remains unclear how these regulatory identity frameworks can be systematically aligned with the specific access control requirements of DPP ecosystems.

Despite ongoing standardisation activities through CEN/CENELEC JTC 24, especially EN 18239 on access rights management, information system security, and business confidentiality, a structured conceptual framework that maps DPP access requirements to digital identity mechanisms has not yet been sufficiently developed in academic literature. Existing discussions often address DPP data governance, interoperability, or technical infrastructure separately, while the combined problem of access rights, entitlement sources, authentication pathways, and regulatory identity infrastructures remains underexplored.

Therefore, this paper addresses the following research question:

How can access rights and digital identity requirements for Digital Product Passports be systematically aligned with emerging EU digital identity regulations to enable secure, role-based, and interoperable access to DPP data?

To answer this research question, a conceptual regulatory analysis is conducted. First, access and identity requirements for DPP ecosystems are derived from the ESPR, the Battery Regulation, and the CEN/CENELEC JTC 24 standard family. Second, three generations of EU digital identity regulation: eIDAS, eIDAS 2.0, and the European Business Wallet are systematically compared against these requirements. Third, the resulting gaps are translated into a hybrid authentication architecture. Finally, the proposed taxonomy and architecture are evaluated using the digital battery passport as the first mandatory DPP implementation case under EU law [1, 2].

2 Background: The DPP as Regulated Technical Infrastructure

The DPP concept is based on the separation between the physical product, its data carrier, and its digital representation. A data carrier, such as a QR code, links the product to a Unique Product Identifier (UPI), which resolves to the DPP through a registry. The DPP itself is hosted by the responsible economic operator or by a DPP service provider and must remain accessible throughout the product lifecycle or regulated end-of-life processing [3].

This infrastructure creates a multi-actor access environment. Economic operators are responsible for creating and maintaining the DPP and managing access rights where discretion is allowed [2]. Market surveillance authorities, customs authorities, and the European Commission derive access rights from statutory mandates. Repairers, recyclers, and refurbishers may access selected data through legally recognised base roles or operator assignment, while consumers and the general public may access only the public part of the DPP without authentication [4].

DPP access control must therefore distinguish between public, controlled, and commercially sensitive data. Access rights depend on the requesting actor, the legal source of the entitlement, the sensitivity of the requested data, and the lifecycle state of the product. This requires fine-granular access mechanisms rather than a single uniform access rule. The technical basis for implementing these mechanisms is provided by the CEN/CENELEC JTC 24 standard family. EN 18219 defines identification schemes for products, economic operators, and facilities [5]; EN 18220 addresses data carrier requirements; and EN 18222 specifies lifecycle, fine-granular, and registry APIs for DPP interaction [6]. These standards form the technical substrate within which access rights management and digital identity mechanisms must be implemented.

3 Regulatory and Standards Landscape

The access rights problem in DPP systems is shaped by product regulation, digital identity regulation, and technical standardisation. Product regulations define which actors are entitled to access specific DPP data, while digital identity regulations define how these actors can prove their identity, roles, and organisational affiliations. The ESPR establishes the general DPP framework and requires public data to remain openly accessible while business confidentiality must be protected [7]. The Battery Regulation introduces the first sector-specific DPP obligation: from 18 February 2027, relevant battery categories must be accompanied by a digital battery passport accessible via QR code [8].

DPP access control also depends on the European digital identity framework. eIDAS provides the basis for cross-border electronic identification and trust services, eIDAS 2.0 introduces the European Digital Identity Wallet and qualified electronic attestations of attributes, and the European Business Wallet extends this landscape towards organisational identity, mandates, and automated B2B/B2G interactions [9–14]. In parallel, CEN/CENELEC JTC 24 is developing harmonised standards for the technical implementation of the DPP. These standards address identifiers, data carriers, APIs, interoperability, data exchange protocols, access rights management, information security, business confidentiality, and data authentication [4–6, 15, 16]. Among them, EN

18239 is particularly relevant because it directly specifies requirements for access rights management, information system security, business confidentiality, and the transfer of responsibilities and access rights between economic operators [4]. Based on this regulatory and technical landscape, the following section analyses whether eIDAS, eIDAS 2.0, and the European Business Wallet can satisfy the identity requirements of DPP access control.

4 Three Generations of EU Digital Identity and the DPP Problem

Every DPP access control system that is deployed before February 2027 will depend on EU digital identity infrastructure to authenticate its actors. The infrastructure has evolved through three legislative generations, each addressing a different problem. A system designer who does not understand these distinctions will make the wrong choices about which identity layer to build on.

Table 1 summarises the three generations and their coverage of DPP identity requirements [9–14].

4.1 Generation 1: eIDAS

The original eIDAS regulation was built around a specific, narrow problem: For example a German citizen needs to log into a Spanish government tax portal using their German national eID. The regulation established mutual recognition of notified electronic identification schemes across Member States and created a legal framework for electronic signatures and trust services. Nothing in the regulation's design anticipated the need to verify that a company holds a waste facility permit in a specific jurisdiction, or that an employee is authorised to execute a deletion operation on behalf of their employer.

eIDAS fails to meet the DPP access control requirements on three structural dimensions. First, it has no organisational identity layer: it can verify that Maria Schmidt is who she claims to be, but not that Schmidt GmbH is the registered Economic Operator responsible for battery type BT-2024-DE-001. Second, it carries no attribute attestations: it provides a binary authenticated/unauthenticated signal with no facility for verifying sector registrations, operating permits, or compliance declarations. Third, it was not designed for the distributed, multi-actor access control choreography the DPP requires: nine actor classes, each with different permissions, interacting across organisational and national boundaries in automated, machine-to-machine flows. Of the core DPP identity requirements, eIDAS meets none.

4.2 Generation 2: eIDAS 2.0

eIDAS 2.0 is a substantial extension of the original eIDAS framework. The European Digital Identity Wallet (EUDIW), which Member States must make available by the end of 2026, introduces capabilities that were absent from the original eIDAS Regulation. First, it creates a framework for electronic attestations of attributes, including Qualified Electronic Attestations of Attributes (QEAAs), which can provide machine-verifiable evidence of specific attributes of a natural or legal person. Second, it supports selective

Table 1. Three-generation comparison of EU digital identity frameworks and their coverage of DPP identity requirements

Dimension	eIDAS	eIDAS 2.0 / EUDIW	EU Business Wallet
Primary subject	Natural persons	Natural persons + legal entities	Legal entities
Identity model	Notified national eID schemes	Mobile wallet + QEAAs	Cloud-based organisational wallet + QEAAs + mandate credential system
Organisational identity	Limited (electronic signatures)	Legal entity possible but person-centric architecture	Native – wallet owned by legal entity; EORI, LEI, sector registrations
Attribute attestations (QEAA)	No	QEAAs issued by trusted public authorities	Extends QEAA to sector-specific registrations and compliance declarations
Mandate / delegation	No	No	Explicit mandate and role-delegation credential system
Automated B2B/B2G flows	No	Partial	Yes
DPP explicit integration	No	No	Yes
DPP identity requirements coverage	0 of 7 core requirements met	Partial – covers attribute attestations; misses mandate, automation, org-native wallet	Near-complete – requires additional technical standards for presentation layer

disclosure, allowing users to disclose only those attributes that are necessary for a specific transaction, rather than exposing the full credential. Third, it strengthens the framework for legal-person identity, representation, and mandates, since powers of representation and e-mandates may be represented as attestable attributes.

Despite these advances, eIDAS 2.0 does not fully resolve the access-control requirements of DPP ecosystems. First, the EUDIW model is primarily designed around wallet-mediated identification, authentication, and attribute presentation by a user. DPP operations, however, may include unattended machine-to-machine lifecycle events, such as deletion confirmations, registry notifications, and synchronisation with backup service providers. These processes require automated authorisation mechanisms that go beyond the ordinary wallet presentation model. Second, while eIDAS 2.0 supports representation and mandates as attestable attributes, it does not define a DPP-specific delegation model that would determine which employee, system, or service provider may execute a particular DPP operation on behalf of a specific economic operator, under defined scope, duration, and revocation conditions. Third, although eIDAS 2.0 establishes the legal and technical framework for QEAAs, it does not itself create the sector-specific credential ecosystem required for DPP access control. In particular, it does not define a harmonised credential for attesting Battery Regulation Responsible Economic Operator status, nor does it designate the competent issuers for such a credential [13, 14]. The framework therefore exists, but the DPP-specific credential and authorisation ecosystem still has to be developed.

4.3 Generation 3: The European Business Wallet

The European Business Wallet proposal, published in November 2025 and currently in first parliamentary reading [11, 12], addresses the organisational and automation gaps in eIDAS 2.0 directly. Four features are critical for DPP. First, the EBW is a cloud-based wallet owned by the legal entity itself not a mobile application held by a person acting on behalf of the entity. Second, it introduces an explicit mandate and role-delegation system: EBW owners can delegate specific operations to authorised representatives through digitally signed mandate credentials with defined scope and revocability [12, 14]. Third, it is designed for automated B2B and B2G flows without requiring human presence at each interaction step. Fourth, and most importantly: the Commission's explanatory memorandum to states that the Digital Product Passport depends on trusted access to conformity and sustainability data and that the Business Wallets proposal can prove legal identity and any granted access rights [8, 12]. The European Parliament's draft report of 1 April 2026 names DPP as a priority use [11].

Even with the EBW, one technical layer remains unspecified in any regulatory instrument: the presentation protocol, the mechanism by which a DPP verifier requests a specific credential presentation from a specific holder in a machine-readable, standardised way. This requires OpenID for Verifiable Presentations (OID4VP), the W3C Verifiable Credentials 2.0 data model [17], the Bitstring Status List for real-time credential revocation [18], and BBS+ or SD-JWT for selective disclosure cryptography. These are not part of the EBW regulation; they are technical standards that the EBW's Architectural Reference Framework references and depends on. The EBW is the regulatory container; these are the technical contents. Identifying this distinction is essential for implementers: no amount of regulatory compliance produces a working DPP authentication system without these additional standards.

Published on 7 April 2026 [14], this regulation lays down the onboarding specifications for the EUDIW at assurance level high, the level that DPP write and delete operations will require. It distinguishes between natural person EUDIW credentials and organisational EBW credentials, confirming that DPP operations authorised at the legal entity level require EBW credentials as the primary authentication mechanism, not personal EUDIW presentations. While Sect. 4 clarifies the identity layer, the following section derives the access rights problem that this identity layer must support within DPP ecosystems.

5 The Access Rights Problem in DPP Ecosystems

The access rights problem in DPP systems is characterized by three structural features that together make it non-trivial to solve through conventional access control models.

First, the actor set is inherently multi-party. Access rights in a DPP system are not solely the prerogative of the manufacturer or the economic operator responsible for the DPP. Market surveillance authorities, customs authorities, and the European Commission hold statutory access rights that derive from regulation rather than from any contractual relationship. These rights cannot be withheld by the economic operator, and they must be technically enforceable regardless of whether the economic operator has pre-authorized the requesting actor [4]. At the same time, economic operators retain discretion over the assignment of access rights to third parties such as professional repairers or logistics providers.

Second, the data is high-dimensional, partially confidential, and dynamic. Battery passport requirements alone enumerate approximately eighty mandatory data attributes, organized into seven thematic clusters: general product information, EU Declaration of Conformity, carbon footprint, due diligence, material composition, circularity, and performance and durability [8]. These attributes differ with respect to their sensitivity: some, such as carbon footprint values and basic product identifiers, are publicly disclosed; others, such as detailed material composition or supplier chain information, may constitute commercially sensitive trade secrets. Additionally, a distinction is drawn between static attributes assigned at manufacture time and not subject to routine changes and dynamic attributes, which are updated as the product is repaired, refurbished, or changes ownership. This combination of dimensional scale, sensitivity heterogeneity, and mutability creates a policy enforcement challenge that cannot be addressed through coarse-grained role assignments alone.

Third, the entitlement source is heterogeneous. Some access rights are defined by delegated acts and are therefore non-negotiable and uniform across all products within a given category. Others are assigned by the economic operator on a product- or actor-specific basis. Still others arise from the lifecycle status of the product itself for example, when ownership is transferred between economic operators, the access rights management responsibilities are transferred accordingly and must be reflected in the system state [4, 19]. A reference architecture must accommodate all three entitlement sources simultaneously, without conflating them. Building on these access-control challenges, the following section proposes a taxonomy that structures DPP access rights along three orthogonal dimensions.

6 A Three-Dimensional Taxonomy of DPP Access Rights

Based on the regulatory analysis presented in Sects. 3 through 5, a taxonomy is proposed that structures DPP access rights along three orthogonal dimensions. Each dimension captures a different aspect of the access rights problem and maps onto distinct technical or governance responses. The authentication column in Table 2 has been updated relative to prior formulations to reflect the three-pathway authentication architecture established in Sect. 7, incorporating the EBW for organisational and automated access scenarios.

6.1 Dimension 1: Data Sensitivity Tier

Three sensitivity tiers are distinguished: public data, controlled data, and confidential-commercial data. Public data includes information that must be accessible to any actor without authentication, such as consumers, non-EU actors, or machines performing automated compliance checks. It should therefore be provided through an unauthenticated access pathway.

Controlled data includes information that is not public and may only be accessed by authenticated and authorised actors. Access depends on a valid entitlement, such as a statutory mandate, a recognised base role, or authorisation by the economic operator. This tier requires identity verification and policy-based access control, but the data is not necessarily commercially sensitive.

Confidential-commercial data is a high-protection subset of controlled data. It includes information that may qualify as a trade secret or commercially sensitive information, such as supplier-related details, proprietary process data, or detailed material composition. The distinction between controlled and confidential-commercial data is therefore not only based on selective access, since both tiers are restricted. Rather, confidential-commercial data requires stronger credential verification, narrower disclosure rules, and stricter auditability because unauthorised disclosure may create competitive, legal, or security-related risks.

6.2 Dimension 2: Lifecycle Mutability

Static attributes are assigned at the point of manufacture or at the time of product placement on the market, and their values are not subject to routine change during normal use. Dynamic attributes, in contrast, are updated as a product is repaired, refurbished, reused, or moved between ownership boundaries. The mutability dimension is significant for access control because write permissions are considerably more restricted than read permissions and are typically limited to the economic operator, designated base-role actors such as recyclers, or the DPP service provider acting under explicit authorisation.

6.3 Dimension 3: Entitlement Source

Three entitlement source categories are identified. Regulatory entitlements derive from primary or secondary EU legislation including the ESPR, the Battery Regulation, and adopted implementing or delegated acts that cannot be overridden at the operator level. Base-role entitlements derive from delegated acts that define recognised actor roles (such as recycler, refurbisher, or professional repairer); holders of these roles do not require individual per-product authorisation from the economic operator. Operator-delegated entitlements are assigned by the economic operator on a discretionary basis for actors falling outside the regulatory and base-role categories. The taxonomy provides the conceptual basis for access classification. The next section translates this classification into a technically implementable authentication and policy architecture.

Table 2. Three-dimensional access rights taxonomy for DPP ecosystems

Sensitivity Tier	Mutability	Entitlement Source	Actor Examples	Authentication Required
Public	Static/Dynamic (Read)	ESPR/Battery Reg.	Consumers, general public, non-authorized actors	None
Controlled (regulatory)	Static/Dynamic (Read)	ESPR/implementing act	Market surveillance authorities, customs, European Commission	eIDAS 2.0 Wallet (non-refutable) EBW for automated/organisational actors
Controlled (base role)	Static/Dynamic (Read + Write)	Delegated acts	Professional repairers, recyclers, refurbishers	eIDAS 2.0 Wallet (role attestation) EBW mandate credential for delegated operations
Controlled (operator-delegated)	Static/Dynamic (per grant)	Operator-delegated	Logistics providers, component suppliers, testing labs	OAuth 2.0 / OpenID Connect (OIDC)
Confidential commercial	Static (typically)	Legal basis or explicit operator authorisation	Notified bodies, qualified auditors, trade secret holders	OAuth 2.0 + additional QEAA attestation (eIDAS 2.0 / EBW)

7 An Updated Hybrid Authentication Architecture for DPP Access Control

The taxonomy developed in Sect. 6 classifies DPP data according to sensitivity, lifecycle mutability, and entitlement source. However, this classification only becomes operational when it is translated into an authentication and policy enforcement architecture. The purpose of the proposed architecture is therefore to connect regulatory access rights with technical identity verification and access-control mechanisms.

The architecture follows an attribute-based access control (ABAC) logic. In ABAC, access decisions are based on attributes of the requesting subject, the requested data object, the intended operation, and the relevant context [20]. This approach is suitable for DPP ecosystems because access decisions cannot be based on actor roles alone. Instead, they must consider several attributes simultaneously, including the actor's organisational identity, legal mandate, role attestation, delegated authorisation, requested data element, sensitivity tier, and lifecycle state.

The proposed architecture consists of three authentication pathways. First, OAuth 2.0 and OpenID Connect are used for operator-delegated access scenarios, where the economic operator or a DPP service provider grants scoped access to business actors such as logistics providers, suppliers, testing laboratories, or selected service partners [21, 22]. This pathway is suitable where access rights are not directly derived from regulation, but from an authorisation granted by the economic operator.

Second, the European Digital Identity Wallet under eIDAS 2.0 is used for individual actors whose access rights depend on verified personal or professional attributes [10]. This includes, for example, authority representatives, professional repairers, recyclers, or refurbishers. Qualified electronic attestations of attributes can support the verification of roles, qualifications, permits, or regulatory mandates. These verified attributes are then mapped to the ABAC policy logic.

Third, the European Business Wallet is used for organisational actors, delegated mandates, and automated business-to-business or business-to-government interactions [11, 12]. This pathway is required where the requesting subject is not only a natural person, but a legal entity or an authorised representative acting on behalf of a legal entity. It is therefore particularly relevant for economic operators, DPP service providers, organisational authority workflows, and machine-to-machine processes.

Access decisions are enforced at the DPP service provider's API layer. Public data is provided through a separate unauthenticated endpoint, while requests for controlled or confidential-commercial data are routed through a policy enforcement point. The policy decision point evaluates whether the actor has the required identity attributes, entitlement source, and authorisation scope for the requested data element and operation. This separation between public and controlled access pathways is consistent with the requirements of EN 18239, which addresses public/controlled data separation, access rights management, information security, and business confidentiality [4].

For controlled and confidential-commercial data, authentication alone is not sufficient. The system must also verify whether the presented credentials are valid, whether the actor is entitled to access the requested data, and whether the requested operation is permitted. In cases involving verifiable credentials, presentation and revocation mechanisms such as OpenID for Verifiable Presentations, the W3C Verifiable Credentials Data Model, and the Bitstring Status List are relevant for ensuring interoperable credential exchange and status checking [17, 18, 23].

Overall, the hybrid architecture links the three dimensions of the taxonomy to suitable authentication mechanisms. Public data requires no authentication. Controlled data requires actor verification through eIDAS 2.0, EBW, or operator-issued OAuth/OIDC credentials, depending on the entitlement source. Confidential-commercial data requires the same mechanisms, but with stronger verification, narrower policy rules, and stricter audit logging. The architecture therefore provides a practical bridge between regulatory access rights and technical implementation.

8 Evaluation: the Battery Passport as a Proof-of-Concept Case

The digital battery passport is used as a proof-of-concept case to evaluate the applicability of the proposed taxonomy and authentication architecture. This case is suitable because the battery passport is the first mandatory DPP under EU law and includes data attributes with different sensitivity levels, lifecycle characteristics, and access requirements.

The evaluation examines whether the seven battery attribute clusters can be assigned to the three taxonomy dimensions: sensitivity tier, lifecycle mutability, and entitlement source. It also assesses whether the resulting access requirements can be linked to one of the authentication pathways introduced in Sect. 7.

Table 3 applies the taxonomy to the seven battery passport attribute clusters. The table shows that each cluster can be assigned to a sensitivity tier, a mutability category, an entitlement source, and a suitable authentication pathway.

Table 3. Application of the access rights taxonomy to DBP attribute clusters

Attribute Cluster	Sensitivity Tier	Mutability	Entitlement Source	Authentication / Access Pathway
General product information	Public	Static	ESPR / Battery Regulation	No authentication; public endpoint
EU Declaration of Conformity	Controlled – regulatory	Static	Delegated or implementing acts	eIDAS 2.0 Wallet for authority actors; EBW for organisational authority access
Carbon footprint	Public	Static	Battery Regulation	No authentication; public endpoint
Due diligence	Controlled / confidential-commercial	Static / dynamic	Delegated acts and operator authorisation	OAuth 2.0 or EBW/eIDAS 2.0 with additional attestation, depending on sensitivity
Material composition	Controlled; partly confidential-commercial	Static	Battery Regulation and delegated acts	eIDAS 2.0 Wallet or EBW, depending on actor role and disclosure level
Circularity	Controlled – base role	Dynamic	Delegated acts defining base-role entitlements	eIDAS 2.0 Wallet with role attestation; EBW mandate credential for organisational or automated updates
Performance and durability	Public summary / controlled detail	Dynamic	Battery Regulation and operator-defined access	Public endpoint for summary data; OAuth 2.0 or EBW for detailed restricted data

(*continued*)

Table 3. (*continued*)

Attribute Cluster	Sensitivity Tier	Mutability	Entitlement Source	Authentication / Access Pathway

The application shows that all seven battery attribute clusters can be covered by the proposed taxonomy without requiring an additional category. Public data can be provided through an unauthenticated pathway, while controlled and confidential-commercial data require authentication, entitlement verification, and policy-based access control.

The circularity cluster illustrates why read and write permissions must be distinguished. Circularity-related data may be updated by recyclers, refurbishers, or repair actors during lifecycle processes. Individual base-role actors can be authenticated through eIDAS 2.0 wallet-based role attestations, while organisational or automated updates require the European Business Wallet.

The performance and durability cluster shows that access rights cannot always be assigned at the cluster level. Some summary data may be public, while detailed test results or state-of-health information may require controlled access. This confirms the need for fine-granular ABAC policies at the level of individual data elements.

Overall, the battery passport case confirms the applicability of the proposed taxonomy and authentication architecture. Each cluster can be mapped to the taxonomy dimensions and linked to a suitable access pathway. The case also shows that separating public and controlled data pathways is necessary because several battery passport clusters contain both public and restricted data elements.

9 Discussion

Five design tensions and implementation risks emerge from the combined analysis.

The first is the tension between regulatory transparency obligations and commercial confidentiality. Certain data classes notably due diligence information covering supply chain sourcing and human rights compliance are subject to competing pressures: their disclosure is mandated in principle by the Battery Regulation, yet the granularity of required disclosure may intersect with information that qualifies as a trade secret. The taxonomy places such data in the confidential-commercial tier, but the precise boundary between the publicly mandated disclosure and the commercially protected remainder will require authoritative clarification through implementing acts and, where necessary, judicial interpretation.

The second is the credential ecosystem gap. The EBW provides the regulatory container for the identity credentials that DPP systems need. However, as of April 2026, no Member State has designated an authority to issue the QEAA needed to attest to Battery Regulation Responsible Economic Operator status under eIDAS 2.0, and the EBW itself remains in parliamentary reading. The battery passport mandate enters into force on 18 February 2027 nine months after the scheduled EU Registry launch in July 2026. This timing creates a real, not hypothetical, implementation risk: DPP service providers designing systems today must plan for an identity layer that is only partially available in the identity generation (eIDAS 2.0 EUDIW) that will be legally operational by the mandate date and must architect for EBW integration that is still being legislated.

The third tension concerns interoperability across product groups. The JTC 24 standardisation stack is designed to be product-group-agnostic at the technical level, but the specific data attributes, access groups, and sensitivity tiers for each product group are defined through product-group-specific delegated acts. A DPP service provider serving multiple product groups must maintain separate policy rulesets for each, while the underlying technical infrastructure remains common. The scalability implications particularly for the Policy Decision Point, which must consult product-group-specific policies for every controlled data request represent an open engineering challenge.

The fourth tension involves the unspecified presentation protocol layer. As established in Sect. 4.3, even the EBW regulation does not specify the presentation protocol (OID4VP), the credential data model (W3C VC 2.0), the revocation mechanism (Bitstring Status List), or the selective disclosure cryptography (BBS+/SD-JWT). These are referenced by the EBW's Architectural Reference Framework but must be tracked separately by implementers. The risk is that different DPP service providers implement incompatible technical stacks that are all EBW-compliant at the regulatory level but non-interoperable at the protocol level.

The fifth tension involves non-EU actors. The proposed architecture relies on the EU Digital Identity Wallet for authenticating authority roles and base-role actors. While the revised eIDAS framework entered into force in May 2024, Member States are required to offer wallets only by 2026, and the supporting trust infrastructure including the certification of wallet providers and the issuance of cross-border role attestations is still being developed. For actors established outside the EU, alternative credential mechanisms compatible with the accountability requirements of EN 18239 will need to be defined, a task that falls beyond the current scope of the JTC 24 standard family.

10 Conclusion

Access rights management in Digital Product Passport ecosystems is not a peripheral implementation detail but a foundational compliance requirement, a governance instrument, and a systems engineering challenge of substantial scope. This paper has made four integrated contributions.

First, a three-dimensional taxonomy of DPP access rights has been developed, mapping data sensitivity tiers, lifecycle mutability, and entitlement sources onto distinct technical and governance responses. Second, a systematic analysis of three generations of EU digital identity regulation has established that eIDAS (2014) meets none of the seven core DPP identity requirements, eIDAS 2.0 meets some but fails on organisational identity, delegation, and automated flows, and the European Business Wallet (2025) is near-complete, subject to the credential ecosystem gap and the unspecified presentation protocol layer. Third, an updated hybrid authentication architecture has been proposed that integrates ABAC policy evaluation with three authentication pathways OAuth 2.0/OIDC for operator-delegated actors, the EUDIW under eIDAS 2.0 for individual authority and base-role actors, and the EBW for legal entities and automated operations. Fourth, the taxonomy and architecture have been evaluated against the battery passport, confirming full coverage of all seven mandatory attribute clusters and alignment with the functional requirements of EN 18239 and the broader JTC 24 standard family.

The identification of the credential ecosystem gap the absence of issued QEAAs for battery-relevant actor roles as of April 2026, nine months before the February 2027 mandate is the most time-sensitive finding. DPP service providers must design their authentication architectures for a transition period in which eIDAS 2.0 EUDIW credentials will be legally available but substantively incomplete, and EBW credentials will be approaching legal availability but not yet deployed at scale. The three-pathway architecture proposed in this paper is designed to accommodate this transition: OAuth 2.0/OIDC provides an operational fallback for operator-delegated actors; eIDAS 2.0 EUDIW handles individual authority and role-based actors when QEAAs are issued; and EBW integration can be activated progressively as the credential ecosystem matures.

The significance of this work extends beyond the battery sector. As ESPR delegated acts expand DPP requirements to textiles, furniture, steel, aluminium, and further product categories between 2026 and 2030, each new product group will require product-group-specific access rights specifications within a shared technical infrastructure. The taxonomy proposed in this paper provides a reusable analytical tool for deriving those specifications systematically from regulatory text, while the updated hybrid architecture offers a reference design that satisfies the core technical requirements across product groups without redesign.

Acknowledgments. The project BatteryPass-Ready (funding period 01 April 2025 – 31 March 2027) is funded by the German Federal Ministry for Economic Affairs and Energy (BMWE) based on a resolution of the German Bundestag under grant agreement No. 16BZF363C.

Disclosure of Interests The authors have no competing interests to declare that are relevant to the content of this article.

References

1. Jensen, S.F., Kristensen, J.H., Christensen, A., et al.: An ecosystem orchestration framework for the design of digital product passports in a circular economy. Bus. Strat. Env. **33**, 7100–7117 (2024). https://doi.org/10.1002/bse.3868
2. Gieß, A., Möller, F.: Exploring the value ecosystem of digital product passports. J. Ind. Ecol. **29**, 561–573 (2025). https://doi.org/10.1111/jiec.13621
3. Fares, N., Islam, M.S., Jauhar, S.K., et al.: Towards an international digital product passport: the new paradigm of a worldwide circular economy. Circ. Econ. Sust. **5**, 5475–5495 (2025). https://doi.org/10.1007/s43615-025-00690-5
4. EN 18239:2026 Digital product passport – Access rights management, information system security, and business confidentiality: English version EN 18239:2026 (2026)
5. EN 18219:2026 Digital product passport – Unique identifiers: English version EN 18219:2026 (2026)
6. EN 18222:2026 Digital product passport – Application Programming Interfaces (APIs) for the product passport lifecycle management and searchability: English version EN 18222:2026 (2026)
7. European Union: Regulation (EU) 2024/1781 of 13 June 2024 establishing a framework for the setting of ecodesign requirements for sustainable products. ESPR (2024)

8. European Union: Regulation (EU) 2023/1542 of 12 July 2023 concerning batteries and waste batteries. Regulation (EU) 2023/1542 / Battery Regulation (2023)
9. European Union: Regulation (EU) No 910/2014 of 23 July 2014 on electronic identification and trust services for electronic transactions in the internal market. eIDAS (2014)
10. European Union: Regulation (EU) 2024/1183 of 11 April 2024 amending Regulation (EU) No 910/2014 as regards establishing the european digital identity framework. eIDAS 2.0 (2024)
11. European Commission: Proposal for a regulation of the european parliament and of the council on the establishment of european business wallets. COM(2025)0838. European Commission, Brussels (2025)
12. European Parliament: Draft Report on COM(2025)0838 – European Business Wallets. 2025/0358(COD), Brussels (2026)
13. Heinäluoma, E.: Draft report on COM(2025)0838 – european business wallets. European Parliament, Committee on Industry, Research and Energy, PE 785.244 (2026)
14. European Commission: Commission implementing regulation (EU) 2026/798 of 7 April 2026 laying down rules for the application of Regulation (EU) No 910/2014 as regards reference standards and specifications for the remote onboarding of users to the European Digital Identity Wallets. Implementing Regulation (EU) 2026/798 (2026)
15. EN 18216:2026 Digital product passport – data exchange protocols: English version EN 18216:2026 (2026)
16. EN 18246:2026 Digital product passport – data authentication, reliability and integrity: English version EN 18246:2026 (2026)
17. W3C: Verifiable credentials data model v2.0. W3C Recommendation (2025). https://www.w3.org/TR/vc-data-model-2.0/
18. W3C: Bitstring status list v1.0: Privacy-preserving status information for verifiable credentials. W3C Recommendation (2025). https://www.w3.org/TR/vc-bitstring-status-list/
19. Ducuing, C., Reich, R.H.: Data governance: digital product passports as a case study. Comput. Regul. Netw. Ind. **24**, 3–23 (2023). https://doi.org/10.1177/17835917231152799
20. Hu, V.C., Ferraiolo, D., Kuhn, R., et al.: Guide to Attribute Based Access Control (ABAC) Definition and Considerations. National Institute of Standards and Technology (2014)
21. Hardt, D.: The OAuth 2.0 Authorization framework. RFC Editor (2012)
22. OpenID Foundation: OpenID connect core 1.0 incorporating errata set 2. OpenID Foundation (2023). https://openid.net/specs/openid-connect-core-1_0.html
23. OpenID Foundation: OpenID for verifiable presentations 1.0. OID4VP. OpenID foundation (2025). https://openid.net/specs/openid-4-verifiable-presentations-1_0.html

Obstacles and Opportunities for the Repair Cycle for Cells and Electronics in EV Batteries

Martin Kurdve[1,2,3](✉) and Emanuel Glans[1]

[1] RISE, Research institutes of Sweden, Göteborg, Sweden
martin.kurdve@ri.se
[2] Chalmers University of Technology TME, Göteborg, Sweden
[3] Mälardalen University, ITV, Eskilstuna, Sweden

Abstract. The value of battery electric systems in both economic and ecologic terms depend on the possibility to keep a long life. Thus, the possibility of repairing faulty batteries is crucial to avoid early disposal of batteries. This study brings up the conflict that may arise between circular economy and ecology on one side, and safety for people handling faulty batteries on the other side. With action research from a repair case of a light electric vehicle battery and with expert interviews the aims of right to repair and battery passport legislation are contrasted against technical possibilities of field diagnostics, safe handling and design. The study shows that several actors along the value chain need to cooperate to enable repair. Development paths of monitoring and failure causes, and reparable design of electronics as well as legal policy are discussed. The paper contributes to scientific knowledge on potential conflicts between various sustainability aims in the development of EV batteries and electronics.

Keywords: Repair · EV batteries and electronics · Battery safety.

1 Introduction

A major issue for electric vehicles (EVs) is how to handle breakdowns of batteries and drivetrain electronics. These parts account for a large share of a vehicle's economic value [1] and thus the owner has an interest in repairing and saving the value, if possible, even after a crash. Also, a large part of the inherent carbon footprint of the vehicle is wasted if these components break down and go to waste [2, 3]. The cells often cover most of a battery's value, but electronics and other parts may also contain retainable value [4]. Here, repair of a component is mainly considered as extension of its current life/use, in contrast to "repair and reuse" which in some literature is considered as refurbishment or remanufacturing [5].

Right to repair (R2R) is a principle implemented in the directive EU 2024/1799 [6] regarding general products, and to some degree for batteries in EU (2023/1542) [7], the Battery Regulation. On the other hand, the handling of faulty batteries entail that electrical, chemical, thermal and fire safety must be considered. People involved in repair

Published by Springer Nature Switzerland AG 2027
G. Pezzotta et al. (Eds.): APMS 2026, IFIP AICT 808, pp. 76–90, 2027.
https://doi.org/10.1007/978-3-032-38594-9_6

refurbishment, or repair logistics are entitled to safe working environments. Transport and handling must consider whether the faulty battery is repairable and considered to be hazardous waste or not [8]. This study aims to map the EV battery repair process actors and related obstacles of repair and transport practice and safety.

Assembly, repair or disassembly of batteries for EVs usually include some challenges. First, the power needed to drive the vehicles often implies a risk of electric shock when handling the battery even when it functions correctly [9]. Handling damaged batteries may include safety risks regarding fire, chemical and electric safety. This study maps actors in the repair cycle who, with legitimate safety or legal concerns, may be hindered to repair faulty batteries. Then the most hazardous fails of a battery, root causes, and detection technologies are investigated. Two research questions are asked:

- RQ1 What main actors need to be involved in the battery repair process and what may their concerns and motivations in repair and safety of faulty batteries be?
- RQ2 What risks and hinders are apparent in handling and repairing faulty batteries, and can they be detected and/or mitigated?

The rest of the article is structured as follows: A broad background narrowing down to battery repair and safety issues is presented in Sect. 2. Then, the dual methodology of this study is presented in Sect. 3, and the results and discussion in Sect. 4 & 5 and conclusions in Sect. 6.

2 Background

2.1 Parts of an EV Battery

An EV battery is a system of electrically and mechanically interconnected battery cells packed in a casing, controlled by electronics in a battery management system (BMS) and power electronics, charging and discharging the battery. Additionally, thermal management with cooling system between cells is often included [9]. Each battery cell contains an anode, a cathode, and an electrolyte separating them. In Li-ion batteries, the anode is typically graphite-based. The cathode is commonly a lithium metal oxide, while the electrolyte composition can vary [2, 10]. There are commercially three main forms of battery cells for EV applications: pouch, cylindrical, and prismatic. The size and number of cells depend on the needed voltage, power and capacity of the EV [9].

Traditionally, battery design has been a cell-module-pack structure [11], but recent developments of EV-packs include cell-to-pack (CTP) and cell-to-chassis (CTC) where cells are directly implemented in the pack or the chassis [12]. In addition to cells and in some cases modules, packs also contain electrical, electronic and structural components such as casing, battery management system (BMS), cooling system and cables [9]. Exact design and composition of a battery are determined by a range of factors, such as cell chemistry, form factor, thermal management strategy and engineering preference [13], consequently requiring repair approaches dependent on the battery design.

With high voltage current can be kept low giving slim cables, and faster charging, but larger risks for arcing when opening and repairing batteries [14]. Power electronics and inverters can be internal or external on the battery pack. Thermal management may use air or fluid cooling [4] and there may be an electric control system and sensors controlling the cooling [9]. The BMS controls function of the battery, keeps charging and discharging within permitted current and voltage levels, and prevents the battery from being overcharged or undercharged [4]. A BMS often also monitors temperature, voltage and state-of-charge (SoC) continuously. State-of-health (SoH) is often dependent on monitoring one or several charging cycles. If charging cannot be performed, SoH may be difficult to determine. Various temperature and individual cells' SoC may make proper SoH estimation challenging. Depending on pack design, several module BMSs can be connected to a central control unit or just one BMS [4].

2.2 Battery Design for Repairability

The design of battery packs is rapidly evolving, with CTP and CTC being two interesting examples from a repairability and recyclability perspective [15, 16]. Design for repairability must be applied, before the battery is put on the market, while the effects of such design come several years later and may benefit other actors than those in charge of the initial design [17]. Circularity may often be divided into three main re-circulations, 3Rs: Reuse, Remanufacturing and Recycling [17]. Further divisions of Rs into 10Rs is often mentioned [18], here Repair is one of the higher R's connected to reuse or prolonging product life. Repair and refurbishment processes are similar [5], with same physical operations, but where repair means that the part is usually reinstalled in the same EV, a refurbished part might be put into another EV, with legal implications. Repair and maintenance are important measures in sustainable design of EVs and battery and drivetrain electronics components [19]. Design for safe dismantling and handling are coupled with labelling standards and information sharing regarding status of battery and repair [17]. In a complete disassembly process, all high and low-value parts are dismantled to be reused or recycled [20]. In repair, only faulty parts are replaced, but some used batteries may give spare parts. When removing or replacing one battery cell, the system needs rebalancing by monitoring the state of single cells [20].

The repairability of a battery pack depends on several factors, with the joining method being particularly important. Welded joints, e.g., make it harder to repair or replace individual parts. On the other hand, such joints may be more robust and reduce the demand for repair [21]. Vehicle and battery manufacturers jointly try to keep centralized control of vehicle battery data and system information, meaning that original equipment manufacturers (OEMs) stay in charge of how to measure the status of the battery, how to repair and disassemble it, and how to decide on wasting it to recycling [17]. This means they may not have business incentives to release such data to repairers. Modularisation and separation of electronic and supportive components are identified as strategies to facilitate disassembly and improve accessibility [12, 16], and may support serviceability and repairability. The number of cells also affects repairability. If a battery pack have cells connected in parallel and packed as a module, then, the module containing a single faulty cell need to be replaced in its entirety [4].

2.3 Batteries and Powertrains Share of Vehicle Value and Footprint

Repairing batteries is an important measure to avoid unnecessary environmental footprint of battery electric vehicles (BEVs), which in turn is strongly dependent on the use stage electricity mix. The avoided tailpipe emissions of BEVs compared to conventional vehicles often result in lower total life cycle impacts, especially in a European context [3, 22]. Several studies investigated the environmental impacts associated with batteries and powertrains and their share of a vehicle's total impact [3, 22–26]. Overall, studies conclude that the contribution from the battery is significant and is the individual component of a BEV with the largest part of the cradle-to-gate footprint [26]. In general, materials in the battery have a larger impact than the impact from energy used in its production [3]. Negri and Bieker [23] show a difference between using EU average electricity mix and renewable mix, and the battery's share of its impact (26 vs. 31% in their baseline). Due to a large share of upstream manufacturing emissions of BEV's total impacts, it is important to keep BEVs and batteries in use and, e.g., extend their lifetime through repair processes, to effectively utilise embodied emissions [27].

The cells often cover most of the battery's economic value, but electronics and other parts may also contain retainable value [4]. If cells are faulty, the electronics may still be functioning and possibly reused as spare parts for the same type of battery. Service, maintenance and/or other circular measures have been found to contribute up to 18% of an EV's total carbon footprint [19, 24], further highlighting that smart design for longevity via easy repair, maintenance and modularity can reduce the footprint by enabling longer service lives. Smart designs should ideally target the environmental hotspots of the EV for largest gains [19], where the battery as mentioned is one such component. Poor component design with respect to repairability may in worst case cause shorter life of the EV and hinder any circularity measures.

2.4 Right to Repair

The right to repair (R2R) directive (EU 2024/1799) [6] has been put in place to strengthen consumers' ability to prolong product life through repair. Here, ethical considerations such as fairness towards the involved actors as well as to the society and planet come into play [28]. Premature obsolescence when a product fails before its expected life is common and the R2R movement means that inability to repair a prematurely failed product means a serious constraint in the product ownership [28]. Meanwhile, safety of repairers and people involved in transporting failed batteries (or failed vehicles) must be ensured according to EU Battery Regulation [7].

For light EVs (light means of transport batteries, i.e. E-bikes and similar) there are requirements on repairability in the EU Battery Regulation [7]. For the batteries it only means that replacement batteries with compatible performance and safety as the original need to be available (EU 2023/1542) [7], not that repair instructions or replacement parts inside the battery must be made available. For car batteries, the regulation puts rights for independent repairers to access information needed to repair the vehicle, but there is no right to open, or right to repair electronics or cooling system inside the battery. On the contrary if such repair is performed, there are obligations to assure safety and that all battery functionality appears as in the original type-approving of the vehicle.

The Ecodesign for Sustainable Products Regulation, ESPR (EU 2024/1781) [29], demands replaceability of electronics in many products. Safety and CE (*Conformité Européenne*) certified functionality is obviously regarded as higher than the right to repair. For battery electronics, the potential risks to affect critical functionality have made the legislator rule that even if it is not illegal to repair batteries there are high demands on proving (testing and documenting) that all critical functionality remains after repair.

The R2R Directive [6] requires spare parts and tools to be offered at "reasonable price" that does not deter repair, and for listed products, producers are not allowed to hinder independent repairers. Batteries are not listed, but "goods incorporating light means of transport batteries" are listed, meaning that replacement batteries must be made available for independent bicycle repairers similarly to the above mentioned.

Vehicles also must abide to the EU Data Act (EU 2023/2854) [30], granting users access to vehicle generated data, who in turn can let independent repairers access this data. The EU Battery Regulation [7] acknowledge the R2R principles by requiring suppliers to offer battery replacement with the same or a functionally equivalent battery and by promoting standards to be developed that facilitate repair of batteries. However, the regulation also put several safety requirements that limits internal repair of batteries. In annex XIV to EU 2023/1542 [7], it is stated that shipping of used batteries requires that they are fully functional, unless it is a used battery sent back to the producer or a third party acting on its behalf. Independent repairers may not ship used batteries that are not fully functional. In sect. (40), the safety requirements of repaired batteries are stating that the original safety of the battery must apply after repair [7]. This may in practice be difficult to test and assure unless original testing software is accessible.

2.5 Safety Hazards in Handling Batteries

Handling Li-ion batteries may introduce hazards to both the personnel involved and the surroundings. For manual battery disassembly, the largest safety risks are associated with the high voltage and the chemicals in the battery cells [31].

A battery is a live object that can give electric shock, even if disconnected from the vehicle. Correct electrical design with regards to electrical safety needs to align with several ISO standards and adhere to CE certification in Europe [9]. High voltage means larger risks of shock and arcing, leading to disconnections or short circuits. Disconnecting batteries and handling these into safe transport storage or opening of batteries require personnel with correct electrical training, regardless of if batteries are fully functional or broken, although the risks increase for damaged or broken batteries.

Batteries are chemical systems that, if physically broken, may emit liquids and/or gases (mainly the electrolyte) that are hazardous to human health and the environment [31]. In functional batteries, the chemicals are enclosed, but for damaged or broken batteries there is a risk that chemicals are released. These may be hazardous for skin and inhaling and may also cause fire for certain chemistries [31].

The lithium metal may, if over-discharged, form lithium dendrites during battery cycling. If the anode is not protected this may lead to short circuits and, in the worst-case scenario, to hazardous side reactions [2]. The chemical cells in the battery pack are also sensitive to high or low temperatures, overcharging, and mechanical stress [2, 10]. In addition to this, many EV batteries are heavy [17] and from an ergonomic perspective the handling of these must be supported by lifting devices.

The safety issue is a major concern when transporting used EV batteries [20]. In Europe, transportation rules are stricter than in e.g. the US [20]. As mentioned, the

Annex XIV to EU Battery Regulation [7] only allows fully functional batteries to be shipped, otherwise it needs to be classified as hazardous waste and transported as such.

3 Method

This study included two types of empirics, first in 2025, a single action research (AR) case on battery electronic repair [32] gave an overview of the repair process (RQ1) and the dilemma to investigate with literature and experts (RQ2). Then followed expert interviews (EI) and literature overview performed 2026 to validate AR findings.

3.1 Empirics Method Part 1 - AR Mapping of Repair Cycle Actors

The first part of the empirics was an exploratory AR-based case where the first author experienced a damaged light EV battery. The AR was used to explore the process first handed, made inquiries in the value chain of how it could be repaired while discussing potential hinders or hazards with the actors personnel (bike repairman, bike repair manager, manufacturer tech. service, battery repairman). Action-oriented circular economy studies are commonly focussing on techno-economic aspects, creating circular material and energy flows and co-design, and organizational aspects of participatory community networks [33]. AR empowers individuals to drive tangible and transformative change, expanding the impact of research [32, 34]. Here the author, as industrial battery value chain researcher and an end user of an EV, experienced how the repair case of a faulty battery was treated by different actors (bicycle repairer, manufacturer, independent battery repairer, and indirect actors) and despite several actors' recommendations, pushed for repair and had a dialogue with each of them to explore this option. This case is used for demonstration of the problem and to get a deeper understanding of the different actors and their relations and concerns. Such AR-empirics may be used to show examples and increase the understanding of complex organizational issues [35] although the collected data have similar weakness as single case studies (it is unknown how generalisable results are) and interviewing (dialogue or open-ended interviews may be susceptible to unintended bias and non-factual opinions).

3.2 Empirics Method Part 2 - Battery Expert Interviews

The second part of the empirics entailed a digital expert interview round [36], performed with battery experts at RISE and three universities found within the RISE Battery research team, XPRES and Chalmers Area of Advance Transport. These research networks are involved in many research projects in battery technologies, chemistry, production, safety, monitoring, maintenance and repair, and disassembly and remanufacturing. A first interview round with two experts, a professor in energy systems at MDU and a senior battery development expert at RISE was performed with ca 45 min each, to set a framework and set questions for following interviews. Then interviews with seven battery research experts (2 from battery development & testing, 3 battery circular business researchers, 1 from heavy EV service development and 1 expert from battery production development) commenced. Interviews were 20–30 min with a focus on the three open questions:

1. *What is your experience of failed/faulty batteries and battery repair?*
2. *What obstacles can you come up with that hinders disassembly, repair and reuse of parts from the battery (not only cells)?*
3. *What conditions and/or monitoring would you recommend for transporting and repairing any faulty batteries?*

A digital whiteboard in Mural was used so that previous answers could be seen and extend the problem mapping, but most interviewees did not use it. To get a generalised picture of the repair process, the interview with a heavy EVs service development expert also included: *What actors exist in your repair process?*

3.3 Literature

No systematic literature review was done in the study. Instead, a background literature overview with repair-relevant papers found in the authors previous studies on battery circularity were used with review papers on design and repair of batteries and electronics [9, 10, 15, 16, 20]. Additional literature, when needed, to explain phenomena found in empirics, was searched through backward (references used in identified papers), and forward search (papers referencing identified papers) in Google Scholar and Scopus. In addition, searches specifically on EU legislations on right to repair and battery regulation were made in grey search on the internet (using EUR-Lex). A systematic literature review is recommended for further studies on right to repair and safety.

4 Results from AR and EI

Action Research Case for Light EV Battery Repair. The AR-case involved the battery of an electric bike with a front wheel motor and a dispatchable battery underneath the rear rack, but in all other parts basically constructed as a normal pedal bike. Price as new was around 1 600€. The extended three-year warranty had run out a year earlier. After a shaky ride in rainy weather there seemed to be a power shortage to the bike, and when trying to charge it later the same day the battery did not seem to take any charge.

The first point of contact in the repair cycle was with the authorized bike repair shop. They had a measuring device testing SoH for the battery at a small cost (around 20–30€). Doing so, the repairman stated that the battery was "broken", i.e. faulty or not fully functional according to the SoH. When the repair shop manager was asked if they could repair the battery, the answer was that they had a "do-not-open policy" enforced in the contract with the manufacturer, and referred to them regarding any repair prescriptions, instructions or specifications. They had spare batteries for sale, at a cost (650–700€), more than a third of the price of the E-bike when new, and offered to send the faulty battery to recycling. When asked about EU regulations such as the right to repair and the battery regulation, coming into force the same month and if that would change their response in future, he said they were worried about safety and did not have personnel with expertise to safely handle neither battery repair, nor electronics repair in the battery.

The manufacturer responded when contacted that they also had a do-not-open policy for failing batteries and they could not repair these. They had no recommended battery repair shops and did not provide instructions or specifications of the battery content for an independent battery repair shop. They did not give out any contact information of the battery supplier for further inquiry and referred to that the battery was sold before the new battery regulations came into force and did not answer how to act with respect to batteries or bikes sold after the new regulation had come into force.

When searching for independent battery repair shops in Sweden, four shops were found on the internet: one in each of the three major cities and on in a smaller town. The closest repair shop was selected. The local trains, used to transport the bike and battery to the battery repair shop, allow electric bikes onboard as long as they are CE marked and not charged onboard [37]. The responsibility of any such transportation lies fully on the passenger, in this case the owner of the bike.

The repair shop had an "opening fee" and then the cost depended on the repair task. Within the same day the repair person had opened the battery and identified the fault, which was a loose cable, and soldered it back. The cost was about 150€, less than a quarter of the cost of a new battery. When asking in general about battery faults, the repairer answered they had mainly different types of bikes, but also some electric lawn mowers and vacuum cleaners. For bikes it was usually easy to determine failing cells and replacing these or mend any failing wiring. The studied battery had standard cells (from Samsung) that were common in many appliances (Fig. 1). For the BMS, large differences applied depending on the manufacturer, where some BMS were available as replacement and some were not. For the battery studied, no repair possibilities would exist if the BMS had been faulty, since no spare BMS was available and special contacts and unknown programming made it difficult to repair. If the fault would have been in the BMS, only a partly repair could have been performed and a "standard" BMS for charging and running the bike could have been used instead. However, the lights would then not have functioned properly, and only full speed would be possible for the bike. In total, the repairer claimed that "around 80% of the batteries" that he opened could be repaired and kept in use. The batteries that could not be repaired had most often been used in the coastline with saltwater sprayed from the sea ruining electronics, and sometimes single cells would be replaced.

Fig. 1. Photo of the inside of the repaired battery from the electric bike

When asked about safety concerns, the repairer said he had been working many years with battery technology at a battery manufacturer and knew how to handle the risks involved. He understood that bike repair shops did not dare to open batteries and thought that they should not, unless they had the right competence and training.

As owner of the battery, the major safety risk in the faulty battery was perceived to be trying to charge the faulty battery. The fault was identified after trying to charge, and if any thermal runaway would have happen, this was probably when, i.e. before any repair shop was contacted. This means the charger needs to stop any risky charge.

Mapping the Battery Repair Process. The process involved the user of the vehicle, the authorised vehicle repair shop, the provider (OEM) of the vehicle, the battery provider, a transporter and an independent repairer of batteries (Fig. 2). They all have different incentives for selling a new battery or repairing the old. When interviewed, an expert of heavy EV service development confirmed the actors although the picture can be somewhat more complex with authorized dealers and OEM controlled battery repairers where only authorized personnel are allowed to perform advanced repair.

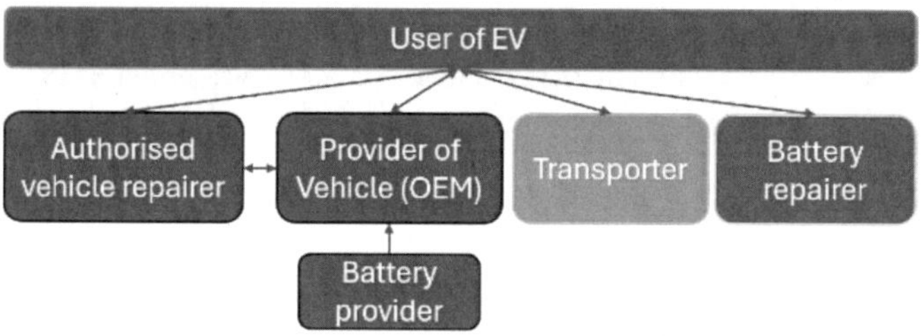

Fig. 2. Actors and dependencies between them in the repair cycle in the case

The most important concerns at the EV repair (mechanical repair) and the battery repair (electronics repair) were competence of the personnel. Transporters and provider of EVs mainly tried to avoid any responsibility for safety issues that could occur. For the transporter, this was not a focused business. The economic incentives to repair instead of providing a new battery seemed low for the battery provider, the EV provider and the EV repair provider, since they would all earn the same or more with less working time involved by just selling a new spare part battery. For the owner, there was a substantial gain at a similar safety risk in repairing instead of replacing the battery. For the battery repair, there was a substantial gain in few working minutes. Looking at sustainability, two main issues were at stake: Environmental loss by scrapping a battery that could be repaired and probably be used twice as long as the current lifetime, and societal risk of a fire accident. Here there were no risk, but the risk was unknown until the battery was opened and the main possible risk was when the fault had occurred but was still unknown to the user and charging was tried at home.

Result of Expert Interviews. The expert interviews with open questions around battery faults, repairs and safety critical faults resulted in a map of faults - critical safety hazards and possible detection methods. Two of the interviewed (circular business) researchers mainly pointed at legislation and contracting as driver and hinder for repair. The waste legislation and Battery Regulation were interpreted by them as an obligation to send batteries for recycling if batteries were faulty. It is obligated to assure CE certification and required SoH testing and documentation after repair. This is difficult to assure for independent repairers and can also be expensive for the battery producer or a third-party repairer operating on behalf of the producer. Transport of a battery to a repair shop is allowed in some cases if battery SoH and function can be proven, while if it is not functional, it has to be transported and dealt with as waste, and in practice one interviewee (development expert) said that all damaged batteries were transported to recycling in a salt water-filled box. Another interviewee (circular business) said that in a case study she had made, damaged EV batteries were stored for 14 days, then either an OEM-authorised repairer comes to inspect the battery, or it is transported in a safe box filled with sand, in case thermal runaway of the battery would occur. Here, safety is critical and faulty batteries may have to be sorted into safe and unsafe faulty batteries, requiring local competence. The heavy EV service expert said most faulty batteries can be serviced/repaired, modular battery design should be done so cooling, connectors etc. can be serviced/repaired from the outside, since most faulty batteries are not due to cell failure, rather failing software or cables/connectors/cooling.

Several of the interviewees discussed safety critical faults and how to detect if a safety hazard had occurred or if a battery is safe. Two types of hazards were regarded as the most critical: thermal runaway and self-ignition, both being hazardous for the surroundings as well as the personnel handling the battery and may cause severe damage to people and property. Three other risks, chemical risks, electric shock and ergonomic risks, were mainly work environmental risks for the personnel handling, transporting or repairing the battery.

Thermal runaway is a self-accelerating failure where heat is generated in the cells faster than it is cooled and the temperature increase then triggers exothermic chemical reactions in the cell. The accelerating heat may then in the end cause fire and/or explosion, and it is difficult to extinguish such a fire. The root causes of thermal runaway can involve external or internal shortcuts, overcharging, overheating or freezing the cells or dendrites/whiskers building up in the cells. The dendrite/whiskers may build up by repeated overdischarging. To detect thermal runaway risks, heat cameras were suggested to be used for external inspection and monitoring of faulty batteries, but one interviewee meant this is not possible for heavier batteries with heavy casing and cooling. Such monitoring only detects when a temperature rise has already occurred, not the cause which involves damaged cell membrane in cells.

Self-ignition is a risk for certain chemistries of batteries, when cells are damaged so that the electrolyte leaks. The electrolyte may then self-ignite if it reaches oxygen in the air and heat or a spark is present. The heat generated may cause thermal runaway in adjacent cells. Again, the cause of leakage may be dendrites/whiskers or cracks in the electrode, or mechanical force, high or low temperatures, from thermal runaway. One researcher mentions trials (not field ready) with HC-gas sensors in battery boxes to detect electrolyte leakage. Transports with non-oxygen atmosphere may limit risks. Another researcher mention that most LFP-chemistry based batteries, hardly have any risk for igniting the electrolyte. Moreover, leaking electrolyte may cause chemical risks.

Chemical risks mainly regard the risk of respiratory or skin exposure if batteries are leaking. One interviewee mentions the importance of caution on electrolyte risks. Proper competence and personal protection equipment can minimise risks for personnel. Again, HC-gas detection may be used to detect leakage. Electric shock is a risk when handling both functional and faulty EV batteries. Volt and current measurement may give indication of the risks. With proper competence and personal protection equipment, the risk for personnel can be limited. EV batteries are often heavy and in e.g. crashed EVs, their weight may risk causing physical injuries. This is a risk similar to many other heavy parts and may be limited by using proper lifting support.

As mentioned above, some hazards are critical for the personnel who tries to handle, open or repair the battery, and include risk for electrical shock, chemical risks and risk of handling heavy materials (see Table 1). Other issues may be totally safe. In a damaged vehicle, for example after an accident, if the SoH measurement is working, it is generally regarded as safe to handle the vehicle and battery in accordance with given safety instructions. However, if SoH measurement outputs are not available, the battery may or may not have a safety critical fault. Sometimes partial information from SoH may be retrieved, still it may be unclear if there is a safety issue or not. Here, increased monitoring of state-of-unhealth, or state-of-safety for damaged batteries may increase the safety assurance for repair. Most of the expert discussed detection in field, but one also mentioned that in repair shops, lab X-ray and CT scan may be used to give better knowledge of the state-of-safety. Also, AI and/or statistical methods could be used to determine if there is higher or lower risk in handling a battery depending on failure.

Table 1. Critical faults, suggested detection and protection

Hazardous fault	Suggested detection	Protection
Thermal runaway	IR, heat camera, temperature monitoring	Safe box, possibly filled with sand
Self-ignition – electrolyte leakage	HC-gas detectors (not field ready)	Non oxygen atmosphere, safe battery chemistries
Chemical emission	HC-gas detectors	PPE, training
Electric shock – also functional batteries	Volt and current measuring	PPE, training
Heavy lifting – also functional batteries	Always present	Training, lifting devices

5 Discussion

What main actors need to be involved in the battery repair process and what may their concerns and motivations in repair and safety of faulty batteries be? As highlighted in the AR bicycle case, battery repair involves several actors along the value chain: provider of vehicle (OEM)/battery, repairers, transporters, and the user/owner. These actors' interests in the R2R principles are mixed, since linear business is profitable, and producers of electronics, batteries or vehicles may earn less on repairing than from selling new batteries as spare parts. For the owner there is a saving in repairing [1], and environmental impact can be reduced by prolonging the life of the battery [19, 24]. The power of the owner in the bicycle case and independent repairer seems low compared to the global companies producing batteries and vehicles. Legal concerns and lack of willingness to take responsibility for any risks is a major bottleneck in the process. A worry about risks could possibly be mitigated by improved monitoring as suggested below, but it also depends on competence and trust from the actor. Lack of competence and training at actors who handle the faulty batteries could be improved together with knowledge of personal protection for different type of chemistries. Meanwhile transporters and logistics providers cannot be expected to be battery experts.

What risks and hinders are apparent in handling and repairing faulty batteries, and can they be detected and/or mitigated? Repairing is an essential measure to lower system cost and environmental footprint of faulty batteries [19]. The AR-empirics indicate that most faulty batteries are repairable and the EI support this. The EI-empiric indicates that technologies are available to monitor safety of faulty batteries that could be used to increase the amounts of damaged batteries that may be rescued to repair. Safety of actors involved is crucial to assure [4, 7]. Here, improved monitoring of state-of-safety involving critical risks of leaking electrolyte and thermal runaway could be developed. Heat and gas monitoring and electrical isolation would cover most if not all safety hazards for safe transport, and in repair shops further instruments could be available. Several safety hazards for personnel can be mitigated by raising battery competence and use of proper PPE in case they are needed. Detection of hazardous versus non-hazardous faults should be further researched. Modular design so that cooling, software and electric connector faults can be determined from outside of pack may help. Design to reduce risks, and design to be able to disconnect and reuse electronics and cells from each other would improve circularity, for example via modularisation [12, 16]. Overall, the seven experts were not fully aligned on all aspects discussed, motivating the need for further research to fully understand how and when a battery can (and should) be repaired.

There is one problem in legislation and design of batteries with regards to repair: a battery that is not faulty obviously does not need repair, but for faulty batteries there are conflicting demands on repairability, safe handling and certification of repaired batteries. In Annex XIV to the Battery Regulation [7], shipment requirements demand documentation that the batteries are fully functional and tested for SoH, unless it is shipped to the producer or third-party acting on the producer's behalf. It is in other words impossible to ship any faulty batteries to any independent repair shop according to current legislation. Changes in technology, design and legislation are needed.

In many cases a failure of the battery and SoH fault may be the result of a non-hazardous fault, such as when a cable is disconnected, or when a non-critical short circuit has occurred in the electronics. In other cases, the lack of SoH may come from a safety critical state, e.g. short circuit or overheating. Therefore, we argue that legislation cannot demand "fully functional" to be able to transport and handle batteries to repair. Instead, the safety of the faulty battery should be tested as state-of-safety where transportation, packaging and handling should be assured. More research may be needed investigating the amount of faulty batteries and the repairability of these.

Even if the vehicle is at a repair shop, or if it is an OEM authorised repair shop, it may be difficult and costly to assure "that the safety of such batteries when repaired can be assessed based on non-destructive tests adapted to them" in accordance with paragraph 40 in EU 2023/1542 [7]. Thus, such testing may also need further research.

The actor map was seen as generisable although in heavy vehicle there are some more optional actors. Some of the detection technologies are only applicable for certain battery designs but it should be possible to develop findings to general design guidance.

6 Contribution and Conclusion

This research contributes with repairability and transport safety in battery and electronic circularity research by investigating the repair circle, its actors and motives that supports and hinders an efficient repair system for EV batteries. It contributes with practical challenges and suggested developments using dual methodology, showing how AR can be used [34]. The paper raises knowledge on managerial conflicts between different sustainability aims such as environmental impact and public safety and health in the development of EV batteries and electronics. Limitations: only a limited AR case and few interviewees in the EI.

Repairing is an essential measure to lower system cost and environmental impacts of faulty batteries. It is indicated that many faulty batteries can be repaired or serviced to their functional state. Often several actors need to be involved and the safety of them is crucial to assure. Overall, design to reduce risks and to disconnect and reuse electronics and cells from batteries and battery packs would improve circularity. Detection of hazardous vs. non-hazardous faults could be further researched to enhance lifetime extension of batteries that are repairable. Improved monitoring of state-of-safety involving critical risks of leaking electrolyte and thermal runaway could be developed. Several safety hazards for personnel can be mitigated by raising battery competence and use of proper PPE in case they are needed. Further in-depth expert interviews especially with electronics and battery repair professionals is recommended for the future.

Acknowledgments. This research was partly performed within the Vinnova funded SusTeq project (2024-00789) within Chalmers Area of Advance Production and Area of Advance Transport. Partly the study was also performed within the Knowledge Foundation funded project Circul8 (project id 20230024_KKS), connected to XPRES, centre of eXellence in Production RESearch, collaboration with KTH, RISE and MDU connected to the Strategic Research Area (No 0219, 201) Excellence in Production Research (XPRES).

Disclosure of Interests. The authors have no competing interests to declare that are relevant to the content of this article. Only public funding as reported in acknowledgements.

References

1. König, A., Nicoletti, L., Schröder, D., Wolff, S., Waclaw, A., Lienkamp, M.: An overview of parameter and cost for battery electric vehicles. World Electr. Veh. J. **12**(1), 21 (2021). https://doi.org/10.3390/wevj12010021
2. Berg, H., Zackrisson, M.: Perspectives on environmental and cost assessment of lithium metal negative electrodes in electric vehicle traction batteries. J. Power Sources. **415**, 83–90 (2019)
3. Hill, N., Raugei, M., Pons, A., Vasileiadis, N., Ong, H., Casullo, L.: Environmental challenges through the life cycle of battery electric vehicles (No. PE 733.112) (2023)
4. Saw, L.H., Ye, Y., Tay, A.A.: Integration issues of lithium-ion battery into electric vehicles battery pack. J. Clean. Prod. **113**, 1032–1045 (2016)
5. Gharfalkar, M., Ali, Z., Hillier, G.: Clarifying the disagreements on various reuse options: repair, recondition, refurbish and remanufacture. Waste Manag. Res. **34**(10), 995–1005 (2016)
6. European Union.: Directive (EU) 2024/1799 of the European Parliament and of the Council of 13 June 2024 on Common Rules Promoting the Repair of Goods and Amending Regulation (EU) 2017/2394 and Directives (EU) 2019/771 and (EU) 2020/1828 (2024).

7. European Union: Regulation (EU) 2023/1542 of the European Parliament and of the Council of 12 July 2023 Concerning Batteries and Waste Batteries, Amending Directive 2008/98/EC and Regulation (EU) 2019/1020 and Repealing Directive 2006/66/EC. (2023).
8. Olsson, L., Fallahi, S., Schnurr, M., Diener, D., Van Loon, P.: Circular business models for extended EV battery life. Batteries. **4**(4), 57 (2018)
9. Haghbin, S., Rezaei Larijani, M., Zolghadri, M., Hedayati Kia, S.: Automotive battery pack standards and design characteristics: a review. Discov. Appl. Sci. **7**(7), 731 (2025)
10. Nitta, N., Wu, F., Lee, J.T., Yushin, G.: Li-ion battery materials: present and future. Mater. Today. **18**(5), 252–264 (2015)
11. Zwicker, M.F.R., Moghadam, M., Zhang, W., Nielsen, C.V.: Automotive battery pack manufacturing–a review of battery to tab joining. J. Adv. Joining Processes. **1**, 100017 (2020)
12. Cicconi, P., Kumar, P.: Design approaches for li-ion battery packs: a review. J. Energy Storage. **73**, 109197 (2023)
13. Paudel, S., Zhang, J., Ayalew, B., Griddaluru, V.Y., Singh, R.: Design, prototyping, and integration of battery modules for electric vehicles and energy storage systems. Electricity. **6**(4), 63 (2025)
14. Rothgang, S., Baumhöfer, T., van Hoek, H., Lange, T., De Doncker, R.W., Sauer, D.U.: Modular battery design for reliable, flexible and multi-technology energy storage systems. Appl. Energy. **137**, 931–937 (2015)
15. Chen, H., Yang, Y., Dong, Z.: The effect of product design on recycling efficiency of lithium-ion batteries through structural equation modeling and life cycle assessment. Sci. Rep. **15**(1), 12352 (2025)
16. Lander, L. et al.: Breaking it down: a techno-economic assessment of the impact of battery pack design on disassembly costs. Appl. Energy. **331**, 120437 (2023)
17. Kurdve, M., Zackrisson, M., Johansson, M.I., Ebin, B., Harlin, U.: Considerations when modelling EV battery circularity systems. Batteries. **5**(2), 40 (2019)
18. Skärin, F., Rösiö, C., Andersen, A.L.: Towards circular production systems: outlining the concept, challenges and future research directions. In: International Conference on System-Integrated Intelligence, pp. 616–625. Springer International Publishing, Cham (2022)
19. Glans, E.: Life cycle assessment of Vidde's pilot snowmobile-today and in future circular production systems. RISE Report. **2025**, 80 (2025) https://urn.kb.se/resolve?urn=urn%3Anbn%3Ase%3Ari%3Adiva-78775
20. Sharmili, N., Nagi, R., Wang, P.: A review of research in the li-ion battery production and reverse supply chains. J. Energy Storage. **68**, 107622 (2023)
21. Rüther, T. et al.: Battery pack states, properties, and characterization techniques beyond cell level. Cell reports physical. Science. **6**(11) (2025)
22. Šimaitis, J., Lupton, R., Vagg, C., Butnar, I., Sacchi, R., Allen, S.: Battery electric vehicles show the lowest carbon footprints among passenger cars across 1.5–3.0° C energy decarbonisation pathways. Commun. Earth Environ. **6**(1), 476 (2025)
23. Negri, M., Bieker, G.: Life-cycle greenhouse gas emissions from passenger cars in the European Union. In: International Council on Clean Transportation (2025)
24. Palm, R., Hagdahl, K.-H., & Dahllöf, L.: Carbon footprint report - carbon footprint of the Volvo EX60. (2026). https://www.volvocars.com/files/cs/v3/assets/blt066aeed1a18c768c/bltc2b3ab4ccf1f617f/volvo_ex60_carbonfootprintreport.pdf?branch=prod_alias
25. IEA. EV Life Cycle Assessment Calculator. 2024. (2024). https://www.iea.org/data-and-statistics/data-tools/ev-life-cycle-assessment-calculator
26. Lombardo, T., Dhir, S.: EV battery supply chain sustainability: life cycle impacts and the role of recycling.: Lombardo, Teo, Dhir, Shobhan. In: EV Battery Supply Chain Sustainability: Life Cycle Impacts and the Role of Recycling. International Energy Agency, Paris (2024)

27. Nguyen-Tien, V., Zhang, C., Strobl, E., Elliott, R.J.: The closing longevity gap between battery electric vehicles and internal combustion vehicles in Great Britain. Nat. Energy. **10**(3), 354–364 (2025)
28. Dalhammar, C., Molnár, M., Maitre-Ekern, E.: From "working with the market" to "challenging the market" in EU product law? Ethical aspects of right-to-repair. In: Vikten av miljörätten & vikten av att vikta rätt: FESTSKRIFT TILL Charlotta Zetterberg (pp. 23-42). Iustus förlag (2025)
29. European Union: Regulation (EU) 2024/1781 of the European Parliament and of the council of 13 June 2024 establishing a framework for setting ecodesign requirements for sustainable products. Off. J. Eur. Union. **L** (2024) https://eur-lex.europa.eu/eli/reg/2024/1781/oj
30. European Union: Regulation (EU) 2023/2854 of the European Parliament and of the council of 13 December 2023 on harmonised rules on fair access to and use of data (data act). Off. J. Eur. Union. (2023) https://eur-lex.europa.eu/eli/reg/2023/2854/oj
31. Wegener, K., Andrew, S., Raatz, A., Dröder, K., Herrmann, C.: Disassembly of electric vehicle batteries using the example of the Audi Q5 hybrid system. Procedia Cirp. **23**, 155–160 (2014)
32. Kuran, O.: Closing the theory-practice gap: socio-economic approach and action research in management. Syst. Pract. Action Res. **37**(6), 783–810 (2024)
33. Dominko, M., Primc, K., Slabe-Erker, R., Kalar, B.: A bibliometric analysis of circular economy in the fields of business and economics: towards more action-oriented research. Environ. Dev. Sustain. **25**(7), 5797–5830 (2023)
34. Johansson, P.E., Wallo, A.: Action researchers' competence-in-use in operations management research. Prod. Plan. Control, 1–16 (2026)
35. Silva, S.C., Neiva, C.R., Dias, J.C.: Action research on circular economy strategies in fashion retail. Int. J. Retail Distrib. Manag. **53**(1), 109–126 (2025)
36. Meuser, M., Nagel, U.: The expert interview and changes in knowledge production. In: Interviewing Experts, pp. 17–42. Palgrave Macmillan UK, London (2009)
37. Västtrafik Webpage regarding bringing electrical vehicles on trains: https://www.vasttrafik.se/en/travel-with-us/during-the-trip/Bike/. Accessed 30 Jan 2026

Forecasting Exogenous Waste Inflow: A Two-Regime Hierarchical Approach for Circular Battery Manufacturing

Ibrahim Teymurlu[1,2(✉)], Quang-Vinh Dang[1], Mehrdad Mohammadi[1], and Ivo Adan[1]

[1] Eindhoven University of Technology, Eindhoven, The Netherlands
{i.teymurlu,q.v.dang,m.mohammadi1,i.adan}@tue.nl
[2] Zhero Systems, Breda, The Netherlands
ibrahim.teymurlu@zhero-systems.nl

Abstract. Waste-based manufacturing operations face a critical forecasting challenge: production planning depends entirely on volatile, uncontrollable supply streams whose volume and quality fluctuate unpredictably. This paper addresses this challenge in the context of circular battery manufacturing, where end-of-life e-bike batteries are repurposed into large-scale energy storage systems. We develop a hierarchical two-regime forecasting approach that accounts for the multi-stage uncertainty inherent in waste streams, where batteries must pass through sequential filtering stages, and the regime-shifting dynamics caused by sporadic high-volume "peak inflow events" Unlike standard time-series models that assume homogeneous behavior, our approach decomposes the supply stream into non-peak and peak regimes and then applies specialized model ensembles to each. Our approach achieves a mean absolute error of around 82 batteries per week, outperforming the best classical cascade approach by 5.0% and the best deep learning approach by 18.6%.

Keywords: Time Series Analysis · Forecasting · Sustainable Manufacturing · Waste-Based Manufacturing · Reverse Logistics

1 Introduction

The global transition to a circular economy has positioned lithium-ion battery recovery and repurposing as a critical pillar of sustainable industrial strategy [5,13]. Within this landscape, our industry partner operates as a circular sustainable energy company that manufactures large-scale energy storage systems by repurposing end-of-life e-bike batteries collected from waste streams. Unlike traditional manufacturing, where raw material procurement is managed through stable supplier contracts, the company's production planning entirely depends on highly volatile and uncontrollable inflow of waste batteries.

While historical time-series data exists, the inherent volatility of battery waste streams presents a compound forecasting challenge that traditional methods struggle to address [4]. The uncertainty is twofold. First, the volumes of

Published by Springer Nature Switzerland AG 2027
G. Pezzotta et al. (Eds.): APMS 2026, IFIP AICT 808, pp. 91–106, 2027.
https://doi.org/10.1007/978-3-032-38594-9_7

processed batteries fluctuate unpredictably due to external disposal behaviors and market dynamics [8], and changes in battery waste regulations [3]. Second, the proportion of batteries passing quality criteria varies substantially between battery models and evolves over time [5]. Consequently, even periods of high processing activity may yield limited usable inventory if acceptance rates are low, meaning that volume forecasts alone are insufficient for production planning. This problem is further compounded by sporadic "Peak Inflow Events"; large, model-specific batch arrivals of usable batteries that deviate sharply from baseline patterns. Although machine learning approaches for rare event prediction exist in the literature [16], the sparse, heterogeneous nature of battery type specific waste data makes such methods impractical in this context. Standard time-series forecasting techniques, when applied directly to such volatile and regime-shifting data, underestimate peak periods and fail to capture the conditional dependencies between processing volumes and acceptance rates [6].

In the context of waste-flow and reverse-logistics, recent forecasting studies use statistical, machine-learning, and deep-learning methods for operational planning. Mohsin et al. [10] propose a seasonal decomposition ensemble for e-waste recovery, using Holt–Winters exponential smoothing and support vector regression (SVR), and compare it with several established benchmarking methods. Mudannayake et al. [11] evaluate models such as autoregressive integrated moving average (ARIMA)-based methods, Light Gradient Boosting Machine (LightGBM), Random Forest, Prophet, long short-term memory networks (LSTM), temporal convolutional networks (TCN), Transformer models, and Neural Basis Expansion Analysis for Time Series (N-BEATS) for municipal solid waste forecasting. Cooijmans [2] studies reverse-supply-chain inflow forecasting for workforce planning. Together, these works motivate benchmark families; ARIMA, SARIMA, Holt–Winters, Prophet, LightGBM, XGBoost, and N-BEATS. However, they mainly forecast aggregate waste or return inflows, rather than jointly modelling the processed–accepted–usable cascade and irregular peak-driven battery inflow events.

Based on these challenges, this study addresses the following research question: *How can a forecasting framework exploit both the hierarchical processing structure and the regime-specific behavior of battery waste inflow to generate reliable forecasts of usable batteries under routine and peak-event conditions?*

This question reflects a gap in waste forecasting and reverse-logistics forecasting literature. Prior work shows that hierarchical or reconciled forecasts can improve accuracy when lower-level series contain useful distinct information [7]. In addition, intermittent and lumpy demand studies show that irregular series can benefit from separating event occurrence from event size, instead of modelling the series as one homogeneous process [2,14].

To address this gap, we develop a hierarchical two-regime forecasting approach. It explicitly models the processed–accepted–usable battery cascade and separates the supply stream into *non-peak* and *peak* components. This supports specialized ensembles: Prophet–LightGBM for regular operations, and Prophet, LightGBM, and XGBoost for peak events [1,9,17]. The main contribution is the integration of cascade-aware forecasting with peak-aware decomposition for waste-based manufacturing inflow.

The remainder of the paper is organized as follows. Section 2 formulates the problem, and Sect. 3 presents our solution methodology. Section 4 discusses the experimental setup and results. Finally, the conclusions are given in Sect. 5.

2 Problem Formulation

In this section, we describe and formulate the problem. Let $\mathbf{D} = \{d_1, d_2, \ldots, d_n\}$ denote a set of n observed business days over a number of years. For each day $d \in \mathbf{D}$, we define the state variables representing the processing cascade: $y^{(\text{proc})}(d)$ is the total batteries processed, $y^{(\text{accepted})}(d)$ is the accepted batteries out of those that are processed, and $y^{(\text{usable})}(d)$ is our target variable, the total count of usable batteries. Given no higher level data, we assume independence for $y^{(\text{proc})}(d)$. The rest are related through:

$$y^{(\text{accepted})}(d) = y^{(\text{proc})}(d) \times y^{a_r}(d) \tag{1}$$

$$y^{(\text{usable})}(d) = y^{(\text{proc})}(d) \times y^{a_r}(d) \times y^{u_r}(d) \tag{2}$$

where $y^{a_r}(d) = \frac{y^{(\text{accepted})}(d)}{y^{(\text{proc})}(d)}$ and $y^{u_r}(d) = \frac{y^{(\text{usable})}(d)}{y^{(\text{accepted})}(d)}$ are acceptance and usability rates respectively. Each of these daily counts are in reality aggregation of counts per battery type. Let $\mathbf{T} = \{t_1, t_2, \ldots, t_m\}$ denote the set of $m \approx 520$ battery types. Then for each daily count $y(d)$ for $d \in D$ we have:

$$y(d) = \sum_{t \in \mathbf{T}} y(d, t), \tag{3}$$

where $y(d,t)$ denotes the count associated with battery type t on day d. Accordingly, the daily acceptance and usability rates are computed from these aggregated counts and are not defined at the level of individual battery types:

$$y^{a_r}(d) = \frac{\sum_{t \in \mathbf{T}} y^{(\text{accepted})}(d,t)}{\sum_{t \in \mathbf{T}} y^{(\text{proc})}(d,t)}, \tag{4}$$

$$y^{u_r}(d) = \frac{\sum_{t \in \mathbf{T}} y^{(\text{usable})}(d,t)}{\sum_{t \in \mathbf{T}} y^{(\text{accepted})}(d,t)}. \tag{5}$$

The objective is to forecast the future number of usable batteries given the historical observations up to day d. Specifically, for a forecast horizon $\mathbf{h} = \{1, 2, \ldots, H\}$, we seek to predict:

$$\hat{\mathbf{y}}^{\text{usable}}(d) = \left[\hat{y}^{\text{usable}}(d+1), \hat{y}^{\text{usable}}(d+2), \ldots, \hat{y}^{\text{usable}}(d)\right] \tag{6}$$

using information about past observations of the processing cascade and any additional covariates.

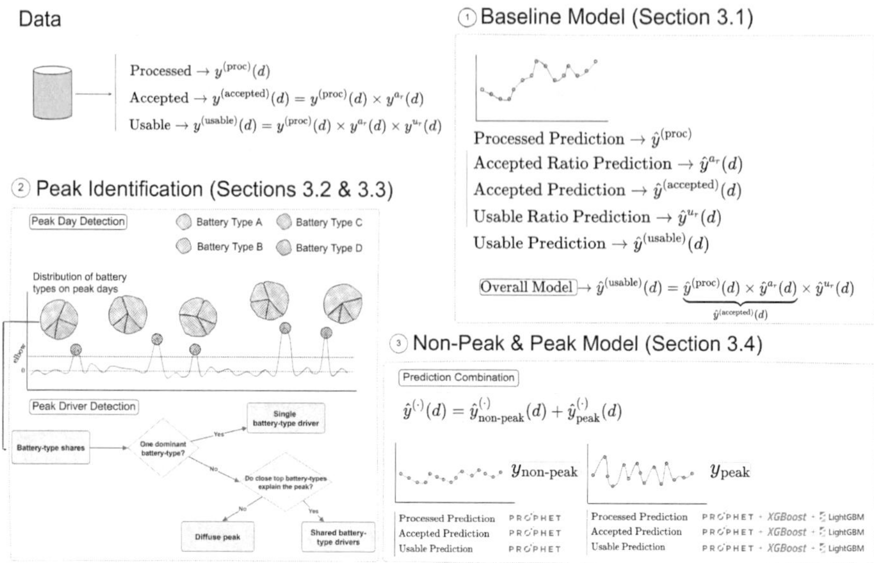

Fig. 1. Schematic overview of the hierarchical peak-adjusted forecasting methodology. (1) The baseline model forecasts the processed, accepted, and usable stages through the processing cascade. (2) Peak days are identified from deviations, and the corresponding battery-type shares are used to select peak drivers. (3) The final model separates non-peak and peak components and recombines them into the peak-adjusted usable inflow forecast.

3 Methodology

In this section, we present the forecasting pipeline, as illustrated in Fig. 1, where we introduce our ensemble approach to make the forecast more reliable and dynamic. Specifically, we incorporate a computationally efficient method to capture the temporal dynamics (Sect. 3.1), which is later used to identify the "peak-event" days and driver models (Sects. 3.2 and 3.3). We then train two separate models on the "non-peak" and "peak" regimes, utilizing both statistical and tree-based machine learning models (Sect. 3.4).

3.1 Baseline Model: Three-Stage Prophet Cascade

To initiate the forecasting pipeline, we look at the prediction objective and the relation of stages of battery count data one onto another; Eqs. (6), (2), and (1), respectively. It is then needless to say that it would be crude to train a forecasting model directly on the usable count data, since then we ignore the dependency of the cascade. Instead, we need to model the relation of each stage.

Mimicking this hierarchy, we define a sequential prediction flow in which each stage of the processing cascade is predicted separately and then combined to produce the final usable battery forecast. Specifically, we first forecast the daily processed battery count $\hat{y}^{(\text{proc})}(d)$, followed by independent forecasts of the acceptance and usability rates, $\hat{y}^{a_r}(d)$ and $\hat{y}^{u_r}(d)$. The predicted usable battery inflow is then obtained by composing these predictions, according to Eq. (2), as follows:

$$\hat{y}^{(\text{usable})}(d) = \underbrace{\hat{y}^{(\text{proc})}(d) \times \hat{y}^{a_r}(d)}_{\hat{y}^{(\text{accepted})}(d)} \times \hat{y}^{u_r}(d) \tag{7}$$

We implement this sequential forecasting flow using Prophet models at each stage of the cascade. Prophet is considered as a benchmark model because of its widespread use in industrial time-series forecasting and its ability to capture trend and seasonality in a flexible manner.

In general, Prophet-based models provide stable and accurate forecasts for the majority of days across all stages of the cascade [6]. However, we observe that the model is prone to larger errors during peak inflow days, when unusually high volumes of batteries arrive in short time windows. These peak events are rare, irregular, and not strongly tied to recurring seasonal patterns, making them difficult to capture.

Rather than treating these errors as model failures, we interpret them as a consequence of the structural uncertainty inherent in waste-based supply streams. In the following sections, we analyze the residual behavior of the Prophet models in detail and propose an extension that explicitly accounts for peak events, enabling the baseline forecasts to be adjusted in a controlled and data-driven manner.

3.2 Peak Day Identification

To better understand the nature of these peak-related errors, we examine the residuals of the baseline Prophet forecasts. Let

$$r_i = y^{(\text{usable})}(d_i) - \hat{y}^{(\text{usable})}(d_i), \tag{8}$$

denote the forecast residual on day d_i, where positive values correspond to an underestimate of the usable battery inflow. Figure 2(a) illustrates both the temporal evolution of these residuals and their empirical distribution. Although most residuals are concentrated around zero, a small number of days exhibit substantially larger positive deviations, forming a sparse right tail.

To characterize this behavior, we focus on the positive residuals and construct the empirical exceedance probability

$$P(r_i > x) = \frac{1}{N} \sum_{i=1}^{N} \mathbb{I}(r_i > x), \tag{9}$$

where N is the total number of residuals and $\mathbb{I}(\cdot)$ denotes the indicator function. Plotting $P(r_i > x)$ on a logarithmic scale reveals a clear change in the decay behavior as the residual magnitude increases, suggesting a transition between regular forecast variability and structurally distinct peak events.

We identify this transition point using an elbow-based changepoint detection approach [15]. Specifically, we fit two linear segments to the log-exceedance curve: one corresponding to the sparse region and the other to the rest. The elbow point, as shown in Fig. 2(b), is defined as the value of x that minimizes the combined fitting error of this piecewise-linear approximation. This point serves as a data-driven threshold separating typical forecast errors from peak inflow days, and is subsequently used to trigger additional analysis and model adjustments in later stages of our approach. The days that have an error above this given threshold for both in-sample and out-of-sample residuals, are marked as $\mathbf{D}_{\text{peak}} \subset \mathbf{D}$.

3.3 Peak Driver Identification

Following the identification of the set of peak days $\mathbf{D}_{\text{peak}} \subset \mathbf{D}$, where the residual r_i exceeds the elbow-derived threshold, we perform a granular decomposition to isolate the specific battery types $t \in \mathbf{T}$ driving these anomalies. For a given peak day $d \in \mathbf{D}_{\text{peak}}$, let $s(d,t)$ denote the fractional contribution of battery type t to the total usable count:

$$s(d,t) = \frac{y^{(\text{usable})}(d,t)}{y^{(\text{usable})}(d)}, \quad \text{where} \sum_{t \in \mathbf{T}} s(d,t) = 1 \tag{10}$$

To identify the primary drivers, we define an ordered set of shares $S_d = \{s_{(1)}, s_{(2)}, \ldots, s_{(m)}\}$ such that $s_{(1)} \geq s_{(2)} \geq \cdots \geq s_{(m)}$, where $s_{(i)}$ represents the i-th largest share on day d (e.g., the left-hand pie in Fig. 3). The selection of the peak driver set $\mathbf{T}_d^* \subset \mathbf{T}$ is governed by two primary heuristic rules. First, under the **Dominance Rule**, if the leading battery type exceeds a threshold, $s_1 > \tau_{\text{leader}} = 0.45$ where 0.45 is decided using expert knowledge and data analysis, it is identified as the sole driver, such that $\mathbf{T}_d^* = \{t_{(1)}\}$.

In cases where no single model dominates, we apply the **Shared Contribution Rule**. Under this rule, we identify a set of candidate drivers by including the top i types, provided that they satisfy a maximum capacity $K = 3$ while maintaining proximity to the leader defined by $s_{(1)} - s_{(i)} \leq \tau_{\text{margin}}$, where $\tau_{\text{margin}} = 0.10$ (decided based on expert knowledge and data analysis). Crucially, to ensure that the selected set is sufficiently representative of the peak events,

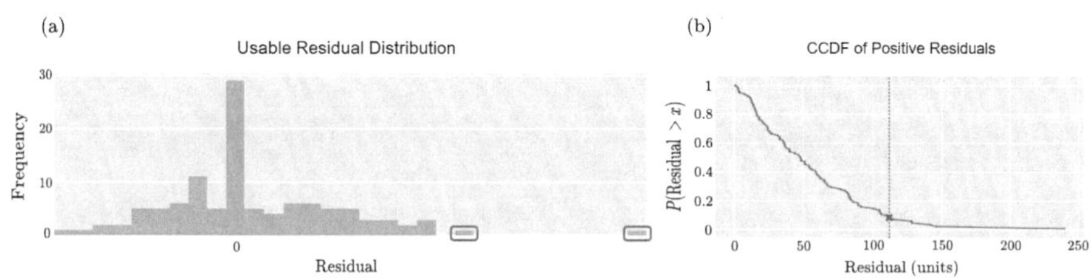

Fig. 2. (a) The residual distribution of the predicted usable count. (b) The illustration of the elbow (red) point. (Color figure online)

Algorithm 1. Peak Driver Selection with Sufficiency Constraint

Input: Ordered shares S_d, Parameters $\tau_{\text{leader}}, \tau_{\text{margin}}, \tau_{\text{cum}}$, and K
$\mathbf{T}_d^* \leftarrow \emptyset$
if $s_{(1)} \geq \tau_{\text{leader}}$ **then**
    $\mathbf{T}_d^* \leftarrow \{t_{(1)}\}$
else
    Candidates $\leftarrow \{t_{(1)}\}$, $C \leftarrow s_{(1)}$
    for $i = 2$ **to** K **do**
        if $(s_{(1)} - s_{(i)} \leq \tau_{\text{margin}})$ **then**
            Candidates $\leftarrow$ Candidates $\cup \{t_{(i)}\}$
            $C \leftarrow C + s_{(i)}$
        else
            break
        end if
    end for
    if $C \geq \tau_{\text{cum}}$ **then**
        $\mathbf{T}_d^* \leftarrow$ Candidates
    end if
end if
return $\mathbf{T}_d^*$

the driver set is only validated if the cumulative share C of these candidates reaches a target $s_1 + s_2 + \cdots + s_i > \tau_{\text{cum}} = 0.60$ (decided based on expert knowledge and data analysis), as exemplified in the right-hand pie of Fig. 3. If the top three battery types do not collectively meet this sufficiency threshold, or if the proximity constraint excludes necessary contributors, the peak is categorized as diffuse and $\mathbf{T}_d^*$ is returned as an empty set. This logic is shown in Algorithm 1.

3.4 Peak-Adjusted Forecast

Following the identification of the peak driver battery types $\mathbf{T}_d^*$, we apply a structural decomposition throughout the entire processing cascade. For each day $d \in \mathbf{D}$, and for each stage of the cascade $y \in \{y^{(\text{proc})}, y^{(\text{accepted})}, y^{(\text{usable})}\}$, the

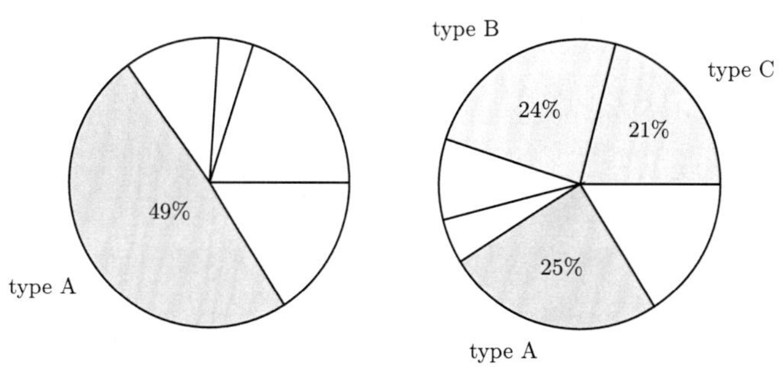

Fig. 3. Two examples of battery type distribution on a peak day.

total daily volume is partitioned into a peak-driven component and a non-peak baseline component:

$$y(d) = y_{\text{peak}}(d) + y_{\text{non-peak}}(d). \tag{11}$$

For days identified as peak events ($d \in \mathbf{D}_{\text{peak}}$), the components are calculated by aggregating the counts of the driver set and its complement, respectively:

$$y_{\text{peak}}(d) = \sum_{t \in \mathbf{T}_d^*} y(d,t), \quad y_{\text{non-peak}}(d) = \sum_{t \notin \mathbf{T}_d^*} y(d,t) \tag{12}$$

Here, two clarifications are necessary. First, throughout the remainder of this work, whenever we mention additivity as in Eq. (11), we refer to counts, not rates. Second, for all regular days $d \notin \mathbf{D}_{\text{peak}}$, the decomposition yields $y_{\text{peak}}(d) = 0$ and $y_{\text{non-peak}}(d) = y(d)$.

Before introducing the peak-adjusted forecasting mechanism, we emphasize that the structural cascade defined earlier remains unchanged across regimes. For both the peak-driven and non-peak components, Prophet based forecasts follow the same three-stage hierarchy consisting of processed volume, acceptance rate, and usability rate. That is, each component is modeled through the sequential structure

$$y^{(\text{proc})}(d) \longrightarrow y^{a_r}(d) \longrightarrow y^{u_r}(d),$$

and differs only in the statistical models used to generate the forecasts, not in the form of the cascade itself.

For each component of the cascade, forecasts are generated separately for the non-peak and peak regimes using model ensembles tailored to their respective statistical characteristics.

For the **non-peak component**, the dynamics is dominated by a smooth seasonal structure with relatively low variance. Accordingly, each stage of the cascade is modeled using a two-model ensemble consisting of Prophet and LightGBM. Let $\hat{y}_{\text{P}}^{(\cdot)}(d)$ and $\hat{y}_{\text{L}}^{(\cdot)}(d)$ denote the Prophet and LightGBM forecasts, respectively, for a given cascade variable $y \in \{y^{(\text{proc})}, y^{a_r}, y^{u_r}\}$. The non-peak forecast is obtained as a convex combination:

$$\begin{aligned} \hat{y}_{\text{non-peak}}^{(\cdot)}(d) &= \alpha_{\text{P}}\, \hat{y}_{\text{P}}^{(\cdot)}(d) + \alpha_{\text{L}}\, \hat{y}_{\text{L}}^{(\cdot)}(d), \\ \alpha_{\text{P}} + \alpha_{\text{L}} &= 1 \end{aligned} \tag{13}$$

For the **peak-driven component**, the forecasting task is more challenging due to abrupt changes in magnitude and limited historical recurrence. To better capture this behavior, we employ a three-model ensemble combining Prophet, LightGBM, and XGBoost. Denoting the corresponding forecasts by $\hat{y}_{\text{P}}^{(\cdot)}(d)$, $\hat{y}_{\text{L}}^{(\cdot)}(d)$, and $\hat{y}_{\text{X}}^{(\cdot)}(d)$, the peak forecast is defined as:

$$\begin{aligned} \hat{y}_{\text{peak}}^{(\cdot)}(d) &= w_{\text{P}}\, \hat{y}_{\text{P}}^{(\cdot)}(d) + w_{\text{L}}\, \hat{y}_{\text{L}}^{(\cdot)}(d) + w_{\text{X}}\, \hat{y}_{\text{X}}^{(\cdot)}(d), \\ w_{\text{P}} + w_{\text{L}} + w_{\text{X}} &= 1 \end{aligned} \tag{14}$$

This ensemble approach allows combining the complementary strengths of the individual models: Prophet provides robustness to calendar effects and long-term trends, LightGBM efficiently captures stable nonlinear interactions, and XGBoost contributes additional robustness under high-variance and irregular conditions typical of peak events.

Finally, for each stage of the cascade, the total forecast is obtained by recombining the regime-specific components:

$$\hat{y}^{(\cdot)}(d) = \hat{y}^{(\cdot)}_{\text{non-peak}}(d) + \hat{y}^{(\cdot)}_{\text{peak}}(d), \tag{15}$$

after which the predicted usable battery inflow is constructed through the cascade composition defined in Eq. (2).

4 Experiments

In this section, we describe the data and experimental setup, perform hyperparameter tuning, and discuss results and findings.

4.1 Data Setup

The dataset utilized for this research is derived from the historical processing logs of our industry partner, which span approximately three years (i.e., $n \approx 750$ business days) from 2022 to early 2026. This temporal scope provides a sufficient window to capture long-term trends and multiple seasonal cycles. The data reflect a complex, multi-level waste stream characterized by the following dimensions:

- *Hierarchical and Cascade Structure:* Data are recorded for $m \approx 520$ distinct battery models. For each business day d, the dataset tracks the battery count through a three-stage processing cascade: total processed $y^{(proc)}(d)$, total accepted $y^{(accepted)}(d)$, and total usable $y^{(usable)}(d)$.
- *Conversion Dynamics:* The processing cascade is defined by a significant volume reduction at each stage. On average, the stream maintains a mean acceptance rate of approximately 46% and a subsequent usability rate of 52%. These rates are not static; they fluctuate according to age, disposal conditions, etc.
- *Extreme Variance and Peak Events:* A defining characteristic of the dataset is its heavy-tailed distribution. While daily inflow is typically stable, "Peak Inflow Events", representing only the top 10% of days by volume, account for more than 16.4% of the total material collected. These peaks are often orders of magnitude higher than the median, creating a sparse right tail that traditional models struggle to capture.
- *Exogenous Seasonality:* Formal statistical testing (Kruskal-Wallis) confirms significant weekly and yearly seasonal patterns. In contrast to traditional manufacturing, these patterns are purely exogenous. They are driven by consumer behavior and third-party waste site operations rather than internal procurement schedules.

4.2 Hyperparameter Tuning

A comprehensive grid search was conducted to identify optimal hyperparameters for all forecasting models. Tables 1, 2, 3, and 4 present the complete search space explored. Table 5 presents the optimal parameters identified within our search space per model. All subsequent experiments in this paper use these values of the parameters.

Tables 1, 2, 3, 4 and 5 summarize the hyperparameter tuning process. Table 1 tunes the Prophet parameters `changepoint_prior_scale`, which controls trend flexibility, and `seasonality_prior_scale`, which controls seasonal strength, for the baseline pipeline. Tables 2 and 3 extend this tuning to the non-peak and peak ensemble models by additionally testing XGBoost and LightGBM parameters: `n_estimators`, `max_depth`, and `learning_rate`, which control the number of trees, tree complexity, and update size. These tables also test ensemble weights, which determine the relative contribution of Prophet, XGBoost, and LightGBM. Table 4 reports the benchmark-model search spaces for SARIMA, Holt-Winters, Seasonal Naive, and N-BEATS, covering their main structure, seasonality, look-

Table 1. Baseline Model (3-Stage Prophet Pipeline) Hyperparameter Search Space

Component	Hyperparameter	Search Space
Processed Count Prophet	changepoint_prior_scale	{0.3, 0.4, 0.5}
	seasonality_prior_scale	{0.03, 0.05, 0.08}
Acceptance Rate Prophet	changepoint_prior_scale	{0.1, 0.15, 0.2}
	seasonality_prior_scale	{0.03, 0.05, 0.08}
Usability Rate Prophet	changepoint_prior_scale	{0.1, 0.15, 0.2}
	seasonality_prior_scale	{0.03, 0.05, 0.08}

Table 2. Non-Peak Model (Hierarchical Ensemble) Hyperparameter Search Space

Component	Hyperparameter	Search Space
Prophet (3-Stage)	changepoint_prior_scale	{0.3, 0.4, 0.5}
	seasonality_prior_scale	{0.03, 0.05, 0.08}
ML Models (XGBoost/LightGBM)	n_estimators	{20, 30, 50}
	max_depth	{3, 4, 5}
	learning_rate	{0.05, 0.1, 0.15}
Ensemble Weights	(Prophet, XGB, LGB)	(0.35, 0.00, 0.65)
		(0.40, 0.10, 0.50)
		(0.30, 0.20, 0.50)
		(0.50, 0.00, 0.50)
		(0.25, 0.25, 0.50)
		(0.60, 0.20, 0.20)

Table 3. Peak Model (3-Stage Hierarchical Ensemble) Hyperparameter Search Space

Stage	Component	Hyperparameter	Search Space
Stage 1: Prophet	Processed Count	changepoint_prior_scale	{0.15, 0.2}
		seasonality_prior_scale	{0.03, 0.05}
	Acceptance Rate	changepoint_prior_scale	{0.1, 0.15}
		seasonality_prior_scale	{0.3, 0.5}
	Usability Rate	changepoint_prior_scale	{0.1, 0.15}
		seasonality_prior_scale	{0.3, 0.5}
Stage 2: ML	XGBoost/LightGBM	n_estimators	{20, 30}
		max_depth	{3, 4}
		learning_rate	{0.03, 0.05}
Stage 3: Ensemble	(Prophet, XGB, LGB)	Ensemble Weights	(0.65, 0.15, 0.25)
			(0.60, 0.20, 0.20)
			(0.40, 0.30, 0.30)
			(0.45, 0.35, 0.20)

Table 4. Individual Model Hyperparameter Grid Search Space

Model	Component	Hyperparameter	Search Space
SARIMA	ARIMA Order	order	{(1,1,1), (1,0,1), (2,1,1), (1,1,2)}
	Seasonal Order	seasonal_order	{(1,0,1,5), (0,1,1,5), (2,0,0,5), (1,1,0,5), (1,0,0,5)}
Holt-Winters	Trend Component	trend	{add, mul, None}
	Seasonal Component	seasonal	{add, mul}
	Damping	damped_trend	{True, False}
	Seasonal Period	seasonal_periods	{15, 30}
Seasonal Naive	Lookback Period	seasonal_period	{5, 10, 15, 20, 25}
N-BEATS	Input Window	input_chunk_length	{20, 30, 40}
	Stack Depth	num_stacks	{5, 10, 15}
	Layer Depth	num_layers	{2, 4}
	Hidden Units	layer_widths	{128, 256}
	Training Epochs	n_epochs	{30, 50}

back, and network-training parameters. Finally, Table 5 lists the selected optimal settings used in the experiments.

4.3 Results and Discussions

We evaluated the proposed hierarchical cascade forecasting approach against 125 alternative model combinations across the three-stage cascade architecture (Volume → Acceptance Rate → Usability Rate). Five individual forecasting models were tested: Prophet, SARIMA, Holt-Winters, Seasonal Naive, and N-BEATS

Table 5. Optimal Hyperparameter Configurations

Model	Component/Parameter	Value
Baseline Prophet Models		
Processed Count	cps/sps	0.4/0.05
Acceptance Rate	cps/sps	0.15/0.05
Usability Rate	cps/sps	0.15/0.05
Non-Peak Ensemble		
Prophet	cps/sps	0.4/0.05
ML	$n/d/\eta$	30/3/0.1
Weights	Prophet/XGBoost/LightGBM	35/0/65%
Peak Ensemble		
Prophet (Proc.)	cps/sps	0.2/0.05
Prophet (Accept./Usab.)	cps/sps	0.15/0.5
ML	$n/d/\eta$	30/3/0.05
Weights	Prophet/XGBoost/LightGBM	65/15/25%
GB Regularization (Fixed)		
All GB models	α/λ	0.5/1.0
All GB models	subsample/colsample	0.8/0.8
Benchmark Models		
SARIMA	order	(1,0,1)
SARIMA	seasonal order	(0,1,1,5)
Holt-Winters	trend/seasonality	mult./add.
Holt-Winters	period	10 days
Seasonal Naive	lookback	25 days
N-BEATS	chunk/stacks	30–40/10–15
N-BEATS	layers/units	2–4/128–256
N-BEATS	epochs	30–50

cps: changepoint prior scale; sps: seasonality prior scale

n: n estimators; d: maxdepth; η: learning rate; α: reg. alpha; λ: reg. lambda

[12]. Each model was independently optimized through grid search, and all possible combinations across cascade stages were evaluated using weekly aggregated metrics on a 20% holdout test set.

Performance Comparison. Table 6 presents the performance comparison between the hierarchical approach, the top classical cascades, and the deep learning-enhanced cascades. The hierarchical model achieves superior performance across most metrics with an MAE (Mean Absolute Error) of 82.29, 5% improvement over the best classical cascade, i.e., Prophet-SARIMA-HoltWinters (MAE = 86.60), and 18.6% improvement over the best N-BEATS cascade (MAE = 101.05). The hierarchical model also shows superior performance in terms of

Table 6. Model Performance Comparison (Weekly Metrics)

Model Combination	MAE	MAPE (%)	R^2
Proposed Approach			
Hierarchical (Non-Peak + Peak)	**82.29**	**25.4**	0.660
Classical Cascade Approaches (Top 5 of 64)			
Prophet-SARIMA-HoltWinters	86.60	25.8	**0.701**
SARIMA-HoltWinters-Prophet	116.55	37.6	0.528
SARIMA-HoltWinters-SARIMA	118.25	40.8	0.493
HoltWinters-HoltWinters-SARIMA	127.88	44.8	0.360
Prophet-SARIMA-Prophet	129.73	28.3	0.309
Deep Learning Cascade Approaches (Top 5 of 61)			
Prophet-NBEATS-HoltWinters	101.05	29.2	0.574
Prophet-NBEATS-Prophet	144.01	30.5	0.132
Prophet-NBEATS-SARIMA	153.48	31.9	0.011
SARIMA-NBEATS-HoltWinters	153.77	32.7	−0.017
HoltWinters-NBEATS-HoltWinters	154.80	34.2	−0.046

MAPE (Mean Absolute Percentage Error), achieving 25.4%, which represents the lowest MAPE among all tested approaches. The classical cascade shows good performance in capturing regular temporal dynamics, as reflected by their competitive MAE and R^2 values. However, visual inspections suggest that this classical model is worse than following the peak pattern compared to the hierarchical approach, especially for a forecast horizon of three months.

Deep Learning Limitations. N-BEATS combinations consistently underperformed classical approaches. The best N-BEATS cascade ranked 16.7% worse than the hierarchical model, with 8 out of 10 best N-BEATS combinations showing MAE values greater than 150 batteries/week and negative R^2 values. The pure N-BEATS cascade performed particularly poorly (MAE = 208.52, R^2 = -0.989).

This failure highlights a fundamental mismatch between N-BEATS's data-driven architecture and the domain's characteristics: limited training data (2 years), strong explicit patterns (5-day work weeks, holidays), and the need for interpretable forecasts. Classical models encoding domain knowledge prove to be more effective than deep learning approaches requiring larger datasets to implicitly learn these patterns.

Classical Cascade Analysis. Among classical cascades, Prophet excelled at volume forecasting (Stage 1), appearing in 7 of 10 top combinations, while SARIMA and Holt-Winters performed better for rate forecasting (Stages 2–3). However, 9 of 10 top classical cascades exhibited MAE values exceeding 115 batteries/week. The fundamental limitation, applying uniform models across heterogeneous demand patterns, prevents them from matching the performance of the hierarchical model.

These results are consistent with prior waste-flow and reverse-logistics forecasting studies, which show that decomposition, model comparison, and operationally oriented inflow forecasting can improve planning performance [2, 10, 11]. Our results extend this literature by showing where the improvement arises in the circular battery manufacturing setting. The largest gains are not obtained simply by replacing one forecasting model with another. Instead, performance improves when the models are embedded in a structure that reflects the processing stages and separates routine inflow from peak-driven events. The hierarchical non-peak and peak model therefore provides empirical evidence that domain-specific forecast structuring can be more important than model complexity alone.

5 Conclusion

This paper addressed the critical forecasting challenges in waste-based manufacturing by developing a hierarchical two-regime approach. By algorithmically decomposing the battery supply stream into non-peak and peak regimes, the proposed approach achieved an MAE of around 82 batteries per week, outperforming the best classical cascade approach by 5.0% and the best deep learning one by 18.6%. The study concludes that specialized ensembles, leveraging the strengths of Prophet, LightGBM, and XGBoost, provide the necessary robustness to handle the structural uncertainty and "Peak Inflow Events" inherent in circular e-bike battery streams. Although the case study focuses on circular e-bike battery manufacturing, the proposed approach combines domain-specific and transferable elements. The specific cascade definition and the interpretation of peak events as battery-type-driven arrivals are particular to the battery repurposing setting. However, the broader framework of modeling uncertain inflows through sequential filtering stages, separating routine and peak-driven regimes, and recombining their forecasts is applicable to other reverse-supply-chain and waste-based manufacturing contexts. Therefore, the method provides not only a solution for usable battery inflow forecasting, but also a general structure for forecasting volatile material streams with quality-dependent conversion processes. The final model is currently being tested and used by our industry partner for operational decision making.

However, there are few limitations in our study. A primary limitation was the sparse and heterogeneous nature of battery-type-specific data, which made standard rare-event machine learning methods impractical for specific model arrivals. In addition, visual inspections indicated that, while the hierarchical approach is superior, there is still room for improvement in capturing the magnitude of peak patterns over extended forecast horizons. Therefore, future research could enhance the model by incorporating additional exogenous covariates, such as changes in battery waste regulations or a shift in consumer disposal behavior.

Acknowledgments. This project is funded by JTF and the European Union through Zhero Systems. Additionally, special thanks to Zhero Systems team for their support and help throughout the project.

Disclosure of Interests. The authors have no competing interests.

References

1. Chen, T., Guestrin, C.: XGBoost: a scalable tree boosting system. In: Proceedings of the 22nd ACM SIGKDD International Conference on Knowledge Discovery and Data Mining, pp. 785–794 (2016). https://doi.org/10.1145/2939672.2939785
2. Cooijmans, S.L.: Forecasting inflows of reverse supply chain to optimize workforce planning at return hub. Master's thesis, Eindhoven University of Technology (2024). https://research.tue.nl/en/studentTheses/0c2750d9-2a92-4ec8-9ad8-8f3e0b5023ac
3. European Parliament and Council: Regulation (EU) 2023/1542 of the European Parliament and of the Council of 12 July 2023 concerning batteries and waste batteries. Off. J. Eur. Union (2023)
4. Guide, V.D.R.: Production planning and control for remanufacturing: industry practice and research needs. J. Oper. Manag. **18**(4), 467–483 (2000). https://doi.org/10.1016/S0272-6963(00)00034-6
5. Harper, G., et al.: Recycling lithium-ion batteries from electric vehicles. Nature **575**(7781), 75–86 (2019)
6. Hyndman, R.J., Athanasopoulos, G.: Forecasting: Principles and Practice, 3rd edn. OTexts (2021). https://otexts.com/fpp3/
7. Hyndman, R.J., Ahmed, R.A., Athanasopoulos, G., Shang, H.L.: Optimal combination forecasts for hierarchical time series. Comput. Stat. Data Anal. **55**(9), 2579–2589 (2011). https://doi.org/10.1016/j.csda.2011.03.006
8. Kampker, A., Heimes, H.H., Offermanns, C., Frank, M., Klohs, D., Nguyen, K.: Prediction of battery return volumes for 3R: remanufacturing, reuse, and recycling. Energies **16**(19), 6873 (2023). https://doi.org/10.3390/en16196873
9. Ke, G., et al.: LightGBM: a highly efficient gradient boosting decision tree. In: Advances in Neural Information Processing Systems, vol. 30 (2017)
10. Mohsin, A., Hongzhen, L., Iqbal, M.M., Salim, Z.R., Hossain, A., Kafy, A.A.: Forecasting e-waste recovery scale driven by seasonal data characteristics: a decomposition-ensemble approach. Waste Manag. Res. **40**(7), 870–881 (2022). https://doi.org/10.1177/0734242X211061443. pMID: 34823396
11. Mudannayake, O., Rathnayake, D., Herath, J.D., Fernando, D.K., Fernando, M.: Exploring machine learning and deep learning approaches for multi-step forecasting in municipal solid waste generation. IEEE Access **10**, 122570–122585 (2022). https://doi.org/10.1109/ACCESS.2022.3221941
12. Oreshkin, B.N., Carpov, D., Chapados, N., Bengio, Y.: N-BEATS: neural basis expansion analysis for interpretable time series forecasting. arXiv preprint arXiv:1905.10437 (2020)
13. Rezaei, M., et al.: A review of lithium-ion battery recycling for enabling a circular economy. J. Power Sources **630**, 236157 (2025). https://doi.org/10.1016/j.jpowsour.2024.236157

14. Rožanec, J.M., Fortuna, B., Mladenić, D.: Reframing demand forecasting: a two-fold approach for lumpy and intermittent demand. Sustainability **14**(15), 1–21 (2022). https://doi.org/10.3390/su14159295. https://ideas.repec.org/a/gam/jsusta/v14y2022i15p9295-d875050.html
15. Satopaa, V., Albrecht, J., Irwin, D., Raghavan, B.: Finding a "Kneedle" in a haystack: detecting knee points in system behavior. In: 2011 31st International Conference on Distributed Computing Systems Workshops, Minneapolis, MN, USA, pp. 166–171. IEEE (2011). https://doi.org/10.1109/ICDCSW.2011.20. http://ieeexplore.ieee.org/document/5961514/
16. Shyalika, C., Wickramarachchi, R., Sheth, A.P.: A comprehensive survey on rare event prediction. ACM Comput. Surv. **57**(3), 1–39 (2024)
17. Taylor, S.J., Letham, B.: Forecasting at scale. Am. Stat. **72**(1), 37–45 (2018)

A Dynamic Premium Pricing of Critical Minerals in EV Battery Supply Chains

Ricky Gao and Shiva Abdoli(✉)

University of New South Wales, Sydney, NSW, Australia
s.abdoli@unsw.edu.au

Abstract. This research proposes a blueprint Dynamic Premium Pricing Model (DPPM) to promote a sustainable and equitable market environment for critical minerals essential to Electric Vehicle (EV) batteries. By integrating principles from economics, engineering and environmental science, this DPPM addresses economic viability, environmental sustainability and social equity within EV battery supply chains. The DPPM is designed to dynamically offer price for critical minerals by integrating factors that drive the market, including government initiatives, Environmental, Social, and Governance considerations. Although the model minimizes selling price under sustainability and risk constraints, this results in a supported premium above current underpriced markets. The model has the potential to adapt to ongoing policy shifts and innovative technologies, serving as a comprehensive blueprint for future advancements. The framework can enhance diversification by improving the financial transparency and bankability of producers, ensure long-term sustainability through efficient resource allocation; and enables stakeholders to capitalize on their competitive advantages by increasing cost-effectiveness and supply chain resilience.

Keywords: Dynamic premium pricing · Battery supply chains · Critical minerals

1 Introduction and Research Scope

A key element underpinning Electric Vehicles (EV) market growth is sustainable management of supply chains for critical minerals essential for EV battery [1]. Production of EV batteries presents complex challenges, with upstream mining activities, and various stages of production. There is a concern regarding geographic concentration of critical mineral reserves and supply chain activities, rendering global supply chain vulnerable to disruptions including geopolitical conflicts or unforeseeable events [2]. This demands a holistic approach to ensure environmental integrity and human rights, alongside securing critical minerals. Transition towards a Circular Economy (CE) for EV batteries could alleviate supply disruptions, reduce environmental footprint and resolve adverse social impacts. Yet, pricing approaches for critical minerals remain underdeveloped with limited standardization and fragmented regional trading. Most market activities are long-term agreements which restrict open trading and weakening price discovery.

Published by Springer Nature Switzerland AG 2027
G. Pezzotta et al. (Eds.): APMS 2026, IFIP AICT 808, pp. 107–121, 2027.
https://doi.org/10.1007/978-3-032-38594-9_8

This leads to price uncertainty, leading investors to perceive critical minerals projects as high-risk. So, there is a need for a pricing model to support investment decisions and reliable valuation of EV battery supply chains. Existing approaches do not provide an integrated mechanism to translate sustainability, risk, and policy factors into actionable pricing signals, limiting their practicality [3]. In this research, we focused on developing a Dynamic Premium Pricing Model (DPPM) that suggests premium prices for these minerals by incorporating market shaping factors. The model can utilise historical data and quantifiable effects of government policies to stabilise prices and encourage sustainable practices. Incorporation of CE benefits, such as recycling efficiencies and ESG compliance, further enhances the model's ability to address stakeholder concerns. The proposed DPPM integrates risk management functions to address macroeconomic and geopolitical uncertainties, ensuring comprehensive coverage of potential challenges to promote supply chain resilience. The model's technical foundation, reinforced by Monte Carlo simulations, enables it to handle market uncertainties and adapt to dynamic conditions. This adaptability ensures that future iterations can adjust to new technologies and datasets, improving decision-making in addressing sustainability and financial concerns. The primary contribution of this work is a computational decision-support framework for dynamic premium pricing of critical minerals under sustainability and geopolitical uncertainty. Application of the proposed framework can provide valuable insights for policymakers and industry stakeholders in supporting strategic decision making in the critical minerals industry.

2 Context, Literature Review, and Research Gap

For energy sector to achieve net zero goals, total number of EV sales is needed to double from 2025–2030, requiring approximately additional 50 lithium, 17 cobalt, and 60 nickel mines (4). Yet, establishing these mines and their supply chain can take more than a decade.

Three-quarters of world's battery cell production capacity is concentrated in China, with 70% of global production capacity for cathodes, 85% for anodes, and 80% in graphite mining [4]. This can discourage potential entrants. A rare exception is Lynas Rare Earths Ltd., a Western Australian enterprise [5]. Democratic Republic of Congo (DRC) controls 70% of global cobalt production heightens geopolitical risks [6]. Concerns of child labour and geopolitical instability make industries worldwide vulnerable to disruptions in supply [7]. In 2014, UNICEF estimated that around 40,000 children worked in cobalt mines [8]. Over 70% of DRC's cobalt goes to China, making it the source of over half of global refined cobalt [9]. Indonesia, the largest nickel producer, faces major environmental issues from deforestation, water pollution, and coal-powered processing [10]. Critical minerals market is hindered by the absence of central spot prices and standardised trading mechanisms, resulting in low liquidity and poor price discovery. Long-term offtake contracts further restrict supply available for open trading, while a lack of product standardisation (except for lithium) creates fragmented regional markets [11]. Index pricing (e.g., Fastmarkets, Benchmark Mineral Intelligence) offers partial clarity but lacks the acceptance required to provide a bankable benchmark [12]. Over-the-counter mineral trading lacks transparency, limiting regulatory oversight and creating inefficiency and systemic risks [11].

Investors view critical minerals projects as high-risk due to price volatility and low transparency, and uncertain demand [11]. Hence, a DPPM is needed to reflect true value of critical minerals by incorporating key factors such as: growing demand and strategic long-term importance, centralized reserves and geopolitical risks, ESG concerns with hidden costs of environmental/social impacts, supply chain vulnerabilities.

Government initiatives increasingly shape critical minerals landscape. An example is U.S. Inflation Reduction Act 2022 (IRA), which incentivizes EV adoption by lowering upfront costs [9, 13]. IRA incentivizes domestic and Free Trade Agreements -country mineral development through strict sourcing requirements for critical minerals to reduce reliance on unstable regions. Although CE principles are new in critical minerals, their integration into DPPM can foster sustainability [14], by supporting reducing demand, extending product lifetimes (e.g., repurposing batteries), recycling materials [15], minimizing waste, and promoting reuse, reducing reliance on new extraction [15, 16].

2.1 Dynamic Pricing Methods

Existing pricing mechanisms in mineral markets primarily rely on long-term bilateral contracts, index-based pricing, and over-the-counter transactions. While these mechanisms provide partial price guidance, they exclude integration of ESG, geopolitical risks, and CE considerations. Existing dynamic pricing literature has focused on retail, energy, and transportation, with limited adaptation to critical mineral characterized by supply and sustainability pressures. Pricing strongly affects profitability, consumer behaviour, and market dynamics. Dynamic pricing, unlike fixed pricing, adjusts in real time based on demand, competition, and inventory, allowing businesses to respond quickly and optimise revenue in a data-driven environment [17]. Artificial Intelligence/Machine learning (AI/ML) can improve pricing by improving predictions of consumer behavior and operational optimization. Various dynamic pricing models have been applied in different contexts, including Competitor-based [18], Behaviour-based [19], Bundle [20], Time-based [21], Peak [22], Segmented [23], and Penetration pricing [24]. Interested readers are referred to literature for their detailed description. Uber uses surge pricing to balance supply and demand in real time, adjusting fares based on time, distance, and rider-to-driver ratios to incentivise drivers and maintain service availability [25]. Amazon uses large-scale dynamic pricing, continuously adjusting prices based on competitors, market trends, and demand [26]. Although these examples are from different industries, they demonstrate how dynamic pricing principles can adapt pricing decisions to rapidly changing market conditions, which motivates their conceptual relevance to critical mineral pricing.

2.2 Research Gap

Literature review highlights a gap in pricing models for critical minerals of EV market. Existing mechanisms overlook strategic importance of minerals, government initiatives, or ESG considerations, while failing to address their geopolitical concentration, environmental, and social costs. Lack of a dynamic pricing framework with stakeholder endorsement undermines supply chain resilience [27]. The research gap addressed in this paper is the absence of an integrated dynamic pricing framework capable of incorporating sustainability, geopolitical, and policy-related factors into pricing decisions for critical mineral. We aimed to address that gap by proposing a DPPM that incorporates key drivers shaping market. DPPM aims to reflect true economic, ethical, and strategic value of critical minerals, promote responsible sourcing and supply chain stability. Beyond theory, it provides foundations for a platform for sustainable critical mineral pricing for EV battery supply chains. Unlike existing pricing approaches, DPPM links sustainability, risk, and policy variables to pricing decisions with an optimization-based and simulation-supported framework.

3 Methodology

The proposed methodology follows a structured pipeline where market/policy inputs are translated to variables evaluated under uncertainty. Building on the identified gaps, we propose a conceptual DPPM by incorporating transferable factors such as market trends, geopolitical risks, and sustainability factors. The framework is implemented as a Python-based model. To validate the model, we applied it on a demonstration case using historical data of natural graphite. As part of the methodology, we conduct Monte Carlo simulations to account for uncertainties/variabilities in market, assigning probability distributions to key parameters. Iterative sampling during simulations generates a spectrum of potential outcomes. This allows ensuring the model provides adaptive and optimal pricing strategies. This enables to move beyond deterministic pricing by capturing probabilistic market behavior, critical for decision-making under uncertainty.

This methodology delivers a blueprint that is theoretically robust and practically validated. The framework optimises price of critical minerals, promoting sustainability, and responsiveness to dynamic market conditions. Framework prioritizes long-term pricing stability and sustainability-oriented cost internalization rather than pure short-term profit maximization. Hence, optimization seeks the minimum viable premium-adjusted price that maintains non-negative profitability under uncertainty. While this study primarily relies on simulation and optimization, it can integrate AI/ML for parameter estimation in future.

3.1 DPPM Formulation

We develop DPPM with a stochastic nature to capture market dynamics and uncertainty. L-BFGS-B optimisation solver is employed to handle the model's complex multi objective function, iteratively refining strategies to optimise prices under multiple constraints. Figure 1a illustrates the model's workflow, including initialization, calculation of penalty and risk values, Monte Carlo simulations, sensitivity analysis, returning an optimized price and profitability assessment report. The dynamic aspect is operationalized through periodic updating of input variables and repeated optimization runs as market conditions evolve.

Objective function, given in (1), determines the minimum feasible premium-adjusted selling price satisfies sustainability/profitability constraints, P_t, over time t. Demand

Pricing Model Implementation Layout
Procedure INPUT(UseCaseParams,SensitivityAnalysisParams) a)
Pricing Model Functions:
  Initialise Pricing Model Class
  Calculate Penalty Value:
    Quantify penalty costs
  Calculate Risk Value:
    Quantify risk cost
  Calculate Demand Forecast:
    Estimate future demand
  Calculate Cost Function:
    Determine total cost
  Apply Optimiser
    Find optimal price
  Calculate Profit:
    Calculate expected profit
Monte Carlo Simulation functions:
  For each simulation iteration:
    Generate simulated parameters
    Calculate simulated price and profit
  Calculate Statistics:
    Calculate mean profit
    Calculate standard deviation of profit
    Calculate 95% confidence interval for profit
  Return: Calculated Values
Sensitivity Analysis with Monte Carlo
  For each simulation iteration:
    Simulate lower and upper parameter values
    Run Monte Carlo for lower/upper values
    Store penalty and risk values for each iteration
  Calculate Statistics:
    Calculate mean profit
    Calculate standard deviation of profit
    Calculate 95% confidence interval for profit
  Return: Sensitivity Results
Report Generation Functions:
  Generate Report:
    Showcase test case results
    Extract sensitivity analysis results
    Format results and recommendations
  Generate Histograms:
    Create subplots for price and profit distributions
Return report

b)

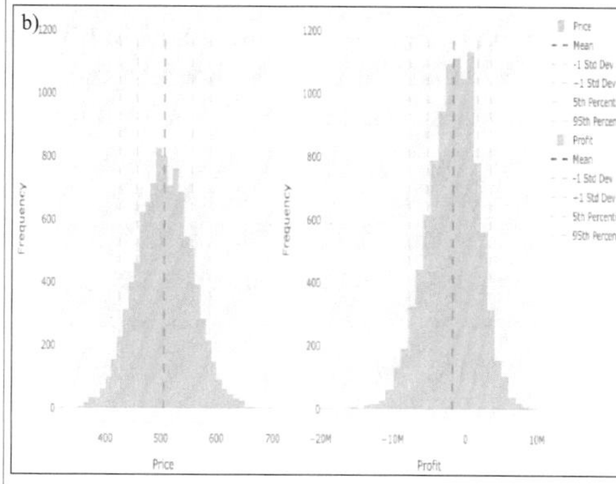

c)

Parameter	Value
Mean Optimal Price	$504.77
Price Range - Confidence Interval (±1 std)	$455.03 to $554.51
Price Range - 5th to 95th Percentile Price	$423.79 to $586.57
Expected Profit	$-1,901,852.56
Profit Confidence Interval (±1 std)	$-5,389,938.32 to $1,586,233.19

Fig. 1 a) Framework workflow b) Natural Graphite Monte Carlo Simulations Price Distribution from Model Report c) Simulation Quantitative Insights from Model Report

forecast $D_t(P_t)$ at time t can be derived from historical data and future market indicators, ensuring the model adapts to market dynamics. $Q_t(D_t(P_t))$ is production quantity at t, influenced by demand forecast. Cost function, $C_t(Q_t(D_t(P_t)))$, reflects production costs as a function of quantity produced, Q_t, and selling price, penalties and risks associated with policy compliance, and market risks. This approach provides an adaptive foundation that allows the model to dynamically adjust the price given real-time market data. Demand forecast function enables embodying how changes in P_t affect the demand. Thus, the model can adjust demand forecasts based on price fluctuations, ensuring that it reflects market responsiveness. Demand forecast function, embodying the elasticity concept, as given in (2). D_{t0} is baseline demand, P_{t0} is the baseline price and ϵ_t is price elasticity of demand at t [28]. Production quantity function Q_t, given in (3), determines the volume of a critical mineral to be produced t. This depends on a company's circumstances, including production capacity, inventory levels, and demand forecast. p represents the company's market share and Q_{max} represents the max production. The cost function $C_t(Q_t)$, given in (4), reflects total cost of production at t. Where $c_{variable}(Q_t(D_t(P_t)))$ represents variable costs that change with Q_t and c_{fixed} represents fixed costs. The penalty, Φ, and risk, Ψ, functions, respectively given in (5) and (6), are crucial for integrating economic, environmental and social considerations into DPPM. Φ quantifies the additional costs of meeting policies, ensuring that the associated costs of compliance are integrated into DPPM. The Ψ quantifies the impact of various risks, highlighting the need for diversified sourcing strategies. These integrated functions provide economic incentives for adherence to ESG and CE principles, influencing suppliers and purchasers within critical minerals market. The penalty and risk terms represent aggregated cost adjustments associated with ESG compliance, CE investments, macroeconomic uncertainty, geopolitical exposure, and supply-chain disruption risks. Although the simplified illustrative formulation omits explicit time subscripts for readability, these parameters can vary dynamically across time periods in practical deployment. The CE factor, given in (7), quantifies the financial impact of implementing CE practices, which can be adjusted depending on the unique circumstances of a stakeholder, where i denotes CE investment categories and r denotes recycling-related cost components.

$$Z = \min_{P_t, \forall t} E\left(\sum_t \left[(P_t \cdot Q_t(D_t(P_t)) - C_t(Q_t(D_t(P_t)))) \cdot (1 - \text{tax})\right]\right) \quad (1)$$

$$D_t(P_t) = D_{t0}\left(\frac{P_{t0}}{P_t}\right)^{\varepsilon_t} \quad (2)$$

$$Q_t(D_t(P_t)) = \min(p \cdot D_t(P_t), Q_{max}) \quad (3)$$

$$C_t(Q_t(D_t(P_t))) = \left(c_{variable}(Q_t(D_t(P_t))) + c_{fixed} + \Phi(CE, ESG) + \Psi(MR, SD, GF)\right) \cdot (1 - \text{subsidy}) \quad (4)$$

$$\Phi(CE, ESG) = \sum_c \nu_c \cdot CE_c + \sum_s \theta_s \cdot ESG_s \quad (5)$$

$$\Psi(MR, SD, GF) = \sum_m \alpha_m \cdot MR_m + \sum_d \beta_d \cdot SD_d + \sum_g \gamma_g \cdot GF_g \quad (6)$$

$$CE_c = CI_i - CR_r - SE_m \quad (7)$$

CE_c: Circular economy factor c, such as waste reduction
ESG_s: ESG factor s, such as emission levels
MR_m: Macroeconomic risk factor m, such as changes in interest rate
SD_d: Supply and demand disruption factor d, such as logistic issues
GF_g: Geopolitical factor g, such as trade tensions
$\lambda_p, \nu_c, \theta_s, \alpha_m, \beta_d, \gamma_g$: Weight coefficients for each factor, their relative importance
CI_i: Upfront and ongoing costs associated with investments made to enable CE practices
CR_r: Costs difference in using recycled materials and new materials over a period
SE_m: Savings from using materials more efficiently, which can reduce overall costs

3.2 Model Implementation

Here, we present core architectural components and their data exchange. The pricing model class initializes parameters, including costs, demand, policy impacts, CE and risk factors, and ESG metrics. It sets initial values for penalties and risks and weightings for each factor that influences the pricing strategy. In practice, these values would be adjusted to reflect the true market circumstances or stakeholder objectives. Demand function forecasts demand by adjusting baseline demand based on the ratio of baseline to current price, raised to the power of the price elasticity of demand. In future applications, if a simulated demand is provided, it can use that instead of baseline demand. The production quantity determines the minimum value out of a company's market share or the maximum amount the company can produce.

Penalty function calculates penalties based on CE factors and ESG metrics by summing the weighted costs associated with each factor. It then updates the penalty breakdown and returns total penalty value. The risk function calculates risks based on macroeconomic, supply and demand, and geopolitical factors by summing the weighted costs associated with each risk factor, proceeding to update the risk breakdown and return the total risk value. Cost function calculates the total cost based on variable costs, fixed costs, penalties and risks. It computes variable costs by multiplying production quantity to variable cost per unit and it uses fixed costs provided as given fixed input cost. Penalties and risks are calculated using their respective functions and any subsidies are applied to the total cost. Profit function calculates profit based on selling price and simulated costs. It determines variable and fixed costs, either from simulated or default values. It calculates demand, finds total cost and calculates pre-tax profit by subtracting total cost from revenue. If pre-tax profit is non-negative, it applies to a tax deduction; otherwise, it returns pre-tax profit.

The core objective of optimisation process is to determine the optimal selling price that factors in penalties and risks, aiming for non-negative profits while justifying a premium. The objective function is used within this process to minimise the adjusted selling price whilst ensuring that the adjusted profit remains non-negative, within a degree of error that is captured by the simulations. The optimization process evaluates only feasible pricing solutions that maintain non-negative expected profit after accounting for penalties and risks.

The L-BFGS-B algorithm is chosen due to its efficiency in handling large-scale problems [29]. This algorithm is ideal for scenarios where the optimization problem involves numerous variables and constraints, making it appropriate for the complex nature of critical mineral pricing. The algorithm begins with an adjustable initial guess set at 150% of initial price and optimization process is constrained between 100%–200% of initial price, providing a flexible range for the search. L-BFGS-B algorithm employs a gradient-based approach, iteratively updating the selling price by calculating the gradient of objective function with respect to the price. This iterative process continues until it converges on an optimal solution. L-BFGS-B is particularly useful for this pricing model due to its limited memory feature, which can dynamically adjust the selling price for future iterations where the prices can change dynamically in accordance with dynamic parameter inputs.

3.3 Monte Carlo Simulation (MCS) and Sensitivity Analysis

MCS allows managing uncertainties by assigning probability distributions to parameters and performing iterative sampling to evaluate variability in optimal pricing and profitability. We used uniform distributions, which is a valid adopted approach in various contexts when there is limited availability of validated probabilistic datasets for a parameter. MCS calculates simulated prices and profits, as well as statistical metrics such as mean profit, standard deviation of profit and confidence intervals for the simulation results. Integrating MCS, scenario, and sensitivity analyses provides probabilistic pricing insights for handling uncertainty. We propose integrating and performing sensitivity analysis on key parameters integrated with MCS's function, such that iterates through each parameter range, adjusting the model with lower/upper values whilst keeping other parameters same as base case and then run simulations to capture the profit distributions. The embedded sensitivity analysis module calculates mean profits, penalty values and risk values for each simulation. It also aggregates penalty and risk breakdowns across all simulations, returning the sensitivity analysis results, mean penalty and risk values and their breakdowns.

4 Demonstration and Results

We applied the proposed approach on natural graphite as an illustrative case, demonstrating its applicability and validating it. While this illustrative case relies on limited data, real-world adoption by governments/approved stakeholders provide access to more diverse data sources, enabling a more informed pricing model. Despite current limitations, this illustrative case shows that model can justify a price premium. The modelled parameters are shown in Table 1. The model is adjustable to accommodate varying scenarios (e.g., cost savings of mining efficiency, changes in logistical costs, new government incentives, or higher recycling rates). All prices are in USD and are estimated. Used sources are:

- Benchmark Mineral Intelligence [30]: provides monthly data on graphite deployment in EV batteries, offering insights into EV-specific demand dynamics.
- Fastmarkets [31]: Delivers market insights for graphite types, informing price trends.
- U.S. Department of Energy [32]: Provides data on critical minerals, including graphite, highlighting regulatory impacts in the energy sector.
- European Commission [33]: Offers guidelines on reuse of critical minerals.
- International Energy Agency [34]: Offers policy analysis on critical minerals, providing insights into global trends or sustainability considerations for the pricing model.
- Tesla [35]: Reports on sustainable practices, examples of quantifying ESG and CE

4.1 Demonstration Case Setup

The optimization process determines the optimal selling price that factors in penalties and risk, aiming for non-negative profits while justifying a premium, using L-BFGS-B algorithm. Price search is constrained between 100%–200% of initial price which is adjustable.

MCS results are shown in Fig. 1b with10,000 simulations. Price and profit distribution graphs illustrate a narrow spread, indicating higher predictability and replicability in results, essential for creating effective pricing models in proving the bankability of companies. Figure 1c demonstrates the mean optimal price, which was identified as \$504.77 per tonne, with an approximate 68% confidence interval ranging from \$455.03 to \$554.51. Evidently, there is a premium applied to hypothetical market price range of

Table 1. Graphite Demonstration Case modelling parameters

Functions	Parameters value
Selling price	P_t: \$(400–500) per ton for natural graphite [36]. This range is based on current market prices by [31].
Demand forecast	D_{t_0}: (1200–1700) kilotons [37, 38], based on historical data and market reports on increasing demand for natural graphite in EV batteries.
	P_{t_0}: \$450 taken as the mid-point of the selling price range.
	ϵ_t: (0.4–0.6), reflecting the relatively inelastic demand due to graphite's criticality in EV batteries and limited substitutes.
Cost	m:(3–7) % represents a relatively small market share for an early-stage company.
	Q_{max}: (50–150) kilotons per annum, based on data from existing companies but varies widely since production depends on stage of development [39].
	$c_{variable}(Q_t(D_t(P_t)))$: 60–80% of price, influenced by mining efficiency logistics.
	c_{fixed}: \$(4,500,000–5,500,000), covering infrastructure and administrative costs.
Penalty	GP_p: (10–30) % of costs as per sections 45X and 48C of IRA.
	CR_r: (2.5–7.5) % of costs due to reduced extraction/processing expenses [33].
	CI_i: (5–15) % of costs represents a discretionary amount for CE investments [35].
	SE_m: (1–4) % of costs, which depends on the extent of CE practices [40].
	ESG_s: (5–20) % of costs depends on consumer demand for sustainable practices.
	λ_p, v_c, θ_s: evenly weighted but can be adjusted for other scenarios.
Risk	MR_m: (5–15) % of costs, accounting for inflation and interest rate changes [41].
	SD_d: (10–30) % of costs, due to market volatility [32].
	GF_g: (5–15) % of costs, reflecting geopolitical risks.
	α_m, β_d, γ_g: evenly weighted but can be adjusted for other scenarios.

\$400.00 to \$500.00. Optimal price confidence interval helps in making realistic pricing strategies by providing a range that optimal price is expected to lie. Also, it highlights the price range within 5th to 95th percentile, extending from \$423.79 to \$586.57, showcasing an alternative metric to assess variability in pricing for stakeholders to understand as it affects formulation of realistic pricing strategies. The profit variability, with an approximate 68% confidence interval of -\$5,389,938.32 to \$1,586,233.19, reflects the expected range of profitability with the current parameters and premium price, aiding in making informed financial risk assessments.

Table 2. Sensitivity Analysis results

Parameter	Value range	Profit range ($)	Value range (±10%)	Profit range
varible_cost per_unit	$360 to $270	−4,178,844.6 to 2,673,878.02	$346.50 to $283.50	−$3,012,163.90 to $1,727,039.39
fixed_cost	$5,500,000 to 4,500,000	−1,108,105.37 to 82,333.06	$5,500,000.00 to 4,500,000.00	−$1,046,302.13 to $85,956.78
P_t0	$425 to $475	v$629,118.46 to 349,031.34	$405.00 to $495.00	−$750,599.89 to $234,499.60
D_t0	1,200,000 to 1,700,000	−$1,399,621.12 to 362,846.13	1,305,000.00 to 1,595,000.00	−$982,839.53 to $503,356.87
epsilon_t	0.60 to 0.40	−$555,776.54 to 399,473.56	0.55 to 0.45	−$524,067.91 to $437,875.55
Q_max	50,000 to 150,000.00	−$1,854,964.32 to 449,498.06	90,000.00 to 110,000.00	−$518,434.49 to $456,881.93
market_share	0.03 to 0.07	−$2,709,293.57 to 1,397,209.79	0.05 to 0.06	−$992,777.20 to $49,466.85
subsidy	0.10 to 0.30	−$4,486,630.38 to 2,889,403.05	0.18 to 0.22	−$1,209,866.04 to $228,375.96
tax	0.3 to 0.10	−$519,816.06 to −275,222.99	0.33 to 0.27	−$565,694.41 to $446,237.06
ce_investments	0.15 to 0.05	−$1,407,800.88 to 402,079.64	0.11 to 0.09	−$629,363.95 to −$332,505.67
ce_recycling	−0.03 to −0.07	−$941,364.58 to −56,807.97	−0.05 to −0.06	−$584,621.92 to −$38,100.70
ce_savings	−0.01 to −0.04	−$748,547.32-(−200,353.46)	−0.02 to −0.03	−$507,317.12 to −$432,301.19
emission_level	0.2- to 0.05	−$3,398,348.05 to −535,635.7	0.06 to 0.05	−$600,317.56 to −$338,600.84
water_usage	0.10 to 0.05	−$1,467,002.87 to −523,626.39	0.06 to 0.05	−$615,155.09 to −$381,781.38
interest_rate	0.07 to 0.02	−$817,434.91 to 36,941.52	0.06 to 0.05	−$588,970.38 to −$355,387.87
inflation_rate	0.08 to 0.03	−$1,078,738.01 to −135,842.51	0.06 to 0.05	−$614,428.71 to −$378,581.94
production_delay	0.18 to 0.07	−$1,014,805.57 to 949,361.34	0.17 to 0.14	−$793,452.75 to −$168,107.00

(continued)

Table 2. *(continued)*

Parameter	Value range	Profit range ($)	Value range (±10%)	Profit range
logistic_issues	0.20 to 0.10	−$1,386,637.3 to 369,879.40	0.17 to 0.14	−$799,083.52 to −$219,512.96
trade_tension	0.07 to 0.02	−$845,001.77 to 18,658.03	0.06 to 0.05	−$600,217.89 to −$400,764.01
regulatory_changes	0.08 to 0.03	−$1,023,976.39 to −135,360.52	0.06 to 0.05	−$600,884.75 to −$354,498.36

Results, Discussion, and Practical Implementation

Table 2 shows how variations in key parameters can affect profitability. For example, adjusting the variable cost per unit between $360.00 and $270.00 results in a profit range of −$4,178,844.60 to $2,673,878.02. This ability to fine-tune parameters in real-time enables companies to optimize their pricing strategies dynamically, respond effectively to changing market conditions and maintain profitability. Table 2 shows how adjusting the parameters values as a percentage of original inputs can impact profitability. So, stakeholders can make informed decisions to achieve optimal financial outcomes. For this illustrative case, 10% was chosen as the percentage-based parameter. This highlights which parameters are most critical for pricing stability and provides guidance for stakeholders on where strategic interventions are most effective.

Table 3 provides an itemized view of how each parameter affects costs and pricing strategies. Penalty value is $5,932,642.55 and risk value is $14,022,609.66, representing additional costs of ESG compliance, CE practices, and risk management. CE initiatives lead to additional costs but result in long-term savings via sustainable practices. Investments in CE practices are quantified at $2,696,655.70, and savings from recycling and other CE practices are estimated at $1,078,662.28 and $808,996.71 respectively, reflecting the expenditure and savings to be expected under current circumstances, which will invariably change as earlier investments start to produce greater long-term financial benefits. For ESG metrics, lower emissions are valued at $3,235,986.84 and efficient water usage is valued at $1,887,658.99, highlighting not only the costs incurred also the improvement in a company's market reputation and investor confidence. This analysis provides stakeholders with actionable insights to refine strategies that account for these diverse influences, ensuring long-term stability and sustainability and can create strategies that reflect the true costs of operations and align with market demands for sustainability and compliance. The proposed DPPM promotes market diversification by integrating sustainability, risk management, and other explained relevant factors. By supporting a broader range of suppliers, especially from IRA-compliant countries—and reflecting a premium price of $504.77 per tonne, DPPM can support mitigating geopolitical risks and supply chain disruptions, by allocating funds to risk mitigation to enhance supplier standards and encourage new market participants.

Table 3. Impact Summaries

Impact	Parameters	Mean value
Circular economy factors	Investments: 0.15 to 0.05, Recycling: −0.03 to 0.07 Savings: −0.01 to −0.04	ce_investments: $2,696,655.70, ce_recycling: $−1,078,662.28, ce_savings: $−808,996.71
ESG metrics	Emission Level: 0.20 to 0.05 Water Usage: 0.10 to 0.05	emission_level: $3,235,986.84 water_usage: $1,887,658.99
Macroeconomic risks	Interest Rate: 0.07 to 0.02 Inflation Rate: 0.08 to 0.03	interest_rate: $1,617,993.42 inflation_rate: $1,348,327.85
Supply-demand risks	Production Delay: 0.18 to 0.07 Logistic Issues: 0.20 to 0.10	production_delay: $3,775,317.99 logistic_issues: $4,044,983.56
Geopolitical factors	Trade Tension: 0.07 to 0.02 Regulatory Changes: 0.08 to 0.03	trade_tension: $1,348,327.85 regulatory_changes: $1,887,658.99

The current state of graphite market shows medium to high levels of environmental and social risks [42]. Reliance on coal-based electricity in mining regions contributes to elevated carbon emissions, worsening environmental risks. The proposed DPPM integrates ESG and sustainability factors to address such risks by offering quantifiable insights, incentivizing suppliers to meet higher standards. For example, we quantifiably demonstrated that investments in emission reduction ($3,235,986.84) and efficient water usage ($1,887,658.99) enhance regulatory compliance and appeal to ESG-conscious stakeholders. These funds can support technologies like blockchain to ensure transparency, boosting investor confidence and market stability. Strong ESG performance might support and justify premium pricing by reflecting the long-term value of reduced environmental impact.

Producers gain a stable premium reflecting ESG compliance and risk management, enhancing financial planning. Off takers receive transparent, dynamic pricing that supports long-term contracts. Investors benefit from improved confidence and project bankability, while governments see alignment with policy incentives and sustainability goals. Overall, the model encourages supply chain diversification, strengthens market resilience, and promotes sustainable industry practices. The proposed DPPM does not directly eliminate supply chain risks or enforce supplier behavior. Rather, it functions as a decision-support framework that enables stakeholders to evaluate pricing implications of ESG performance, geopolitical exposure, and circular economy initiatives when comparing sourcing and investment alternatives.

5 Conclusion

In this research, we developed a Dynamic Premium Pricing Model to integrate economic, environmental, and social factors into the pricing of critical minerals. We demonstrated, through a graphite study as an illustrative case, that the model can support premium pricing by reflecting true costs of sustainable sourcing, incorporating risk adjustments, and promoting supply chain diversification. We validated the model's adaptability using Monte Carlo simulations and sensitivity analysis, confirming its robustness under uncertainty. In practice, the proposed DPPM can be used by producers, investors, or policymakers as a decision-support tool to evaluate pricing implications associated with sustainability compliance, geopolitical exposure, recycling investments, and sourcing diversification strategies. As a future research direction, the model can be expanded to other critical minerals, integrate real-time market data, and leverage advanced technologies such as AI/ML and blockchain. This can strengthen the model's predictive capabilities and improve supply chain traceability in the path towards transitioning to sustainable and equitable mineral markets.

Disclosure of Interests. The authors have no competing interests to declare that are relevant to the content of this article.

References

1. Dou, S., Xu, D., Zhu, Y., Keenan, R.: Critical mineral sustainable supply: challenges and governance. Futures. **146**, 103101 (2019)
2. Agusdinata, D.B., Eakin, H., Liu, W., Romero, H.: Governance of sustainable critical-minerals supply chain: a telecoupled network-of-networks framework. Appl. Geogr. **191**, 104023 (2026)
3. Wang, J., Zhou, Z., Yu, M.S.: Pricing models in a sustainable supply chain with capacity constraint. J. Clean. Prod. **222**, 57–76 (2019)
4. IEA: Global Supply Chains of EV Batteries [Online]. IEA (2022) https://www.iea.org/reports/global-supply-chains-of-ev-batteries
5. Halton, B., Beazley, K.: AUKUS and Critical Minerals: Hedging Beijing's Pervasive, Clever and Coordinated Statecraft [Online]. Australian Strategic Policy Institute (2023) https://www.aspi.org.au/report/aukus-and-critical-minerals-hedging-beijings-pervasive-clever-and-coordinated-statecraft
6. Liu, Z.Z.: Critical Minerals and the New Cold War. Tribune Content Agency LLC, Tokyo (2023)
7. Human Rights Watch: Child Labor and Human Rights Violations in the Mining Industry of the Democratic Republic of Congo [Online]. Human Rights Watch (2022) https://www.hrw.org/news/2022/07/14/child-labor-and-human-rights-violations-mining-industry-democratic-republic-congo
8. Cordos, A., Dodita, A.: Cobalt ESG Risks Threaten Electric Vehicle Supply Chain [Online]. Sustainalytics (2022) https://www.sustainalytics.com/esg-research/resource/investors-esg-blog/cobalt-esg-risks-threaten-electric-vehicle-supply-chain
9. S&P Global: Inflation Reduction Act: Impact on North America Metals and Minerals Market. [Online]. S&P Global (2023) https://cdn.ihsmarkit.com/www/prot/pdf/0823/Impact-IRA-Metals-Minerals-Report-FINAL-August2023.pdf
10. ABC News: Indonesia's Electric Vehicle Battery Nickel Rush. [Online]. ABC News (2023) https://www.abc.net.au/news/2023-10-22/indonesias-electric-vehicle-battery-nickel-rush/102862362
11. State of Play: 2023 Critical Minerals: Developing Price Transparency. [Online]. State of Play (2023) https://stateofplay.org/download/2023-critical-minerals-developing-price-transparency/

12. Krol-Sinclair, M.: Bring, Commodities Market Regulators into the Critical Minerals Discussion. [Online]. Center for Strategic & International Studies (2023) https://www.csis.org/analysis/bring-commodities-market-regulators-critical-minerals-discussion
13. The White House: Inflation Reduction Act Guidebook [Online]. The White House (2023) https://www.whitehouse.gov/wp-content/uploads/2022/12/Inflation-Reduction-Act-Guidebook.pdf
14. Abbitt, C., et al.: The role of design in circular economy solutions for critical materials. B3 One Earth. **4**, 353–362 (2021)
15. Nurdiawati, A., Agrawal, T.K.: Creating a circular EV battery value chain: end-of-life strategies and future perspective. Resour. Conserv. Recycl. **185**, 106484 (2022)
16. Graedel, T.E., et al.: Criticality of metals and metalloids. Proc. Natl. Acad. Sci. U.S.A. **112**(14), 4257–4262 (2015)
17. Akbari, K.: Innovation in pricing mechanisms: an analysis of the emergence of dynamic and fixed pricing in five countries. J. Eur. Lang. Lit. **20**, 37–87 (2023)
18. Fisher, M., Gallino, S., Li, J., et al.: Competition-based dynamic pricing in online retailing: a methodology validated with field experiments. Manag. Sci. **64**, 2496–2514 (2018)
19. Liu, K., et al.: Optimal strategies of green product supply chains based on behaviour-based pricing. J. Clean. Prod. **335**, 130288 (2022)
20. Abdallah, T., Asadpour, A.: Large-scale bundle-size pricing: a theoretical analysis. Oper. Res. **69**(4), 1158–1185 (2021)
21. Eid, C., et al.: Time-based pricing and electricity demand response: existing barriers and next steps. Util. Policy. **40**, 15–25 (2016)
22. Guda, H., Subramanian, U.: Your Uber is arriving: managing on-demand workers through surge pricing, forecast communication, and worker incentives. Manag. Sci. **65**(5), 1995–2014 (2019)
23. Bolton, R.N., Myers, M.B.: Price-based global market segmentation for services. J. Mark. **67**(3), 108–128 (2003)
24. Gerard, J., Spann, M., Fischer, M., Tellis, G.J.: Skimming or penetration? Strategic dynamic pricing for new products. Mark. Sci. **34**(2), 235–249 (2015)
25. Phillips, J.: How Uber's dynamic pricing model works [Online]. Uber. https://www.uber.com/en-GB/blog/uber-dynamic-pricing/
26. Gao, R., Abdoli, S.: Investigating and proposing a framework for sustainable supply chains of critical minerals in electric vehicle batteries. In: Proceedings of the International Conference on Industrial Engineering and Operations Management (2024)
27. Hao, C.H., et al.: Dynamic pricing in consumer-centric electricity markets: a systematic review and thematic analysis. Energ. Strat. Rev. **52**, 101349 (2024)
28. Price Elasticities of Demand for Individual Commodities Imported into the United States: International Monetary Fund. Research Dept. 1. IMF Staff Papers (1951)
29. Zhu, C., et al.: Algorithm 778: L-BFGS-B: Fortran subroutines for large-scale bound-constrained optimization. ACM Trans. Math. Softw. **23**(4), 550–560 (1997)
30. Benchmark: Natural Graphite Price Assessment. [Online]. Benchmark (2024) https://www.benchmarkminerals.com/price-assessments/natural-graphite/
31. Fastmarkets: Graphite [Online]. Fastmarkets (2024) https://www.fastmarkets.com/insights/category/commodity/graphite/
32. U.S. Department of Energy: Critical Materials Assessment. U.S. Department of Energy (2023)
33. European Commission: European Critical Raw Materials Act. [Online]. European Commission (2024) https://commission.europa.eu/strategy-and-policy/priorities-2019-2024/european-green-deal/green-deal-industrial-plan/european-critical-raw-materials-act_en
34. International Energy Agency: Global Critical Minerals Outlook 2024. International Energy Agency (2024)

35. Tesla: Tesla 2023 Impact Report. s.l. Tesla (2023)
36. Fastmarkets. Graphite Buyers Are Willing to Pay IRA Premium. [Online]. (2024). https://www.fastmarkets.com/insights/graphite-buyers-are-willing-to-pay-ira-premium/.
37. Fastmarkets: Graphite Market Outlook: Five Key Factors to Watch. [Online]. Fastmarkets (2023) https://www.fastmarkets.com/insights/graphite-market-outlook-five-key-factors-to-watch/
38. Global Data: Graphite Mining Market Analysis by Reserves, Production, Assets, Demand Drivers and Forecast to 2030 [Online]. Global Data (2024) https://www.globaldata.com/store/report/graphite-mining-market-analysis/
39. Ian, H., et al.: Recycling and reusing of graphite from retired Lithium-ion batteries: a review. Adv. Mater. **36**(13), e2308494 (2024)
40. Tesla: Tesla Impact Report 2023. Tesla (2023)
41. Trading Economics: United States Inflation Rate. [Online]. Trading Economics (2024) https://tradingeconomics.com/united-states/inflation-cpi
42. International Energy Agency: Global Critical Minerals Outlook 2024. s.l. International Energy Agency (2024)

Battery Swapping Business Models for Heavy-Duty Machines in Road Construction and Quarry Operations

Koteshwar Chirumalla[1,2(✉)], Stavros Vouros[1], and Bobbie Frank[3,4]

[1] Digital and Circular Industrial Services (DigiCircle) Research Group, Department of Engineering Sciences, Mälardalen University, Eskilstuna 63217, Sweden
koteshwar.chirumalla@mdu.se
[2] Åbo Akademi University, Åbo 20500, Finland
[3] Volvo Construction Equipment AB, Eskilstuna 63185, Sweden
[4] Lund University, Lund 22100, Sweden

Abstract. Battery swapping has been discussed as a potential approach to support the electrification of heavy-duty machines in road construction and quarry operations. These applications require high energy use, continuous operation, and reliable uptime, which can make conventional charging challenging to implement. At the same time, battery swapping is not widely adopted in these sectors, and there is limited understanding of suitable business models across different operational scenarios. The purpose of this paper is to examine battery swapping business models for heavy-duty machines in road construction and quarry operations under different operational conditions. The study considers five operational scenarios, ranging from single-machine use to multi-machine and high-intensity operations, including synchronized fleets, off-grid construction sites, and large quarry environments. The analysis focuses on four main criteria: machine utilization, project duration, energy infrastructure, and number of subcontractors. These criteria influence the design of battery swapping systems and the corresponding business models. Based on this analysis, the paper proposes a continuum framework of business models, ranging from simple battery rental solutions to more integrated energy-as-a-service approaches. The results show how different operational conditions may require different configurations, from flexible and low-investment solutions to more advanced and service-based models. The findings provide a structured way to explore how battery swapping could be implemented in different construction and quarry settings. The paper contributes to the literature on battery-based business model innovation and servitization, with a specific focus on heavy-duty machine industry.

Keywords: Battery Swapping · Business Model Innovation · Electrification · Battery-as-a-Service · Energy-as-a-Service

G. Pezzotta et al. (Eds.): APMS 2026, IFIP AICT 808, pp. 122–136, 2027.
https://doi.org/10.1007/978-3-032-38594-9_9

1 Introduction

Zero-emission heavy machinery refers to equipment such as construction, mining, material handling, and industrial machines that operate using battery-electric, hydrogen-based, or other non-combustion powertrains, thereby avoiding direct tailpipe emissions [1]. The adoption of such machines is driven by stricter environmental regulations, increasing pressure to lower carbon emissions, and the need to improve environmental performance in energy-intensive industries [1]. In this context, the electrification of heavy-duty machines is gaining attention in road construction and quarry operations as part of efforts to improve energy efficiency and reduce environmental impact [2, 3].

Electric machines are gradually being introduced in several markets, supported by policy initiatives and pilot projects [4]. However, the market is still developing, and electrified equipment represents a relatively small share of the overall heavy-duty machinery fleet. Most currently available machines are based on built-in battery solutions, reflecting the early stage of heavy-duty electrification [5, 6]. At the same time, alternative system configurations are still being explored [7]. As a result, different technical pathways for electrification, such as direct charging, battery swapping, and alternative energy carriers, remain under consideration [7–9].

At present, most original equipment manufacturers (OEMs) focus on machines with integrated batteries, both in construction equipment and heavy-duty trucks [5, 6, 10]. Battery swapping, in contrast, remains relatively unexplored in these sectors [11, 12]. While some early developments can be observed, for example in Chinese truck applications [13] and in construction equipment Limach in the Netherlands [14], battery swapping is not yet widely implemented in heavy-duty machinery.

In other industries, different approaches to battery systems have emerged over time. In handheld power tools, battery swapping has become widely adopted [15]. A similar development can be observed in micro-mobility applications such as electric scooters, e-bikes, and mopeds [16], where built-in batteries have increasingly replaced by swappable battery systems [17, 18]. Battery swapping has also been explored in the passenger vehicle segment, for example through NIO's battery swapping ecosystem [19, 20]. These developments suggest that multiple technological pathways can coexist and evolve under different operational and business conditions [21].

This raises an important question: if similar transitions were to occur in heavy-duty construction and quarry operations, what would this mean for battery swapping and its associated business models? In particular, how could battery swapping be configured in such contexts, and what implications might it have for system design and business models? While battery swapping has developed in several industries, its role in heavy-duty applications remains unclear. Electrification in these sectors is still at an early stage, and most current solutions rely on built-in battery systems. In addition, operational conditions such as high energy demand, continuous machine use, and varying environments introduce additional complexity compared to other applications.

Existing research on battery systems has mainly focused on technical performance, infrastructure planning, and optimization aspects [22, 23]. Less attention has been given to how different system configurations influence business models in heavy-duty applications. At the same time, research on business model innovation [24], servitization [25], and circular business models [26] has shown that battery technologies can reshape value creation, delivery, and capture across industrial ecosystems. Previous studies have explored business model configurations for battery circularity, second-life applications, and electric mobility systems. For example, Olsson et al. [27], Wrålsen et al. [28], Jiao [29], Chirumalla et al. [26], Xu et al. [30], and Kulkov [31] examined different business model archetypes related to battery ecosystems, service-based solutions, and electric mobility. Research has also emphasized the importance of system-level approaches and servitization in electric mobility business models [32].

However, these studies mainly focus on passenger vehicles, battery circularity, or general electric mobility systems. There is still limited understanding of how battery swapping business models could be configured in heavy-duty construction and quarry operations. In particular, there is a lack of structured frameworks linking operational scenarios with possible business model configurations in such contexts.

This study addresses this gap by taking an exploratory perspective on battery swapping in heavy-duty construction and quarry operations. The purpose of this paper is to examine battery swapping business models for heavy-duty machines in road construction and quarry operations under different operational conditions. The study is guided by the following research question (RQ): *What types of battery swapping business models are suitable for heavy-duty machines in road construction and quarry operations under different operational conditions?*

The paper contributes to research on business model innovation, servitization, and electrification by proposing a continuum framework that connects operational conditions with possible business models configurations. The results identify five operational scenarios ranging from single-machine use to large-scale operations, showing how different conditions may require different technical and business model configurations.

2 Theoretical Background

Electrification of heavy-duty machines introduces not only technical changes but also new organizational and business model challenges. In construction and quarry operations, operational conditions such as high energy demand, long operating hours, temporary worksites, and constrained infrastructure create uncertainty regarding how electrification solutions should be configured and managed [2, 5, 33]. As a result, different approaches to energy supply and battery management, including battery swapping, are currently being explored [7, 9, 11].

Battery swapping differs from conventional charging by separating charging activities from machine operation through replacement of depleted batteries with charged ones [34]. While this approach may reduce downtime and enable more centralized energy management, it also requires additional coordination, infrastructure, standardization, and ecosystem integration [9, 21]. This suggests that the feasibility of battery swapping depends not only on technology, but also on how value creation, delivery, and capture are organized across actors.

In this context, research on business model innovation [24, 26] and servitization [25] provides an important conceptual lens. Electrification shifts traditional ownership-oriented models toward more service-oriented and performance-based approaches [35, 36]. Instead of owning both the machine and the battery, customers may access batteries, charging, or uptime through leasing, battery-as-a-service, or energy-as-a-service models [26]. These approaches redistribute risks, responsibilities, and revenue streams between manufacturers, service providers, contractors, and energy actors.

Previous studies have explored business model configurations related to battery ecosystems, circularity, and electric mobility. For example, Kulkov [31] identified several battery swapping business model archetypes, including integrated provider and battery-as-a-service models. Research on circular business models has further emphasized lifecycle thinking, collaboration, and service integration in battery ecosystems [26–31]. Similarly, Kley et al. [32] proposed a system-level framework combining vehicle, infrastructure, and service dimensions in electric mobility business models. Recently, Huijssoon et al. [37] has also highlighted the importance of ecosystem mapping and iterative modelling in designing circular battery business models and identifying coordination challenges between actors. Together, these studies indicate that electrification involves broader socio-technical and organizational transformations rather than isolated technological change.

3 Research Methodology

3.1 Research Approach

This study is based on a qualitative case study [38] conducted in collaboration with a machine manufacturer in the heavy-duty machine industry. A case study approach [38] was chosen to gain a deeper understanding of how battery swapping can be explored in real operational contexts and how different business model configurations may be applied under varying conditions. The case company is actively engaged in the electrification of heavy-duty machines, primarily focusing on solutions with integrated batteries. At the same time, battery swapping is considered as part of ongoing research and exploratory activities. This provides a relevant context to study battery swapping without assuming its implementation as a dominant or preferred solution. The case study allows for an in-depth examination of operational conditions and the exploration of alternative configurations, including battery swapping. Rather than evaluating a fully implemented system, the study focuses on analyzing potential scenarios and their implications for system design and business models.

3.2 Data Collection

Data was collected from multiple sources within the case study to capture both practical insights and ongoing discussions related to electrification and battery swapping in heavy-duty operations. The data collection included semi-structured interviews, bi-weekly project meetings with researchers and industry representatives, and a site visit to a construction environment.

Two semi-structured interviews were conducted. The first interview involved a customer specialist from the OEM side, and the second interview involved a site manager from the customer side. Both respondents had more than 10 years of experience in their respective fields and were selected based on their involvement in electrification initiatives and operational decision-making. Each interview lasted approximately 45 min. The interviews focused on operational challenges related to electrification, including energy supply, machine utilization, charging limitations, project conditions, and perspectives on battery swapping solutions.

In addition to the interviews, the study included continuous participation in 20 bi-weekly project meetings. These meetings involved six researchers with expertise in business models, simulation, life cycle assessment (LCA), and energy management. The meetings also included three representatives from the OEM side, covering project management, machine concepts, and customer applications, as well as two representatives from the customer side responsible for site and machine operations. The meetings enabled ongoing discussions, idea development, and validation of assumptions throughout the study. A site visit to a construction environment was also conducted to improve understanding of practical operating conditions, machine workflows, and energy-related challenges. Observations from the site visit were documented through field notes and discussed during project meetings. The use of multiple data sources supported triangulation between interviews, observations, and project discussions, which contributed to the consistency and credibility of the findings.

3.3 Data Analysis

The collected data were analyzed using an iterative and exploratory process. The analysis started with reviewing interview notes, observations from the site visit, and documentation from project meetings. Initial coding focused on identifying recurring themes related to electrification challenges, operational conditions, battery usage, infrastructure limitations, and possible battery swapping configurations. Through this process, key operational criteria influencing battery swapping systems were identified, including machine utilization, project duration, energy infrastructure, and the number of subcontractors involved on site. These criteria were used to structure the analysis and explore how different operational conditions may influence battery swapping solutions and business model configurations.

Based on the identified criteria, different machine setups and operational scenarios were gradually developed during the bi-weekly meetings. The scenarios were not predefined but emerged through repeated discussions, reflections, and feedback between researchers and industry participants. Early scenario concepts were continuously refined and validated through additional discussions in the project meetings. This iterative process resulted in five operational scenarios ranging from single-machine operations to large-scale and high-intensity environments, including off-grid construction sites and quarry operations. In the next step, the scenarios were compared against the identified operational criteria to examine how battery swapping could potentially be configured under different conditions. The analysis focused on system characteristics such as battery capacity, charging approach, swapping frequency, level of automation, and infrastructure requirements. Based on this comparison, corresponding business model dimensions were analyzed, including value proposition, value creation, value delivery, and value capture.

The analysis also applied a pattern matching logic [38] by comparing operational conditions, scenario characteristics, and business model dimensions across the identified scenarios. This supported the identification of recurring relationships and patterns between operational conditions and possible business model configurations. These patterns contributed to the development of the proposed continuum framework for battery swapping business models, illustrating how configurations may vary depending on operational conditions and system complexity. The iterative interaction between interviews, project meetings, site observations, and scenario discussions supported continuous validation of the findings throughout the research process. This approach strengthened the reliability and practical relevance of the developed scenarios and framework.

4 Results

4.1 Criteria Influencing Battery Swapping Business Models

The analysis identified four main criteria that influence the design of battery swapping systems and the selection of suitable business models. These criteria are machine utilization, project duration, electrical infrastructure, and the number of subcontractors on site. Each of these factors affects how battery swapping can be implemented in practice.

Machine utilization refers to how intensively the machines are used during operation. It can range from low to high. In low-utilization cases, such as a single machine used intermittently, battery demand is limited and simple battery rental solutions can be sufficient. In contrast, high-utilization scenarios, such as continuous multi-shift operations in quarry sites, require frequent battery swaps, a larger number of batteries, and more advanced service-based business models to ensure uptime.

Project duration describes the length of the construction or quarry project. Short-term projects may last only a few weeks or months, while long-term projects can continue for several years. In short-duration projects, temporary and mobile battery swapping solutions are more suitable, often based on rental or leasing models. For long-term projects, it becomes more feasible to invest in permanent infrastructure and more integrated business models, such as energy-as-a-service.

Electrical infrastructure is a critical factor that determines how energy can be supplied and managed. Sites with access to a strong electrical grid can support direct charging and relatively simple swapping setups. In off-grid locations, alternative solutions such as diesel generators or hybrid systems are needed, increasing system complexity. In some cases, battery energy storage systems (BESS) can be used to manage energy supply and enable efficient charging. For example, an off-grid bridge construction site may require a mobile swapping station combined with BESS, which affects both technical design and the business model.

The **number of subcontractors** on site also influences the organization of battery swapping. In sites with few subcontractors, coordination is easier, and a single business model can be applied across all machines. In contrast, sites with many subcontractors involve multiple actors with different needs and contracts. This requires more flexible and scalable business models, such as shared battery pools or pay-per-use systems. For example, a large construction site with several subcontractors may require a centralized swapping service that can be accessed by different users.

These four criteria interact with each other and shape the operational conditions of each site. Understanding their impact is important for selecting appropriate battery swapping solutions and developing suitable business models.

4.2 Battery Swapping Business Models Across Operational Scenarios

This section presents five operational scenarios identified in the analysis and examines the corresponding battery swapping business models. The scenarios represent different combinations of the four operational criteria and illustrate how these criteria influence both the design of battery swapping systems and the choice of business models. The presented scenarios should be understood as empirically informed operational configurations developed through an iterative and collaborative analysis process. The following subsections describe each scenario and its associated business model configuration.

Scenario 1: Rental-Based Battery Swapping for Single-Machine, Short-Duration Operations

This scenario represents a basic use case where a single machine is operated on a short-duration project. The site typically has access to the electrical grid or requires only a low level of energy. The machine is owned by the customer or dealer, while additional batteries are provided through rental by the OEM or dealer. Battery swapping is performed manually or with simple tools such as a forklift. Charging is supported by small, portable chargers, and no dedicated swapping station is required.

This setup requires low capital investment and is relatively easy to deploy. It is particularly suitable for pilot projects or small contractors who want to test electric machines without committing to large infrastructure investments. At the same time, the approach is labor-intensive and not suitable for scaling to larger operations.

The value proposition in this scenario is a low-risk entry into electrification, offering operational flexibility for small-scale users. Value is created through a limited number of additional battery packs, portable charging equipment, and basic service support. Value delivery is based on shipping batteries to the site, combined with on-demand support and short-term contractual arrangements. Value capture is achieved through battery rental fees (weekly/monthly), charging fees based on energy consumption (per kWh), and service-related fees.

The business model in this scenario can be described as a **combination of battery rental and usage-based energy billing**. This model aligns well with the operational conditions, as it minimizes upfront investment and allows flexible use. However, due to its manual nature and limited scalability, it is mainly suitable for low-utilization and short-duration projects. As operational intensity or project complexity increases, more structured and automated solutions become necessary.

Scenario 2: Shared Battery Swapping for Small Multi-Machine Operations

This scenario represents operations with two to three machines working on a site over a medium to long project duration. The site typically has access to the electrical grid, supported by a small battery energy storage system (BESS) to manage energy demand. Battery swapping is organized through a semi-automated and modular system, which can be delivered to the site as a plug-and-play unit. A small pool of shared spare batteries, typically one to two units, is used to support operations.

This setup is able to handle moderate workloads efficiently while maintaining relatively low system complexity. The shared infrastructure reduces the need for individual investments in batteries and charging equipment. However, the system requires coordination between users, especially when multiple subcontractors are involved.

The value proposition in this scenario is improved machine uptime and reduced downtime related to charging. By sharing infrastructure, the cost per machine is reduced, making electrification more accessible for small to medium-sized operations. Value is created through a modular swapping station, a shared battery pool, and a basic energy management system that supports charging and battery availability.

Value delivery is organized through subscription-based access to the swapping system, combined with managed charging schedules and maintenance services. This ensures that batteries are available when needed and that the system operates reliably. Value capture is based on a combination of subscription fees per machine or battery usage, energy pricing based on actual consumption (kWh), and pay-per-swap fees. Additional performance-based services can also be offered.

The business model in this scenario can be described as a **basic or light battery-as-a-service (BaaS) model**. This model is well suited for medium-utilization and medium-duration projects, where shared infrastructure improves cost efficiency without requiring large investments. Compared to the single-machine scenario, this model provides better scalability and operational efficiency, while still maintaining relatively low complexity.

Scenario 3: Fleet-Based Battery Swapping with Full Energy-as-a-Service for Synchronized Operations

This scenario represents operations with four to five machines working synchronously over a long project duration. Such operations are typically characterized by high machine utilization and continuous workflows, where interruptions can significantly affect productivity. The setup includes an automated battery swapping station supported by an integrated BESS. Battery usage and charging are managed through dynamic scheduling software, and operations are supported by performance-based contracts with defined uptime targets.

This configuration enables near zero-downtime operations, as battery swaps are automated and optimized across the fleet. The integrated BESS allows high-power charging even in locations with limited grid capacity. However, this setup requires careful site planning, higher upfront investment, and long-term operational commitments.

The value proposition in this scenario is based on guaranteed uptime and zero waiting time for battery replacement. This is critical for synchronized operations, where delays in one machine can affect the entire workflow. Value is created through support for multi-shift operations, automated swapping infrastructure, integrated energy storage, and software systems for fleet-level energy optimization. In addition, predictive battery health management helps ensure reliability and reduce unexpected failures.

Value delivery is organized through continuous service provision, including 24/7 operational support, digital monitoring dashboards, and service level agreement (SLA)-based contracts. These elements ensure transparency and performance tracking throughout the project. Value capture is based on availability-oriented pricing, such as cost per operating hour, combined with energy-as-a-service contracts that include availability (uptime) guarantees. Long-term service agreements are typically required to support this model.

The business model in this scenario can be described as a **full energy-as-a-service model**. This model is well suited for high-utilization, long-duration projects where operational reliability is critical. Compared to previous scenarios, it offers a higher level of integration and performance, but also requires greater coordination, investment, and long-term commitment.

Scenario 4: Mobile Battery Swapping Solutions for Off-Grid Construction Sites

This scenario represents construction projects located in remote areas, such as bridge construction or road infrastructure sites, where access to the electrical grid is limited or unavailable. The setup is based on a mobile and containerized battery swapping solution, which can be deployed as a battery trailer or swap-truck. Energy supply is provided through a hybrid system that combines BESS, solar generation, and diesel generator sets. These components are integrated into a mobile energy hub with microgrid control to manage energy flows.

This configuration enables electrification in locations where conventional charging infrastructure cannot be installed. It allows multiple subcontractors with different types of machines to operate on the same site. However, the system involves complex operations and logistics, including transport, setup, and energy management. The cost per unit of energy (kWh) is also typically higher compared to grid-connected solutions.

The value proposition in this scenario is the ability to support electrification without dependence on grid infrastructure. This reduces the need for diesel fuel logistics and supports lower emissions, which is particularly important for public infrastructure projects with sustainability requirements. Value is created through mobile swapping units, hybrid energy systems, and microgrid-based energy balancing.

Value delivery is based on a fully managed mobile energy hub, provided as a turnkey solution to the site. This includes deployment, operation, and maintenance of the system, as well as support for multiple users. Value capture is based on energy delivery pricing, typically at a premium per kWh, combined with infrastructure leasing fees. In some cases, additional value can be captured through carbon reduction incentives or green contract premiums.

The business model in this scenario can be described as a **mobile energy hub-as-a-service model**. This model is well suited for off-grid and high-complexity sites where flexibility and mobility are critical. Compared to previous scenarios, it offers greater independence from infrastructure constraints, but at the cost of increased system complexity and higher operational expenses.

Scenario 5: Infrastructure Concession Model for Large-Scale Quarry and Long-Duration Operations

This scenario represents large-scale operations with six to fifteen machines working over a long project duration, such as quarry sites or major construction projects. These operations are characterized by very high machine utilization and continuous production requirements. The setup includes a permanent and fully automated high-capacity battery swapping station, supported by a multi-megawatt charging yard and a large BESS.

In addition, digital tools such as digital twin are used for energy forecasting, route optimization, and battery lifecycle management.

This configuration enables extremely high productivity and supports full electrification of operations. It allows large fleet owners to optimize total cost of ownership (TCO) compared to diesel-based systems. However, the setup requires significant upfront investment and is only suitable for long-duration projects where such investments can be justified.

The value proposition in this scenario is based on industrial-scale uptime, predictable energy costs, and compliance with environmental and sustainability requirements. Value is created through permanent automated infrastructure, large-scale energy storage, strong grid connections, and advanced software systems for energy and fleet optimization. In this model, the provider delivers a comprehensive offer that includes guaranteed machine uptime, energy supply, maintenance and service, and battery lifecycle management.

Value delivery is organized through long-term agreements, typically structured as concession models over five to ten years. These agreements include guaranteed uptime, integrated fleet optimization, and management of batteries throughout their lifecycle, including end-of-life handling. Value capture is based on multi-year energy-as-a-service contracts, performance-based pricing, and shared savings compared to diesel operations. In addition, value can be captured through monetization of emission reductions.

The business model in this scenario can be described as an **infrastructure concession model**. This represents the most advanced form of battery swapping business model, combining energy supply, infrastructure ownership, and operational services into a single integrated offering. It is best suited for high-utilization, long-duration operations where scale and stability enable efficient implementation.

5 Proposal of a Continuum Framework for Battery Swapping

The five scenarios presented in this study (Scenario 1–5) illustrate how battery swapping solutions and corresponding business model configurations may vary under different operational conditions. When viewed together, they form a continuum ranging from simple and flexible solutions to more integrated and capital-intensive systems. This paper therefore proposes a continuum framework of battery swapping business models, showing how different configurations may be considered across operational contexts, from basic rental models to more integrated infrastructure-based approaches (see Table 1). The framework summarizes key dimensions of battery swapping business models and the configurations observed across the five scenarios. It provides a structured way to describe and explore business model options based on operational conditions. The framework is organized along six main dimensions: setup, value proposition, value creation, value delivery, value capture, and business model type. Each dimension reflects progression from simpler to more advanced configurations across Scenario 1 to 5.

In terms of setup, configurations range from single-machine operations with portable charging in Scenario 1 to large-scale sites with permanent automated swapping stations and integrated energy systems in Scenario 5. Intermediate configurations include shared modular systems (Scenario 2), automated energy-supported operations (Scenario 3), and mobile energy hubs for off-grid environments (Scenario 4).

Table 1. A continuum framework for battery swapping business models

Dimension	Scenario 1	Scenario 2	Scenario 3	Scenario 4	Scenario 5
Setup	Single machine	2-3 machines	4-5 fleet	Off-grid mobile	Large-scale site
Value proposition	Flexibility	Cost sharing	Uptime guarantee	Energy independence	TCO optimization
Value creation	Battery rental	Shared infrastructure	Automation + Software	Mobile energy hub	Integrated platform
Value delivery	Transactional	Subscription	SLA	Managed service	Concession
Value capture	Rental fee	Subscription	Availability pricing	Energy premium	Performance/Shared savings
Business model	Rental	Light BaaS	Full EaaS	Mobile EaaS	Concession

The **value proposition** evolves from flexibility and low-risk electrification in Scenario 1 to cost efficiency and uptime improvements in Scenarios 2 and 3, energy independence in Scenario 4, and industrial-scale performance and total cost of ownership optimization in Scenario 5.

Value creation progresses from basic hardware provision, such as battery rental, to shared infrastructure, automated systems with software support, mobile hybrid energy solutions, and more integrated energy platforms. Similarly, **value delivery** evolves from transactional rental and on-demand support to subscription-based services, SLA-based arrangements, managed energy services, and long-term contractual agreements.

Value capture mechanisms also vary across the continuum, from rental and usage-based fees in Scenario 1 to subscription revenue, availability-based pricing, energy-based pricing, and performance-related or shared savings models in the more advanced scenarios.

Finally, the **business model types** can be described along a continuum, from rental-based models to shared battery-as-a-service, more integrated energy-as-a-service approaches, mobile energy hub solutions, and infrastructure-oriented concession models. The continuum framework highlights that battery swapping business models are not fixed solutions but depend on operational conditions and system requirements. It provides a practical tool for industry actors to explore and compare different configurations based on site-specific conditions, project characteristics, and system complexity.

6 Discussion

6.1 Theoretical Implications

This study contributes to research on business model innovation, servitization, and electrification by proposing a continuum framework for battery swapping in heavy-duty machine applications. Previous research has highlighted the importance of business models in enabling electrification and battery ecosystems [37, 33, 36]. Existing studies have explored battery swapping archetypes [31], circular battery business models [26–30], and system-level electric mobility frameworks [32]. However, most of this research focuses on passenger vehicles, battery circularity, or general electric mobility systems, with limited attention to heavy-duty construction and quarry operations.

The findings extend this literature by showing how business model configurations may vary depending on operational conditions such as machine utilization, project duration, energy infrastructure, and site complexity. Rather than presenting a fixed business model archetype, the proposed continuum framework illustrates how different configurations may emerge across operational scenarios. In this way, the study complements earlier framework-based research on electric mobility and circular business models by linking operational conditions to value creation, value delivery, and value capture configurations in heavy-duty applications.

The results also relate to research on servitization [25] and energy-as-a-service [26], where value increasingly shifts from product ownership toward integrated and performance-based offerings [26, 35]. Similar to findings in previous servitization research [25], the scenarios in this study illustrate progression from transactional and ownership-oriented models toward service-based and infrastructure-oriented configurations. The study therefore supports the view that electrification may drive broader socio-technical and organizational transformations rather than only technological change.

In addition, the study contributes to research on battery swapping and energy infrastructure, which has mainly focused on technical optimization and operational efficiency [22, 23]. By combining operational scenarios with business model dimensions, the paper complements existing technical research with a business perspective. The proposed framework should therefore be understood as an exploratory analytical tool rather than a validated predictive model. Its contribution lies in structuring and comparing possible configurations under different operational conditions, thereby supporting future empirical and theoretical development in heavy-duty electrification research.

6.2 Practical Implications

The findings of this study provide practical insights for industry actors involved in the electrification of construction and quarry operations. The proposed continuum framework can support decision-making by helping companies explore how different system configurations and business models may fit specific operational conditions.

For *equipment manufacturers and dealers*, the framework highlights the need to consider a range of business model options rather than a single standardized approach. Depending on customer needs and project conditions, different configurations may be relevant. For example, simpler rental-based models may be suitable for small-scale applications or pilot projects, while more integrated and service-based approaches may be explored for high-utilization and long-duration operations. This suggests that flexibility in both technical solutions and business models is important. For *contractors and fleet operators*, the framework provides a structured way to assess different electrification options. It shows how operational factors such as machine utilization and energy infrastructure can influence system design and business model choices. This can support planning and reduce uncertainty when evaluating alternative approaches, including both built-in battery systems and potential battery swapping configurations.

For *energy providers and service companies*, the results indicate opportunities to develop integrated energy and service offerings. Depending on site conditions, this may include solutions such as managed charging, energy-as-a-service, or mobile energy systems in off-grid environments. The framework can help identify where such approaches may be relevant and how they could be organized. Rather than promoting a specific solution, the framework can inform procurement strategies that allow for different technical and business model configurations. This may support innovation and enable actors to explore solutions that meet both operational and sustainability requirements.

7 Conclusions, Limitations, and Future Work

This paper explored battery swapping business models for heavy-duty machines in road construction and quarry operations. Based on a case study, five operational scenarios were identified and analyzed. The results show that different system configurations and business model options may be relevant depending on machine utilization, project duration, energy infrastructure, and site conditions. Rather than assuming a specific technological direction, the study provides a structured and exploratory way to examine how battery swapping could be configured under different operational contexts.

The main contribution of the paper is the proposed continuum framework, which links operational conditions with possible battery swapping business model configurations. The framework illustrates how business model configurations may evolve from simple rental-based approaches to more integrated and infrastructure-oriented models. In contrast to previous research that mainly focuses on passenger vehicles, technical optimization, or battery circularity, this study specifically addresses heavy-duty construction and quarry operations and highlights how operational conditions influence both technical system design and business model choices.

The study has some limitations. First, the analysis is mainly qualitative and does not include detailed quantitative evaluation of costs, energy performance, or system efficiency. Second, the scenarios are conceptual and may not capture the full complexity and variation of real-world operations. Future work can build on this study in several ways. The proposed continuum framework can be further validated through empirical studies with a case company and one of its customers to assess its applicability in real operational settings. In addition, quantitative analysis of costs, energy use, and performance can provide a deeper understanding of the economic and operational implications of different business model configurations. Future research can also combine life cycle assessment (LCA) with the proposed framework across the five scenarios to evaluate environmental impacts alongside economic and operational performance.

Acknowledgments. This work was supported by Converge II (A solution for energy distribution in road construction & quarrying), funded by the Swedish Energy Agency in Sweden (2024–201967) and Circul8 (Smart Battery Circularity), funded by the Knowledge Foundation in Sweden (2019–1602).

Disclosure of Interests The authors have no competing interests to declare that are relevant to the content of this article.

References

1. Fortune Business Insights: Zero-Emission Heavy Machinery Market Size and Future Outlook. https://www.fortunebusinessinsights.com/zero-emission-heavy-machinery-market-115429. Accessed 9 Apr 2026
2. Beltrami, D., Iora, P., Tribioli, L., Uberti, S.: Electrification of compact off-highway vehicles—overview of the current state of the art and trends. Energies. **14**, 5565 (2021)
3. Perugu, H., Collier, S., Yoon, S., Barth, M., Boriboonsomsin, K.: Off-road construction and agricultural equipment electrification: review, challenges, and opportunities. Vehicles. **4**, 780–807 (2022)
4. Zero Emission Resource Organisation: Policy insights and recommendations: Cleaner Construction Machines in Europe. https://zero.no/wp-content/uploads/2025/12/Report_CleanerConstructionMachinesEU_11-2025_web-o.pdf. Accessed 9 Apr 2026
5. Sharma, R.: Electric Construction Equipment Market Research Report 2033. Market Intelo Report ID:CM-743 (2025)
6. Bhardwaj, S., Mostofi, H.: Technical and business aspects of battery electric trucks: a systematic review. Future Transp. **2**(2), 382–401 (2022)
7. Hacker, F., et al.: Electrification of heavy duty vehicles and development of charging infrastructure - development perspectives and recommendations for action from the perspective of heavy duty vehicle manufacturers and charging infrastructure experts. In: 1st Subreport of the ELV LIVE Research Project. Öko-Institut (2024)
8. Sharma, R.: Battery-Electric Construction Equipment Market Research Report 2033. Market Intelo Report ID:CM-23969 (2025)
9. Adu-Gyamfi, G.: Determinants of adoption intention of battery swap technology for electric vehicles. Energy. **251**, 123862 (2022)
10. Shoman, W., Yeh, S., Sprei, F., Plötz, P., Speth, D.: Battery electric long-haul trucks in Europe: public charging, energy, and power requirements. Transp. Res. Part D: Transp. Environ. **121**, 103825 (2023)
11. Nåbo, A., et al.: Battery Swapping for Heavy Duty Vehicles: A Feasibility Study on Up-Scaling in Sweden. VTI report 1199A (2024). https://doi.org/10.13140/RG.2.2.17552.17927
12. Zhao, P., et al.: Challenges and opportunities in truck electrification revealed by big operational data. Nat. Energy. **9**, 1427–1437 (2024)
13. Li, Y., et al.: Electrifying heavy-duty truck through battery swapping. Joule. **8**, 1556–1561 (2024)
14. LIMACH Homepage.: https://www.limach.nl/en/products/e881/. Accessed 10 Apr 2026
15. CISIVIS Homepage.: Are Power Tool Batteries Interchangeable?. Accessed 10 Apr 2026
16. Zhang, F., et al.: The battery-swapping revolution: exploring user preferences in electric micro-mobility sector. Transp. Res. A Policy Pract. **194**, 104416 (2025)
17. Tycorun.: How Long Does It Take To Swap A Battery?. https://www.tycorun.com/blogs/industry-insights/how-long-does-it-take-to-swap-a-battery. Accessed 10 Apr 2026
18. Electreefi.: Battery swapping solution: fast-tracking EV adoption. https://electreefi.com/battery-swapping-solution-fast-tracking-ev-adoption/. Accessed 10 Apr 2026
19. Wang, F., Zhang, Q.: The development of China's new energy vehicle charging and swapping industry: review and prospects. Energies. **18**, 4548 (2025)
20. Pisano, A., Saba, M., Baldovino, J.A.: A critical review of NIO's business model. World Electr. Veh. J. **14**, 251 (2023)
21. Pradhan, R., et al.: Factors influencing battery swapping adoption of electric vehicles: using structural equation modelling approach. In: 4th Australian International Conference on Industrial Engineering and Operations Management, November, Melbourne (2025)

22. Zhan, W., et al.: A review of siting, sizing, optimal scheduling, and cost-benefit analysis for battery swapping stations. Energy. **258**, 124723 (2022)
23. Feng, Y., Lu, X.: Construction planning and operation of battery swapping stations for electric vehicles: a literature review. Energies. **14**(24), 8202 (2021)
24. Teece, D.J.: Business models, business strategy and innovation. Long Range Plan. **43**(2–3), 172–194 (2010)
25. Baines, T., Lightfoot, H., Benedettini, O., Kay, J.: The servitization of manufacturing: a review of literature and reflection on future challenges. J. Manuf. Technol. Manag. **20**(5), 547–567 (2009)
26. Chirumalla, K., et al.: Enabling battery circularity: unlocking circular business model archetypes and collaboration forms in the electric vehicle battery ecosystem. Technol. Forecasting Soc. Change. **199**, 123044 (2024)
27. Olsson, L., et al.: Circular business models for extended EV battery life. Batteries. **4**, 57 (2018)
28. Wrålsen, B., et al.: Circular business models for lithium-ion batteries—stakeholders, barriers, and drivers. J. Clean. Prod. **317**, 128393 (2021)
29. Jiao, N.: Business Models for Second-life Electric Vehicle Battery Systems (thesis). University of Cambridge, UK (2019)
30. Xu, M., et al.: Developing a holistic circular business model framework for the EV battery closed-loop supply chain: a data-driven approach. Technovation. **152**, 103487 (2026)
31. Kulkov, I., Chirumalla, K.: Business model archetypes and deployment strategies for EV battery swapping–preliminary insights. In: IFIP International Conference on Advances in Production Management Systems, pp. 387–401 (2025)
32. Kley, F., et al.: New business models for electric cars—a holistic approach. Energy Policy. **39**, 3392–3403 (2011)
33. Chirumalla, K., Klaff, S., Zako, R., Sannö, A.: Elevating B2B mobility with sharing autonomous electric vehicles: exploring prerequisite criteria and innovative business models. Sustainability. **15**, 13757 (2023)
34. Ho-Yin, M.: Infrastructure planning for electric vehicles with battery swapping. Manag. Sci. INFORMS. **59**(7), 1557–1575 (2013)
35. Kindström, D.: Towards a service-based business model – key aspects for future competitive advantage. Eur. Manag. J. **28**(6), 479–490 (2010)
36. Bohnsack, R.: Business models for sustainable technologies: exploring business model evolution in the case of electric vehicles. Res. Policy. **43**(2), 284–300 (2014)
37. Huijssoon, H., et al.: An iterative framework for circular business models: insights from mapping and modelling. In: IFIP International Conference on Advances in Production Management Systems, pp. 459–473 (2025)
38. Yin, R.K.: Case Study Research: Design and Methods. Sage Publications, CA (2009)

Identifying Key Decisions in Battery Lifecycles and the Role of Blockchain Technology

Moshkan Ebrahimi(✉), Koteshwar Chirumalla, and Anas Fattouh

Engineering sciences, Mälardalens University, Eskilstuna, Sweden
moshkan.ebrahimi@mdu.se

Abstract. The accelerating transition toward electric mobility is largely driven by the widespread adoption of electric vehicle batteries (EVBs). This shift requires systematic management of EVBs throughout their entire lifecycle, including design, production, first-life operation, transition, second-life use, and end-of-life treatment. Effective EVB lifecycle management is essential to ensure technical reliability, economic viability, environmental safety, and circular economy performance. Managing EVBs involves a series of critical decisions across the lifecycle that depend on the availability of structured and reliable data. In this context, Blockchain Technology (BCT) is not envisioned as a standalone solution but as a governance layer integrated within broader technical architecture. Existing research highlights the potential of BCT for traceability, decentralization, smart contracts, and consensus mechanisms; however, the literature remains fragmented and largely conceptual. There is still limited understanding of how key decisions are made across the EVB lifecycle in real-world multi-actor contexts and how BCT features can systematically support data-driven, coordinated, and transparent decision-making. This paper aims to identify key decisions across the EVB lifecycle that enable circularity and to examine the role of BCT in supporting these decisions. We conducted an exploratory qualitative study involving seven companies across the EVB lifecycle. The findings show that BCT, through its key features, enhances transparency and coordination across the EVB lifecycle, enabling evidence-based, auditable, and trustworthy decision-making that supports circular economy strategies. The study contributes to the literature on the circular economy and blockchain-enabled circularity, particularly in the context of EVB lifecycle management.

Keywords: Battery lifecycle · Battery circularity · Data-driven lifecycle decision-making · Blockchain technology

1 Introduction

The global shift toward electric mobility is accelerating through the widespread adoption of EVBs, which form the backbone of decarbonized transport systems [1].

This transition underscores the need for systematic battery lifecycle management spanning design, production, first-life operation, transition, second-life use, and end-of-life (EoL) treatment. Effective lifecycle management supports technical reliability,

Published by Springer Nature Switzerland AG 2027
G. Pezzotta et al. (Eds.): APMS 2026, IFIP AICT 808, pp. 137–151, 2027.
https://doi.org/10.1007/978-3-032-38594-9_10

economic and environmental performance, and alignment with circular economy (CE) principles [2]. However, current EVB lifecycle practices remain constrained by fragmented datasets, limited traceability, and insufficient information sharing among actors [3, 4], resulting in uncertainty regarding ownership, value, and lifecycle coordination [1, 3]. To address these challenges, digital technologies are increasingly being explored. BCT provides a decentralized and cryptographically secured ledger capable of recording real time and verifying near real time lifecycle data in [5–7]. Its core features, traceability, decentralization, smart contracts, and consensus mechanisms are suggested to improve transparency, automation, and trust in inter-organizational networks [3]. Rather than functioning as a standalone solution, BCT operates as a governance layer within a broader digital infrastructure [8], enabling verified data exchange, access control, and coordination among actors [3, 4]. With clear responsibilities and interoperability standards, it can support transparent lifecycle transitions across production, reuse, repurposing, and EoL recovery [9, 10]. The importance of traceability is further reflected in the EU Battery Regulation (EU) 2023/1542 and emerging Digital Battery Passport (DBP) requirements for batteries above 2 kWh. While the DPP defines regulatory requirements for lifecycle data and traceability, this study positions BCT as a complementary governance and implementation layer enabling tamper-resistant data sharing across ecosystems [11]. Existing literature on EVB lifecycle management focuses mainly on CE strategies such as reuse, second-life applications, and recycling, while highlighting persistent challenges related to fragmented data, limited transparency, and unclear governance structures [1, 12]. Although prior studies recognize the importance of lifecycle data, they often rely on incomplete or laboratory-based information, providing limited insight into real-world multi-actor decision-making [13, 14].

Research on BCT remains fragmented and conceptual, focusing on technical capabilities or isolated applications without systematically linking BCT features to lifecycle decision processes [15, 16]. Consequently, there is limited understanding of how lifecycle decisions are structured and how BCT can support data-driven decision-making in practice. The purpose of this paper is to identify key decisions across the EVB lifecycle that enable circularity and to examine the role of BCT in supporting these decisions. The following research question is formulated:

RQ: What role do BCT features play in supporting key decisions across the EVB lifecycle?

This study serves as a preliminary foundation for more comprehensive investigations and future applications of BCT in support of EVB lifecycle management.

The remainder of this paper is structured as follows. Section 2 presents the theoretical background, Sect. 3 outlines the methodology, Sect. 4 reports the empirical findings, Sect. 5 describes the theoretical and managerial implications with suggestions of future research directions.

2 Theoretical Background

2.1 Battery Lifecycle Management and Key Decisions

The EVB lifecycle is commonly described as a sequence of interconnected stages, although the level of detail varies across studies. In general, the lifecycle includes design, production, first-life, potential second-life applications, and EoL management [17]. Some studies adopt a broader CE perspective, emphasizing value-retention strategies across the lifecycle, including repair, reuse, remanufacturing, repurposing, and recycling, often categorized into short-, medium-, and long-loop strategies [4, 18]. Effective EVB lifecycle management is essential for enabling CE, as it supports lifespan extension through maintenance, restoration, reuse, refurbishment, and remanufacturing [4, 13]. The performance and durability of EVBs depend on the characteristics of the raw materials used during production, which affect key performance metrics, lifespan, and degradation [2, 16, 19]. Decisions on selecting sustainable raw materials, coupled with enhanced recovery and recycling initiatives, are essential for CE strategies [3]. Degradation occurs at both cell and pack levels due to electrochemical aging, influenced by thermal conditions, charging patterns, and user driving, affecting State of Health (SOH), State of Charge (SOC), and State of Aging (SOA) [13]. Typically, an EVB reaches the end of its first life when capacity declines to 70–80% of its original maximum [1]. Maintaining performance, safety, and range becomes challenging, though residual capacity enables second-life applications, such as stationary energy storage for renewable energy [20]. Continuous monitoring of aging profiles and SOH helps determine secondary use. When further use is unfeasible, recycling reclaims valuable raw materials for next-generation batteries. Effective lifecycle decision-making depends on accurate and reliable data to assess battery condition and remaining value. Continuous monitoring of SOH and degradation profiles supports decisions regarding reuse, repurposing, and transition to EoL recovery [21]. In this context, traceability, data governance, and coordination among actors are essential to support informed decision-making across lifecycle stages [3, 22]. Collaboration among actors enables more informed assessment of battery condition and supports evidence-based decisions regarding maintenance, repurposing, and EoL recovery pathways [3, 4]. Digital technologies such as BCT are increasingly explored to enhance data integrity, traceability, and information sharing across actors, thereby supporting coordinated lifecycle decisions and enabling circular economy implementation.

2.2 Blockchain Technology and Data-Driven Decisions

BCT is a cryptographically secured, decentralized distributed ledger designed to enable traceability through real-time, immutable data entries. It can be deployed in public, private, consortium, or hybrid environments, depending on data ownership structures and permission rules governing participation, including reading, writing, and validation rights [5]. Literature commonly identifies four core features of BCT: traceability, decentralization, smart contracts, and consensus mechanisms which are suggested to support data integrity, collaboration, and trust among actors [3]. Within EVB ecosystems, BCT is increasingly discussed in combination with IoT technologies and Digital

Product Passports (DPPs) and AI to enable real-time battery tracking, improved lifecycle visibility, and enhanced service management [23, 24]. Improved analytics remain essential for predicting battery behaviour and estimating battery lifetime. However, these analytics depend on the availability of reliable, complete, and trustworthy lifecycle data. Operating in distributed networks involving multiple and potentially untrusted actors, BCT organizes information into cryptographically secured blocks distributed across network participants. In this context, decentralization is argued to reduce dependence on centralized intermediaries while addressing challenges related to ownership, control, privacy, and transparency. By distributing data across participating actors, decentralized architectures are suggested to improve coordination, governance transparency, and trust throughout ecosystem [25]. Furthermore, real-time data integration within decentralized infrastructures can improve data accessibility and support more efficient information sharing and traceability [3, 6, 26]. Data quality is managed through governance protocols and cryptographic mechanisms embedded in smart contracts and consensus processes, thereby linking technical mechanisms to governance and decision-support structures in multi-actor systems. Consensus mechanisms are collectively applied by network participants to validate data, supporting consistency and contributing to system security [10]. Smart contracts, defined as self-executing programs operating according to predefined rules, are further described as enabling automated verification, protocol-compliant actions, and reduced reliance on manual intervention [3]. In EVB lifecycle management, smart contracts are suggested to support functions such as anomaly detection, automated approvals, and predefined operational agreements [26, 27], particularly in structured decision-making processes involving multiple stakeholders. The literature further suggests that BCT can support monitoring, predictive assessment, and lifecycle decision-making by improving the integrity, accessibility, and continuity of battery-related data [1, 3, 24]. Battery condition and operational data are recorded on decentralized ledgers and validated through consensus mechanisms, improving the reliability of data used for decision-making [10, 13]. Traceability is suggested to enable continuous monitoring of key battery parameters and support predictive analytics and performance assessment across the lifecycle [1, 3, 5, 6]. Furthermore, decentralization is suggested to enhance data sharing and coordination among actors [3, 6], while smart contracts support automated rule-based actions such as anomaly detection and predefined agreements, reducing reliance on manual intervention [26, 27]. Overall, the integration of decentralization, traceability, smart contracts, and consensus mechanisms complements data-driven and analytical approaches. Together, these features support more reliable, transparent, and efficient decision-making across EVB lifecycle stages, particularly in multi-actor governance environments where data ownership and decision rights are distributed.

3 Methodology

3.1 Research Approach and Data Collection

This study employed an exploratory qualitative research design, which is particularly well-suited for investigating emerging and underexplored phenomena [28]. It engaged key actors across the EVB lifecycle to develop a comprehensive understanding of the role of BCT in enabling circularity. Seven companies were purposively selected to capture diverse perspectives across the battery lifecycle, including a battery cell manufacturer with recycling capabilities, two OEMs, an energy service company, a public transport operator managing electric buses, and two IT firms specializing in BCT solutions. Semi-structured interviews were used as the sole data collection method. Interview participants were selected purposively to ensure representation across key EVB lifecycle stages, different actor categories within the EVB ecosystem, and multiple functional roles within organizations. This approach enabled the capture of both cross-organizational and intra-organizational perspectives on EVB lifecycle decision-making processes and supports participant co-creation of knowledge in complex and evolving settings. The research was conducted in two stages. In the first stage, semi-structured interviews explored the potential role of BCT in enabling battery circularity, guided by a literature-informed interview protocol focusing on lifecycle management, circularity, and BCT features. Findings from this stage informed a second round of interviews, refined to identify key EVB lifecycle decisions and examine the role of BCT in supporting these decisions. Open-ended questions allowed exploration of participant perspectives across lifecycle stages, balancing structure with flexibility to capture emerging themes in a relatively underexplored field. In total, 13 semi-structured interviews were conducted. Table 1 shows respondent diversity across organizational roles, lifecycle stages, and actor categories within the EVB ecosystem. Representation across manufacturing, operation, recycling, energy, and digital technology enabled triangulation of both technical and governance perspectives in EVB lifecycle decision-making. Although some actor categories were represented by a single respondent, potential bias was mitigated through cross-organizational comparison, multi-stage interviews, and functional diversity among participants. The study primarily focused on companies operating within Swedish EVB ecosystem, enabling direct access to actors involved in EVB lifecycle management and blockchain-related activities. The inclusion of manufacturing, operational, recycling, energy, and digital technology perspectives enabled triangulation across both technical and governance-related dimensions of EVB lifecycle decision-making. Although some actor categories were represented by a single respondent, potential single-respondent bias was mitigated through cross-organizational comparison, multi-stage interviews, and the inclusion of participants with diverse functional responsibilities.

3.2 Data Analysis

The empirical material was analyzed using thematic analysis, a structured approach to identifying, organizing, and interpreting patterns within qualitative data, particularly suitable for complex and emerging topics [29]. All interviews were transcribed and repeatedly reviewed to gain familiarity with participants' perspectives. Relevant data segments were identified, and initial codes were generated to capture key ideas, recurring expressions, and meaningful concepts. These codes were then examined to identify patterns and relationships, which were grouped into broader categories reflecting key EVB lifecycle decisions, the data required to support these decisions, and the role of BCT in enabling data access, coordination, and governance. Categories were refined into themes representing the decision-making and governance logic of the EVB lifecycle, considering evolving decision criteria, performance indicators, and traceability requirements across design, operation, second-life transition, and end-of-life management. Themes were further interpreted to ensure conceptual clarity and alignment with the research purpose and theoretical framing [30].

Table 1. Interviewee companies and representative job roles of respondents (stage 1,2)

Actors in battery ecosystem	Number of interview Stage 1	Number of interview Stage 2	Duration (Minutes)	Organizational role of interviewees
Battery cell manufacturer and recycler	1		120	Project manager
Battery pack and EV manufaturer (OEM)	1	1	120/ 90	1. Data analytics lead
EV manufaturer (OEM)	2	1	150/120/90	1. Test Leader 2. R&D manager 3. Electromobility engineer
Energy service company and digital platform		1	120	Technical aggregator
Public transport company	1	1	120 /90	Head of sustainability and innovation
IT company	2	1	120 /90 /120	1. Principal technology specialist 2. Technical sales
IT company	1		90	Blockchain technology lead

4 Results

In this section, we present findings based on interviews related to key decisions that arise at different stages of the EVB lifecycle. We then illustrate how BCT features, decentralization, traceability, smart contracts, and consensus mechanisms can support and enhance these decisions.

4.1 Battery Lifecycle Decisions

4.1.1 Design and Production Stage

Design Strategy Decisions: The design and production stages are critical decision points that influence how circularity can be embedded across the EVB lifecycle. Several key decisions made during these stages directly influence the technical, economic, and environmental performance of future EVBs. The first decision concerns the early integration of circularity principles into design. This requires engineers to anticipate lifecycle pathways and design EVBs that are easier to disassemble, repair, remanufacture, or recycle. The second key decision involves creating structured to design criteria and review gates to guide development choices, ensuring that circularity, cost, and performance targets are reviewed systematically. A third decision involves balancing circularity-related environmental considerations with technical robustness to ensure reliable performance across different operating environments. As the Head of Sustainability remarks, "*Battery should be sustainable but also robust and function across different temperatures.*" Maintaining this balance often requires trade-offs between energy density, weight, and recyclability, which must be explicitly evaluated at the design stage. A fourth decision relates to the validation of design choices through verification and simulation, which help confirm performance, safety, and recyclability before batteries reach production. These processes provide evidence to support data-informed decision-making and reduce costly redesigns later in the development process. A fifth decision concerns how multiple lifecycle phases are prioritized. As the Data Analytics Lead explains, *"Designing for multiple usage phases introduces both environmental and business risks."* Finally, decisions regarding system architecture and standardization are important for simplifying reconfiguration, repair, and recycling, thereby supporting circular flexibility. The Electromobility Engineer points out that *"Current battery systems often require significant manual work to enable new functionality."*

Performance and Economic Trade-off Decisions: At the design and production stages, a central challenge is determining how to balance economic, operational, and environmental goals. One key decision concerns how far to pursue circularity when cost pressures are high. Integrating design features that enable easier repair, second-life applications, or improved recyclability often increases production costs, influencing manufacturers' willingness to adopt them. As the Electromobility Engineer reflects, *"Implementing features for second-life applications and recycling would require additional costs, and manufacturers are generally reluctant to include them in designing their products."* These perspectives illustrate that decisions regarding circularity are not purely technical but are shaped by cost constraints and market viability.

Data, Transparency, and Standardization Decisions: The findings highlight several key decisions related to transparency regarding materials, technical requirements, and engineering processes. Early transparency supports internal coordination, while extending it beyond design ensures downstream actors can access critical information. Second, actors must decide on the scope and structure of data-sharing documentation, which affects battery reuse and recycling. The Principal Technologist observes, *"Initially, this transparency may be internal to the design unit. As the product moves into operation, transparency must extend beyond the design function."* Third, decisions on standardization and interoperability are important, as standardized and compatible designs enhance scalability and circularity. Finally, actors must establish verification processes and structured design approaches. The Principal Technologist emphasizes, *"Verification and simulation processes must demonstrate that performance and quality requirements have been met before the product transitions into operations."*

4.1.2 First-Life, Transition, and Second-Life Phases

Data Management Decisions: The first critical decision concerns how to collect and monitor data during first-life operation. Continuous data capture supports both performance optimization and future reuse. As Head of Sustainability emphasizes, *"Providing as many insights as possible from first-life use... enhances its potential for second-life applications."* The second decision involves assessing battery health and determining how to evaluate key indicators such as SOH, remaining useful life (RUL), and operational conditions, often using model-based approaches. The third decision focuses on lifecycle transitions. When a battery reaches the end of its first life, actors must determine whether it should be reused, remanufactured, or recycled. Principal Technologist highlights, *"The most important decision point occurs during the transition from first life to second life."* The fourth decision addresses handling of incomplete or fragmented data. Actors must decide how to make lifecycle decisions when service histories or operational records are incomplete or unavailable. Head of Sustainability observes, *"Without a service history… it is difficult to determine a battery's value."*

Lifecycle and Business Decisions: Transitioning batteries from first-life to second-life applications requires an explicit cost–benefit evaluation. The first decision concerns evaluating the economic viability of second-life applications. Actors must determine whether remanufacturing or repurposing justifies the associated time, effort, and costs.

The second decision involves defining governance structures and allocating responsibilities across lifecycle stages. Actors must decide how to document ownership transfers, assign accountability, and coordinate across actors, while Head of Sustainability highlights, *"The first-life user often works with other actors to facilitate the transfer to second-life use."* Electromobility Engineer further notes, *"The OEM [should] take responsibility according to extended producer responsibility (EPR),"* although *"Manufacturers generally do not want to take responsibility for second life applications."* The third decision relates to the scalability of second-life applications. Actors must assess whether second-life solutions can be implemented at scale within existing business models. Electromobility Engineer observes, *"Second life applications are typically small scale… not compatible with a global manufacturer."*

Data and Performance Verification: Ensuring reliability and trust in battery performance requires a set of critical verification-related decisions across the lifecycle. The first decision concerns how to verify and ensure the credibility of battery data. Actors must determine appropriate verification mechanisms to validate sensor data and support reliable assessments. As Data Analytics Lead emphasizes, *"Verification and comparison ensure the credibility of the sensor data."* The second decision concerns how to validate battery performance for second-life applications. Actors must decide how to assess whether batteries meet the functional requirements of a new application.

Principal Technologist states, *"A documented quality validation confirming that it meets the functional requirements of the new application effectively acts as a certified quality guarantee."*

4.1.3 End-of-Life Phase

Safety and Compliance Decisions: EoL management requires decisions to ensure compliance with safety, environmental, and regulatory requirements, including how batteries are handled and processed in accordance with appropriate procedures to mitigate risks associated with hazardous materials and stored energy. The second decision involves determining environmentally responsible disposal and treatment strategies. Actors must aim to minimize environmental impact while recovering valuable materials. The third decision relates to defining decommissioning requirements and processes. Actors must establish criteria that integrate technical, safety, environmental, and logistical considerations. Principal Technologist explains, *"Decommissioning must be based on technical requirements, safety, environmental standards, and logistical factors."* The fourth decision concerns managing uncertainty due to insufficient regulatory guidance and documentation. Principal Technologist observes, "There were insufficient specifications defining how to safely dismantle batteries."

EoL Assessment and Recovery Decisions: Effective EoL management depends on data-driven decisions that determine appropriate recovery pathways and economic outcomes. The first decision concerns what data to collect and share to support EoL processing. Actors must determine the scope of information on battery composition, origin, and lifecycle history required for downstream activities such as recycling. The second decision involves assessing the condition of the EVB to determine the most appropriate EoL pathway. Head of Sustainability observes, *"The EVB's state of health is critical for determining its suitability for recycling."* The third decision relates to evaluating the economic feasibility of recycling. Head of Sustainability highlights, *"Recycling is a cost–benefit consideration… more attractive for high-value materials, such as cobalt."*

4.2 Blockchain Technology

Interviewees highlighted BCT as potentially relevant for supporting decision-making across the battery lifecycle, particularly in contexts characterized by fragmented data, limited transparency, and unclear governance structures. Interviewees perceived BCT as contributing to visibility and coordination across the battery lifecycle when integrated within broader digital infrastructures. The Principal Technologist described it *as "A service layer at the top of the architecture, indexing and governing all critical data packages."* Furthermore, interviewees associated BCT with the coordination of decisions across lifecycle stages, particularly at key transition points. As the Principal Technologist noted, *"The blockchain should govern the entire lifecycle handovers, managing the contractual, legal, and data traceability across actors."*

4.2.1 Decentralization

Decentralized Governance and Lifecycle Decision-Making: Decentralization was described by interviewees as a governance mechanism enabling distributed yet coordinated decision-making across actors in the EVB lifecycle, particularly in complex and fragmented contexts. The Principal technologist emphasized that *"Decentralization represents a well-thought-of architecture to improve transparency across multiple players within that lifecycle."* Interviewees further explained that decentralization allows actors to share data through distributed ledgers, supporting decisions based on shared and verified information rather than isolated data silos. This was considered particularly important when batteries move across lifecycle stages and organizational boundaries. In addition, decentralization was associated with improved tracking and tracing capabilities, operational efficiency, and the ability to identify the correct and up-to-date battery information, ownership transfer, and redeployment decisions.

Strategic and Market-Based Decision-Making: Interviewees highlighted decentralization in relation to strategic decisions on battery allocation and market opportunities. The R&D Manager explained that EVBs are distributed across multiple markets and applications, making centralized systems less effective in handling diverse scenarios, while decentralized systems enable participation from multiple actors and create opportunities for selling or repurposing battery packs. The Technical Aggregator further emphasized that sharing data on battery placement across markets can enable more flexible lifecycle considerations beyond rigid classifications such as first-life, second-life, and end-of-life. The R&D Manager stated, *"Since EVBs are distributed across various markets and applications, a centralized system would struggle to cover all these different scenarios effectively. A decentralized system ensures that multiple actors can participate, creating diverse opportunities to sell or repurpose battery packs."* In addition, decentralization was associated with reduced inefficiencies in data handling. The Project Manager noted that information is often repeatedly shared across entities, leading to redundancy and inefficiency, and that decentralized data management can streamline operations while maintaining security and reducing duplication.

4.2.2 Traceability

Lifecycle Monitoring and Performance Decisions: Traceability was consistently described by interviewees as a fundamental enabler of decision-making across the battery lifecycle. The Principal Technologist emphasized its role in supporting transparency and structured information flow across complex lifecycle processes, stating, *"This is where we recognize the need for traceability and transparency... across a smart workflow and multi-faceted lifecycle."* Interviewees further explained that traceability provides information on material composition and origin, including details on cell generation and constituent materials. It was also described as supporting monitoring of battery performance and condition through transparent usage information. In addition, traceability was associated with risk management through faster identification of potential issues, as well as reduced uncertainty in second-life applications by providing confidence in the integrity and history of battery assets.

Value, Second-Life, and End-of-Life Decisions: Interview findings indicate that traceability plays an important role in informing lifecycle value and second-life decisions. The R&D Manager explained that avoiding rapid battery degradation is important for retaining battery value over time. It was further noted that assigning value in second-life applications requires assessment of battery SOH and access to relevant condition and usage data, which can be recorded to improve transparency for involved actors. At the EoL, traceability was described as supporting recycling and recovery decisions by providing information on recoverable material content. It was also associated with potentially more efficient operational processes, as prior data availability can reduce analysis time during dismantling. In addition, the Principal Technologist emphasized the importance of transparency and accountability across actors, stating, *"An intelligent blockchain system is essential to ensure transparency and accountability for all parties involved."*

4.2.3 Smart Contracts

Automated and Real-Time Decision-Making: Smart contracts were described by interviewees as supporting automated decision-making and facilitating verification processes. The Technical Aggregator explained that automation can enable faster data sharing and more efficient exchange of information between specific partners in an automated manner. It was further noted that collaboration is not solely dependent on smart contracts themselves, but also on the quality and structure of the shared information. Certification was also described as a mechanism for performance verification that can streamline processes that would otherwise require manual assessment. In addition, smart contracts were associated with improved tracking, ownership transparency, and accountability. The R&D Manager emphasized this aspect, stating: *"Access to previous smart contracts related to the same battery pack allows tracing its history as it moves through different second-life applications... provides a comprehensive history, including descriptions of services, ownership changes, and applications."*

Accountability, and contract-level verification in decisions: The Principal Technologist highlighted the importance of contractual transparency in smart contracts for defining and tracking ownership. Interviewees further emphasized that embedding certifications within smart contracts can enhance transparency, enforceability, and accountability by integrating verification mechanisms directly into digital agreements. Access to certifications and audit information was also described as improving transparency, while verifiable certificates were associated with validating battery handling practices across actors. In addition, smart contracts were described as supporting more dynamic decision-making processes through real-time data integration, enabling proactive responses to operational conditions. The Principal Technologist stated, *"A smart contract must function as a living contract... ensuring its integrity throughout its lifespan."* Real-time data inputs were further linked to the possibility of triggering preventive actions in safety-critical situations, such as rising battery temperatures.

4.2.4 Consensus Mechanisms

Data Reliability and Collaborative Decision-Making: Consensus mechanisms were described by interviewees as relevant for ensuring agreement on shared data in multi-actor environments within the battery lifecycle. The Principal Technologist emphasized that *"Where the lifecycle depends on shared information, the ability to reach a common agreement on data accuracy is essential."* Interviewees further noted that consensus mechanisms can support validation of data quality when multiple actors are involved, enabling alignment of shared information used in decision-making processes. This was linked to the importance of reliable data for assessing key lifecycle indicators such as SOH, RUL, and traceability records, which are relevant for decisions related to reuse and recycling. In addition, consensus mechanisms were associated with improved coordination of decision-making across actors by supporting shared agreement on validated information used in lifecycle transitions such as refurbishment, reuse, and end-of-life processing. Table 2 presents the decisions identified across the EVB lifecycle and illustrates how BCT features may relate to these decision areas based on the interview findings.

Table 2. Lifecycle decisions supported by BCT features include 1. Decentralization, 2. Traceability, 3. Smart contracts and 4. Consensus mechanisms

Lifecycle stage	Theme	Key decisions	1	2	3	4
Design and production stages	Design strategy decisions	Decision on integration of circularity principles into design	x		x	
		Decision on structured tollgates and design criteria				
		Decision on balancing circularity-related environmental considerations with technical robustness				
		Decision on design choices		x		
		Decision on prioritizing multiple lifecycle phases				
		Decisions on system architecture and standardization	x	x	x	x
	Performance and economic trade-off decisions	Decision on balancing cost pressures with the integration of circular design features				
		Decision on the trade-off between system performance and cost				
	Data, Transparency, and standardization decisions	Decision on transparency regarding materials, technical requirements	x	x	x	
		Decision on scope and structure of technical data-sharing documentation		x	x	
		Decisions on standardization and interoperability	x			
		Decision on verification processes and structured design approaches			x	
First life, transition, and second life stages	Data management decisions	Decision on how to collect and monitor data during first-life operation	x	x		x
		Decision on assessing battery health to evaluate key indicators		x		
		Decision on transition to different lifecycle	x	x	x	
		Decide how to handle incomplete or fragmented data	x			x
	Lifecycle and business decisions	Decision concerns evaluating the economic viability of second-life applications				
		Decision relates to the scalability of second-life applications	x			
	Data and performance verification	Decision on how to verify and ensure the credibility of battery data	x			x
		Validate battery performance		x		x
End of life stage	Safety and regulatory compliance	Decision concerns how to handle and process batteries in accordance with safety and environmental standards				
		Decision on determining environmentally responsible disposal and treatment strategies				
		Decision relates to defining decommissioning requirements and processes				
		Decision concerns managing uncertainty due to insufficient regulatory guidance and documentation				
	Operational, recycling, and EoL strategic decisions	Decision concerns what data to collect and share to support EoL processing	x		x	x
		Decision involves assessing EVB condition to determine its appropriate EoL pathway		x		x

5 Discussion and Conclusions

While this study examines the role of BCT in EVB lifecycle management, the findings do not suggest that BCT directly enables circularity outcomes. Rather, BCT is conceptualized as an enabling digital infrastructure that supports transparency, coordination, verification, traceability, and data governance across multiple actors. Further, it can reduce uncertainty in lifecycle decisions related to battery monitoring, ownership transfer, second-life allocation, reuse, remanufacturing, and EoL processing.

However, the findings also indicate that not all EVB lifecycle decisions can be equally supported by BCT and its associated features. Its contribution is strongest in governance- and information-related decision structures, whereas decisions dependent on physical, technical, and economic processes such as material quality assessment, battery condition evaluation, recycling operations, and regulatory compliance continue to rely on empirical measurements, laboratory testing, engineering expertise, and context-specific operational assessments. These processes remain outside the digital information layer and therefore cannot be fully enabled or automated by BCT alone.

Theoretical Implications: This study contributes to research on EVB circularity by adopting a lifecycle- and decision-oriented perspective on BCT. While prior studies have primarily emphasized traceability and data-sharing capabilities [1, 6, 8, 9], the findings suggest that BCT may also support a broader set of lifecycle decisions, including design, first-life operation, second-life allocation, and EoL processing. By linking decision-making challenges such as uncertainty in battery condition, limited lifecycle data, and difficulties in value assessment [2, 5, 13] to digital enabling mechanisms, the study suggests that traceability and immutable records may help reduce uncertainty in estimating parameters such as SOH and RUL. These interpretations are based on the analytical lens of BCT capabilities rather than on direct causal evidence from the empirical material and should therefore be understood as context-specific insights from a qualitative study. Beyond data provision, BCT is also perceived as a coordination and governance mechanism in multi-actor ecosystems. Decentralization and consensus mechanisms are seen as supporting shared validation of data and alignment of responsibilities, which are particularly relevant in cross-organizational transitions such as second-life deployment and recycling [4, 11]. However, the study does not model or validate formal governance structures, which remain an important area for future technical and organizational research. Furthermore, data standardization and interoperability emerge as key preconditions for effective digital governance in EVB lifecycle management. In this context, BCT is positioned as a supporting infrastructure that enhances data integrity, accessibility, and auditability in fragmented and multi-actor ecosystems [9]. Overall, the study positions BCT as part of a broader digital governance layer that supports, rather than determines, circular decision-making across the EVB lifecycle, while recognizing that real-world implementation and governance design require further empirical and technical investigation.

Managerial Implications: This study offers practical insights for battery manufacturers, OEMs, recyclers, energy and utility providers, grid operators, and other stake-holders involved in EVB lifecycle management. The findings suggest that BCT may support decision-making across battery lifecycles by improving data transparency, traceability, and standardization from first-life operation through second-life applications and EoL processing. Improved data visibility may support managerial decisions related to battery allocation, performance monitoring, value assessment, and recycling strategies. In multi-actor ecosystems, enhanced data sharing and coordination may also help reduce inefficiencies, strengthen accountability, and improve alignment with evolving regulatory requirements. From a managerial perspective, these capabilities may contribute to the development of more transparent and potentially more circular business models not only in battery sector but also in other industries with complex lifecycle governance requirements, such as electronics, automotive, and pharmaceuticals. At the same time, the findings highlight that the practical implementation of BCT in EVB ecosystems involves technical and organizational challenges, which should be carefully considered when evaluating its feasibility and scalability in real-world applications. In addition, other decentralized digital approaches, such as IoT, AI, and federated learning models (FLM), are increasingly relevant in multi-actor EVB environments. The potential integration of BCT with FLM may represent a promising direction for enabling secure, privacy-preserving, and collaborative lifecycle management.

Given the potential of BCT to support key decision-making across EVB lifecycles, challenges and feasibility considerations in its implementation within EVB ecosystems underscore the need for further research into its technical feasibility and practical deployment.

Acknowledgments. This work was supported by Circul8 (Smart Battery Circularity) funded by the Knowledge Foundation in Sweden (0024, 2023), and SmartCharg (Smart and Circular Battery Charging Solutions) funded by Vinnova in Sweden (00814, 2023).

Disclosure of Interests The authors declare that there is no conflict of interest regarding the publication of this paper.

References

1. da Silva, E.R., et al.: Unleashing the circular economy in the electric vehicle battery supply chain: a case study on data sharing and blockchain potential. Resour. Conserv. Recycl. **193**, 106969 (2023)
2. Júnior, C.A.R., et al.: Towards a business model for second-life batteries: barriers, opportunities, uncertainties, and technologies. J. Energy Chem. **78**, 507–525 (2023)
3. Ebrahimi, M., Chirumalla, K., Fattouh, A.: Enabling battery circularity with blockchain technology: an exploratory study of key benefits. In: IFIP International Conference on Advances in Production Management Systems. Springer (2025)
4. Chirumalla, K., et al.: Enabling battery circularity: unlocking circular business model archetypes and collaboration forms in the electric vehicle battery ecosystem. Technol. Forecast. Soc. Chang. **199**, 123044 (2024)
5. Perez, A., Gallo, P., Sanseverino, E.R.: Blockchain and nested tokens for tracking, reusing, and recycling batteries. In: 2023 Asia Meeting on Environment and Electrical Engineering (EEE-AM). IEEE (2023)
6. Xiao, L., et al.: Research on the construction of a blockchain-based industrial product full life cycle information traceability system. Appl. Sci. **14**, 4569 (2024)
7. Luca, C.: How Real-Time Blockchain Data Streams Transform Evidence Collection in External Audits. ResearchGate (2025)
8. Sekar, A., Tech, D., Noteboom, C.: Integrating AI and Blockchain in Supply Chains: An SDRT-Based Resilience Framework. ResearchGate (2025)
9. Jaiman, V., Pernice, L., Urovi, V.: User incentives for blockchain-based data sharing platforms. PLoS One. **17**(4), e0266624 (2022)
10. Yadav, A.K., et al.: A comparative study on consensus mechanism with security threats and future scopes: blockchain. Comput. Commun. **201**, 102–115 (2023)
11. European Union, E. Regulation (EU) 2023/1542 of the European Parliament and of the Council. European Union. 2023. https://eur-lex.europa.eu/legal-content/EN/TXT/?uri=CELEX%3A02023R1542-20250731. Accessed 20 May 2026
12. Zhang, X., et al.: A blockchain-enabled framework for reverse supply chain management of power batteries. J. Clean. Prod. **415**, 137823 (2023)
13. Jin, R., et al.: Blockchain-based data collection with efficient anomaly detection for estimating battery state-of-health. IEEE Sensors J. **21**, 13455–13465 (2021)
14. Gao, Y.-L., et al.: The behavioural evolution of the smart electric vehicle battery reverse supply chain under government supervision. Ind. Manag. Data Syst. **123**(10), 2577–2606 (2023)

15. Feng, Z., et al.: The influence of carbon emission reduction instruments on blockchain technology adoption in recycling batteries of the new energy vehicles. Int. J. Prod. Res. **62**(3), 891–908 (2024)
16. Júnior, C.A.R., et al.: Blockchain review for battery supply chain monitoring and battery trading. Renew. Sust. Energ. Rev. **157**, 112078 (2022)
17. Gianvincenzi, M., et al.: Systematic review of battery life cycle management: a framework for European regulation compliance. Sustainability **16**, 10026 (2024)
18. Rönkkö, P., et al.: The circular economy of electric vehicle batteries: a Finnish case study. Environ. Syst. Decis. **44**(1), 100–113 (2024)
19. Rahman, T., Alharbi, T.: Exploring lithium-ion battery degradation: a concise review of critical factors, impacts, data-driven degradation estimation techniques, and sustainable directions for energy storage systems. Batteries **10**(7), 220 (2024)
20. Li, Z., Zhong, X., Xu, X.: The mechanism of retired power batteries recycling through blockchain token incentives. J. Clean. Prod. **415**, 137560 (2023)
21. John, J., Kudva, G., Jayalakshmi, N.: Secondary life of electric vehicle batteries: degradation, state of health estimation using incremental capacity analysis, applications and challenges. IEEE Access. **12**, 63735–63753 (2024)
22. Wrålsen, B., O'Born, R.: Use of life cycle assessment to evaluate circular economy business models in the case of Li-ion battery remanufacturing. Int. J. Life Cycle Assess. **28**(5), 554–565 (2023)
23. Augello, A., et al.: Tracing battery usage for second life market with a blockchain-based framework. In: 2021 IEEE International Conference on Environment and Electrical Engineering and 2021 IEEE Industrial and Commercial Power Systems Europe (EEEIC/I&CPS Europe), pp. 1–6 (2021)
24. Faria, F.L., de Oliveira, A.K., Rüther, R.: A sustainable blockchain-based framework to develop the Li-ion second-life batteries market. Energy. **316**, 134603 (2025)
25. Raouf, M.A.: Decentralizing IoT data ownership and control with blockchain technology. In: 2024 8th International Conference on Smart Cities, Internet of Things and Applications (SCIoT). IEEE (2024)
26. Duan, K., et al.: Unlocking blockchain's potential in collaborative remanufacturing and data sharing: a case study on electric vehicle batteries. Ind. Manag. Data Syst. **125**(7), 2321–2347 (2025)
27. Alqaryuti, A., et al.: Blockchain-based traceability, certification, and maintenance of FCEV components. Green Technol. Sustainability. **4**, 100396 (2026)
28. Stebbins, R.A.: Exploratory Research in the Social Sciences, vol. 48. Sage (2001)
29. Boyatzis, R.E.: Transforming Qualitative Information: Thematic Analysis and Code Development. Sage (1998)
30. Elliott, V.: Thinking about the coding process in qualitative data analysis. Qual. Rep. **23**(11), 2850–2861 (2018)

Lithium-ion Batteries' Lifecycle Mapping and Their Environmental Assessment: Academic Versus Grey Literature

Nour El Houda Mezni[1(✉)], Valérie Botta-Genoulaz[1], Taha Arbaoui[1], and Giulio Mangano[2]

[1] INSA Lyon, Université Lumière Lyon 2, Université Claude Bernard Lyon 1, Université Jean Monnet Saint-Etienne, DISP UR4570, 69621 Villeurbanne, France
{nour-el-houda.mezni,valerie.botta,taha.arbaoui}@insa-lyon.fr
[2] Department of Management and Production Engineering, Politecnico di Torino, 10129 Turin, Italy
giulio.mangano@polito.it

Abstract. This paper analyzes electric vehicle lithium-ion battery supply chains and their environmental assessment from two complementary viewpoints, addressing the misalignment between academic and industrial approaches. Academic literature is examined through a systematic literature review, while industrial practices are assessed using grey literature. A lifecycle mapping of the supply chain is first developed and compared across both sides. The analysis then examines environmental indicators and identifies key similarities and divergences. Results reveal inconsistencies in indicator selection and scope, with industrial reporting lacking comprehensiveness and standardization compared to academic frameworks that generally rely on lifecycle assessment. The results underline the need for standardized lifecycle assessment-based reporting to improve transparency and data quality across lithium-ion battery supply chains.

Keywords: Supply Chain · Environmental Assessment · Systematic Literature Review · Electric Vehicle Lithium Battery

1 Introduction

Transitioning to cleaner mobility solutions is one of the main challenges of this decade. Electric vehicles (EVs) are often presented as an alternative to internal combustion engine vehicles because they can reduce greenhouse gas (GHG) emissions and limit the use of fossil fuels. However, EVs are not impact-free [1]. Their overall environmental performance depends on many factors across their lifecycle. In particular, EV batteries represent the main contributor of EV lifecycle impacts [2]. Moreover, batteries differ in materials, production processes, and performance, which immensely varies their impacts [3]. Therefore, it is still unclear to what extent EVs can truly be considered a cleaner solution. Furthermore, Lithium-ion batteries (LIBs) are currently the main technology

Published by Springer Nature Switzerland AG 2027
G. Pezzotta et al. (Eds.): APMS 2026, IFIP AICT 808, pp. 152–166, 2027.
https://doi.org/10.1007/978-3-032-38594-9_11

used in EVs: They offer high energy density, good performance, and relatively long lifetimes and the breakthroughs in their technologies directly pushes the development of EVs [4]. However, their increasing demand raises environmental concerns. LIB supply chains (LIBSC) are complex, globally scattered, and resource-intensive [5]. They rely on critical materials such as lithium, cobalt, and nickel etc. where the extraction and processing of these materials are often concentrated in a few regions and can cause environmental and social issues [6]. In addition, growing demand and geopolitical tensions increase supply risks. As a result, many stakeholders are trying to secure raw materials, develop local production, and improve the sustainability of LIBSCs. At the same time, regulations worldwide are being implemented to address these issues. For example, batteries in the European union market are now required to report their environmental footprint. Such measures aim to improve transparency, encourage greener production, and promote a circular economy [7]. In this context, developing an accurate and comprehensive representation of the full lifecycle of LIBs, along with a robust assessment of their environmental performance is a central issue. Existing literature tends to focus on isolated segments of the supply chain, which limits the development of a holistic approach [8, 9]. As a result, there is still a need for integrated approaches that capture the full complexity of LIBSCs. Such an approach is essential to identify key environmental hotspots and to better understand how these impacts are measured and assessed across different stages. This in turn requires a clear and structured view of the entire supply chain, including its stages, key actors, and associated challenges. At the same time, the battery market is evolving rapidly [10], raising questions about the alignment between academic research and industrial practices, which may not always fully converge. For this reason, this paper aims to answer the following research question: "How do academic and industrial approaches differ and align in their representation of the LIB lifecycle and indicator selection for environmental assessment, and what implications arise from these differences?". Therefore, it is important to consider both academic and industrial viewpoints to obtain a more realistic and complete understanding of LIBSCs. To address this gap, this paper combines a review of academic literature with an analysis of grey literature to better capture real-world industrial practices. The objective is to compare these two points of view and highlight potential discrepancies and complementarities, ultimately providing a comprehensive understanding of LIBSCs and their environmental assessment.

This paper is structured as follows. Section 2 presents the methodology used to analyze both academic and grey literature. Section 3 introduces the battery lifecycle mapping from both viewpoints, followed by a comparative analysis. Section 4 focuses on the environmental assessment of LIBSC, again comparing both viewpoints and finally Sect. 5 concludes provides the conclusions and perspectives of this work.

2 Methodology

The first part consists of reviewing the scientific literature. A systematic literature review (SLR) aims to answer a research question by synthesizing scientific evidence in a transparent and reproducible manner. In this case, an SLR was chosen to ensure comprehensive coverage of the academic literature and to identify potential gaps. Consequently, a

SLR was conducted following PRISMA guidelines [11]. The review process included database selection, definition of keywords and search queries, application of inclusion and exclusion criteria, and snowballing. The Web of Science database was used, with searches performed across titles, abstracts, and keywords using terms such as lithium-ion batteries, electric vehicles, battery supply chain, lifecycle assessment, sustainability, simulation, risk, and resilience. Studies published in English up to 2025 were included. Knowing that these queries would generate many results, the strategy was to recover all potentially relevant papers and then to exclude papers after screening to be more precise. The screening removed papers that were too broad (circular economy, lifecycle assessment), too narrow (single processes or components), or focused solely on battery performance (weight, charging), as well as those addressing policies, regulations, or consumer perceptions. This resulted in 67 studies from an initial 88. Forward and backward snowballing identified 132 additional studies. Here, The Web of Science "electrochemistry" meso-topic was used as an exclusion filter. By experimenting, this filter was the only one that guaranteed the exclusion of irrelevant papers. In the end, a total of 199 papers were included in the final corpus. These papers span from the year 2010 until 2025 and the three main journals are *Journal of Cleaner Production*, *Resources, Conservation and Recycling*, and *Sustainability*.

At the same time, grey literature complemented these findings. The analysis focused exclusively on industrial sources to reflect the views of the companies themselves and their publicly disclosed practices; academic publications were therefore not taken into account. The searches were conducted between November 2025 and March 2026 using the Google search engine. The keyword combinations followed the general structure "name of the LIB lifecycle stage" + "electric vehicle companies", with the lifecycle stages identified in the previous sections. Websites listing companies within each lifecycle stage were used for compiling the list of companies to be considered. These were included if they operated at least at one LIB lifecycle stage and had sufficient public information relevant to the study's objectives. Companies with no connection to EV or LIBs were also excluded. The search process continued until further research no longer yielded any substantially new information. The final sample consisted of 40 companies. Afterwards, an analysis of each company's official website and documents was conducted. The companies 'websites were prioritized as primary sources of information as they are published directly by the companies themselves. Information was systematically collected in tabular form, detailing on the company characteristics, their geographical location, their operational activities, the stages of LIB lifecycle with which they are associated, and their environmental performance indicators. Environmental data were primarily obtained from Environmental, Social and Governance (ESG) reports, sustainability reports (mainly from 2024), and other corporate documents. Companies operating across multiple lifecycle stages were assigned to all relevant stages.

3 Battery Lifecycle Mapping

A central concept in this work is the lifecycle of LIB for EVs. While many sources provide lifecycle mappings, these often differ in structure, terminology, and level of detail, making comparisons and synthesis challenging. To address this, a lifecycle mapping was identified based on the SLR.

3.1 Academic LIB Lifecycle Mapping

According to the results of the SLR, the representation of the lifecycle of a LIB is illustrated in Fig. 1. It undergoes the following stages:

- **Raw material extraction** Involves mining the natural resources needed for the manufacturing. It covers the mining of metals such as lithium, cobalt, nickel, manganese, copper, and aluminum, as well as the extraction of natural graphite [12].
- **Raw material processing** is where extracted natural resources are processed and purified into high-quality materials suitable for battery manufacturing. Essentially converting mined ores or brines into compounds [13].
- **Battery component manufacturing** is where refined raw materials are transformed into the key components that will make up a LIB. This includes producing the active materials for the cathode and anode, preparing electrolytes and separators etc. [14].
- **Battery cell manufacturing** is where all the main components are brought together to create the final cells. It includes preparing the electrodes, assembling them with separators and electrolyte into a sealed unit, and then stabilizing the cell [14].
- **Module and pack assembly** means individual battery cells are combined into larger units that can power EVs. First, cells are grouped into modules then, these modules are then assembled into a full battery pack together with the battery management system, thermal regulation and other components [14].
- **EV use** is the operational lifetime of LIBs when installed in EVs. After their use, batteries may no longer meet automotive standards but can still have residual value.
- **Collection and logistics after End-of-Life (EoL)** is for when LIBs are retrieved from vehicles and transported to facilities for further treatment. This stage includes the safe removal of batteries from vehicles, temporary storage, and transport to specialized centers [15].
- **Pre-processing after EoL** focuses on determining the condition of LIBs and the appropriate EoL route. It includes diagnostic testing, and sorting operations to assess state of health and safety. These evaluations enable the classification of battery packs, modules, or cells according to their suitable application. This ends by allocating each battery to its corresponding EoL pathway among the following [16].
- **Recycling** aims to recover valuable metals and reuse them. There are multiple recycling processes such as pyrometallurgy, hydrometallurgy, or direct recycling. Finally, the recovered metals undergo refining, where they are purified to battery-grade quality to reintegrate the manufacture of new batteries [17].
- **Remanufacturing** involves restoring spent or degraded batteries to a usable condition by repairing or replacing components. Unlike recycling, it seeks to maintain the original function of the battery to reintegrate in EVs [8].
- **Second use** refers to extending the service life of EV batteries by redeploying them in less demanding applications. Typical uses include stationary energy storage, grid support, or backup power systems [18]. Meaning that LIBs are no longer for EV use.
- **Disposal** is for batteries that cannot be economically or technologically recovered.

3.2 Industrial LIB Lifecycle Mapping and Key Actors

Consulting grey literature enabled reconstruction of the LIB lifecycle from an industrial perspective. Figure 2 is presented in two parts: LIBs first life in EVs and then the EoL.

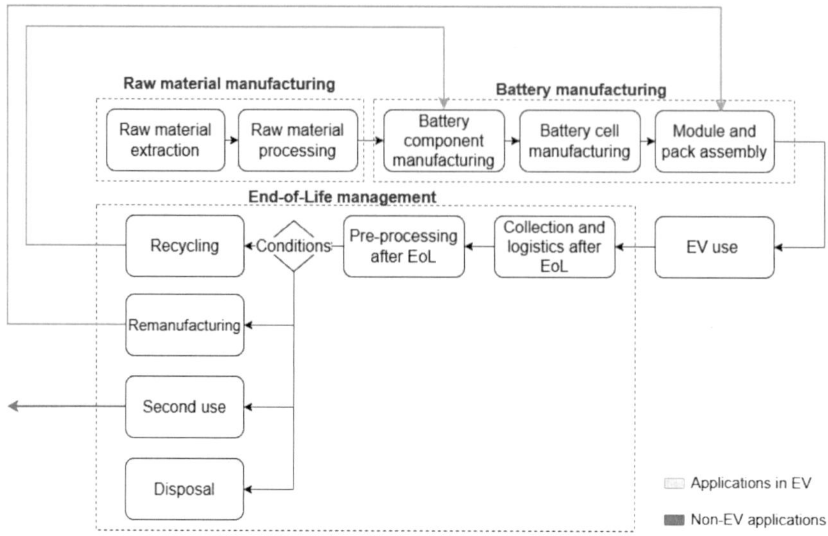

Fig. 1. Academic lifecycle mapping.

Lifecycle stages and key actors (identified companies) are shown and then compared with the previously presented academic mapping in Fig. 1. Overall, this industrial mapping is not fundamentally different, the main divergence lies in the level of detail. The industrial mapping breaks down stages into more granular stages, whereas the academic mapping is more aggregated. Overall, the differences are: Battery Active Materials Manufacturing which is essentially the same stage as in academic Battery component manufacturing but industrials use a more technical name. Battery Module assembly and Battery Pack assembly are two separate stages in industrial mapping because they are not necessarily done by the same actor. Battery Integration in EV is also separated as a single step that was in the aggregated academic step Module and pack assembly**.**

The stages of raw material extraction and processing seem to be closely related, as all identified companies operate across both stages. As illustrated in Fig. 2, these nine companies report engaging in both mining and refining activities [19]. The companies identified can be regarded as dominant upstream producers [20], which helps explain their integration of both activities to maximize added value. Since refining requires important capital investment and technological capacities, it is handled by large companies. Moreover, the vertical integration of these two stages is attractive because it secures feedstock for refining, reduces costs and increases bargaining power for the companies [21]. The main raw materials involved here are lithium, cobalt, nickel, and copper. Five of the companies focus exclusively on lithium, while the rest operate on diverse minerals [22]. Active material manufacturing represents more than 35% of the value-added transformation after refining and constitutes the technological core of LIBs. At this stage, refined chemical precursors are converted into cathode and anode materials that ultimately determine battery performance [23]. The mapping identified companies specifically specialized in this segment, such as Umicore and Nichia [24]. Unlike mining and refining, cathode and anode manufacturing depend on long R&D investment.

This helps explain why few companies extend into active materials manufacturing. This stage requires strong technical expertise to compete. Next, batteries undergo Cell manufacturing, Module assembly, Pack assembly and Integration in EV. Companies display different degrees of participation across these stages. There is the type of manufacturers that deal with Battery cell manufacturing until Battery pack assembly then supplying packs to Original Equipment Manufacturers (OEM). For example, we have Panasonic, LG Energy Solution etc. [25]. Besides, companies such as ACC, Verkor, Northvolt stop at Module assembly leaving the rest to OEMs [26]. In contrast, BYD combines all 4 stages which is an example of a highly integrated strategy that can reduce costs and mitigate dependence on external suppliers [27]. These are advantages that are particularly valuable in context of LIBSC disruptions. Many automotive manufacturers, such as Tesla, Ford, BMW, and General Motors, do not manufacture cells. Instead, they source cells and focus on assembly and integration within vehicles [28]. This model allows companies to retain control over vehicle-specific features without bearing the high capital and technological costs of cells.

The lower part of industrial lifecycle mapping is identical to the academic one except for the stage of Disposal. None of the key actors identified mention offering this option. This can be explained by the prioritization of circular economy pathways and diverting batteries from going to waste. For the stages Collection and logistics after EoL and Pre-processing after EoL, few companies describe in detail the operations they perform (diagnostics, discharging, dismantling, shredding) therefore it was not possible to further detail the specialized activities. However, the EoL mapping reveals several the emerging circular ecosystem for LIBs. First, the distribution of activities suggests a tendency toward vertical integration, as many companies operate across multiple stages rather than specializing in a single activity. Companies involved in Collection and pre-processing often extend their operations to reuse or recycling, indicating recycling and second use companies tend to also do the collection and pre-processing of spent batteries within their operations. This may reflect both economic and operational considerations, including the need to secure supply. Furthermore, Remanufacturing seems to be underrepresented. The limited presence of specialized remanufacturing actors may be explained by the high level of technical expertise required to repair EV batteries and by the strategic importance of this activity for OEMs, who may prefer to retain these capabilities internally. Additionally, some key actors on Recycling are the same for Battery Active Materials Manufacturing thereby recovering materials that can be reintegrated into upstream production [29]. Overall, these observations suggest that the industrial ecosystem for battery EoL management is in an early stage of development. The circular economy landscape appears to be developing in Europe and North America, where many actors involved in recycling have established large-scale facilities [30]. European companies play a prominent role in developing recycling and refining capacities, pushed by regulations encouraging circularity. In North America, companies such as Redwood Materials aim to recover and refine battery materials to reintegrate into domestic LIBSC. This reflects strategic efforts to reduce dependence on external suppliers for critical materials, particularly given the dominance of Asian countries.

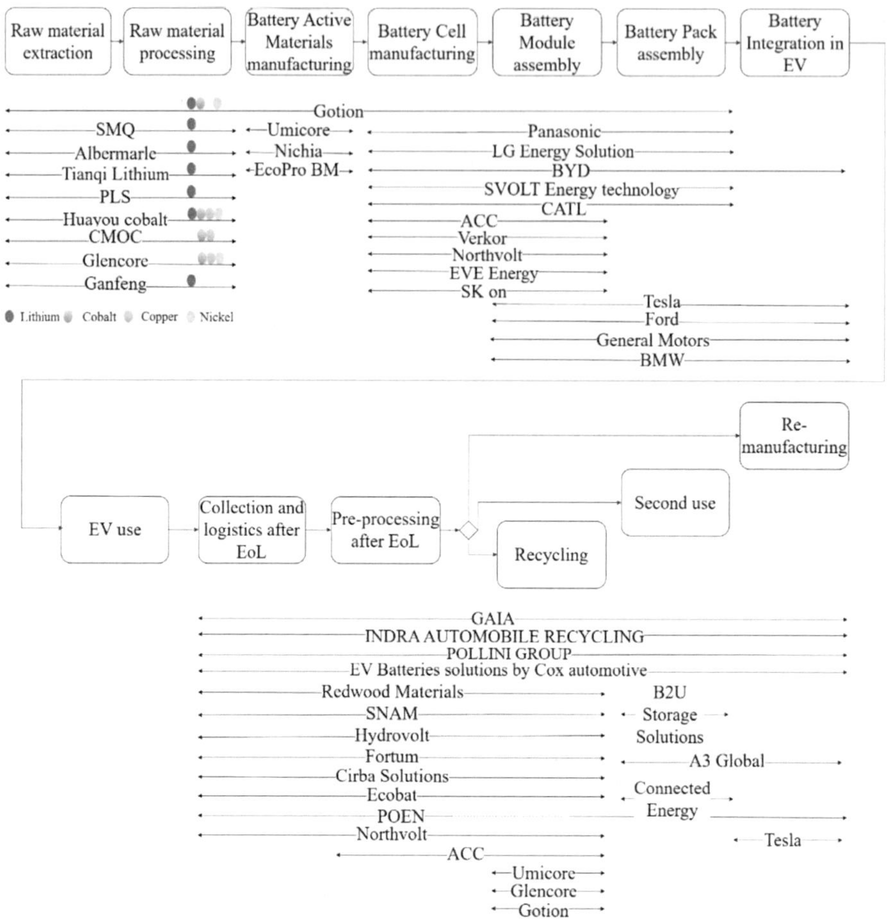

Fig. 2. Industrial lifecycle mapping.

4 Environmental Assessment of LIBSC

The aim of this section is to analyze how the environmental dimension is addressed in the academic and grey literature by examining and comparing the indicators used.

4.1 Academic Point of View

Out of 199 papers obtained through the SLR, 114 assessed the environmental performance of LIBSCs. LCA was the most commonly used method, using quantitative indicators corresponding to LCA impact categories. A smaller number of studies employed alternative indicators, such as Product Circularity Indicator, green performance criteria, recycling rate etc. [31]. In order to identify the most commonly used environmental indicators, all indicators mentioned in the SLR articles were listed and their frequency analyzed. Due to the large variety of LCA impact categories, the analysis was simplified by grouping conceptually similar indicators into broader categories. These categories were based on the International Reference Life Cycle Data System (ILCD), which provides a consistent methodological framework for LCA in the European context. The impact categories considered are: Climate change, Resource depletion, Land use, Particulate matter, Eutrophication, Acidification, Human toxicity, Ecotoxicity, Ionizing radiation, Ozone depletion, and Photochemical ozone formation. Indicator distribution in Fig. 3 shows that Climate change is the most frequently addressed category, appearing 104 times. This focus aligns with decarbonization and carbon neutrality targets, and reflects the energy-intensive nature of battery production, particularly material extraction, refining, and cell manufacturing, which are major contributors to GHG emissions and environmental impacts throughout the lifecycle of LIBs [17]. However, this should be interpreted with caution. Prioritizing Climate change as the primary indicator may encourage a narrow assessment and increase the risk of environmental burden shifting [32]. By concentrating primarily on GHG emissions, other impact categories may receive less attention and this can potentially lead to incomplete assessments. Resource depletion of materials appears 48 times, which may reflect concerns regarding mineral depletion and the criticality of raw materials. Since the rapid growth in EVs deployment has led to an increase in the demand for critical materials, Iulia et al. [33] have highlighted the need to more systematically integrate resource criticality considerations into LCA studies of EVs. In particular, it has been argued that criticality should be consistently accounted for to better assess the potential supply risks associated with specific materials [33]. Additionally, Toxicity-related categories such as Ecotoxicity (42 occurrences) and Human toxicity (39 occurrences) are also frequently considered after the first two, suggesting a growing awareness of the environmental and health implications associated with LIBs [34]. The other impact categories receive less attention, suggesting that they may be incorporated as secondary considerations rather than as primary focus of environmental assessment.

4.2 Industrial Point of View

Grey literature was consulted for 33 companies among the identified in the previous section, primarily consisting of ESG and sustainability reports [35, 36]. Among these, only 20 companies disclosed publicly available environmental data. This fact shows a lack of transparency and introducing a potential bias. For the companies with available data, the reported indicators largely align with categories defined by the Global Reporting Initiative (GRI), which provides standardized frameworks to measure and communicate environmental, social, and economic impacts in a consistent and comparable manner [37]. The GRI categories used in this analysis are detailed in Table 1. In addition, a category named Other was introduced to capture indicators that do not clearly fit within the chosen categories. Figure 4 presents the distribution of environmental indicators across these categories using two ways: the total number of indicator occurrences and the number of companies reporting at least one indicator within each category. The first metric provides insight into reporting intensity, while the second helps reduce bias related to differences in reporting granularity, as some companies disclose highly detailed indicators. The results show that Emissions is the most frequently reported category in terms of occurrences, reflecting the detailed reporting (the various scopes for GHG

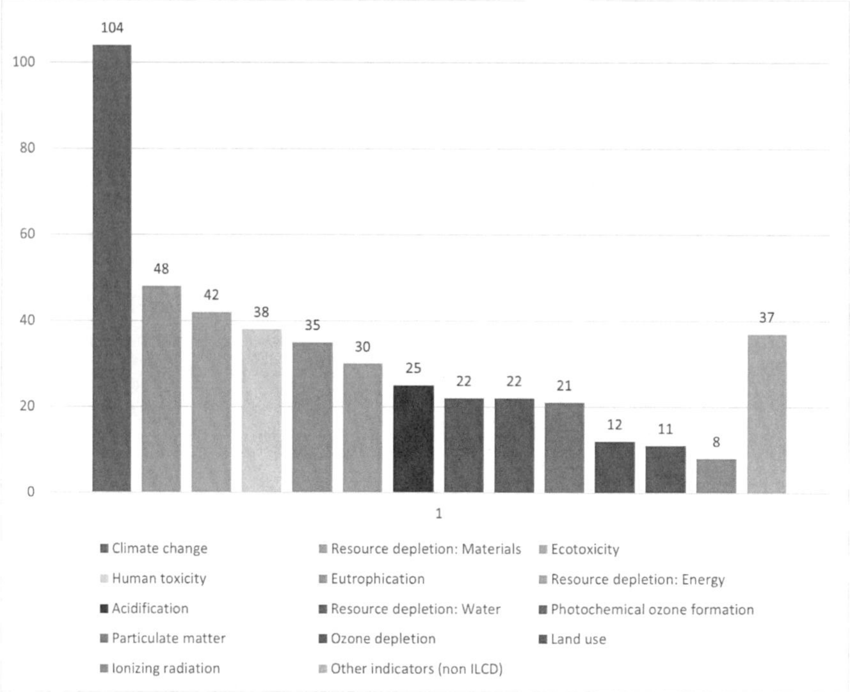

Fig. 3. Environmental indicators in academia.

emissions) and the central role of climate-related indicators. Water and Effluents and Energy emerge as the next most frequently reported categories, followed by Waste, while Materials is less frequently disclosed. Biodiversity is by far the least reported category, both in terms of occurrences and number of reporting companies. The Other category includes items such as environmental investments, environmental performance indices, and number of environmental incidents, which don't fit into any category but still need to be reported by companies, which explains the important number in this category. When considering the number of companies, most categories show relatively similar coverage, with the notable exceptions of Other and Biodiversity, which remains marginal. The predominance of emissions-related indicators can be explained by strong regulatory pressure and increasing stakeholder focus on climate change, making GHG reporting a priority for companies. Similarly, Energy, Water and Effluents, and Waste indicators are closely tied to operational processes and are relatively easy to quantify, which facilitates their disclosure. In contrast, Biodiversity impacts are complex to assess which explains their limited reporting. Materials related indicators may also be underrepresented due to challenges in tracking material flows across complex LIBCSs and the lower regulatory pressure.

Table 1. GRI environmental standards indicators.

GRI standard	Topic disclosures
GRI 301: Materials	- Materials used by weight or volume - Recycled input materials used - Reclaimed products and their packaging materials
GRI 302: Energy	- Energy consumption within the organization - Energy consumption outside of the organization - Energy intensity - Reduction of energy consumption - Reductions in energy requirements of products and services
GRI 303: Water and Effluents	- Water withdrawal - Water discharge - Water consumption
GRI 304: Biodiversity	- Operational sites owned, leased, managed in, or adjacent to, protected areas and areas of high biodiversity value outside protected areas - Significant impacts of activities, products and services on biodiversity - Habitats protected or restored - International Union for Conservation of Nature Red List species and national conservation list species with habitats in areas affected by operations
GRI 305: Emissions	- Direct GHG emissions - Energy indirect GHG emissions - Other indirect GHG emissions - GHG emissions intensity - Reduction of GHG emissions - Emissions of ozone-depleting substances - Nitrogen oxides, sulfur oxides, and other significant air emissions
GRI 306: Waste	- Waste generated - Waste diverted from disposal - Waste directed to disposal

4.3 Differences and Similarities

When comparing environmental indicators from academic and industrial viewpoints, many common themes emerge, like climate change, energy, water, and air pollutants. However, key differences can be identified along two dimensions: system boundaries and the nature of the indicators used (inventory-based vs. impact-based). For instance, academic papers use indicators such as Climate change, GHG emissions and Carbon footprint. These are generally calculated over the entire lifecycle of LIBs. In contrast, companies primarily report this within organizational boundaries, through indicators such as Direct GHG emissions, Energy indirect GHG emissions, and Other indirect GHG emissions. While other indirect GHG emissions aims to capture upstream and

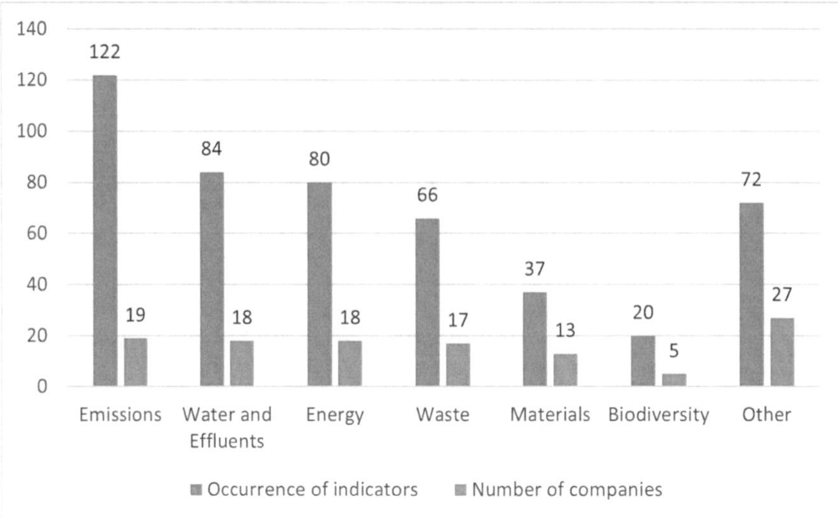

Fig. 4. Environmental indicators in grey literature.

downstream emissions, it is subject to higher uncertainty. Moreover, many of the companies considered in the analysis have several products and activities, consequently the reported indicators are not exclusively focused on LIBs. The same goes for Energy related indicators. Industrial reporting focuses on operational indicators such as Energy consumption within and outside the organization, Energy intensity, and Reductions in energy consumption typically at the facility level. In contrast, LCA evaluates energy use across the entire lifecycle through indicators such as Cumulative energy demand, which accounts for the total primary energy required to produce a product or service. For Water, both approaches use volumetric indicators such as Water withdrawal and Water consumption. However, LCA extends beyond these measures by incorporating impact-based indicators that quantify environmental consequences like aquatic Eutrophication, and Ecotoxicity. These consequences are generally not captured in industrial reporting, which tends to focus on physical quantities rather than associated impacts. In the case of air pollutants, companies typically report the quantities of emitted substances such as Nitrogen oxides and Sulfur oxides. In LCA, these emissions are first quantified as inventory flows and then translated into impact categories like Particulate matter formation for example which assess their potential effects on human health [38]. The same goes for the impact category Ozone depletion in LCA, that assesses the potential impact on the ozone layer and convert emissions into a potential impact score. Whereas, according to GRI 305: Emissions, companies report Emissions of ozone-depleting substances only as a physical quantity.

Several LCA impact categories have no similar indicators in industrial reporting, including Resource depletion of materials, Eutrophication, Acidification, Ecotoxicity, Human toxicity, Ionizing radiation, Photochemical ozone formation, and Land use. These LCA indicators reflect impact-based assessments that rely on environmental modelling at regional or global scales and therefore cannot be directly captured through company-level indicators. For instance, resource depletion is increasingly recognized as a critical issue in the context of LIBs [33] due to the reliance on critical materials. However, companies typically report indicators under GRI 301: Materials like Materials used by weight or volume or the Recycled input materials used, without explicitly addressing resource criticality. Similar limitations apply to impact categories such as Eutrophication, Acidification, and Photochemical ozone formation, which depend on complex modelling of emission pathways and their interactions within ecosystems and the atmosphere. Likewise, Ecotoxicity and Human toxicity require fate and exposure modelling to assess how pollutants affect living organisms, making these impacts difficult to attribute directly to a single company's activities [39]. Other categories, such as Ionizing radiation, are generally driven by upstream processes like electricity production for example nuclear energy production [40]. Land use on the other hand involves spatial and long-term impacts on ecosystems, such as biodiversity loss and soil degradation, which are not captured through standard reporting [41]. Conversely, Waste appears as a recurrent category in industrial reporting but does not correspond to a standalone LCA impact category. In LCA, waste is not treated as an impact but is accounted for through its contributions to other impact categories, such as Climate change, Ecotoxicity or Resource depletion. In contrast, companies report waste for regulatory compliance.

A discrepancy is observed in environmental assessment. Academic studies rely on LCA, a systematic and comprehensive method, whereas industrial reporting remains selective and not fully standardized. Industrial reporting depends on data availability and the company's strategic objectives leading to selective disclosures. This misalignment limits the comparability and reliability of industrial environmental assessments.

5 Conclusion and Perspectives

Both academic and grey literature were analyzed to compare environmental indicators from these two perspectives and to examine indicator reporting practices within the LIBSC. The results reveal a mismatch between academic and industrial approaches. In particular, the indicators reported by industry lack standardization and comprehensiveness, whereas academic approaches largely rely on LCA, which remains a complex and resource-intensive methodology to implement in practice. These findings highlight the need for closer collaboration between academia and industry. This could involve initiatives that promote knowledge exchange through open data practices, encourage industrial participation in research programs as part of corporate sustainability efforts. Such collaboration would also ensure that research results are applicable to industry in practice. Besides, researchers could contribute by seeking to reduce excessive data requirements and simplify complex modelling approaches whilst maintaining scientific rigor. In particular, environmental indicators that have been found to be lacking in industrial reporting practices – such as resource depletion of materials, eutrophication, acidification, ecotoxicity, human toxicity, ionizing radiation, photochemical ozone formation, and land use – could be further developed to result in simplified, practical assessments tailored to the industrial sector. This could facilitate the development of hybrid reporting integrating both GRI and LCA indicators. Furthermore, there is a need to establish a set of environmental indicators specifically adapted to the battery sector.

Likewise, industries could progressively expand their assessment practices beyond simply reporting carbon footprints, by incorporating broader assessments of environmental impact at the product-level using the tools and methodologies developed by researchers. In this context, emerging initiatives related to ESG standardization and battery passports may also help address current discrepancies in sustainability reporting. Battery passports, for instance, could facilitate a more standardized exchange of environmental information, including material sources, carbon footprint, recycled content, and life-cycle impact indicators. Finally, policymakers also have an important role in supporting this transition through regulations that encourage standardized reporting requirements and stronger collaboration between industry and research institutions.

Acknowledgements. All research data can be shared with readers upon request. This research is funded by the French Agence Nationale de la Recherche within the CPJ framework. The authors thank Jacob Walter, Michel Kayal, and Angela Criado-Molina for their contributions to this work.

Disclosure of Interests. The authors have no competing interests to declare.

References

1. Li, P., Xia, X., Guo, J.: A review of the life cycle carbon footprint of electric vehicle batteries. Sep. Purif. Technol. **296**, 121389 (2022)
2. Temporelli, A., Carvalho, M.L., Girardi, P.: Life cycle assessment of electric vehicle batteries: an overview of recent literature. Energies. **13**(11), 2864 (2020)
3. McManus, M.C.: Environmental consequences of the use of batteries in low carbon systems: the impact of battery production. Appl. Energy. **93**, 288–295 (2012)
4. Kwade, A., Diekmann, J.: Recycling of lithium-ion batteries. In: The LithoRec Way, Sustainable Production, Life Cycle Engineering and Management, vol. 53, pp. 53–81. Springer (2018)
5. ANRT: Association Nationale Recherche Technologie, Groupe de travail "Transition énergétique": Les enjeux industriels et technologiques des minerais et métaux pour la transition énergétique et numérique. ANRT (2025)
6. Pol, V.G.: Lithium-ion battery critical materials sustainability. ACS Energy Lett. **10**(5), 2553–2558 (2025). https://doi.org/10.1021/acsenergylett.5c01018
7. Melin, H.E., Rajaeifar, M.A., Ku, A.Y., Kendall, A., Harper, G., Heidrich, O.: Global implications of the EU battery regulation. Science. **373**(6553), 384–387 (2021)
8. Neri, A., Butturi, M.A., Gamberini, R.: Sustainable management of electric vehicle battery remanufacturing: a systematic literature review and future directions. J. Manuf. Syst. **77**, 859–874 (2024)
9. Hanna, F., Somers, C., Anctil, A.: Life cycle assessment of lithium-ion battery recycling: evaluating the impact of recycling methods and location. Environ. Sci. Technol. **59**(28), 14432–14443 (2025)
10. IEA: Global Battery Markets Are Growing Strongly – and So Are the Supply Risks. IEA, Paris (2026) https://www.iea.org/commentaries/global-battery-markets-are-growing-strongly-and-so-are-the-supply-risks. Accessed 6 Apr 2026
11. Page, M.J. et al.: PRISMA 2020 explanation and elaboration: updated guidance and exemplars for reporting systematic reviews. BMJ. **372**, n160 (2021)
12. Barbosa, J.C. et al.: Batteries and sustainability: the relevance of life cycle assessment. Sustain. Energy Technol. Assess. **82**, 104488 (2025)

13. Yang, Z., Huang, H., Lin, F.: Sustainable electric vehicle batteries for a sustainable world: perspectives on battery cathodes, environment, supply chain, manufacturing, life cycle, and policy. Adv. Energy Mater. **12**(26) (2022). https://doi.org/10.1002/aenm.202200383
14. Chordia, M., Nordelöf, A., Ellingsen, L.A.: Environmental life cycle implications of upscaling lithium-ion battery production. Int. J. Life Cycle Assess. **26**(10), 2024–2039 (2021)
15. Mohiuddin, M.D., Bai, L., Mo, W.: Reverse logistics for electric vehicle batteries: a systematic review. Comput. Ind. Eng. **208**, 111327 (2025)
16. Popien, J.L., Thies, C., Spengler, T.S.: Exploring recycling options in battery supply chains–a life cycle sustainability assessment. Procedia CIRP. **105**, 434–439 (2022)
17. Yang, Z., Huang, H., Lin, F.: Sustainable electric vehicle batteries for a sustainable world: perspectives on battery cathodes, environment, supply chain, manufacturing, life cycle, and policy. Adv. Energy Mater. **12**(26), 2200383 (2022)
18. Yu, W., Zheng, Y., Zhang, Y.: Carbon emission reduction by echelon utilization of retired vehicle power batteries in energy storage power stations. World Electr. Veh. J. **13**(8), 144 (2022)
19. Albemarle: Innovating from Mine to Market: Lithium for Energy Storage. Albemarle (2026)
20. Farmonaut: Largest lithium & diamond companies and mines worldwide. https://farmonaut.com/mining/largest-lithium-diamond-companies-mines-worldwide. Accessed 6 Apr 2026
21. Gultom, T.H.: Integrated vertical mining and processing for critical mineral: a case study in Obi Island, North Maluku Province. IOP Conf. Ser. Earth Environ. Sci. **1422**(1), 012023 (2024)
22. Glencore: Metals and Minerals. https://www.glencore.com/what-we-do/metals-and-minerals. Accessed 19 May 2026
23. Altilium: The missing link in EV supply chains: cathode active material – Altilium's mission to localise production for a greener, stronger UK. https://altilium.tech/2025/07/27/the-missing-link-in-ev-supply-chains-cathode-active-material-altiliums-mission-to-localise-production-for-a-greener-stronger-uk/. Accessed 6 Apr 2026
24. Nichia Corporation: Cathode Materials. https://www.nichia.co.jp/en/product/battery.html. Accessed 1 Apr 2026
25. Panasonic Energy: Pack Modules. https://energy.panasonic.com/eu/business/products/pack-module. Accessed 19 May 2026
26. Verkor: Our Cells and Modules. https://verkor.com/en/our-cells-and-modules/. Accessed 19 May 2026
27. EVBoosters: The blueprint of an EV empire: how BYD built global dominance through vertical integration. https://evboosters.com/ev-charging-news/the-blueprint-of-an-ev-empire-how-byd-built-global-dominance-through-vertical-integration/. Accessed 6 Apr 2026
28. Ford: Ford Commits to Manufacturing Batteries. https://corporate.ford.com/articles/electrification/ford-commits-to-manufacturing-batteries/. Accessed 19 May 2026
29. Umicore: Battery Recycling Solutions. https://www.umicore.com/en/about/battery-materials-solutions/battery-recycling-solutions/start/. Accessed 19 May 2026
30. Electric Drives TV: Europe now has 30 EV battery gigafactories in operation. https://electricdrives.tv/europe-now-has-30-ev-battery-gigafactories-in-operation/. Accessed 6 Apr 2026
31. Picatoste, A., Schulz-Mönninghoff, M., Niero, M., Justel, D., Mendoza, J.M.F.: Comparing the circularity and life cycle environmental performance of batteries for electric vehicles. Resour. Conserv. Recycl. **210**, 107833 (2024)
32. Chordia, M., Nordelöf, A., Ellingsen, L.A.-W.: Environmental life cycle implications of upscaling lithium-ion battery production. Int. J. Life Cycle Assess. **26**(10), 2024–2039 (2021)
33. Dolganova, I., Rödl, A., Bach, V., Kaltschmitt, M., Finkbeiner, M.: A review of life cycle assessment studies of electric vehicles with a focus on resource use. Resources. **9**(3), 32 (2020)

34. Richa, K., Babbitt, C.W., Gaustad, G.: Eco-efficiency analysis of a lithium-ion battery waste hierarchy inspired by circular economy. J. Ind. Ecol. **21**(3), 715–730 (2017)
35. Tesla: Impact Report 2024 – Extended Version. https://www.tesla.com/ns_videos/2024-tesla-impact-report.pdf. Accessed 19 May 2026
36. ACC: Rapport RSE 2024. https://www.acc-emotion.com/sites/default/files/media/files/RA%20RSE%20EN%20Double%20page.pdf. Accessed 19 May 2026
37. Global Reporting Initiative: How to use the GRI standards. https://www.globalreporting.org/how-to-use-the-gri-standards/gri-standards-english-language/. Accessed 6 Apr 2026
38. van Zelm, R. et al.: European characterization factors for human health damage of PM10 and ozone in life cycle impact assessment. Atmos. Environ. **42**(3), 441–453 (2008)
39. Saouter, E. et al.: Environmental footprint: update of life cycle impact assessment methods – ecotoxicity freshwater, human toxicity cancer, and non-cancer. In: EUR 29495 EN. Publications Office of the European Union, Luxembourg (2020)
40. United Nations Economic Commission for Europe: Life Cycle Assessment of Electricity Generation Options. United Nations, Geneva (2021)
41. Vidal-Legaz, B. et al.: Land-Use Related Environmental Indicators for Life Cycle Assessment. JRC Technical Report. Publications Office of the European Union, Luxembourg (2016)

Adoption of Battery Electric Trucks: A Review on Transport Companies' Perspectives

Matteo Capolli[1], Alessandro Creazza[2], Pietro Evangelista[3], and Claudia Colicchia[1](✉)

[1] Department of Management, Economics and Industrial Engineering, Politecnico di Milano, Via Lambruschini 4/b, 20156 Milan, Italy
claudia.colicchia@polimi.it

[2] LIUC University, Castellanza, VA, Italy
acreazza@liuc.it

[3] National Research Council (CNR), Institute for Studies on the Mediterranean (ISMed), Naples, Italy
pietro.evangelista@ismed.cnr.it

Abstract. The transition to battery electric trucks is widely recognized as a promising step toward decarbonizing road freight, yet adoption remains limited outside a few leading markets. While considerable attention has been devoted to modeling the performance of battery electric trucks, much less is known about how electrification is experienced by transport-owning logistics operators. This review addresses that gap by focusing on studies that provide insight into the implications of adopting battery electric trucks with stationary charging for transport owners. The results show that the literature continues to pay limited attention to the motivations and pressures shaping adoption, as well as to the organizational and business-model changes required to integrate battery electric trucks into logistics operations. In addition, there is a clear opportunity for further research on how these pressures evolve in response to changing and often inconsistent policy signals.

Keywords: Battery electric trucks · Electrification · Freight transport · Literature review

1 Introduction

In 2023, global greenhouse gas emissions from the transport sector reached 8.4 $GtCO2_e$ [1]. Of these, one quarter came from heavy-duty trucks, despite these accounting for only 6% of road transport vehicles [2]. Their presence is ubiquitous in the movement of goods, and global road freight transport activity is expected to double by 2050 [3]. Without significant action, this trend will cause the sector to have a greater emissions impact, which pursuing engine efficiency alone will not be able to offset. One possible action is the substitution of carbon-intensive diesel used to fuel trucks. This transition can be pursued through biofuels, which are often considered bridge solutions because the availability of sustainable biogenic feedstocks is limited and expected to decline in

Published by Springer Nature Switzerland AG 2027
G. Pezzotta et al. (Eds.): APMS 2026, IFIP AICT 808, pp. 167–180, 2027.
https://doi.org/10.1007/978-3-032-38594-9_12

the future [4], or through the adoption of zero-emission trucks, such as fuel cell electric trucks and battery electric trucks. Among the zero-emission alternatives, heavy-duty battery electric trucks (BETs) stand out as the most readily available technology. The reason lies in the greater availability of models on the market and a projected improvement in terms of battery energy density and costs (€150/kWh by 2035) [5]. From an environmental perspective, BETs powered by renewable sources represent the solution with the lowest overall greenhouse gas emissions, outperforming even green hydrogen trucks, while boasting a higher energy conversion efficiency than internal combustion vehicles [6]. Despite their leading position in driving decarbonization, today heavy-duty BETs do not seem to be truly taking off, at least not in the European or American markets, when compared with the far more virtuous Chinese case: sales shares stop at 2% for the heavy-duty segment ($>$12 tons) in Europe and the United States, versus a 29% sales share in the same segment in China [7]. Some authors attribute this to the lack of demand-side measures: while OEMs are forced to reduce average fleet emissions [8], fleet operators, for example through the European Clean Vehicles Directive, have been given the possibility of accessing public procurement channels using multiple alternative fuels, including natural gas and biofuels [9]. Moreover, previously approved measures to sustain the uptake of heavy-duty electric vehicles have been progressively watered down in the United States, causing the U.S. zero emission truck market to plummet, with sales falling by about 80% in the first half of 2025 [9]. In any case, it is particularly demanding to facilitate adoption in such a fragmented transport sector, with more than 500,000 freight transport firms operating in Europe, with an average fleet of around 12 trucks [10]. Any hope of scaling up electric road freight requires consideration of both large and small transport owners' perspectives, along with their relationship with all the other actors with whom they form a complex ecosystem: on the demand side, shippers (transport buyers); on the supply side, OEMs and asset financiers; and, as enablers, charge point operators and grid operators [9]. Prior contributions reviewing how electrification was treated in the literature revealed that empirical evidence collected up to now on heavy-duty freight transport electrification has relied predominantly on secondary transport data (e.g., databases, previous research, or data generated artificially for mathematical models and optimizations), while primary data sources, such as interviews and workshops, were comparatively limited [11]. Addressing this gap, this paper advances existing reviews by focusing specifically on how the literature addresses the adoption and implementation of heavy-duty electric freight vehicles from an actor-oriented perspective. In doing so, it assesses whether recent research has moved beyond technical and model-based feasibility analyses towards a deeper understanding of the barriers, drivers, enablers and conditions shaping the transition to electric trucks.

Accordingly, the review is guided by the following research question: How does the existing literature address the adoption and implementation of heavy-duty electric freight vehicles, and to what extent does it account for the conditions, perceptions and actions of the actors involved in this transition?

2 Methodology

2.1 Material Collection

Scopus was used for its broad multidisciplinary coverage of peer-reviewed literature relevant to this study. The search was limited to journal articles to ensure academic quality, consistency, and comparability across the selected studies. No year limit was applied, as the aim was to capture the full evolution of the topic over time. The search query and refinement process were conducted in November 2025.

Inputted keywords are presented in four distinct groups (combined through the AND operator), reflecting the search strategy.

- **Group 1**: (haul* OR truck* OR freight*)
- **Group 2:** ("commercial electric vehicle*" OR "electric commercial vehicle*" OR "electric freight vehicle*" OR "electric truck*" OR "battery electric")
- **Group 3:** (owner* OR provider* OR compan* OR operator* OR firm* OR user* OR actor*)
- **Group 4:** (adopt* OR uptake OR implement* OR transition* OR deploy* OR barrier* OR enabler* OR driver* OR challenge* OR factor* OR obstacle* OR potential* OR feasibl* OR viabl*)

TITLE-ABS-KEY((haul* OR truck* OR freight*) AND ("commercial electric vehicle*" OR "electric commercial vehicle*" OR "electric freight vehicle*" OR "electric truck*" OR "battery electric") AND (owner* OR provider* OR compan* OR operator* OR firm* OR user* OR actor*) AND (adopt* OR uptake OR implement* OR transition* OR deploy* OR barrier* OR enabler* OR driver* OR challenge* OR factor* OR obstacle* OR potential* OR feasibl* OR viabl*) AND NOT (rail* OR air* OR sea* OR bike*)) AND (LIMIT-TO (SRCTYPE,"j"))

Group 1 defines the **transport activity**, restricting the search to freight transport, haulage, and trucking, and therefore excluding passenger transport. Group 2 specifies the **vehicle type**, focusing on electric commercial vehicles used for freight operations. Group 3 introduces the **actor dimension**, ensuring that the retrieved studies refer to or involve organizational actors such as companies, operators, or logistics providers. Finally, Group 4 limits the scope to the **issue of adoption**, capturing studies addressing the implementation, uptake, barriers, drivers, and other factors influencing the transition to electric trucks. In addition, rail, air, sea, and bike transport were excluded from the search.

This research query led to the retrieval of 158 contributions, which were screened through a step-by-step selection process structured according to the PRISMA flow diagram.

2.2 Exclusion Criteria

Starting from 158 records retrieved from Scopus, 56 records were excluded after title screening, 20 after abstract screening, and 20 after full-text assessment. Three reports were not retrieved. This resulted in 59 publications from the database search. Three additional publications were identified through backward and forward snowballing, leading to a final sample of 62 studies. The selection process is done by three reviewers to remove the selection bias associated with the subjective judgment of the inclusion/ exclusion process. The complete PRISMA flow diagram is available in our public repository.

The main, non-exhaustive reasons for exclusion across the title, abstract, and full-text screening stages include papers referring exclusively to fuel cell electric trucks powered by hydrogen (14), battery electric trucks used in applications other than road freight transport, such as mining, forestry transportation, or waste collection (10), focused on vehicle-level engineering and technical design aspects (e.g., component design, vehicle subsystems, safety engineering, or mechanical optimization) (10), evaluating charging methods other than stationary charging, such as overhead catenary systems, wireless charging, or battery swapping (8), papers targeting exclusively light-duty vehicles (< 3.5 tons) in order to remain coherent with the objective of this work, which is focused on heavy-duty road freight transport vehicles (9), addressing autonomous logistics equipment or automated terminal operations (4), addressing alternative fuel vehicles, with limited attention to battery electric trucks (12). Methodological heterogeneity was therefore not treated as a limitation to be eliminated, but as a feature of the evidence base. Model-based studies were used to identify the techno-economic, environmental and infrastructural conditions that shape adoption, whereas actor-based studies were used to examine how these conditions are perceived and implemented by firms involved in electric heavy-duty road freight.

3 Descriptive Analysis

3.1 Years, Journals and Geographical Distribution

Contributions prior to 2021 are scarce, with the earliest paper in the review dating back to 2013 and reflecting an early phase of battery-electric truck research, focused primarily on technical and economic feasibility. At that stage, deployments were still limited, and much of the available evidence concerned pilot projects and early user experiences rather than widespread commercial deployment [12, 13]. From 2021 onward, publications addressing this topic increased markedly (data for 2025 are partial, as the year was not yet complete when the review was conducted). This acceleration in research activity coincides with growing regulatory attention to transport decarbonization, including truck-specific policy initiatives such as the EU heavy-duty vehicle CO_2 standards adopted in 2019 and California's Advanced Clean Trucks regulation, adopted in 2020.

More than 50% of total publications in the review sample were published in Transportation Research Part D, Applied Energy, World Electric Vehicle Journal, Sustainability (Switzerland), Energies, Cleaner Logistics and Supply Chain (decreasing order of frequency), reflecting the interdisciplinary nature of freight electrification, which involves not only transport-environment concerns, but also energy-system integration, operational logistics, and sustainability-oriented transition pathways.

In terms of geographical distribution, the majority of the articles in the sample are linked to the United States, followed by Sweden and Germany, with some cases of contributions adopting an explicitly international perspective, such as assessments across European countries [14] or literature reviews aiming to collect evidence globally [11, 15].

3.2 Research Methods Used in the Review Sample

The methodological profile of the review sample is dominated by quantitative studies, which account for 39 of the 62 papers considered. These are followed by conceptual - empirical contributions (9 papers), qualitative case studies (6 papers), surveys (5 papers), literature reviews (2) and a conceptual paper (1) (more details in our **repository**). Overall, the evidence base is therefore characterized by two main methodological streams: on one hand, a predominantly modelling-oriented quantitative literature (total cost of ownership, life cycle assessments, optimization problems, simulations, scenario and sensitivity analyses) focused on assessing the technical, economic and environmental implications of truck electrification; on the other hand, a smaller body of empirical qualitative, survey-based studies, in some cases applying a conceptual lens, including but not limited to business model frameworks [16, 17], multilevel perspective [18], coordination theory [19] and a typology based on organizational structure and external network heterogeneity [20].

3.3 Keyword Co-occurrence Analysis

Keyword co-occurrence was employed in this literature review to examine the relatedness of keywords and whether they present any clustering. In this analysis each keyword is treated as a node and each co-occurrence of a pair of words in two papers as a link between those two words. Keywords were extracted from the Author Keywords in the Scopus database of the review sample and pre-processed in order to reduce noise and avoid fragmentation of the map (Fig. 1). The result is the division of keywords into four clusters covering four themes: Economics (blue), Charging (green), Impact (yellow), and Transition Barriers (red)

4 Content Analysis

This literature review combines the thematic structure derived from the keyword co-occurrence analysis with a methodological distinction between model-based contributions and studies involving direct actor perspectives. Quantitative studies are discussed first, as they provide analytical background on the technical, economic, and operational conditions affecting freight operators. Studies involving direct actor perspectives, although fewer in number, are then examined in greater depth because they are better suited to understanding decision-making dynamics, perceived barriers and implementation practices (Fig. 2).

4.1 Quantitative Studies

Cost. The total cost of ownership (TCO) of trucks is one of the main decision-making factors for logistics operators evaluating battery electric trucks, as it allows them to go beyond the initial purchase cost (CAPEX) and include the operating costs accumulated over the vehicle life (OPEX), such as fuel/energy, maintenance, tolls, and insurance [15]. This is of utmost importance, as in freight transport OPEX is found to be approximately

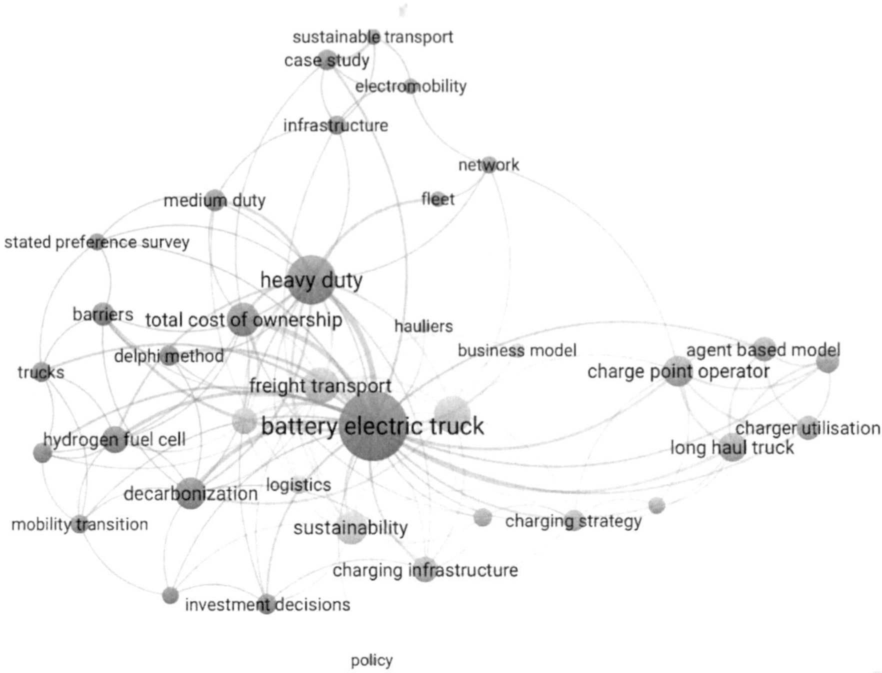

Fig. 1. Keyword co-occurrence

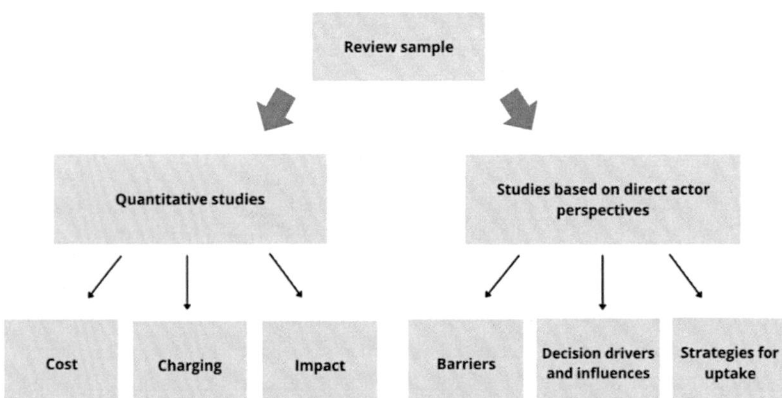

Fig. 2. Structure of the literature review

75% of TCO on average, and for this reason evaluating only the initial purchase cost would heavily mislead the assessment [14]. Results suggest that cost competitiveness varies significantly across regions, largely due to differences in diesel prices and taxation schemes, but this must be read with care, as the data employed for estimation come from different studies and assumptions, including different truck lifespans and ownership periods. A key consequence is that TCO cannot be discussed without more specific details on the vehicle operational mission profile, namely average annual mileage traveled and load weight transported [21]. Even so, some variables are still characterized by high uncertainty, such as residual value due to an immature second-hand market [15] and real battery lifespan under real-world degradation patterns [22]. In general, the key principle for making the case in favor of electric trucks is that operating costs must be high enough to compensate for the higher purchase cost [13], mainly attributable to battery costs, which means that the battery must be pushed to operate close to the limits of its design; otherwise, it becomes underutilized capital [23]. Some contributions have also attempted to factor into the total cost of ownership the intangible costs specific to operating electric trucks, such as recharging downtime, range anxiety, and cargo capacity limitations due to the higher weight of electric trucks compared to conventional trucks, showing that these additional costs account for more than 35% of the perceived ownership cost of BETs [24]. Policy can improve the total cost of ownership of BETs because their competitiveness against diesel is highly sensitive to the gap between electricity and diesel running costs. Measures that increase diesel operating costs, such as fuel taxes, can therefore significantly strengthen the cost position of BETs relative to diesel [14]. A crucial theme in the review concerns the timing of the transition to electric trucks: cost-optimal scenarios imply partial electrification of fleets, where electric trucks are employed in settings that guarantee high utilization, such as line-haul settings, while diesel trucks may be retained to serve distant customers even after 2040 [25]. Looking more closely at the financial feasibility of fleet replacement, an analysis of the balance sheets of transport firms in Sweden, one of Europe's leading markets for electric truck adoption, suggests that the level of financial stress put on companies transitioning to electric trucks makes them unfit to access traditional financing options (internal, debt, and equity) for acquiring one truck, let alone new ones that would really allow scaling up [26].

Charging. When it comes to deciding whether to rely on private depot charging or public charging, the literature has mainly shifted toward the inclusion of investment costs in the total cost that transport companies must incur. In fact, public charging infrastructure, in times of initial demand uncertainty, risks being underutilized, leading to excessively high charging costs for users and greater profitability risks for investors [27]. On the other hand, in fleet replacement problems, logistics companies that can supply their customers without needing public charging demonstrate a fast transition to BETs in regional case applications [25]. Accessibility to high-power-output chargers also has the effect of decreasing the upfront purchase costs for companies [28], as, instead of investing in onboard battery capacity to cover the full daily range, vehicles can recharge during operations. Additionally, the opportunity to employ the idle capacity of electric trucks for regulation purposes supporting grid stability [29], or in integration with smart manufacturing facilities [30], is explored.

Impact. Employing electric trucks is not necessarily a guarantee of reducing environmental impact. In fact, the choice of where, when, and how trucks are configured and charged plays a role. Use-phase electricity emissions were found to dominate battery-related life-cycle emissions [31]. For this reason, relying on carbon-intensive grids or following low-price signals can ultimately undermine improvements in freight CO_2 emissions [32]. Here too, the choice of charging strategy matters: larger batteries can be environmentally preferable when they enable a higher share of charging at a cleaner home depot rather than at more carbon-intensive public chargers. At the same time, larger batteries may reduce payload and yearly freight mileage, thereby increasing the number of vehicles required to deliver the same transport performance [33].

4.2 Studies Based on Direct Actor Perspectives

Barriers. Quantitative studies on barriers already highlight several issues that may arise for those operating electric trucks, such as high upfront purchase costs, uncertain residual values, and uncertainty around battery lifetime. However, several authors agree that these implications alone are not sufficient for a comprehensive analysis of barriers. Transitions require, alongside analytical perspectives focused on technological and economic aspects, a multidimensional perspective that also includes the social dimension, which is considered a key element in supporting the market acceptance of technological innovations [18]. Several studies included in this review move in this direction by collecting perceived barriers not only through interviews with logistics companies and hauliers, but also by involving researchers, representatives of sectoral associations, truck manufacturers, and shippers. A first element that emerges from these contributions is that barriers related to charging infrastructure are not generic, but can be broken down into more specific issues, such as insufficient charger coverage along freight routes, inadequate charging speed in relation to operational time windows, site constraints, and limited grid capacity [18, 34, 35]. More broadly, the issue concerns how to plan, execute, and manage mixed fleets, and how to address the operational difficulty of integrating battery-electric trucks into existing logistics systems [36]. On the economic side, the case for electric trucks remains highly uncertain, particularly with regard to financing conditions, expectations of cost neutrality, and the distribution of costs and benefits across different actors [37]. This, in turn, requires coordination among multiple stakeholders, which may translate into the co-development of complementary investments such as charging infrastructure and grid capacity [16]. Fleet operators also report a lack of support from customers, governments, and truck manufacturers. In particular, low customer willingness to pay for electrified transport and low acceptance of new delivery times are frequently mentioned as relevant barriers [36]. At the same time, there is high uncertainty surrounding the durability of subsidy schemes [34], also due in some cases to low political stability and short-term legislative periods [18]. In addition, some studies report the unavailability of electric truck models for specific use cases [35]. Another recurring issue is first-mover reluctance and a process of deferred commitment among fleet operators. This contributes to a broader lack of industry-wide knowledge on electrified freight transport [34] and points to the need for a wider process of competence building [37]. The barrier landscape evolves with market maturity: while some factors, such as the need for planning and management tools, remain constant, others, such as charging availability, may gradually become less relevant [37]. In addition, a DEMATEL-based contribution shows that, while cost is certainly a matter of concern for users, the barriers with higher leverage may lie elsewhere, especially in the challenges associated with transitioning to new business models and partnerships [38]. A useful way to interpret these findings is to distinguish between fleets with and without direct experience of electric trucks. Firms without experience tend to emphasize technological uncertainty and feasibility concerns before adoption, whereas firms with direct experience highlight barriers more closely related to implementation and market conditions. Nevertheless, some structural constraints remain relevant in both cases, including charging infrastructure, range, charging time, vehicle availability, and purchase cost [34, 38].

Decision Drivers and Influences. Fleet operators' decisions to acquire electric trucks have been influenced by both internal and external factors. Internal factors include the opinions of direct users of electric trucks (the drivers), the company's strategic business motives (e.g., reputational benefits, positioning for public contracts), and intrinsic beliefs and values (e.g., environmental consciousness, corporate social responsibility) [39]. Internal factors also include decision-makers' and companies' intrinsic characteristics, with adoption shown to vary based on the degree of formalization and centralization within a firm [20]. Additionally, higher purchase intentions were recorded among firms with higher revenues and larger fleets [40], while they were lower among older decision-makers and those in smaller freight operations [41]. External factors range from technology supplier support efforts, such as trialability offered by OEMs, to customer demand for electrified transport [20, 39, 42]. Customers may also become bottlenecks, however, if they hinder adoption by refusing to adapt schedules and pricing arrangements to the operational changes that electrification could entail [20]. The role of external actors can also shift in decisions on the acquisition of electric trucks. For example, dealers may be less influential in the early stages, whereas utilities, landowners, and local governments can become more important when depot charging and site constraints come into play.

Strategies for Uptake. A few particularly interesting contributions focus entirely on strategies and implications for uptake, rather than primarily on listing barriers. New business models can become a vehicle for overcoming barriers to electric vehicle adoption and for moving commercial fleets towards a more sustainable system, especially when they consider the complex interdependencies between actors in an electrified ecosystem. These include leasing, to reduce customer acquisition costs, and energy-oriented solutions, such as employing electric truck batteries as mobile energy storage for grid management and peak correction [17]. In particular, with regard to the relationship between shippers and LSPs, more detailed and transparent information from logistics service providers (LSPs) on the reasons behind cost increases may make shippers more willing to accept higher service prices. This collaboration could also extend to the exchange of more detailed information on goods flows in order to support charging planning. At the same time, shippers need a better understanding of delivery plans and of how operational routines could be adapted to facilitate charging, for example through dedicated time slots or by combining loading and unloading with charging [19]. As regards charging, new opportunities have emerged: providers of charging services no longer need to be the same actors that traditionally supplied diesel; this role may also be taken on by logistics companies themselves. For instance, companies can share charging infrastructure, helped by reservation mechanisms [43]. Important insights come from the first companies using electric trucks more extensively, showing that disruptions to transport operations have so far been limited, provided that vehicle redundancy is maintained, proprietary charging infrastructure is in place, ideally combined with energy storage to ensure operational continuity, and relatively easy transport assignments are selected, such as short routes requiring no charging during operations [44].

5 Discussion and Research Agenda

Consistent with its actor-oriented focus, this literature review shows that barriers to freight truck electrification have been widely discussed from two complementary perspectives. Quantitative studies mainly make visible the techno-economic and environmental conditions that may limit adoption, especially those related to cost, charging and emissions performance. Studies directly involving actors confirm that these dimensions are perceived as concrete barriers by transport operators, but also enrich the picture by highlighting additional social, market and coordination barriers that are less easily captured through modelling approaches. What emerges more clearly from studies directly involving actors is that, according to early adopters, barriers are no longer perceived primarily as relating to poor technological reliability, but increasingly as stemming from broader forms of uncertainty linked to both demand [36] and policy [34], particularly with regard to the subsidies on which some actors have relied to support fleet electrification. Despite these uncertainties, the directly interviewed companies (mainly in the USA and Nordic countries) still decided to deploy electric trucks. Yet surprisingly few of the contributions reviewed in this work have examined the motivations and/or pressures behind such decisions. Likewise, the literature has developed several theoretically grounded strategies for making electric trucks competitive, such as more flexible delivery windows, depot charging, the integration of charging time into scheduling, collaboration, and co-investment in charging infrastructure. However, very few studies examine how actors implement these changes in practice. At the same time, a growing number of companies are building experience, which highlights the value of exploring which implementation strategies have moved from theory into practice during the ongoing transition, and for identifying which aspects of electrification still clash with transport operators' operational realities.

Based on these findings, a research agenda can be outlined around three main directions for future studies. First, future studies should examine more systematically the drivers, motivations, and pressures behind the adoption of heavy-duty electric trucks in the road freight sector. Existing contributions have only marginally addressed this issue and often within broader analyses of heterogeneous heavy-duty alternative-fuel vehicles used in different operational contexts, such as public services, refuse collection, and school transport [39, 42]. Conducting an exploratory study focused on heavy-duty electric trucks in the road freight sector, and conducted in an institutional context other than the US and Nordic countries, would therefore represent a relevant opportunity, especially if it employed a theoretical lens able to assess in a coherent and systematic way the pressures faced by companies and their responses to them amid the uncertainty currently characterizing the transition to road freight electrification. Second, future research should investigate the practical implementation strategies through which electrification is integrated into logistics operations. Past contributions addressing this topic have focused predominantly on changes in the decision-making processes of companies that adopted electric trucks, leaving underexplored the changes in the use phase [20], the mitigation strategies some companies implement [44], and the forms of collaboration developed, which are often hard-won because they require continuous mutual adjustment [19]. Third, future studies should address how firms react to uncertain, inconsistent, or ambiguous policy frameworks. This dimension has remained largely unexplored, yet it appears increasingly relevant in a context where company investments are often shaped by expectations regarding subsidies, regulation, and long-term institutional commitment [18, 34]. Research in this area could help clarify the relationship between policy design and company uptake, while exploring the conditions that risk undermining ongoing electrification processes.

6 Conclusions and Limitations

Understanding the motivations that have led some companies to adopt battery electric trucks, together with the strategies they have used to make them operational, represents a key priority for future research and could offer a concrete point of reference for a freight transport industry that still struggles with limited confidence and insufficient capabilities for electrification. Such evidence would also be valuable for the broader ecosystem of actors with a stake in this transition, including truck manufacturers, charge point operators, shippers, and public authorities. As the number of battery electric trucks adopted continues to increase, examining the barriers that still prevent these vehicles from moving beyond pilot projects or symbolic initiatives and becoming workable, scalable solutions could help unlock the broader benefits of road freight electrification. This study should be interpreted in light of some methodological boundaries. The review focused on peer-reviewed journal articles indexed in Scopus, which ensured a consistent and academically validated source base but may have excluded relevant insights from other databases or non-journal sources. In addition, limiting the review to English-language publications may have reduced the visibility of context-specific studies published in other languages.

Supplementary Materials. The complete PRISMA flow diagram, the summary table of the included studies, and other supplementary materials of this review are available in the public repository.

Disclosure of Interests. The authors have no competing interests to declare that are relevant to the content of this article.

References

1. Olhoff, A., et al.: Emissions Gap Report 2024: no more Hot Air … Please! With a Massive Gap between Rhetoric and Reality, Countries Draft New Climate Commitments. United Nations Environment Programme (2024). https://doi.org/10.59117/20.500.11822/46404
2. Alfaro-Pelico, R., et al., Policies for advancing the renewables-based electrification of road transport [Online]. 2025. www.irena.org
3. OECD: ITF Transport Outlook 2023. OECD Publishing (2023). https://doi.org/10.1787/b6cc9ad5-en

4. Carraro, C., Searle, S., Baldino, C.: Waste and residue availability for advanced biofuel production in the European Union and the United Kingdom. Int. Counc. Clean Transp. **2050**(11), 1–9 (2021)
5. Link, S., Stephan, A., Speth, D., Plötz, P.: Rapidly declining costs of truck batteries and fuel cells enable large-scale road freight electrification. Nat. Res. (2024). https://doi.org/10.1038/s41560-024-01531-9
6. O'Connell, A., Pavlenko, N., Bieker, G., Searle, S.: A Comparison of the Life-Cycle Greenhouse Gas Emissions of European Heavy-Duty Vehicles and Fuels, pp. 1–36. International Council on Clean Transportation, Washington, DC (2023)
7. Sen, A., Teter, J., Kreutzfeldt, S., Miller, J.: Vision 2050 Update on the Global Zero-Emission Vehicle Transition in 2025 [Online]. International Council on Clean Transportation, Washington, DC (2026) www.theicct.org
8. European Parliament and Council: Regulation (EU) 2024/1610 of the European Parliament and of the Council of 14 May 2024 amending Regulation (EU) 2019/1242 as regards strengthening the CO2 emission performance standards for new heavy-duty vehicles and integrating reporting obligations, amending Regulation (EU) 2018/858 and repealing Regulation (EU) 2018/956 [Online] (2024). European Parliament and Council, Official Journal of the European Union. Available: https://eur-lex.europa.eu/eli/reg/2024/1610/oj
9. Smart Freight Centre: Accelerating ZET Deployment: Complementary Demand-Side Measures to Strong CO_2 Standards Authored by SFC with Contributions from ACEA and AllChiefs [Online]. Smart Freight Centre (2025) www.smartfreightcentre.org
10. Ragon, P.-L., Rodríguez, F.: Road Freight Decarbonization in Europe Readiness of the European Fleets for Zero-Emission Trucking [Online]. International Council on Clean Transportation, Washington, DC (2022) www.clean-trucking.eu
11. Gillström, H., Jobrant, M., Sallnäs, U.: Towards Building an Understanding of Electrification of Logistics Systems – A Literature Review and a Research Agenda. Elsevier Ltd. (2024). https://doi.org/10.1016/j.clscn.2023.100134
12. Hovi, I.B., Pinchasik, D.R., Figenbaum, E., Thorne, R.J.: Experiences from battery-electric truck users in Norway. World Electr. Veh. J. **11**(1) (2020). https://doi.org/10.3390/WEVJ11010005
13. Davis, B.A., Figliozzi, M.A.: A methodology to evaluate the competitiveness of electric delivery trucks. Transp. Res. E Logist. Transp. Rev. **49**(1), 8–23 (2013). https://doi.org/10.1016/j.tre.2012.07.003
14. Noll, B., del Val, S., Schmidt, T.S., Steffen, B.: Analyzing the competitiveness of low-carbon drive-technologies in road-freight: a total cost of ownership analysis in Europe. Appl. Energy. **306** (2022). https://doi.org/10.1016/j.apenergy.2021.118079
15. Danielis, R., Niazi, A.M.K., Scorrano, M., Masutti, M., Awan, A.M.: The economic feasibility of battery electric trucks: a review of the total cost of ownership estimates. Energies. **18**(2), 429 (2025). https://doi.org/10.3390/en18020429
16. Dehkordi, R., Ahokangas, P., Evers, N., Sorvisto, M.: Legitimacy challenges in emerging electric commercial vehicle (ECV) ecosystem. Energy. **322** (2025). https://doi.org/10.1016/j.energy.2025.135626
17. Dehkordi, R., Ahokangas, P., Evers, N., Sorvisto, M.: Business model design for electric commercial vehicles (ECVs): an ecosystemic perspective. Energy Policy. **186** (2024). https://doi.org/10.1016/j.enpol.2023.113971
18. Müller, C.: Transition to battery-electric and fuel cell heavy-duty trucks: a multi-level, multi-dimensional approach. Transp. Res. D Transp. Environ. **127** (2024). https://doi.org/10.1016/j.trd.2024.104052
19. Jobrant, M., Sallnäs, U., Gillström, H.: Commercial freight electrification: unravelling inter-firm coordination between logistics service providers and shippers. Int. J. Log. Res. Appl. (2025). https://doi.org/10.1080/13675567.2025.2473595

20. Sugihara, C., Hardman, S., Kurani, K.: Who decides which trucks to buy? Implications for electrifying freight fleets. Transp. Res. D Transp. Environ. **126** (2024). https://doi.org/10.1016/j.trd.2023.104015
21. Winkelmann, J., Spinler, S., Neukirchen, T.: Green transport fleet renewal using approximate dynamic programming: a case study in German heavy-duty road transportation. Transp. Res. E Logist. Transp. Rev. **186** (2024). https://doi.org/10.1016/j.tre.2024.103547
22. Taefi, T.T., Stütz, S., Fink, A.: Assessing the cost-optimal mileage of medium-duty electric vehicles with a numeric simulation approach. Transp. Res. D Transp. Environ. **56**, 271–285 (2017). https://doi.org/10.1016/j.trd.2017.08.015
23. Vijayagopal, R., Rousseau, A.: Electric truck economic feasibility analysis. World Electr. Veh. J. **12**(2) (2021). https://doi.org/10.3390/wevj12020075
24. Hao, X., et al.: Evaluating the current perceived cost of ownership for buses and trucks in China. Energy. **254** (2022). https://doi.org/10.1016/j.energy.2022.124383
25. Bakker, J., Lopez Alvarez, J.A., Veldman, J., Buijs, P.: Strategic fleet replacement for the electrification of heavy-duty road freight transportation. Appl. Energy. **391** (2025). https://doi.org/10.1016/j.apenergy.2025.125935
26. Parviziomran, E., Elliot, V., Bergqvist, R.: Financing dynamics in sustainable heavy-duty road transport: an agent-based modeling approach. Transp. Res. D Transp. Environ. **132** (2024). https://doi.org/10.1016/j.trd.2024.104258
27. Alonso-Villar, A., Davíðsdóttir, B., Stefánsson, H., Ásgeirsson, E.I., Kristjánsson, R.: Optimising fast-charging infrastructure for long-haul electric trucks in remote regions under adverse climate conditions. eTransportation. **24** (2025). https://doi.org/10.1016/j.etran.2025.100414
28. Kin, B., Hopman, M., Quak, H.: Different charging strategies for electric vehicle fleets in urban freight transport. Sustainability (Switzerland). **13**(23) (2021). https://doi.org/10.3390/su132313080
29. Zhao, Y., Noori, M., Tatari, O.: Vehicle to grid regulation services of electric delivery trucks: economic and environmental benefit analysis. Appl. Energy. **170**, 161–175 (2016). https://doi.org/10.1016/j.apenergy.2016.02.097
30. Karmali, L.P., Gholami, A., Nezamoddini, N.: Integrated optimization of production planning and electric trucks charging and discharging scheduling. Sustain. Energy Grids Netw. **39** (2024). https://doi.org/10.1016/j.segan.2024.101397
31. Schneider, J., Wolff, S., Seidenfus, M., Lienkamp, M.: Sizing up sustainability: Influence of battery size and cell chemistry on battery-electric trucks' life-cycle carbon emissions. e-Prime Adv. Electr. Eng. Electron. Energy. **9** (2024). https://doi.org/10.1016/j.prime.2024.100656
32. Piepenbrink, H., Flämig, H., Menger, A.: CO2e life-cycle assessment: twin comparison of battery–electric and diesel heavy-duty tractor units with real-world data. Future Transp. **5**(1) (2025). https://doi.org/10.3390/futuretransp5010012
33. Syré, A.M., Göhlich, D.: Decarbonization of long-haul heavy-duty truck transport: technologies, life cycle emissions, and costs. World Electr. Veh. J. **16**(2) (2025). https://doi.org/10.3390/wevj16020076
34. Sugihara, C., Hardman, S., Kurani, K.: Social, technological, and economic barriers to heavy-duty truck electrification. Res. Transp. Bus. Manag. **51** (2023). https://doi.org/10.1016/j.rtbm.2023.101064
35. Tanco, M., Cavallieri, S., Levy, M., Rossi, S., Jurburg, D.: Barriers towards the adoption of battery electric trucks-an exploratory study in Uruguay. Int. J. Electr. Hybrid Veh. **15**, 292–317 (2023)
36. Melander, L., Nyquist-Magnusson, C.: Drivers for and barriers to electric freight vehicle adoption in Stockholm. Transp. Res. D Transp. Environ. **108** (2022). https://doi.org/10.1016/j.trd.2022.103317

37. Gillström, H., Björklund, M., Stahre, F., Abrahamsson, M.: Wired for change: sustainable business models in the transition towards electrified road freight transport. Cleaner Logist. Supply Chain. **13** (2024). https://doi.org/10.1016/j.clscn.2024.100185
38. Konstantinou, T., Gkritza, K.: Examining the barriers to electric truck adoption as a system: a Grey-DEMATEL approach. Transp. Res. Interdiscip. Perspect. **17** (2023). https://doi.org/10.1016/j.trip.2022.100746
39. Bae, Y., Mitra, S.K., Rindt, C.R., Ritchie, S.G.: Factors influencing alternative fuel adoption decisions in heavy-duty vehicle fleets. Transp. Res. D Transp. Environ. **102** (2022). https://doi.org/10.1016/j.trd.2021.103150
40. Konstantinou, T., Gkritza, K.: Are we getting close to truck electrification? U.S. truck fleet managers' stated intentions to electrify their fleets. Transp. Res. Part A Policy Pract. **173** (2023). https://doi.org/10.1016/j.tra.2023.103697
41. Moglia, M., Tapsuwan, S., Ghaderi, H., Nygaard, C.A., Dia, H., Smith, D.A.: Who doesn't like a battery electric truck? Heterogeneous motivations in the uptake of low-emissions trucks in Australia. Transp. Res. Part A Policy Pract. **193** (2025). https://doi.org/10.1016/j.tra.2025.104396
42. Mohammed, L., Niesten, E., Gagliardi, D.: Adoption of alternative fuel vehicle fleets – a theoretical framework of barriers and enablers. Transp. Res. D Transp. Environ. **88** (2020). https://doi.org/10.1016/j.trd.2020.102558
43. Govik, L.: Digital platforms for sharing and booking electrical vehicle charging infrastructure. Int. J. Sustain. Transp. **18**(9), 777–790 (2024). https://doi.org/10.1080/15568318.2024.2407139
44. Björklund, M., Gillström, H., Stahre, F.: Resilient electrified freight transport: disruptions and mitigation strategies. Cleaner Logist. Supply Chain. **14** (2025). https://doi.org/10.1016/j.clscn.2025.100211

Sustainability in Critical Raw Materials for Energy Transition: Identification of Sustainability Indicators and Categories Through a Systematic Literature Review

Francisco Encina-Mansilla(✉) and Christian Thies

Resilient and Sustainable Operations and Supply Chain Management Group, Hamburg University of Technology, Hamburg, Germany
francisco.encina@tuhh.de

Abstract. The global energy transition is driving rapidly increasing demand for critical raw materials (CRMs) used in electric mobility, renewable energy generation, and other low-carbon production systems. While these materials are essential for decarbonization, their extraction and supply chains are associated with significant environmental and social impacts and are characterized by high geopolitical and supply risks. At the same time, sustainability-related evidence for CRM supply chains remains fragmented across studies, indicators, and assessment approaches, limiting comparability and integration into manufacturing-oriented decision support. This paper addresses this gap by identifying and structuring sustainability indicators for CRM supply chains. A systematic literature review of peer-reviewed studies is conducted following a PRISMA-based selection process. Based on this analysis, the study derives a harmonized set of core environmental and social indicators and examines how their relevance varies across materials, with a particular focus on lithium, cobalt, and neodymium. The results show that environmental indicators are more mature and consistently operationalized than social indicators, while material-specific differences remain important, particularly for lithium, cobalt, and neodymium. Building on these findings, the paper proposes a two-layer indicator framework consisting of a general baseline enabling cross-material comparability and a material-specific layer capturing dominant sustainability hotspots. The framework provides a structured and reusable basis for data extraction, model development, life cycle assessment, supply risk analysis, and decision-support for sustainable manufacturing and CRM supply chains.

Keywords: Critical Raw Materials · Sustainable Manufacturing · Supply Chain Management · Sustainability Assessment · Systematic Literature Review

1 Introduction

In 2019, the European Commission launched the European Green Deal, setting the goal of achieving climate neutrality in the European Union by 2050 [1]. Reaching this target requires the rapid expansion of clean energy technologies such as wind turbines, solar

Published by Springer Nature Switzerland AG 2027
G. Pezzotta et al. (Eds.): APMS 2026, IFIP AICT 808, pp. 181–194, 2027.
https://doi.org/10.1007/978-3-032-38594-9_13

photovoltaic systems, and electric vehicles. These technologies, however, rely heavily on critical raw materials (CRMs), making secure access to these resources essential for sectors including clean energy, mobility, defence, and digital technologies [2].

Compared to fossil-based systems, low-carbon technologies are significantly more material-intensive, which shifts the energy system from being fuel-based to resource-based and increases global demand for minerals [3, 4]. This growing demand is especially evident for materials such as lithium, cobalt, nickel, and rare earth elements. Their supply chains are highly concentrated in a small number of countries, which increases exposure to geopolitical risks, trade restrictions, and price volatility [3, 4]. For the European Union, this creates a strategic vulnerability, as it relies heavily on imports while also facing environmental and social risks linked to extraction and processing activities [5].

Within this policy context, the EU has further specified how critical raw materials are identified and monitored. In the 2023 assessment, 87 materials were evaluated based on Economic Importance (EI) and Supply Risk (SR), of which 34 were classified as critical [6]. A smaller subset, referred to as Strategic Raw Materials (SRMs), is considered particularly important for the EU's green, digital, defence, and space sectors and for strengthening Europe's resilience and strategic autonomy. An overview of CRMs and SRMs is provided in Fig. 1.

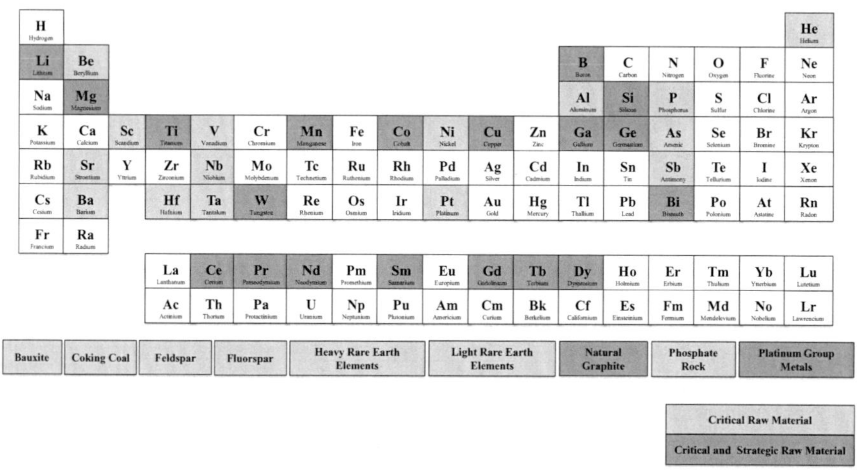

Fig. 1. Overview of CRM and SRM based on Annex I (Strategic raw materials) and Annex II (Critical raw materials) of Regulation (EU) 2024/1252 of the European Parliament and of the Council (2024)

To address these challenges, the European Union adopted the Critical Raw Materials Act (CRMA) in 2024. This regulation aims to ensure a secure and sustainable supply of CRMs by strengthening domestic capacities, diversifying supply sources, and promoting recycling and circularity across value chains [7, 8]. These developments reflect a broader understanding of resource criticality that includes not only economic factors but also geopolitical, environmental, and social dimensions [9].

At the same time, new digital tools such as Digital Product Passports (DPPs) are being introduced to improve transparency and traceability in CRM-intensive supply chains. The Battery Passport is one example, aiming to provide structured lifecycle data to support sustainability reporting and traceability in the electric mobility sector [10]. However, despite these policy and technological developments, sustainability data related to CRM supply chains remain fragmented and difficult to access. In particular, social aspects are still underrepresented, with gaps in stakeholder coverage, indicator selection, and data availability [11]. These limitations hinder effective life cycle assessment (LCA) and supply risk analysis, especially in regions where weak governance, environmental degradation, and geopolitical instability increase supply risks [3].

Against this background, existing research provides extensive insights into sustainability impacts and risks in critical raw material value chains. However, the underlying evidence remains fragmented across studies, with considerable variation in how indicators are defined, selected, and operationalized. This limits comparability across materials and contexts and constrains the integration of sustainability considerations into manufacturing-oriented decision support, life cycle assessment, and supply risk analysis.

To address this gap, this paper presents a systematic literature review of peer-reviewed studies on sustainability in critical raw material supply chains. The objective is to identify and structure the sustainability indicators most consistently applied in literature and to analyze how their relevance varies across materials. Based on this analysis, the paper derives a harmonized set of core environmental and social indicators and proposes a two-layer indicator framework consisting of a general baseline for cross-material comparability and a material-specific layer capturing dominant sustainability hotspots. This structured approach provides a reusable basis for data extraction, modelling, and decision-support applications in sustainable manufacturing and CRM supply chain management.

Existing sustainability assessment approaches often remain either too generic, applying similar indicators across different CRMs, or too case specific, focusing on individual materials without supporting broader comparison. The proposed framework addresses this limitation by combining harmonized indicators with material-sensitive assessment criteria derived from the literature.

2 Methodology

2.1 Preliminary Scoping Phase: Development of the Data Extraction Matrix

Before starting the systematic literature review, a preliminary scoping review was carried out as part of a broader umbrella analysis of review papers on critical raw materials (CRMs) and the energy transition. The aim of this phase was to examine how sustainability dimensions were addressed in existing review studies, identify the most frequently discussed sustainability themes, and support the development of the preliminary data extraction matrix. Six key review papers were analyzed in this phase (see Table 1). Using an adapted methodology based on Thies et al. [12], the papers were reviewed to identify publication trends, relevant journals, and the main technologies, sustainability dimensions, and indicators discussed in literature.

Table 1. Scoping Papers for Review Database

	Document title	Authors	Year	Source
1	Critical minerals for electric vehicles: A telecoupling review.	Agusdinata, D. B., Eakin, H., & Liu, W.	2022	Environmental Research Letters, 17(1), 013005 [13].
2	Minerals and energy interface in energy transition pathways: A systematic and comprehensive review	Srivastava, N., & Kumar, A.	2022	Journal of Cleaner Production, 376, 134354 [14].
3	Critical elements for a successful energy transition: A systematic review	Kamran, M., Raugei, M., & Hutchinson, A.	2023	Renewable and Sustainable Energy Transition, 4.0 [15].
4	Critical mineral mining in the energy transition: A systematic review of environmental, social, and governance risks and opportunities	Carr-Wilson, S., Pattanayak, S. K., & Weinthal, E	2024	Energy Research and Social Science, 116.0 [16].
5	Low-carbon transition risks in the energy sector: A systematic	Sun J., Yang, Y., & Zhou, P.	2024	Environmental Research Letters, 17(1), 013005 [17].
6	S-LCA of lithium mining in Chile and its potential impacts on water and the local community	Roche, L.; Link, A.; Marinova, S.; Coroama, V.; Finkbeiner, M.	2024	International Journal of Life Cycle Assessment [18]

This initial step helped clarify how sustainability impacts and issues were addressed in review-based studies and provided valuable insight into the key sustainability aspects discussed in the literature. The scoping phase showed that sustainability was widely discussed in the literature, but the way indicators or analytical categories were defined, selected, and structured varied across studies. Some papers explicitly referred to established frameworks or organizing approaches, such as UNEP-based S-LCA guidance, ESG framing, or other conceptual structures, while others used different approaches or provided less detail on the basis for indicator selection and organization. To support a more consistent organization of the extracted information, established international frameworks were used, including the UNEP Guidelines for Social Life Cycle Assessment (S-LCA) [19], the Global Guidance for Life Cycle Impact Assessment Indicators and Methods (GLAM) [20], and the JRC Environmental Footprint (EF) 3.1 method [21]. These frameworks provided the conceptual basis for defining sustainability dimensions, impact categories, and indicators. By combining elements from these sources, a preliminary data extraction matrix was developed to support the systematic identification of social and environmental indicators in literature. This scoping phase established the methodological basis for the subsequent systematic literature review and indicator selection process.

The following presents the main characteristics of the review database:

- **Environmental Sustainability (GLAM/EF JRC):** Climate change, particulate matter (PM2.5), ozone depletion, ionising radiation (human health), photochemical ozone formation, water use and scarcity, water-related human health, land use and biodiversity, soil quality (SOC), acidification, eutrophication terrestrial, eutrophication freshwater, eutrophication marine, human toxicity (cancer and non-cancer), ecotoxicity (freshwater), resource use minerals and metals, resource use fossil, waste* and other environmental categories or indicators.
- **Social Sustainability (UNEP):** Freedom of association, child labour, fair salary, working hours, forced labour, equal opportunity and non-discrimination, health and safety, social benefits and security, technology (TE), employment relationship, sexual harassment, smallholders, access to material resources, access to immaterial resources, delocalization and migration, cultural heritage, safe and healthy living conditions, Indigenous rights, community engagement, local employment, secure living conditions, fair competition, promoting social responsibility, supplier relationships, intellectual property rights, wealth distribution, feedback mechanisms, consumer privacy, transparency, end-of-life responsibility, public commitments to sustainability, economic development, prevention of armed conflicts, technology development, corruption, ethical treatment of animals, poverty alleviation, education in local community, health issues for child consumers, marketing to children and others social sustainability categories or indicators.
- **Country:** Countries discussed in the reviewed Papers.
- **Topic:** Geopolitics (GE), economics (EC), sustainability (SU), risk (RI), governance (GO), supply chain (SC).
- **Supply Chain Phase:** Mining – Upstream, Refining – Midstream, Downstream – Manufacturing and End-of-life & Circularity.
- **Technology:** Batteries, solar PV, wind turbines, electric vehicles (EVs), hydro, nuclear, electricity networks, geothermal, carbon capture, heat pumps, fuel cells, hydrogen, PV inverters and energy transition.
- **EU CRMs List:** Antimony, arsenic, baryte, bauxite, beryllium, bismuth, boron/borate, cobalt, coking coal, copper, feldspar, fluorspar, gallium, germanium, hafnium, heavy rare earth elements, helium, light rare earth elements, lithium, magnesium, manganese, natural graphite, nickel, niobium, phosphate rock, phosphorus, platinum group metals, scandium, silicon metal, strontium, tantalum, titanium metal, tungsten, vanadium, neodymium.

2.2 Systematic Literature Review

This systematic literature review was conducted following the methodological approach proposed by Sauer and Seuring [22], which is widely applied in sustainability and supply chain research. This approach provides structured guidance for identifying, evaluating, and synthesizing relevant academic literature. The aim was to select studies that meaningfully address critical raw materials (CRMs) within the context of the energy transition.

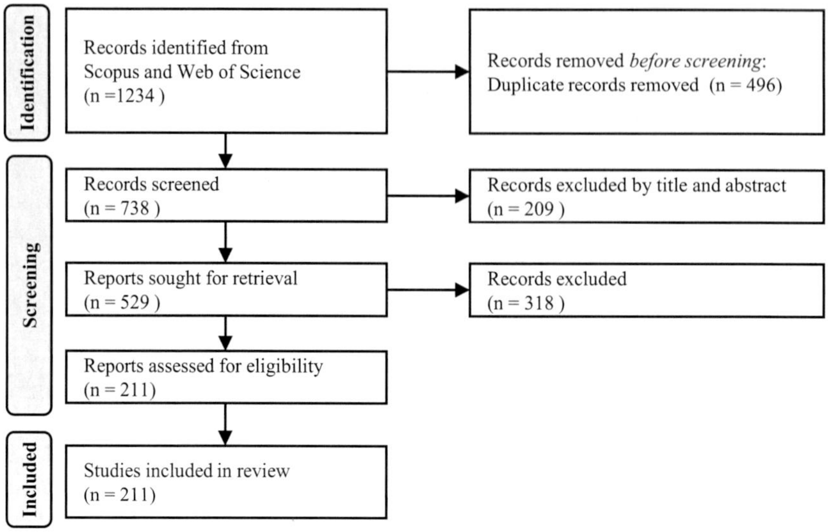

Fig. 2. Adapted PRISMA [23] flow diagram for the SLR

The literature search was performed using Scopus and Web of Science, two well-established academic databases with broad coverage of peer-reviewed research. The search identified 1,234 records in total, including 635 records from Scopus and 599 records from Web of Science (see Fig. 2). The search strings and keywords used in the literature review are presented in Table 2. After removing 496 duplicate records, 738 unique studies remained for further screening. In order to transparently document the screening process and the number of studies at each stage, the study selection followed the reporting structure of the PRISMA [23] Statement. A title and abstract screening was conducted for the 496 studies. During this stage, 209 articles were excluded because they were not related to CRMs or did not address topics relevant to the energy transition.

The remaining 529 studies were then assessed through full-text review. During this phase, predefined exclusion criteria (see Table 3) were applied to ensure relevance and quality. Non-academic sources, non-English publications, studies lacking sustainability considerations (environmental, social, or governance aspects), and purely theoretical studies without practical relevance were excluded. Additional exclusions were applied to remove duplicate publications and studies with an overly narrow technical or chemical focus.

After completing all screening stages, a final set of 211 studies met all inclusion criteria and were included in the systematic literature review. These studies formed the basis for the qualitative and quantitative analyses presented in the subsequent sections.

The Fig. 3 present the annual distribution of articles included in this review from 2019 to 2025. Between 2019 and 2021, only a few studies were published each year. Starting in 2022, the number of papers began to grow quickly. The largest increase happened between 2020 and 2024, showing that researchers are paying more attention to this area. The number of publications in 2025 was lower, but the analysis for this

Table 2. Search strings and keywords used in the systematic literature review

Strings	Keywords used
Critical raw material	TITLE-ABS-KEY ("critical raw material*" OR "critical Material*" OR "critical mineral*" OR "Strategic mineral*" OR "Strategic metal*" OR "critical metal*" OR "strategic material*")
Critical raw materials list of the EU	OR antimony OR arsenic OR bauxite OR alumina OR aluminium OR baryte OR beryllium OR bismuth OR boron OR cobalt OR "coking coal" OR copper OR feldspar OR fluorspar OR gallium OR germanium OR hafnium OR helium OR "rare earth*" OR lithium OR magnesium OR manganese OR graphite OR nickel OR niobium OR phosphate OR phosphorus OR platinum OR "platinum group metals" OR scandium OR "silicon metal" OR strontium OR tantalum OR titanium OR tungsten OR vanadium OR neodymium OR praseodymium OR terbium OR dysprosium OR gadolinium OR samarium OR cerium) AND
Sustainability, social environmental	("sustain*" OR "social*" OR "environ*") AND
Energy transition	"Energy Transition*" OR "clean Energy Technolog*" OR "low-carbon transition"

Table 3. Exclusion Criteria

Category	Exclusion criteria
Source type	Blogs, news articles, editorials, unverified web content
Language	Non-English publications
Relevance	Not related to CRMs in the context of energy transition
Lifecycle stage	Focus only on end-use consumption or post-use behavior
Sustainability scope	Lacks ESG (Environmental, Social, Governance) indicators or assessment
Time frame	Published before 2010 (unless foundational and widely cited)
Practical relevance	Purely theoretical/speculative with no decision-making relevance
Duplication	Duplicate sources (e.g., preprints later published or reissued reports)
Technical/chemical focus	Focused only on chemistry, lab extraction methods, or process engineering

review was done at the end of March. Therefore, it is not clear from the data whether the number of studies will continue to increase during the rest of the year.

Out of the 211 papers reviewed, 115 (about 55%) are published in just 15 main journals, out of a total of 96 sources. The most frequent are Resources, Conservation and Recycling (16 papers), Extractive Industries and Society (14), and Journal of Cleaner Production (12). Other important journals include Resources Policy and Sustainability (Switzerland) (11), followed by Energy Research and Social Science (9), Environmental Science and Technology (8), and Energies (7). This concentration shows that research on sustainability and critical raw materials is primarily discussed within a few leading journals that shape the main directions of the field.

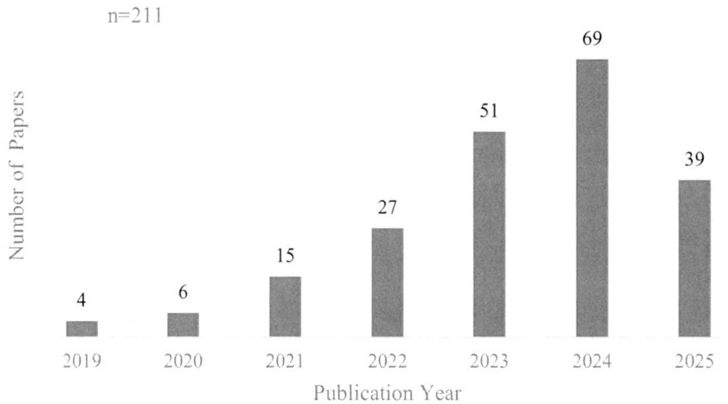

Fig. 3. Distribution of reviewed articles by publication year

The word cloud presented in Fig. 4 provides an overview of the dominant themes appearing across the reviewed literature. A number of keywords can be singled out, for instance, energy transition, life cycle assessment, critical minerals, lithium, and sustainability. The fact that these words feature so prominently is indicative of the reviewed papers focusing mainly on the sustainability aspects of using metal and minerals as the core of energy systems instead of just taking technologies or materials separately. Besides these essential terms, the word cloud still has words like mining, circular economy, recycling, and resources. This suggests that besides energy, related applications, there is also a significant interest in material supply chains and end of life issues. So, the word cloud is instrumental in framing the analysis as it lays out the initial sketch of the main themes surfaced in the reviewed studies.

The keyword co-occurrence network illustrate in Fig. 5, shows the connections between the related topics in the literature. Energy transition is the most prominent and central keyword, appearing in combination with a wide range of associated terms. Several of these connections relate to mining and critical minerals, highlighting the material dimension of the energy transition as a major focus within the literature. In particular, many studies address resource extraction and material availability, while lithium and associated minerals receive especially strong attention.

Following the study selection process, the sustainability indicators identified in the selected studies were grouped according to recurring environmental, social, governance, and lifecycle related themes. Indicators referring to similar sustainability aspects but

Fig. 4. Word Cloud of Most Relevant Keywords in the Reviewed Papers

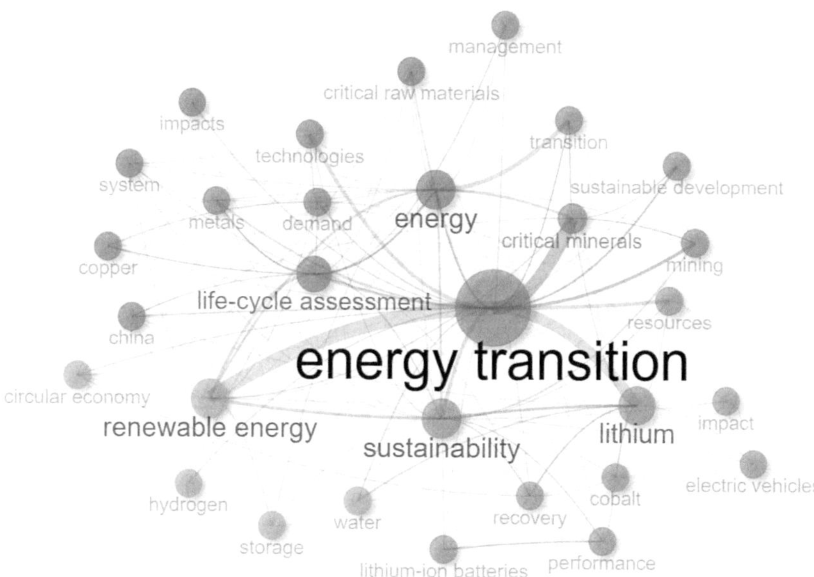

Fig. 5. Keyword Co-occurrence Network

using different terminology were consolidated to improve comparability, while material-specific indicators were retained where the literature identified distinct sustainability concerns associated with particular CRMs or lifecycle stages.

3 Results and Discussion

3.1 Analysis of SLR Data and Identification of Indicators

The analysis of the systematic literature review (SLR), as structured in the review database, shows that sustainability in critical raw material supply chains is addressed through many indicators, but only a limited subset is applied consistently across the coded records. Environmental indicators are used more frequently and more systematically than social indicators, reflecting the strong influence of life cycle assessment approaches. A stable environmental core emerges: climate change dominates, followed by mineral and metal resource use, water use and scarcity, and land use and biodiversity; human toxicity also appears relatively often. Other impact categories (e.g., acidification, particulate matter, fossil resource use) are used less regularly and therefore contribute less to cross-study comparability.

Social indicators show a different pattern. They are more unevenly applied and form a weaker shared core across studies. The most recurring social themes focus on communities and governance, including community engagement, public commitments to sustainability, access to material resources, and indigenous rights, often alongside local employment, economic development, and conflict-related risks. Many labour-rights indicators appear far less consistently, and several downstream-facing topics are absent from the coded corpus. Overall, the SLR suggests that fragmentation reflects differences in indicator selection and data availability: a small set of recurring indicators supports comparison and systematic extraction, while many additional indicators remain case specific. The predominance of environmental indicators can be explained by the maturity of life cycle assessment methods, the availability of standardized environmental assessment frameworks, and the existence of more accessible environmental databases. In contrast, social indicators remain more difficult to quantify because they are highly context dependent, less harmonized across studies, and often limited by data availability and supply chain transparency (Table 4).

Table 4. Core Environmental and Social Sustainability Indicators

Environmental indicators	Social indicators
Climate change	Community engagement
Resource use - minerals & metals	Public commitments to sustainability
Water use & scarcity	Access to material resources
Land use & biodiversity	Indigenous rights
Human toxicity - cancer & noncancer	Economic development

The indicator framework is therefore intentionally organised in two layers. The first layer is a fixed baseline set used for cross-material comparability and consistent screening. The second layer captures material-specific emphasis, allowing the framework to reflect the different sustainability hotspots that dominate for different CRMs. In downstream use, the baseline layer supports consistent comparison across materials and countries, while the material-specific layer supports more targeted interpretation, prioritisation and decision-support in relation to particular supply chains.

3.2 Analysis of Lithium, Cobalt, and Neodymium

Across the full SLR, the same baseline set of environmental and social indicators was applied to all records. When the database is examined by material, the same indicators recur, but their relative importance is shifted in a consistent way.

For lithium, the environmental discussion is centred on climate change and resource use for minerals and metals, and it is repeatedly made concrete through water use and scarcity and land use and biodiversity. On the social side, lithium papers lean toward community-facing indicators, especially access to material resources, together with signals that reflect how projects affect local people and local rights. In practice, lithium is most often operationalised through a water, land, and community pathway, where the key sustainability tensions are framed around local limits and local impacts.

The focus of cobalt remains broadly similar, in the environmental, again centred on climate change and mineral resource use, with water and land concerns also present. The social profile shifts more clearly toward workplace and labour risks. In the cobalt subset, health and safety and child labour stand out as the strongest recurring social signals, while corruption appears as a governance-related concern.

For neodymium, the evidence base is smaller and therefore less stable, but the subset generally keeps climate change and mineral resource use as core themes and adds broader resource and energy concerns. Social indicators appear more lightly and tend to be expressed through general governance or community topics, rather than the specific labour-risk framing that characterises cobalt.

The findings highlight the importance of material-sensitive sustainability assessment approaches, particularly in the context of battery value chains. Although the reviewed materials contribute to the energy transition, the literature shows that their sustainability priorities differ consistently across environmental, social, and governance dimensions. These differences support the need for sustainability frameworks that combine harmonized baseline indicators with material-sensitive assessment criteria capable of reflecting the distinct sustainability concerns associated with different CRMs and lifecycle stages. The proposed framework may support practical applications in sustainability monitoring, ESG assessment, decision support, and policy-oriented evaluation of CRM supply chains. In addition, the increasing implementation of Digital Product Passports and Battery Passports may further increase the need for harmonized and traceable sustainability information across material supply chains. The framework may therefore contribute to future reporting, traceability, and assessment systems within battery and energy transition contexts (Table 5).

Table 5. Li-Co-Nd Indicator Emphasis

Dimension	Indicator	Lithium	Cobalt	Neodymium
Environmental	Climate change	●	●	●
Environmental	Resource use - minerals & metals	●	●	●
Environmental	Water use & scarcity	●	●	●
Environmental	Land use & biodiversity	●	●	●

(continued)

Table 5. (*continued*)

Dimension	Indicator	Lithium	Cobalt	Neodymium
Environmental	Human toxicity - cancer & non-cancer	●	●	◐
Social	Community engagement	●	●	●
Social	Indigenous rights	●	●	●
Social	Public commitments to sustainability	●	●	◐
Social	Access to material resources	●	●	○
Social	Economic development	◐	◐	●

4 Conclusion

This paper presented a systematic literature review of sustainability indicators in critical raw material (CRM) supply chains in the context of the energy transition. Based on the analysis of 211 peer reviewed studies, the results show that environmental indicators are more clearly defined and more consistently applied across the literature. This is mainly linked to the widespread use of life cycle assessment approaches. In contrast, social indicators are less consistent, with differences in scope, data availability, and methods.

The review identified a stable set of key environmental indicators, including climate change, resource use, water use, and land use. Social indicators are more often related to community impacts, governance, and labour conditions. At the same time, the results show that sustainability priorities vary across materials. In particular, lithium, cobalt, and neodymium present different sustainability priority, which means that some indicators require more attention depending on the material.

The findings also show that sustainability is widely discussed in the literature, but the way indicators are defined and structured is not consistent across all studies. Some papers clearly apply established frameworks, such as the JRC Environmental Footprint (EF) 3.1 method, while others use different approaches or provide less detail. This highlights the need for a more consistent and transparent way to organize sustainability related information. To address this, the paper proposes a two layer indicator framework. The first layer is a general baseline that supports comparison across different materials. The second layer includes material specific indicators that reflect the main sustainability risks of each material. This structure helps improve data consistency while still capturing important differences between materials.

Overall, this study provides a structured and reusable baseline of sustainability indicators that supports future work in data extraction, modelling, and decision support applications in sustainable manufacturing and CRM supply chain management. While the broader research project also includes data extraction activities, this paper focuses specifically on the identification and structuring of sustainability indicators to support future assessment and data extraction processes. The results contribute to improving transparency and comparability in sustainability assessment and support the integration of sustainability into manufacturing-oriented decision making.

The proposed framework may also support future traceability and reporting systems, including Digital Product Passports and Battery Passports, by providing a more structured and harmonized approach to sustainability information across CRM supply chains. It may further contribute to sustainability assessment, risk assessment, modelling, and indicator selection processes in manufacturing and supply chain decision making.

Acknowledgments. This study is part of the project "MAnufacturing as a service And Supply chain predictIVE TWIN for critical raw materials", which is funded by the European Union's HORIZON-CL4-2023-TWIN-TRANSITION-01-07 Programme under the grant agreement No. 101138334.

Disclosure of Interests. The authors have no competing interests to declare that are relevant to the content of this article.

References

1. European Commission: The European Green Deal COM(2019) 640 Final (2019). https://eur-lex.europa.eu/legal-content/EN/TXT/HTML/?uri=CELEX:52019DC0640
2. European Commission: Directorate-General for Internal Market, Industry, Entrepreneurship and SMEs: Critical Raw Materials for Strategic Technologies and Sectors in the EU: A Foresight Study. Publications Office (2020) https://data.europa.eu/doi/10.2873/58081
3. UN-Energy: UN-Energy Policy Brief: Aligning Critical Raw Materials Development with Sustainable Development. UN-Energy (2023) https://unece.org/sustainable-energy/publications/un-energy-policy-brief-aligning-critical-raw-materials-development
4. International Energy Agency: IEA: The Role of Critical Minerals in Clean Energy Transitions. IEA, Paris (2021) https://www.iea.org/reports/the-role-of-critical-minerals-in-clean-energy-transitions
5. University of Cambridge Institute for Sustainability Leadership (CISL) and the Wuppertal Institute: Embracing Circularity: A Pathway for Strengthening the Critical Raw Materials Act. CLG Europe, Cambridge, UK (2023)
6. European Commission: Study on the Critical Raw Materials for the EU 2023 - Final Report. European Commission (2023). https://doi.org/10.2873/725585
7. European Parliament, & Council of European Union: Regulation (EU) 2024/1252 of the European Parliament and of the Council of 11 April 2024 establishing a framework for ensuring a secure and sustainable supply of critical raw materials and amending Regulations (EU) No 168/2013, (EU) 2018/858, (EU) 2018/1724 and (EU) 2019/1020Text with EEA relevance, European Parliament, & Council of European Union (2024). http://data.europa.eu/eli/reg/2024/1252/oj
8. Hool, A., Helbig, C., Wierink, G.: Challenges and opportunities of the European critical raw materials act. Miner. Econ. **37**, 661–668 (2024). https://doi.org/10.1007/s13563-023-00394-y
9. Hofmann, M., Hofmann, H., Hagelüken, C., Hool, A.: Critical raw materials: a perspective from the materials science community. Sustain. Mater. Technol. **17**, e00074 (2018). https://doi.org/10.1016/j.susmat.2018.e00074
10. Battery Pass Consortium: Battery Passport Content Guidance - Executive Summary. Battery Pass Consortium (2023) https://thebatterypass.eu/assets/images/content-guidance/pdf/2023-Battery_Passport_Content_Guidance_Executive_Summary.pdf
11. Zafar, I., Stojceska, V., Tassou, S.: Social sustainability assessments of industrial level solar energy: a systematic review. Renew. Sust. Energ. Rev. **189**, 113962 (2024). https://doi.org/10.1016/j.rser.2023.113962

12. Thies, C., Kieckhäfer, K., Spengler, T.S., Sodhi, M.S.: Operations research for sustainability assessment of products: a review. Eur. J. Oper. Res. **274**(1), 1–21 (2019). https://doi.org/10.1016/j.ejor.2018.04.039
13. Agusdinata, D.B., Eakin, H., Liu, W.: Critical minerals for electric vehicles: a telecoupling review. Environ. Res. Lett. **17**(1), 013005 (2022). https://doi.org/10.1088/1748-9326/ac4763
14. Srivastava, N., Kumar, A.: Minerals and energy interface in energy transition pathways: a systematic and comprehensive review. J. Clean. Prod. **376**, 134354 (2022). https://doi.org/10.1016/j.jclepro.2022.134354
15. Kamran, M., Raugei, M., Hutchinson, A.: Critical elements for a successful energy transition: a systematic review. Renew. Sustain. Energ. Transit. **4** (2023). https://doi.org/10.1016/j.rset.2023.100068
16. Carr-Wilson, S., Pattanayak, S.K., Weinthal, E.: Critical mineral mining in the energy transition: a systematic review of environmental, social, and governance risks and opportunities. Energy Res. Soc. Sci. **116** (2024). https://doi.org/10.1016/j.erss.2024.103672
17. Sun, J., Yang, Y., Zhou, P.: Low-carbon transition risks in the energy sector: a systematic review. Sustainable Prod. Consumption. **50**, 115–127 (2024). https://doi.org/10.1016/j.spc.2024.07.025
18. Roche, L., Link, A., Marinova, S., Coroama, V., Finkbeiner, M.: S-LCA of lithium mining in Chile and its potential impacts on water and the local community. Int. J. Life Cycle Assess. (2024). https://doi.org/10.1007/s11367-024-02378-8
19. UNEP: In: Benoît Norris, C., Traverso, M., Neugebauer, S., Ekener, E., Schaubroeck, T., Russo Garrido, S., Berger, M., Valdivia, S., Lehmann, A., Finkbeiner, M., Arcese, G. (eds.) Guidelines for Social Life Cycle Assessment of Products and Organizations 2020. United Nations Environment Programme (2020) https://www.lifecycleinitiative.org/wp-content/uploads/2021/01/Guidelines-for-Social-Life-Cycle-Assessment-of-Products-and-Organizations-2020-22.1.21sml.pdf
20. UNEP/SETAC Life Cycle Initiative: Global Guidance for Life Cycle Impact Assessment Indicators. Volume 1: Framework, Goal and Scope Definition. United Nations Environment Programme (2016) https://www.lifecycleinitiative.org/training-resources/global-guidance-lcia-indicators-v-1/
21. Andreasi Bassi, S. et al.: Updated Characterisation and Normalisation Factors for the Environmental Footprint 3.1 Method. Publications Office of the European Union, Luxembourg (2023). https://doi.org/10.2760/798894
22. Sauer, P.C., Seuring, S.: How to conduct systematic literature reviews in management research: a guide in 6 steps and 14 decisions. Rev. Manag. Sci. **17**(5), 1899–1933 (2023). https://doi.org/10.1007/s11846-023-00668-3
23. Page, M.J. et al.: The PRISMA 2020 statement: an updated guideline for reporting systematic reviews. BMJ. **372**, n71 (2021). https://doi.org/10.1136/bmj.n71. http://creativecommons.org/licenses/by/4.0/

From Aging-Aware Operation to Circular Value Retention: A Circular Battery Digital Twin for Electric Bus Fleets

Anas Fattouh(✉), Erik Dahlquist, and Koteshwar Chirumalla

DigiCircle Research Group, Mälardalen University, Eskilstuna, Sweden
anas.fattouh@mdu.se

Abstract. The electrification of public transport has introduced new challenges in managing lithium-ion battery degradation, operational efficiency, and lifecycle sustainability. While battery digital twins (BDTs) have emerged as a promising solution for monitoring and prediction, most existing approaches remain limited to short-term state estimation and do not exploit lifecycle data for circular decision-making. This paper proposes a Circular Battery Digital Twin (CBDT) framework that integrates aging-aware operation, predictive lifecycle modeling, and circular value retention within a unified architecture. The framework combines real-world operational, environmental, and maintenance data to continuously calibrate a semi-empirical degradation model supporting multiple use cases, including route reassignment and second-life assessment. The framework is demonstrated using a multi-year dataset from a real electric bus operating in Sweden. The bus operates with a 60 kWh LFP battery pack and relies exclusively on pantograph charging at terminus stops. The results show that CBDT enables consistent degradation estimation, supports cost-aware operational decisions, and provides a pathway toward circular battery management. The framework successfully identified an optimal reassignment threshold at 70% load that extends operational life by 45%. The study demonstrates how integrating multi-source data and lifecycle intelligence enables the transition from reactive battery management to proactive and circular decision-making.

Keywords: Battery Digital Twin · Electric Bus Fleet · Lithium-Ion Battery Degradation · State of Health · Remaining Useful Life · Second-Life Batteries · Circular Value Retention · Route Reassignment · Uncertainty Quantification

1 Introduction and Related Work

The global transition toward sustainable transportation has accelerated the adoption of electric buses in urban mobility systems. These vehicles offer significant environmental benefits by reducing greenhouse gas emissions and improving air quality [1]. However, the performance, reliability, and economic viability of electric bus fleets are strongly dependent on the behavior and degradation of lithium-ion batteries, which represent a major portion of the total cost of ownership [2]. Over time, batteries experience capacity

Published by Springer Nature Switzerland AG 2027
G. Pezzotta et al. (Eds.): APMS 2026, IFIP AICT 808, pp. 195–210, 2027.
https://doi.org/10.1007/978-3-032-38594-9_14

fade and internal resistance growth due to complex interactions between electrochemical processes, temperature variations, and operational conditions [3]. These degradation mechanisms not only reduce vehicle range but also increase operational uncertainty and maintenance costs [4].

1.1 Battery Degradation Modeling

Battery degradation models have evolved significantly over the past decade, ranging from simple empirical equations to advanced physics-informed and data-driven approaches. Pelletier et al. [5] developed empirical relationships between cycle life and depth of discharge (DoD) and C-rate, providing tractable models for transportation applications. Maheshwari [6] contributed to modeling, aging, and optimal operation of lithium-ion batteries, while Ahmadian et al. [7] explored resistance growth as a function of state of charge (SoC) and degradation over time. Lam and Bauer [8] proposed a practical capacity fading model for lithium iron phosphate (LFP) batteries in electric vehicles, based on extensive cycling experiments with current profiles containing regenerative braking. More recently, Wildfeuer et al. [9] conducted teardown analysis and characterization of commercial lithium-ion batteries, providing open-source datasets for advanced algorithms. Zhang et al. [10] experimentally studied degradation characteristics of LFP and nickel manganese cobalt (NMC) batteries during overcharging at low temperatures. Birkl et al. [2] presented degradation diagnostics for lithium-ion cells, identifying three primary degradation modes: loss of lithium inventory, loss of active positive electrode material, and loss of active negative electrode material. Waldmann et al. [3] investigated temperature-dependent aging mechanisms, revealing two distinct regimes: below 25 °C where lithium plating dominates, and above 25 °C where cathode degeneration and SEI layer growth accelerate.

Despite these advances, most studies focus on isolated aging phenomena rather than integrating them into broader decision-making frameworks. Berecibar et al. [11] provided a critical review of state of health (SoH) estimation methods, noting that accurate and reliable SoH estimation remains challenging for real applications. The authors emphasized that combining multiple approaches may yield better results than any single method. A key gap is the absence of degradation models that are simultaneously calibrated from real-world fleet data and connected to circular economy decisions.

1.2 Digital Twins for Battery Systems

The concept of the digital twin has gained significant attention as a means of bridging the gap between physical systems and digital models. Singh et al. [12] presented an implementation approach for battery digital twins, identifying functionalities such as degradation evaluation, usage optimization, and second-life application possibility. Renold and Kathayat [13] provided a comprehensive review of machine learning, deep learning, and digital twin data-driven approaches in battery health prediction for electric vehicles. Li et al. [14] proposed an intelligent digital twin model for battery management systems using back propagation neural networks, achieving over 95% prediction accuracy. Naseri et al. [15] conducted a comprehensive review of digital twin applications for electric vehicle battery systems, identifying use cases, requirements, and platforms, and highlighted that digital twins enable real-time connectivity, intelligence, and analytical capabilities for batteries.

However, existing digital twin implementations for batteries are predominantly focused on operational aspects such as state estimation and fault diagnosis [14]. They do not fully address lifecycle management or circular economy considerations. Table 1 summarizes the key distinctions between representative existing BDT approaches and the proposed CBDT, highlighting the contributions of this work.

Table 1. Comparison of existing Battery Digital Twin approaches with the proposed CBDT.

Feature	State-estimation BDTs [14, 15]	Lifecycle BDTs [12]	CBDT (this work)
Primary focus	Real-time SoH, SoC	Degradation prediction	Full lifecycle, circularity
Data sources	Electrical signals	Electrical + limited thermal	Operational, thermal, maintenance
Decision time horizon	Short-term (seconds–minutes)	Medium-term (months)	Long-term (years)
Decision scope	Operational	Operational + some tactical	Operational + Strategic (demonstrated); Tactical (architectural)
Circular economy integration	None	None	Second-life (demonstrated); remanufacturing, recycling (architectural)
Calibration approach	Lab-parameterized	Lab + field	Field first + literature
Validation	Lab/synthetic data	Partial real-world	Demonstration on multi-year fleet data (74 operational days)

1.3 Fleet-Level Decision Support

Several researchers have developed methods and frameworks to support decision-making in transport applications at various levels. At the operational level, Zhang et al. [16] researched energy consumption laws and charging strategies for electric buses based on real operation data from 48 electric buses, proposing a multi-condition two-level nested optimization method. Wang et al. [17] developed a real-time synchronous dispatching and recharging strategy for multi-line electric bus systems using deep reinforcement learning.

At the tactical level, Wang et al. [18] proposed optimal scheduling for electric bus fleets based on dynamic programming considering battery capacity fade, demonstrating a 20% reduction in battery replacement investments. Schmidt et al. [19] developed decision support strategies for commercial fleet electrification, analyzing 81 empirical mobility patterns and providing a decision mechanism for assessing smart charging potential.

At the strategic level, Aishwarya et al. [20] conducted a systematic review of sustainability integration across electric vehicle battery lifecycles, identifying 10 major challenges and 8 core technologies supporting circular economy principles. Koroma et al. [21] performed life cycle assessment of battery electric vehicles, examining implications of future electricity mix and different battery end-of-life management strategies.

1.4 Research Gap and Contribution

Despite the growing body of literature, a critical gap remains: the lack of integration between aging-aware operation, data-driven calibration, and circular value retention within a single digital twin framework. Most studies treat degradation modeling, operational optimization, and end-of-life decisions as separate problems without considering their interdependencies. Furthermore, existing BDTs (as summarized in Table 1) do not incorporate circular economy considerations and rely predominantly on laboratory-calibrated parameters rather than real-world operational data. In the context of electric bus fleets operating under challenging conditions, such as high-rate pantograph charging or extreme climates, this gap is particularly significant.

This paper addresses the gap by proposing a Circular Battery Digital Twin (CBDT) that extends traditional digital twin concepts to include lifecycle and circular economy dimensions. The research question guiding this work is: *How can a circular battery digital twin that integrates degradation-aware updating with lifecycle information to support first-life value retention and second-life transition decisions for electric bus fleets?*

To answer this question, a CBDT framework extending traditional BDT is developed to include circular economy dimensions and fleet-level decision support. Moreover, a data-driven calibration pipeline that continuously estimates degradation model parameters from real-world fleet data is proposed. The framework has been demonstrated using a multi-year dataset from an electric bus in Sweden, covering two distinct use cases and providing insights into how pantograph charging conditions affect the practical applicability of the results.

2 Methodology

2.1 Design Science Research Approach

An iterative Design Science Research (DSR) methodology was employed in the development of the proposed framework, following the approach of Peffers et al. [22]. The DSR process combined a systematic literature review and continuous validation using real-world operational data from a public electric bus service in Sweden. The use case played a central role throughout the research process, serving both as a source of empirical input and as a practical testbed for iterative design and evaluation. This approach ensured both scientific rigor and practical relevance in addressing the challenges of battery degradation and circularity in electric vehicle operations.

2.2 Circular Battery Digital Twin Framework

The CBDT framework is defined as a lifecycle-oriented digital representation that links a physical battery system, logged operational data, executable models, state updates, uncertainty handling, and circular decision services. Battery digital twin literature identifies monitoring, state estimation, prediction, and decision support as central battery DT functions [12, 15]. Circular digital twin literature extends this logic by emphasizing the use of product and lifecycle information to support circular economy decisions such as life extension, reuse, remanufacturing, and recycling [23].

The proposed CBDT framework, therefore, combines three information dimensions across all layers: technical information, economic information, and environmental information. The technical dimension represents battery structure, states, operating conditions, degradation behavior, and model outputs. The economic dimension represents cost, residual value, replacement timing, degradation cost, and second-life value. The environmental dimension represents energy consumption, electricity mix, avoided emissions, material recovery, and lifecycle impacts. This three-dimensional structure is necessary because circular battery decisions are not determined by technical health alone; they also depend on economic feasibility and environmental consequences.

The framework is structured into nine layers. The physical asset layer represents the battery pack, cell/module/pack hierarchy, chemistry, nominal capacity, internal resistance, and BMS constraints. The operational context layer represents the bus or fleet, route profile, duty cycle, charging profile, ambient conditions, and maintenance context. The measurement and data layer represents voltage, current, temperature, SoC, charging events, equivalent full cycles, depth of charge, C-rate, data-quality flags, cost-relevant operational data, and environmental factors. The battery state layer represents SoC, SoH, temperature state, resistance state, remaining usable capacity, remaining useful life, residual value state, and environmental utility. The model layer contains modular technical, economic, and environmental models. The orchestration and synchronization layer coordinates model selection, model initialization, parameter updating, shared states, validation, and cross-layer updates. The scenario and decision-service layer evaluates route reassignment, charging strategy, maintenance planning, RUL forecasting, second-life suitability, economic feasibility, and environmental consequences. The circular lifecycle layer links first-life operation, value retention, second-life assessment, repurposing, recycling, and material recovery. The KPI layer converts technical, economic, and environmental information into decision indicators.

2.3 Circular Battery Digital Twin Architecture

The Circular Battery Digital Twin (CBDT) architecture operationalizes the framework through five functional blocks: physical system and operational context, data acquisition and preprocessing, CBDT core, analytics/simulation/prediction, and decision services. The physical system and operational context define the observable counterpart of the twin, including the electric-bus fleet, battery packs, routes, duty cycles, charging infrastructure, ambient conditions, and maintenance context [4].

The CBDT core consists of an information/state layer, a modular model layer, and a model orchestration/coupling layer. The information/state layer stores shared states such as SoC, SoH, temperature, internal resistance, remaining capacity, and RUL. The model layer may contain equivalent-circuit models, thermal models, degradation models, range/energy models, parameter-evolution models, uncertainty models, economic models, and environmental models. The orchestration layer selects, initializes, and couples the models required by a selected service or scenario [24].

The analytics, simulation, and prediction block uses the CBDT core to support monitoring, state estimation, forecasting, scenario analysis, and uncertainty propagation. The decision-service block translates these outputs into route reassignment, charging strategy assessment, maintenance planning, second-life assessment, and repurpose-or-retire decisions. Feedback loops are part of the architecture as implemented decisions affect future operation and new logged data updates the twin state and identifiable parameters [25].

2.4 Model Stack and Information Model

The general framework includes ECM, thermal, degradation, range/energy, uncertainty, economics, and environmental models. However, the present demonstrator focuses on the degradation-aware pathway as the available dataset supports health-state updating and degradation-oriented decision services more directly than full electro-thermal-ageing co-simulation. This boundary is consistent with battery digital twin implementation studies that treat DTs as modular systems whose models and functions depend on the available data, target use case, and required decision service.

The model stack used in the demonstrator consists of four connected components. First, a semi-empirical degradation model represents capacity-loss or SoH-decline behavior as a function of cycle usage and stress indicators such as equivalent full cycles, depth of charge, temperature, and C-rate. Semi-empirical and empirical degradation models are widely used when computational tractability and operational interpretability are required. Second, a two-phase baseline degradation representation distinguishes early break-in behavior from steady-state degradation, allowing the baseline degradation term to change with accumulated cycling. Third, a Bayesian parameter layer represents uncertain or weakly identifiable parameters as prior distributions when the available data do not provide sufficient excitation for reliable estimation. Fourth, a stochastic RUL and uncertainty layer propagates measurement, parameter, model, and forecast uncertainty into health and remaining-life indicators.

The information model connects the model stack to the CBDT layers. Logged data are transformed into SoC-ceiling indicators, EFC, DoD, C-rate, temperature exposure, route-energy indicators, and data-quality flags. These features update battery states and the identifiable degradation parameters. The updated states and parameter distributions are then used by scenario evaluation to estimate the consequences of route reassignment and second-life transition decisions. The information model therefore links technical battery health, economic value retention, and environmental circularity indicators rather than treating degradation as an isolated engineering calculation.

The model stack is recursive. New logged operation updates the preprocessing layer; the preprocessing layer updates stress indicators and SoH proxies; the model stack updates the battery state and identifiable parameters; the uncertainty layer updates prediction intervals; and the decision services influence future operation. This recursive structure is necessary because battery health prediction from field data depends on continuous updating and because field data may not excite all degradation factors sufficiently for full parameter identification. In the current demonstrator, the degradation-aware pathway represents a partial implementation of the CBDT framework. A complete circular battery digital twin that fully captures electro-thermal-ageing interactions remains a direction for future work.

3 Use Case Demonstration

3.1 Dataset Description and Preprocessing

The use-case demonstration is based on logged electric-bus fleet data for one LFP battery pack operating under real bus-service conditions. The available data include state-of-charge observations, current and voltage-related operation records, battery temperature, route-operation information, charging events, and maintenance-related records. The dataset is used to construct a degradation-aware demonstrator.

The preprocessing step converts raw logged operation into monthly health-update information. Operating days are retained only when the data contains sufficient within-day observations and a non-trivial daily SoC swing. For the considered bus, 74 valid operating days were retained after filtering. The daily SoC swing used in the demonstrator is approximately 19.1 percentage points, corresponding to about 11.46 kWh per day for the corrected 60 kWh pack capacity. This gives an average throughput of approximately 0.191 equivalent full cycles per operating day.

The battery pack is represented as an LFP pack with corrected nominal capacity C_{nom} = 60 kWh. The bus is charged by high-power pantograph charging, and the nominal charging power used in the demonstrator is 400 kW. This gives an effective C-rate charging of 6.67C. The observed temperature interval used in the demonstrator is narrow, approximately 22.5–25.5 °C, and the observed daily depth of cycle is below the high-DoC stress threshold used in the semi-empirical model. Therefore, the dataset supports updating the baseline degradation state and the C-rate-related term more directly than the temperature or depth-of-cycle terms.

The main degradation-state indicator extracted from the available data is a monthly SoC-ceiling proxy. The proxy is used because the logged operational dataset does not provide repeated laboratory-grade capacity tests at each update step. This is a typical challenge in field-data battery prognostics, where partial cycling, incomplete observations, and operational noise must be transformed into health indicators before model correction and decision support.

3.2 Degradation Model and Parameters Update

The proposed CBDT framework was applied to above dataset to demonstrate its capabilities across six use cases. The simulation environment was configured using the calibrated degradation model and the operational data described in Sect. 3.1.

The demonstrator uses a semi-empirical degradation model as the executable degradation component. The model is intentionally interpretable: it separates a baseline degradation term from stress terms associated with depth of cycle, temperature, and C-rate. For interval i, the degradation rate per equivalent full cycle is defined as [26]:

$$\begin{aligned} d_i = {} & \mathrm{SoH}_{\mathrm{base}}(i) + k_{\mathrm{DoC}} \max(0, \mathrm{DoC}_i - 60) \\ & + k_T \max(0, |T_i - 20| - 10) + k_C \max\big(0, C_{\mathrm{rate},i} - 0.5\big) \end{aligned} \tag{1}$$

where d_i is the SoH loss rate per EFC in interval i, $\mathrm{SoH}_{\mathrm{base}}(i)$ is the baseline degradation term, DoC_i is the depth of cycle, T_i is the battery temperature, $C_{rate,i}$ is the charge/discharge rate indicator, and k_{DoC}, k_T, and k_C are stress-sensitivity coefficients. The battery health state is propagated as:

$$\mathrm{SoH}_{i+1} = \mathrm{SoH}_i - d_i\, \mathrm{EFC}_i \tag{2}$$

where EFC_i is the equivalent full cycles accumulated in interval i. In the present dataset, the DoC and temperature stress terms are weakly informative because the observed DoC is below the adopted stress threshold and the temperature range is narrow. Therefore, these coefficients are treated as fixed or prior quantities rather than claimed to be estimated from the bus data. The C-rate term is more relevant because the pantograph charging condition excites the C-rate stress term.

The baseline degradation term is represented with a two-phase structure to distinguish early break-in behavior from later steady-state degradation [27]:

$$\mathrm{SoH}_{\mathrm{base}}(i) = \begin{cases} \mathrm{SoH}_{\mathrm{base,break-in}}, & \mathrm{EFC}_{\mathrm{cum},i} < \mathrm{EFC}^* \\ \mathrm{SoH}_{\mathrm{base,steady}}, & \mathrm{EFC}_{\mathrm{cum},i} \geq \mathrm{EFC}^* \end{cases} \tag{3}$$

where $\mathrm{EFC}_{\mathrm{cum},\,i}$ is cumulative EFC and EFC* is the phase-transition point. In the demonstrator, the transition is anchored at 50 EFC, corresponding to day 262 under the adopted average EFC/day. This structure avoids forcing a single degradation baseline over the whole horizon.

For update window k, the SoC-ceiling health proxy is computed from the daily energy throughput and SoC swing as:

$$y_k = \frac{E_{\mathrm{daily,kWh},k}}{(\Delta \mathrm{SoC}_k/100) C_{\mathrm{nom}}} \times 100 \tag{4}$$

where y_k is the SoH proxy, $E_{daily,kWh,k}$ is the daily energy throughput in the window, $\Delta\mathrm{SoC}_k$ is the corresponding SoC swing, and C_{nom} is the nominal battery capacity. The proxy is averaged over the update window to reduce day-to-day variability before state correction.

The steady-state degradation trend is updated by anchored cumulative least squares after the break-in anchor. Let x_j be the cumulative EFC at observation j, y_j the corresponding SoH proxy, and (x^*, y^*) the phase-transition anchor. The slope estimate is:

$$\hat{\beta} = \frac{\sum_j \left(x_j - x^*\right)\left(y_j - y^*\right)}{\sum_j \left(x_j - x^*\right)^2} \tag{5}$$

The steady-state baseline term is then corrected for the active C-rate stress term:

$$\hat{\text{SoH}}_{\text{base,steady}} = -\hat{\beta} - k_C \Delta C, \qquad \Delta C = \max(0, C_{\text{rate}} - 0.5) \tag{6}$$

The update is limited to quantities that are identifiable from the observed operating envelope. This means that the degradation model is re-run with new data at each update window, the health state is recursively updated, and identifiable parameters are corrected, but the full model structure is not retrained at every window [28].

Uncertainty is propagated using a scalar recursive state estimator. Let H_k denote the latent SoH state in update window k and y_k the SoH proxy. The process and measurement equations are:

$$H_k = H_{k-1} - \delta_k + w_k, \qquad w_k \sim \mathcal{N}(0, Q_{\text{noise}}) \tag{7}$$

$$y_k = H_k + v_k, \qquad v_k \sim \mathcal{N}(0, R_{\text{noise}}) \tag{8}$$

where δ_k is the predicted SoH loss in window k, Q_{noise} represents process uncertainty, and R_{noise} represents measurement uncertainty. The recursive prediction and correction equations are:

$$\hat{H}_{k|k-1} = \hat{H}_{k-1} - \delta_k, \qquad P_{k|k-1} = P_{k-1} + Q_{\text{noise}} \tag{9}$$

$$K_k = \frac{P_{k|k-1}}{P_{k|k-1} + R_{\text{noise}}} \tag{10}$$

$$\hat{H}_k = \hat{H}_{k|k-1} + K_k\left(y_k - \hat{H}_{k|k-1}\right), P_k = (1 - K_k)P_{k|k-1} \tag{11}$$

The filtered health estimate is reported with a model-conditional 95% interval $\hat{H}_k \pm 2\sqrt{P_k}$. Kalman filtering is a standard recursive method for updating a hidden state from a process model and noisy measurements [29]. The interval is used to avoid reporting deterministic threshold times when the health signal is inferred from operational data rather than measured by repeated capacity tests.

For a selected health threshold H_{thr}, the projected remaining useful life is:

$$\text{RUL}_k = \frac{\hat{H}_k - H_{\text{thr}}}{\hat{\delta}_{\text{daily}}}, \qquad \sigma_{\text{RUL},k} = \frac{\sqrt{P_k}}{\hat{\delta}_{\text{daily}}} \tag{12}$$

The projected threshold-crossing day is therefore $d_k + RUL_k \pm 2\sigma_{RUL,k}$. This formulation is used for reassignment timing and second-life threshold projection.

Figure 1 shows that the filtered SoH trajectory follows the reference two-phase degradation trend while smoothing the monthly SoH proxy observations. The confidence bands remain narrow in the plotted back-test, indicating that the recursive estimator constrains uncertainty when the process and measurement noise assumptions are fixed. The Kalman gain decreases after the initial windows, which means the estimator gradually shifts from high reliance on observations toward a more balanced weighting of the process model and the noisy SoH proxy. The projected reassignment day converges toward the reference 80% threshold-crossing day as additional update windows become available. The temporary disturbance in the projection near the phase-transition region reflects the limited information available to the early steady-state regression, not a separate physical degradation mode.

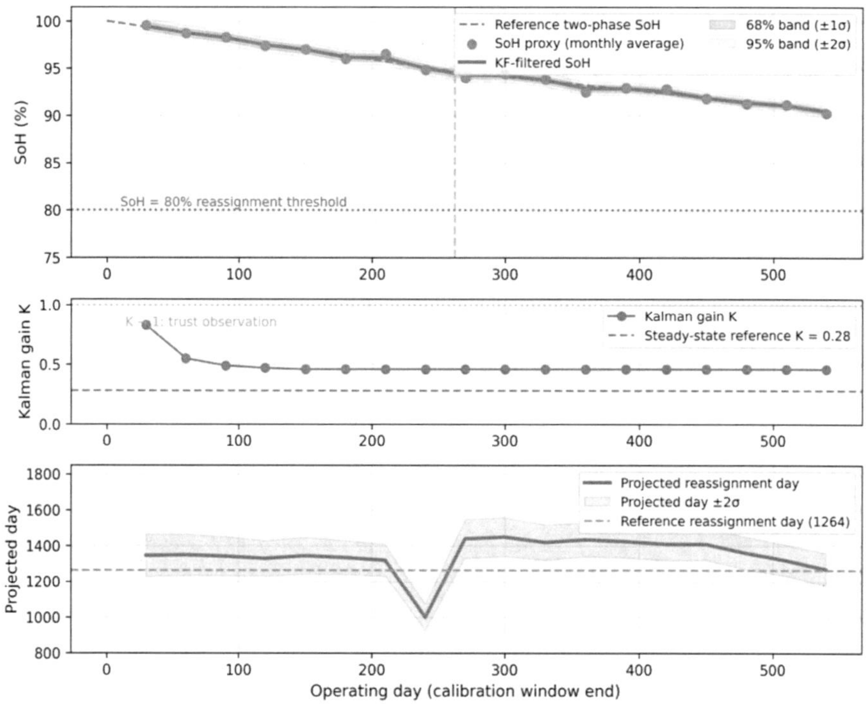

Fig. 1. Recursive SoH estimation and uncertainty propagation.

3.3 Use Case 1: Route Reassignment for First-Life Value Retention

The first use case evaluates route reassignment as a first-life value-retention service. The service is activated when the filtered or projected health trajectory reaches the first-life threshold used in the demonstrator. The reassignment day is defined as:

$$d_{80} = \min\{d : \mathrm{SoH}(d) \leq 80\} \tag{13}$$

The operational benefit of a reassignment scenario s is measured by the relative extension of the day at which the end-of-day SoC reaches the lower feasibility boundary:

$$\mathrm{LifeExtension}_s = \frac{d_{\mathrm{depletion},s} - d_{\mathrm{depletion},0}}{d_{\mathrm{depletion},0}} \times 100 \tag{14}$$

where $d_{\mathrm{depletion},\,0}$ is the depletion day under the original route and $d_{\mathrm{depletion},\,s}$ is the depletion day after reassignment. This use case links technical health state to circular value retention because a less demanding route can preserve operational usefulness after the first-life health threshold has been reached.

Figure 2 compares the original route with two lower-load reassignment scenarios. The reassignment occurs on day 1264, when the SoH trajectory reaches 80%. Under the original route, the end-of-day SoC trajectory reaches the lower feasibility boundary at day 5202. Reassignment to a 70% load route extends the operating window to day 7543, corresponding to a 45.0% life extension relative to the original route. Reassignment to an 85% load route extends the operating window to day 6166, corresponding to an 18.5% life extension. The larger benefit of the 70% scenario is consistent with the lower daily energy demand and larger end-of-day SoC margin after reassignment.

The result supports the use of route reassignment as a first-life retention service, but it should not be interpreted as a general optimization rule for all fleets. The result is conditional on the adopted battery capacity, route-load assumptions, C-rate stress representation, and threshold definition. A fleet-level implementation would need multiple vehicles, route demand constraints, charging availability, and service-scheduling constraints.

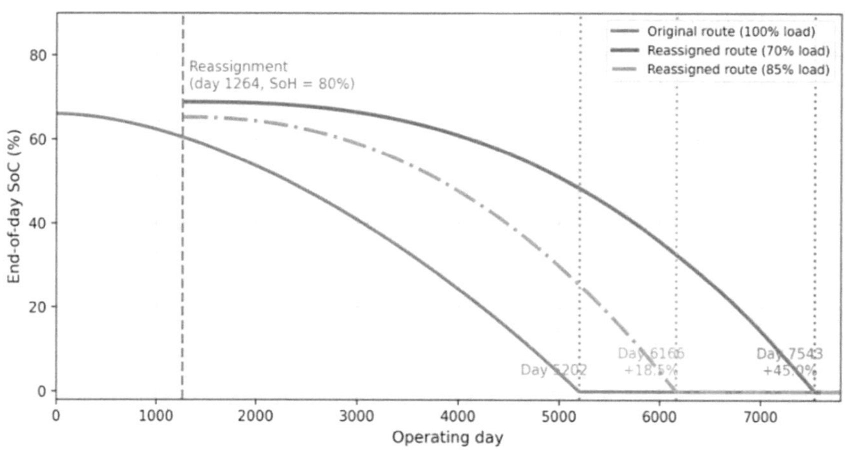

Fig. 2. Use Case 1: route reassignment comparison between the original route and reassigned 70% and 85% load scenarios.

3.4 Use Case 2: Second-Life Assessment for Circular Transition

The second use case evaluates a threshold-based circular transition service. The purpose is not to certify the battery for a specific second-life application, but to show how the CBDT can estimate the time window between the end of first-life vehicle use and a lower second-life threshold. The second-life threshold day is defined as:

$$d_{70} = \min\{d : \mathrm{SoH}(d) \leq 70\} \tag{15}$$

The threshold-based second-life window is:

$$\mathrm{SecondLifeWindow} = d_{70} - d_{80} \tag{16}$$

The 80% and 70% thresholds are used as demonstrator decision thresholds. Second-life literature commonly discusses remaining capacity, SoH, RUL, safety, and application requirements as screening criteria; therefore, the thresholds should be interpreted as simplified decision boundaries rather than complete qualification tests.

Figure 3 shows that the SoH trajectory crosses the 80% first-life threshold on day 1264 and the 70% second-life threshold on day 1947. Equation (16) gives a threshold-based second-life window of 683 days, approximately 1.87 years. The blue region represents first-life bus service, the green region represents the simplified second-life assessment window, and the red region represents the end-of-life or recycling phase. The result demonstrates how the degradation-aware CBDT can convert a health trajectory into a circular transition decision. However, a complete second-life decision would also require safety screening, power capability, resistance growth, economic value assessment, environmental benefit assessment, and application-specific duty-cycle matching.

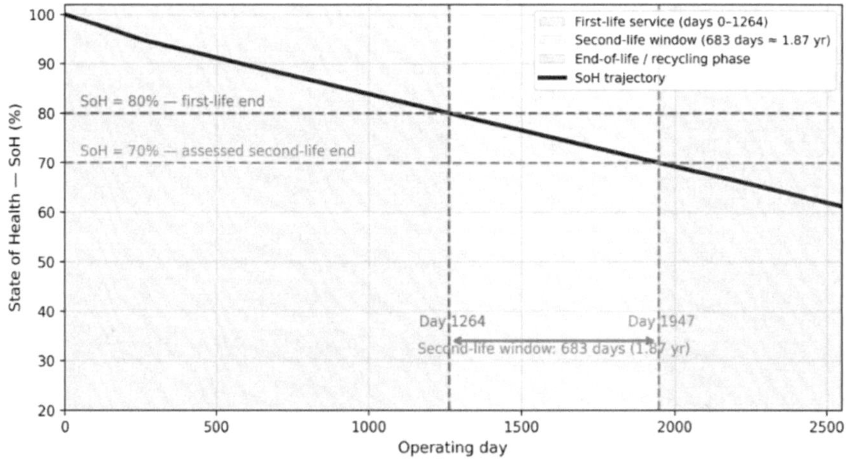

Fig. 3. Use Case 2: second-life assessment using SoH trajectory.

3.5 Discussion and Limitations

The two use cases are sufficient to demonstrate the proposed CBDT framework as a degradation-aware circular decision-support demonstrator when the scope is stated precisely. Use Case 1 demonstrates first-life value retention by using the updated health trajectory to evaluate route reassignment. Use Case 2 demonstrates a circular transition decision by estimating the window between first-life end and a lower second-life threshold. Together, the use cases connect aging-aware operation with circular value retention, which is the intended positioning of the paper.

The results also show why the demonstrator should not be described as a static degradation model. The recursive SoH update in Fig. 1 corrects the health state from logged data and propagates uncertainty into the projected reassignment day. This recursive correction is the element that makes the demonstrator closer to a digital-twin service than a one-time degradation simulation. At the same time, the implementation remains partial because it does not yet couple ECM, thermal, degradation, range, economic, and environmental models at runtime.

The route reassignment curves show that less demanding operation can extend the feasible operating window after the 80% health threshold. The 70% load scenario produces a larger life extension than the 85% load scenario because the lower load increases the end-of-day SoC margin and delays the point where the route becomes infeasible. This result demonstrates the principle of first-life retention, but the numerical extension should be interpreted as scenario-specific rather than fleet-general.

The second-life curve shows that threshold-based assessment can provide a first estimate of the transition window from vehicle use to lower-demand applications. However, threshold-based SoH alone is not a complete second-life assessment. The circular decision should also include power capability, resistance growth, safety status, residual value, environmental value, and the requirements of the intended second-life application.

The main limitation is the boundary of the implemented demonstrator. The paper proposes a generic CBDT framework, while the implemented part focuses on degradation-aware state estimation, identifiable parameter updating, uncertainty propagation, and two circular decision services. The ECM, thermal, economic, environmental, and full lifecycle models are included in the framework but are not fully implemented in the demonstrator. Future work should therefore integrate coupled electro-thermal-ageing simulation, multi-bus fleet data, economic value models, environmental impact models, independent capacity-test validation.

4 Conclusion and Future Work

This paper proposed a Circular Battery Digital Twin (CBDT) framework for electric bus fleets and demonstrated it through degradation-aware implementation. The framework was positioned as an integrated information model that links technical, economic, and environmental information across battery operation, model updating, circular lifecycle stages, and decision services. This positioning follows circular-digital-twin research, where digital twins are used to connect lifecycle information with circular decision-making and value-retention processes.

The implemented demonstrator focused on the degradation-aware part of the framework. It combined a semi-empirical degradation model, a two-phase baseline aging representation, Bayesian treatment of weakly identifiable parameters, filtered SoH correction, and uncertainty-aware RUL projection.

Two use cases were presented. The first use case demonstrated first-life value retention through route reassignment and the second use case demonstrated circular transition decision-making by estimating the operating interval between the 80% first-life threshold and the 70% second-life boundary.

Future work will first validate the degradation-aware update loop on additional buses and, where possible, against independent capacity or diagnostic tests. Second, the CBDT will be extended from a degradation-centered demonstrator toward a coupled electro-thermal-aging and range-aware twin. Third, the circular part of the framework will be strengthened by adding explicit economic and environmental models, including degradation cost, residual value, second-life value, avoided-emissions estimation, and recycling or material-recovery indicators.

Acknowledgments. This work was supported by Circul8 (Smart Battery Circularity), funded by the Knowledge Foundation (2023-0024), and SmartCharg (Smart and Circular Battery Charging Solutions), funded by the Vinnova FFI Circularity program (2023-00814) in Sweden. It was also supported by the TESTED-SOS (Tested Site Optimization Solutions).

Disclosure of Interests. The authors have no competing interests to declare that are relevant to the content of this article.

References

1. Chirumalla, K. et al.: Smart battery circularity: towards achieving climate-neutral electrification. In: Thürer, M., Riedel, R., von Cieminski, G., Romero, D. (eds.) Advances in Production Management Systems. Production Management Systems for Volatile, Uncertain, Complex, and Ambiguous Environments (APMS2024), pp. 187–201. Springer, Cham (2024)
2. Birkl, C.R., Roberts, M.R., McTurk, E., Bruce, P.G., Howey, D.A.: Degradation diagnostics for lithium ion cells. J. Power Sources. **341**, 373–386 (2017)
3. Waldmann, T., Wilka, M., Kasper, M., Fleischhammer, M., Wohlfahrt-Mehrens, M.: Temperature dependent ageing mechanisms in Lithium-ion batteries – a post-mortem study. J. Power Sources. **262**, 129–135 (2014)
4. Sulzer, V. et al.: The challenge and opportunity of battery lifetime prediction from field data. Joule. **5**(8), 1934–1955 (2021)
5. Pelletier, S., Jabali, O., Laporte, G., Veneroni, M.: Battery degradation and behaviour for electric vehicles: review and numerical analyses of several models. Transp. Res. B Methodol. **103**, 158–187 (2017)
6. Maheshwari, A.: Modelling, Aging and Optimal Operation of Lithium-Ion Batteries. Ph.D. thesis. Eindhoven University of Technology, Eindhoven, Netherlands (2018)
7. Ahmadian, A., Sedghi, M., Elkamel, A., Fowler, M., Golkar, M.A.: Plug-in electric vehicle batteries degradation modeling for smart grid studies: review, assessment and conceptual framework. Renew. Sust. Energ. Rev. **81**, 2609–2624 (2018)
8. Lam, L., Bauer, P.: Practical capacity fading model for Li-ion battery cells in electric vehicles. IEEE Trans. Power Electron. **28**(12), 5910–5918 (2013)

9. Wildfeuer, L., Wassiliadis, N., Karger, A., Bauer, F., Lienkamp, M.: Teardown analysis and characterization of a commercial lithium-ion battery for advanced algorithms in battery electric vehicles. J. Energy Storage. **48**, 103909 (2022)
10. Zhang, X., Sun, P., Wang, S., Zhu, Y.: Experimental study of the degradation characteristics of LiFePO4 and LiNi0.5Co0.2Mn0.3O2 batteries during overcharging at low temperatures. Energies. **16**(6), 2786 (2023)
11. Berecibar, M., Gandiaga, I., Villarreal, I., Omar, N., Van Mierlo, J., Van Den Bossche, P.: Critical review of state of health estimation methods of Li-ion batteries for real applications. Renew. Sust. Energ. Rev. **56**, 572–587 (2016)
12. Singh, S., Weeber, M., Birke, K.P.: Implementation of battery digital twin: approach, functionalities and benefits. Batteries. **7**(4), 78 (2021)
13. Renold, A.P., Kathayat, N.S.: Comprehensive review of machine learning, deep learning, and digital twin data-driven approaches in battery health prediction of electric vehicles. IEEE Access. **12**, 43984–43999 (2024)
14. Li, H., Kaleem, M.B., Chiu, I.J., Gao, D., Peng, J., Huang, Z.: An intelligent digital twin model for the battery management systems of electric vehicles. Int. J. Green Energy. **21**(3), 461–475 (2024)
15. Naseri, F. et al.: Digital twin of electric vehicle battery systems: comprehensive review of the use cases, requirements, and platforms. Renew. Sust. Energ. Rev. **179**, 113280 (2023)
16. Zhang, Z. et al.: Research on energy consumption law and charging strategies design of electric buses. Energy. **322**, 135327 (2025)
17. Wang, W., Yu, B., Zhou, Y.: A real-time synchronous dispatching and recharging strategy for multi-line electric bus systems. Transp. Res. Part E Logist. Transp. Rev. **185**, 103516 (2024)
18. Wang, J., Kang, L., Liu, Y.: Optimal scheduling for electric bus fleets based on dynamic programming approach by considering battery capacity fade. Renew. Sust. Energ. Rev. **130**, 109978 (2020)
19. Schmidt, M., Staudt, P., Weinhardt, C.: Decision support and strategies for the electrification of commercial fleets. Transp. Res. Part D: Transp. Environ. **97**, 102894 (2021)
20. Aishwarya, V.M., Ekren, B.Y., Singh, T., Singh, V.: Integrating sustainability across the life-cycle of electric vehicle batteries: circular supply chain challenges, innovations, and global policy impacts. Renew. Sust. Energ. Rev. **216**, 115671 (2025)
21. Koroma, M.S. et al.: Life cycle assessment of battery electric vehicles: implications of future electricity mix and different battery end-of-life management. Sci. Total Environ. **831**, 154859 (2022)
22. Peffers, K., Tuunanen, T., Rothenberger, M.A., Chatterjee, S.: A design science research methodology for information systems research. J. Manag. Inf. Syst. **24**(3), 45–77 (2007)
23. Preut, A., Kopka, J.-P., Clausen, U.: Digital twins for the circular economy. Sustainability. **13**, 10467 (2021)
24. Pasdarshahri, H., Veilleux, É., Mooney, W., Fréchette, L.G., Grondin, F., Rancourt, D.: Coupled electro-thermal-aging battery pack modeling—part 1: cell level. Batteries. **10**, 404 (2024)
25. Mügge, J., Seegrün, A., Hoyer, T.-K., Riedelsheimer, T., Lindow, K.: Digital twins within the circular economy: literature review and concept presentation. Sustainability. **16**, 2748 (2024)
26. Dahlquist, E., Azaza, M., Vasquez, J.R., Majidiezhad, M., Fattouh, A., Fentaye, A.D.: A battery model for transportation and stationary applications. In: 65th International Conference of Scandinavian Simulation Society (SIMS2024) (2024)
27. Wang, R., Zhu, M., Zhang, X., Pham, H.: Lithium-ion battery remaining useful life prediction using a two-phase degradation model with a dynamic change point. J. Energy Storage. **59**, 106457 (2023)

28. Gismero, A., Schaltz, E., Stroe, D.-I.: Recursive state of charge and state of health estimation method for lithium-ion batteries based on coulomb counting and open circuit voltage. Energies. **13**, 1811 (2020)
29. Plett, G.L.: Extended Kalman filtering for battery management systems of LiPB-based HEV battery packs: part 3. State and parameter estimation. J. Power Sources. **134**, 277–292 (2004)

Navigating Complexity in the Circular Economy: A Systems Perspective on Scotch Whisky

Isabel DiPirro[1], Agnessa Spanellis[1], and Melissa Marques-McEwan[2](✉)

[1] University of Edinburgh Business School, University of Edinburgh, Edinburgh, Scotland
[2] Edinburgh Business School, Heriot-Watt University, Edinburgh, Scotland
M.Marques-McEwan@hw.ac.uk

Abstract. Despite ambitious circular economy (CE) policies in Scotland, translating national commitments into effective industrial implementation remains a critical challenge. This study examines how Scotland's emerging CE policies enable or constrain CE adoption within Scotch whisky - an industry characterized by export orientation, premium packaging, and untapped potential to valorize by-products. Drawing on systems thinking, we apply causal loop diagrams (CLDs) to analyze qualitative data from semi-structured interviews with stakeholders, using a four-step coding process to translate interview data into feedback structures. Our analysis reveals twelve interconnected feedback loops across three thematic domains: bio-based distilling resource circularity, product packaging circularity, and industry-wide knowledge-sharing dynamics. The findings demonstrate how operational priorities, brand heritage, and export-oriented business models create distinct barriers for the CE transition of Scotch whisky. This research contributes an empirical systems analysis of CE adoption in Scotch whisky and a methodological pathway for systems-based CE research applicable to other industrial sectors.

Keywords: circular economy · systems thinking · whisky manufacturing

1 Introduction

The circular economy (CE) has gained traction over the past decade, globally and in Scotland, which has committed to becoming circular by 2045 [1]. In 2024, the Scottish Parliament enacted the CE (Scotland) Act [2], signaling its national commitment to sustainable consumption, production, and resource management, followed by the publications of Scotland's CE and Waste Route Map to 2030 and Scotland's CE strategy outlining priority actions [1, 3]. Whereas generally there is support for CE in principle, translating policy into effective industrial implementation remains a critical challenge.

CE is not yet widespread across key industrial sectors, especially whisky manufacturing. Whisky is key to the Scottish economy, with over 150 malt and grain distilleries

G. Pezzotta et al. (Eds.): APMS 2026, IFIP AICT 808, pp. 211–228, 2027.
https://doi.org/10.1007/978-3-032-38594-9_15

accounting for £5.4bn worth of Scotch exports [4]. The industry has established its sustainability ambitions, committing to net zero by 2045 and aligning its CE goals with SDGs, particularly SDG 12 on responsible consumption and production. Distilleries promote CE ambitions, but questions remain about how systematically these principles are being embedded in daily operations and whether policy can support key circular innovations such as optimized valorization pathways from grain to bottle.

CE policy has faced contention in the whisky industry. The CE (Scotland) Act 2024 has been criticized for primarily addressing waste while neglecting higher-priority practices such as reuse, repair, and reducing systemic over-consumption, and the CE Strategy does not prioritize whisky manufacturing [3]. When it comes to packaging, a recent Deposit Return Scheme (DRS) policy was initially rejected in Scotland, with clear opposition from the whisky industry, including the Scottish Whisky Association (SWA) lobbying against the scheme. The Scottish DRS was eventually passed in the Scottish Parliament but only after it aligned with the UK-wide scheme and excluded glass, raising skepticism about the policy's effectiveness.

In this context of rising CE policies, their broader systemic impacts on Scottish whisky are not well understood, preventing wider industrial adoption. Addressing this requires examining the economic, policy, and systemic mechanisms that shape CE adoption at the sector level - an analysis that existing research, focused primarily on macro-level policy or established valorization pathways in isolation, has not yet undertaken for Scotch whisky. Therefore, this paper explores: *How do Scotland's emerging CE policies enable or constrain the Scotch whisky manufacturing sector's transition toward circularity?*

This study employs a qualitative inductive approach, using semi-structured interviews with key stakeholders across three archetypes: distilleries, CE solution providers, and CE ecosystem enablers. Transcripts were analyzed through a four-step process - open coding, axial coding, causality coding, and causality mapping - to develop causal loop diagrams (CLDs) that identify reinforcing and balancing feedback mechanisms shaping CE adoption. The system boundary encompasses Scotland's whisky sector, with three thematic domains emerging inductively from the data: bio-based distilling resource circularity, product packaging circularity, and industry-wide knowledge-sharing dynamics. By grounding CLD construction in a four-step coding process, this paper contributes both an empirical systems analysis of CE barriers and enablers in Scotch whisky manufacturing and a methodological pathway for systems-based CE research applicable to other traditional, export-oriented industrial sectors.

2 Literature Review

A CE designs waste out of the system and reduces emissions by moving towards closed-loop production-consumption patterns, increasing the efficiency of resource use across an economic system [5]. CE as an interdisciplinary field draws from several schools of thought, including environmental economics, industrial ecology, and product-service systems [6]. This diversity of thought fosters holistic and innovative approaches to addressing complex challenges. However, it also creates ambiguity in the development and implementation of circular policies and strategies [5, 7].

Recognizing the importance of CE for a more sustainable and resilient society, many policies are being designed at the macro level, particularly in Scotland. The CE (Scotland) Act 2024 introduced national commitments to CE, accompanied by a CE Strategy and a Waste Route Map to 2030 [1–3]. In practice, however, policy initiatives have often faced industry resistance. The Deposit Return Scheme (DRS), which proposed a £0.20 refundable deposit on drinks containers, was initially rejected in Scotland due to conflicts with the UK Internal Market Act, and only eventually accepted when it aligned with England's approach of excluding glass. Extended Producer Responsibility (EPR) regulations shifted financial responsibility for packaging waste from consumers to producers by requiring large organizations to report packaging data and pay material- and weight-based fees [6]. These obligations operate alongside recovery targets, with compliance achievable through Packaging Recovery Notes (PRNs) and Packaging Export Recovery Notes (PERNs).

Despite whisky being a key export sector deeply linked to Scottish heritage, the CE Strategy has not included interventions aimed directly at this industry [3]. Most CE policy has so far focused on providing direction rather than co-creating specific plans with industry. Nevertheless, research is increasingly demonstrating the dangers of neglecting the nuance of local industries [8]. For Small and Medium Enterprises (SMEs), this is even more relevant as the contribution of CE to social, environmental, and economic outcomes can vary reflecting regional nuances [9], and SMEs rely more on their stance within the local community. It has been found that SMEs that leverage a place-based CE in their sustainability strategies can more effectively navigate trade-offs to maximize business, society, and ecosystem value, overall creating greater resilience for the broader systems in which they operate [10]. While the value of applying a local or regional lens to CE is clear, formal research in this space remains limited [11].

Within the Scotch whisky sector, there is potential to increase circularity, with studies showing the carbon and water implications of valorizing the by-products of a distillery, such as draff, pot ale, and spent lees [11, 12]. While these studies acknowledge environmental trade-offs, they primarily evaluate established pathways (animal feed and bioenergy) and do not examine how evolving policies shape industry-level decision-making. Consequently, there is limited research that holistically integrates the evolving CE policy landscape with sectoral dynamics to identify leverage points.

Addressing this gap requires engagement across the broader stakeholder ecosystem in which distilleries operate. A CE is enabled by an alliance of stakeholders and their technological innovations and capabilities [5]. It requires engagement across a network of manufacturers, retailers, supply chain partners, communities, governments, NGOs, and end users, as these interventions generate impact beyond a company's operations [13]. CE requires collaboration across circular "adopters" and "natives" alike, both of whom face unique challenges and who have distinct pathways towards circularity [13]. CE "adopters" are companies that face the challenge of transitioning away from linear practices deeply entrenched in legacy linear systems. While established firms have the experience and market foothold to influence system change, they typically pursue circularity incrementally [14]. CE "natives", on the other hand, are founded on CE principles. Often, new ventures have the agility to pursue disruptive models but lack the resources and partnerships to effectively scale up and integrate into incumbent systems [14]. Challenges include access to capital, the need to orchestrate complex and collaborative relationships across diverse actors, and the difficulty of navigating changing or unsupportive regulatory environments [14, 15].

Given the breadth of stakeholders and complexity in CE, systems thinking represents a valuable approach for navigating implementation and avoiding unintended consequences [16]. It is widely acknowledged that CE is a concept rooted in systems thinking [6, 16]. Nevertheless, only recently systems thinking approaches have started to be applied across diverse CE empirical studies, for example using Viable System Models to surface the mechanisms that enable or hinder an organization's adaptation to changing environments [17]. Effective systems analysis requires a comprehensive understanding of the relationships and structures that shape a complex system, to identify leverage points capable of triggering system-wide change [18]. System Dynamics (SD) focuses on the dynamic behavior of a system over time to understand feedback loops between different stakeholders and mechanisms within a system and to simulate the temporal impact of interventions [18]. SD has been applied in CE research to simulate transitions at micro-, meso-, and macro-system levels, with bottom-up and top-down interventions [19–21]. However, most applications use quantitative simulation; qualitative CLD construction from primary interview data - offering a more accessible entry point for exploratory, sector-specific analysis - remains less developed, particularly in traditional manufacturing contexts [21, 22]. This gap is particularly acute for Scotch whisky, where the interdependencies between innovative by-product valorization, packaging waste, and industry knowledge-sharing, and their impact on delivering CE policies in an export-focused industry have not previously been examined as an integrated system.

3 Methods

This study follows a qualitative inductive approach, framed by subjective ontology and interpretivist epistemology. The system boundary was defined as the Scotch whisky manufacturing sector, including distilleries, their ecosystem partners, and the broader policy environment. To understand the interdependencies in the Scottish whisky manufacturing ecosystem [22], data was collected through semi-structured interviews across three key stakeholder archetypes that holistically represent diverse perspectives on CE adoption: Distilleries, CE Solution Providers, and CE Ecosystem Enablers. Stakeholder archetypes were informed by prior literature [13, 23], with Table 1 outlining the selection criteria and summarizing participant engagement.

Data was collected through semi-structured interviews enabling the use of consistent, pre-formulated questions while retaining flexibility to explore emergent themes. Interviews focused on infrastructure, economic, and policy enablers and included specific questions that distinguished CE adoption across bio-based and finite-resource loops. Overall, 13 stakeholders were interviewed.

The data analysis of textual interview transcripts was informed by systems thinking literature, combining qualitative thematic coding and causal mapping to enable a structured approach to capturing depth and dynamic data interpretation [24, 25]. This four-step process included two stages of thematic coding, followed by the identification of causal relationships and aggregation into broader feedback loops: (1) open coding,

Table 1. Summary of stakeholder groups and selection criteria

Stakeholder Group	Selection Criteria	N. Interviews
Distilleries	Whisky manufacturing firms	6
CE Solution Providers	Stakeholders from the value chain providing CE solutions for both finite and/or biobased resources (e.g., packaging, bio-upcycling)	5
CE Ecosystem Enablers	Stakeholders from organizations representing the broader interests of Scotch whisky. They act as intermediary between macro-level and enterprise action.	2
Total		13

(2) axial coding, (3) causality coding, and (4) causality mapping [23, 24]. MAXQDA24 was used as a computer-aided qualitative data analysis software (CAQDAS) to support inductive thematic analysis. Previous studies demonstrated that using CAQDAS to develop coding trees for constructing CLDs simultaneously can strengthen the rigor of both methodologies, adding dynamic sensibility and providing a more rigorous approach to developing CLDs [26]. Once the causality mapping was complete, the identified feedback loops were aggregated iteratively to develop a final CLD, constructed in an online systems visualization tool (Kumu). Table 2 illustrates this coding process for one cluster (Brand Influence on CE Packaging Design) showing how textual interview data was progressively structured, leading to causal mapping in Balancing Loop B3: Distilleries & Brands Maturity → Premium Product Positioning → Consumer Expectations of Brand Consistency → (−) Flexibility in CE-aligned Changes to Brand Design & Messaging → Distillery Willingness to Invest in CE Changes.

Table 2. Example of representative quotes leading to (a), (b), (c) coding, creating (d) B3

Representative Quote	(a) Open Coding	(b) Axial Coding	(c) Causality coding
"Members are very protective of their branding... you would never get a situation where every single distillery agrees to the same format of bottle because that loses individuality" [CE Ecosystem Enabler 1]	Brand Protection & Consumer Expectations	Effect of distillery's market position on consumer expectations of brand consistency	Mature & Established Distillery & Brand → (+) Premium Product Positioning

(continued)

Table 2. (*continued*)

Representative Quote	(a) Open Coding	(b) Axial Coding	(c) Causality coding
"Brand1 is considered our experimental brand - it gives us license to do things that are a little bit more unexpected" [Distillery 2]	Brand Protection & Consumer Expectations	Ability to de-risk brand experimentation with multiple product lines	Premium Product Positioning → (+) Consumer Expectations of Brand Consistency
"I think the industry has almost given itself the problem because we've historically told everybody that luxury is [heavy packaging]... we're still tied to these maybe incorrect perceptions" [Distillery 4]	Brand Protection & Consumer Expectations	Tension between brand consistency and sustainability decision-making	Consumer Expectations of Brand Consistency → (−) Flexibility in CE-aligned Changes to Brand Design and Messaging
"Luxury is heavy and chunky... you need more backing from the brand and marketing side that you can change, but it doesn't have to be at the detriment of luxury" [Distillery 5]	Sustainability Branding	Influence of CE adoption on distillery sustainability brand affinity	Flexibility in CE-aligned Changes to Brand Design & Messaging → (+) Distillery Willingness to Invest in CE Changes

4 Findings: Systems Dynamics of Circular Scotch Whisky

Through the analysis, three distinct yet interconnected themes emerged: (1) Bio-Based Distilling Resource Circularity, (2) Product Packaging Circularity, and (3) Circular Economy Innovation and Knowledge Sharing. These themes were not predefined but emerged through thematic analysis and mapping. The three themes are presented separately because of their distinct dynamics across material characteristics, business priorities, legislative relevance, and consumer perception. Figure 1 illustrates a section of CLD (full loop definitions are provided in Table 3)

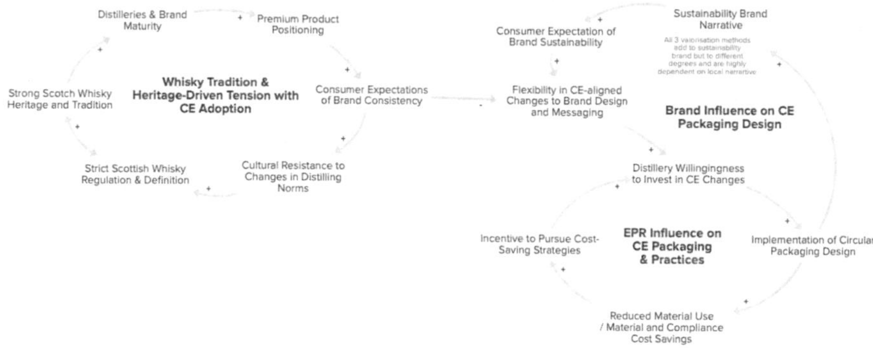

Fig. 1 Section of CLD system mapping of CE adoption in Scotch Whisky

(1) Bio-Based Distilling Resource Circularity refers to the management of bio-based by-products of whisky production, including draff, pot ale, and spent lees. Participants emphasized that distilleries prioritize efficiency of their core operations, treating by-product management as a cost-disposal function rather than a value-creation opportunity. Animal feed and bioenergy are common co-products, but new emerging technologies could reduce material use in complementary industries (e.g., aquaculture, food) or improve the efficiency of existing bioenergy processes. For bio-based distillery materials, the analysis maps out (1.a) decision-making tradeoffs and (1.b) financial constraints that limit capital investment in valorization technologies.

(1.a) Tradeoffs of Different Valorization Methods and Crowd-Out Dynamics

Animal feed remains a traditional valorization pathway among smaller distilleries, valued for its logistical convenience with nearby agricultural demand and the cultural importance of maintaining long-standing relationships with local farmers embedded in whisky heritage narratives. However, as distilleries scale, supply-demand misalignments grow, exacerbated by the seasonality of local agriculture, costs of managing materials beyond local farms, and strict SEPA regulations on product quality and storage - collectively making this pathway challenging at volume. Overall, distilleries' rationale for adopting valorization technology is less focused on circular hierarchy and more on cost efficiency, sustainability goals, and energy access. Thus, bioenergy, particularly anaerobic digestion (AD), has emerged as the dominant valorization pathway, despite ranking lower in the waste hierarchy than higher-value recovery options, e.g., bio-ingredients (protein concentrates, polyphenols, yeast extracts) for diverse applications.

AD adoption is incentivized by subsidies, which reinforces its perception as an established technology with low risk. As AD dominates the market, onsite and offsite options are readily available, giving distilleries flexibility to outsource. Bioenergy was frequently identified as the priority technology due to its ability to address multiple sustainability targets – a "catch-all" option that is promoted by SWA and broader national standards. With net zero positioned as a key competitive indicator, bioenergy is perceived as a way to satisfy decarbonization targets despite only nominally meeting CE criteria in standards that still lack consideration of consequential life-cycle carbon impact. Bioenergy is also seen to improve resilience for remote regions such as the Highlands and Islands which have limited grid infrastructure.

From a CE perspective, higher valorization pathways would be preferred to AD. However, they are constrained by limited market maturity, technical feasibility challenges, and risk asymmetries: smaller distilleries adopt a wait-and-see approach pending commercial proof, while larger producers are reluctant to assume operational risk at scale. Moreover, the attractiveness of AD will persist as long as it remains subsidized, which structurally crowds out investment in alternative technologies. As a result, distilleries tend to favor AD as a single, proven technology with an established commercial and sustainability case. **(R1, R2, B1)**

(1.b) Financing Capital Investment for Enhanced Valorization Technology

For a circular native technology to compete with basic valorization methods (i.e., AD, biomass, or animal feed), it must demonstrate economic value. Yet the challenge lies in demonstrating economic value through cost-efficient scale-up and matching supply with demand. Distilleries act at the supply side, typically paying for the removal of their "waste", which then serves as inputs for co-product generation, generally for food and agriculture industries. UK support for scaling capital-intensive technologies remains limited, however, diluted by greater emphasis on constantly developing new solutions rather than scaling existing ones. A dynamic forms as private-backed capital infrastructure is required to achieve cost-efficient, consistent by-product removal, which incentivizes distilleries to adopt new technology. Yet distillery appetite drives private investors' willingness to invest in this capital. Schemes like those from Scottish Enterprise use buy-side champions to spur demand but alone cannot sufficiently drive scale.

Funding and ownership of shared infrastructure remain a central tension. Scotland's remoteness favors hub-and-spoke models, channeling byproducts from nearby distilleries to a single facility. The challenge remains in determining who will fund the infrastructure. In many cases, circular natives own and operate the facility, managing resource removal directly or via partners, while bearing the burden of securing funding, positioning their services similarly to traditional waste operators. In the case of anaerobic digestion (AD), some distilleries have explored hosting on-site plants and licensing capacity to nearby distilleries. Even when publicly or privately funded, disputes over cost-sharing, ownership, and community benefit dilute responsibility and hinder coordination. **(R3, B2)**

(2) Product Packaging Circularity emerged as a second subsystem. While there is a range of finite materials that span the Scotch whisky value chain, glass accounts for the majority. As an export-oriented industry, products reach their end-of-life beyond UK boundaries, limiting the scope of UK legislation's direct influence on post-consumer resource management. For distillery packaging materials, this analysis explored (1) the influence of brand on implementing circular packaging and (2) the intended and unintended consequences of UK CE legislation.

(2a) Brand Influence on CE Packaging Design

A distillery's willingness to invest in circular packaging is influenced by its brand flexibility and affinity with sustainability. Mature, established distilleries resist visual brand changes that could compromise consumer perceptions of product quality and consistency, given the long-standing heritage their brands embody. Newer distilleries are less constrained by legacy expectations and are more likely to innovate and experiment through special releases and diversified product lines. Where sustainability underpins brand differentiation, investment in circular packaging design is framed as strategic commercial investment rather than added cost, with newer distilleries better placed to embed CE processes from the outset. Diversified brand portfolios enable experimentation: circular changes can be tested on entry-level products like blended malts before scaling across premium lines, making it more financially feasible to update multiple brands. Once a company decides to pursue circular design for one product, it typically has a wider-spread impact on its other brands as it is more financially feasible to explore packaging updates for multiple brands at once rather than pursuing each line separately.

The export nature of Scotch whisky has a major influence on CE adoption in packaging, as end-user markets dictate brand decisions. For example, Asian markets constitute a critical demand segment, where gift box packaging is frequently perceived as a signal of prestige. Therefore, the decision to remove gift boxes could potentially undermine a brand's competitive position in different locations. **(R4, B3)**

(2b) The Intended and Unintended Consequences of UK Packaging Legislation

EPR was identified by the distilleries as the policy most likely to impact their operations. By introducing weight- and material-based fees, EPR incentivizes producers to redesign bottle packaging to reduce material intensity and increase recycled content, embedding circular considerations into product design decisions. Fees collected through the scheme are intended to fund public recycling initiatives. Several stakeholders emphasized the importance of awareness campaigns in supporting this transition. However, interviewees raised concerns about the effective distribution and use of these funds by local authorities. Yet, the inclusion of PERNs in policy design perpetuates the export of recycled materials rather than strengthening domestic recycling infrastructure, perpetuating the insufficient supply of recycled glass in the UK. In parallel, Scotland's DRS was initially intended to include glass but was rejected and replaced by a UK-wide scheme that excludes glass.

While whisky would not be the primary source of glass in the UK as most is exported, the industry would have benefited from improved infrastructure and overall increase in the local supply of higher-quality recycled glass at volume. While the industry resists some CE legislation, participants generally expressed support for CE policies in principle, albeit with skepticism about feasibility. EPR fees create a tangible basis for cost–benefit analysis, helping to justify investment in circular packaging. Although brand identity constrains packaging flexibility, if circular design becomes the industry standard, regulatory compliance will drive consistent changes across competitors, reducing reputational risk for individual brands. While EPR applies only to UK sales, global brand consistency means circular packaging changes would extend across markets. Given the Scottish heritage in whisky production, this is a key sector where a change in Scottish regulations can improve circularity globally. **(R5, B4, B5)**

(3) CE Innovation and Knowledge Sharing was the final thematic domain. This analysis shows how the industry's ability to pursue CE innovation is impacted by its alignment with (1) Scotch whisky tradition and heritage, and (2) existing industry knowledge sharing dynamics and competitive positioning.

(3.a) Tension between CE Adoption and Whisky Tradition

To ensure the long-standing reputation of the industry, various standards have been established to strictly define what constitutes Scotch Whisky. These regulations dictate that sourcing, distilling, maturation and bottling are completed in Scotland, that material additives are prohibited during distilling, and that maturation is completed within certain capacity limits. These standards influence premium brand positioning, as consumers associate this certification with quality. In turn, consumer brand expectations regarding the consistency of legacy brands contribute to cultural resistance to changes in distilling norms, reinforcing the stringent regulations governing whisky production. These regulations can limit the ability to implement certain CE practices. For example, as an export-heavy industry, distilleries face the challenge of adopting take-back models that require bottling outside Scotland, as well as the technicalities of bulk maturation and shipping. The strict regulations create cultural rigidity that is, at times, upheld more by tradition than law. For instance, Scotch whisky is one of the few alcoholic beverages where gift packaging is the norm. Over time, this has set a customer expectation that makes it risky for companies to move away from. However, many distilleries acknowledge that the industry lacks robust consumer research to confirm whether such changes would meaningfully impact customer loyalty or brand equity. **(B6)**

(3.b) Industry-Wide Knowledge Sharing Dynamics

Given the long maturation periods, many distilleries spoke to the collaborative culture in Scotch whisky, especially in by-product management, which is not closely tied to brand identity and thus is less associated with competitive differentiation. As most distilleries do not have formal R&D departments, they rely on research and knowledge-sharing support from third parties, such as the SWA. This trade association offers a range of resources, including industry working groups focused on water and effluent, packaging, and net zero. These groups enable members to convene and discuss legislative and technical challenges related to the adoption of practice. Through these working groups, the SWA also helps spearhead knowledge sharing and industry experimentation aligned with the collective interests of distilleries, including industry-wide LCA assessments. Nevertheless, competition law limits the level of collaboration among distilleries and the extent to which the SWA can offer recommendations on specific CE technologies and solutions. SWA initiatives and targets are driven by the collective consensus of its membership; consequently, some stakeholders expressed a lack of ambition in some of the SWA's targets, and others spoke to a disproportionate prioritization of energy or packaging over distilling by-products.

Many distilleries look to one or two of the industry's largest players to observe which innovations they adopt. However, the leading firms often withhold developments, seeking to secure intellectual property exclusivity before sharing innovations more widely. This approach allows them to capitalize on first-mover benefits. Some distilleries spoke to the benefits of outsourcing their circular innovation to external partners, as with off-site bioenergy technology which has increased the industry's collective capacity to adopt the innovation. However, this decreased visibility and control around the level of valorization and circularity achieved. **(R6, B7)**

The systems dynamics across the three themes are identified in Table 3.

Table 3. Identified system dynamics

Theme	Sub-system	Feedback Loop	Key variables in the loop
(1) Bio-Based Distilling Resource Circularity	(1.a) Trade-Off and Crowding-Out Dynamics in New Valorization Methods	Reinforcing (R1)	AD Subsidies → Adoption of Basic VT (Bioenergy Technology) → Industry-Wide Prioritization of Net Zero → AD Subsidies
		Reinforcing (R2)	Cost Efficiency of Enhanced VT → Distillery Incentive to Adopt → Adoption of Enhanced VT → (+) Cost Efficiency of Enhanced VT
		Balancing (B1)	Adoption of Basic VT → (−) Ease of Switching to Enhanced VT → (+) Adoption of Enhanced VT → (−) Adoption of Basic VT
	(1.b) Financing Capital Investment for Enhanced Valorization Technology	Reinforcing (R3)	Distillery Incentive to Adopt CE Technology → Willingness for Private Investment in CE Emerging Tech Infrastructure → Investment Capacity for CE Emerging Tech → Ability for CE Natives to Scale → Local Infrastructure Capacity to Support New CE Technology → Cost Efficiency of By-Product Removal → Distillery Incentive
		Balancing (B2)	Shared Capital Infrastructure Models Development & Participation → Local Infrastructure Capacity → Feasibility / Attractiveness of Participation → Shared Capital Infrastructure Models Development & Participation
(2) Product Packaging Circularity	(2.a) Brand Influence on CE Packaging Design	Reinforcing (R4)	Sustain. Brand Narrative → Consumer Expectation of Brand Sustain. → Distillery's Willingness to Invest in Circular Design → Implementation of Circular Packaging → Sustain. Brand Narrative

(*continued*)

Table 3. (*continued*)

Theme	Sub-system	Feedback Loop	Key variables in the loop
		Balancing (B3)	Distilleries & Brands Maturity → Premium Product Positioning → Consumer Expectations of Brand Consistency → (−) Flexibility in CE-aligned Changes to Brand Design & Messaging → Distillery Willingness to Invest in CE Changes
	(2.b) The Intended and Unintended Consequences of UK Packaging Legislation	Reinforcing (R5)	EPR Implementation → Weight- and Material-Based Fees → Incentive to Pursue Cost-Saving Strategies → Distillery's Willingness to Invest in Circular Design → Implementation of Circular Packaging Design → Reduced Material Use / Material and Compliance Cost Savings → [loop reinforces]; also: Funding for Public Recycling Campaigns → Public Awareness → UK Domestic Recycling Rates → Local Supply of Recycled Glass
		Balancing (B4)	EPR Implementation → PERNs → Exported Recycling Processing → Glass Leakage out of UK → (−) UK Domestic Recycling Rates → (−) Local Supply of Recycled Glass; also: Poor UK Recycling Infrastructure → Demand for Imported Recycled Glass → Packaging Carbon Intensity

(*continued*)

Table 3. (*continued*)

Theme	Sub-system	Feedback Loop	Key variables in the loop
		Balancing (B5)	High Exports → (−) Industry Influence in UK Regulation → (+) Industry Incentive to Engage in Local Policy → (+) Industry Influence & Engagement in UK Regulation → (+) Policy Alignment with Industry Needs → (+) Industry Receptivity to New Policy → (+) Success of DRS → (+) UK Domestic Recycling Rates; also: DRS Exclusion of Glass → (+) Quality of Recycled Glass → (+) Improvements to UK Glass Recycling Infrastructure
(3) CE Innovation & Knowledge Sharing	Tension between CE Adoption and Whisky Tradition	Balancing (B6)	Strong Scotch Heritage & Tradition → Strict Scotch Regulation & Definition → Consumer Expectations of Brand Consistency → Cultural Resistance to Changes in Distilling Norms → (reinforces) Strict Scotch Regulation & Definition → Strong Scotch Heritage & Tradition
	Industry-Wide Knowledge Sharing Dynamics	Reinforcing (R6)	Industry-Wide Net Zero → Third Party Support (e.g., SWA) → Industry Collaboration Working Groups → CE Knowledge Sharing and Experimentation → Collective Capacity of CE Innovation → (reinforces) CE Knowledge Sharing; also: Collaborative Culture in Scotch Whisky Distilling → Collective Capacity of CE Innovation

(*continued*)

Table 3. (*continued*)

Theme	Sub-system	Feedback Loop	Key variables in the loop
		Balancing (B7)	Size and Capacity of Distillery → In-house R&D Investment → IP Exclusivity Around CE Innovation → (−) Distillery Willingness to Share CE Innovation → (−) CE Knowledge Sharing and Industry Experimentation; also: Competition Law → (−) Third Party Support & Guidance (SWA) → (limits) Industry Collaboration Working Groups

5 Discussion

The CLDs reveal a Scotch whisky sector navigating CE transition within a policy environment that is, at best, partially effective. Across all three thematic domains, a consistent pattern emerges: macro-level interventions are designed with broad sustainability intent but lose traction when they meet the realities of an export-oriented, heritage-constrained industry [21]. Industry-wide sustainability targets (e.g., decarbonizing operations by 2040 and net zero by 2045), coordinated through the SWA, have been effective in aligning distilleries around shared goals. However, these targets (and the carbon accounting standards that underpin them) prioritize net zero over CE, inadvertently reinforcing AD. Because AD impacts can be more readily claimed toward climate targets, it remains the dominant pathway, subsidized and de-risked, even though higher-value bio-based pathways offer greater environmental benefits [11]. This mirrors the broader tension between net zero and CE, where alignment is assumed but not guaranteed [7]. Resolving this requires sustainability standards that explicitly integrate CE considerations, so that AD is evaluated not as a default but against the full spectrum of valorization options. Such standards are not present in the Scottish CE strategy.

EPR represents the most commercially meaningful packaging intervention, creating genuine financial logic for circular design through cascading effects across supply chains. Yet, its impact is undermined by PERNs, which incentivize the export of recyclable material rather than building domestic infrastructure, perpetuating the recycled glass supply gap that distilleries depend on resolving - a concern consistent with broader critiques of UK EPR governance [27]. This reflects a systemic design flaw: the reinforcing loop driving circular packaging investment (R5) is simultaneously counteracted by a balancing loop that exports rather than retains recovered material (B4), structurally limiting the domestic glass supply that EPR itself depends on. DRS compounds this by removing glass from its scope entirely, severing a potential lever for improving domestic recycled glass supply precisely when EPR is increasing demand for it. While DRS may lay the groundwork for future inclusion of glass, there is a risk that progress will stall, leaving a critical gap in enabling circular packaging at scale.

In parallel, the product stewardship plan does not apply to distilleries, focusing on consumer-facing sectors such as textiles [6]. Across these policies, a secondary failure emerges as distilleries were not substantively engaged in early consultation for EPR or DRS. This generates resistance, skepticism, and a disconnect between policy intent and where materials actually flow [8]. Given the economic importance of whisky to Scotland, this exclusion risks the sector's potential as a driver of CE across global markets.

The most structurally underserved dimension, however, is interventions to scale higher-value CE solutions for bio-based by-products. With little rigor in direct circular policy for bio-based materials [1, 3], circularity is treated as a secondary outcome, relying on indirect alignment with broader policies rather than on dedicated CE mechanisms. With limited policy explicitly targeting bio-based materials beyond food production and waste, outcomes are largely shaped by general regulation and subsidies. For example, SEPA constraints on storage can limit scalable uses such as animal feed [11], while anaerobic digestion (AD) incentives are primarily driven by Net Zero goals. As a result, bio-based materials are often considered "managed" rather than maximally valorized. Without EPR-like mechanisms to introduce cost–benefit trade-offs across valorization pathways, there is little incentive to prioritize higher-value circular uses, risking systematic underperformance in bio-based circularity [23].

The findings indicate that the key barriers to CE in Scotch whisky are not technological, matching findings in different contexts across the literature [14]. Instead, circularity is limited by the absence of financially viable business models to support shared capital investment across distilleries and complementary industries [13, 15]. Circular native companies face a deadlock: private investors require demonstrated distillery demand, while distilleries require proven, cost-efficient removal before committing. Bio-based innovations are generally positioned as enabling technologies rather than core levers of production and consumption, which results in limited direct policy influence. Scotland's CE strategy and Waste Route Map have so far focused on recycling and waste infrastructure [1, 3], failing to include meaningful actions in a sector where Scotland has significant global influence. Stronger, more explicit policy mechanisms are therefore needed to embed commercial validation and financial incentives into valorization decisions and drive higher-value circular outcomes [14, 20].

The systems approach adopted in this study reveals why these barriers persist and interact. By mapping feedback structures across the three thematic domains, the CLDs make visible the self-reinforcing nature of AD dominance (R1), the structural tension between EPR's intent and PERNs' unintended consequences (R5, B4), and the deadlock between distillery demand and private investment in bio-based infrastructure (R3, B2). These are interdependent mechanisms that amplify one another across the system, and potential leverage points where targeted interventions could trigger system-wide change [22]. It also exposes where policies designed in isolation produce contradictory effects when they interact within the same system [16, 24].

6 Conclusion

This research examines how macro-level interventions shape the commercial attractiveness of CE resource valorization in the Scottish whisky context. It builds on existing scholarship applying causal loop mapping as an effective tool for unpacking system complexity in CE transitions within regional contexts [23, 24]. In doing so, it contributes to the still-emerging field of regional CE research and providing a foundation for future work to validate and simulate these interactions through system dynamics modelling.

Effective CE implementation depends on supportive policy frameworks and infrastructure that enable firms to pursue CE initiatives aligned with business environmental and economic objectives. The findings highlight the need for more proactive and inclusive CE policy design in Scotland – including standards that integrate CE criteria alongside net zero, EPR-style mechanisms for bio-based valorization pathways, and earlier industry consultation in policy design. Although export-oriented, Scotch whisky remains economically central to the country, making early engagement critical to securing industry buy-in and ensuring that regulatory structures and fee mechanisms are effective. If whisky producers are not involved from the outset, as demonstrated in the DRS, CE policymakers risk resistance, ineffective implementation, and significant delays in addressing essential CE and net zero goals established for the country.

The limitations of this study include reliance solely on qualitative interviews from a limited sample, which capture a subset of perspectives and might be prone to bias. Future research can benefit from incorporating other perspectives, including upstream packaging design and production, bioenergy service companies (e.g., anaerobic digestion), and CE policy advisors for the Scottish and UK governments. At the micro level, future work could explore and test specific business models for shared valorization infrastructure, pilot collaborations between distilleries and CE native companies, and refill or take-back schemes suited to export-oriented supply chains.

Disclosure of Interests. The authors have no competing interests to declare that are relevant to the content of this article.

References

1. The Scottish Government: Scotland's Circular Economy and Waste Route Map to 2030. The Scottish Government (2024)
2. The Scottish Government: Circular Economy (Scotland) Act 2024 (2024)
3. Scottish Government: A Circular Economy Strategy for Scotland. Scottish Government, Edinburgh (2026) https://www.gov.scot/publications/circular-economy-strategy-scotland/. Accessed May 2026
4. SWA: Scotch Whisky Industry Records £5.4bn Global Exports in 2024 amid Turbulent Global Trading Conditions. Scotch Whisky Association (2025) https://scotch-whisky.org.uk/newsroom/2024-export-figures/. Accessed Mar 2026
5. Kirchherr, J., Yang, N.-H.N., Schulze-Spüntrup, F., Heerink, M.J., Hartley, K.: Conceptualizing the circular economy (revisited): an analysis of 221 definitions. Resour. Conserv. Recycl. **194**, 107001 (2023). https://doi.org/10.1016/j.resconrec.2023.107001

6. Ghisellini, P., Cialani, C., Ulgiati, S.: A review on circular economy: the expected transition to a balanced interplay of environmental and economic systems. J. Clean. Prod. **114**, 11–32 (2016). https://doi.org/10.1016/j.jclepro.2015.09.007
7. Murray, A., Skene, K., Haynes, K.: The circular economy: an interdisciplinary exploration of the concept and application in a global context. J. Bus. Ethics. **140**, 369–380 (2017). https://doi.org/10.1007/s10551-015-2693-2
8. Arsova, S., Genovese, A., Ketikidis, P.H.: Implementing circular economy in a regional context: a systematic literature review and a research agenda. J. Clean. Prod. **368**, 133117 (2022). https://doi.org/10.1016/j.jclepro.2022.133117
9. Dey, P.K., Malesios, C., Chowdhury, S., Saha, K., Budhwar, P., De, D.: Adoption of circular economy practices in small and medium-sized enterprises: evidence from Europe. Int. J. Prod. Econ. **248**, 108496 (2022). https://doi.org/10.1016/j.ijpe.2022.108496
10. Howard, M., Böhm, S., Eatherley, D.: Systems resilience and SME multilevel challenges: a place-based conceptualization of the circular economy. J. Bus. Res. **145**, 757–768 (2022). https://doi.org/10.1016/j.jbusres.2022.03.014
11. Duffy, C. et al.: Optimising sustainability: circular pathways for scotch whisky distillery co-products. J. Clean. Prod. **395**, 136436 (2023). https://doi.org/10.1016/j.jclepro.2023.136436
12. Leinonen, I., MacLeod, M., Bell, J.: Effects of alternative uses of distillery by-products on the greenhouse gas emissions of Scottish malt whisky production: a system expansion approach. Sustainability. **10**, 1473 (2018). https://doi.org/10.3390/su10051473
13. Rovanto, I.K., Bask, A.: Systemic circular business model application at the company, supply chain and society levels—a view into circular economy native and adopter companies. Bus. Strat. Env. **30**, 1153–1173 (2021). https://doi.org/10.1002/bse.2677
14. Kanda, W., Klofsten, M., Bienkowska, D., Henry, M., Hjelm, O.: Challenges of circular new ventures: an empirical analysis of 70 cases. J. Clean. Prod. **442**, 141103 (2024). https://doi.org/10.1016/j.jclepro.2024.141103
15. Han, D., Konietzko, J., Dijk, M., Bocken, N.: How do circular start-ups achieve scale? Sustain. Prod. Consump. **40**, 363–375 (2023). https://doi.org/10.1016/j.spc.2023.06.007
16. Robinson, S.: A systems thinking perspective for the circular economy. In: Circular Economy and Sustainability, pp. 35–52. Elsevier (2022)
17. Adamides, E.D., Georgousoglou, K., Mouzakitis, Y.: Designing a flexible and adaptive municipal waste management organisation using the viable system model. Sustainability. **15**, 13323 (2023). https://doi.org/10.3390/su151813323
18. Sterman, J.: System Dynamics: Systems Thinking and Modeling for a Complex World. MIT Sloan School of Management (2002). https://doi.org/10.1287/420a0422-8060-4775-b8d7-a8f01fa36ffe
19. Franco, M.A.: A system dynamics approach to product design and business model strategies for the circular economy. J. Clean. Prod. **241**, 118327 (2019). https://doi.org/10.1016/j.jclepro.2019.118327
20. Gao, C., Gao, C., Song, K., Fang, K.: Pathways towards regional circular economy evaluated using material flow analysis and system dynamics. Resour. Conserv. Recycl. **154**, 104527 (2020). https://doi.org/10.1016/j.resconrec.2019.104527
21. Guzzo, D., Pigosso, D.C.A., Videira, N., Mascarenhas, J.: A system dynamics-based framework for examining circular economy transitions. J. Clean. Prod. **333**, 129933 (2022). https://doi.org/10.1016/j.jclepro.2021.129933
22. Meadows, D.: Leverage Points: Places to Intervene in a System. The Sustainability Institute (1999)
23. Manolchev, C., Cherrington, R., Crabolu, G.: Untangling circularity: transitioning to a regional circular economy in the clothing and textile sector in England. J. Clean. Prod. **482**, 144188 (2024). https://doi.org/10.1016/j.jclepro.2024.144188

24. Crabolu, G., Font, X., Eker, S.: Evaluating policy complexity with causal loop diagrams. Ann. Tour. Res. **100**, 103572 (2023). https://doi.org/10.1016/j.annals.2023.103572
25. Kim, H., Andersen, D.F.: Building confidence in causal maps generated from purposive text data: mapping transcripts of the Federal Reserve. Syst. Dyn. Rev. **28**, 311–328 (2012). https://doi.org/10.1002/sdr.1480
26. Yearworth, M., White, L.: The uses of qualitative data in multimethodology: developing causal loop diagrams during the coding process. Eur. J. Oper. Res. **231**, 151–161 (2013). https://doi.org/10.1016/j.ejor.2013.05.002
27. Ramasubramanian, B., Tan, J., Chellappan, V., et al.: Recent advances in extended producer responsibility initiatives for plastic waste Management in Germany and UK. Mater. Circ. Econ. **5**, 6 (2023). https://doi.org/10.1007/s42824-02-00076-8

Reconfiguring Power in Food Supply Chains: Governance Mechanisms and Food Waste Across Stages of the Relationship

Claudia Colicchia[1], Attilia Imbriani[1(✉)], Gerardo Rosciano[1], and Alessandro Creazza[2]

[1] Department of Management, Economics and Industrial Engineering, Politecnico di Milano, Via Lambruschini 4/b, 20156 Milan, Italy
{claudia.colicchia,attilia.imbriani}@polimi.it, gerardo.rosciano@mail.polimi.it
[2] LIUC University, Castellanza (VA), Italy
acreazza@liuc.it

Abstract. This study investigates how buyer power is enacted through governance mechanisms in food supply chains and with what implications for food waste prevention and valorisation. Building on a literature review and a multiple case study of four companies operating in the Italian grocery sector, the paper adopts a processual perspective to examine how power levers shift across stages of definition, enforcement, and revision of standards and terms in buyer–supplier relationships. Findings show that power is not a static attribute but is reconfigured across governance episodes. Structural and contractual levers dominate the definition of standards, while enforcement relies on gatekeeping, monitoring, and selective use of coercive and informational mechanisms. Revision episodes of standards and terms, in turn, reveal how sustainability priorities can reshape the use of power, either reinforcing commercial objectives or enabling more collaborative approaches to food waste management. The study further demonstrates that product heterogeneity, particularly perishability, substitutability, and brand architecture, affects the feasibility and impact of different power levers. In highly perishable categories, stricter controls tend to shift waste risk upstream, whereas information sharing and joint practices support more balanced outcomes. By conceptualising food waste as the outcome of how power is exercised across sequential governance episodes, the paper contributes to both supply chain power literature and food waste research, offering a process-oriented framework linking governance choices to sustainability outcomes.

Keywords: Food supply chains · Buyer–supplier relationships · Food waste · Power · Governance

Published by Springer Nature Switzerland AG 2027
G. Pezzotta et al. (Eds.): APMS 2026, IFIP AICT 808, pp. 229–243, 2027.
https://doi.org/10.1007/978-3-032-38594-9_16

1 Introduction

Supply chains are not only systems for the exchange of goods, but also arenas in which actors negotiate control over decisions, risks, and outcomes (Emerson, 1962; Pfeffer & Salancik, 1978). In supply chain management, power asymmetries have long been recognised as a central determinant of coordination, collaboration, and performance (Maloni & Benton, 2000; Nyaga et al., 2013). Food supply chains (FSCs) provide a particularly salient context, where retailers often act as dominant actors, able to shape product specifications, service levels, and contractual terms (Hingley, 2005; Maglaras et al., 2015). At the same time, these governance choices have been increasingly linked to food waste (FW) generation along the chain. Empirical studies show that strict private standards, uncompensated risk-transfer mechanisms, and asymmetric contractual arrangements can contribute to upstream losses, particularly in fresh categories (Herzberg et al., 2022; Pietrangeli et al., 2023), while information sharing and collaborative practices may mitigate mismatches and reduce waste (Malik & Hingley, 2021). Despite this growing body of research, two limitations remain. First, power is often treated as a relatively static attribute of buyer–supplier relationships, typically captured through structural asymmetries or governance modes. Second, FW is frequently analysed as the outcome of operational inefficiencies, with limited attention to how it is shaped by the governance mechanisms embedded in commercial relationships. As a result, the link between power, governance processes, and FW outcomes remains underexplored.

This paper addresses these limitations by adopting a processual perspective on power in FSCs. Rather than viewing power as a fixed characteristic of the dyad, we conceptualise it as enacted through specific governance levers that shift across sequential episodes of the relationship, namely, the definition, enforcement, and revision of standards and terms. Building on a literature review and a multiple-case study of four companies operating in the Italian grocery sector, the study investigates how these levers are mobilised at different decision points and how their use is conditioned by product characteristics.

In doing so, the paper makes two main contributions. First, it reconceptualises power in supply chains as a dynamic phenomenon, linking structural roots and classic power bases to concrete governance mechanisms. Second, it frames FW not merely as an operational by-product, but as the cumulative outcome of how power is exercised across governance episodes. By integrating insights from power and FW literatures, the study offers a process-oriented framework to understand how governance choices shape sustainability outcomes in food supply chains.

2 Theoretical Background

2.1 Power in Supply Chains

Power is a foundational concept in supply chain research and is commonly defined as the ability of one actor to influence the behaviour and decisions of another (Emerson, 1962). Classical work conceptualises power as rooted in dependence: an actor becomes powerful when it controls critical resources that others need and cannot easily substitute (Pfeffer & Salancik, 1978). The mechanisms through which power is exercised have been extensively theorised through the five bases of power, i.e., coercive, reward, legitimate, expert, and referent (French & Raven, 1959). These bases can be operationalised through both mediated instruments, such as contractual clauses and penalties, and non-mediated mechanisms, such as expertise, reputation, and relational influence (Maloni & Benton, 2000; Nyaga et al., 2013).

Complementary theoretical lenses further explain how power emerges and operates in inter-organisational relationships. Resource Dependence Theory (RDT) links power to asymmetries in resource control and availability (Emerson, 1962; Pfeffer & Salancik, 1978). Transaction Cost Economics (TCE) emphasises the role of contracts and governance structures in managing uncertainty, asset specificity, and opportunism (Williamson, 1993). Social Exchange Theory (SET), in turn, highlights how trust, reciprocity, and relational norms shape whether power is exercised in coercive or collaborative ways (Cook et al., 2013; Nyaga et al., 2013).

2.2 Power in Food Supply Chains

FSCs amplify power dynamics due to a combination of structural and product-related characteristics. Retail concentration, combined with fragmented upstream supply, positions large retailers as channel leaders with significant control over market access and product flows (Hingley, 2005). This structural position allows retailers to shape product specifications, private standards, and operational processes across the chain (Maglaras et al., 2015). In this context, power is often exercised through contractual and operational levers embedded in day-to-day interactions. Private standards, service-level agreements, and minimum shelf-life requirements define acceptable product characteristics and performance thresholds, effectively acting as gatekeeping mechanisms for market access (Herzberg et al., 2022; Pietrangeli et al., 2023). These levers translate structural power into concrete governance practices that regulate supplier behaviour. Product characteristics further reinforce these dynamics. Perishability compresses decision cycles and increases exposure to quality and timing risks, making compliance with standards more critical and enhancing the effectiveness of coercive and legitimate power bases (Maglaras et al., 2015). At the same time, brand strength and substitutability condition bargaining positions: strong national brands can counterbalance retailer power, while private-label products typically reinforce retailer control over specifications and processes (Hingley, 2005).

2.3 Power and Food Waste

Recent literature has increasingly linked power asymmetries in FSCs to FW generation. Empirical evidence suggests that strict quality standards, aesthetic requirements, and contractual clauses can contribute to waste, particularly at the supplier–retailer interface (Herzberg et al., 2022; Pietrangeli et al., 2023). When suppliers face limited bargaining power, they may accept conditions that shift the risk of unsold or non-compliant products upstream, resulting in higher levels of waste. Conversely, more collaborative governance mechanisms can mitigate these effects. Information sharing, joint planning, and data-driven coordination have been shown to improve demand matching and reduce mismatches that lead to waste (Malik & Hingley, 2021; Nyaga et al., 2013).

Institutional frameworks increasingly reinforce these dynamics: the 2025 amendment to the EU Waste Framework Directive introduced binding FW reduction targets, explicitly positioning retailers as pivotal actors in prevention and valorisation (European Parliament & Council of the European Union, 2025).

Table 1 synthesizes prior literature by grouping recurring patterns that link sources of power to the power bases and governance levers through which they are enacted. It highlights how these mechanisms influence both the distribution of risks and the management of food waste along the chain.

Table 1. Power, governance mechanism and their effects in food supply chains

Source of power	Power bases	Effects	References
Retailer structural dominance	Coercive and legitimate (delisting, SLAs, unilateral changes)	Risk shifted upstream; over-sorting; rejections	(Herzberg et al., 2022; Pietrangeli et al., 2023)
Supplier-controlled strategic assets	Expert and referent (specification control, co-design)	High quality and innovation; potential downstream hold-up risks	(Belaya et al., 2009; Kim & Oh, 2005; Maloni & Benton, 2000)
Complementary structural resources (retailer + supplier)	Expert and legitimate (know-how; retailer's brand)	Jointly upgrades; need of aligned incentives	(Belaya et al., 2009; Kim & Oh, 2005)
Institutional frameworks	Legitimate (rules, audits, standards)	High compliance; less opportunism; upstream waste	(Carbone, 2017; Marques et al., 2022)
Contractual arrangements	Coercive and legitimate (SLAs, penalties, return clauses)	Demand mismatches; upstream risk	(Carbone, 2017; Herzberg et al., 2022; Pietrangeli et al., 2023)
Relational and capability-based coordination	Reward, expert, referent (joint planning, incentives)	Improved coordination; reduced defects and FW	(Malik & Hingley, 2021; Nyaga et al., 2013)
Digital and informational capabilities	Legitimate and reward (data sharing, platform access)	Improved coordination and reduced FW	(Brinker & Haasis, 2022; Fang et al., 2024)

3 Research Gaps and Research Questions

Although prior research has extensively examined power in supply chains and, more recently, its implications for FW in FSCs, several limitations remain.

First, existing studies predominantly conceptualise power as a structural and relatively static attribute of buyer–supplier relationships. Power is typically inferred from asymmetries in size, resource control, or market position, and analysed in terms of "power regimes" or governance modes (Cox, 2001; Maloni & Benton, 2000). While this perspective has generated valuable insights, it provides a limited understanding of how power is concretely enacted in practice and how it evolves over time within ongoing relationships.

Second, research on FW in FSCs has largely focused on operational drivers, such as forecasting errors, demand variability, and inventory management (Mena et al., 2011). Although recent studies highlight the role of private standards and contractual practices in generating upstream waste (Herzberg et al., 2022; Pietrangeli et al., 2023), these contributions tend to examine isolated mechanisms rather than the broader governance processes through which such practices are defined, enforced, and revised.

Third, limited attention has been paid to the role of product heterogeneity in shaping the exercise of power. While emerging research has started to classify food products based on their intrinsic characteristics and their implications for food waste generation and recovery (Viscardi & Colicchia, 2023), these insights have not yet been integrated into analyses of power and governance in supply chains.

Taken together, these limitations point to the need for a process-oriented perspective that connects power, governance mechanisms, and FW outcomes. For these reasons, this study adopts an episodic view of governance and distinguishes three key phases in buyer–supplier relationships: (i) the definition of standards and contractual terms, (ii) their enforcement in day-to-day operations, and (iii) their revision over time.

Accordingly, the study is guided by the following research questions:

RQ1: How do power levers shift across episodes of definition, enforcement, and revision of standards and terms in buyer–supplier relationships in food supply chains, and at which decision points are they most salient?
RQ2: How does product heterogeneity affect the choice and effectiveness of these power levers, and with what perceived effects on food waste prevention and valorisation?

By addressing these questions, the paper aims to advance existing literature by (i) reconceptualising power as a dynamic and processual phenomenon, (ii) linking governance mechanisms to FW outcomes, and (iii) integrating product-level characteristics into the analysis of power in FSCs.

4 Methodology

This study adopts a qualitative multiple-case study design to investigate how power is enacted through governance mechanisms in buyer–supplier relationships and how these mechanisms relate to FW. Case studies are particularly suitable for examining complex, processual phenomena in real-world contexts and for uncovering underlying mechanisms that are difficult to capture through quantitative approaches (Yin, 2009).

4.1 Research Design and Case Selection

A purposive sampling strategy was used to select information-rich cases relevant to the research questions (Yin, 2009). The study focuses on the Italian grocery sector, a context characterised by strong retail concentration and significant power asymmetries.

Four companies were selected to capture variation in organisational structure and governance among downstream actors: three grocery retailers and one independent food wholesaler. This focus allows addressing a relatively underexplored perspective, as prior research has predominantly examined power dynamics from the point of view of manufacturers or producers.

This design enables analytical replication by comparing organisations with different roles and levels of influence within the supply chain (Eisenhardt & Graebner, 2007). In particular, the inclusion of a wholesaler provides insight into a configuration in which bargaining power is more constrained and often shaped by upstream conditions.

The selected cases differ in size, format, and degree of vertical coordination, allowing the identification of both recurring patterns and context-specific dynamics. For confidentiality reasons, companies are anonymised as Cases A–D. Table 2 provides an overview of the main characteristics of the case companies, including size, role, and key informants interviewed in each case, as detailed in Sect. 4.2.

Table 2. Overview of the case companies

Case	Type	Turnover	Employees	Role in SC	Key informant(s)
A	Retailer	€1.1B	3650	Channel leader	Supply Chain Manager
B	Retailer	€4.2B	10000	Multi-format retailer	Head of Procurement; Sustainability Manager
C	Retailer	€9.2B	28000	Integrated retailer	Business Development Coordinator; Chief Sustainability Officer
D	Wholesaler	€9 M	20	Intermediary	Chief Operating Officer

The study does not restrict analysis to a specific product category: informants were asked to reflect across the full range of categories they manage, allowing product heterogeneity to emerge as an analytical dimension rather than being held constant by design.

4.2 Data Collection

Primary data were collected through four semi-structured interviews with key informants directly involved in supplier relationship management and sustainability practices, conducted between April and September 2025, approximately 60 min each. The interview protocol covered five thematic areas: company profile and role in the supply chain; sustainability priorities; governance of supplier relationships; contractual and operational levers; and perceived links between these levers and FW outcomes. In some cases, multiple informants participated in a single interview to provide complementary functional perspectives, as detailed in Table 2. All interviews were recorded, transcribed verbatim, and complemented by field notes capturing contextual observations and preliminary insights. Secondary data, including company reports and publicly available documents, were used to contextualise the cases and triangulate factual information.

4.3 Data Analysis

Data were analysed using the Gioia methodology, which enables systematic inductive theory building from qualitative data (Gioia et al., 2013). The analysis proceeded in three steps. First, interview transcripts were coded using informant-centric terms (first-order codes), remaining close to participants' language. This phase produced 36 first-order codes. Second, codes capturing related practices were iteratively clustered into 12 s-order themes through constant comparison within and across cases. Third, aggregate dimensions were derived to capture higher-level theoretical constructs: company context and sustainability, power-shaping governance mechanisms, power asymmetries and risk governance, and critical resources and dependencies. To strengthen reliability, coding was conducted independently by two researchers; disagreements were resolved through discussion until consensus was reached (Gioia et al., 2013). A high-resolution version of the data structure is available as supplementary material at: https://osf.io/a5euk/files/q8wxs.

To address the research questions, identified themes were mapped onto three governance episodes: definition, enforcement, and revision of standards and terms. In parallel, product-related characteristics (e.g., perishability, shelf life, branding) were used as analytical lenses to examine how product heterogeneity conditions the activation of specific power levers and their perceived effects on FW.

Cross-case comparison enabled the identification of recurring patterns and differences across organisational contexts, strengthening the robustness of the findings. Throughout the analysis, traceability between empirical evidence and theoretical constructs was maintained to ensure transparency and reliability (Gioia et al., 2013).

5 Findings

The findings show that power in buyer–supplier relationships is not static but is enacted through different governance levers that vary across contexts and decision points. Table 3 summarises the cross-case patterns emerging from the analysis, showing the salience of each theme across the four cases. Salience ratings (strong, moderate, weak) reflect the frequency and centrality of related first-order codes in the interview data and the extent to which informants explicitly linked the mechanism to food waste outcomes. A "strong" rating indicates that the theme was recurrently described as a key governance lever; "moderate" indicates partial or context-dependent relevance; "weak" indicates that the theme was mentioned but played a marginal or indirect role.

Table 3. Cross-case comparison of governance mechanisms, power configurations, and their perceived effects on food waste

2nd-order codes	Case A	Case B	Case C	Case D
Company priorities	● Profit-first logic	● PL commercial logic	● Sustainability integrated	● Profit first

(continued)

Table 3. (*continued*)

2nd-order codes	Case A	Case B	Case C	Case D
Sustainability efforts	◑ Selective initiatives	● Formal agenda	● Structured plan	◑ Secondary channel halted
Causes of FW	● Service guarantee; overhang	● Low rotation; forecasting	◑ In-store prep; broad assortment	● Promotions; order constraints
Negotiation	● Formal	● Multi-level	● Long-term; asymmetric	◑ Informal
Power moderator	● Perishability	● SL thresholds for risky items	● Strict PL specs	● Fresh categories; operational urgency
Upstream power	● Brand pull dominates	◑ Muscular; continuous	◑ Brand moderates leverage	● Limited vs. brands
Power asymmetry	● Rare penalties; retailer-dictated PL	● Logistics & PL specs imposed	● Contract legitimises termination	○ Unfavourable clauses accepted
Gatekeeping	● PL & fresh	● Tight inbound on PL	◑ Prior qualification	◑ Strong; auth. required
Risk & cost allocation	● Seasonal returns; shifting	○ Suppliers fund recall & shrinkage	● Return & donation upstream	◑ Overstock on wholesaler
Critical resources	◑ External innovation	● Rich data & analytics	● Internal know-how; logistics	○ Know-how consolidating
Mutual dependencies	◑ Partnerships & secondary channels	● Data sharing: co-investment	● Donation network; logistics	◑ Re-routing; donations
Dependency structure	◑ Packaging lock-in;	○ Multi-source; low lock-in	◑ Dual sourcing	● Packaging PL lock-in

Legend: ● strong, ◑ moderate, ○ weak

Building on this empirical structure, the findings are presented by focusing on how these mechanisms combine and evolve throughout three key moments (definition, enforcement, and revision of standards and terms). Across cases, the salience and effects of these levers are consistently shaped by product characteristics, particularly perishability, shelf life, and brand architecture.

5.1 Power in the Definition of Standards and Terms

At the definition stage, power is primarily exercised through structural and contractual levers that determine the initial allocation of responsibilities, risks, and decision rights.

Across all retailer cases, this stage is characterised by the design of detailed product specifications, service-level agreements, and contractual clauses regulating delivery conditions, shelf life, and risk allocation. Private-label (PL) products represent the context in which retailer power is most pronounced. Retailers define product characteristics, packaging, and quality standards through formal specifications, effectively controlling both product design and supply conditions. These specifications often extend beyond legal requirements and embed operational constraints, such as minimum life on receipt (MLOR) and delivery calendars, which directly affect suppliers' production and logistics decisions. Across cases, this translates differently: in Case A, requirements escalate with perishability ("*the closer we get to deli counter products, the more stringent the rules become...There is no compromise on quality*"); in case B, MLOR thresholds are differentiated by product risk (66% standard, 75% for slow moving items); in case C, the contract is framed as "an agreement between two parties", a narrative that legitimises rules largely drafted unilaterally. In case D, power is inverted: suppliers impose order minimums that constrain the wholesaler ("*if we don't order the whole pallet, they won't ship it to us, even if we then risk having leftover goods*").

Across all cases, the definition stage also embeds mechanisms that pre-allocate FW risk. Contractual clauses, such as return agreements, penalties, and service-level requirements, effectively determine ex ante how unsold or non-compliant products will be managed and who will bear the associated costs. As a result, FW outcomes are partially shaped at this stage, before any operational execution takes place.

5.2 Power in the Enforcement of Standards

During the enforcement stage, power is operationalised through a combination of gatekeeping, monitoring, and selective use of sanctions. The most salient mechanism is gatekeeping at goods receipt, where buyers decide whether products meet contractual and quality standards.

Retailers exercise strong gatekeeping power, particularly in fresh and PL categories. In case A, daily enforcement relies primarily on delivery calendars adherence and refusal of non-conforming goods, with penalties available but seldom activated. In case C, the *capitolato* legitimises penalties or termination for specification deviations, though packaged products are accepted based on prior qualification and intensive inspection is reserved for fresh categories.

However, enforcement is not purely coercive. In case B, buyers share granular performance data, including per-store rotations, shrinkage, and markdown outlays, to renegotiate MLOR thresholds; for selected partners, the firm enables real-time data access through vendor-managed inventory arrangements, shifting stock responsibility upstream while providing richer visibility in return. In the wholesaler case, enforcement is more informal and relational, with limited use of formal penalties.

Product characteristics strongly influence enforcement dynamics. In highly perishable categories, stricter acceptance criteria and tighter control mechanisms increase the likelihood of product rejection and upstream risk exposure. Conversely, in longer shelf-life or brand-dominated categories, enforcement focuses more on commercial performance than on technical compliance.

5.3 Power in the Revision of Standards and Terms

Revision episodes reveal a third configuration of power, in which governance mechanisms are renegotiated and adapted over time. Across cases, revision is triggered by a combination of periodic processes (e.g., annual negotiations) and event-driven factors, such as performance issues, regulatory changes, or innovation opportunities.

Data-driven renegotiation is particularly evident in case B, where detailed operational analytics justify changes in conditions, such as stricter shelf-life requirements or pricing structures. As one informant noted, "*if the product does not rotate, the problem remains*", signalling that optimal flow design alone cannot substitute for demand-side interventions such as price repositioning and assortment pruning.

Sustainability considerations emerge most clearly at this stage. In case C, packaging innovation is a recurrent revision trigger, with the retailer also acting as an "*educator*" for small suppliers ("*we explain to them what is needed to comply*"). In case A, revision episodes are slower due to packaging lock-in, while in case D it is largely supplier-led, leaving the wholesaler with minimal influence over specification content.

Overall, revision episodes illustrate that power is not only used to enforce existing conditions but also to reshape governance structures over time, either reinforcing existing asymmetries or enabling more collaborative arrangements.

5.4 The Role of Product Heterogeneity

Across all episodes, product characteristics act as key moderators of how power is exercised. Perishability, shelf life, substitutability, and brand architecture jointly determine both the feasibility and the effects of different power levers.

In highly perishable categories, coercive and risk-shifting mechanisms are amplified, increasing the likelihood of rejection and upstream FW. However, perishability does not mechanically generate waste: in Cases B and C, informational and expert power, sophisticated demand forecasting, inventory analytics, enable more collaborative outcomes, while in Case A coercive enforcement with limited data sharing pushes unsold risk back upstream. The same structural asymmetry can thus support either FW prevention or risk transfer, depending on how power is exercised.

Finally, where substitutability is high, buyers impose stringent requirements and shift risks upstream; in low-substitutability contexts, governance relies more on relational and incentive-based mechanisms.

Taken together, these findings show that power is enacted through a dynamic combination of levers that vary across governance episodes and product contexts, with direct implications for how FW risks are distributed and managed along the supply chain.

6 Discussion and Propositions

6.1 Power as a Processual and Episodic Phenomenon

Prior research has predominantly conceptualised power as a structural attribute of buyer–supplier relationships, rooted in asymmetries in resource dependence and market position (Emerson, 1962; Pfeffer & Salancik, 1978; Cox, 2001). While this perspective explains who holds power, it provides limited insight into how power is enacted in practice. The findings show that power is not exercised uniformly but is reconfigured across three governance episodes: definition, enforcement, and revision of standards and terms.

This dynamic view complements Resource Dependence Theory (RDT) by showing how dependence is operationalised through specific governance mechanisms rather than remaining an abstract structural condition (Emerson, 1962; Pfeffer & Salancik, 1978). It also extends Transaction Cost Economics (TCE), which emphasises the role of contracts in managing uncertainty (Williamson, 1993), by demonstrating that contracts are not static safeguards but are continuously reinterpreted and adapted through enforcement and revision practices. Finally, it aligns with Social Exchange Theory (SET), which highlights that the effects of power depend on how it is exercised within ongoing relationships (Cook et al., 2013; Nyaga et al., 2013).

These insights address RQ1 by showing how power levers vary across episodes, leading to the following propositions:

P1a. Structural and contractual power levers dominate the definition of standards and terms, translating dependence asymmetries into formal specifications and risk-allocation mechanisms.
P1b. Enforcement relies primarily on contractual and informational levers, often expressed through coercive and legitimate power bases.
P1c. Revision episodes are characterised by a greater role of informational and expert levers, which are used to adapt and reshape governance arrangements over time.

6.2 Power, Governance, and Food Waste Outcomes

Existing literature has begun to link buyer power and governance practices to FW, particularly through the role of private standards and contractual clauses in shaping upstream losses (Herzberg et al., 2022; Pietrangeli et al., 2023). However, these studies typically focus on isolated mechanisms rather than on how governance processes as a whole influence FW outcomes.

The findings suggest that FW is not simply an operational by-product but is partially determined by how power is exercised across governance episodes.

Importantly, the way power is exercised varies with organisational priorities. In contexts where sustainability is more institutionalised, revision episodes are used to introduce practices such as improved data sharing, packaging innovation, and structured valorisation channels. In more commercially driven contexts, power is primarily used to protect margins, often reinforcing risk transfer upstream. This finding is consistent with SET, which suggests that the relational use of power can foster cooperation and joint value creation, while coercive use may lead to opportunistic or defensive behaviours (Nyaga et al., 2013; Huo et al., 2017). It also extends existing FW literature by showing that waste outcomes emerge from the cumulative effect of governance choices rather than from isolated operational inefficiencies.

Accordingly, these insights lead to the following proposition:

P2. Food waste outcomes in supply chains are shaped by how power is exercised across governance episodes. The same structural asymmetries can lead to either risk-shifting or more balanced food waste management, depending on how contractual, informational, and relational levers are combined.

6.3 The Role of Product Heterogeneity

While prior research acknowledges that product characteristics influence both supply chain dynamics and FW (Mena et al., 2011), their role in shaping the exercise of power has received less attention. The findings show that product heterogeneity is a key moderator of both the choice and the impact of power levers.

In highly perishable categories, short shelf life and high uncertainty increase dependence on timely coordination and amplify the effectiveness of coercive and legitimate levers. Buyers are more likely to impose strict specifications and acceptance criteria, which can shift FW risk upstream, consistent with evidence on fresh produce supply chains (Herzberg et al., 2022; Maglaras et al., 2015). However, the findings also show that these effects are not deterministic. When buyers complement control mechanisms with information sharing and collaborative practices, perishability can be managed more effectively, reducing FW. Substitutability and brand architecture further affect power dynamics. In private-label contexts, where buyers control product design and have access to multiple suppliers, structural power is reinforced and more likely to be exercised through formal contractual and technical levers. Conversely, in categories dominated by strong national brands or limited supplier alternatives, power is more balanced, and governance relies more on relational and incentive-based mechanisms.

These insights address RQ2, leading to three additional propositions:

P3. In highly perishable categories, buyers are more likely to deploy coercive and risk-shifting power levers at the definition and enforcement stages, increasing the likelihood of upstream food waste unless these levers are complemented by information sharing and collaborative practices.

P4a. In contexts where buyers control private-label products and have access to multiple sourcing options, power is more likely to be exercised through formal contractual and structural levers.

P4b. In brand-dominated or low-substitutability contexts, power is more balanced and governance relies more on relational and incentive-based mechanisms.

7 Conclusions

This study, integrating insights from a literature review and a multiple-case study, develops a processual perspective on power, showing how it is mobilised across the definition, enforcement, and revision of standards and terms.

These mechanisms influence FW not only at the operational level but also through the allocation of risks and responsibilities embedded in contractual and organisational choices. Product heterogeneity (perishability, shelf life, substitutability) and brand architecture, further condition the selection and the effectiveness of power levers such that similar operational conditions can lead to different FW outcomes depending on how power is exercised and coordinated.

From a theoretical perspective, the study contributes to the literature in three ways: reconceptualising power as a dynamic and episodic phenomenon; framing FW as the outcome of governance processes rather than as a purely operational issue; and integrating product heterogeneity into the analysis of power in FSCs.

From a managerial standpoint, the findings suggest that companies can actively shape FW outcomes by reconfiguring governance mechanisms across relationship episodes. At the definition stage, buyers should design contractual clauses, including MLOR thresholds, return agreements, and service-level penalties, with explicit attention to how risk is allocated: clauses that shift unsold or non-compliant product risk entirely upstream tend to generate defensive supplier behaviour and higher FW, particularly in perishable categories. Differentiated MLOR thresholds by product risk profile (as in Case B) represent a practical tool to balance freshness control with upstream feasibility. At the enforcement stage, complementing gatekeeping with data sharing enables suppliers to anticipate and prevent non-conformities rather than merely absorb their consequences. Buyers with advanced informational capabilities should consider VMI-style arrangements or structured performance dialogues as alternatives to purely coercive enforcement. At the revision stage, governance review cycles should be used proactively to introduce FW-oriented practices rather than limiting revision to commercial renegotiation. Supplier development programmes, as observed in Cases B and C, can build upstream capabilities that make compliance more feasible and reduce structural sources of waste. Finally, the wholesaler case highlights that actors with limited bargaining power need targeted support to access the informational and contractual tools that make collaborative FW management possible.

This study is subject to some limitations. The empirical analysis is based on a limited number of cases within the Italian grocery sector, which may affect the generalisability of the findings. In addition, the evidence primarily reflects the perspective of buying organisations in the downstream stages of the supply chain (i.e., grocery retailers/ wholesalers). While this addresses an underexplored perspective, it means that supplier-side experiences of governance mechanisms, risk allocation, and FW outcomes remain unobserved. The same contractual clause or gatekeeping practice may be perceived and enacted differently by upstream actors, potentially leading to different FW implications than those reported here. Future research should incorporate supplier perspectives through dyadic or multi-actor designs to capture the full relational dynamics through which power shapes FW outcomes.

Disclosure of Interests.. The authors have no competing interests to declare that are relevant to the content of this article.

References

Belaya, V., Gagalyuk, T., Hanf, J.: Measuring asymmetrical power distribution in supply chain networks: what is the appropriate method? J. Relat. Mark. **8**(2), 165–193 (2009)

Brinker, J., Haasis, H.-D.: Power in the context of SCM and supply chain digitalization: an overview from a literature review. Logistics. **6**(2), 25 (2022)

Carbone, A.: Food supply chains: coordination, governance and other shaping forces. Agric. Food Econ. **5**(1), 21 (2017)

Cox, A.: The power perspective in procurement and supply management. J. Supply Chain Manag. **37**(2), 4–7 (2001)

Cook, K.S., Cheshire, C., Rice, E.R.W., Nakagawa, S.: Social exchange theory. In: Handbooks of Sociology and Social Research, pp. 61–88 (2013)

Eisenhardt, K.M., Graebner, M.E.: Theory building from cases: opportunities and challenges. Acad. Manag. J. **50**(1), 25–32 (2007)

Emerson, R.M.: Power-dependence relations. Am. Sociol. Rev. **27**(1), 31–41 (1962)

European Parliament & Council of the European Union: Directive (EU) 2025/1892 Amending Directive 2008/98/EC as Regards Food Waste and Textile Waste, pp. 1–31. Official Journal of the European Union (2025)

Fang, M., Yu, Y., Park, K., Liu, F., Xiao, S.S., Shi, Y.: Supply chain relationship dependencies and circular economy performance: the contingency role of digitalization capability. J. Purch. Supply Manag. **30**(4), 100936 (2024)

French, J.R.P., Raven, B.: The bases of social power. In: Cartwright, D. (ed.) Studies in Social Power, pp. 150–167 (1959)

Gioia, D.A., Corley, K.G., Hamilton, A.L.: Seeking qualitative rigor in inductive research. Organ. Res. Methods. **16**(1), 15–31 (2013)

Herzberg, R., Schmidt, T., Keck, M.: Market power and food loss at the producer–retailer interface. Sustain. Sci. **17**(6), 2253–2267 (2022)

Hingley, M.K.: Power imbalanced relationships: Cases from UK fresh food supply. Int. J. Retail Distrib. Manag. **33**(8), 551–569 (2005)

Huo, B., Flynn, B.B., Zhao, X.: Supply chain power configurations and their relationship with performance. J. Supply Chain Manag. **53**(2), 88–111 (2017)

Kim, B., Oh, H.: The impact of decision-making sharing between supplier and manufacturer on their collaboration performance. Supply Chain Manag. **10**(3), 223–236 (2005)

Maglaras, G., Bourlakis, M., Fotopoulos, C.: Power-imbalanced relationships in the dyadic food chain: an empirical investigation of retailers' commercial practices with suppliers. Ind. Mark. Manage. **48**, 187–201 (2015)

Malik, S.A., Hingley, M.K.: Consumer demand information as a re-balancing tool for power asymmetry between food retailers and suppliers. Econ. Agro-Aliment. **23**(2), 1–26 (2021)

Maloni, M., Benton, W.C.: Power influences in the supply chain. J. Bus. Logist. **21**, 49–73 (2000)

Marques, L., Lontra, P., Wanke, P., Antunes, J.J.M.: Governance modes in supply chains and financial performance at buyer, supplier and dyadic levels: the positive impact of power balance. Benchmarking. **29**(1), 255–284 (2022)

Mena, C., Adenso-Diaz, B., Yurt, O.: Causes of food waste at the supplier–retailer interface: evidences from the UK and Spain. Resour. Conserv. Recycl. **55**(6), 648–658 (2011)

Nyaga, G.N., Lynch, D.F., Marshall, D., Ambrose, E.: Power asymmetry, adaptation and collaboration in dyadic relationships involving a powerful partner. J. Supply Chain Manag. **49**(3), 42–65 (2013)

Pfeffer, J., Salancik, G.R.: The External Control of Organizations: a Resource Dependence Perspective. Harper & Row (1978)

Pietrangeli, R., Herzberg, R., Cicatiello, C., Schneider, F.: Quality standards and contractual terms affecting food losses: the perspective of producer organisations in Germany and Italy. Foods. **12**(10), 2064 (2023)

Viscardi, S., Colicchia, C.: A classification of food products to enhance circular economy and reduce waste: a systematic literature review. Resour. Conserv. Recycl. **23**, 200229 (2023)

Williamson, O.E.: Transaction cost economics and organization theory. Ind. Corp. Change. **2**(2), 107–156 (1993)
Yin, R.K.: Case Study Research: Design and Methods, vol. 5. sage (2009)

Nutrient Value Loss Framework for Supply Chain Management

Silvia Cardini(✉), Anna Savio, Beatrice Marchi, Simone Zanoni, and Lucio Enrico Zavanella

University of Brescia, Via Branze 38, 25123 Brescia, Italy
{silvia.cardini,anna.savio,beatrice.marchi,simone.zanoni, lucio.zavanella}@unibs.it

Abstract. Food waste in supply chains is still predominantly assessed through mass-based indicators, which implicitly treat equal discarded quantities as equivalent losses. In food systems, however, this assumption is weak, since the consequences of waste depend not only on quantity, but also on nutritional composition, target population needs, replacement conditions, and downstream health implications. This paper proposes a functional loss value perspective for food waste assessment, replacing the conventional mass-based view with a multidimensional evaluation of the function no longer delivered by discarded products. The framework is operationalised through three complementary dimensions: Nutrient Loss Value (*NLV*), which measures nutritional content weighted by its relevance for a specific population group; Substitution and Replacement Cost (*SRC*), which captures the economic, temporal, and environmental effort required to restore the unavailable food function; and Preventable Health Impact (*PHI*), which translates nutritional loss into potential health consequences through DALY-based coefficients derived from epidemiological and dietary reference data. These dimensions are integrated into a composite Lost Value Index (*LVI*), proposed as an exploratory prioritisation metric for supply chain decision support. An illustrative application involving spinach, eggs, and salmon across two target populations demonstrates how physically equivalent waste events may generate different priorities when assessed in functional terms. The results reveal rank reversals that remain invisible under conventional mass- or expiry-based logic and indicate the potential relevance of prioritisation rules that consider a value perspective.

Keywords: Food waste · Nutrient loss · Supply chain management · Lost value index

1 Introduction

In recent years, the transition toward sustainable and resilient production and supply systems has become a central priority for both academia and industry, driven largely by the European policy agenda, including the Farm-to-Fork Strategy and the Circular Economy Action Plan [1, 2]. In this context, food supply chains are no longer assessed

Published by Springer Nature Switzerland AG 2027
G. Pezzotta et al. (Eds.): APMS 2026, IFIP AICT 808, pp. 244–259, 2027.
https://doi.org/10.1007/978-3-032-38594-9_17

solely in terms of economic efficiency but increasingly in relation to environmental performance, waste reduction, and nutritional outcomes [3]. Despite this shift, food losses and waste are still predominantly measured through mass-based indicators, such as kilograms or units discarded [4, 5]. While these measures are easy to aggregate and operationally convenient, they assume that equal physical losses generate equal consequences.

In food systems, the value delivered by a product cannot be reduced to its mass alone [6]. Food primarily performs a nutritional function, and the loss of this function depends on the product composition, the nutritional need of the target population, and the effort required to restore the unavailable value [7]. As a result, two waste events with identical mass may generate substantially different consequences [8]. This limitation is especially relevant in perishable food supply chains, where time-temperature exposure, storage conditions, and processing decisions can progressively affect product quality before physical disposal occurs [9]. A purely mass-based representation of waste therefore overlooks an important part of the actual loss generated along the supply chain [10].

Previous research has significantly advanced the analysis of food losses and waste, but the relevant literature remains fragmented [11]. Studies on food waste often focus on discarded quantities and economic losses; quality-oriented supply chain models mainly address shelf life, freshness, or safety; and nutrition-oriented research rarely enters operational decision-making [12, 13]. Consequently, the functional dimension of food remains underrepresented in supply chain management [14]. What is still missing is a structured framework capable of translating a physical waste event into the loss of the function that the product would have delivered, together with the broader operational and health-related implications of that loss.

Based on this gap, the objective of this paper is to develop and demonstrate a structured framework that translate physical food waste into functional value loss for supply chain decision making. The study is guided by the following research questions:

- **RQ1**. How can a physical food waste event be conceptually reframed as the loss of the function that the product would have delivered?
- **RQ2**. Which dimensions are needed to operationalise functional value loss in food supply chains, considering nutritional relevance, replacement effort, and preventable health implications?
- **RQ3**. How does the proposed framework change waste prioritisation compared with conventional mass-based or expiry-based assessment in an illustrative application?

To answer these questions, this study proposes a functional value loss perspective for food waste assessment. Rather than interpreting waste as discarded mass, the framework evaluates waste according to the delivered function that becomes unavailable when the product is discarded. The conceptual shift from mass-based loss to functional value loss is addressed by RQ1. The framework is then operationalised through three complementary dimensions: Nutrient Loss Value (*NLV*), which captures nutritional content in relation to population-specific relevance; Substitution and Replacement Cost (*SRC*), which represents the economic, temporal, and environmental effort required to restore the unavailable food function; and Preventable Health Impact (*PHI*), which translates nutritional loss into potential health consequences. These dimensions are integrated into the Lost Value Index (*LVI*), an exploratory decision-support metric for waste prioritisation. Finally, the illustrative application addresses RQ3 by showing how the framework modifies prioritisation compared with conventional mass-based logic. The application is intended as a structured demonstration of the framework, not as empirical validation in a real supply chain setting.

To clarify the position of the study, Table 1 compares the proposed *LVI* framework with existing food waste assessment approaches. While previous research has contributed through macro-level nutritional evaluations, waste management hierarchies, and cause-effect logistic models, these approaches generally treat waste as discarded physical mass. By contrast, the proposed framework reframes waste as a functional value loss and integrates nutritional relevance, replacement effort, and preventable health impacts into a supply chain decision-support structure [11].

Table 1. Comparison of the proposed Lost Value Index framework with existing literature

Assessment Dimension	Existing Frameworks in Literature	Proposed Framework	Key Existing Reference
Primary Assessment Metric	Physical mass, monetary value, or generic shelf-life indicators. Implicitly assumes equal physical losses have equal consequences	*NLV*(Nutrient Loss Value)	[3, 10, 14]
Supply Chain Focus	Focus on disposal (waste hierarchy), or mapping the root causes of inefficiencies across the supply chain	Preventive Prioritization: extension of FEFO logic toward more value sensitive prioritisation for operational inventory and batch management (*SRC*)	[11, 13]
Integration of Health	Macro-level assessments: used primarily to guide national policies or evaluate global food supply against population dietary gaps.	Operational: Translates nutritional density and preventable DALYs (*PHI*)	[8, 14]

The contribution of the paper is threefold. First, it advances a functional interpretation of food waste, in which the relevance of waste event depends on the value no longer delivered rather than on the mass discarded. Second, it proposes an operational framework for the food domain that combines nutritional loss, substitution and replacement effort, and preventable health consequences within a unified assessment structure. Third, it demonstrates, through an application, how this logic may generate different managerial priorities from conventional mass-based approaches, supporting more value sensitive waste management and inventory decisions. Although the framework is specialised for food systems, the underlying methodological logic is not sector specific and can be transferred to other domains by redefining the relevant function delivered by the product or service.

The remainder of the paper follows the research logic introduced above. Chapter 2 develops the conceptual rationale of the functional value loss perspective and then operationalises it through the *LVI* components. Chapter 3 presents the illustrative application, separating the application design, the descriptive results, their interpretation, and the resulting managerial implications, limitations and future research directions. Chapter 4 concludes the paper by summarising the main findings and contributions.

2 Conceptual Framework and Methodological Approach

This section develops the conceptual rationale of the proposed framework and translates it into an operational assessment structure for food waste. The starting point is the shift from conventional mass-based waste assessment to a functional value loss perspective. Waste in production and supply chain systems is commonly measured through mass-based indicators, such as kilograms or units discarded. While simple to aggregate, these indicators fail to capture the significance of losses when the value of what is discarded depends on its specific function. Two physically equivalent losses may generate radically different consequences in terms of service delivery, social impact, or replacement effort.

The core methodological premise of this study is therefore to assess waste according to the function no longer delivered rather than the physical quantity discarded. This perspective acknowledges that the relationship between physical quantity and functional content is non-linear and context dependent. A discarded product may represent a limited physical loss but a substantial functional loss when it is difficult to replace, when it addresses critical needs, or when its absence generates relevant downstream consequences.

Although the framework is developed in the food domain, the underlying logic is not sector specific. Its application requires identifying the function delivered by a product or service and defining the dimensions through which the loss of that function can be assessed. In food systems, this means linking physical waste to nutritional relevance, replacement effort, and potential health consequences. These dimensions are operationalised in the following section through the Nutrient Loss Value, the Substitution and Replacement Cost, and the Preventable Health Impact, which are then integrated into the Lost Value Index.

2.1 A Three-Level Framework for Food Waste Assessment

In the food domain, functional value loss cannot be inferred directly from the mass of discarded products, because the consequences of waste depend on nutritional content, population vulnerability, and replacement conditions. This study proposes a three-level framework that transforms physical waste into three complementary dimensions of loss:

1. Nutrient Loss Value (*NLV*): Captures nutritional content weighted by functional relevance for a target population.
2. Substitution and Replacement Cost (*SRC*): Quantifies the economic and operational burden required to compensate for functional value loss.
3. Preventable Health Impact (*PHI*): Translates nutritional loss into measurable health outcomes using Disability-Adjusted Life Years (DALYs).

2.1.1 Nutrient Loss Value (NLV)

The *NLV* shifts the focus from raw weight to the specific nutrients (e.g., protein, vitamins, minerals) most critical in a given context [7]. For an item i and a given target group g, the index is calculated as:

$$NLV(i, g) = \sum_{k} w(k, g) \times n(i, k) \tag{1}$$

where $n(i, k)$ is the amount of nutrient k in item i per 100 g. Nutritional data are sourced from CREA Food Composition Tables, maintained by the CREA Research Centre for Food and Nutrition, which provides standardized food composition data and reports that the database has been revised and updated according to current international standards [15].The term $w(k, g)$ represents the weight for a specific nutrient k and a target group g. This weight is defined as the normalized average of three scores: clinical importance, observed population deficiency, and substitution difficulty. Clinical importance and observed population deficiency are estimated based on standardized nutritional reference sources and population-level evidence, while substitution difficulty is defined through the assessment framework adopted in this study.

2.1.2 Substitution and Replacement Cost (SRC)

While *NLV* captures the intrinsic nutritional value of food, *SRC* internalizes the systemic effort required to restore the unavailable food function. This layer is important because products with a similar nutritional loss may generate very different operational consequences once replacement is considered [16]. *SRC* is an independent layer in respect of population concerns and needs, it reflects the supply chain friction, calculated as the average of three normalized sub-components: procurement cost, replenishment lead time, and associated environmental burdens, in this case linked with Climate Change.

$$SRC_i = \frac{Cost_{norm} + LT_{norm} + CC_{norm}}{3} \tag{2}$$

2.1.3 Preventable Health Impact (PHI)

The third component of the framework, *PHI*, represents a fundamental shift in the assessment logic, moving from the food product's properties to the actual human outcomes. While *NLV* captures the intrinsic nutritional value and *SRC* reflects the systemic effort required to restore it, *PHI* quantifies the health consequences of failing to deliver that nutrition to the intended population [17]. In this sense, food waste is interpreted as a missed health opportunity: if the discarded food had been consumed by the intended target population, a measurable portion of disease that are related to nutrition, could have been prevented.

To make this layer operational, the framework bridges clinical epidemiology with supply chain events through a health conversion factor $\theta(k, g)$ which represents the marginal health impact per nutrient unit. This factor is defined as:

$$\theta(k, g) = \frac{DB(k, g)}{RDI(k, g) \bullet 365 \bullet 100,000} \tag{3}$$

Where $DB(k, g)$ is the annual disease burden, expressed in *DALY* per 100,000 people, associated with nutrient k for group g, and $RDI(k, g)$ is the Recommended Daily Intake for the same nutrient and group. Disease Burden estimates are obtained from the IHME Global Burden of Disease (GBD) Results Tool, while nutrient reference values are derived from the EFSA Dietary Reference Value (DRVs), accessed through the DRV Finder. Since EFSA defines DRVs as an umbrella framework including different index, for this study we considered Population Reference Intake as our RDI value [18, 19].

The *PHI* associated with a specific waste event is then calculated by multiplying this conversion factor by the total amount of nutrient lost:

$$PHI(i, g) = \sum_{k} \theta(k, g) \bullet (\mathrm{n(i, k)} \bullet Q_i \bullet 10) \tag{4}$$

In this formulation $n(i, k)$ represents the nutrient content per 100 g of products, while Q_i is the wasted quantity in kilograms, the constant factor 10 is applied to align the mass units, ensuring full transparency in the conversion from physical waste to health prevention capacity.

2.1.4 Lost Value Index (LVI)

The three dimensions are integrated into a final composite metric, the *LVI*, which is proposed as an exploratory decision-support metric governance metric:

$$LVI = \varphi \bullet (\alpha \bullet NLV_{norm} + \beta \bullet SRC_{norm} + \gamma \bullet PHI_{norm}) \tag{5}$$

where:

$$\varphi = \frac{\mathrm{RSL_{min}}}{\mathrm{RSL_i}}$$

In this formulation *NLV*, *SRC*, *PHI* represent the normalized value of Nutrient Loss Value, Substitution and Replacement Cost, and Preventable Health Impact, respectively. To ensure mathematical consistency and allow the aggregation of heterogeneous metrics, nutritional density, health outcomes (*DALYs*), and logistical costs, the components are transformed into dimensionless values. Specifically, each component is normalized relative to the maximum observed impact within the analysed scenario, mapping the results onto a scale from 0 to 1. This linear scaling preserves the relative ratios between products while ensuring that no single dimension dominates the index due to its unit of measurement.

The term φ_i represents a relative remaining shelf-life factor. RSL_i indicates the remaining shelf life of product or batch i, while RSL_{min} is the minimum remaining shelf life observed among the products or batches compared within the same decision context. The factor φ_i ranges as well from 0 to 1 and assigns maximum temporal priority to the batch with the shortest remaining shelf life. In this way, the *LVI* incorporates not only the functional value potentially lost, but also the urgency with which that value must be preserved before the product become unsuitable for use.

The coefficient $\alpha, \beta, \gamma \geq 0$ (with $\alpha + \beta + \gamma = 1$) represent weighting factors calibrated to the strategic priorities of the decision context. For instance, a configuration that assigns greater weight to *SRC* prioritizes supply chain resilience, while a setup that assign greater value to *PHI* emphasizes public health outcomes. Since these coefficients influence the final ranking, their selection must be transparent, justified, and tested through sensitivity analysis. In this paper, the adopted weights are illustrative and are used to demonstrate the functioning of the framework rather than to prescribe a general standard.

This formulation also allows the framework to preserve the operational rationale of First-Expire, First-Out (FEFO), while extending it through a value sensitive logic. Conventional FEFO rules prioritise products according to their expiration date or remaining shelf life, meaning that the product closest to expiration is moved first out of inventory toward sale, donation, processing, or consumption [20]. In this sense, "out" does not refer to disposal, but to prioritise allocation before the product loses its suitability for use. The proposed First-Value, First-Out (*FVFO*) logic adopts the same interpretation of "out" but ranks products according to their expected functional value loss, as captured by the *LVI*. Therefore *FVFO* does not replace safety or expiry constraints but complements them by integrating temporal urgency with nutritional relevance, replacement burden, and preventable health impact.

Figure 1 summarizes the proposed three-level framework and illustrates how a physical food waste event is translated into three complementary dimensions of functional value loss, namely NLV, SRC, and PHI, which are then integrated into the composite Lost Value Index (LVI).

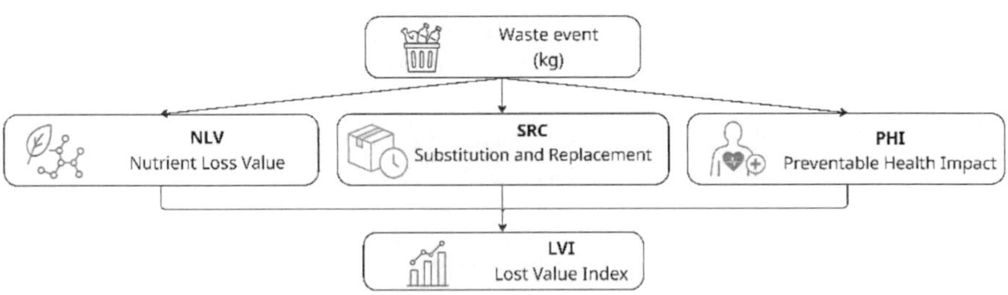

Fig. 1. Conceptual overview of the proposed food waste assessment framework

2.2 Transferability of the Methodology in Different Sectors

Although the structure proposed in this paper is specialized for food waste, the underlying methodological logic is not specific to one sector. The same interpretative shift, from physical loss to functional value loss, can be transferred to other sectors, provided that the dimensions of value are redefined according to the function delivered in each context. What is transferable is not necessarily the specific structure used for food, but the methodological process through which a physical loss is translated into a structured assessment of functional impact. This applicability relies on identifying the specific functional unit that characterizes the output of a given system. In healthcare, for instance, expired pharmaceutical doses or cancelled procedures could be interpreted not only as physical or organisational losses, but as missed treatment or patients left untreated. In the energy sector, distribution losses expressed in kilowatt-hours could be reframed as missed decarbonisation targets. Similarly, in industrial production, scrapped batched and unplanned downtime could be assessed as lost output capacity, delayed deliveries, or unmet service commitments.

In each case, the structural logic is preserved: a context-dependent weighting function assigns differential relevance to each unit of physical loss, enabling managers to prioritise interventions based on the real-world consequence of a waste event.

3 Illustrative Application: Design, Results, and Discussion

3.1 Illustrative Scenario and Application Scope

The role of this application is illustrative. It is used to demonstrate the operational steps of the framework and to explore whether the proposed metrics produce different prioritisation outcomes from mass-based assessment. It should not be interpreted as empirical validation of the framework, since it is based on a simplified scenario and selected products rather than on longitudinal data from an actual supply chain.

To transition from a mass-based to a functional perspective, it is first necessary to identify the primary function that the product is intended to deliver. In the food sector, the main function is the provision of nutrients. Therefore, while current waste management is anchored to mass, the transition to a functional assessment must start from the nutritional composition of the product. However, this nutrition value is only a starting baseline, the proposed framework wants to consider a broader context, health consequences, and replacement effort. What matters with decision making is not only how nutrients can be transferred by a product, but also who loses access to it, how critical those nutrients are in that context, and how difficult it is to compensate for that loss.

To demonstrate the limitations of mass-based indicators in Sustainable and Waste management, we analyse a scenario where three different products, green spinach (i_1), fresh eggs (i_2), and frozen salmon (i_3), reach the end of their shelf life. In traditional logistic, these events are recorded as a loss of 100 kg, suggesting an identical failure in supply chain efficiency. However, their functional impact is fundamentally different when evaluated through the proposed framework. This analysis considers two target populations to test the model's sensitivity: group 1 (g_1), representing the elderly population where protein is clinically prioritized, and group 2 (g_2), representing women of childbearing age, where iron deficiency is the primary concern.

3.2 Descriptive Application Results

This Section reports the numerical outputs generated by applying each layer of the framework to the illustrative scenario. The interpretation of their implications for prioritisation is developed afterwards, in order to distinguish evidence generated by the application from the managerial reading of such evidence.

The analysis begins with the parametrization of the *NLV* layer. The nutritional data $n(i, k)$ and the context weights ($w(k, g)$) are summarized in Table 2. The nutritional data $n(i, k)$ are sourced from the CREA database [15], ensuring the empirical reliability of analysis and the weights, as formalized in the methodology, are not arbitrary managerial choices but are derived from standardized clinical guidelines and public health targets.

Table 2. Nutritional content and weights

Nutrient k	Unit	Green spinach i_1	Fresh egg i_2	Salmon i_3	$w(k, g_1)$	$w(k, g_2)$
Protein	g/100 g	3.4	12.4	18.4	0.8	0.2
Iron	mg/100 g	2.9	1.5	0.7	0.2	0.8

The resulting *NLV* values, calculated for a 100 kg waste event, are presented in Table 3. The results highlight the framework's sensitivity to the target population: for group 1, salmon generates an *NLV* roughly 4.5 times higher than spinach reflecting its superior protein density. Conversely, for group 2, the gap narrows significantly as spinach gains relevance due to its higher iron content.

Table 3. Resulting *NLV*

Metric	Green Spinach i_1	Fresh egg i_2	Salmon i_3
Mass loss (kg)	100	100	100
$NLV(i, g_1)$	3.27	9.49	13.68
$NLV_{norm}(i, g_1)$	0,239	0,694	1,00
$NLV(i, g_2)$	2,99	3,50	3,95
$NLV_{norm}(i, g_2)$	0,758	0,887	1,00

At this stage the *NLV* valued provide a more granular description of waste impact than mass alone, but they remain a static measure of nutritional content and do not account for the operational effort required to restore such value.

While *NLV* captures the nutritional value lost with waste, *SRC* internalizes the systemic effort required to restore the unavailable food function. This difference does not depend solely on market price but reflects a complex interaction between resources, time and logistics.

To quantify this friction, we consider three components: procurement cost, replenishment lead time, and associated environmental burdens in this case linked with Climate

Change (CC). The unit cost values were defined as representative average retail prices for fresh products in Norther Italy while CC impacts were derived from the AGRIBALYSE food life cycle inventory database [21]. Replenishment lead times were not intended to represent measured supplier-specific data but were introduced as illustrative scenario parameters reflecting increasing replacement complexity across the selected products. In this sense, spinach represents a product with short replenishment time, eggs an intermediate case, and salmon a product associated with higher procurement and cold-chain complexity. The inclusion of lead time as a critical variable allows for a transition from a static view of waste to a dynamic assessment of supply chain vulnerability. A discarded product with a long replenishment cycle, such as salmon compared to spinach, imposes a larger functional gap on the system, increasing the risk of failing to meet the target population's needs. The data used for the calculation are summarized in Table 4.

Table 4. Data for *SRC*

Product i	Unit Cost (€/kg)	Lead Time $days$	CC impact ($kgCO_{2,\,eq}$/kg)
Green spinach	3.78	1	0.42
Fresh egg	4.45	2	1.88
Salmon	30	5	5.50

As shown in Table 5, the disparity in replacement burden is substantial. Salmon carries the maximum *SRC* value (1.00) because its procurement cost is nearly eight times that of spinach and its replenishment cycle is five times longer.

Table 5. Normalized *SRC* components and final index

Product i	Cost normalized (C')	Lead Time (LT')	CC normalized (CC')	*SRC*
Green spinach	0.126	0.200	0.077	0.134
Fresh egg	0.148	0.400	0.342	0.297
Salmon	1.000	1.000	1.000	1.00

The *SRC* layer also incorporates sustainability information and metrics. Replacing a discarded product implies additional environmental burden associated with producing and transporting its replacement. By including these environmental costs, the framework captures a component of the ecological friction that is often decoupled from economic value in traditional reporting. Since the values adopted in this illustrative application combine environmental indicators with scenario-based assumptions on replenishment complexity, the resulting *SRC* values should be interpreted as a demonstration of the framework logic rather than as product-specific empirical benchmarks.

The third component of the framework, *PHI*, shifts the assessment from the product to the human outcome, interpreting food waste as a missed health opportunity. To operationalize this layer, *DALY* coefficients are derived from the Global Burden of Disease (GDB) data and translated into nutrient specific marginal impact factors ($\theta(k, g)$).

For this application, "protein-energy malnutrition" was used as a proxy disease for protein deprivation, while "dietary iron deficiency" served as the proxy for iron deprivation. The health conversion factors were calculated using *DALY* rates from the IHME results platform and nutritional requirements from EFSA Population Reference Intake values. Since these parameters mainly support the calculation procedure rather thank the interpretation of the results, they are not reported in a separate table.

The *PHI* for the three waste events was calculated and normalized. The results, presented in Table 6, highlight a critical divergence from the mass-based and even the nutritional (*NLV*) perspective.

Table 6. *PHI* results for a 100 kg waste event

Product i	Quantity lost (kg)	Protein lost (g)	Iron lost (mg)	$PHI_{norm}(i, g_1)$	$PHI_{norm}(i, g_2)$
Green spinach	100	3,400	2,900	1.00	1.00
Fresh egg	100	12,400	1,500	0.931	0.713
Salmon	100	18,400	700	0.925	0.565

Under the PHI layer, spinach generates the highest impact in both target groups, although for different underlying reasons. In Group 2, this result is consistent with the high disease burden associated with iron deficiency in women of childbearing age, which amplifies the value of the iron content in spinach. More interestingly, spinach also ranks first in Group 1 (the elderly population), despite the initial clinical parameterization that prioritized protein intake for this demographic. This finding emerges because the PHI layer is not driven by nutrient density alone, but by the interaction between the specific nutrient content of the food and the disease burden coefficients derived from epidemiological data. In other words, the DALY-normalized health significance of iron loss remains sufficiently high to offset the superior protein density of salmon even in a population group where protein is clinically critical.

Taken together, the PHI results show that a mass-based metric can hide the distribution of potential health consequences across populations. A 100 kg loss may represent not only a logistical issue; it may also a measurable loss in potential health benefits, depending on where discarded food would have generated the largest reduction in nutrition-related disease burden.

To account for temporal urgency, the final *LVI* also incorporates the relative remaining shelf-life factor introduced in Sect. 2.2.4. In this illustrative application, the remaining shelf-life values were defined according to consumer-use assumptions rather than supplier operational data: 4 days for fresh spinach, 10 days for fresh eggs, and 5 days for vacuum-packed salmon. These assumptions allow the example to compare the prioritisation obtained through the value-sensitive *LVI* with the prioritisation that would emerge from a purely expiry-based logic. The results are reported in Table 7 where the FEFO rank is based only on the remaining shelf life, while the final *LVI* rank is based on the proposed index.

Table 7. Comparative *LVI* result

Product i	Target Group	RSL (days)	φ	*LVI*	FEFO rank	*LVI* Rank
Green spinach	g_1	4	1.00	0.522	1	2
	g_2			0.730		1
Fresh egg	g_1	10	0.400	0.284	3	3
	g_2			0.280		3
Salmon	g_1	5	0.800	0.777	2	1
	g_2			0.661		2

3.3 Discussion of Prioritisation Effects

The following Section interpret the descriptive outputs in relation to the study objective. The focus is not on claiming statistical validation, but on showing how the framework changes the decision logic when the same waste events are evaluated in functional rather than physical or purely expiry-based terms.

The final *LVI* ranking already incorporates the relative remaining shelf-life factor, together with nutritional relevance, replacement burden, and preventable health impact. A purely FEFO-based rule would prioritise products only according to their remaining shelf life: in the illustrative scenario, spinach would be selected first, followed by salmon and then eggs. This logic captures temporal urgency but does not distinguish between products with different nutritional roles, replacement complexity, or potential health-related consequences.

The *LVI* results show that this additional information can change the prioritisation logic. In Group 1, salmon emerges as the highest-priority product ($LVI(3, g_1) = 0.777$), despite not having the shortest remaining shelf life. Spinach, although the most urgent product under FEFO, ranks second ($LVI(1, g_1) = 0.522$), while eggs rank third ($LVI(2, g_1) = 0.284$). This result highlights that a product with a slightly longer remaining shelf life may still deserve priority when its expected functional value loss is substantially higher. In Group 2, spinach remains the highest-priority product ($LVI(1, g_2) = 0.730$), followed by salmon ($LVI(3, g_2) = 0.661$) and eggs ($LVI(2, g_2) = 0.280$. In this case, the FEFO and LVI rankings partially converge for the first position, but for different reasons: FEFO prioritises spinach because it expires first, whereas the LVI prioritises it because temporal urgency is reinforced by its functional relevance for iron-related nutritional needs.

These results illustrate the core rationale of the proposed First-Value, First-Out (FVFO) logic: expiry date matters, but it should not be the only criterion for prioritisation.

FVFO therefore extends FEFO by combining temporal urgency with nutritional relevance, replacement burden, and preventable health impact. This logic is operationalised through the Functional Priority Dispatching (FPD) rule: when facing potential waste, logistics providers could prioritise the batch that maximises the functional value delivered to its destination. The approach extends waste management beyond physical efficiency and connects it with the human-centric and data-driven objectives of Industry 5.0.

3.4 Managerial Implications, Limitations, and Future Research

The transition from a mass-based assessment to the *LVI* can support more value-sensitive waste management decisions, shifting the framework from a retrospective reporting logic into a proactive Decision Support System (DSS). From a managerial perspective, the main potential contribution lies in the operationalisation of the FPD rule. Under this logic, scarce resources, such as limited transport capacity or specialised workforce for last minute rescue operations, could be allocated according to the functional impact of a product rather than its physical mass alone. This approach is particularly relevant in perishable supply chains, where real-time monitoring of the cold chain could trigger automated interventions based on the functional sensitivity of the batch. However, practical implementation would require data interoperability between digital supply networks, nutritional databases, and, where relevant, public health data sources.

For the *LVI* to become as a rigorous tool for industrial governance, the selection of weighting coefficients (w, α, β, and γ) must also be transparent and empirically justified. In critical sectors like food and healthcare, these parameters should not rely solely on arbitrary managerial preferences, but should be refined through sensitivity analysis, stakeholder consultation, empirical calibration, and, where possible, alignment with open-access clinical or regulatory data sources. In the present paper, these coefficients are used for demonstration purposes only.

The illustrative nature of the application also represents the main limitation of this study. The numerical example demonstrates the internal logic and managerial potential of the proposed framework, but it does not validate the model using real operational data, nor does it assess its performance against observed supply chain outcomes. For this reason, the framework should be interpreted as a conceptual and methodological contribution that requires empirical validation before being used as a prescriptive decision rule in industrial context. A further simplifying assumption is that product quality and nutritional composition are considered fixed until the consumption event occurs, whereas in real cold supply chains product quality progressively deteriorates over storage time and, particularly for chilled products, as a function of storage temperature and environmental conditions [22].

Future research should move the framework from illustrative prioritisation to operational decision support by testing it in pilot settings, such as grocery stores, fresh-food supply chains, or other contexts where perishable food waste is directly managed. These applications would make it possible to compare *LVI* prioritisation with existing disposal routines, while evaluating data requirements, sensitivity to weighting choices, ease of use for practitioners, and compatibility with real inventory and waste management processes. A particularly relevant extension concerns the dynamic nature of product quality, where the residual value of a product progressively changes with storage time and, especially for chilled or frozen products, with temperature conditions. Future developments could therefore consider the nutrient condition of product as a time-temperature-dependent quality degradation function, allowing the functional value of a product to evolve dynamically. This would also support the integration of functional loss risk into inventory models, including Economic Order Quantity (EOQ) formulations, replenishment adjustment, and technological trade-offs between chilled and frozen preservation. Finally, future studies could investigate whether the framework can be adapted from population level target to more specific consumer or patient groups.

4 Conclusion

This paper proposed a functional value loss perspective for food waste assessment, replacing the conventional mass-based interpretation of waste with a multidimensional evaluation of the function no longer delivered. In response to RQ1, the study reframed food waste as a loss of delivered function rather than as a loss of physical quantity. In response to RQ2, this perspective was operationalised through three complementary dimensions, *NLV*, *SRC*, and *PHI* integrated into the *LVI*. The framework provides a structured way to connect nutritional relevance, replacement burden, and health consequences within a single assessment logic. In response to RQ3, the illustrative scenario showed that physically equivalent waste events may generate different impacts when evaluated in functional terms. Products with the same mass loss differed in their contribution to nutritional loss, replacement complexity, and potential health outcomes across target populations. As a result, the proposed framework reveals distinctions that are not captured by traditional mass-based or expiry-based approaches. The application should not be read as a demonstration of the framework, not as empirical validation in real supply chain conditions. Within this scope, the results also support the transition from conventional FEFO logic towards a more value-sensitive FVFO policy, operationalized through the FPD rules.

From a managerial perspective, the *LVI* can support waste prioritisation and more informed supply chain decisions in contexts where sustainability and public health objectives are relevant, redefining the relevant delivered function. However, the framework remains at a conceptual and illustrative stage. Future research should therefore prioritise empirical validation through pilot studies in grocery stores, fresh-food factories, or comparable perishable-food supply chains, followed by sensitivity analysis, parameter refinement, and integration into practical decision-support models.

Disclosure of Interests. The authors have no competing interests to declare that are relevant to the content of this article.

References

1. European Commission: Farm toFork Strategy: For a fair, healthy and environmentally-friendly food system #EUGreenDeal F (2020)

2. European Commission: Circular Economy Action Plan (2020)
3. Akkerman, R., Farahani, P., Grunow, M.: Quality, safety and sustainability in food distribution: a review of quantitative operations management approaches and challenges. OR Spectr. **32**, 863–904 (2010). https://doi.org/10.1007/s00291-010-0223-2
4. FAO: Integration of Environment and Nutrition in Life Cycle Assessment of Food Items: Opportunities and Challenges (2021). https://doi.org/10.4060/cb8054en
5. Xue, L. et al.: Missing food, missing data? A critical review of global food losses and food waste data. Environ. Sci. Technol. **51**, 6618–6633 (2017). https://doi.org/10.1021/acs.est.7b00401
6. Conrad, Z., Niles, M.T., Neher, D.A., Roy, E.D., Tichenor, N.E., Jahns, L.: Relationship between food waste, diet quality, and environmental sustainability. PLoS One. **13**, e0195405 (2018). https://doi.org/10.1371/journal.pone.0195405
7. Beal, T., Massiot, E., Arsenault, J.E., Smith, M.R., Hijmans, R.J.: Global trends in dietary micronutrient supplies and estimated prevalence of inadequate intakes. PLoS One. **12**, e0175554 (2017). https://doi.org/10.1371/journal.pone.0175554
8. Spiker, M.L., Hiza, H.A.B., Siddiqi, S.M., Neff, R.A.: Wasted food, wasted nutrients: nutrient loss from wasted food in the United States and comparison to gaps in dietary intake. J. Acad. Nutr. Diet. **117**, 1031–1040.e22 (2017). https://doi.org/10.1016/j.jand.2017.03.015
9. Marchi, B., Zanoni, S.: Cold chain energy analysis for sustainable food and beverage supply. Sustainability. **14**, 11137 (2022). https://doi.org/10.3390/su141811137
10. Chaboud, G., Daviron, B.: Food losses and waste: navigating the inconsistencies. Glob. Food Secur. **12**, 1–7 (2017). https://doi.org/10.1016/j.gfs.2016.11.004
11. Garcia-Garcia, G., Woolley, E., Rahimifard, S., Colwill, J., White, R., Needham, L.: A methodology for sustainable management of food waste. Waste Biomass Valor. **8**, 2209–2227 (2017). https://doi.org/10.1007/s12649-016-9720-0
12. Elbiyad, J. et al.: Quantitative and qualitative assessment of food waste in rural markets in Morocco. North African J. Food Nutr. Res. **8**, 130–139 (2024). https://doi.org/10.51745/najfnr.8.18.130-139
13. Mohammed, A., de Sousa, L., Jabbour, A.B., Zubairu, N., Chiappetta Jabbour, C.J., Al Naabi, H.: Food waste in the era of e-commerce: a novel farm-to-fork management methodology. Int. J. Prod. Econ. **285**, 109603 (2025). https://doi.org/10.1016/j.ijpe.2025.109603
14. Alexander, P., Brown, C., Arneth, A., Finnigan, J., Moran, D., Rounsevell, M.D.A.: Losses, inefficiencies and waste in the global food system. Agric. Syst. **153**, 190–200 (2017). https://doi.org/10.1016/j.agsy.2017.01.014
15. CREA: AlimentiNUTrizione (2019). https://www.alimentinutrizione.it/
16. Poore, J., Nemecek, T.: Reducing food's environmental impacts through producers and consumers. Science. **360**, 987–992 (2018). https://doi.org/10.1126/science.aaq0216
17. Afshin, A., et al.: Health effects of dietary risks in 195 countries, 1990–2017: a systematic analysis for the global burden of disease study 2017. Lancet. **393**, 1958–1972 (2019). https://doi.org/10.1016/S0140-6736(19)30041-8
18. European food safety authority (EFSA): dietary reference values for nutrients summary report. EFS3. **14** (2017). https://doi.org/10.2903/sp.efsa.2017.e15121
19. Global Burden of Disease Collaborative Network: Global Burden of Disease Results Tool https://vizhub.healthdata.org/gbd-results Accessed 09 Apr 2026
20. Grunow, M., Piramuthu, S.: RFID in highly perishable food supply chains – remaining shelf life to supplant expiry date? Int. J. Prod. Econ. **146**, 717–727 (2013). https://doi.org/10.1016/j.ijpe.2013.08.028

21. Colomb, V., Amar, S.A., Mens, C.B., et al.: AGRIBALYSE® , the French LCI database for agricultural products: high quality data for producers and environmental labelling. OCL. **22**(1), D104 (2015). https://doi.org/10.1051/ocl/20140047
22. Zanoni, S., Cardini, S., Marchi, B., Zavanella, L.E.: Lot sizing problem for cold supply chain with energy and quality considerations. Energies. **19**, 1360 (2026). https://doi.org/10.3390/en19051360

From Desert to Field: Environmental Corporate Social Responsibility as a Driver of Sustainable Technological Innovation in the UAE Agriculture Sector

Nilakshi W. K. Galahitiyawe[1](✉), Mohamad Al Atta[2], and Muhammad Shujaat Mubarik[1]

[1] Heriot-Watt University, Edinburgh, UK
{n.galahitiyawe,M.Mubarik}@hw.ac.uk
[2] Valmont Industries, Dubai, UAE

Abstract. Environmental sustainability has become a strategic priority in operations and production management, particularly in environmentally constrained sectors such as agriculture. In arid regions, sustainable technological innovation is essential for long-term sectoral viability and food security. This study examines how Environmental Corporate Social Responsibility (ECSR) functions as a driver of Sustainable Technological Innovation (STI) in the agriculture sector of the United Arab Emirates (UAE). Drawing on Stakeholder Theory and Innovation Diffusion Theory, the research investigates how environmental responsibility practices influence the adoption, diffusion, and sustained use of innovative agricultural technologies. A qualitative methodology was adopted, combining semi-structured interviews and ethnographic observations from a large-scale agricultural project. Findings indicate that ECSR plays a critical enabling role by legitimising long-term investment, aligning stakeholder expectations, and embedding sustainability within operational decision-making. However, diffusion remains constrained by high capital costs, harsh climatic conditions, and capability gaps. The study offers theoretical and practical insights for managers, policymakers, and researchers seeking to develop resilient, sustainable, and technology-enabled agricultural systems in arid environments.

Keywords: Environmental Corporate Social Responsibility · Sustainable Technological Innovation · Agriculture · UAE

1 Introduction

Sustainability has emerged as one of the most significant challenges facing modern organisations as they respond to escalating environmental, social, and economic pressures [1, 2]. Climate change, resource depletion, and increasing stakeholder scrutiny have compelled firms to reassess how production systems are designed, operated and governed [3]. In this context, Environmental Corporate Social Responsibility (ECSR) has evolved

Published by Springer Nature Switzerland AG 2027
G. Pezzotta et al. (Eds.): APMS 2026, IFIP AICT 808, pp. 260–274, 2027.
https://doi.org/10.1007/978-3-032-38594-9_18

from a compliance-oriented obligation into a strategic mechanism shaping investment decisions and technological trajectories [4, 5]. Parallel to this transformation, Sustainable Technological Innovation (STI) has become central to achieving operational efficiency while reducing environmental impact [6]. Technologies such as Internet of Things (IoT), artificial intelligence (AI), renewable energy systems, and precision automation have enabled organisations to optimise resource use and improve resilience [7, 8]. These developments are particularly critical in agriculture, one of the world's most resource-intensive sectors [9]. The challenges of agricultural sustainability are amplified in arid regions such as the United Arab Emirates (UAE), where extreme temperatures, limited rainfall, saline soils, and chronic water scarcity constrain domestic food production [10, 11]. Historically, these limitations have resulted in high dependency on food imports, exposing the UAE to supply-chain vulnerabilities [12]. In response, national strategies have increasingly emphasised Agri-technology adoption and environmental responsibility [13]. Despite this, empirical research examining the relationship between ECSR and technological innovation in agriculture, particularly in arid contexts, remains limited [14]. However, existing studies on ECSR and sustainable innovation have largely examined their relationship in broader corporate, manufacturing, or agribusiness contexts, with limited attention to how environmental responsibility shapes technology adoption in highly resource-constrained agricultural systems. This gap is important because the diffusion of sustainable technologies in agriculture is not determined by technological availability alone. It also depends on stakeholder expectations, institutional support, perceived economic feasibility, and the compatibility of innovations with local environmental conditions. In arid economies like UAE, where water scarcity, saline soils, high temperatures, and food-security concerns create both pressure for innovation and barriers to implementation, ECSR may operate less as a direct trigger of technological adoption and more as an enabling framework that legitimises investment, aligns stakeholders, and supports the diffusion of sustainable technologies. Therefore, the UAE context provides a theoretically useful setting to examine how ECSR, stakeholder alignment, and innovation diffusion interact in shaping sustainable technological innovation in agriculture. This study addresses this gap by analysing ECSR enables stakeholder alignment and supports the diffusion technological innovation in the UAE agriculture sector. To this end, the study seeks to address following research questions:

1. Who are the key internal and external stakeholders involved in environmental corporate social responsibility in the UAE agriculture sector, and how do they influence the adoption and implementation of sustainable technological innovations?
2. How do stakeholders perceive and what do they expect from environmental corporate social responsibility practices in relation to sustainable technological innovation in the UAE agriculture industry?
3. What challenges and opportunities are associated with integrating environmental corporate social responsibility practices with sustainable technological innovation in the UAE agriculture sector, as explained through innovation diffusion theory?
4. What recommendations can be proposed for organisations and researchers to promote the adoption and implementation of sustainable technological innovations through environmental corporate social responsibility practices in the UAE agriculture industry?

To address above research questions, this study adopts an ethnographic research strategy employed to gain an in-depth and contextually rich understanding of how ECSR initiatives and technologies are enacted within real agricultural operations. Data collection combined semi-structured interviews with naturalistic observations, enabling triangulation and enhancing the credibility of the findings. This Study contributes to the body of knowledge in at least three ways. First, the study enhances the contextual understanding on the STI in the context of agriculture's sector of UAE. This sector, despite its significant strategic importance, has remained under-represented in the extant literature. Secondly, the study provides a novel theoretical understanding by integrating Stakeholder theory with Diffusion of Innovation Theory study to explain as to legitimacy, stakeholders pressure, and diffusion conditions combinedly form the sustainability-oriented innovation. Thirdly, the study provides empirically grounded (qualitative) insights into the drivers and barriers of STI-ECSR integration. The rest of the paper is organized in 5 sections. Following section provides brief review of literature on the topics. Subsequent section, i.e., Sect. 3, illustrates methodology adopted in the study. Section 4 details the findings of the study followed by detailed discussion on the findings in Sect. 5. Last section, i.e., Sect. 6 concludes the paper.

2 Literature Review

2.1 Sustainable Technological Innovation in Operations Management

Sustainable Technological Innovation (STI) refers to the development and application of technologies that create economic value while simultaneously reducing environmental impact and supporting long-term ecological sustainability [15]. Within the field of operations management, STI is closely associated with process optimisation, emissions mitigation, waste reduction, and organisational resilience [16]. Advances in digital technologies, including the Internet of Things (IoT), artificial intelligence (AI), and data analytics, enable real-time monitoring and optimisation of resource utilisation, thereby improving both operational efficiency and environmental performance [17]. As a result, STI is increasingly viewed as inseparable from sustainability performance and long-term competitive advantage [18]. Despite its benefits, the adoption of STI presents significant challenges. Research indicates that organisations often face high capital requirements, uncertainty regarding return on investment, technological complexity, and organisational resistance to change when implementing sustainable technologies [19]. These barriers are particularly pronounced in sectors characterised by thin margins and high environmental uncertainty, such as agriculture. Consequently, many organisations struggle to move beyond pilot projects or symbolic adoption toward full operational integration of sustainable technologies. This highlights the importance of institutional support, stakeholder alignment, and governance mechanisms in enabling sustained technological innovation [20].

2.2 Sustainable Technological Innovation in Agriculture

The agriculture sector is among the most severely affected by climate change and environmental degradation. Agriculture encompasses a wide range of practices through which crop plants and domesticated animals provide food, fibre, and other essential products needed to sustain the global human population [21]. Climate-induced pressures, including increased water salinity, more frequent droughts and floods, and rising incidences of pests and invasive species, are disrupting agricultural ecosystems and threatening long-term food security [22]. These challenges contribute to ecological imbalance and pose significant risks to sustainable development worldwide. In response, scholarly attention has increasingly shifted toward STI as a critical mechanism for safeguarding global food systems and nutritional security [23]. Technologies such as IoT-enabled sensors, AI-driven analytics, automation, and precision machinery are being deployed to optimise resource use, stabilise yields, and enhance agricultural resilience under conditions of environmental uncertainty. These innovations support real-time sensing, predictive modelling, and adaptive decision-making, reducing waste while improving environmental and operational performance [24].

At a systemic level, researchers emphasise the importance of stakeholder engagement in accelerating the adoption and diffusion of sustainable agricultural technologies [25]. Meaningful involvement of employees, consumers, investors, and supply chain partners strengthens acceptance of innovation and facilitates behavioural change. Trust building through transparency in supply, production, and management processes is also critical in supporting long-term technological integration rather than short-term or symbolic adoption [26]. At the national level, the United Arab Emirates (UAE) provides a salient example of the promotion of STI in response to climate change and global disruptions such as the COVID-19 pandemic. The UAE has invested heavily in smart greenhouses, AI powered agricultural systems, controlled-environment farming, and data-driven management platforms to mitigate environmental constraints and supply-chain vulnerabilities [27]. These initiatives align with national priorities related to food and water security within an arid and import dependent context. Furthermore, policy initiatives such as Agri-tech accelerators, unified agricultural licensing frameworks, and cost reduction measures aim to lower entry barriers and broaden stakeholder participation in sustainable innovation [28]. Collectively, these efforts underscore the importance of STI as a strategic response to environmental threats in agriculture.

2.3 Environmental Corporate Social Responsibility

Environmental Corporate Social Responsibility (ECSR) refers to voluntary organisational commitments that extend beyond regulatory compliance to proactively address environmental challenges [29]. Typical ECSR initiatives include emissions reduction, resource conservation, renewable energy adoption, biodiversity protection, and transparent environmental reporting [30]. From an operations perspective, ECSR may influence strategic decisions related to process design, technology investment, supplier selection, and performance measurement [31]. Empirical research consistently demonstrates that ECSR enhances corporate reputation, stakeholder trust, and employee engagement, while supporting long-term organisational performance [32]. Although CSR has long historical roots, contemporary ECSR is increasingly understood as a strategic environmental practice that shapes stakeholder relationships, operational decisions, and innovation-related investments [33, 34]. Stakeholders play a particularly central role in shaping the execution and impact of ECSR. Research highlights that environmental responsibility is not solely determined by internal managerial values but is co-constructed through engagement with external stakeholders such as governments, communities, customers, and investors [35]. Studies further demonstrate that ECSR may function as a strategic marketing and communication mechanism capable of generating long-term reputational and financial benefits [36]. In this sense, ECSR is increasingly recognised not merely as a philanthropic or compliance-based activity, but as a strategic organisational practice with enduring operational and competitive implications.

Previous research suggests that CSR/ECSR can support sustainable innovation by enhancing stakeholder trust, legitimacy, long-term investment, and sustainability alignment, particularly in agricultural contexts. However, the relationship is not automatic, as high costs, uncertain returns, limited technical capabilities, weak institutional support, and resistance to change can hinder technology adoption. This study extends existing knowledge by examining ECSR as an enabling framework for stakeholder alignment and STI diffusion in the UAE's arid agricultural environment. While the literature highlights interconnections between ECSR, stakeholder engagement, and innovation, the underlying mechanisms remain underexplored. Stakeholder Theory and IDT together provide a useful lens for explaining these relationships.

2.4 Theoretical Underpinnings

This study draws on Stakeholder Theory (ST) and Innovation Diffusion Theory (IDT) to explain how ECSR supports stakeholder alignment and the diffusion of sustainable technological innovation (STI) in the UAE agricultural sector. ST argues that organisational success depends on recognising and responding to the interests of diverse stakeholders, including governments, communities, customers, suppliers, and the natural environment [37]. Such influences are particularly significant in agriculture due to environmental externalities, food security concerns, and regulatory oversight [38, 39]. IDT explains how innovations spread through social systems and identifies barriers to adoption such as financial constraints, risk aversion, limited knowledge transfer, and institutional challenges [40]. Since diffusion requires sustained implementation rather than initial adoption alone, ECSR is conceptualised as an enabling framework that legitimises investment, aligns stakeholder expectations, and supports STI diffusion within the UAE's arid agricultural environment [41].

3 Research Methodology

This study adopts a qualitative research methodology grounded in interpretivist and pragmatic philosophical perspectives to explore how Environmental Corporate Social Responsibility (ECSR) influences Sustainable Technological Innovation (STI) in the UAE agriculture sector [42–44]. A qualitative approach is appropriate given the exploratory and context-specific nature of the research and the need to capture stakeholders' perceptions, experiences, and practices surrounding sustainability-driven innovation [45]. An ethnographic research strategy was employed to gain an in-depth and contextually rich understanding of how ECSR initiatives and technologies are enacted within real agricultural operations [46, 47]. Since ECSR-driven technological adoption is shaped by contextual factors such as water scarcity, climatic conditions, stakeholder interactions, operational routines, and institutional expectations, field-based observation provides insights that could not be captured through interviews alone. This approach therefore enabled the researchers to examine the lived and operational context within which sustainable technologies are adopted, resisted, or adapted.

Data collection combined semi-structured interviews and naturalistic observations to enable methodological triangulation and strengthen the credibility of the findings [48, 50]. Interviews explored ECSR practices, technology adoption processes, perceived benefits and challenges, and the role of institutional and governmental support. Observations were undertaken during the implementation and operational phases of the large-scale Maliha Farm project in the UAE and focused on farming practices, stakeholder interactions, and environmental conditions using systematic field notes and digital recording tools [21, 49, 51]. A purposive sampling strategy was adopted to recruit participants with direct involvement in, or informed perspectives on, ECSR and technological innovation in the UAE agricultural sector [52]. Participants were selected based on their relevance to the research objectives, including involvement in agricultural production, decision-making responsibilities related to technology or sustainability, policy expertise, and experience with ECSR-related initiatives as depicted in Table 1.

Table 1. Respondents' profile

Organisation	Designation	Count
Valmont Industries	Operation Director, Commercial Director, Regional Vice President, Project Manager	04
Jenan Investment LLC	CEO Business Development and planning	01
Department of Agricultural and Livestock	Farm Manager Engineer- water resources Environmental Engineer	02
Dubai Municipality		02
Total		09

The Maliha Farm project, sponsored by the Department of Agriculture and Livestock in Sharjah and supported technologically by Valmont Industries, provided the primary research context. Data were collected through online and face-to-face interviews and analysed using thematic analysis following Braun and Clarke's framework [54, 56]. Frequency analysis was used to complement thematic findings and improve analytical transparency by identifying dominant stakeholder concerns and priorities [58, 59].

4 Analysis and Findings

4.1 Stakeholders and ECSR-Driven Technologies

The findings indicate the presence of clearly identifiable internal and external stakeholders who influence the adoption and implementation of ECSR-driven technological innovation. Internal stakeholders include farmers and agricultural companies, while external stakeholders consist of government entities, consumers, and community representatives. This stakeholder structure is consistent with Stakeholder Theory, which emphasises the role of multiple actors in shaping organisational decision-making and sustainability outcomes [60]. Stakeholders identified four major categories of technologies through which ECSR is operationalised: sustainable farming techniques, input-conservation technologies, renewable energy technologies, and remote-sensing technologies. As illustrated in Fig. 1, sustainable farming techniques such as vertical farming, greenhouse agriculture, and aquaculture represent the most frequently mentioned category, reflecting their perceived importance in addressing water scarcity and climatic constraints. Input conservation technologies, including water-efficient irrigation systems and optimised use of fertiliser and pesticides, further highlight stakeholder concern for efficient resource utilisation in an arid environment [61]. The prominence of these technologies demonstrates that ECSR within the UAE agriculture sector is closely linked to practical, technology driven sustainability initiatives rather than symbolic commitments [53, 55]. The technology categories shown in Fig. 1 were derived from the thematic coding process. Interview and observation data were coded for references to technologies associated with ECSR-oriented agricultural practices. Related codes were then grouped into four broader categories: sustainable farming techniques, input-conservation technologies, renewable energy technologies, and remote-sensing technologies. The percentages indicate the relative frequency of coded references to each category across the qualitative dataset.

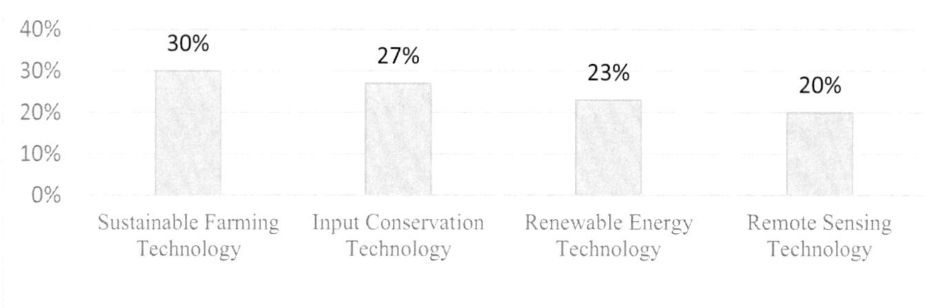

Fig. 1. ECSR-driven technologies supporting sustainable innovation in UAE agriculture

4.2 Stakeholder Perceptions and Expectations of ECSR

The findings reveal divergent stakeholder perceptions regarding the effectiveness of ECSR in fostering sustainable technological innovation. One group of stakeholders' views ECSR as a strong enabler that encourages agricultural companies and farmers to adopt sustainable technologies aligned with the UAE's national vision for food and water security. This perspective emphasises the role of ECSR in motivating proactive engagement with innovation and achieving both tangible benefits such as cost efficiency and improved productivity and intangible benefits, including enhanced organisational reputation and social value [62]. The distribution of these perceptions is presented in Fig. 2, which illustrates the relative balance between positive and sceptical stakeholder views.

Fig. 2. Perceived effectiveness of ECSR in fostering sustainable technological innovation

Stakeholder perceptions indicate that ECSR is viewed as an enabling condition rather than a direct mechanism that automatically produces technological adoption. Supportive stakeholders associated ECSR with long-term investment, reputational value, food-security objectives, and resource efficiency. More sceptical stakeholders emphasised that ECSR alone cannot overcome structural barriers such as high capital costs, harsh climatic conditions, and uncertainty around returns on investment. This distinction is important because it shows that ECSR supports sustainable technological innovation primarily by creating legitimacy, alignment, and motivation, while actual diffusion depends on economic, technical, and institutional conditions. In contrast, another group of stakeholders perceives ECSR as having limited impact on technological innovation, citing the relatively small size of the UAE agriculture sector and the challenges posed by harsh climatic conditions. Importantly, these opposing perspectives are not contradictory but rather complementary. The structural constraints identified by sceptical stakeholders simultaneously reinforce the necessity of technological innovation to enhance agricultural resilience, improve food security, and reduce dependence on imports. These findings suggest that ECSR functions more as an enabling framework guiding environmental practices than as a direct driver of immediate innovation outcomes [57, 63].

4.3 Challenges and Opportunities for ECSR-STI Integration

As depicted in Fig. 3, there were three dominant challenges emerging from the analysis: financial constraints, harsh environmental conditions, and perceived gaps in governmental support. Financial challenges, particularly high capital costs and uncertainty regarding return on investment were frequently cited as major barriers to adopting sustainable technologies. These concerns are intensified by the high cost of essential resources, especially water, within the UAE farming context [49]. Environmental challenges, including extreme heat and limited water availability, increase technological complexity and perceived risk. Alongside these challenges, several opportunities supporting ECSR-driven STI were identified. Resource-saving technologies, alternative farming techniques suitable for arid conditions, and alignment with the UAE's sustainability vision were perceived as key enabling factors. As illustrated in Fig. 3, government leadership plays a critical role in this process.

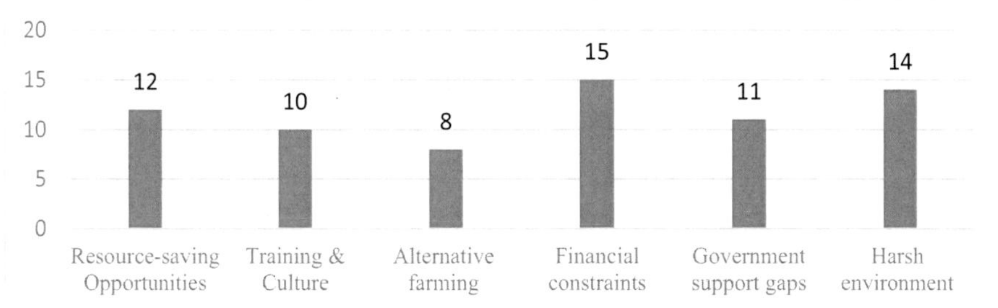

Fig. 3. Key challenges for sustainable technological innovation

Stakeholders acknowledged that rulers and public institutions act as innovators and opinion leaders, enhancing the observability and legitimacy of sustainable technologies and accelerating diffusion [65]. However, the findings also reveal a perception-policy gap, whereby existing governmental initiatives are not always experienced as sufficient or accessible at the operational level. To avoid conflating constraints with enabling conditions, the analysis distinguishes between barriers that restrict STI diffusion and factors that may enable wider adoption. Barriers refer to conditions that increase perceived risk, cost, complexity, or uncertainty. Enabling conditions refer to mechanisms that improve feasibility, legitimacy, trialability, observability, or stakeholder confidence in sustainable technologies. Overall, the findings show that ECSR contributes to sustainable technological innovation by aligning stakeholder expectations, legitimising investment in resource-efficient technologies, and creating a broader sustainability rationale for agricultural transformation. However, the diffusion of these technologies remains conditional rather than automatic. High capital costs, environmental severity, capability limitations, and uneven access to institutional support continue to restrict adoption. The analysis therefore suggests that ECSR is most effective when supported by practical mechanisms such as financial incentives, demonstration projects, training, cross-sector collaboration, and clearer translation of national policy into farm-level support.

4.4 Recommendations and Enabling Conditions

This study also identified some recommendations to promote technological innovations in Agri-culture sector in UAE. The analysis highlighted a clear distinction between tangible benefits, such as productivity gains, cost savings, and improved resource efficiency, and intangible benefits, including enhanced organisational culture, stakeholder trust, and social legitimacy associated with ECSR-driven innovation. As illustrated in Fig. 4, stakeholders consistently emphasised collaboration between agricultural firms, research institutions, and government bodies as a critical enabler of sustainable innovation. Mechanisms such as demonstration farms, financial support schemes, and awareness campaigns were identified as effective in reducing uncertainty and encouraging adoption [66].

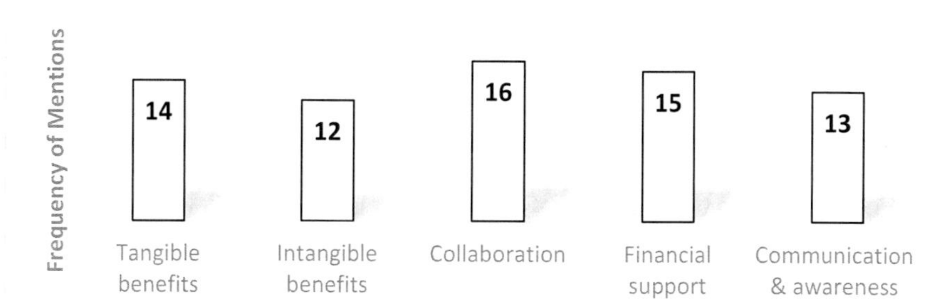

Fig. 4. Recommendations to promote the adoption of sustainable technological innovation

Additional enabling conditions include user training to improve technological competence, automated alert systems to enhance human–technology interaction, and regulatory oversight to ensure the health and safety of food produced using advanced technologies. The frequency analysis indicates that, while some scepticism toward ECSR persists, supportive attitudes and sustainability-oriented solutions dominate stakeholder discourse, suggesting readiness for transformation when enabling conditions are strengthened [62]. Taken together, the findings demonstrate that ECSR can function as a strategic enabler of sustainable technological innovation in the UAE agriculture sector. However, its effectiveness depends on multi-level alignment among stakeholders, economic incentives, institutional support, and technological capability.

5 Discussion

This study examined how Environmental Corporate Social Responsibility (ECSR) facilitates stakeholder alignment and influences the diffusion of Sustainable Technological Innovation (STI) within the UAE agricultural sector. The findings indicate that ECSR should not be viewed as a direct trigger of technological adoption but rather as an enabling framework through which stakeholder expectations, institutional priorities, environmental pressures, and technological opportunities become aligned. While ECSR creates legitimacy and motivation for sustainable innovation, successful diffusion remains dependent on economic feasibility, technological capability, institutional support, and the suitability of technologies for arid agricultural environments. The stakeholder categories identified in this study closely reflect the foundations of Stakeholder Theory, highlighting the importance of employees, customers, suppliers, communities, and shareholders in shaping organisational strategies and innovation outcomes [63]. Participants demonstrated relatively high familiarity with ECSR concepts, based on self-reported ratings on a 10-point scale, and identified practical initiatives such as vertical farming, greenhouse agriculture, solar energy systems, and water-saving technologies. This suggests that ECSR is increasingly perceived not as an abstract sustainability principle but as an operational framework closely associated with technological adoption and environmental performance [64, 65]. These findings reinforce the argument that sustainability-driven innovation emerges when stakeholder expectations, organisational capabilities, and environmental constraints are effectively aligned [66, 67], particularly in the UAE where food security and resource scarcity are national priorities. The study also identified contrasting stakeholder perceptions regarding the effectiveness of ECSR in promoting sustainable innovation. Senior managers and community representatives largely viewed ECSR as a positive catalyst encouraging the adoption of water-efficient, energy-saving, and digitally enabled technologies. This supports previous research positioning ECSR as a legitimacy-building mechanism capable of encouraging long-term sustainability investments [68, 69]. In contrast, several decision-makers within agricultural firms expressed scepticism regarding ECSR's practical influence on innovation, citing the small scale of the UAE agricultural sector, harsh climatic conditions, and uncertain financial returns. Similar tensions have been reported in previous CSR and innovation studies, where misalignment between sustainability goals and short-term economic performance constrains innovation outcomes [68, 69]. This divergence highlights an important contextual paradox: the environmental challenges that constrain agricultural production simultaneously create a greater need for technological innovation. Consequently, ECSR alone is insufficient to generate innovation outcomes and must be complemented by supportive governance structures and economic incentives [58]. Three principal barriers to ECSR-driven innovation diffusion were identified: financial constraints, perceived limitations in governmental support, and environmental challenges associated with arid farming conditions. Concerns regarding implementation costs, uncertain returns on investment, and the high cost of desalinated water mirror barriers identified in international studies on sustainable agriculture [65, 66]. Interestingly, stakeholder perceptions of inadequate governmental support contrast with existing UAE policy initiatives and incentives, suggesting the existence of a perception-policy gap that warrants further investigation.

Drawing on IDT, the study highlights the role of UAE rulers and government institutions as innovators and opinion leaders who influence technology adoption through demonstration and example [63, 64]. However, diffusion remains constrained by perceptions of complexity, uncertainty, and limited trialability, particularly among smaller farms with restricted financial and technical capacity. Demonstration farms, collaborative research initiatives, financial incentives, training programmes, and awareness campaigns emerged as important mechanisms for improving observability and trialability and accelerating adoption [65, 69]. Finally, the findings emphasise the need to balance affordability with environmental sustainability. Although consumers remain price-sensitive, evidence suggests increasing acceptance of moderate price premiums for sustainably produced food when environmental benefits are transparent and credible [69, 70]. While the findings are not statistically generalisable, they may be analytically transferable to other arid, water-scarce, and import-dependent agricultural systems where sustainable technology adoption depends on stakeholder alignment, policy support, and economic feasibility.

6 Conclusion

This study examined the role of Environmental Corporate Social Responsibility (ECSR) in promoting Sustainable Technological Innovation (STI) in the UAE agricultural sector. The findings indicate that ECSR can serve as an important catalyst for sustainable innovation in arid and resource-constrained environments. Internal and external stakeholders significantly influenced technology adoption, although perceptions of ECSR effectiveness varied among groups. Financial limitations, harsh climatic conditions, and insufficient governmental support emerged as major barriers; however, these challenges also highlighted the importance of technological solutions for improving agricultural resilience, food security, and reducing reliance on imports. The study demonstrates that ECSR extends beyond symbolic sustainability commitments and can act as a meaningful driver of sustainable technological innovation when supported by favourable institutional, technological, and economic conditions. Recommended practices include adopting recyclable materials, smart monitoring systems, and solar-powered technologies, alongside user training, automated alerts, and food safety testing for technologies designed for extreme climates. ECSR initiatives are most effective when aligned with national priorities and supported through collaboration among government, industry, and research institutions. Although the study provides valuable context-specific insights, its qualitative design limits statistical generalisability and highlights opportunities for future comparative, longitudinal, and quantitative research.

Disclosure of Interests. The authors have no competing interests to declare that are relevant to the content of this article.

References

1. Agudelo, M.A.L., Jóhannsdóttir, L., Davídsdóttir, B.: A literature review of the history and evolution of corporate social responsibility. Int. J. Corp. Soc. Responsib. **4**(1), 1–23 (2019). https://doi.org/10.1186/s40991-018-0039-y
2. Bowen, H.R.: Social Responsibilities of the Businessman. Harper & Row, New York (1953)
3. Afeltra, G., Alerasoul, S.A., Strozzi, F.: The evolution of sustainable innovation: from the past to the future. Eur. J. Innov. Manag. **26**(2), 386–421 (2023). https://doi.org/10.1108/EJIM-02-2021-0113
4. Blakeney, M.: Agricultural innovation and sustainable development. Sustainability. **14**(5), 2698 (2022). https://doi.org/10.3390/su14052698
5. Harris, D.R., Fuller, D.Q.: Agriculture: definition and overview. In: Smith, C. (ed.) Encyclopedia of Global Archaeology, pp. 104–113. Springer, New York (2014). https://doi.org/10.1007/978-1-4419-0465-2_64

6. Khan, N. et al.: Potential role of technology innovation in transformation of sustainable food systems. Agriculture. **11**(10), 984 (2021). https://doi.org/10.3390/agriculture11100984
7. Takshe, A.A., Lyra, D.A., Alkhani, F., Mendoza, N., Talli, M.: An initial reading into the UAE's food security response during COVID-19. PalArch's J. Archaeol. Egypt/Egyptol. **18**(2), 336–352 (2021)
8. Food Security Office UAE: The ag-tech government accelerators program (2023). https://foodsecurity.gov.ae
9. Freeman, R.E.: Strategic Management: a Stakeholder Approach. Cambridge University Press, Cambridge (2010). https://doi.org/10.1017/CBO9781139192675
10. Borger, F.G., Kruglianskas, I.: Corporate social responsibility and environmental and technological innovation performance. Int. J. Technol. Policy Manag. **6**(4), 399–413 (2006). https://doi.org/10.1504/IJTPM.2006.011724
11. Cillo, V., Petruzzelli, A.M., Ardito, L., Del Giudice, M.: Understanding sustainable innovation. Corp. Soc. Responsib. Environ. Manag. **26**(5), 1012–1025 (2019). https://doi.org/10.1002/csr.1783
12. Jia, Y., Gao, X., Billings, B.A.: Corporate social responsibility and technological innovation. J. Manag. Account. Res. **34**, 163–186 (2021). https://doi.org/10.2308/JMAR-2020-048
13. Liu, Y., Chen, Y., Ren, Y., Jin, B.: Impact mechanism of CSR on sustainable technological innovation performance. J. Clean. Prod. **308**, 127345 (2021). https://doi.org/10.1016/j.jclepro.2021.127345
14. Rashid, N.R.N.A., Khalid, S.A., Rahman, N.I.A.: Environmental corporate social responsibility and customer loyalty. Procedia Econ. Finance. **31**, 705–713 (2015). https://doi.org/10.1016/S2212-5671(15)01159-4
15. Mazur-Wierzbicka, E.: The application of corporate social responsibility in European agriculture. Misc. Geogr. **19**(1), 19–23 (2015). https://doi.org/10.1515/mgrsd-2015-0001
16. Biró, K., Szalmáné Csete, M.: Corporate social responsibility in agribusiness: climate-related empirical findings from Hungary. Environ. Dev. Sustain. **23**, 5647–5674 (2020). https://doi.org/10.1007/s10668-020-00838-3
17. Chen, Y., Jin, S.: Corporate social responsibility and green technology innovation. Sustainability. **15**(10), 8164 (2023). https://doi.org/10.3390/su15108164
18. De Nieves-Nieto, C., Bernal-Conesa, J.A., Juan, A., Peñalver, B., Santos, C.: CSR and sustainability effects on stakeholder–performance relationships. J. Sci. Ind. Res. **77**, 570–574 (2018)
19. Rogers, E.M.: Diffusion of Innovations, 4th edn. Simon & Schuster, New York (2010)
20. Dearing, J.W., Cox, J.G.: Diffusion of innovations theory, principles, and practice. Health Aff. **37**(2), 183–190 (2018). https://doi.org/10.1377/hlthaff.2017.1104
21. Chen, X., Li, T.: Diffusion of agricultural technology innovation. Sustainability. **14**(22), 15008 (2022). https://doi.org/10.3390/su14221500
22. Asemah, E., Okpanachi, R., Edegoh, L.: Business advantages of corporate social responsibility practice. New Media Mass Commun. **18**, 45–54 (2013)
23. Deloitte: Citizenship and Employee Engagement Survey. Deloitte Insights (2011)
24. Easterby-Smith, M., Thorpe, R., Lowe, A.: Management Research. Sage, London (1999)
25. Saunders, M., Lewis, P., Thornhill, A.: Research Methods for Business Students. Pearson, London (2007)
26. Saunders, M., Lewis, P., Thornhill, A., Bristow, A.: Research Philosophy and Theory Development. Pearson, London (2019)
27. Dissanayake, E.V.A.: Research onion: A systematic approach for designing research methodology. ResearchGate (2023). https://doi.org/10.13140/RG.2.2.24466.12489
28. Taherdoost, H.: What are different research approaches? SSRN. (2022). https://doi.org/10.30564/jmser.v5i1.4538

29. Aspers, P., Corte, U.: What is qualitative in qualitative research. Qual. Sociol. **44**, 599–608 (2021). https://doi.org/10.1007/s11133-021-09497-w
30. Gobo, G.: Ethnography. Sage, London (2011). https://doi.org/10.4135/9780857028976
31. Campbell, S., Greenwood, M., Prior, S., et al.: Purposive sampling: complex or simple? J. Res. Nurs. **25**(8), 652–661 (2020). https://doi.org/10.1177/1744987120927206
32. Braun, V., Clarke, V.: Using thematic analysis in psychology. Qual. Res. Psychol. **3**(2), 77–101 (2006). https://doi.org/10.1191/1478088706qp063oa
33. Mihas, P.: Qualitative, multimethod, and mixed methods research. Int. Encycl. Educ. **12**, 302–313 (2023)
34. Li, Y., Zhang, S.: Qualitative data analysis. In: Applied Research Methods, pp. 149–165. Springer (2022). https://doi.org/10.1007/978-3-030-93574-0
35. Sutherland, S., Katz, S.: Concept mapping methodology: a catalyst for organisational learning. Eval. Program Plann. **28**(3), 257–269 (2005). https://doi.org/10.1016/j.evalprogplan.2005.04.017
36. Smith, J.A.: Qualitative Psychology. Sage, London (2015)
37. Moon, K., Blackman, D.: A guide to ontology, epistemology, and philosophical perspectives for interdisciplinary researchers. Conserv. Biol. **28**, 1167–1177 (2017). https://doi.org/10.1111/cobi.12326
38. Al-Ababneh, M.M.: Linking ontology, epistemology and research methodology. ResearchGate (2020). https://doi.org/10.23756/sp.v8i1.500
39. Al-Saadi, H.: Demystifying ontology and epistemology in research methods. ResearchGate (2014)
40. Rahman, S.: Advantages and disadvantages of qualitative and quantitative approaches. J. Educ. Learn. **6**(1), 102–112 (2020). https://doi.org/10.5539/jel.v6n1p102
41. Remenyi, D., Williams, B., Money, A., Swartz, E.: Doing Research in Business and Management. Sage, London (2005)
42. Zangirolami-Raimundo, J., Echeimberg, J.O., Leone, C.: Research methodology topics: Cross-sectional studies. ResearchGate (2018). https://doi.org/10.7322/jhgd.152198
43. Thomas, L.: Cross-Sectional Study Definitions, Uses and Examples. Scribbr (2020)
44. World Bank: World Bank open data – UAE imports of goods and services (2023). https://data.worldbank.org
45. Global Innovation Index: Creating Healthy Lives – the Future of Innovation. WIPO, Cornell University, INSEAD (2019)
46. UAE Government Portal: Agriculture and animal wealth (2023). https://u.ae
47. UAE Government Portal: Innovation in the UAE (2023). https://u.ae
48. UAE Government Portal: Wheat farm in Sharjah (2023). https://u.ae
49. Valmont Industries: Sustainability and innovation practices (2023). https://ww2.valmont.com
50. Department of Agriculture and Livestock, Sharjah: Official portal (2023). https://dal.shj.ae
51. Chen, Y., Jin, S.: Corporate social responsibility and green technology adoption. Sustainability. **15**(10), 8164 (2023). https://doi.org/10.3390/su15108164
52. De Nieves-Nieto, C., et al.: CSR and sustainability performance linkages. J. Sci. Ind. Res. **77**, 570–574 (2018)
53. Jia, Y., Gao, X., Billings, B.A.: CSR and technological innovation. J. Manag. Account. Res. **34**, 163–186 (2021). https://doi.org/10.2308/JMAR-19-241
54. Liu, Y., et al.: CSR and sustainable innovation performance. J. Clean. Prod. **308**, 127345 (2021). https://doi.org/10.1016/j.jclepro.2021.12734555
55. Khan, N., et al.: Technology innovation in food systems. Agriculture. **11**(10), 984 (2021). https://doi.org/10.3390/agriculture1110098456
56. Dearing, J.W., Cox, J.G.: Innovation diffusion in practice. Health Aff. **37**(2), 183–190 (2018). https://doi.org/10.1377/hlthaff.2017.1104

57. Asemah, E., et al.: Business advantages of CSR. New Media Mass Commun. **18**, 45–54 (2013)
58. Mazur-Wierzbicka, E.: CSR and agriculture. Misc. Geogr. **19**(1), 19–23 (2015). https://doi.org/10.1515/mgrsd-2015-0003
59. Chen, Y., Jin, S.: CSR–innovation relationship. Sustainability. **15**(10), 8164 (2023). https://doi.org/10.3390/su15108164
60. De Nieves-Nieto, C., et al.: CSR and stakeholder performance. J. Sci. Ind. Res. **77**, 570–574 (2018)
61. Borger, F.G., Kruglianskas, I.: CSR and environmental innovation. Int. J. Technol. Policy Manag. **6**(4), 399–413 (2006). https://doi.org/10.1504/IJTPM.2006.011172
62. Jia, Y., Gao, X., Billings, B.A.: CSR and innovation legitimacy. J. Manag. Account. Res. (2021). https://doi.org/10.2308/JMAR-19-241
63. Cillo, V., et al.: Innovation tensions in sustainability. CSR Environ. Manag. **26**(5), 1012–1025 (2019). https://doi.org/10.1002/csr.1732
64. Liu, Y., et al.: CSR and innovation constraints. J. Clean. Prod. **308**, 127345 (2021). https://doi.org/10.1016/j.jclepro.2021.127345
65. Blakeney, M.: Innovation barriers in agriculture. Sustainability. **14**(5), 2698 (2022). https://doi.org/10.3390/su14052698
66. Khan, N., et al.: Technological adoption challenges. Agriculture. **11**(10), 984 (2021). https://doi.org/10.3390/agriculture11100984
67. Rogers, E.M.: Opinion Leadership and Innovation Diffusion. Simon & Schuster (2010)
68. Chen, X., Li, T.: Innovation diffusion determinants. Sustainability. **14**(22), 15008 (2022). https://doi.org/10.3390/su142215008
69. Asemah, E., Okpanachi, R., Edegoh, L.: CSR as moral and economic strategy. New Media Mass Commun. **18**, 45–54 (2013)
70. Rashid, N.R.N.A., Khalid, S.A., Rahman, N.I.A.: CSR loyalty and long-term value. Procedia Econ. Finance. **31**, 705–713 (2015). https://doi.org/10.1016/S2212-5671(15)01158-4

Collaborative Manufacturing, Service Systems and Lifecycle Management

Managing Openness in Collaborative Innovation Projects of Manufacturing Companies

Djerdj Horvat[1(✉)] and Torben Schubert[1,2]

[1] Fraunhofer Institute for Systems and Innovation Research (ISI), Breslauer Str. 48, 76139 Karlsruhe, Germany
djerdj.horvat@isi.fraunhofer.de

[2] Centre for Innovation Research (CIRCLE), Lund University, Instrumentmakaregränden 1, Lund, Sweden

Abstract. The literature emphasizes the importance of openness in innovation projects as a mechanism for accessing knowledge not available within firms. At the same time, scholars have highlighted the open innovation paradox, whereby increased collaboration raises the risk of knowledge leakage to partners, potentially undermining firms' ability to capture value from their innovations. These risks are particularly pronounced in traditional manufacturing sectors, where firms rely on physical products and knowledge leakage may directly affect revenue streams. Despite these concerns, it remains an open question how firms in such contexts can effectively manage innovation partnerships to navigate this paradox. To address this research gap, we combine the profiting-from-innovation framework with a comparative case study of four German manufacturing firms to develop an integrated model. Based on three contingency dimensions – product-market competition, technological dynamism, and appropriability regime strength – the model explains how firms can capture the benefits of open innovation while maintaining control over knowledge leakage risks. Our findings suggest that innovation partnerships in manufacturing are likely to be conditional on low mutual threat of product market competition. When competitive pressures are non-negligible, firms tend to introduce restrictions on knowledge flows, resulting in what we conceptualize as semi-open collaborative strategies. Furthermore, we identify first-mover advantages, and the strength of the appropriability regime as key contingency factors shaping the design of such semi-open strategies. These strategies combine mechanisms such as lead-time advantages, formal intellectual property rights, and trust-based governance to balance openness and protection in innovation partnerships.

Keywords: open innovation paradox · innovation collaboration strategies · manufacturing

1 Introduction

Literature increasingly underscores the importance of integrating open innovation strategies into innovation processes to tap into knowledge beyond firm boundaries [1]. At the same time, several authors have highlighted the so-called open innovation paradox,

Published by Springer Nature Switzerland AG 2027
G. Pezzotta et al. (Eds.): APMS 2026, IFIP AICT 808, pp. 277–292, 2027.
https://doi.org/10.1007/978-3-032-38594-9_19

which arises from the simultaneous increase in the risks of knowledge leakage to partners, potentially undermining firms' ability to appropriate returns from their innovations [2, 3]. This challenge is particularly pronounced for manufacturing companies, as their innovation processes often rely on technologies developed collaboratively in innovation projects with external partners, in contexts where knowledge cannot be fully protected by patents or other legally enforceable exclusion mechanisms [4]. Against this backdrop, an important yet insufficiently addressed question emerges: how can manufacturing firms design collaborative innovation projects that (a) leverage the benefits of openness in technology development while (b) mitigating the risks of knowledge leakage [2, 5–7].

In this paper, we contribute to answering this question by developing an explanatory framework that (1) identifies firm **strategies** governing the openness of collaborative innovation projects, (2) describes **central contingency factors** affecting strategic choices about collaboration patterns, and (3) maps contingencies to strategies to derive **predictions about decisions** under given conditions.

To develop our framework, we adopt a combination of deductive and inductive reasoning, integrating theory development with a multiple case study design [8]. From a theoretical perspective, we draw on the profiting from innovation (PFI) literature [9–11], which identifies the key factors shaping a firm's ability to capture value from its innovations. These factors form the core categories structuring our integrative theoretical framework. Empirically, we employ a comparative case study design involving four German manufacturing firms to develop an in-depth understanding of heterogeneous strategies related to openness in collaborative innovation projects.

2 Theoretical Background

The profiting-from-innovation (PFI) framework provides a conceptual lens for explaining the fundamental factors that shape a firm's ability to capture value from its innovations. Originally developed by Teece (1986), the framework has been adapted to evolving business environments [9, 10]. More recent contributions have explicitly incorporated the role of business model design [11, 12], which we use as theoretical fundament for explaining the mechanisms for crafting innovation partnerships in manufacturing.

According to PFI framework, following factors play a central role in capturing value from innovation: importance of access to complementary assets, the strength of the intellectual property rights (IPR), and technological dynamism, especially in terms of first-mover advantages. Furthermore, PFI ephasizes the role of underlying dynamic capabilities required to leverage these factors effectively.

First, **access to complementary assets** through external partners constitutes a primary rationale for engaging in innovation collaborations. In the specific case of technology-oriented innovation, a number of authors have highlighted that the search for complementary resouces is a major driving force of the initial decision to form collaborative partnerships [13] when firms find it difficult to develop them in-house [14]. However, such collaborations inherently involve the risk of knowledge leakage, which may outweigh the initially anticipated benefits. This tension gives rise to the open innovation paradox [2, 3], requiring firms to design and implement appropriate protection strategies. As outlined by the PFI framework, the effectiveness of these strategies depends on specific contextual contingency factors.

Second, the **appropriability regime** determines the extent to which intellectual property, e.g. the economic value of innovation, can be protected [9]. It encompasses a range of protection instruments, including formal IPR as well as formal and informal secrecy. The strength of the appropriability regime may vary considerably across industries and institutional contexts. In open innovation, firms must actively manage the risk of knowledge leakage. Mechanisms such as patents or formal secrecy agreements (e.g., NDA) can partially mitigate these risks. Importantly, these mechanisms do not necessarily restrict knowledge sharing per se, but rather regulate the permissible use of knowledge ex post through legal means.

Third, when the appropriability regime is weak, protection strategies based primarily on formal IPR are unlikely to be effective. In such contexts, the PFI framework points to alternative, less formal mechanisms that leverage technological dynamism. High-tech environments, characterized by rapid technological progress and short innovation cycles, create conditions in which firms must rely on timing advantages [15, 16]. From its original formulation, the PFI framework has emphasized the importance of developing capabilities that enable firms to continuously reconfigure their processes and products [9, 10]. When successfully implemented, such capabilities allow firms to pursue competitive strategies based on timing advantages, socalled **first-mover advantages** [17].

In explaining innovation partnerships, especially in manufacturing context, two key gaps emerge from the PFI framework. First, it provides limited guidance on how firms respond to situations characterized by both low technological dynamism and weak appropriability regimes. In such contexts, neither IPR-based protection nor lead-time strategies are likely to be effective. It therefore remains unclear whether firms are effectively constrained from engaging in collaborative innovation partnerships, or whether alternative mechanisms - largely overlooked by the PFI framework - exist that enable them to manage value appropriation under these conditions. Second, the PFI framework implicitly assumes that addressing the open innovation paradox in collaborative settings requires restricting knowledge flows to prevent leakage. However, empirical evidence of more open knowledge-sharing strategies suggests that restrictive approaches may not be the only viable option. This raises the question of whether the PFI framework overlooks important mechanisms that enable firms to balance openness and value appropriation without relying primarily on knowledge protection. To address these gaps, we employ a comparative case study design [8, 18] aimed at developing an in-depth understanding of different strategic approaches to managing openness and value capture in collaborative innovation contexts of manufacturing companies.

3 Methodology

To empirically explore and refine our framework, we conducted case studies in four highly innovative German manufacturing firms (see Table 1). Case selection followed a theoretical sampling approach [19]. The case (A) involves a technology company in the automotive industry that develops software-based platforms for a global automotive group. The firm collaborates extensively with high-tech start-ups and software companies across national boundaries and regularly faces challenges related to knowledge sharing. The case (B) focuses on a high-tech company in the medical industry, representing a highly regulated environment. Given the combination of high unit costs driven by substantial innovation investments and intense market competition, effective management of knowledge in collaborative innovation is critical. The case (C) examines a company in the chemical industry, where product innovation processes rely heavily on knowledge complementarities arising from close collaboration with research institutions and other firms. The case (D) is a manufacturing SME specializing in customer-specific electric heating components. Its business model is characterized by close and long-term collaboration with customers, which creates particular challenges in maintaining the confidentiality of innovation-relevant knowledge within projects.

Table 1 Case study overview

Characteristics/Cases	A	B	C	D
Employees	500	750	75	60
Manufacturing sector	Automotive	Medical	Chemical	Electrical equipment
Main product	Automotive software and technology	Medical technologies and devices	Powder and intelligent coating	Customer-tailored electric heating components
Major competitive factor	Unified technology	Unified technology, quality	Quality, Innovation	Short delivery time, flexibility

Primary data collection was based on semi-structured, face-to-face interviews with key personnel involved in innovation and collaboration activities. Interviews lasted between one and two hours. Rather than aiming for a large number of respondents, we focused on individuals with substantial decision-making authority, meaning Senior and C-level employees (see Table 2)

We conducted three rounds of interviews, aimed at capturing a comprehensive view of strategic decision-making in collaborative innovation projects. First, we focused on identifying and understanding the factors influencing firms' willingness to engage in innovation collaborations with external partners, as well as the criteria guiding partner selection. In addition, we explored the knowledge-related challenges inherent in such collaborations. Second, we shifted our attention to the strategies firms employ to balance knowledge sharing and knowledge absorption, as well as the challenges associated with achieving the required complementarities in innovation projects. To guide this phase, we developed our interview protocol based on the PFI framework, enabling us to systematically capture knowledge exchange strategies in projects. We also examined the mechanisms used to protect strategically relevant knowledge and the associated challenges in collaborative settings. Third, we validated and further refined the patterns of strategies that had been identified inductively in the second phase. To complement the interview data and enhance construct validity [20], we additionally analyzed firm-specific secondary data, including presentations, project documentation, and information available on the websites of the focal companies and their innovation partners.

Table 2 Interviews

Cases	Interview rounds		
	Initial round	Main round	Model validation round
A	Chief of Innovation Group (CIG)	Chief of Innovation Group (CIG)	Chief of Innovation Networks (CIN), Research Funding Manager (CRF)
B	Senior Project manager (SPM)	Senior Project manager (SPM)	Chief of Research and Development (CRD)
C	Chief Technology Officer (CTO)	Chief Executive Officer (CEO)	Chief Executive Officer (CEO) and Chief Technology Officer (CTO)
D	Chief Operations Manager (COM)	Chief Executive Officer (CEO)	Chief Technology Officer (CTO)

In data analysis, we employed a combination of deductive and inductive reasoning [21], allowing us to balance theoretical structure with openness to emergent insights. We began by deriving the main analytical categories deductively from our theoretical framework, which combines different degrees of openness with key contingency factors based on the PFI framework. Subsequently, we conducted a detailed within-case analysis by examining the interview transcripts. The aim of this step was to understand the underlying rationales for diverse strategies in collaborative innovation projects. We also performed a cross-case analysis to identify patterns of similarity and difference across cases, thereby developing a more comprehensive understanding of how firms approach openness in collaborative innovation. Finally, we linked the deductively derived categories with the inductively identified patterns and their underlying rationales. These patterns, which represent distinct strategies of openness, emerged as higher-order conceptual themes within the theoretical framework.

4 Results

Following the basic notion of the PFI-framework, we start with the central role of mutual access to complementary assets that a partnership in innovation-based collaboration offers to partners [9, 10, 13]. Our interview partners described the crux of complementary assets, particularly knowledge, in the sense of filling the gaps that are essential for finishing the innovation projects. One example is:

> *"When we search for our partners, which is often a long process, we try to find the right partner which means companies with resources that we really need because we don't have them. But not only this. At the very beginning, we have to consider also the resources that we are willing to share in projects. [...]But, when we start a partnership, we share very strongly, because then something also comes back. It's no use if they all close down."* (CEO, Case C)

However, they also state the value of the core knowledge and the issues for sharing it with partners, particularly due to the risk of knowledge leakage and fear of competition. It appears to be a general pattern that companies are ready to share their non-core knowledge while at the same time they are looking for external knowledge which is difficult to generate in-house. Otherwise, if there is no complementarity in knowledge which companies search for and are willing to share in projects, it is unlikely that the companies would start a collaborative project [13]. One interview partner explained:

> *"We need knowledge that we don't have. For example, in my area, I have suppliers of welding machines who are collaborating with me in my projects, because we need a very high quality welding, and in most of the cases it depends on the knowledge that we build together, something like mixing our knowledge"*(SPM, Case B)

Parallel to reaping benefits from openness in collaborative projects resulting from asset complementarity, we identified in our data a significant relevance of potential risks of knowledge leakage resulting from the threat of product market competition between the partners in projects. Researching the activities of companies in this respect in-depth, we understood that companies generally analyze the potential competitive situation with the selected companies and use the outcome as a prerequisite for setting the collaboration strategy. If there is no threat of product market competition because the companies, for instance, serve very different markets, they are willing to share assets in innovation-based collaboration more openly. On the other hand, high threat of market competition between the partners, resulting from, for example, offering products or services for the same market, will result in rather cautious asset exchange strategies.

> *"Our company is involved in projects with research institutions, in which we work closely together to develop innovative and sometimes unconventional technical solutions. There is no competition among the project partners; instead, we are involved in a partnership. Outside of the project work, each partner is doing its own business. [...] This is why I feel free to communicate openly with them."* (COM, Case D)

We learned from case studies that companies tend to be more willing to collaborate in a true open, as it were limitless, knowledge exchange solely in the instance of both high asset complementarity and low threat of product market competition. Otherwise, for example in case of high asset complementarity combined with risks of knowledge leakage resulting from market competition, companies rather carefully navigate the knowledge flows inside the partnership. We call this kind of restricted or "semi-open" innovation collaborations. In our case studies, we were able to identify four main types of strategies in such semi-open innovation collaborations. Table 3 summarizes the relevance of these strategies for our four case studies.

The first type is relevant for highly competitive markets with pronounced technological dynamisms, in which the first mover advantage plays a central strategic role for competitiveness. Implementing the so-called ***lead-time strategy***, companies rely on their capabilities and knowledge that enable them to take advantage of first-mover advantages. Hence, they select very carefully the technology or product related knowledge they are

Table 3 Relevance of strategies in case studies

Collaboration strategy	Case Study			
	A	B	C	D
(1) Lead-time-strategy	X	X		
(2) Patent-dominated strategy		X	X	
(3) Joint lead-time/patent-based strategy	X			
(4) Trust-based strategy			X	X

ready to share with innovation partners due to the high risk of competition on the market; namely the partners can theoretically misuse this core knowledge for creating their own lead-time advantages. A typical case comes from the automotive industry, in which the company that offers a certain innovative technology in vehicles takes the leading position on the market as a pioneer.

> *"Who is first on the market is the key success factor. Look at Tesla with their electronic cars; everybody would say Tesla is the pioneer in this segment, it is the brand maker, let's bay one. Or look at Apple with iPhone; why is this product so successful, among others I would say because of the first mover advantage."* (CIG, Case A)

Nevertheless, due to the essential role of partners' complementary assets for the success of innovation in collaborative projects, companies following a lead-time strategy have to make compromises over sharing non-core knowledge for external knowledge which is difficult to generate in-house. In order to precisely regulate the rules of knowledge exchange, companies use formal secrecy as a protection mechanism in collaborative innovation projects, like e.g. a NDA.

> *"Our company has a standard NDA [...]. That's why it always takes a while until the other side has checked it legally and is ready to sign. But there are also cases where the other side does not accept the NDA and has amendments. Sometimes we come to a conclusion and sometimes we don't, in which case the project doesn't take place"* (CIG, Case A)

Simultaneously, since the core knowledge, which is essential for first-mover advantages, quickly becomes obsolete in the regime of high technological dynamism and short technology life cycles. Formal IPR like patents play a rather marginal role for those companies, at least in the invention phase. The main reason for that are slow examinations, and thus long administrative processes concerning patents. Additionally, industries like chemistry face unique challenges in the patenting process due to the explicit nature of chemical formulations. As a result, patents may not always provide complete protection from imitations. Therefore, companies in this segment often opt to introduce innovative products as pioneers in the market, relying on achieving high visibility and establishing a recognizable brand instead of focusing on protective measures using e.g. patents.

> *"[...] obtaining a patent for a smal company like us is already quite complex and we only resort to patents in extreme cases. This is also because the technology or products in our segment are rely hard to protect using patents; competitors can even use the patent do develop their own products. We prefer to take advantage of a half-year head start from a good idea instead of focusing on potential benefits we might gain from a patent in the future."* (CEO, Case D)

However, our case studies also provide ample evidence that forward-thinking companies recognize the importance of effectively combining lead time advantages with IPR protection. By doing so, they gain a competitive edge and can swiftly bring their innovative products or services to market. Coupled with robust IPR protection, these companies ensure that their pioneering ideas remain safeguarded from unauthorized use or imitation by competitors. Notably, this ***joint lead-time /patent-based strategy*** emphasis on lead time and IPR protection is not a blanket strategy but rather tailored to specific instances. Innovative solutions with significant disruptive potential warrant greater attention to both elements, as they face higher risks of being copied or lagging behind competitors if not implemented swiftly. In contrast, more incremental innovations might not demand the same level of urgency in integrating lead time and IPR protection. As technology continues to shape the business landscape, this combination of strategies remains a potent method for companies to not only thrive but also shape the future of their respective industries. A similar scenario arises when companies collaborate with external partners who possess specialized knowledge or technology. Instead of purchasing licenses for this valuable intellectual property, they engage in innovative joint projects, leveraging these assets collectively.

> *"This is always when we work on products with a compelling* "game-changing" *character, and with them our primary goal is to create new spaces in the market. We are determined to be the first to introduce these innovative products, thereby establishing ourselves as trailblazers in the field. [...] but given the significant strategic importance of these products, especially considering the advanced technologies and technical solutions that underpin them, we are taking proactive steps to safeguard them through the process of patenting."* (CRD, Case B)

In contrast, there are situations where the first-mover advantage does not have a critical strategic role. Instead, other factors, like unique technical features combined with high quality, become more important. In such cases, the lead time strategy loses its significance. Nevertheless, due to the high relevance of these innovative features, which define the cutting-edge technology in the industry, formal IPR, such as patents, plays a central role as a protecting instrument, thus we call this ***patent-dominated strategy.*** These collaboration strategy is particularly important for innovation projects that lead to technological milestones in terms of quality, rather than creating entirely new products or technologies for the industry. Our interviewee from the medical company, for instance, explains their preference for focusing on quality rather than always being the first on the market. They also emphasize the significance of considering the high sensitivity of their products when making decisions about sharing knowledge in collaborative innovation projects.

> *"Our main USP is our very trustable and highly qualitative product. We have very often the situation in which the life of a patient in the hospital depends on our product, therefore we have to offer 100% quality without compromise. How fast we come with our products is I think rather insignificant in contrast to trustworthiness resulting from our quality and technology."* (SPM, Case B)

Finally, the fourth type pertains to strategies that are applicable to segments with lower technological dynamism and weaker appropriability regimes. In such scenarios, traditional methods like IPR and lead-time strategies prove ineffective. Instead, the primary means of safeguarding against inadvertent knowledge leakage in these collaborations is by fostering a sense of trust, which emerges from extensive experience gained through long-term engagement in joint projects. Furthermore, the cornerstone of successful innovation lies in the ability to deliver top-notch quality products and services that consistently meet and exceed customer expectations, foster unwavering customer loyalty. One interview partner explained:

> *"We have two types of partners, these who we know very well from past projects and completely new partners. With old partners, we have a very open communication because we trust them."* (CEO, Case C)

While the timeline for developing and delivering innovative solutions is essential, it takes a backseat compared to the paramount importance of trust representing a pivotal factor that companies must earn in the market through collaborative efforts with innovative enterprises and clients alike. Thereforem we call this ***trust-based strategy.***

5 Discussion

According to the classic open innovation literature, openness in innovation projects enables firms to access and absorb innovation-relevant assets, such as knowledge from external sources [1]. The focus is thereby on complementarity in assets as prominently discussed in the PFI framework [9, 11]. Our case-study analyses confirm likewise that without significant knowledge complementarities, there will be no or only very limited knowledge exchange between the parties. By comparison, complementary knowledge assets, which are difficult to build in-house but can be absorbed through collaboration with external partners in innovation projects. This argument is in line with the classical resource-based motives for collaboration [10, 13] affirming thereby the basic criteria for opening up innovation processes for collaborations.

Nevertheless, referring to the risks of uncontrolled knowledge leakage [2, 3], we questioned whether companies, which manufacture and sell highly innovative physical products, are willing to engage in truly open innovation partnerships without limitations on inbound and outbound knowledge flows, as the traditional open innovation literature propagates. Our comparative case study analyses show that such very open business models are usually unlikely to be implemented, because of the risk of knowledge leaking to partners, which are usually competitors at the same time. Thus, truly open strategies occurred only if there was no perceived risk of product market competition between the partners. In such cases, further exploitation of knowledge absorbed from partners did not represent a threat to the original business of neither party in the project. Hence, we observed instances where firms were willing to share knowledge more openly without putting too much effort into protecting their knowledge positions. However, in situations with a certain level of product market competition, companies implemented partial restrictions on innovation partnerships in order to mitigate the risks of knowledge leakage. Based on this finding, we develop our Proposition 1:

Proposition 1*: Truly open collaboration strategies with absent or very low limitations on mutual knowledge flows between partners occur in the manufacturing sector only if partners are not simultaneously relevant product market competitors. In contrast, any kind of product market competition between the partners calls for different knowledge sharing restrictions in innovation partnerships, and thus for semi-open collaboration strategies in innovation projects of manufacturing companies.*

Importantly, these findings suggest that partner type, specifically whether a partner is also a product-market competitor, acts as a boundary condition for Proposition 1. This has direct implications for partner selection in practice, as the feasibility of open collaboration strategies depends on the absence of competitive overlap between partners. Where such overlap exists, firms shift toward more restricted forms of knowledge sharing and thus toward semi-open collaboration strategies in innovation partnerships.

Relying on the PFI-framework [9, 11], we assume that companies decide upon the level of openness considering potential first mover advantages and the strength of IPR protection as contingencies that trigger protection strategies and thus can help to craft the openness, i.e. to navigate the open innovation paradox [12, 22, 23]. We were particularly inspired by the understanding that the utilization of these two triggers depends heavily on the sector affiliation, market characteristics, as well as the nature of the product or technology innovation.

First mover advantage holds significant strategic relevance in industries characterized by rapid technological progress, fast innovation cycles, and intense competition [15]. In such dynamic environments, companies that are early to introduce novel products or technologies often gain a competitive edge. Our results show that, on the one hand, keeping the core knowledge secret within innovation processes using formal secrecy, and thus mitigating the risk of its uncontrolled knowledge outflows, is a prerequisite for achieving first-mover advantages on the market and thus for business success in general [17]. However, in order to implement an effective lead-time strategy, companies have to ensure that the very core of their dynamic capabilities, which they use for creating lead-time advantages on the market, remains completely secret, because otherwise partners could potentially copy it [24, 25]. In other words, companies have to put restrictions not only on the permissible use of shared knowledge, but also on what is shared in the collaborative innovation projects. This is why formal secrecy in form of NDA, particularly in a very explicit form, is used as a primary protection mechanism in these realms [26]. In contrast, in market segments with extremely high requirements in terms of technological performance, the first-mover advantage has a rather marginal character in comparison to high quality and trustworthiness of customers. Based on these results we developed our Proposition 2.1:

Proposition 2.1: *High relevance of first mover advantage combined with a low to medium levels of effectiveness of formal IPR calls for a lead-time strategy in collaborative innovation projects of manufacturing companies.*

On the other hand, the relevance of appropriability regimes, particularly IPR strategies, increases with sensitivity and strategic importance of the knowledge shared in the innovation projects, as we can see in our case studies as well. This is equally in accordance with Teece's PFI-framework, in which the IPR regime represents a fundamental determinant of return from innovation. Our results show, however, a certain level of heterogeneity in strategies which implement IPR protection. On the one hand, innovative solutions with significant disruptive potential require greater attention to both elements, lead-time advantage and IPR regime, due to higher risks of being copied or falling behind competitors if not implemented swiftly. This leads us to our Propositon 2.2:

Proposition 2.2*: High relevance of first mover advantage combined with a high level of effectiveness of formal IPR calls for following a joint patent and lead-time strategy in collaborative innovation projects of manufacturing companies.*

On the other hand, the first-mover advantage is not always the key determinant of strategic success in certain scenarios. Instead, unique technical features combined with high quality take precedence as crucial factors. In such cases, the lead time strategy loses its significance as innovation projects aim to achieve technological milestones in terms of quality rather than being the first to market entirely new products or technologies. In these situations, IPR plays a central role as a protective instrument for the innovative features that define cutting-edge technology in the industry. Hence we conclude that in contexts where unique technical features and high-quality innovations define the competitive landscape, collaborative strategies and formal IPR play critical roles in protecting and promoting success in the market. Being a first-mover, however, may not be as significant in comparison to delivering superior quality and cutting-edge advancements. These findings lead us to our Propositions 2.3.

Proposition 2.3*: Low relevance of first mover advantage combined with high level of effectiveness of formal IPR protection calls for a patent-based collaboration strategies in innovation projects of manufacturing companies.*

Finally, we aimed at understanding the market setting with lower technological dynamisms combined with weak appropriability regimes. Generally, in such situations, neither the first mover advantage nor the use of IPR can enable an appropriate strategy. Teece (2017) calls it a "weak" appropriability regime in which the protection of innovation is difficult due to the fact that knowledge as the main resource for its creation can be easily codified and transfered. Products and technologies that are relatively easy to copy thanks to the rather explicit nature of the core knowledge used for innovation. Moreover, instead of focusing on the advantages of the lead-time strategy, companies put the quality and the confidence of customers in the focus of their innovation strategy. Therefore, there is no real possibility for an effective implementation of any well-known formal protection mechanism, we discussed above. We identified a situation like this in our case study from the electrical equipment industry where the main product are traditional electric heating components. As the core technology and the related knowledge for products are highly explicit in nature, resulting from detailed product specifications they develop with their customers, they can be theoretically easily absorbed by every single partner in the collaborative project and further used for developing similar products for the same market. The only way to protect the core knowledge in the innovation collaboration from uncontrolled leakage represents thereby the trust among the partners. When partners trust each other, they are more willing to share knowledge, resources, and strategic information without relying heavily on detailed legal agreements or strict control mechanisms [27, 28]. Trust reduces concerns about opportunistic behavior, lowers transaction and coordination costs, and facilitates open communication and joint problem-solving [29]. As a result, collaborative processes become more flexible and efficient, which is particularly important in innovation projects characterized by uncertainty, complexity, and evolving objectives [27]. This leads us to our last Proposition 2.4:

Proposition 2.4*: Low relevance of first mover advantages combined with low effectiveness in terms of formal IPR calls for trust- based collaboration strategies in innovation projects of manufacturing companies.*

Put together, our four propositions stand for four different strategies of openness in collaborative innovation projects, which can be systematized using a three-dimensional framework (see Fig. 1). The dimensions, which we derived using a mix of deductive and inductive reasoning, represent three central contingency factors affecting a strategic choice about collaboration patterns. On the one hand, threat of product market competition shapes how companies decide upon various degrees of openness (see Proposition 1). On the other hand, the relevance of a technological first mover advantage and the strength of the IPR regime frame various semi-open collaboration strategies that companies follow with respect to their specific constellations (see Propositions 2.1–2.4).

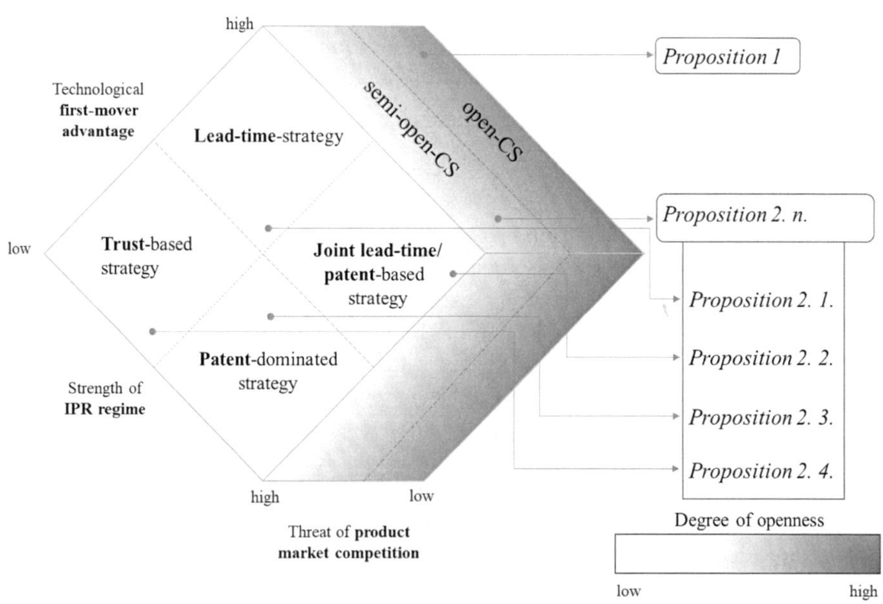

Fig. 1. An integrated framework of collaboration strategies in manufacturing innovation projects

6 Conclusions

Drawing from the existing body of research on the open innovation paradox and knowledge leakage in innovation partnerships [2, 3, 5–7, 30], as well as the role of protection mechanisms derived from the PFI-framework [9–12], our study aimed to shed light on the strategic decisions made by manufacturing firms concerning the openness in their innovation partnerships. By doing so, we sought to offer insightful and exploratory perspectives on the ways these firms craft their approaches to collaboration and openness in the context of innovation. We contribute thereby to the literature in four important ways.

First, by systematically integrating key insights from the profiting from innovation literature [10, 11], we explain the conditions under which openness in collaborative projects captures value of innovation. Specifically, our integrated model defines conditions under which, even in traditional manufacturing that relies on selling physical goods, firms will enter open collaborative innovation partnerships. So far, the innovation collaboration literature had a specific focus on the digital economy, which actually provides some intriguing examples of very open collaborations, e.g. in software development [31]. However, it remained unclear whether for firms which rely on selling physical (technology-based) products truly open innovation partnerships are a viable option. Our results imply that this can be the case if the threat of product market competition by partners is low. In that respect, our insights extend the scope of the PFI literature by introducing product market competition, which has so far only received scant attention, as an important contingency factor.

Second, we highlighted that in many cases, innovation partnerships in manufacturing will be semi-open rather than fully open, because partners with a sufficient degree of asset complementary will often also be or at least may become important competitors on the focal firm's product market. In this case, manufacturing firms will have to navigate the open innovation paradox [2, 5, 6] by designing semi-open collaboration strategies putting partial restrictions on knowledge sharing with or use by partners.

Third, in the process of examining semi-open strategies in-depth, we could identify two types of strategies under conditions when either the appropriability regime is strong (IPR-based strategy) or technological dynamism gives rise to first mover advantages (lead-time-based strategy). Moreover, striving to understand the strategic choice of manufacturing companies under opposite conditions, low technological dynamism and weak appropriability regime, we could identify another strategy relying on trust as a protecting mechanism against knowledge leakage [32] that was neglected in the PFI-framework. We learned from our data that companies are inclined towards establishing durable collaborations with partners and select very carefully with whom they build a supportive and trust-based relationship, on which they can both depend. Hence, companies rely on trust as a surrogate protection mechanism against non-permissible use of the knowledge shared within the partnership.

Fourth, our model provides practical guidance for managers in manufacturing companies on designing the mode of open-innovation partnerships for firms relying on selling technology-based physical goods. We unveil conditions under which firms may seek very open partnerships with few restrictions on knowledge flows and delineate these from situations under which firms should aim to implement (variegated types of) semi-open collaborations.

We recognize that our analysis suffers from some limitations which could serve as the starting points for future research in this area. Firstly, given the inherent restrictions of the in-depth case study method, the developed model is valid only in the context of manufacturing companies. While the firms were carefully selected to account for a broad coverage of different size categories, industries, positions in the value chain, and levels of product complexity, it is unclear to what degree the model presented in this paper can be applied to other industries. Furthermore, the study is primarily based on a specific geographic and sectoral context, namely German manufacturing firms. As such, the findings may be shaped by country-specific institutional and industrial conditions, and future research could examine different national contexts to assess whether the observed effects are consistent or differ across countries and institutional environments. Furthermore, although our model integrates different levels of technological dynamism, it does not account for different environmental settings in which the collaboration takes place. For instance, the innovation project might vary across different types of external partners or different institutional frameworks. Thirdly, we do not know about the effects chosen strategies have on innovation and business performances, which future studies could examine using quantitative methods. Finally, future research might explore the dynamics within collaborative strategies under changing conditions through in-depth, long-term analyses. Particularly interesting in these terms would be to understand why and how firms change or modify the type of their collaborative strategy.

Disclosure of Interests. The authors have no competing interests to declare that are relevant to the content of this article.

References

1. Chesbrough, H.: Open Business Models: how to Thrive in the New Innovation Landscape. Harvard Business Press (2006)
2. Bogers, M.: The open innovation paradox: knowledge sharing and protection in R&D collaborations. Eur. J. Innov. Manage. **14**, 93–117 (2011). https://doi.org/10.1108/14601061111104715
3. Vanhaverbeke, W.: The interorganizational context of open innovation. In: Open Innovation: Researching a New Paradigm, pp. 205–219 (2006)
4. Schubert, T.: Infringement of intellectual property in innovation partnerships. R&D Manage. **46**, 241–254 (2016). https://doi.org/10.1111/radm.12128
5. Bhatnagar, B., Dörfler, V., MacBryde, J.: Navigating the open innovation paradox: an integrative framework for adopting open innovation in pharmaceutical R&D in developing countries. J. Technol. Transf. **48**, 1121–1149 (2022). https://doi.org/10.1007/s10961-022-09958-6
6. Foege, J.N., Lauritzen, G.D., Tietze, F., Salge, T.O.: Reconceptualizing the paradox of openness: how solvers navigate sharing-protecting tensions in crowdsourcing. Res. Policy. **48**, 1323–1339 (2019). https://doi.org/10.1016/j.respol.2019.01.013
7. Laursen, K., Salter, A.J.: The paradox of openness: appropriability, external search and collaboration. Res. Policy. **43**, 867–878 (2014). https://doi.org/10.1016/j.respol.2013.10.004

8. Eisenhardt, K.M.: Building theories from case study research. AMR. **14**, 532–550 (1989). https://doi.org/10.2307/258557
9. Teece, D.J.: Profiting from technological innovation: implications for integration, collaboration, licensing and public policy. Res. Policy. **15**, 285–305 (1986). https://doi.org/10.1142/9789812796929_0001
10. Teece, D.J.: Reflections on profiting from innovation. Res. Policy. **35**, 1131–1146 (2006). https://doi.org/10.1016/j.respol.2006.09.009
11. Teece, D.J.: Profiting from innovation in the digital economy: standards, complementary assets, and business models in the wireless world. Res. Policy. **47**, 1367–1387 (2017). https://doi.org/10.1016/j.respol.2017.01.015
12. Desyllas, P., Sako, M.: Profiting from business model innovation: evidence from pay-as-you-drive auto insurance. Res. Policy. **42**, 101–116 (2013). https://doi.org/10.1016/j.respol.2012.05.008
13. Rothaermel, F.T.: Incumbent's advantage through exploiting complementary assets via interfirm cooperation. Strateg. Manag. J. **22**, 687–699 (2001). https://doi.org/10.1002/smj.180
14. Colombo, M.G., Grilli, L., Piva, E.: In search of complementary assets: the determinants of alliance formation of high-tech start-ups. Res. Policy. **35**, 1166–1199 (2006). https://doi.org/10.1016/j.respol.2006.09.002
15. Bourgeois III, L.J., Eisenhardt, K.M.: Strategic decision processes in high velocity environments: four cases in the microcomputer industry. Manag. Sci. **34**, 816–835 (1988). https://doi.org/10.1287/mnsc.34.7.816
16. Meyer, N., Horvat, D., Hitzler, M., Doll, C.: Business models for freight and logistics services. Work. Pap. Sustain. Innov. **S04/2018**, 1–55 (2018). https://doi.org/10.24406/publica-fhg-299025
17. Teece, D., Pisano, G.: The dynamic capabilities of firms: an introduction. In: Handbook on Knowledge Management, pp. 195–213. Springer (2003)
18. Yin, R.K.: RK.: Case Study Research: Design and Methods. Sage Publications, Thousand Oaks, CA (2009)
19. Seawright, J., Gerring, J.: Case selection techniques in case study research: a menu of qualitative and quantitative options. Political Res. Q. **61**, 294–308 (2008). https://doi.org/10.1177/1065912907313
20. Gibbert, M., Ruigrok, W., Wicki, B.: What passes as a rigorous case study? Strateg. Manag. J. **29**, 1465–1474 (2008). https://doi.org/10.1002/smj.722
21. Gioia, D.A., Corley, K.G., Hamilton, A.L.: Seeking qualitative rigor in inductive research: notes on the Gioia methodology. Organ. Res. Methods. **16**, 15–31 (2013). https://doi.org/10.1177/1094428112452151
22. Vecchiato, R.: Creating value through foresight: first mover advantages and strategic agility. Technol. Forecast. Soc. Change. **101**, 25–36 (2015). https://doi.org/10.1016/j.techfore.2014.08.016
23. Markides, C., Sosa, L.: Pioneering and first mover advantages: the importance of business models. Long Range Plan. **46**, 325–334 (2013). https://doi.org/10.1016/j.lrp.2013.06.002
24. de Faria, P., Sofka, W.: Knowledge protection strategies of multinational firms—a cross-country comparison. Res. Policy. **39**, 956–968 (2010). https://doi.org/10.1016/j.respol.2010.03.005
25. Gallié, E.-P., Legros, D.: French firms' strategies for protecting their intellectual property. Res. Policy. **41**, 780–794 (2012). https://doi.org/10.1016/j.respol.2011.12.008
26. Bos, B., Broekhuizen, T.L.J., de Faria, P.: A dynamic view on secrecy management. J. Bus. Res. **68**, 2619–2627 (2015). https://doi.org/10.1016/j.jbusres.2015.04.009
27. Dyer, J.H., Singh, H.: The relational view: cooperative strategy and sources of interorganizational competitive advantage. AMR. **23**, 660–679 (1998)

28. Poppo, L., Zenger, T.: Do formal contracts and relational governance function as substitutes or complements? Strateg. Manag. J. **23**, 707–725 (2002). https://doi.org/10.1002/smj.249
29. Zaheer, A., McEvily, B., Perrone, V.: Does trust matter? Exploring the effects of interorganizational and interpersonal trust on performance. Organ. Sci. **9**, 141–159 (1998). https://doi.org/10.1287/orsc.9.2.141
30. McEvily, S.K., Eisenhardt, K.M., Prescott, J.E.: The global acquisition, leverage, and protection of technological competencies. Strateg. Manag. J. **25**, 713–722 (2004). https://doi.org/10.1002/smj.425
31. Teece, D.J.: Business models and dynamic capabilities. Long Range Plan. **51**, 40–49 (2018). https://doi.org/10.1016/j.lrp.2017.06.007
32. Granovetter, M.: The impact of social structure on economic outcomes. In: The Sociology of Economic Life, pp. 46–61. Routledge (2018)

Stereo-Vision-Based Part Classification for Brownfield Assembly Using a Low-Cost Camera

Max-Heiner Birk[1,2](✉), Andreas Gaus[2], Christoph Reich[1], and Ing. Michael Engler[1]

[1] Furtwangen University, Robert-Gerwig-Platz 1, 78120 Furtwangen, Germany
max-heiner.birk@bosch.com

[2] Bosch Rexroth AG, Anden Kelterwiesen 14, 72160 Horbam Neckar, Germany

Abstract. Variant-rich brownfield assembly environments require reliable part identification as a basis for downstream automation steps. In many existing production settings, however, the integration of high-end measurement technology is limited by cost, installation effort and compatibility with established system structures. This paper presents a low-cost stereo-vision-based approach for classifying piston housings by their inner bore diameter using a ZED 2 camera. The proposed method combines RGB image processing with stereo-derived depth information to obtain a metric diameter estimate from image observations. Circle candidates are first detected in the image domain and subsequently validated using geometric and depth-based criteria. These criteria include edge coverage along the bore contour, depth consistency on the detected ring structure and plausibility checks derived from the expected diameter ranges of the target part classes. The resulting diameter estimate is used to assign parts to predefined size categories relevant for subsequent assembly operations. To improve temporal stability, the approach further incorporates track-based measurement smoothing, local re-detection within a region of interest and confirmation logic across multiple frames. The overall concept is motivated by an industrial brownfield use case in hydraulic component assembly and is investigated in a prototype experimental setup. The results indicate that the combination of geometry-constrained detection and depth-based validation enables practical and reproducible part classification using cost-efficient sensing. The paper therefore demonstrates how low-cost stereo vision can provide a technically feasible perception module for feature-based automation in existing assembly environments.

Keywords: Stereo vision · Brownfield assembly · Part classification · Depth-based measurement · Low-cost sensing

1 Introduction

Brownfield assembly environments are characterized by existing equipment, established process structures and limited freedom for extensive hardware modifications. At the same time, many such environments must cope with increasing product variety and the

Published by Springer Nature Switzerland AG 2027
G. Pezzotta et al. (Eds.): APMS 2026, IFIP AICT 808, pp. 293–307, 2027.
https://doi.org/10.1007/978-3-032-38594-9_20

resulting need for flexible and reliable automation. In these settings, the identification of variant-relevant part features is a key prerequisite for downstream handling, process parameterization, and automated decision-making. However, this task is often challenging because product variants cannot always be distinguished by explicit coding or easily accessible identifiers. Instead, relevant differences are frequently reflected in geometric properties of the physical part.

This challenge is particularly evident in the assembly of hydraulic components, where geometric differences influence both handling strategies and subsequent assembly operations. In the use case addressed in this paper, the inner bore diameter of a piston housing serves as a variant-relevant characteristic. The bore diameter is not only technically meaningful from an assembly and measurement perspective, but also sufficiently distinctive to enable a simplified yet practically relevant class assignment. In the investigated prototype scenario, the classification task is deliberately reduced to two dominant part classes with small and large inner bores.

A robust determination of such a feature from camera data is not trivial. A circular structure may be detectable in the image plane, but the observed pixel radius depends directly on the distance between camera and object. As a result, image-based circle detection alone is insufficient for deriving a metric diameter that remains valid across varying object distances. To overcome this limitation, image geometry must be combined with depth information. This motivates the use of stereo vision, which provides both RGB image data and depth measurements and therefore enables the estimation of real-world geometric quantities from visual observations.

Against this background, this paper presents a low-cost stereo-vision-based approach for classifying piston housings by their inner bore diameter using a ZED 2 camera. The proposed method combines image-based circle detection with geometry- and depth-based validation as well as metric diameter estimation. In addition, the approach incorporates temporal stabilization mechanisms to improve reproducibility across image sequences. The overall concept is motivated by a brownfield assembly use case from hydraulic component production, while the present investigation is conducted in a prototype experimental setup under varying distance, motion, and illumination conditions.

The contribution of the paper is threefold. First, it proposes a practically implementable stereo-vision pipeline for bore-based part classification using cost-efficient sensing. Second, it introduces a validation strategy that combines geometric edge support, local depth consistency, and metric plausibility checks for robust bore detection and classification. Third, it shows how temporal stabilization can support more reproducible feature-based class assignment under prototype conditions relevant to brownfield deployment.

To structure the investigation more explicitly, the paper addresses the following research questions:

RQ1: Can a low-cost stereo-vision setup be used to derive a metrically interpretable inner bore diameter for piston housing classification under varying working distances in a brownfield-oriented prototype scenario?

RQ2: Does the proposed combination of geometrically constrained candidate detection, depth-based validation and temporal stabilization provide a technically robust basis for class assignment under realistic fluctuations in pose, motion and illumination?

The remainder of the paper is structured as follows. Section 2 reviews related work on retrofit-capable sensing, stereo-vision-based measurement, and feature-based part classification in manufacturing. Section 3 introduces the industrial motivation and prototype context. Section 4 presents the proposed method. Section 5 describes the experimental setup, while Sect. 6 reports the results, which are subsequently discussed in Sect. 7. Section 8 concludes the paper and outlines future work.

2 Related Work

The gradual enhancement of existing production systems is one of the key challenges in modern manufacturing environments. In brownfield settings in particular, new functionalities must be integrated into already established system structures without substantially disturbing ongoing processes or requiring extensive hardware modifications. As a result, retrofit-capable, economically feasible, and preferably non-intrusive sensing and automation solutions have become increasingly important [1–3].

In this context, industrial machine vision has become a central building block of data-driven manufacturing systems. Camera-based approaches are widely used for quality inspection, defect detection, feature extraction, and dimension-related assessment [4–6]. At the same time, many of these applications remain primarily focused on 2D image data and surface-related inspection tasks. Whenever real geometric features of physical parts must be determined in a robust and reproducible way, purely image-based methods often reach their limits, especially when the apparent feature size varies with the acquisition geometry [5, 7].

This has increased the relevance of optical 3D metrology. Such methods make it possible to evaluate visual information not only qualitatively, but also metrically. For industrial deployment, however, suitability is not determined by measurement accuracy alone. Calibration effort, working distance, surface properties, integration effort, and economic viability are equally important. Especially in brownfield environments, this creates a trade-off between highly accurate specialized metrology systems and flexible, cost-efficient sensing solutions that can be integrated into existing processes with reasonable effort [2, 3, 7].

Stereo vision is particularly relevant in this context. By combining two camera views, depth information can be estimated and image observations can be translated into real geometric quantities. This is especially useful when a feature is clearly visible in the image but its metric interpretation depends on the object distance. Circular structures such as bores are a typical example, since their apparent size in pixels changes with the distance to the camera [8–11]. This requirement is further reinforced by the intended application perspective of the present work, in which the camera is planned as part of a robot-supported perception setup. As a result, the working distance cannot be assumed to remain constant during operation. Under such conditions, the apparent size of circular features in the image cannot be interpreted reliably on the basis of pixel measurements alone. A depth-supported diameter estimation is therefore essential to ensure robust feature extraction despite distance variations [8, 11, 12].

Stereo-vision-based measurement has already been applied to precise dimensional inspection tasks, for example for the measurement of 3D holes and small mechanical components [8–11]. These studies indicate that measurement quality depends not only on depth reconstruction itself, but also on its geometrically consistent use. Important factors include system calibration, robust extraction of suitable image features, and plausibility assessment of the resulting measurements [7, 9–11]. At the same time, many existing contributions focus either on high-accuracy metrology scenarios or on comparatively controlled acquisition conditions. For brownfield-oriented perception tasks, however, additional requirements arise from limited integration freedom, variable distances, fluctuating illumination and the need for robust operation with cost-efficient hardware.

For the present paper, an important observation is that industrial usefulness does not always require full 3D reconstruction of complex parts. In many assembly-related tasks, it is sufficient to extract a single functionally relevant feature in metric form, provided that this extraction is robust against distance changes, local depth noise, and short-term visual disturbances [11, 12]. This is precisely the perspective adopted here. The present work therefore does not aim at general-purpose 3D measurement, but at the robust extraction of one assembly-relevant geometric feature that can support downstream automation decisions in a brownfield context.

Overall, the reviewed literature highlights a gap between general-purpose machine vision on the one hand and highly specialized 3D metrology on the other. Brownfield applications require an intermediate class of solutions: sensing approaches that are metrically meaningful, technically manageable, economically integrable, and sufficiently robust under variable acquisition conditions. The present paper addresses this gap by developing and investigating a low-cost stereo-vision pipeline for bore-based classification of piston housings in an industrially motivated brownfield context.

3 Industrial Motivation and Prototype Context

This work is motivated by a brownfield use case from the assembly of hydraulic components. In such environments, the demand for automation often arises because variant-relevant information for handling and assembly decisions is generally available in principle, but is not yet provided in a directly usable form for automated execution. Long-established production structures already include fixed processes, installed equipment, and existing information flows. Any additional automation functionality should therefore be integrated with minimal intervention into the installed system.

Within this context, the piston housing represents a part whose geometric characteristics are relevant for downstream process steps. Of particular interest is the inner bore diameter, because it provides a simple, visually accessible, and functionally meaningful basis for distinguishing between variants. For the present investigation, the classification problem is deliberately reduced to two dominant size classes. Although simplified, this scenario remains technically meaningful and allows the feasibility of camera-based feature determination for subsequent automation steps to be examined in a controlled and transparent way.

To investigate this idea, the method is examined in a prototype experimental setup. This setup serves as an intermediate step between conceptual method development and later transfer to a production-related context. Its purpose is to assess whether the relevant feature can be derived robustly from the proposed combination of image processing and stereo-derived depth information and whether it can be used for a practically meaningful classification task.

For this purpose, a ZED 2 camera provides both color image data and depth information. The study covers a variable acquisition range with camera distances of approximately 0.3 m to 1.0 m. During image acquisition, the parts were moved manually, so that the evaluation is based on image sequences with changing position and perspective. In addition, foreground and background brightness varied due to sunlight conditions. As a result, the prototype setup already includes practically relevant variations in distance, motion, perspective, and illumination.

In this context, functional reliability is understood as the repeated detection of the relevant inner bore, rejection of implausible circle candidates, derivation of a metrically plausible diameter estimate and assignment of a locked track to the correct target class under the investigated prototype variations. These variations refer to the previously described changes in distance, lateral position, moderate perspective, manual motion and foreground/background brightness. The term is therefore used in a prototype-oriented sense and does not imply full industrial process capability.

4 Proposed Method

4.1 Measurement Principle and Parameterization

The proposed method determines the inner bore diameter of a piston housing from color and depth data provided by a stereo camera and uses this information to assign the part to one of two size classes, small or large. The overall approach is organized as a multi-stage processing pipeline. First, circle candidates are detected in the image domain. These candidates are then validated by geometric and depth-based checks. Subsequently, a metric diameter is computed and compared with predefined class bands. Finally, a tracking stage stabilizes the result over multiple frames. The methodological core lies in the combination of image geometry, local depth information, and temporal consistency, since the apparent size of a bore in the image depends directly on the distance between camera and object.

A ZED 2 camera is used as the sensing device. The prototype implementation was realized in Python using OpenCV for image preprocessing, edge extraction and Hough-based circle detection, NumPy for numerical operations and robust statistical calculations and the ZED SDK interface for synchronized RGB/depth data and camera calibration parameters. The camera was operated in PERFORMANCE depth mode with millimeter output, HD720 image resolution, and 120 fps. For feature extraction, synchronized RGB and depth data were evaluated jointly. In addition, the effective focal length f_x of the left camera was read directly from the intrinsic calibration parameters of the ZED camera system rather than being hard-coded. This quantity is expressed in pixel units and is required for diameter estimation.

Diameter estimation is based on the relation between image radius, depth and focal length. If a bore is detected in the image as a circle with radius r_{px} and if a representative depth value Z is available for this structure, a real diameter can be determined. For the present application, the following relation is used:

$$d_{mm} = \frac{2r_{px}Z}{f_x} \tag{1}$$

Here, d_{mm} denotes the real diameter in millimeters, r_{px} the circle radius in pixels, Z the corresponding depth in millimeters and f_x the effective focal length of the camera in pixels. The accuracy of this computation directly depends on a correctly estimated circle radius and a stable depth estimate along the bore structure.

For subsequent classification, two predefined diameter bands are used. In the current implementation, the small class is represented by 29.0–32.0 mm and the large class by 59.0–63.0 mm. In addition, a tolerance margin of ± 0.6 mm is applied. The method further uses a globally admissible diameter range of 28.0–70.0 mm and a valid working depth interval of 100.0–1200.0 mm. These parameters integrate prior geometric knowledge about the target parts into the evaluation. At the same time, they reduce the search space, focus circle detection on physically plausible candidates, and lower the number of implausible detections.

The parameterization was chosen in an application-oriented manner on the basis of preliminary experimental testing. In particular, the thresholds and search ranges were selected such that a practical balance was achieved between sensitivity to valid bore candidates and robustness against false detections caused by weak contours, unstable depth values, or irrelevant round structures. The aim was therefore not universal parameter optimality, but robust behavior under the acquisition conditions relevant for the prototype scenario.

Prior geometric knowledge is therefore used not only for class assignment after detection, but already beforehand to constrain the search space in a physically plausible way, thereby reducing spurious circle hypotheses and improving subsequent validation.

4.2 Circle Detection and Geometry–/Depth-Based Validation

For each incoming frame, the color image is processed first. The image is converted into grayscale. Histogram equalization and median filtering are then applied in order to reduce the influence of local brightness differences while suppressing image disturbances and preserving relevant contours. In the current implementation, grayscale equalization is followed by median filtering with a kernel size of 5.

In the next step, an edge image is generated using Canny thresholds of 60 and 160. This image serves as the basis for the subsequent circle search. In addition, a downscaled image version with a scale factor of 0.5 is used for candidate detection. This reduces computational effort and improves the stability of the Hough-based search.

Before circle detection is carried out, a coarse depth estimate of the current frame is computed. For this purpose, all valid depth values in the scene are evaluated and their median is calculated. This value does not represent the final bore depth, but serves as an auxiliary quantity for adapting the search space. Minimum and maximum pixel radii are then calculated from the expected diameter band of a class, the coarse depth estimate, and the focal length f_x. These limits define a plausible radius interval for the Hough transform. Circle detection therefore does not operate with freely chosen radius bounds, but is adapted to the current geometric scale of the scene.

Detection is performed first for the small class. If a plausible candidate is found, its radius can also be used to constrain the search for the large class by means of an expected radius ratio. This couples the second search to the geometry already observed. If no small candidate is available, the radius bounds for the large class are derived directly from its diameter band. In this way, geometric prior knowledge is already incorporated into candidate generation before the actual classification step.

Circle candidates are generated by the Hough circle transform. In the current implementation, both class-specific searches use $dp = 1.2$, $minDist = 22$, $param1 = 120$ and $param2 = 40$. Here, dp controls the inverse resolution ratio of the accumulator, $minDist$ defines the minimum distance between detected circle centers, $param1$ corresponds to the upper threshold of the internal Canny edge detection and $param2$ specifies the accumulator threshold for accepting circle candidates. Together, these parameters determine the internal search resolution, the separation of neighboring detections, and the acceptance sensitivity of the detector. The result of this step is a set of possible circle structures in the image. These candidates represent initial hypotheses only. For reliable classification, this step alone is insufficient because circle detectors may also respond to accidental round patterns or weak local structures. For this reason, a multi-stage validation follows.

The first validation stage checks whether the detected circle is supported by a ring-shaped edge structure. To this end, 120 support points are sampled uniformly along the circumference. For each point, the local neighborhood is examined for edge evidence within a tolerance window of ± 2 px. The ratio between confirmed support points and all tested points defines the edge coverage of the ring. In the current implementation, a candidate is retained only if its coverage exceeds 50%. This step removes candidates that are formally circular but only weakly supported geometrically.

After geometric validation, the method performs depth-based validation. For this purpose, the depth distribution on a narrow ring of ± 2 px around the detected circle is evaluated. The method therefore does not rely on a single depth value at the circle center. Instead, it collects multiple depth values along the bore structure. Two robust quantities are computed from these values. The median describes the representative ring depth, while the median absolute deviation (MAD) describes the spread of the depth values. In the current implementation, a candidate remains valid only if at least 60 valid depth samples are available, the median lies inside the admissible working range of 100.0–1200.0 mm, and the MAD does not exceed 4.0 mm. This evaluation improves the stability of the method because individual erroneous depth values have less influence. At the same time, it checks whether the depth information along the bore is internally consistent. Such consistency is crucial for metric diameter estimation.

This two-stage validation strategy is central to the method. Edge coverage ensures that a candidate is supported by image geometry, whereas ring-based depth evaluation ensures that the associated metric interpretation is based on locally consistent depth information rather than on isolated or unstable pixel values.

4.3 Metric Classification and Temporal Stabilization

The real diameter is computed only after successful geometric and depth-based validation. For this purpose, the validated circle radius and the representative ring depth are inserted into the metric model. The result is a diameter value in millimeters. This measurement is then compared with the predefined class bands. At the frame level, the validated diameter estimate provides a provisional class hypothesis. The final class label reported by the system is derived from the temporally smoothed diameter estimate of a confirmed and locked track. Raw single-frame classifications are therefore not treated as final class decisions before temporal confirmation. If the value lies inside the band of the small class, the part is assigned to small. If it lies inside the band of the large class, it is assigned to large. In addition, the measurement must lie inside the globally admissible diameter range. In this way, classification is linked directly to depth-based diameter estimation and is not derived from image-based circle detection alone.

Since the evaluation is based on image sequences with varying distance and moving parts, the method extends single-frame detection by a tracking stage. Each valid detection is assigned to an existing track or used to initialize a new one by nearest-neighbor matching. In the current implementation, assignment is accepted only if the spatial distance remains within 40 px. For confirmed tracks, position and radius are updated by exponential smoothing with $\alpha = 0.3$ and the metric diameter estimate is smoothed with the same factor. This reduces short-term fluctuations of individual measurements.

A track is regarded as stable only after several successful assignments. In the current implementation, tracks become visible after 4 persistent hits and enter a lock state after 5 confirmed assignments. This state marks observations that have been detected consistently over multiple frames. In addition, a track may remain active for a limited number of frames without a direct new assignment. In the present implementation, unmatched tracks are retained for up to 12 frames, or for up to 45 frames once they are locked. This increases robustness in the presence of short-term failures of circle detection.

For locked tracks, the method also performs local re-detection. If no direct assignment is obtained in a new frame, a new circle search is carried out in the vicinity of the last known position. The local search range is adapted to the previously observed radius and constrained to an expected radius interval of $\pm 15\%$. This re-detection step again passes through geometric and depth-based validation. Temporal stabilization therefore does not merely smooth individual measurements, but also supports continuity of class assignment in the presence of moderate motion, changing viewing conditions, and occasional detection failures.

Overall, the proposed processing chain combines three tightly coupled levels: geometrically guided candidate generation, local image- and depth-based plausibility validation, and temporally stabilized metric classification. The deliberate focus on a single assembly-relevant feature keeps the system technically manageable while still yielding information that is directly usable for downstream automation. Within the scope of the investigated prototype scenario, this indicates that the method may be a promising perception module for variant-rich brownfield applications requiring integration-light feature extraction. Broader industrial suitability requires further validation under production-near operation conditions.

Figure 1 summarizes the proposed stereo-vision-based pipeline, including candidate generation, geometric and depth-based validation, metric diameter estimation, classification and temporal stabilization.

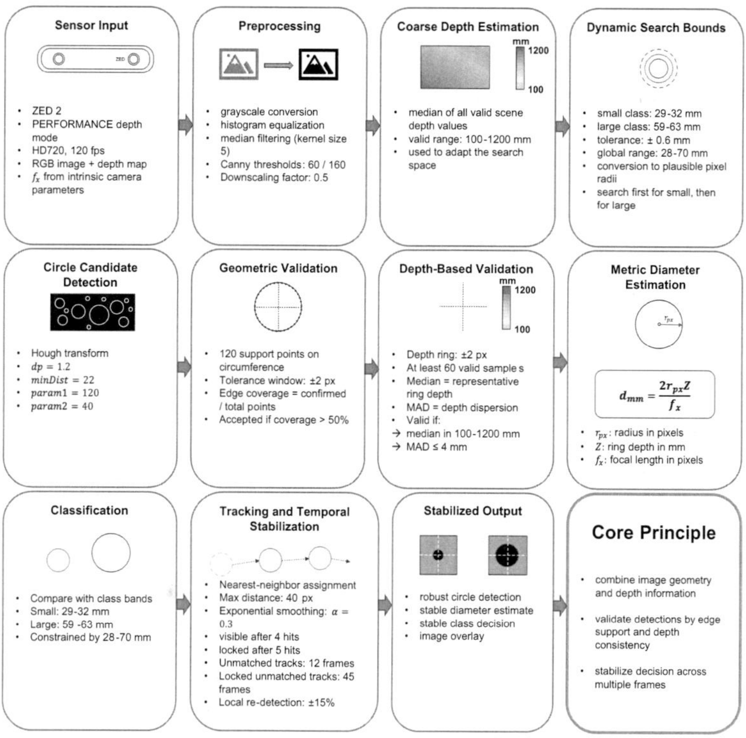

Fig. 1. Overview of the proposed stereo-vision-based processing pipeline for bore-based part classification

5 Experimental Setup

5.1 Setup and Acquisition Conditions

The experimental setup was designed to investigate the proposed method under prototype conditions with practical relevance. The aim of this stage was not yet full industrial validation, but a structured feasibility assessment of whether the inner bore diameter of piston housings can be derived robustly from low-cost stereo-vision data and used for class assignment under varying acquisition conditions.

The sensing configuration and processing parameters are introduced in Sect. 4. The present section therefore focuses on the acquisition conditions and evaluation setting relevant to the prototype assessment.

The investigation was carried out in repeated prototype image sequences rather than isolated single images. Distances, lateral position, moderate perspective, manual motion and brightness varied during acquisition.

Both target classes were considered repeatedly under these varying acquisition conditions. In this way, the setup was intended to avoid a one-sided qualitative assessment and to examine whether the proposed processing chain remained functionally reliable across different observations of both small and large piston housings. Since the recordings consisted of successive frames, the setup also allowed the temporal stabilization behavior of the method to be examined in addition to single-frame detectability.

5.2 Parts, Classes and Evaluation Objective

The investigated objects were piston housings from the context of hydraulic component assembly. For the present study, two dominant target classes were considered. These classes differ in their inner bore diameter and are referred to in this paper as small and large. Assignment relied exclusively on the bore-related feature derived from visual and depth information. External labels or additional identification features were not used.

The evaluation was based on image sequences in which the parts were observed successively within the field of view of the camera. Across the investigated prototype recordings, approximately 100 locked detection instances were considered across repeated image sequences of both target classes. The recordings covered distances between approximately 0.3 m and 1.0 m and included repeated manual repositioning, resulting in variations in lateral position, apparent scale and moderate perspective. Illumination varied naturally due to changing sunlight conditions. The evaluation did not follow a fully factorial design, but was structured as a prototype-oriented feasibility assessment under practically varied acquisition conditions. Ground truth class labels were assigned on the basis of the known part type and the corresponding reference bore diameter. A class decision was counted as correct if the stable class label of a locked track matched the known target class of the observed piston housing. Observations before track confirmation were not treated as final class decisions, because the proposed method explicitly uses temporal confirmation before entering the lock state. For each frame, the color image and depth map were processed by the proposed pipeline. Circle candidates were generated, validated and transformed into metric diameter estimates. These measurements formed the basis for classification into the two target classes. In addition, the sequence-based setup allowed temporally successive observations to be linked by tracking.

Table 1 summarizes the main characteristics of the prototype evaluation setting and the basis on which final class decisions were interpreted.

The experimental investigation pursued three objectives. First, it aimed to assess whether the inner bore can be detected reliably as the relevant geometric feature in the available RGB and depth data. Second, it examined whether the resulting metric diameter estimates remained sufficiently separable for the two target classes under varying acquisition conditions. Third, it considered whether temporally successive observations could be combined into a more stable overall classification by means of the proposed tracking and smoothing mechanisms.

Table 1. Summary of the prototype evaluation setting

Evaluation aspect	Result
Investigated classes	2(small, large)
Camera-to-object distance	approx. 0.3–1.0 m
Detection instances	approx. 100
Evaluation basis	repeated image sequences
Ground truth assignment	known part type / reference bore diameter
Final class decision	stable locked track label
Evaluation focus	bore detection, class separability, temporal stablity
Evaluation type	prototype-oriented feasibility assessment

6 Results

6.1 Classification Results and Stability Across Image Sequences

Within the investigated prototype setup, the proposed method enabled repeated discrimination between the two considered target classes on the basis of the estimated inner bore diameter.

The evaluation of the image sequences showed that both target classes remained distinguishable within the investigated distance range of approximately 0.3 m to 1.0 m. Although the apparent bore size in the image changed with camera-to-object distance, the integration of depth information allowed this scale dependency to be compensated in the diameter estimation. On this basis, the resulting diameter estimates remained interpretable for the intended two-class discrimination task within the evaluated prototype sequences.

A central observation of the investigation concerns the stabilizing effect of the sequence-based tracking logic across successive frames. Consecutive observations of the same bore were combined into more consistent measurement profiles, which reduced short-term label fluctuations within the evaluated sequences.

Representative detection results under varying acquisition conditions are shown in Fig. 2. The examples were selected to illustrate the behavior of the proposed method for different lateral object positions, different camera-to-object distances and moderate pose variations. In the context of the present study, these images are intended primarily as qualitative illustrations of the pipeline behavior for both target classes under the evaluated prototype acquisition conditions.

Although the displayed diameter values show some variation across individual observations, the examples indicate that the proposed processing chain remained operational for the intended two-class discrimination task. In the present context, the primary objective was therefore not high-precision metrology, but robust bore-based classification under practically relevant variations in position, distance and pose. The labels shown in Fig. 2 indicate stable class assignment within the sequence-based tracking logic of the prototype implementation.

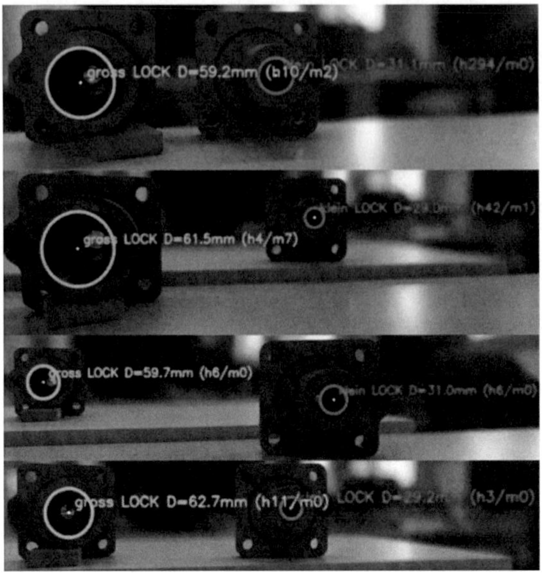

Fig. 2. Representative detection results under varying acquisition conditions. The annotations show the final locked track-level class label and the corresponding smoothed diameter estimate

6.2 Influence of Parameterization and Interpretation of the Results

In addition to the overall functionality of the method, the investigation showed that result quality depends on appropriate parameterization of the processing chain. This applies in particular to the settings of the Hough-based-circle search, the minimum edge coverage required for geometric validation, the admissible depth dispersion in the ring-based depth evaluation and the parameters governing tracking, locking and local re-detection. Parameter tuning therefore forms an important part of practical deployment.

The experiments indicated that parameterization determines the balance between sensitivity and robustness. Beyond candidate selectivity, parameter variation also influenced how quickly a stable lock state was reached. More restrictive settings tended to delay stable confirmation, whereas more permissive settings produced faster detections at the cost of less stable intermediate hypotheses. In this respect, the performance of the proposed pipeline depends not only on the design of its individual processing stages, but also on application-oriented tuning of the involved thresholds and search ranges.

From a methodological point of view, these observations are consistent with the structure of the proposed approach. Since the method combines image-based candidate generation, geometric plausibility checks, local depth consistency assessment and temporal stabilization, parameter choices affect several stages simultaneously. For example, search-space restriction influences the number of initial circle hypotheses, geometric validation affects candidate selectivity, while depth-based thresholds determine whether metric estimation remains stable and tracking parameters govern how strongly short-term measurement fluctuations are suppressed over time.

The reported results should therefore be interpreted as a prototype-oriented assessment of technical feasibility and methodological suitability rather than as a statistically comprehensive benchmark study. Within this scope, the findings indicate that robust class assignment depends on the interaction of candidate detection, local depth consistency checks and temporal stabilization.

7 Discussion

The results indicate that the proposed approach is technically suitable for the considered task and relevant primarily because it determines an assembly-relevant feature with comparatively low sensing and integration effort. This is particularly important in brownfield contexts, where additional automation functions must be connected to existing structures while economic cost and technical intervention remain limited.

A major strength of the method lies in its deliberate focus on a single geometric feature. This keeps the processing chain manageable and functionally well aligned with the intended application. At the same time, the inner bore diameter represents a characteristic that can directly support downstream decisions. In this sense, the approach does not aim at universal 3D measurement, but at application-oriented feature determination. Within the present context, this reduction should not be regarded as a limitation in itself, but as a deliberate design decision that limits complexity and facilitates integration into existing processes.

The investigation further shows that robustness does not result from circle detection alone. Practical usefulness emerges only when image-based candidate generation is combined with local depth validation and temporal stabilization. Unlike a purely image-based radius interpretation, the proposed method compensates distance-dependent scale effects through depth-supported diameter estimation and sequence-based confirmation. From a methodological perspective, this suggests that the decisive factor in low-cost stereo-vision-based perception for brownfield scenarios is less the isolated performance of a single processing step than the coordinated interaction of geometric constraints, depth consistency checks, metric interpretation and sequence-based confirmation.

At the same time, the limits of the investigation must be stated clearly. The evaluation was carried out in a prototype setup and therefore does not yet represent full industrial validation. In addition, the present study focused on a deliberately reduced two-class scenario based on a single geometric feature. This was suitable for investigating technical feasibility in a transparent manner, but it also limits the generalizability of the current results. Transfer to additional part variants, more complex geometries or multi-feature classification tasks would require adapted candidate models, extended validation logic and broader evaluation under more diverse operating conditions.

A further limitation concerns the current evaluation depth. The reported results support the feasibility of the proposed processing chain under varying distance, pose, motion and illumination conditions, but they do not yet constitute a comprehensive benchmark study. In particular, more extensive quantitative analysis, comparison with alternative baseline approaches and systematic parameter sensitivity investigations remain part of future work. These aspects are especially relevant if the method is to be transferred from a prototype scenario to production-near operation.

Future work should focus on production-near validation, extension toward additional feature types and systematic coupling with robotics or decision-making modules.

8 Conclusion

This paper presented a stereo-vision-based approach for classifying piston housings by their inner bore diameter in a brownfield-oriented assembly context. The objective was to capture an assembly-relevant geometric feature with cost-efficient sensing in a way that allows reliable discrimination between two variant classes under practically relevant variations in acquisition conditions.

The investigation showed that the combination of image-based circle detection, geometry- and depth-based validation, metric diameter estimation and temporal stabilization can provide a technically feasible basis for bore-based part classification. In particular, the results indicate that low-cost stereo vision can support robust two-class discrimination even when distance, pose, motion and illumination vary within the considered prototype scenario. The approach should be understood as a prototype-oriented feasibility assessment.

Future work should therefore focus on broader quantitative evaluation, more systematic parameter sensitivity analysis, extension toward additional features and part variants and validation under more production-near and robot-supported deployment conditions. In this sense, the proposed method should be interpreted as a viable perception module for subsequent automation steps rather than as a final end-to-end solution.

Acknowledgements. The authors would like to thank all contributors for their technical support and constructive exchange in the context of the underlying industrial use case.

Disclosure of Interests. The authors have no competing interests to declare that are relevant to the content of this article.

References

1. Słowik, M., Sierocka, H.: Manufacturing equipment retrofitting towards industry 4.0 standards — a systematic overview of the literature. Eng. Manage. Prod. Serv. **15**, 14–26 (2023). https://doi.org/10.2478/emj-2023-0017
2. Jaspert, D., Ebel, M., Eckhardt, A., Poeppelbuss, J.: Smart retrofitting in manufacturing: a systematic review. J. Clean. Prod. **312**, 127555 (2021). https://doi.org/10.1016/j.jclepro.2021.127555
3. García, Á., Bregon, A., Martínez-Prieto, M.A.: A non-intrusive industry 4.0 retrofitting approach for collaborative maintenance in traditional manufacturing. Comput. Ind. Eng. **164**, 107896 (2022). https://doi.org/10.1016/j.cie.2021.107896
4. Werheid, J. et al.: Machine vision in manufacturing SMEs: a review. Discov. Appl. Sci. **7**, 371 (2025). https://doi.org/10.1007/s42452-025-06923-4
5. Gao, Y., Li, X., Wang, X.V., Wang, L., Gao, L.: A review on recent advances in vision-based defect recognition towards industrial intelligence. J. Manuf. Syst. **62**, 753–766 (2022). https://doi.org/10.1016/j.jmsy.2021.05.008

6. Di Leo, G., Liguori, C., Pietrosanto, A., Sommella, P.: A vision system for the online quality monitoring of industrial manufacturing. Opt. Lasers Eng. **89**, 162–168 (2017). https://doi.org/10.1016/j.optlaseng.2016.05.007
7. Catalucci, S., Thompson, A., Piano, S., Branson, D.T., Leach, R.: Optical metrology for digital manufacturing: a review. Int. J. Adv. Manuf. Technol. **120**, 4271–4290 (2022). https://doi.org/10.1007/s00170-022-09084-5
8. Pai, W., Liang, J., Zhang, M., Tang, Z., Li, L.: An advanced multi-camera system for automatic, high-precision and efficient tube profile measurement. Opt. Lasers Eng. **154**, 106890 (2022). https://doi.org/10.1016/j.optlaseng.2021.106890
9. Malassiotis, S., Strintzis, M.G.: Stereo vision system for precision dimensional inspection of 3D holes. Mach. Vis. Appl. **15**, 101–113 (2003). https://doi.org/10.1007/s00138-003-0132-3
10. Ren, Z., Liao, J., Cai, L.: Three-dimensional measurement of small mechanical parts under a complicated background based on stereo vision. Appl. Opt. **49**(10), 1789–1801 (2010). https://doi.org/10.1364/AO.49.001789
11. Tao, L. et al.: A high-accuracy circular hole measurement method based on multi-camera system. Measurement. **207**, 112361 (2023). https://doi.org/10.1016/j.measurement.2022.112361
12. Meng, F. et al.: A visual measurement method for deep holes in composite material aerospace components. Sensors. **24**, 3786 (2024). https://doi.org/10.3390/s24123786

From Disruption to Decision: Toward Resilient Integrated Process Planning and Scheduling

Filip Dzigurski(✉), Casper Schou, and Ole Madsen

Department of Materials and Production, Aalborg University, Aalborg, Denmark
fidz@mp.aau.dk

Abstract. This paper reviews how resilience is reflected in Integrated Process Planning and Scheduling (IPPS) research under disturbance-driven manufacturing conditions. Although resilience is widely discussed in manufacturing, IPPS studies rarely address it explicitly, instead embedding it through modelling assumptions, disturbance response mechanisms and performance indicators. A structured literature review of 90 papers was conducted to examine which resilience attributes are used in IPPS research, how they are operationalised, and how their relationships with disturbance types and performance indicators reveal patterns relevant to resilient IPPS. The results identify eight resilience attributes grouped into three clusters: structural, operational and proactive information. Operational attributes dominate the reviewed IPPS literature, while structural and proactive information attributes are represented to a lesser extent. Overall, the findings indicate that resilience in IPPS remains fragmented and is mostly measured indirectly through conventional KPIs. The paper therefore points toward future work on Resilient Integrated Process Planning and Scheduling (RIPPS) through explicit disturbance modelling, resilience-oriented measurement and multi-objective optimisation.

Keywords: Integrated Process Planning and Scheduling · Resilience · Disturbances · Manufacturing

1 Introduction

Manufacturing systems increasingly operate under conditions of uncertainty, variability and structural interdependencies [36]. Frequent changeovers, dynamic order arrivals, machine breakdowns and processing time deviations destabilise planned schedules and amplify ripple effects across manufacturing operations [41], often requiring replanning and rescheduling [42]. However, traditional approaches treat process planning and scheduling as sequential and independent problems despite their interdependence, leading to sub-optimised decisions [37].

G. Pezzotta et al. (Eds.): APMS 2026, IFIP AICT 808, pp. 308–323, 2027.
https://doi.org/10.1007/978-3-032-38594-9_21

Within this context, Integrated Process Planning and Scheduling (IPPS) has emerged as a widely adopted framework for integrating process planning, resource allocation and scheduling into a unified decision-making structure [10, 59]. Nevertheless, classical IPPS approaches primarily optimise efficiency under static conditions, limiting their ability to address persistent uncertainty and variability [60] and highlighting the need for more disturbance-aware planning logic.

Under these circumstances, resilience has gained attention as a system property that extends beyond robustness [45], encompassing resistance to disturbances, recovery [41], adaptation [40] and learning over time [12]. Rather than a single attribute, resilience represents an intrinsic capability emerging from multiple interrelated attributes embedded within manufacturing systems [1,2,40]. Although widely discussed at system and supply-chain levels [34], resilience is rarely addressed explicitly in IPPS studies [19,52]. Instead, it is often reflected implicitly through robustness to disruptions [56], flexible rescheduling [14] and reduced recovery times [15]. As a result, resilience in IPPS remains fragmented and difficult to assess as a capability shaped through modelling choices, disturbance handling and performance evaluation.

This fragmentation highlights the need for a structured review of how resilience is conceptualised and operationalised in IPPS. In particular, there is limited synthesis linking resilience attributes with disturbance types, algorithmic approaches and performance indicators, leaving resilience treated as a loosely defined objective rather than as a system capability shaped by multiple design and decision-making elements. This paper therefore reviews and synthesises the literature to develop a coherent perspective on resilience in IPPS by identifying resilience attributes, examining how they are reflected under different disturbances, and consolidating recurring links between disturbances, algorithms and KPIs into a conceptual framework. To achieve these objectives, the paper addresses the following research questions:

- Research Question 1 (RQ1): Which resilience attributes are used within IPPS research?
- Research Question 2 (RQ2): How are resilience attributes operationalised in mechanisms for handling disturbances?
- Research Question 3 (RQ3): Do the relationships among resilience attributes, disturbance types and performance indicators contribute to a resilient IPPS framework?

The remainder of this paper is organised as follows. Section 2 reviews the theoretical foundations of manufacturing resilience and IPPS. Section 3 describes the research methodology. Section 4 presents the results, Sect. 5 discusses their implications, and Sect. 6 concludes with recommendations for future research.

2 Theoretical Foundations of Resilience in IPPS

2.1 Manufacturing Resilience

The concept of resilience originates from ecological systems theory, where it was defined as the ability of systems to absorb environmental changes and persist [26]. In manufacturing research, resilience was initially treated as a structural property concerned with withstanding disruptions through attributes such as robustness and redundancy. Gu et al. [21] defined resilience as the ability of a system to mitigate or absorb disruptions and recover to normal conditions through built-in redundancy or flexibility enabled by Reconfigurable Manufacturing Systems (RMS). Similarly, Kristianto et al. [32] described resilient manufacturing as an extension of responsive manufacturing, achieved by balancing responsive and robust attributes supported by redundancy and flexibility. In these interpretations, resilience is largely reactive and performance-oriented. Malshe et al. [40] extended this view by framing resilience as the intrinsic property of a system to resist, recover or adapt to a new and improved state under perturbations, thereby moving beyond simple recovery and linking resilience to measurable system characteristics. With increasing digitalisation and system interconnectivity, resilience research shifted towards transparency-enabled and dynamically managed systems [5]. Li et al. [36], Manupati et al. [41] and Park et al. [45] emphasised visibility, traceability, performance measurement and real-time reaction as key conditions for resilient production systems. More recent contributions further highlight proactive and anticipatory dimensions. Duchek [12] conceptualised resilience through anticipation, coping and adaptation, while Alexopoulos et al. [2] argued that resilience must be assessed quantitatively to be integrated into system design. Studies, such as [1,15], also show a shift from single-metric recovery assessment towards multi-objective evaluation incorporating performance loss, recovery time, cost, adaptability and system stability.

Across these perspectives, resilience emerges as a configuration of interrelated attributes rather than a single property. The literature highlights a recurring set of resilience-related attributes, among the most prominent being flexibility, robustness, redundancy, visibility, adaptability and recoverability. However, these attributes are typically analysed at system or plant level, while their operational realisation through planning and scheduling decisions remains less explicitly examined. For a structured analysis of resilience within IPPS research, these attributes must therefore be synthesised and categorised as analytical criteria. This enables the investigation of how resilience is constructed through decision-making mechanisms, how attributes are enhanced under disturbances and how they are measured through performance indicators.

2.2 IPPS as an Operational Interface of Resilience

IPPS extends traditional production planning by generating process plans and schedules simultaneously rather than sequentially [6]. By capturing the interdependencies between alternative process plans and temporal resource allocation, it improves coordination across manufacturing operations and supports more responsive decision-making under dynamic conditions while generating executable process plans for the shop floor [44]. From a resilience perspective, the availability of alternative process plans and machine assignments contributes to routing flexibility and functional redundancy [6], while dynamic rescheduling mechanisms support recoverability by adjusting schedules in response to disturbances. Although these mechanisms do not explicitly optimise resilience as an objective, they reflect resilience attributes through operational configuration. IPPS can eliminate schedule conflicts, reduce process flow times and increase responsiveness to irregular fluctuations [25]. Recent studies have further advanced IPPS by formulating it as a Markov Decision Process, enabling Reinforcement Learning models to represent complex relationships among operations, machines and jobs, and support scheduling strategies for intelligent manufacturing systems [18,35]. Despite these advancements, IPPS research still evaluates performance mainly through indicators such as makespan [3], total tardiness [14] and cost [54]. While such metrics may indirectly reflect aspects of robustness, recovery or flexibility, resilience attributes are rarely conceptualised explicitly or assessed systematically. Consequently, it remains unclear how resilience, understood as an intrinsic capability composed of multiple attributes, is constructed through IPPS methodologies and decision structures.

3 Research Methodology

This study adopts a modified structured literature review methodology guided by the three-phase framework proposed by Snyder [49]:

1. Review design
2. Literature collection
3. Literature analysis and synthesis

Given the implicit treatment of resilience within IPPS research, a semi-systematic review logic was selected to enable conceptual synthesis across heterogeneous studies while maintaining transparency. To ensure methodological rigour, elements of the PRISMA protocol were incorporated to document search strategy, screening procedures and inclusion criteria.

3.1 Phase 1: Review Design

The review was designed to address the research questions formulated in Sect. 1. Preliminary scoping indicated heterogeneity in resilience definitions and limited explicit linkage between resilience theory and IPPS methodologies. Consequently, the resilience attributes synthesised in Sect. 2.1 were adopted as analytical criteria for examining IPPS literature. The search strategy did not include resilience as a primary search term, since the review aimed to capture the broader IPPS literature in which resilience is often reflected implicitly rather than explicitly. Accordingly, studies were first identified through a broad IPPS-oriented search and subsequently examined through a resilience lens based on the synthesised attributes. The literature search was conducted using Elsevier's Scopus and Clarivate's Web of Science databases due to their comprehensive coverage of peer-reviewed engineering research [24]. The search was restricted to English-language engineering publications from 2015 to 2026, with 2015 selected as the starting year to cover a ten-year review period prior to the review process. The applied search string was:

("Integrated production planning and scheduling" OR "Planning and scheduling" OR "Manufacturing orchestration" OR "Production orchestration" OR "IPPS" OR "PPS") AND ("manufactur*" OR "production system*" OR "shop floor" OR factory) AND NOT ("Supply chain" OR "Logistics")

3.2 Phase 2: Literature Collection and Screening

Literature selection was performed as a six-phase process, as outlined in Table 1, starting from the initial database searched. Moreover, the initial database is refined to the final amount of papers by using the PRISMA screening procedure.

Table 1. Literature screening and selection process

Phase	Description	Results
Database search	Initial database search based	731
Keyword search	Python-based keyword filtering applied to paper titles and abstracts	302
Title screening	Paper relevance assessed based on titles and alignment with the research scope	158
Abstract reading	Further refinement through abstract reading and internal relevance grading	71
Snowballing	Backward and forward snowballing applied to identify additional relevant publications	19
Considered papers	Final set of papers included in the literature review	90[a]

[a] Full list of analysed papers - https://github.com/Dziga1603/Resilience-in-IPPS

The keyword search was automated using Python code[1]. The automated screening was based on a predefined set of keywords derived from the resilience attributes introduced in Sect. 2.1. These included terms such as resilience, flexibility, redundancy, robustness, awareness, and adaptability, together with close linguistic variants and related expressions (e.g., coordination and cooperation). This step served as an initial inclusion filter intended to capture papers reflecting

[1] Python code for keyword search going through paper abstracts - same repository.

resilience-relevant production capabilities, including studies that did not explicitly use the term resilience. Subsequently, titles and abstracts were assessed manually based on their alignment with the review scope, meaning that papers were qualified if they were related to integrated planning and scheduling in industrial production contexts, and disqualified if they fell outside the IPPS context or addressed unrelated planning or scheduling activities. To make this stage more transparent, each paper was assigned an internal relevance score from 1 to 10 based on its conceptual and methodological alignment with the review scope and research questions. Papers scoring 6 or higher were retained for final consideration, while papers below this threshold were excluded. This scoring procedure supported the reduction from 158 title-screened papers to 71 papers after abstract reading. Snowballing was then performed once in both backward and forward directions to identify additional relevant publications.

For analytical purposes, the selected papers were classified into two primary groups:

- Attribute papers - studies defining, conceptualising or decomposing resilience attributes within manufacturing and IPPS context; 21 papers identified
- Algorithmic papers - studies proposing optimisation or decision-support approaches addressing disturbances, uncertainty or dynamic scheduling within IPPS frameworks; 69 papers identified

3.3 Phase 3: Literature Analysis

Firstly, attribute papers were analysed to establish a structured reference set of resilience attributes relevant to IPPS. These studies were synthesised to clarify how resilience is defined, decomposed and measured across domains. This analysis addresses RQ1 by identifying and consolidating resilience attributes that form the analytical basis for examining IPPS research.

Secondly, algorithmic IPPS papers were examined to determine how resilience attributes are operationalised within planning and scheduling mechanisms under disturbance conditions. Since resilience terminology is often absent, attributes were identified based on operational behaviour, modelling assumptions and performance objectives. To address RQ2, each study was coded according to:

- Resilience attributes addressed
- Disturbance type considered
- Algorithmic approach
- Performance indicator used

Finally, a cross-synthesis of the IPPS studies was conducted to identify recurring patterns across the literature rather than within individual papers. This phase focused on how resilience attributes, disturbance types, algorithmic approaches and KPIs were associated across studies, making it possible to identify dominant relationships, recurring combinations and conceptual gaps in the field. In this way, the analysis addresses RQ3 and supports the development of a resilient conceptual framework for IPPS.

4 Analysis and Synthesis of Resilience in IPPS

4.1 Identification of Resilience Attributes

To address RQ1, the review identifies recurring attributes that provide a structural basis for interpreting resilience in planning and scheduling. As shown in Table 2, eight attributes are grouped into three clusters according to their functional role of resilience. Of these, 18 papers were associated with structural, 41 with operational, and 25 with proactive information attributes. The categories are not mutually exclusive, since individual papers may reflect attributes from more than one cluster. Among the algorithmic papers, 27 referred to disturbances only conceptually, for example in the motivation or contextual framing, without embedding them in model formulation, model logic or decision-making mechanisms. These papers were excluded from the operationalisation mapping, as the analysis focuses on mechanisms through which disturbances are handled and resilience attributes are operationalised, rather than on disturbance acknowledgement alone.

4.2 Operationalisation of Resilience Attributes in IPPS

The structural cluster captures resilience through robustness and redundancy, operationalised in IPPS through mechanisms that preserve system stability [11] and continuity under disturbances [22]. The operational cluster reflects resilience through flexibility, adaptability, recoverability and responsiveness, expressed through the system's ability to adjust [15], reorganise [51], restore execution under disruption [29], and react in a timely manner to changing production conditions [53]. The proactive information cluster is represented by anticipatory and visibility, which contribute to resilience through prediction [8] and situational awareness [60]. Although these attributes can be distinguished analytically by their primary resilience function, they do not operate independently in IPPS. In practice, resilience emerges through their interaction, as the same planning and scheduling mechanism may support several attributes at once. This is particularly evident in the relationship between redundancy and flexibility, where redundant resources such as alternative machines or parallel capacity expand system flexibility by increasing the number of feasible routing, allocation and sequencing options under disruption [28]. Visibility also supports responsiveness through timely detection of system changes [56], while flexibility strengthens recoverability by enabling affected operations to be reorganised and restored [51]. However, these relationships are not exclusively reinforcing, as improving one resilience attribute may reduce another or introduce operational trade-offs. Increasing flexibility in routing and scheduling through additional alternative routes may strengthen adaptability, but it can also reduce responsiveness and stability by introducing greater variability into system execution [23].

4.3 Mapping Resilience Across Disturbances, Algorithms and KPIs

To address RQ3, the reviewed IPPS literature was cross-synthesised by linking the three resilience attribute clusters to the disturbance types they address, the

Table 2. Resilience attributes in IPPS literature. *Note:* Values in parentheses indicate the number of reviewed papers associated with each cluster or attribute. The cited sources are a representative subset of the total, which have been selected as they most clearly describe the respective operationalisations.

Cluster	Attribute	Operationalisation	Resilience Mechanism	Resilience Contribution	Source
Structural Attributes (18)	Robustness (16)	Stability-oriented schedule design under uncertainty	Disturbance absorption through stable schedule structures	Reduces performance degradation when disruptions occur	[7,11,15,22] [28,48,60]
		Scenario- or simulation-based robustness assessment	Robustness evaluation under uncertain conditions	Supports selection of schedules that remain effective under disruptions	[7,8,20,29]
	Redundancy (4)	Backup production resources or parallel resource capacity	Reserve capacity and substitute resource availability	Preserves production continuity when primary resources are disrupted	[13,55]
Operational Attributes (41)	Flexibility (38)	Process and routing flexibility in production planning	Alternative process and routing choices	Enables re-routing and process substitution under changing conditions	[3,30,37,39, 51] [53,54,58,61]
		Operational sequencing flexibility in scheduling	Dynamic rescheduling of jobs and operations	Improves short-term adjustment while limiting disruption impact	[4,9,14,25,27] [47,56]
		Resource reconfiguration capability	Functional reallocation or reconfiguration of production resources	Supports adjustment of production capabilities of disruption conditions	[18,29,46,60]
	Adaptability (29)	Rolling or iterative planning revision	Continuous plan revision with updated information	Sustains alignment between plans and current system conditions	[8,9,25,27]
		Dynamic schedule adjustment during execution	Real-time adaptation of planning and scheduling decisions	Maintains feasible schedules as operating conditions evolve	[4,7,15,52,58]
		Data-driven or learning-based planning adaptation	Analytics-enabled adaptive decision support	Improves the quality and speed of adjustment under uncertainty	[18,29,42,46]
	Recoverability (15)	Targeted rescheduling and restoration of disrupted operations	Recovery planning for affected tasks and production flow	Restores workflow continuity while limiting disruption propagation	[9,18,29,31, 61]
	Responsiveness (19)	Reactive and event-driven planning adjustment after disruption detection	Rapid replanning triggered by operational events	Enables timely reaction to disruptions and reduces downtime	[9,22,29,30, 52] [53,58]
		Closed-loop decision feedback between system and planner	Feedback-based adjustment of planning decisions	Improves responsiveness through continuous sensing, evaluation and correction	[8,42,46,47, 57]
Proactive Information Attributes (25)	Anticipatory (15)	Forecast-based production planning	Prospective assessment of future production states	Enables earlier preventive action against disruptions	[8,16,20,28, 31]
		Predictive analytics for operational risks	Data-driven estimation of disruption likelihood	Supports proactive mitigation of emerging operational risks	[7,11,15,29, 42]
		Forward planning under uncertainty	Explicit incorporation of expected future conditions into planning	Improves preparedness and planning robustness over time	[18,29,30,46, 57]
	Visibility (20)	Real-time production data integration	Continuous situational awareness from current shop-floor data	Aligns planning decisions with actual operating conditions	[9,18,29,33, 60]
		Digital information sharing across planning layers	Cross-layer transparency and information consistency	Improves coordination between planning and scheduling functions	[8,22,27,39, 51]
		System-state monitoring for decision support	Continuous tracking of machines, jobs and resources	Allows timely detection of deviations and supports informed intervention	[15,20,58,61]

KPIs they optimise and the algorithmic approaches they employ. To enable cross-study comparison, the specific disruptions and performance measures reported in the literature were consolidated into broader analytical categories. Disturbances were grouped into machine failure, job disturbance, time uncertainty and resource disruption, while KPIs were grouped into time-related, performance, cost and energy, and stability categories.

Structural attributes are most often associated with disturbances that threaten schedule feasibility, continuity and production stability. In the reviewed studies, robustness is examined under machine failures [7,11,52], new job insertions [15,18,30], uncertain processing times [16,28,51] and staffing issues [16,20]. Redundancy is addressed where continuity is preserved through backup equipment [28]. These attributes are evaluated mainly through time-related KPIs, particularly makespan [31,52,58]; delivery-performance KPIs such as on-schedule completion rate [16], customer satisfaction [51] and backorders [20]; cost- and energy-related KPIs, including production cost [15,27,60] and energy consumption [8]; and stability-oriented KPIs such as deviation metrics [30,52,60] and stability under breakdown [48]. Across this cluster, robustness is typically handled through robust or dynamic optimisation models solved by metaheuristics [11], hybrid heuristics [52] or DRL [60]. Monte Carlo simulation [16,20] is also used to assess the effect of uncertainty on delivery and time-related performance, while [28] applies robust bi-objective optimisation to balance reliability and cost under disruption risk.

Operational attributes are most commonly associated with machine failures [46,48,53,56], followed by order-related disturbances such as new job arrivals, rush orders and order cancellations [14,22,53]. The reviewed studies also emphasise resource and execution variability, including machine-tool wearing, machine availability, transport-resource constraints, multiple project release dates and execution modes [3,39,46,47]. These attributes are evaluated largely through time-related KPIs, particularly makespan and related measures such as processing or completion time [39,46,48,53,56]; performance KPIs such as tardiness and earliness/lateness [38,39,47]; cost- and energy-related KPIs including energy consumption [39,50], production cost [9,27] and inventory-related costs [46]; and stability KPIs captured through deviation measures [4,47]. These KPIs are optimised primarily through genetic and hybrid metaheuristics, including GA-based rescheduling [3,48,53,56], co-evolutionary search [39] and greedy-enhanced population methods [47]. In this cluster, responsiveness is reflected through rapid replanning and feedback-based adjustment during execution, allowing the system to react to disruptions in a timely manner [22].

Proactive information attributes differ from the previous two clusters in their emphasis on information quality, state awareness, forecasting and feedback-driven adaptation. In the reviewed studies, they are linked to disturbances such as demand uncertainty and forecast variation [17,33], shifting market demands [23,54] and changing shop-floor conditions [11,43]. Their KPI focus is centred on makespan [33,43,54], but also includes computation or response speed [23], demand fulfilment rate, backlog and service-sensitive planning outcomes [33], project-level delivery performance and profit implications [47], as well as production cost [50] and energy consumption [61]. Stability is reflected through solution feasibility under changing conditions [17], the quality of data for rescheduling [54], and the ability to revise plans continuously through real-time state updates and rolling forecasts [33]. These KPIs are supported through multi-objective optimisation, Petri-net and holonic coordination models, DT-enabled DRL planning, genetic hyper-heuristics and adaptive deep reinforcement learning approaches [17, 23, 33, 43, 54]. Unlike the structural and operational clusters, this group improves resilience primarily by strengthening how the system monitors and predicts evolving production conditions.

These relationships are summarised in Fig. 1 as a three-layer matrix, where each layer represents one attribute cluster and the cell values indicate how many papers link a given disturbance type to a given KPI category within that cluster. Overall, resilience in IPPS is not represented through a single modelling logic, but through complementary attribute clusters with different roles. Structural attributes mainly preserve feasibility and continuity under uncertainty, operational attributes dominate execution-time adjustment, recovery and timely response, and proactive information attributes strengthen resilience through visibility, anticipation and data-driven support. Together, these findings indicate that resilience in IPPS emerges from the combination of stable system design, adaptive execution and timely information use rather than from any single attribute in isolation.

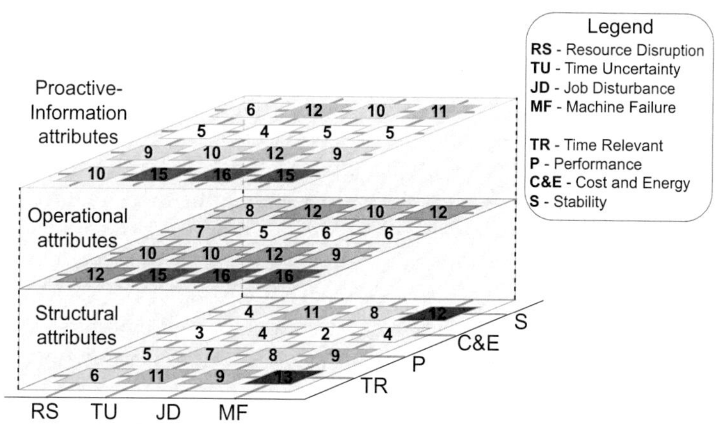

Fig. 1. Layered representation of the relationships between resilience attribute clusters, disturbance types, and performance indicator categories identified in the reviewed intelligent production planning and scheduling literature.

5 Toward Resilient Integrated Process Planning and Scheduling - RIPPS

The review indicates that resilience in production planning and scheduling is not yet represented through a coherent modelling logic, but rather through a fragmented combination of structural, operational and proactive information attributes. In most reviewed studies, these attributes remain embedded implicitly rather than formulated as an explicit resilience-oriented design logic for IPPS. At the same time, close to half of the literature refers to disturbances only at a conceptual level, without incorporating them directly into model formulation or solution procedures, suggesting that disturbance-aware IPPS remains only partially developed. The findings further show that the literature has focused more on conceptualising resilience than on measuring it in IPPS. Although attributes such as robustness, flexibility, adaptability and responsiveness are frequently discussed, they are only rarely translated into explicit and consistent measurement logic. Instead, resilience is typically assessed indirectly through conventional production KPIs such as makespan, tardiness, cost and energy consumption. While these indicators capture relevant performance effects, they do not make trade-offs among resilience attributes explicit, limiting comparability across studies and constraining cumulative development of the field.

To address this gap, future research needs to embed resilience more explicitly within IPPS modelling and decision logic. This includes incorporating disturbances directly into model formulations and solution procedures, while developing ways to measure how resilience attributes are represented, prioritised and balanced in planning and scheduling activities. Since resilience in IPPS cannot be reduced to a single optimisation objective, such development must reflect its multidimensional nature and the trade-offs across attributes and performance dimensions. Improving one aspect of resilience, such as robustness, responsiveness or recoverability, may come at the expense of cost, energy use or scheduling efficiency. From this perspective, the review contributes by identifying recurring resilience attributes, structuring them into three clusters, and showing how they interact across IPPS studies. On this basis, the results provide a conceptual foundation for future work on Resilient Integrated Process Planning and Scheduling (RIPPS) as a more explicit direction for embedding resilience into IPPS through disturbance-aware modelling, multi-objective decision logic, and stronger integration of real-time and predictive information.

6 Conclusion

This paper reviewed how resilience is reflected in IPPS by identifying the main resilience attributes in the literature, examining how they are operationalised in reviewed studies, and analysing recurring relationships between disturbance types, KPIs and algorithmic approaches. The results show that resilience in IPPS is currently represented through fragmented structural, operational and proactive information attributes, often addressed implicitly rather than through an explicit resilience-oriented design logic.

Based on these findings, the paper points toward RIPPS as a future direction for embedding resilience more explicitly in IPPS. Future work should translate resilience into measurable and operational decision logic through explicit disturbance modelling, resilience-oriented performance assessment and multi-objective optimisation supported by real-time and predictive information.

Acknowledgements. This research was supported by MADE REACT, funded by Innovation Fund Denmark under grant number 4354-00008B.

Disclosure of Interests. The authors have no competing interests to declare that are relevant to the content of this article.

References

1. Abimbola, M., Khan, F.: Resilience modeling of engineering systems using dynamic object-oriented bayesian network approach. Comput. Ind. Eng. **130**, 108–118 (2019). https://doi.org/10.1016/j.cie.2019.02.022
2. Alexopoulos, K., Anagiannis, I., Nikolakis, N., Chryssolouris, G.: A quantitative approach to resilience in manufacturing systems. Int. J. Prod. Res. **60**(24), 7178–7193 (2022). https://doi.org/10.1080/00207543.2021.2018519
3. Awad, M., Abd-Elaziz, H.: An efficient modified genetic algorithm for integrated process planning-job scheduling. In: Proc. Int. Mob. Intell. Ubiquitous Comput. Conf. (MIUCC), pp. 319–323 (2021). https://doi.org/10.1109/MIUCC52538.2021.9447610
4. Bahroun, Z., Shamayleh, A., Zakaria, R.: Dynamic and flexible scheduling for a single machine. In: Proc. Int. Conf. Control Decis. Inf. Technol. (CoDIT), pp. 616–621 (2018). https://doi.org/10.1109/CoDIT.2018.8394866
5. Barata, J., Kayser, I.: Industry 5.0 - past, present, and near future. Procedia Comput. Sci. **219**, 778–788 (2023). https://doi.org/10.1016/j.procs.2023.01.351
6. Barzanji, R., Naderi, B., Begen, M.A.: Decomposition algorithms for the integrated process planning and scheduling problem. Omega **93**, 102025 (2020). https://doi.org/10.1016/j.omega.2019.01.003
7. Bazargan-Lari, M., Taghipour, S., Zaretalab, A., Sharifi, M.: Planning and scheduling of a parallel-machine production system subject to disruptions and physical distancing. IMA J. Manag. Math. **34**(4), 721–744 (2023). https://doi.org/10.1093/imaman/dpac010
8. Chen, Y., Huang, X., Yi, W., Pei, Z., Wang, C., Ji, Z.: Bi-level collaborative day-ahead optimization scheduling of manufacturing-energy system targeting energy cost reduction. Energy **338**, 138672 (2025). https://doi.org/10.1016/j.energy.2025.138672
9. Chen, Z., Zou, J., Wang, W.: Digital twin-oriented collaborative optimization of process planning and scheduling in a flexible job shop. Int. J. Ind. Eng. Theory Appl. Pract. **31**(3), 483–505 (2024). https://doi.org/10.23055/ijietap.2024.31.3.9823
10. Chryssolouris, G., Chan, S., Cobb, W.: Decision making on the factory floor: an integrated approach to process planning and scheduling. Robot. Comput.-Integr. Manuf. **1**(3–4), 315–319 (1984)

11. Duan, J., Wang, J.: Robust scheduling for flexible machining job shop subject to machine breakdowns and new job arrivals considering system reusability and task recurrence. Expert Syst. Appl. **203**, 117489 (2022). https://doi.org/10.1016/j.eswa.2022.117489
12. Duchek, S.: Organizational resilience: a capability-based conceptualization. Bus. Res. **13**(1), 215–246 (2019). https://doi.org/10.1007/s40685-019-0085-7
13. Duran, E., Ozturk, C., O'Sullivan, B.: Exact and heuristic methods for planning and scheduling collaborative manufacturing systems. In: IFIP Adv. Inf. Commun. Technol., vol. 727, pp. 53–68 (2024). https://doi.org/10.1007/978-3-031-71743-7_4
14. Erden, C., Demir, H., Canpolat, O.: A modified integer and categorical PSO algorithm for solving integrated process planning, dynamic scheduling, and due date assignment problem. Sci. Iran. **30**(2), 738–756 (2023). https://doi.org/10.24200/sci.2021.55250.4130
15. Feng, Q., et al.: Time-based resilience metric for smart manufacturing systems and optimization method with dual-strategy recovery. J. Manuf. Syst. **65**, 486–497 (2022). https://doi.org/10.1016/j.jmsy.2022.08.010
16. Franke, S., Franke, F., Riedel, R.: Robustness evaluation of production plans using Monte Carlo simulation. Procedia Manuf. **54**, 130–135 (2021). https://doi.org/10.1016/j.promfg.2021.07.021
17. Gamboa Quintanilla, F., Cardin, O., L'Anton, A., Castagna, P.: A petri net-based methodology to increase flexibility in service-oriented holonic manufacturing systems. Comput. Ind. **76**, 53–68 (2016). https://doi.org/10.1016/j.compind.2015.09.002
18. Ghaleb, M., Namoura, H., Taghipour, S.: Reinforcement learning-based real-time scheduling under random machine breakdowns and other disturbances: a case study. In: Proc. Annu. Reliab. Maint. Symp. (RAMS) (2021). https://doi.org/10.1109/RAMS48097.2021.9605791
19. Gong, J., You, F.: A resilience analysis approach for process design, integration and optimization. Chem. Eng. Trans. **70**, 1681–1686 (2018). https://doi.org/10.3303/CET1870281
20. Grimm, B., Lambert, M., Rakurty, C.: Using Monte Carlo simulations and little's law to improve process planning. In: Proc. Conf. Prod. Syst. Logist. pp. 799–805 (2024). https://doi.org/10.15488/17767
21. Gu, X., Jin, X., Ni, J., Koren, Y.: Manufacturing system design for resilience. In: Procedia CIRP, vol. 36, pp. 135–140 (2015). https://doi.org/10.1016/j.procir.2015.02.075
22. Guizzi, G., Revetria, R., Vanacore, G., Vespoli, S.: On the open job-shop scheduling problem: a decentralized multi-agent approach for the manufacturing system performance optimization. In: Procedia CIRP, vol. 79, pp. 192–197 (2019). https://doi.org/10.1016/j.procir.2019.02.045
23. Guo, H., Li, K., Liu, J., Zhuang, C., Pei, F.: Dynamic integrated process planning and scheduling under multi-resource constraints in workshops with reconfigurable manufacturing cells: a novel hyper-heuristic approach. Expert Syst. Appl. **289**, 128337 (2025). https://doi.org/10.1016/j.eswa.2025.128337
24. Gusenbauer, M.: Google Scholar to overshadow them all? Comparing the sizes of 12 academic search engines and bibliographic databases. Scientometrics **118**(1), 177–214 (2018). https://doi.org/10.1007/s11192-018-2958-5
25. Haro, E., Avalos, O., Gálvez, J., Camarena, O.: An integrated process planning and scheduling problem solved from an adaptive multi-objective perspective. J. Manuf. Syst. **75**, 1–23 (2024). https://doi.org/10.1016/j.jmsy.2024.05.018

26. Holling, C.: Resilience and stability of ecological systems. Annu. Rev. Ecol. Syst. **4**, 1–23 (1973). https://doi.org/10.1146/annurev.es.04.110173.000245
27. Imsetif, J., Nezamoddini, N., Aqlan, F.: Job shop planning and scheduling of reconfigurable manufacturing systems. Oper. Manag. Res. **18**(3), 891–912 (2025). https://doi.org/10.1007/s12063-025-00551-2
28. Jafar-Zanjani, H., Zandieh, M., Sharifi, M.: Robust and resilient joint periodic maintenance planning and scheduling in a multi-factory network under uncertainty: A case study. Reliab. Eng. Syst. Saf. **217**, 108113 (2022). https://doi.org/10.1016/j.ress.2021.108113
29. Javaid, W., Ullah, S.: Data driven simulation based optimization model for job-shop production planning and scheduling: an application in a digital twin shop floor. J. Simul. (2025). https://doi.org/10.1080/17477778.2025.2469687
30. Jin, L., Zhang, C., Shao, X., Yang, X.: A study on the impact of periodic and event-driven rescheduling on a manufacturing system: an integrated process planning and scheduling case. Proc. Inst. Mech. Eng. B **231**(3), 490–504 (2017). https://doi.org/10.1177/0954405416629585
31. Jin, L., Zhang, C., Wen, X., Christopher, G.: A neutrosophic number-based memetic algorithm for the integrated process planning and scheduling problem with uncertain processing times. IEEE Access **8**, 96628–96648 (2020). https://doi.org/10.1109/ACCESS.2020.2996496
32. Kristianto, Y., Gunasekaran, A., Helo, P.: Building the "triple r" in global manufacturing. Int. J. Prod. Econ. **183**, 607–619 (2017). https://doi.org/10.1016/j.ijpe.2015.12.011
33. Kuo, H.A., Hong, T.Y., Chien, C.F.: A deep reinforcement learning based digital twin framework for resilient production planning under demand uncertainty and an empirical study in semiconductor wafer fabrication. Comput. Ind. Eng. **208**, 111389 (2025). https://doi.org/10.1016/j.cie.2025.111389
34. Leng, J., et al.: Resilient manufacturing: a review of disruptions, assessment, and pathways. J. Manuf. Syst. **79**, 563–583 (2025). https://doi.org/10.1016/j.jmsy.2025.02.006
35. Li, H., et al.: Solving integrated process planning and scheduling via graph neural network based deep reinforcement learning. arXiv (2024)
36. Li, M., et al.: Out-of-order architecture for real-time data-driven resilient planning and scheduling of cyber-physical manufacturing systems. IEEE Trans. Autom. Sci. Eng. **23**, 2983–2994 (2026). https://doi.org/10.1109/TASE.2025.3563084
37. Lin, C.S., Li, P.Y., Wei, J.M., Wu, M.C.: Integration of process planning and scheduling for distributed flexible job shops. Comput. Oper. Res. **124**, 105053 (2020). https://doi.org/10.1016/j.cor.2020.105053
38. Liu, N., Zhang, Y.F., Lu, W.F.: Improving energy efficiency in discrete parts manufacturing system using an ultra-flexible job shop scheduling algorithm. Int. J. Precis. Eng. Manuf.-Green Technol. **6**(2), 349–365 (2019). https://doi.org/10.1007/s40684-019-00055-y
39. Liu, Q., Wang, C., Li, X., Gao, L.: A multi-population co-evolutionary algorithm for green integrated process planning and scheduling considering logistics system. Eng. Appl. Artif. Intell. **126**, 107030 (2023). https://doi.org/10.1016/j.engappai.2023.107030
40. Malshe, A., Bapat, S., Rajurkar, K., Melkote, S.: Biological strategies from natural structures for resilience in manufacturing. CIRP J. Manuf. Sci. Technol. **34**, 146–156 (2021). https://doi.org/10.1016/j.cirpj.2020.10.010

41. Manupati, V., Putnik, G., Jacob, S., Chiramal, A., Sooraj, N.: A social network and simulation-based optimization approach for manufacturing resilience in a distributed manufacturing system. IFAC-PapersOnLine **58**(27), 1221–1226 (2024). https://doi.org/10.1016/j.procir.2024.10.231
42. Marzia, S., Azab, A., Vital-Soto, A.: Integrated process planning and scheduling framework using an optimized rule-mining approach for smart manufacturing. Mathematics **13**(16), 2605 (2025). https://doi.org/10.3390/math13162605
43. Mohapatra, P., Nayak, A., Kumar, S., Tiwari, M.: Multi-objective process planning and scheduling using controlled elitist non-dominated sorting genetic algorithm. Int. J. Prod. Res. **53**(6), 1712–1735 (2015). https://doi.org/10.1080/00207543.2014.957872
44. Naderi, B., Begen, M.A., Zaric, G.S.: Type-2 integrated process-planning and scheduling problem: Reformulation and solution algorithms. Comput. Oper. Res. **142**, 105728 (2022). https://doi.org/10.1016/j.cor.2022.105728
45. Park, K.T., Lee, J.Y., Park, M.W., Park, Y., Lee, J.Y., Choi, Y.H.: Models and p4r asset description for digital twin-based advanced planning and scheduling using cyber-physical integration for resilient production operation. J. Manuf. Syst. **77**, 127–153 (2024). https://doi.org/10.1016/j.jmsy.2024.08.030
46. Ramya, G., Chandrasekaran, M., Shankar, E.: Case study analysis of job shop scheduling and its integration with material requirement planning. Mater. Today Proc. **16**, 1034–1042 (2019). https://doi.org/10.1016/j.matpr.2019.05.192
47. Rauf, M., Guan, Z., Yue, L., Guo, Z., Mumtaz, J., Ullah, S.: Integrated planning and scheduling of multiple manufacturing projects under resource constraints using raccoon family optimization algorithm. IEEE Access **8**, 151279–151295 (2020). https://doi.org/10.1109/ACCESS.2020.2971650
48. Sajadi, S.M., Alizadeh, A., Zandieh, M., Tavan, F.: Robust and stable flexible job shop scheduling with random machine breakdowns: multi-objectives genetic algorithm approach. Int. J. Math. Oper. Res. **14**(2), 268–289 (2019)
49. Snyder, H.: Literature review as a research methodology: an overview and guidelines. J. Bus. Res. **104**, 333–339 (2019). https://doi.org/10.1016/j.jbusres.2019.07.039
50. Wang, H.: Manufacturing workshop multi-objective dynamic scheduling problem and model establishment. Acad. J. Manuf. Eng. **17** (2019)
51. Wen, X., Li, X., Gao, L., Wang, K., Li, H.: Modified honey bees mating optimization algorithm for multi-objective uncertain integrated process planning and scheduling problem. Int. J. Adv. Robot. Syst. **17**(3) (2020). https://doi.org/10.1177/1729881420925236
52. Wen, X., Lian, X., Qian, Y., Zhang, Y., Wang, H., Li, H.: Dynamic scheduling method for integrated process planning and scheduling problem with machine fault. Robot. Comput.-Integr. Manuf. **77**, 102334 (2022). https://doi.org/10.1016/j.rcim.2022.102334
53. Xia, H., Li, X., Gao, L.: A hybrid genetic algorithm with variable neighborhood search for dynamic integrated process planning and scheduling. Comput. Ind. Eng. **102**, 99–112 (2016). https://doi.org/10.1016/j.cie.2016.10.015
54. Yu, M., Zhang, Y., Chen, K., Zhang, D.: Integration of process planning and scheduling using a hybrid GA/PSO algorithm. Int. J. Adv. Manuf. Technol. **78**(1-4), 583–592 (2015). https://doi.org/10.1007/s00170-014-6669-7
55. Zanjirani, D., Esmaelian, M.: An integrated approach based on fuzzy inference system for scheduling and process planning through multiple objectives. J. Ind. Manag. Optim. **16**(3), 1235–1259 (2020). https://doi.org/10.3934/JIMO.2018202

56. Zhang, L., Wong, T.: An object-coding genetic algorithm for integrated process planning and scheduling. Eur. J. Oper. Res. **244**(2), 434–444 (2015). https://doi.org/10.1016/j.ejor.2015.01.032
57. Zhang, S., Wong, T.N.: Integrated process planning and scheduling: an enhanced ant colony optimization heuristic with parameter tuning. J. Intell. Manuf. **29**(3), 585–601 (2014). https://doi.org/10.1007/s10845-014-1023-3
58. Zhang, S., Xu, Y., Yu, Z., Zhang, W., Yu, D.: Combining extended imperialist competitive algorithm with a genetic algorithm to solve the distributed integration of process planning and scheduling problem. Math. Probl. Eng. **2017**, 9628935 (2017). https://doi.org/10.1155/2017/9628935
59. Zhang, W.J., van Luttervelt, C.A.: Toward a resilient manufacturing system. CIRP Ann. - Manuf. Technol. **60**(1), 469–472 (2011). https://doi.org/10.1016/j.cirp.2011.03.041
60. Zhang, Y., Zhu, H., Tang, D., Zhou, T., Gui, Y.: Dynamic job shop scheduling based on deep reinforcement learning for multi-agent manufacturing systems. Robot. Comput.-Integr. Manuf. **78**, 102412 (2022). https://doi.org/10.1016/j.rcim.2022.102412
61. Zheng, J., Kobayashi, Y., Takahashi, Y., Yanagida, T., Sato, T., Hitaka, D.: MLCP: a framework integrating with machine learning and optimization for planning and scheduling in manufacturing and services. In: Proc. IEEE Int. Conf. Syst. Syst. Eng. (SoSE), pp. 123–128 (2020). https://doi.org/10.1109/SoSE50414.2020.9130560

Human-Centric Phased Deployment of Auditable Warranty and After-Sales Workflows: An AHP-Based Portfolio Method for Product and Asset Lifecycle Management

Vicente González-Prida[1](✉), Bernal Picado[1], Antonio J. Guillén López[2], and Adolfo Crespo Márquez[1]

[1] University of Seville, Higher Technical School of Engineering, Seville, Spain
{vgonzalezprida,adolfo}@us.es, berpicarg@alum.us.es
[2] Complutense University of Madrid, Department of Business Organization, Madrid, Spain
anguil02@ucm.es

Abstract. Warranty and after-sales processes are not merely post-sale support activities; in asset-intensive and servitized settings they shape lifecycle decision-making, data capture, organizational learning, and can indirectly support product and asset life extension. However, once a target workflow has been defined, organizations still face a practical question that the literature rarely addresses: what should be implemented first under limited capacity, uneven digital maturity, and heterogeneous contractual contexts? This paper proposes a human-centric multicriteria method for the phased deployment of auditable warranty and maintenance workflows in Product and Asset Lifecycle Management (PALM). Building on a workflow baseline aligned with maintenance documentation principles, the method separates mandatory process requirements from selectable deployment modules. Criteria weights are obtained through an Analytic Hierarchy Process (AHP), while the final deployment plan is selected through a multi-period portfolio model with capacity and precedence constraints. A synthetic illustrative case is used because no expert panel was available at this stage; it is intended to demonstrate the internal logic of the method rather than to provide empirical validation. Under the assumed architectural dependencies, the illustration suggests that governance and evidence modules should precede heavier systems integration. The contribution is threefold: a deployment-oriented decision model for human-centric after-sales governance, a practical taxonomy of workflow modules, and a bridge between workflow design and deployable PALM implementation.

Keywords: human-centric lifecycle management · warranty management · after-sales service · multicriteria decision-making · asset management · servitization

Published by Springer Nature Switzerland AG 2027
G. Pezzotta et al. (Eds.): APMS 2026, IFIP AICT 808, pp. 324–338, 2027.
https://doi.org/10.1007/978-3-032-38594-9_22

1 Introduction

Industry 5.0 has moved the debate on lifecycle management beyond efficiency-centric digitalization and towards human-centred, resilient, and organizationally grounded approaches [1–3]. In this view, product and asset lifecycle management (PALM) is no longer limited to engineering design, operations, or maintenance in isolation. Lifecycle performance emerges from the interaction of technical systems, data and knowledge assets, contractual structures, human work systems, and governance routines. This has direct implications for asset-intensive manufacturers and service providers operating under servitized business models, where after-sales and warranty processes become a key locus of lifecycle decision-making rather than a residual support function [4–7].

Warranty and after-sales workflows influence whether anomalies are triaged consistently, whether coverage decisions are auditable, whether evidence is captured in a reusable form, whether customer communication is timely and contractual, and whether resolved cases feed back into service adaptation and future design. These mechanisms matter for service continuity, trust, and lifecycle decision quality, and can indirectly support product and asset life extension. They also influence whether digital tools and enterprise systems improve or merely complicate operational practice [5, 8, 9]. Yet organizations rarely struggle with defining a desirable end-state only; they more often struggle with deciding what to implement first when resources, digital maturity, and internal alignment are limited.

This practical gap is amplified in servitized contexts. Recent studies show that servitization efforts are undermined by low commitment, slow capability development, and low scalability when organizational routines and operational capabilities are not sequenced appropriately [6]. Similarly, human-centred Industry 5.0 literature highlights tensions associated with automation, wellbeing, skills, responsibility, and value creation [1, 2]. In maintenance and asset management, data-driven decision support is increasingly available, but cross-functional coordination and implementation remain uneven [4, 5]. What is still missing is a decision model that takes an auditable target workflow as given and then helps managers determine which deployment modules should be activated first, second, and postponed. This shift towards human-centred and governance-oriented lifecycle management implies that decision-making structures, rather than technological solutions alone, become critical design elements. In this context, the challenge is not only to define target workflows, but to structure how their implementation is progressively deployed in a way that ensures accountability, traceability, and coordination across the lifecycle.

This paper addresses that gap. It does not redesign a warranty/after-sales workflow from scratch. Instead, it formulates the subsequent deployment problem: given a human-centric and auditable workflow baseline, which implementation modules should be deployed under limited organizational capacity? The aim of the paper is to provide a deployment-oriented decision framework for prioritising and sequencing workflow modules in human-centric PALM under practical industrial constraints. In this context, implementation modules—referred to in this paper as deployment modules—are defined as discrete implementation units associated with the target workflow. These modules do not redefine the process logic, but represent how key capabilities, such as governance structures, evidence management, role accountability, system integration, and learning mechanisms, are progressively established in practice. Deployment modules constitute the decision units through which workflow implementation is structured and sequenced. The present study assumes a workflow baseline already exists. That baseline corresponds to an auditable warranty and maintenance workflow in which the core logic includes case intake, triage, contractual screening, evidence consolidation, work-order release, execution, closure, and learning feedback.

The baseline is informed by earlier warranty-management work [13, 17], by maintenance documentation principles in EN 13460 [16], and by more recent workflow design efforts in servitized settings [12]. The contribution of the present paper is an AHP-based multi-period portfolio method that separates mandatory process requirements from selectable deployment modules, assigns weights to lifecycle, governance, human-centric, and deployability criteria, and generates a phased deployment roadmap. Rather than proposing a new process map, the contribution lies in structuring the decision layer that governs how workflow capabilities are deployed under real-world constraints. The proposed method is particularly suited to asset-intensive settings in which lifecycle decision quality depends on how warranty, maintenance, customer interaction, and learning loops are operationalized. From this perspective, deployment modules operationalize the human-centric and governance dimensions of asset management by structuring how decisions are made, how responsibilities are assigned, and how information is captured and reused across the lifecycle. This connects deployment sequencing with lifecycle decision quality in asset-intensive systems.

2 Literature Background and Gap

Recent PALM and Industry 5.0 research has clarified that human-centricity is not a soft complement to digitalization but a design principle affecting decision quality, responsibility allocation, learning, and acceptance [1–3]. Pacheco and Iwaszczenko identify multiple human-centric tensions in the move toward Industry 5.0, especially around automation, wellbeing, education, safety, and value creation [1]. Hermawati et al. show that even the notion of human-centricity itself remains fragmented, which complicates implementation and readiness assessment [2]. In parallel, Passalacqua et al. demonstrate that human-centred AI in Industry 5.0 is still underdeveloped on psychosocial dimensions such as autonomy, motivation, and trust, despite the rapid expansion of technical AI applications [3].

For PALM, this means that workflow digitalization cannot be assessed only by its functional performance; it must also be assessed by the way it shapes human roles and decision authority. A second relevant stream concerns maintenance and asset management decision support. Naqvi et al. propose a human knowledge-centred maintenance decision support service in a digital twin environment, showing that maintenance work orders contain reusable human knowledge that can support new maintenance decisions [4]. Hinrichs et al. likewise emphasize that data-driven decision-making in maintenance is valuable not only for local maintenance scheduling but also for cross-functional coordination across asset, production, and logistics responsibilities [5]. These contributions point to the strategic value of data and knowledge assets in PALM, but they do not solve the deployment sequencing problem that emerges once organizations decide to operationalize those capabilities in concrete processes. A third stream concerns servitization and digital servitization. Minaya et al. synthesize three decades of servitization and digital servitization research and argue that the transition depends on strategic adaptability and technological alignment rather than on isolated digital initiatives [7]. Chen et al. show that digital servitization advances through discontinuous and continuous interplay between business model elements and digital technologies [8], while Coreynen et al. describe spiraling dynamics of learning and alignment in digital service innovation [9]. Most recently, Sun and Oliva explain why servitization efforts fail when capability development and scaling dynamics are not aligned over time [6]. Together, these studies reinforce a central point for the present paper: the order in which capabilities are activated matters. However, they do not offer a deployment model specifically tailored to auditable warranty and maintenance workflows.

Warranty and after-sales literature provides another essential foundation. Earlier work in this line proposed a reference framework for warranty management in industrial assets and positioned after-sales as an integrated process linked to quality, logistics, reliability, maintenance, and ICT-enabled coordination [13, 17]. The same line also showed that AHP can improve warranty-related prioritization decisions and that dynamic AHP becomes relevant when implemented decisions alter the subsequent decision context [14, 15]. More recent warranty research has focused on optimization of warranty servicing policies, such as condition-based maintenance and inspection scheduling under extended warranty [11, 18]. Those studies are highly valuable but operate at the policy-optimization level rather than at the process-deployment level. They help determine what a provider should do to minimize expected servicing cost, but not what organizational module should be deployed first so that an auditable, human-centric process can work in practice.

Finally, maintenance documentation standards remain relevant because workflow deployment is ultimately materialized through records, work orders, and information objects. EN 13460 makes explicit that maintenance requires adequate information flow, defines work-order information elements, and distinguishes between preparatory and operational documentation [16]. This is especially pertinent for after-sales governance because auditable coverage assessment, work-order traceability, closure, and lessons learned all depend on the quality and consistency of those information objects. The literature therefore converges on a useful but incomplete picture. We know that human-centric PALM requires better alignment between technologies, people, and organizational routines; that data and knowledge assets matter; that servitization success depends on sequencing capabilities; and that warranty/after-sales management is structurally relevant to lifecycle performance. What remains underdeveloped is a practical, formal method for deciding which workflow-enhancement modules should be deployed first once an auditable target process has already been defined. This paper addresses precisely that gap.

3 Research Framing and Baseline Workflow

Building on this perspective, the focus shifts from process definition to the structuring of deployment decisions under real-world constraints. This naturally leads to a sequencing problem, where the challenge is not only which modules to implement, but in which order they should be activated to ensure feasibility, coherence, and lifecycle decision quality. In this context, the workflow defines the operational logic of the process, while deployment modules define how this logic is progressively implemented in practice. Deployment modules are understood as discrete implementation units that strengthen, formalize, or scale specific capabilities of the workflow, including governance structures, evidence management, role accountability, system integration, and learning mechanisms. Figure 1 and Table 1 summarize the coarse-grained workflow baseline and illustrate how deployment modules M1–M6 interact with specific workflow blocks. Rather than being tied to single steps, modules may support multiple parts of the workflow, reinforcing their interpretation as cross-cutting implementation capabilities.

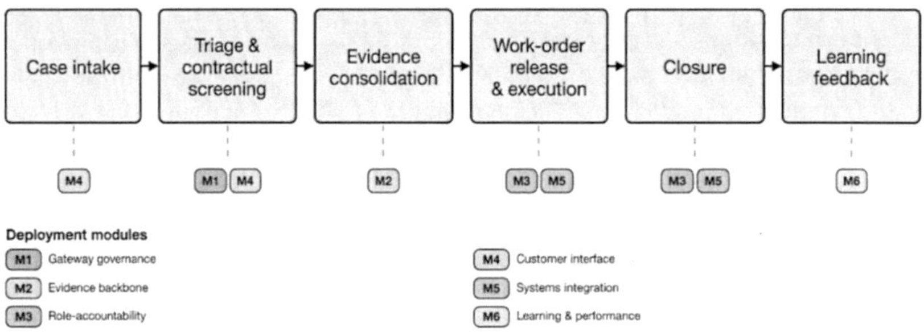

Fig. 1. Simplified baseline workflow and module mapping

The mapping highlights that deployment modules are not confined to individual workflow steps, but may span multiple stages, reinforcing their role as cross-cutting implementation capabilities.

This distinction is important. Several elements of the workflow are mandatory by contractual or governance logic and cannot be treated as alternatives in the deployment model. Examples include documented work-order traceability, explicit service closure, or customer authorization when contractually required. In this paper, such requirements are assumed to be minimally satisfied by the baseline workflow. The actual decision concerns optional implementation modules that strengthen, formalize, or scale those baseline requirements (Fig. 2). That shift—from mandatory requirements to selectable deployment modules—also resolves a common methodological confusion in multicriteria studies of workflows, namely, the incorrect treatment of process obligations as if they were competing alternatives.

Table 1. Short mapping between baseline workflow blocks and deployment modules

Baseline workflow block	Main operational purpose	Related deployment module(s)
Case intake	Captures the initial service event, request, or incident trigger.	M4
Triage & contractual screening	Checks coverage, escalation logic, remote-handling eligibility, and customer-facing gating.	M1, M4
Evidence consolidation	Defines the minimum evidence package and the traceability record supporting the decision.	M2
Work-order release & execution	Assigns responsibility, authorizes intervention, and connects execution with system support.	M3, M5
Closure	Documents completion, confirms accountable handoff, and records formal closure information.	M3, M5
Learning feedback	Captures lessons learned and feeds improvement/performance loops for future cases.	M6

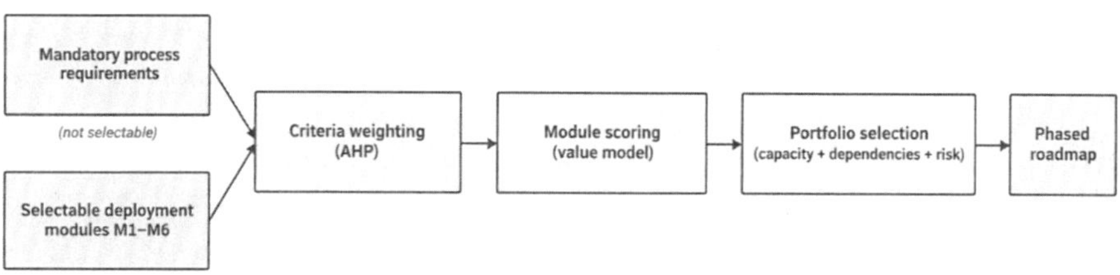

Fig. 2. Conceptual bridge from an auditable workflow baseline to phased deployment portfolios for PALM

4 Methods

4.1 Decision Setting and Module Derivation

The method combines two layers. First, a multicriteria weighting layer based on the Analytic Hierarchy Process (AHP) is used to quantify the relative importance of deployment criteria. Second, a multi-period portfolio model selects the deployment sequence of workflow modules under capacity and precedence constraints. Candidate deployment modules were derived from the workflow architecture and grouped into six modules: M1 gateway governance, M2 evidence backbone, M3 role-accountability, M4 customer interface, M5 systems integration, and M6 learning and performance. Table 2 distinguishes mandatory workflow requirements from these selectable modules. The derivation followed six workflow areas that are already present in the baseline logic: decision gateways map to M1, evidence and decision records to M2, role ownership and sign-off to M3, customer communication and approval handling to M4, CMMS/ERP handshake to M5, and closure and learning loops to M6 (Table 2).

Table 2. Mandatory workflow requirements versus selectable deployment modules

Mandatory requirement	Why it is not an alternative	Deployment modules most related
Traceable case intake and work-order record	Minimal traceable intake is assumed in the baseline; the deployment decision concerns how evidence and systems support are strengthened and scaled	M2, M5
Explicit coverage/authorization decision	A coverage/authorization decision must exist when contractually required; the deployment decision concerns how gateways and customer-interface mechanisms formalize it	M1, M4
Auditable service closure	Minimal closure evidence is assumed in the baseline; the deployment decision concerns how accountable handoff, formal service closure, and their system-supported recording are strengthened and scaled	M3, M5
Named human responsibility point	An accountable role must exist in the baseline even if lightly defined; module M3 formalizes, clarifies, and scales responsibility	M3
Feedback capture for future cases	Minimum closure coding is assumed in the baseline; module M6 enriches, structures, and reuses learning information	M6

4.2 Evaluation Criteria and AHP Weighting

Deployment modules are evaluated using six criteria: lifecycle service impact (C1), traceability and accountability gain (C2), contractual/compliance risk reduction (C3), human-centric fit (C4), implementation feasibility (C5), and scalability/transferability (C6). Table 3 summarizes the criteria and their decision logic. In practice, the human-centric fit criterion can be assessed through expert judgement, role-clarity indicators, perceived cognitive coordination burden, accountability transparency, and the degree to which AI or digital tools support rather than replace human decision-making. To avoid collapsing all deployability concerns into a single score, C5 captures relative deployability under local organizational conditions, whereas absolute implementation load is modeled separately in the portfolio layer as a scarce-capacity constraint.

Table 3. Evaluation criteria used in the AHP weighting layer

Criterion	Meaning in the deployment problem	Direction
C1 Lifecycle service impact	Expected effect on service continuity, resolution quality, and lifecycle performance	Max
C2 Traceability/accountability gain	Improvement in evidence quality, auditability, and explicit responsibility	Max
C3 Contractual/compliance risk reduction	Reduction of exposure to coverage disputes, ambiguity, and non-conformity	Max
C4 Human-centric fit	Expected reduction in role ambiguity, cognitive coordination burden, and opacity of responsibility handoffs	Max
C5 Implementation feasibility	Relative deployability under local organizational conditions, distinct from absolute resource consumption	Max
C6 Scalability/transferability	Ability to reuse the module across assets, customers, and contracts	Max

Let $A = [aij]$ denote the pairwise comparison matrix for the criteria, with $aii = 1$, $aij > 0$ and $aij = 1/aji$. The criteria weights vector is $w = (w1, \ldots, w6)T$ with $\Sigma c\ wc = 1$. We use the geometric mean procedure, because it is robust and transparent for synthetic or aggregated judgments. The geometric mean for criterion i is $g_{\mathrm{i}} = (\Pi_{\mathrm{j}}\ a_{\mathrm{ij}})^{1/6}$, and the normalized weight is $wi = gi/\Sigma r\ gr$. The consistency of the matrix can be checked through $CI = (\lambda max - n)/(n - 1)$ and $CR = CI/RIn$, where $\mathrm{n} = 6$ and $\mathrm{RI_n}$ is Saaty's random index [14].

$$A = \left[aij\right] a_{ii} = 1, a_{ij} > 0, a_{ij} = \frac{1}{a_{ji}} \tag{1}$$

$$\mathrm{w} = (w_1, \ldots, w_6)^{\top}, \sum_{c=1}^{6} w_c = 1,\ \ A\mathrm{w} = \lambda_{\max}\mathrm{w} \tag{2}$$

$$g_i = \left(\prod_{j=1}^{6} a_{ij}\right)^{1/6}, w_i = \frac{g_i}{\sum_{r=1}^{6} g_r} \tag{3}$$

$$CI = \frac{\lambda_{\max} - n}{n - 1}, CR = \frac{CI}{RI_n} \tag{4}$$

Because no expert panel was available at this stage, the illustrative case uses a synthetic consensus judgment setting. This is stated explicitly as methodological demonstration rather than empirical validation. The synthetic criteria weights are fixed at w = (0.24, 0.18, 0.18, 0.14, 0.16, 0.10), corresponding respectively to C1–C6 (Table 4). A perfectly consistent synthetic pairwise matrix may then be generated through aij = wi / wj, which yields CR = 0 by construction. This choice is appropriate here because the objective of the illustrative case is to reveal the behaviour and internal consistency of the deployment model without elicitation noise, not to claim field-tested parameter values.

Table 4. Synthetic criteria weights used in the illustrative case

Criterion	Synthetic weight
C1 Lifecycle service impact	0.24
C2 Traceability/accountability gain	0.18
C3 Contractual/compliance risk reduction	0.18
C4 Human-centric fit	0.14
C5 Implementation feasibility	0.16
C6 Scalability/transferability	0.10

4.3 Module Scoring

Let rjc ∈ {1, ..., 9} be the rating of module j under criterion c. Ratings are normalized as qjc = (rjc - 1)/8 ∈ [0, 1]. The intrinsic deployment value of module j is then vj = Σc wc qjc. For interpretability, we also report the equivalent weighted score on the original 1–9 scale. Ratings are assigned synthetically but coherently with the logic of the modules: for example, systems integration (M5) scores high on lifecycle effect and scalability but lower on feasibility; role-accountability (M3) scores especially high on human-centric fit; and gateway governance (M1) scores high on compliance and traceability. In the synthetic case, human-centric fit was rated according to expected reduction in role ambiguity, cognitive coordination burden, and opacity of responsibility handoffs.

$$qjc = (rjc - 1)/8, vj = \Sigma c\ wc\ qjc \tag{5}$$

4.4 Multi-Period Deployment Portfolio Model

The general deployment model is multi-period. Let the planning horizon be divided into T waves, $T = \{1, ..., T\}$. Binary variable $z_{jt} = 1$ if module j is deployed in wave t and 0 otherwise. Each module may be deployed at most once, so $\Sigma_t\ z_{jt} \leq 1$ for all j. Define the cumulative activation variable $x_{jt} = \Sigma_{\tau = 1..t}\ z_{j\tau}$, which equals 1 if module j is active by the end of wave t. Let e_j be the nominal implementation effort of module j and B_t the available capacity in wave t. Capacity feasibility is enforced by $\Sigma_j\ e_j\ z_{jt} \leq B_t$ for all t.

$$\Sigma t\ zjt \leq 1,\quad xjt = \Sigma\tau = 1..t\ zj\tau \tag{6}$$

$$\Sigma j\ ej\ zjt \leq Bt \quad \forall t \qquad (7)$$

Some modules require others to be active beforehand. Let P be the set of precedence relations, where (i, j) ∈ P means that module i must be active no later than module j. Precedence is enforced through $x_{jt} \leq x_{it}$ for all (i, j) ∈ P and all t. In the synthetic case, the precedence set is P = {(1,4), (2,4), (1,5), (2,5), (3,5), (2,6)}, meaning that customer-interface functions cannot be stabilized before governance and evidence foundations are in place, and that systems integration is architecturally dependent on prior governance, evidence, and role-accountability modules.

$$xjt \leq xit \quad \forall (i, j) \in P, \quad \forall t \qquad (8)$$

Let δ ∈ (0,1] be a discount factor that rewards earlier activation. The baseline deterministic deployment problem maximizes the discounted cumulative value of active modules across waves: maximize Σt δt-1 Σj vj xjt, subject to the capacity and precedence constraints above. This formulation is considered sufficient for the present level because it directly produces a phased deployment roadmap under explicit constraints.

$$\max \sum_{t \in \mathcal{T}} \delta^{t-1} \sum_{j \in \mathcal{J}} v_j x_{jt} \qquad (9)$$

More elaborate extensions could incorporate module complementarities and downside implementation risk, for instance through synergy terms or CVaR-type penalties. These extensions are not activated in the synthetic illustration, so that the present contribution remains focused on the managerial logic of phased deployment.

Figure 3 presents the hierarchical structure used to evaluate the deployment modules. The precedence relations considered in the synthetic case are shown in Fig. 4.

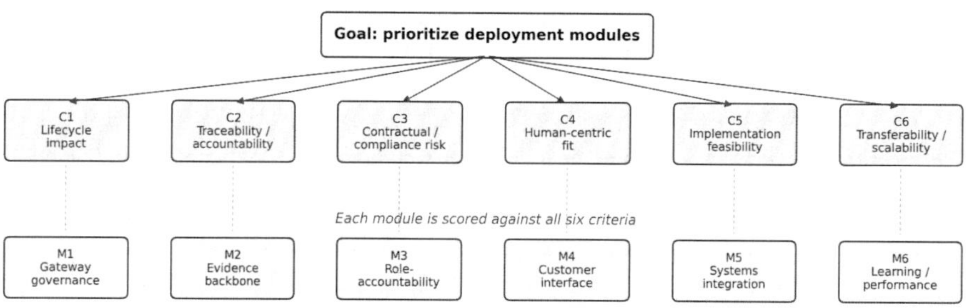

Fig. 3. AHP hierarchy and deployment-module taxonomy

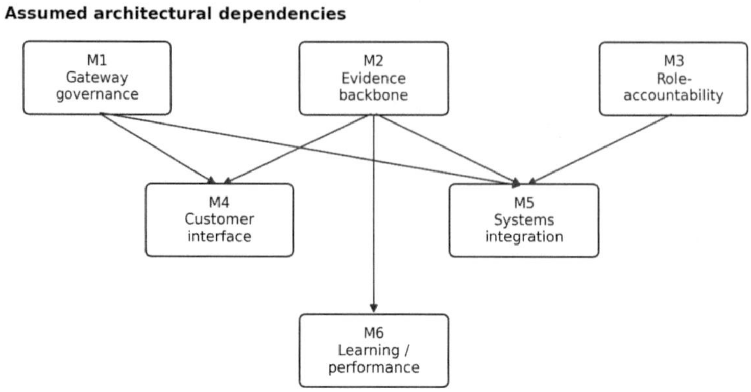

Fig. 4. Precedence relations among deployment modules in the synthetic case

5 Synthetic Illustrative Case and Results

The synthetic illustrative case represents a medium-sized industrial OEM/service provider operating under servitized after-sales arrangements and moderate digital maturity. The organization already recognizes the need for an auditable workflow, but it cannot deploy all modules at once. The nominal implementation efforts are set at e = (2, 3, 2, 2, 5, 3) for M1–M6, respectively. Three deployment waves are considered with capacities B = (5, 4, 5). The ratings assigned to each module under the six criteria are shown in Table 5. The resulting criteria weights are shown in Table 4. Lifecycle service impact receives the highest synthetic weight, followed by traceability/accountability and contractual/compliance risk reduction. Human-centric fit remains substantial, while scalability receives a smaller but still meaningful weight. This weighting pattern is used only to illustrate the method and is consistent with the idea that a PALM-oriented warranty workflow must first work operationally and contractually, but also remain understandable and acceptable to the humans who operate and govern it.

Table 5. Synthetic ratings of deployment modules, weighted score, and implementation effort

Module	C1	C2	C3	C4	C5	C6	Weighted score	Effort
M1	8	8	9	7	8	7	7.94	2
M2	8	9	8	7	6	8	7.72	3
M3	7	8	7	9	7	7	7.46	2
M4	7	7	8	8	6	6	7.06	2
M5	9	8	8	6	3	9	7.26	5
M6	8	7	7	7	5	9	7.12	3

Table 5 shows that M1 gateway governance obtains the highest weighted score, closely followed by M2 evidence backbone and M3 role-accountability. M5 systems integration receives a high service-impact score but is penalized by low implementation feasibility and high effort. M6 learning-and-performance is moderately attractive and portable, but not urgent in the first wave. Given the assumed weights, capacity limits and precedence structure, the resulting base-case portfolio is therefore intuitive but not trivial: Wave 1 deploys M1 and M2; Wave 2 deploys M3 and M4; Wave 3 deploys M5; and M6 is deferred beyond the horizon. Fig. 5 illustrates this roadmap.

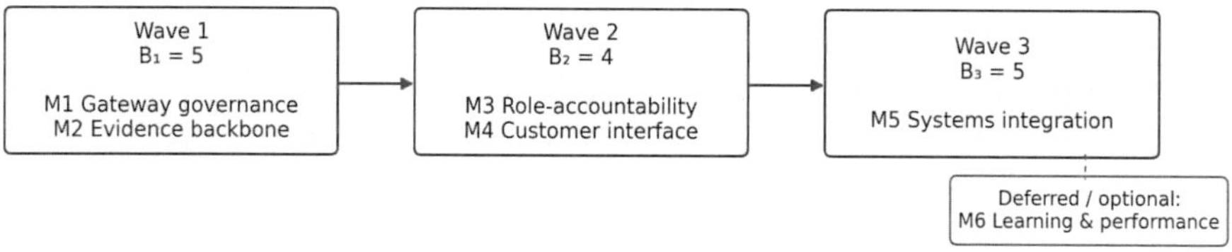

Figure 5. Base-case phased deployment roadmap obtained under the deterministic illustrative formulation

Under the assumed precedence structure, two insights emerge from the base portfolio. First, governance and evidence modules dominate the first deployment wave. In the synthetic instantiation, this suggests that human-centric PALM in after-sales may begin with clarified decision gateways, minimum evidence packages, and accountable roles rather than with software integration. Second, systems integration becomes attractive only after those human and governance foundations exist in the modeled architecture. In other words, digitalization is sequenced around people and accountability rather than being treated as a first-wave substitute for them.

Sensitivity analysis was performed under three alternative weighting logics: governance-oriented, human-oriented, and feasibility-oriented. The resulting deployment portfolios under the different weighting scenarios are summarized in Table 6. The governance-oriented scenario preserves the base roadmap. By contrast, both the human-oriented and the feasibility-oriented scenarios replace M5 with M6 in Wave 3, meaning that learning and closure feedback are prioritised ahead of deeper systems integration when organizations care more about adoption and local deployability than about immediate digital connectivity. The top two waves remain stable across all scenarios, which indicates that M1 and M2 are robust first-wave choices.

Table 6. Selected deployment portfolios under alternative weighting logics

Scenario	Wave 1	Wave 2	Wave 3	Deferred
Base	M1 + M2	M3 + M4	M5	M6
Governance-oriented	M1 + M2	M3 + M4	M5	M6
Human-oriented	M1 + M2	M3 + M4	M6	M5
Feasibility-oriented	M1 + M2	M3 + M4	M6	M5

This result should be interpreted as a design-oriented indication rather than as a field-validated prescription. It suggests that the first deployment wave should focus on the minimal socio-technical conditions that make the workflow reliable and reviewable: explicit gateways, explicit evidence, and explicit responsibility (Fig. 6).

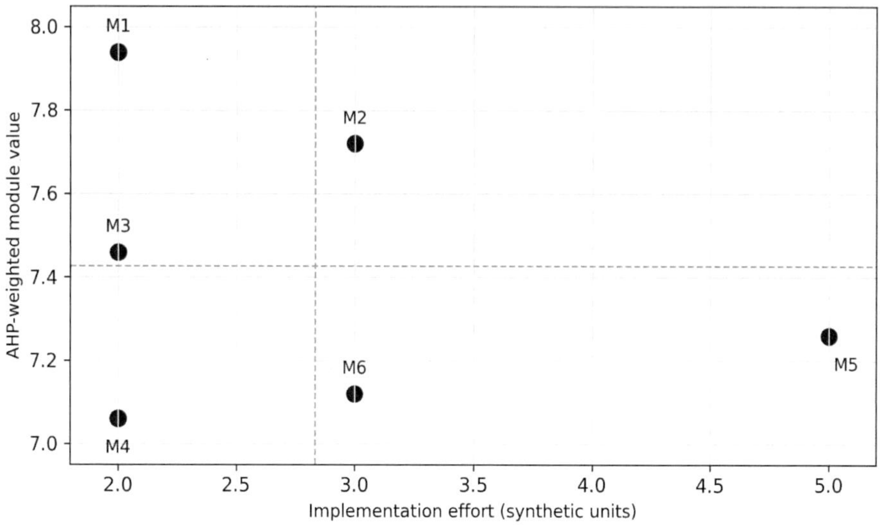

Fig. 6. Synthetic value-effort view of the deployment modules; M5 is attractive but effort-intensive, which explains its delayed activation

More advanced digital features may create value later, but only if the organization first builds a stable human-centric governance layer.

6 Discussion

The paper contributes to the PALM agenda in three ways. First, it treats warranty and after-sales not as a narrow support process but as a lifecycle governance mechanism that affects diagnosis, repair decisions, service closure, knowledge capture, and future adaptation. Second, it places human-centricity at the centre of deployment logic rather than only at the level of user interfaces. Third, it addresses a concrete adoption problem: how to deploy a workflow in phases under limited capacity. This deployment-oriented perspective complements previous work that focused on the design and governance of auditable warranty and after-sales workflows. Rather than redefining the workflow itself, the present contribution addresses the subsequent implementation problem by supporting the prioritisation and phased deployment of workflow modules under practical industrial constraints [19]. This directly answers the interest in how asset management principles and practices can be advanced, deployed, scaled, and adopted in industry. Methodologically, the study also clarifies why a pure AHP would be insufficient in this setting. The candidate objects of choice are not mutually exclusive technologies but compatible deployment modules. AHP is therefore most useful in weighting criteria and deriving module value, while the final sequencing problem must be solved as a constrained portfolio-selection problem. This distinction resolves the frequent confusion between mandatory process obligations and genuine alternatives. The paper also remains coherent with earlier warranty-management research while avoiding simple repackaging. Earlier work in this line proposed integrated warranty frameworks, workflow representations, quality and contractual perspectives, and AHP-based prioritization in warranty contexts [13–15, 17]. The present paper moves one level downstream: from framework or process definition to deployment sequencing. Its limits are equally clear. The illustration is synthetic and should be read as a design-oriented proof of concept. Industrial validation with expert elicitation and post-deployment performance evidence remains necessary before making claims about practical effectiveness.

7 Conclusions

This paper proposed a human-centric multicriteria method for phased deployment of auditable warranty and after-sales workflows in PALM. The method combines AHP-based criteria weighting with a multi-period portfolio model, thereby separating the valuation of deployment modules from the choice of deployment sequence. More fundamentally, the paper frames workflow implementation as a structured decision problem, in which deployment modules act as decision units and sequencing becomes the central mechanism through which organizational capabilities are progressively activated. The synthetic case suggests that, under the assumed dependencies and capacity limits, gateway governance, evidence backbone, and role-accountability may reasonably precede heavier system-integration investments. The central implication is clear: in asset-intensive and servitized settings, after-sales digitalization should be sequenced around human accountability and auditable information objects, not around software integration alone. This makes the workflow more reviewable, more adoptable, and more likely to support lifecycle decision quality. Empirical validation with practitioner panels, richer industrial cases, and post-deployment performance indicators remains a priority for future work.

Acknowledgements. This research was supported by the Spanish Ministry of Science and Innovation under project "Asset Management in the New Digital Twin Environment" (PID2022-137748OB-C32).

Disclosure of Interests The authors have no competing interests to declare that are relevant to the content of this paper.

References

1. Pacheco, de J., D.A., Iwaszczenko, B.: Unravelling human-centric tensions towards industry 5.0: literature review, resolution strategies and research agenda. Digit. Bus. **4**(2), 100090 (2024). https://doi.org/10.1016/j.digbus.2024.100090
2. Hermawati, S., Correa, R., Mohan, M., Lawson, G., Houghton, R.: Defining human-centricity in industry 5.0 and assessing the readiness of ergonomics/human factors communities in UK. Ergonomics. **68**(6), 857–876 (2025). https://doi.org/10.1080/00140139.2024.2343947

3. Passalacqua, M. et al.: Human-centred AI in industry 5.0: a systematic review. Int. J. Prod. Res. **63**(7), 2638–2669 (2025). https://doi.org/10.1080/00207543.2024.2406021
4. Naqvi, S.M.R., Ghufran, M., Meraghni, S., Varnier, C., Nicod, J.-M., Zerhouni, N.: Human knowledge centered maintenance decision support in digital twin environment. J. Manuf. Syst. **65**, 528–537 (2022). https://doi.org/10.1016/j.jmsy.2022.10.003
5. Hinrichs, M., Prifti, L., Schneegass, S.: Data-driven decision-making in maintenance management and coordination throughout the asset life cycle: an empirical study. J. Qual. Maint. Eng. **30**(1), 202–220 (2024). https://doi.org/10.1108/JQME-04-2023-0038
6. Sun, X., Oliva, R.: Failure modes in servitization: a process theory. J. Oper. Manag. **72**(1), 42–63 (2026). https://doi.org/10.1002/joom.70009
7. Minaya, P.E., Avella, L., Trespalacios, J.A.: Synthesizing three decades of digital servitization: a systematic literature review and conceptual framework proposal. Serv. Bus. **18**(2), 193–222 (2024). https://doi.org/10.1007/s11628-024-00559-x
8. Chen, Y., Visnjic, I., Parida, V., Zhang, Z.: On the road to digital servitization – the (dis)continuous interplay between business model and digital technology. Int. J. Oper. Prod. Manag. **41**(5), 694–722 (2021). https://doi.org/10.1108/IJOPM-08-2020-0544
9. Coreynen, W., Matthyssens, P., Struyf, B., Vanhaverbeke, W.: Spiraling between learning and alignment toward digital service innovation. J. Serv. Manage. **35**(2), 306–331 (2024). https://doi.org/10.1108/JOSM-12-2022-0400
10. Rodríguez, M., Crespo, A., González-Prida, V.: Enhancing prescriptive capabilities in electrical substations: a systemic impact factor approach for failure impact analysis. Energies. **17**(4), 770 (2024). https://doi.org/10.3390/en17040770
11. Zheng, R., Fang, H., Hu, C.: Joint optimization of inspection and condition-based maintenance for a deteriorating product under extended warranty. Reliab. Eng. Syst. Saf. **245**, 110043 (2024). https://doi.org/10.1016/j.ress.2024.110043
12. Zani, V. et al.: Designing smart product-service systems: the SEEM-smart methodology and its application in the electrical industrial sector. IFAC-PapersOnLine. **58**(8), 318–323 (2024). https://doi.org/10.1016/j.ifacol.2024.08.140
13. González-Prida, V., Crespo Márquez, A.: A framework for warranty management in industrial assets. Comput. Ind. **63**(9), 960–971 (2012). https://doi.org/10.1016/j.compind.2012.09.001
14. González-Prida, V., Gómez Fernández, J., Crespo Márquez, A.: Practical application of an analytic hierarchy process for the improvement of the warranty management. J. Qual. Maint. Eng. **17**(2), 163–182 (2011). https://doi.org/10.1108/13552511111134592
15. González-Prida, V., Viveros, P., Barberá, L., Crespo Márquez, A.: Dynamic analytic hierarchy process: AHP method adapted to a changing environment. J. Manuf. Technol. Manag. **25**(4), 457–475 (2014). https://doi.org/10.1108/JMTM-03-2013-0030
16. European Committee for Standardization: EN 13460:2009. Maintenance. Documentation for maintenance. CEN, Brussels (2009). https://doi.org/10.31030/1493965
17. Murthy, D.N.P., Jack, N.: Extended Warranties, Maintenance Service and Lease Contracts: Modeling and Analysis for Decision-Making. Springer, London (2014). https://doi.org/10.1007/978-1-4471-6440-1
18. Murthy, D.N.P., Jack, N.: EWs/MSCs: An Overview. In: Extended Warranties, Maintenance Service and Lease Contracts, pp. 91–125. Springer, London (2014). https://doi.org/10.1007/978-1-4471-6440-1_5
19. González-Prida, V., Guillén López, A.: An auditable process framework for governing after-sales service cases and maintenance execution in servitized asset-intensive systems. Discov. Sustain. (2026). https://doi.org/10.1007/s43621-026-03865-8

The Role of Serious Games for Boundary-Object Negotiation in Innovation Projects

Giacomo Barbieri(✉), Maricruz Solera Jimenez, and Jan Braaksma

Department of Design, Production and Management, University of Twente, Drienerlolaan 5, 7522 NB Enschede, The Netherlands
{g.barbieri,m.solerajimenez,a.j.j.braaksma}@utwente.nl

Abstract. Innovation projects that span multiple disciplines and organizations depend on cross-functional collaboration and knowledge integration to succeed. Boundary objects—shared artifacts, models, or methods that enable coordination across different social and knowledge domains—are key means for realizing such collaboration and integration. However, boundary objects are rarely self-explanatory or automatically accepted. To become effective, they must undergo negotiation cycles through the active participation of the actors involved in the collaboration. This negotiation process is difficult to achieve, yet essential for developing shared understanding, fostering collective sensemaking, and enabling the effective use of boundary objects. To facilitate this process, this paper explores Serious Games (SGs)—structured, goal-oriented games designed for purposes beyond entertainment—as potential mechanisms for boundary-object negotiation. Guided by a Research through Design perspective—where knowledge emerges through the design and application of artifacts—an SG workshop was developed and implemented within a European rail innovation project, where a Business Case methodology acted as a boundary object for integrating domain-specific knowledge. Drawing on design-thinking principles, the SG enabled participants to understand, analyze, and negotiate the selected boundary object. The study demonstrates how the SG acted as a catalyst for cross-functional dialogue, facilitating shared understanding and collective sensemaking around the boundary object. The findings highlight how playful, participatory, and human-centered interventions can enhance boundary-object negotiation and strengthen methodological alignment, especially in complex innovation environments.

Keywords: Innovation Management · Project Management · Asset Management · Cross-Functional Collaboration · Design Thinking

1 Introduction

Innovation in today's technology-intensive environment increasingly depends on complex knowledge work, where experts from diverse domains must collaborate to combine and apply specialized expertise. Such collaboration requires

Published by Springer Nature Switzerland AG 2027
G. Pezzotta et al. (Eds.): APMS 2026, IFIP AICT 808, pp. 339–353, 2027.
https://doi.org/10.1007/978-3-032-38594-9_23

spanning multiple types of boundaries—disciplinary, organizational, cognitive, and social—to share information, coordinate tasks, and integrate heterogeneous knowledge [10]. Boundary spanning facilitates the division of work necessary to solve complex organizational problems; however, the diversity of boundaries can also inhibit experts from coordinating tasks, sharing knowledge, and brokering expertise [15]. Therefore, successful innovation projects demand effective *Cross-Boundary Spanning* mechanisms capable of linking multiple domains and fostering integration across disciplinary and organizational divides.

A key mechanism that supports cross-boundary spanning and knowledge integration in innovation projects is the use of *Boundary Objects* [26]. These establish a shared syntax or language for individuals to represent their knowledge across boundaries [10], enabling collaboration among actors who possess distinct expertise, goals, and vocabularies. Boundary objects can take multiple forms [9], such as prototypes, drawings, sketches, designs, simulation models, databases, or software platforms. Rather than requiring participants to fully transfer or assimilate one another's domain-specific knowledge, boundary objects act as knowledge catalysts, fostering cross-functional discussion and coordination around a shared representation of the problem at hand [22].

Building on this perspective, negotiation can be broadly defined as "a discussion between parties in order to reach an agreement" [12]. In collaborative innovation settings where knowledge and expertise are dispersed, effective project coordination depends on the actors' ability to negotiate and reconcile their different understandings [23]. Within such contexts, boundary objects play a crucial mediating role by enabling individuals at the interface of different domains to represent, clarify, and translate knowledge across boundaries [11]. Empirical studies have shown that boundary objects act as key enablers of *Knowledge Negotiation*, particularly in complex design environments [2].

While extensive research has examined how boundary objects facilitate the negotiation of knowledge across disciplinary and organizational domains, little attention has been paid to the negotiation of the boundary object itself. As highlighted by Bechky (2003) [7] and Tuertscher et al. (2014) [27], boundary objects do not automatically generate shared understanding; they must be continuously discussed, challenged, and refined by the actors involved in the collaboration. Despite these insights, to the best of the authors' knowledge, no study has systematically examined how the negotiation of boundary objects unfolds in practice or the mechanisms that can facilitate it. This need becomes particularly salient when the boundary object is not a well-established or standardized tool—such as a BIM model or a shared software repository—but a novel or project-specific artifact, as is often the case in innovation projects [9]. This highlights the need for empirical and methodological research on approaches that support *Boundary-Object Negotiation* in innovation settings.

In this context, Kilis et al. (2025) [18] emphasize that social interaction and active engagement are essential to generating the 'creative tension' required for boundary-object negotiation. *Serious Games* (SGs), understood as structured and goal-oriented activities designed for purposes beyond entertainment [1], offer participatory and experiential formats that inherently support such dynamic collaborative processes. However, while SGs have been used as boundary objects to support knowledge negotiation [17], they have not been examined as a means to facilitate the processes of boundary-object negotiation. This gap motivates the following research question (RQ):

How can Serious Games facilitate the process of Boundary-Object Negotiation in Innovation Projects?

To address this RQ, this study adopts a *Research through Design* (RtD) approach, in which knowledge is generated through the creation and evaluation of artifacts, with the design process itself serving as a means of inquiry [28]. Within this perspective, *The BuCa Restaurant* game was developed and implemented through a series of sessions within an innovation consortium. The experience was then analyzed to reflect on the role of SGs in supporting boundary-object negotiation. The remainder of the paper is structured as follows: Sect. 2 presents the theoretical background used to develop the SG. Section 3 details its design process. Section 4 outlines its application in multiple game sessions. Section 5 reports the results and addresses the RQ. Finally, Sect. 6 offers concluding reflections and directions for future research.

2 Theoretical Framework

In this section, the theoretical concepts underpinning the development of the SG are presented.

2.1 Design Science

Design Science Research Methodology (DSRM) is a research approach aimed at creating and evaluating artifacts designed to solve identified problems [24]. It is particularly suitable for applied fields such as information systems, engineering, and management, where bridging theory and practice through the development of innovative tools or frameworks is essential. In this work, DSRM is adopted as the overarching *Methodological Approach* to guide the design of the SG.

DSRM comprises six steps, each of which is instantiated in this paper: (1) *Problem Identification* is addressed in the Introduction (Sect. 1), where the need for approaches that support boundary-object negotiation is established; (2) *Objective Definition* is detailed in Sect. 3.2, outlining the design requirements for the SG; (3) *Design and Development* is described in Sect. 3.3; (4) *Demonstration* is presented in Sect. 4, through the application of the SG in multiple game sessions; (5) *Evaluation* is provided in Sect. 5, assessing the SG's ability to support boundary-object negotiation; and (6) *Communication* of results is embedded throughout the paper, with conclusions summarized in Sect. 6.

2.2 Experiential Learning

Experiential learning is a pedagogical approach that emphasizes learning through direct experience, reflection, and active engagement. At its core lies *Kolb's Experiential Learning Cycle*, which comprises four stages [19]: concrete experience, reflective observation, abstract conceptualization, and active experimentation. Learners first engage in a concrete activity, reflect on that experience, derive conceptual insights, and then test these insights through further action. This iterative process not only deepens understanding but also fosters adaptability, critical thinking, and meaningful knowledge transfer [25] [5]. In this study, the SG served as the concrete experience that prompted participants to reflect on the boundary object, generate conceptual insights about its structure and use, and iteratively refine it prior to its application in the project setting.

2.3 Design Thinking

Design Thinking is a practical methodological approach that extends design beyond physical and aesthetic concerns, integrating scientific knowledge and creative practices to address complex problems [8]. This interdisciplinary approach combines *Divergent Thinking*, which supports creativity and the exploration of alternatives, with *Convergent Thinking*, which emphasizes analysis and synthesis. In this work, Design Thinking provides a structured yet flexible, participatory, and human-centered toolkit for navigating the complexity of boundary-object negotiation.

Beyond its underlying principles, DT also offers a set of practical tools [21]. In particular, *analogy* was employed to situate participants in a simplified and risk-free scenario—distinct from their actual work context—thereby enabling them to engage with the boundary object without organizational pressures or domain-specific constraints. Furthermore, *visualization* techniques supported the externalization of ideas, enabling participants to collectively envision the boundary object and negotiate its structure and meaning.

3 Design Process

This section outlines the project context and the design process of *The BuCa Restaurant*, including its core objectives and methodological development steps.

3.1 Project Context

The Europe's Rail Joint Undertaking (ERJU) is the EU's main instrument for coordinating research and innovation in the rail sector, aiming to deliver a high-capacity, integrated, and digital European rail network. Within this framework, Flagship Project 2 (FP2)—titled *Rail to Digital Automated up to Autonomous Train Operation* (R2DATO) (https://rail-research.europa.eu/pages/fp2-r2dato/deliverables)—focuses on advancing automation and digitalisation in both passenger and freight transport. FP2-R2DATO seeks to develop and deploy scalable Digital and Automated (up to Autonomous) Train Operation (DATO) technological solutions, contributing to the modernization and capacity enhancement of the existing rail infrastructure.

Within FP2-R2DATO, Work Package 32 (WP 32)—*DATO Assessment and Potential Identification*—plays a central role in bridging technical innovation with strategic deployment. This work package is tasked with integrating insights from diverse research streams into a cohesive and generalizable Business Case (BuCa) methodology aimed at assessing DATO technologies [4]. WP 32 brings together a diverse consortium, including national autorities (DLR, NRD and Trafikverket), train operators (NS and RENFE), freight operators (DB Cargo), infrastructure managers (ProRail and ADIF), and academic partners (NTNU, LTU, KTH, TU Delft, and the University of Twente).

In this context, the *Value-based Multi-Criteria Decision Analysis* method presented in [6] was selected as a blueprint for the BuCa methodology due to its ability to function as a boundary object by integrating multiple knowledge dimensions. However, rather than being used to compare alternative options (e.g. DATO technologies), the methodology was adapted to compare the impacts on different stakeholders within a specific application scenario—that is, a given DATO technology and set of network characteristics. This adaptation necessitated a negotiation process within the consortium to establish shared understanding, collective sensemaking, and effective use of the boundary object.

3.2 SG Objectives

The development of the SG was guided by three primary objectives, aimed at ensuring its relevance, applicability, and effectiveness in supporting boundary-object negotiation. These objectives are:

- *Obj1) Boundary Object*: the core steps of the selected boundary object had to be implemented within the SG to allow participants to enact and explore the BuCa methodology in practice;
- *Obj2) Analogy*: the SG had to implement an analogy-based scenario that mirrors the structural logic of the methodology while remaining sufficiently detached from the real project context, thereby providing a simplified, safe, and cognitively accessible environment in which participants could understand, experiment with, and reflect on the approach;
- *Obj3) Negotiation*: in line with [20], the SG needed to enable boundary-object negotiation through iterative processes of: (i) *Articulation*—expressing and externalizing domain-specific knowledge through the boundary object; (ii) *Alignment*—connecting and adjusting these articulations with those of others; (iii) *Contestation*—identifying and debating conflicts or differences in how the boundary object is interpreted, represented, or operationalized; and (iv) *Transformation*—adapting the boundary object to incorporate collective insights.

3.3 SG Design

In accordance with *Obj1*, the SG had to implement the steps of the methodology presented in [6], adapted to compare the impacts on different stakeholders within a specific application scenario. These steps are as follows:

1. *Application Scenario*: consists in specifying the considered DATO technologies and the network characteristics in which they will be applied, as well as identifying the relevant stakeholders involved in or affected by their implementation;
2. *Value Drivers and Metrics*: in Asset Management (AM), value represents the result of considering both positive and negative impacts, as well as financial and non-financial effects, on stakeholders [16]. In this context, value can be expressed as performance less cost in relation to the associated risks [14]. Within each of these three dimensions, value drivers (or enablers) are factors that significantly influence the realization of value, while value metrics (indicators) are the performance measures used to assess these drivers [13]. In this step, a hierarchical tree of value drivers and their corresponding metrics is built for each value dimension;
3. *Utility functions*: a utility function is associated to each metric enabling the representation of the impacts on different stakeholders within a specific application scenario;
4. *Weights*: weights are assigned enabling the expression of the relative importance of drivers and metrics in the aggregation of overall value;
5. *Value Model*: the overall additive utility functions are computed using the individual utility functions formulated in step 3 and the weights assessed in step 4.
6. *Validation*: a sensemaking exercise is conducted to discuss, interpret, and critically reflect on the results of the value model.

In accordance with *Obj2*, the SG had to be based on an analogy that mirrors the structural logic of the BuCa methodology while remaining sufficiently detached from the real project context. A culinary analogy was selected for this purpose, as it had already been employed within the consortium to build a shared vision [4], and participants were therefore familiar with it.

The narrative of *The BuCa Restaurant* game was designed to mirror the consortium task of developing a BuCa methodology to support the adoption and implementation of DATO technologies. In the game scenario, BuCa is portrayed as a well-established and rapidly growing chain of restaurants whose expanding customer base has begun to strain its operational capacity. Despite its commercial success, the company faces increasing labor shortages and operational inefficiencies, limiting its ability to meet rising demand. To address these challenges, BuCa seeks to explore digitalization and automation as strategic enablers of improved performance and resilience. In this context, a governmental "Angel Program" is available to support businesses like BuCa willing to experiment with innovative digital solutions. To access this funding, applicants must submit a compelling illustration of the business case for the proposed digitalization technologies, thereby framing the core challenge of the game.

The project consortium comprised three domain-specific teams—capacity, human factors, and cost—which can be aligned, respectively, with the three AM value dimensions of performance, risk, and cost considered in AM. The participants involved in these teams came from diverse organizational and professional backgrounds, including infrastructure managers, train operators, national authorities, and academic institutions participating in the consortium. To preserve this domain-specific structure and maintain manageable group sizes, three separate game sessions were designed. Furthermore, given that the full application of the BuCa methodology would have required more time than was available within a single game session, only the impact assessment was implemented during the domain-specific sessions. The remaining misalignment assessment and reflective components—namely, the *Obj3* negotiation process—were conducted in a subsequent plenary session involving all three teams. This division is illustrated in Table 1.

Table 1. Mapping of the BuCa methodology steps across the game (domain-specific) sessions and the subsequent reflection (plenary) session.

BuCa Methodology	Game Sessions	Game Reflection
Application Scenario	Meet BuCa	/
Value Drivers and Metrics	Hierarchical Trees	Value Framework
Utility Functions	Semaphore-based Assessments	Metric-level Misalignments
Weights	/	Weighted Metrics
Value Model	Impact Visualizations	Driver-level Misalignments
Validation	/	Boundary-Object Negotiation

4 The BuCa Restaurant Game

The game sessions of *The BuCa Restaurant* are presented in Sect. 4.1, while Sect. 4.2 describes the subsequent reflection session.

4.1 Game Sessions

Each session consisted of four phases designed to enable participants to: (i) understand the BuCa methodology and how their team could contribute to assessing the impacts of a given technology on different stakeholders; and (ii) propose visualizations to highlight these impacts. These phases are described below (Table 1):

1. *Meet BuCa*: the application scenario described in Sect. 3.3 was introduced, including the restaurant's demand-related challenges, the potential culinary digital technologies, and the stakeholders involved in or affected by the decision problem;
2. *Hierarchical Trees*: prior to the game sessions, the main metrics identified during earlier project activities by the domain-specific teams were clustered into value drivers to construct hierarchical trees—one for each team. These railway-based metrics were then translated into the culinary context, as illustrated in Fig. 1. During the game session, the resulting hierarchical trees were presented to the participants as the basis for the subsequent assessment;

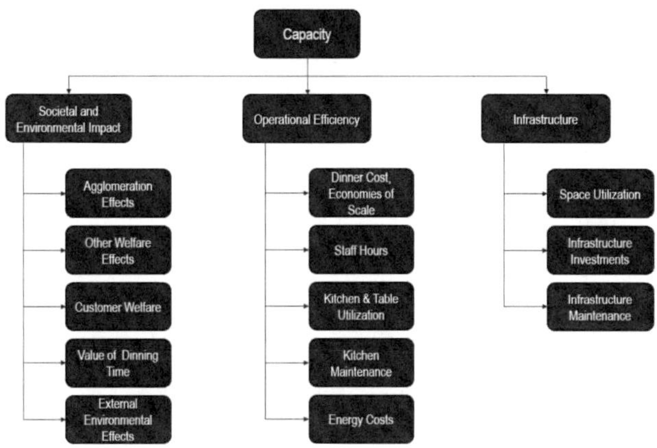

Fig. 1. Hierarchical tree for the Capacity value dimension used in *The BuCa Restaurant* game, including three value drivers and thirteen metrics.

3. *Semaphore-based Assessments*: in this phase, participants were asked to assess the impacts on different stakeholders with respect to each metric. To facilitate this, a semaphore-based assessment (green, yellow, red) was adopted, enabling players to grasp the underlying logic of the evaluation process, which in the real project context would be implemented through formal utility functions. Each team focused on assessing stakeholder impacts within its respective value dimension: the capacity team examined performance-related (gain) impacts, the cost team focused on cost-related impacts, and the human factors team addressed impacts related to the allocation of responsibility for mitigating technology adoption risks (see Fig. 2);
4. *Impact Visualizations*: in the final phase, participants were asked to propose visualizations to highlight the impacts on different stakeholders, considering that four key variables could be represented: stakeholders, technology, value drivers/metrics, and assessment results. This divergent activity served two purposes. First, it supported the acceptance of the proposed BuCa methodology by allowing participants to shape how their outcomes would be commu-

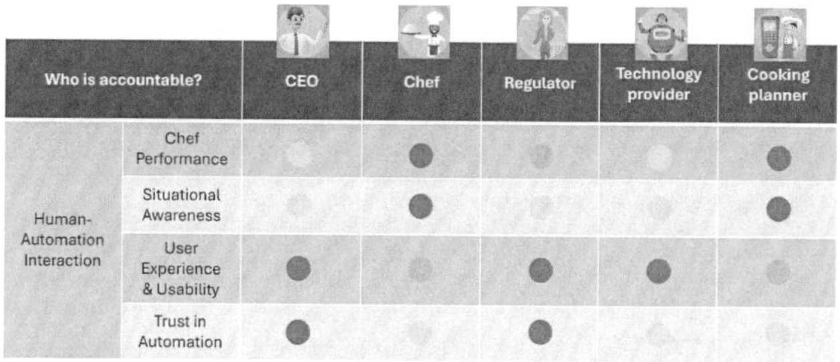

Fig. 2. Excerpt of the semaphore-based assessment for the human factors team. Value drivers are listed in the first column and their corresponding metrics in the second, while the colored indicators represent stakeholder accountability levels (red = high, yellow = medium, green = low). (Color figure online)

nicated. Second, visualizing the expected outputs of the assessment helped clarify what each team would need to produce in the real project context.

The game sessions took place in Utrecht (The Netherlands) on 17 February 2025 (cost team), 25 February 2025 (human factors team), and 13 March 2025 (capacity team), respectively. Each session lasted approximately 2.5 h and was conducted in a hybrid format, enabling participants located abroad to take part in the game. *Miro* (https://miro.com/) was used as the primary platform, allowing players to perform the assessment and develop the impact visualizations, examples of which are illustrated in Fig. 3.

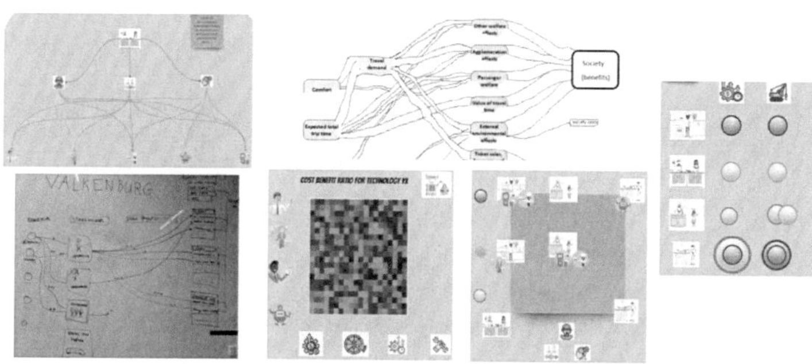

Fig. 3. Examples of illustrations developed during the *Impact Visualizations* phase.

After the game sessions, the visualizations were reviewed and synthesized through a convergence process, leading to the selection of the visualization depicted in Fig. 4 to represent stakeholder impacts within each value dimension. This visualization contains a *Value Curve* for each stakeholder and was selected because it effectively integrates the four key variables—stakeholders, technology, value drivers/metrics, and assessment results—into a single representation.

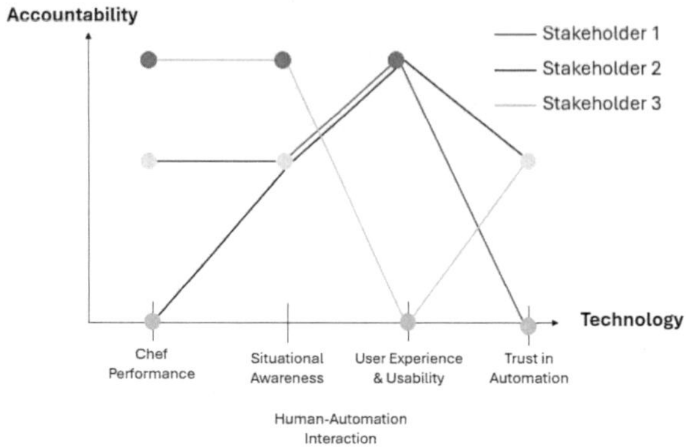

Fig. 4. Example of the selected visualization used to represent the impacts of a given technology on different stakeholders across the metrics of the Human–Automation Interaction value driver.

4.2 Game Reflection

The reflection session took place in Utrecht on 24 March 2025. It included members of the three teams—capacity, cost, and human factors—and had the following purposes: (i) *Integrated results*: illustrate how the different domain-specific impact assessments could be integrated to highlight potential stakeholder misalignments; and (ii) *Boundary-object negotiation*: negotiate the proposed BuCa methodology based on the provided overview. It is worth noting that the utility values and weights used in the examples were illustrative and assigned solely to demonstrate the aggregation process and resulting misalignment visualizations. The following elements were presented to the participants (Table 1):

1. *Value Framework*: in AM, a Value Framework (VF) defines the value elements of an organization [13]; that is, the elements that deserve proper attention and control because they influence value realization. According to [3], a VF comprises distinct value dimensions, each encompassing multiple value elements represented as tuples of value drivers and value metrics. Because the hierarchical trees resemble the structure of a VF, this tool was selected to integrate the three value dimensions (Fig. 5);
2. *Metric-level Misalignments*: by assessing stakeholder impacts for each metric through utility functions and integrating the resulting value curves, a representation like the one shown in Fig. 6 can be obtained. This representation enables the identification of stakeholder misalignments at the metric level. In this context, misalignment refers to potential trade-offs among stakeholders regarding benefits, costs, and risks. For example, a stakeholder who obtains limited gains, faces high costs, and bears high responsibility for mitigating risks would likely oppose the considered technology;
3. *Weighted Metrics*: as can be observed from Fig. 6, the large number of metrics makes the identification of stakeholder misalignments difficult. To synthesize

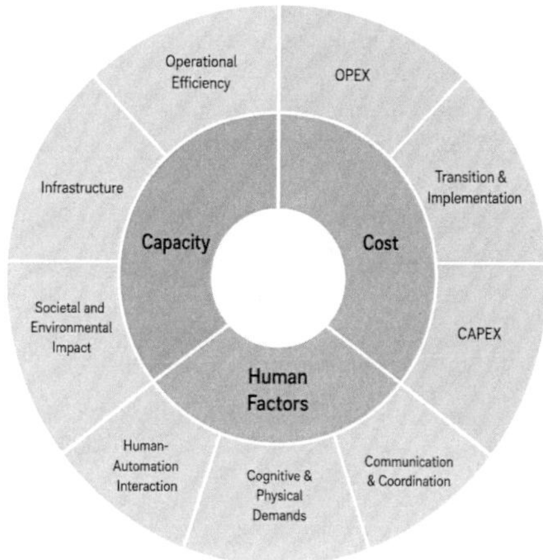

Fig. 5. Value framework for the DATO BuCa project. The figure illustrates three value dimensions and nine value drivers. Metrics are associated with each driver to complete the framework as illustrated in Fig. 1 for the capacity dimension.

the results, weights can be assigned to the different metrics according to their relative importance within each value driver;

4. *Driver-level Misalignments*: then, a weighted sum can be applied to the utility functions of the metrics associated with each value driver; see [6] for details. This aggregation enables the assessment of stakeholder impacts at the driver level, producing a more compact representation of potential stakeholder misalignments (Fig. 7).

Following the presentation of these elements, participants engaged in a discussion aimed at negotiating the proposed BuCa methodology.

5 Results and Discussions

Section 5.1 presents the results of applying the SG within the project context, while Sect. 5.2 discusses how SGs can facilitate boundary-object negotiation.

5.1 BuCa Methodology: Boundary-Object Negotiation

Feedback was collected during the reflection session through guided discussions. Participants indicated that the SG contributed to a clearer *understanding* of the BuCa methodology through hands-on application. For instance, the Human Factors team noted that "the SG helped define the relationship between the domain-specific metrics, the methodology, and stakeholder perspectives," while the Cost team highlighted that "the SG helped clarify the detail required for metric assessment." This improved understanding supported cross-functional dialogue during the reflection session, leading to deeper *analysis* and *negotiation* of the boundary object. As a result, the following decisions were made:

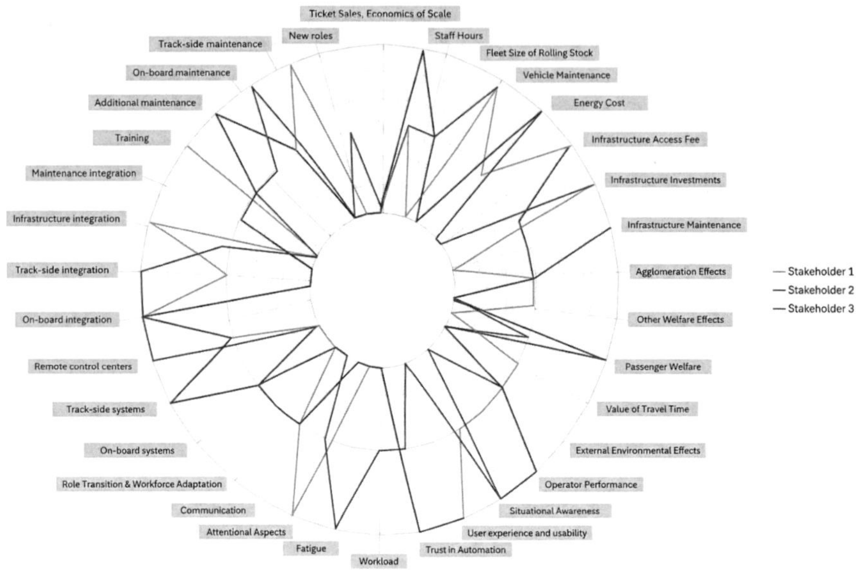

Fig. 6. Metric-level misalignment visualization. The figure integrates metrics from the capacity, cost, and human factors value dimensions, while the value curves represent stakeholder impacts across these metrics, enabling the identification of potential trade-offs. Metric labels are indicative and should not be interpreted in detail, as the focus of this paper is on illustrating the methodological approach.

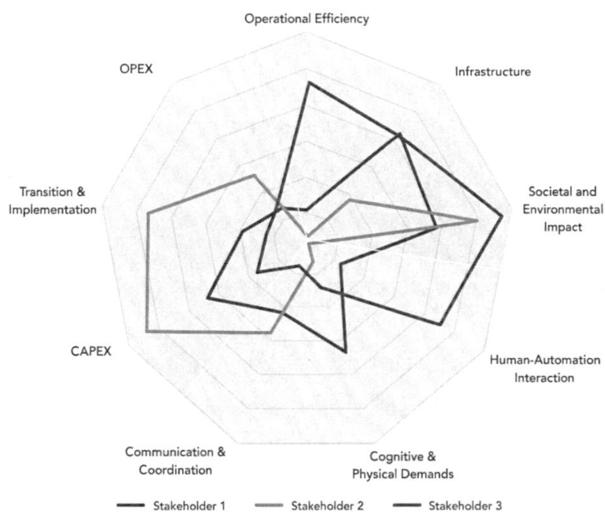

Fig. 7. Driver-level misalignment visualization. Driver labels are indicative and should not be interpreted in detail, as the focus of this paper is on illustrating the methodological approach.

- *BuCa methodology*: the proposed methodology was accepted as the boundary object, including the use of qualitative assessment scales for stakeholder impact assessment and visualizations to highlight potential misalignments;
- *Visualizations*: a linear, hierarchy-based layout similar to Fig. 4 (rather than a circular/radial representation) was selected for both the VF and misalignment plots. The rationale is that circular representations may suggest a comprehensive visualization of all benefit, cost, and risk elements, whereas this study focuses only on the capacity, cost, and human factors dimensions;
- *Time dimension*: although the temporal dimension (e.g., technology roadmap and dependencies) was outside the scope of the current game design, the reflection session highlighted its importance as future work.

Finally, although the use of analogy generated mixed reactions—some participants initially felt unfamiliar with the culinary domain—the strength of the approach lies in enabling teams to *anticipate* and *negotiate* the integration of domain-specific outcomes before they fully materialize, within a simplified and safe environment. In doing so, the SG: (i) helps overcome potential cognitive inertia through its hands-on approach; and (ii) reflects the principles of iterative innovation practices, such as Agile frameworks like Scrum, where shared understanding develops through cycles of experimentation, feedback, and refinement.

5.2 Serious Games for Boundary-Object Negotiation

To address the RQ and in line with the RtD approach, we now illustrate how SGs can facilitate boundary-object negotiation by reflecting on the experiences gained during the game and reflection sessions and relating them to the four negotiation processes identified by [20]. In particular, this exploratory case suggests that SGs can support:

- *Articulation*: by creating controlled, analogy-based settings in which participants externalize their knowledge through the boundary object, making tacit assumptions visible to others;
- *Alignment*: by creating situations in which the domain-specific knowledge of different teams is integrated through the boundary object toward a shared goal;
- *Contestation*: by creating experiential situations in which participants reflect on the game outcomes and debate differences in how the boundary object is interpreted, represented, or operationalized;
- *Transformation*: by enabling participants to modify the boundary object based on the collective insights generated through the game experience and subsequent reflection.

In conclusion, this exploratory case suggests that, especially in complex innovation consortia—where participants and knowledge are distributed across disciplinary and organizational boundaries and the boundary object is not a standardized tool—such experiential practices can act as catalysts for cross-functional dialogue, supporting shared understanding, fostering collective sense-making, and paving the way for the effective use of boundary objects.

6 Conclusion and Future Work

This paper examined how SGs can facilitate boundary-object negotiation in innovation projects. Following a Research through Design perspective, an SG was developed and applied within a European rail innovation project to support the negotiation of a Business Case (BuCa) methodology that acted as a boundary object. The findings indicate that the game facilitated participants' understanding of the methodology through hands-on experimentation and acted as a catalyst for cross-functional dialogue. In particular, it enabled processes of articulation, alignment, contestation, and transformation, thereby supporting collective sensemaking and refinement of the methodology. These results suggest that playful, participatory, and human-centered interventions can facilitate boundary-object negotiation in complex innovation consortia. Future research should investigate the approach transferability to other collaborative innovation settings and evaluate its long-term impact within the current project context.

Acknowledgments. Funded by the European Union. Views and opinion expressed are however those of the authors only and do not necessarily reflect those of the European Union. Neither the European Union nor the granting authority can be held responsible for them. The project FP2-R2DATO is supported by the Europe's Rail Joint Undertaking and its members.

Disclosure of Interests. The authors have no competing interests.

References

1. Abt, C.: Serious Games. University Press of America (1987)
2. Alin, P., Iorio, J., Taylor, J.E.: Digital boundary objects as negotiation facilitators: Spanning boundaries in virtual engineering project networks. Proj. Manag. J. **44**(3), 48–63 (2013)
3. Barbieri, G., Benavides, A.M., Esteves, L.A., Olaya, C., Zapata, F.: Organizational value framework for asset management decision-making. IFAC-Papersonline **58**(8), 395–400 (2024)
4. Barbieri, G., Jimenez, M.S., Braaksma, J.: From cooking to consensus: Using analogy to build shared vision in inter-organizational innovation projects. In: International Conference on Technology Management, Operations and Decisions (ICT-MOD), pp. 1–8. IEEE (2025)
5. Barbieri, G., Sanchez-Londoño, D., Cattaneo, L., Fumagalli, L., Romero, D.: A case study for problem-based learning education in fault diagnosis assessment. IFAC-PapersOnLine **53**(3), 107–112 (2020)
6. Barbieri, G., Vega, A.S., Gutierrez, J., Laserna, J., Mateus, L.M.: Strategic capital investments in asset management: a value-based approach. J. Qual. Maint. Eng. **31**(5), 1–22 (2025)
7. Bechky, B.A.: Sharing meaning across occupational communities: the transformation of understanding on a production floor. Organ. Sci. **14**(3), 312–330 (2003)
8. Brown, T., Katz, B.: Change by design. J. Prod. Innov. Manag. **28**(3), 381–383 (2011)

9. Caccamo, M., Pittino, D., Tell, F.: Boundary objects, knowledge integration, and innovation management: a systematic review of the literature. Technovation **122**, 102645 (2023)
10. Carlile, P.R.: A pragmatic view of knowledge and boundaries: boundary objects in new product development. Organ. Sci. **13**(4), 442–455 (2002)
11. Carlile, P.R.: Artifacts and knowledge negotiation across domains. In: Artifacts and Organizations, pp. 101–118. Psychology Press (2013)
12. Carnevale, P.J., Pruitt, D.G., et al.: Negotiation and mediation. Annu. Rev. Psychol. **43**(1), 531–582 (1992)
13. Crespo Márquez, A., Macchi, M., Parlikad, A.K.: Fundamental concepts and framework. In: Crespo Márquez, A., Macchi, M., Parlikad, A.K. (eds.) Value Based and Intelligent Asset Management, pp. 3–38. Springer, Cham (2020). https://doi.org/10.1007/978-3-030-20704-5_1
14. GFMAM: The Value of Asset Management to an Organization. Tech. rep., Global Forum on Maintenance & Asset Management (2016)
15. Hsiao, R.L., Tsai, D.H., Lee, C.F.: Collaborative knowing: the adaptive nature of cross-boundary spanning. J. Manage. Stud. **49**(3), 463–491 (2012)
16. ISO55000: Asset Management - Overview, Principles and Terminology. Standard, International Organization for Standardization (2024)
17. Jean, S., Medema, W., Adamowski, J., Chew, C., Delaney, P., Wals, A.: Serious games as a catalyst for boundary crossing, collaboration and knowledge co-creation in a watershed governance context. J. Environ. Manage. **223**, 1010–1022 (2018)
18. Kilis, E., Adamsone-Fiskovica, A., Stræte, E.P., Värnik, R., Kriipsalu, M.: The curious ambivalence of working with boundary objects: Interdisciplinarity, circularity, and processual alignment of perspectives. J. Environ. Stud. Sci., 1–14 (2025)
19. Kolb, D.A.: Experiential learning: Experience as the source of learning and development. FT Press (2014)
20. Lee, C.P.: Boundary negotiating artifacts: unbinding the routine of boundary objects and embracing chaos in collaborative work. Comput. Support. Cooperative Work (CSCW) **16**(3), 307–339 (2007)
21. Liedtka, J., Ogilvie, T.: The designing for growth field book: a step-by-step project guide. Columbia University Press (2019)
22. Nicolini, D., Mengis, J., Swan, J.: Understanding the role of objects in cross-disciplinary collaboration. Organ. Sci. **23**(3), 612–629 (2012)
23. Okhuysen, G.A., Bechky, B.A.: 10 coordination in organizations: an integrative perspective. Acad. Manag. Ann. **3**(1), 463–502 (2009)
24. Peffers, K., Tuunanen, T., Rothenberger, M.A., Chatterjee, S.: A design science research methodology for information systems research. J. Manag. Inf. Syst. **24**(3), 45–77 (2007)
25. Rojas, A.M., Barbieri, G.: A low-cost and scaled automation system for education in industrial automation. In: 24th IEEE International Conference on Emerging Technologies and Factory Automation (ETFA), pp. 439–444. IEEE (2019)
26. Star, S.L.: The structure of ill-structured solutions: boundary objects and heterogeneous distributed problem solving. In: Distributed Artificial Intelligence, pp. 37–54. Elsevier (1989)
27. Tuertscher, P., Garud, R., Kumaraswamy, A.: Justification and interlaced knowledge at atlas, cern. Organ. Sci. **25**(6), 1579–1608 (2014)
28. Zimmerman, J., Forlizzi, J., Evenson, S.: Research through design as a method for interaction design research in hci. In: Proceedings of the SIGCHI Conference on Human Factors in Computing Systems, pp. 493–502 (2007)

FlowExtract: Procedural Knowledge Extraction from Maintenance Flowcharts

Guillermo Gil de Avalle[1(✉)], Laura Maruster[1], Eric Sloot[2], and Christos Emmanouilidis[1]

[1] University of Groningen, Nettelbosje 2, Groningen, The Netherlands
{g.gil.de.avalle,l.maruster,c.emmanouilidis}@rug.nl
[2] Philips Consumer Lifestyle B.V., Oliemolenstraat 5, Drachten, The Netherlands
eric.sloot@philips.com

Abstract. Maintenance procedures in manufacturing facilities are often documented as flowcharts in static PDFs or scanned images. They encode procedural knowledge essential for asset lifecycle management, yet inaccessible to modern operator support systems. Vision-language models, the dominant paradigm for image understanding, struggle to reconstruct connection topology from such diagrams. We present *FlowExtract*, a pipeline for extracting directed graphs from ISO 5807-standardized flowcharts. The system separates element detection from connectivity reconstruction, using YOLOv8 and EasyOCR for standard domain-aligned node detection and text extraction, combined with a novel edge detection method that analyzes arrowhead orientations and traces connecting lines backward to source nodes. Evaluated on industrial troubleshooting guides, FlowExtract achieves very high node detection and substantially outperforms vision-language model baselines on edge extraction, offering organizations a practical path toward queryable procedural knowledge representations. The implementation is available at https://github.com/aixpert-rug/FlowExtract.

Keywords: Procedural knowledge · Knowledge extraction · Maintenance documentation · Flowchart understanding · Computer vision

1 Introduction

Flowcharts encode procedural knowledge as step-by-step instructions representing decision logic and action sequences, in a visual format that humans parse effortlessly. We trace arrows between boxes, interpreting shapes as actions or decisions and connections as control flow. This understanding relies on both semantic interpretation of node content and spatial reasoning about how elements relate [1]. Automated systems face a harder task: parsing flowcharts requires text recognition, identification of visual elements, and reconstruction of the connections between them [2]. Although standards such as ISO 5807 [3] define unambiguous symbol conventions, procedural documentation often remains as

Published by Springer Nature Switzerland AG 2027
G. Pezzotta et al. (Eds.): APMS 2026, IFIP AICT 808, pp. 354–369, 2027.
https://doi.org/10.1007/978-3-032-38594-9_24

scanned images or static PDF files, posing challenges for organizations seeking to extract the knowledge encoded within [4].

This challenge is particularly acute for asset lifecycle management. Maintenance procedures guide operators and technicians through equipment diagnostics, corrective actions, or preventive routines, encoding operational knowledge developed over decades of experience [5]. However, this knowledge typically remains trapped in vast libraries of unorganized documentation that staff must manually navigate [4]. Converting these procedures into queryable knowledge representations would enable intelligent decision support [6], but manual digitization is prohibitively expensive at scale [5], creating demand for automated extraction methods that can reliably parse the flowchart structure.

Vision-language models (VLMs) have emerged as the dominant paradigm for joint document and image understanding [7], encoding visual features and textual information through transformer architectures. VLMs demonstrate strong visual analysis capabilities, and can even interpret basic diagrams [2]. However, when applied to flowcharts with dense layouts, overlapping arrows, and/or complex branching structures, performance suffers substantially. Systematic evaluation reveals that while VLMs handle node and text detection reasonably well, they consistently fail to reconstruct the connection topology [2]. Pipeline approaches combining object detection with language models face similar limitations, as converting spatial layouts into textual descriptions discards positional information essential for determining connectivity [8]. The conclusion is clear: connectivity extraction remains an important bottleneck in flowchart digitization, one that semantic understanding alone cannot resolve.

Recognizing these limitations, prior work on engineering diagram digitization suggests an alternative. Hybrid architectures separate element detection from connectivity reconstruction, reserving neural methods for discrete objects, while using classical techniques for line tracing [9,10]. We implement this principle in *FlowExtract*, combining YOLOv8 [11] for node detection and EasyOCR [12] for text extraction with a novel edge detection method. Where prior approaches detect line networks first and attach directional information afterward [10], our method anchors on arrowheads as hooks for connection detection. It analyzes their orientations to determine the direction of the edges, and then traces the connecting lines backward to identify the source nodes. This design prioritizes precision over recall, proposing edges only where directional indicators have been detected rather than inferring connectivity from generic line extraction alone.

We evaluate FlowExtract on industrial troubleshooting diagrams from a consumer electronics manufacturing facility. These documents present challenges including dense technical terminology, tightly spaced nodes, and overlapping edges. FlowExtract achieves near-perfect node detection and substantial improvements over baselines on edge extraction, with a precision-oriented profile where detected connections are typically correct. This profile fits well within human-in-the-loop digitization workflows [13], where the system provides a reliable structural skeleton as a directed graph, allowing human validators to extend the extraction rather than detect and correct errors that could propagate into the final knowledge base [14]. Overall, this evaluation addresses the research question of whether a hybrid architecture separating element detection from connectivity reconstruction can substantially outperform VLMs on procedural flowchart digitization.

Our contributions are twofold. First, we introduce a novel arrowhead-anchored edge detection method for flowchart digitization that prioritizes precision over recall, producing directed graph representations where detected connections are reliable. Second, we provide empirical evidence that hybrid architectures separating element detection from connectivity reconstruction substantially outperform vision-language models on procedural flowcharts. Taken together, these contributions offer a starting point for organizations seeking to unlock procedural knowledge from legacy maintenance documentation, enabling its integration into modern decision support systems. The remainder of this paper is organized as follows. Section 2 reviews related work on vision-language models, spatial structure extraction, and human-in-the-loop workflows. Section 3 describes the dataset, pipeline architecture, and evaluation methodology. Section 4 presents the results, followed by discussion in Sect. 5 and conclusions in Sect. 6.

2 Background

2.1 Vision-Language Model-Based Extraction

Vision-language models have achieved strong performance in combined document-image interpretation, inferring semantically meaningful descriptions of visual content [7]. However, this semantic focus encounters challenges when connection topology becomes complex. Systematic evaluation on a dataset of 13,858 flowcharts, comprising both scientific diagrams and synthetic examples, reveals a consistent pattern across both closed models (GPT-4V, Claude-3, Gemini-Pro) and open models (LLaVA, Qwen-VL, InternLM, DeepSeek). Although VLMs handle node and text detection reasonably well, they consistently fail to reconstruct connection topology, with edge-level F1 scores remaining below 0.30 in all tested architectures [2]. These limitations persist amid strong performance on related tasks, which also require visual reasoning and text recognition.

Hybrid approaches, which combine the analytical abilities of VLMs or text-only LLMs with other methods that provide enhanced visual cues, also face similar limitations. A representative example uses the Segment Anything Model for zero-shot segmentation, OCR for text extraction, and GPT-3.5-Turbo for graph reconstruction from element descriptions [8]. This conversion from spatial layout to unordered textual descriptions discards the essential positional information to determine connectivity. Arrow-guided prompting takes an alternative approach by explicitly encoding arrow directions into VLM prompts [15], demonstrating improvements over unaugmented baselines. However, even with explicit directional cues, VLMs struggle with overlapping or densely packed arrow patterns. The common limitation across these approaches is the reliance on language models to infer connection topology from representations that encode spatial information implicitly or incompletely. Textual descriptions inherently lose the precise positional relationships of 2D layouts, and proximity becomes ambiguous when elements are described sequentially rather than spatially.

One noteworthy exception applies the Relationformer neural architecture to jointly extract symbols and connections from piping and instrumentation diagrams, outperforming modular baselines by more than 25% in edge detection [16]. However, this study pre-trained on around 170,000 samples and fine-tuned on tens of thousands more, with ablation studies showing catastrophic performance degradation when training data was reduced. Such data requirements are infeasible in most industrial digitization projects, where labeled diagrams are much more limited. These constraints motivate approaches that leverage characteristics of the domain knowledge for methodological design, rather than learning connectivity patterns from data alone.

2.2 Spatial Structure Extraction

Where language models infer connectivity using their internal understanding and/or fine-tuning, alternative approaches usually exploit the geometric structure of diagrams directly. Diagrams across technical domains share a common visual grammar wherein discrete nodes are joined by connections, generally lines or arrows. This convention appears in flowcharts standardized under ISO 5807 [3], in piping and instrumentation schematics, and in hand-drawn sketches alike. *Nodes* can be understood as bounded regions with characteristic shapes and fixed aspect ratios. This is where neural network architectures excel, given their capacity for learned pattern matching in symbol detection and text recognition tasks [9]. *Edges* or *Connecting lines*, by contrast, vary in length and orientation but can be compactly described by geometric parameters, making them amenable to line tracing techniques such as the Hough transform [17] that follow paths through pixel space rather than recognizing learned patterns. Recognizing this asymmetry, recent systems have adopted hybrid architectures, reserving neural networks for discrete elements while relying on classical image processing techniques for line extraction [10].

Within this decomposition, different methods emphasize different elements, although arrowhead detection has emerged as a particularly effective strategy. Arrowheads can be treated as nodes themselves, since they are bounded regions with characteristic shapes amenable to pattern recognition. Work on handwritten diagram recognition has demonstrated that extending object detectors with keypoint predictors to localize arrowheads and tails as spatial coordinates can double the overall edge accuracy to 78.6% [18]. Even the pipeline approach described in the previous section employed arrows as explicit cues for vision-language models, though without achieving comparable performance [15]. The consistency of these results likely stems from the ubiquity of arrowheads as standardized directional cues, which justifies their use as explicit anchors from which the remainder of each connection can be inferred, thereby improving overall directed graph extraction.

2.3 Human-in-the-Loop Extraction

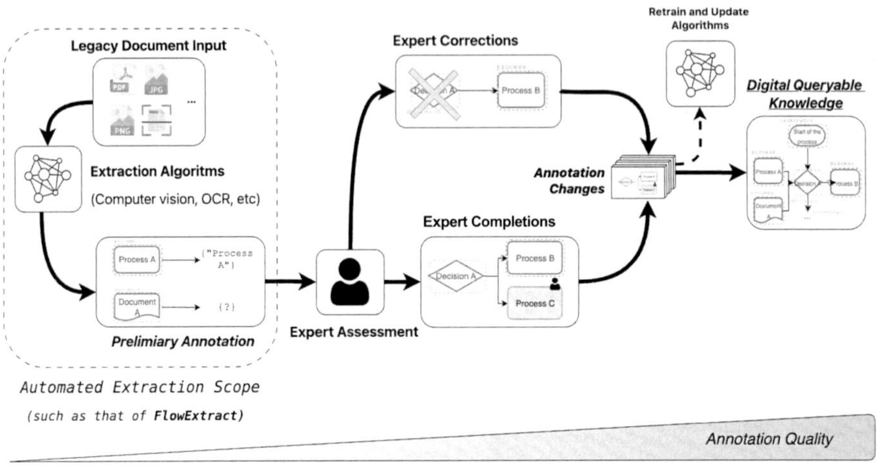

Fig. 1. Human-in-the-loop workflow for knowledge extraction from legacy maintenance documentation.

Even where decomposition approaches prove more effective, they do not guarantee operational reliability. In industrial maintenance contexts, where extracted procedural knowledge informs decisions with safety consequences on top of effectiveness and efficiency requirements, fully automated extraction alone remains insufficient to obtain the data quality that would effectively mitigate such risks [6]. *Human-in-the-loop* workflows address this gap by positioning domain experts that validate outputs and contribute contextual knowledge, which automated methods cannot reliably capture [5,13], thus maximizing the quality of extraction. Figure 1 illustrates such workflow, in which automated extraction provides a preliminary extraction that experts correct and complete to obtain the final *digital queryable knowledge* that may be used in operator support systems.

However, effective oversight of automated AI systems presents cognitive challenges that constrain how such human-in-the-loop workflows should be designed, even in the conception of the initial automated extraction. Research on *automation bias*, the tendency to over-rely on automated recommendations, demonstrates that validators often accept incorrect outputs without sufficient verification [14]. This bias manifests itself asymmetrically. Commission errors, where validators accept incorrect outputs, prove harder to detect than omission errors, where validators notice missing information [19]. Training interventions can reduce commission errors but show limited effectiveness against omission errors [14]. Systems producing false positives therefore impose heavier cognitive burdens than systems producing false negatives; the former requires

Table 1. Class Distribution Across Dataset Splits

Class	Training	Validation	Test	Total
Arrowhead	357	48	93	498
Process	177	23	45	245
Document	119	11	38	168
Decision	118	15	29	162
Terminator	35	4	9	48
Connector	17	2	5	24
Total	823	103	219	1145

detecting errors embedded within plausible outputs, while the latter requires extending an incomplete but reliable skeleton. We therefore posit that extraction systems designed to fit within human-in-the-loop workflows should adopt conservative extraction strategies, prioritizing precision over recall to position validators where human cognitive abilities excel.

3 Methodology

3.1 Dataset

The present study involves a collection of troubleshooting maintenance diagrams collected from an operational consumer electronic domestic devices manufacturing facility. Using real-world operational data ensures our evaluation reflects the actual challenges of production environments, including authentic visual characteristics and domain-specific terminology. The dataset comprises 35 diagrams written in Dutch, consisting of 1145 nodes (flowchart elements, such as process boxes, decision diamonds, and terminators), edges (directional arrows connecting nodes), and decision labels (text annotations "ja"/"nee" in Dutch, appearing along edge paths to indicate branching logic).

This dataset was manually annotated using Label Studio [20], an open-source data labeling tool, for bounding box detection of all element types and ground truth specifying node connection and edge labels. In total, 1145 node instances were captured across all diagrams, plus an extra 62 "ja"/"nee" annotations. We split the dataset into 25 training images (823 instances, Table 1), 3 validation images (103 instances), and 7 test images (219 instances). The test set is held out during training and used only for final evaluation. Note that although the operational dataset is small, each image provides multiple instances of symbols, offering a somewhat richer basis for training, validation, and testing.

3.2 FlowExtract Pipeline

Our pipeline processes troubleshooting diagram images and outputs directed graphs representing procedural flow. Figure 2 illustrates the processing workflow:

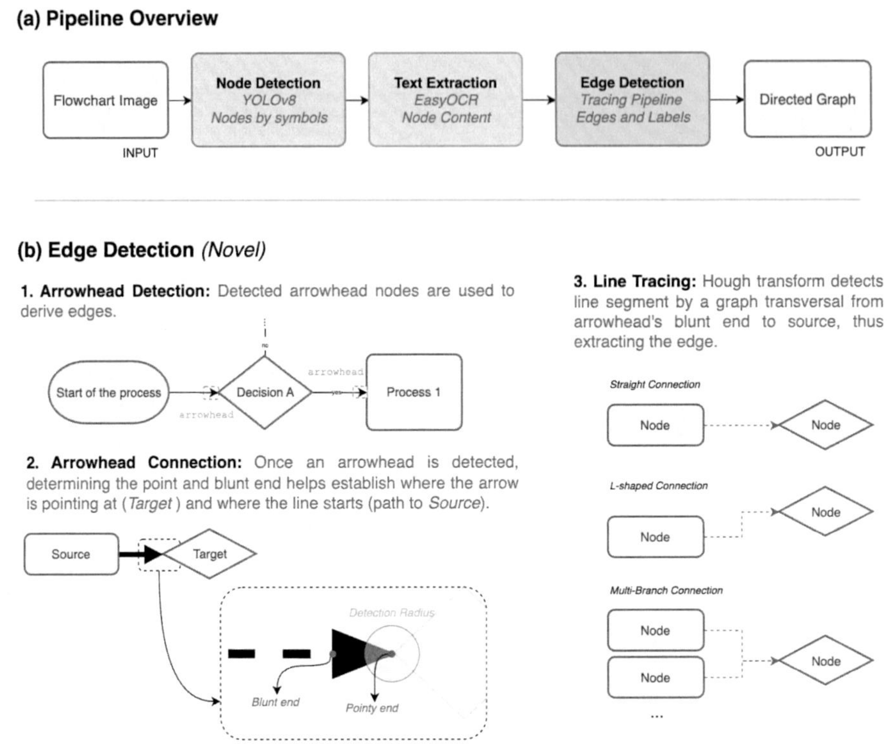

Fig. 2. FlowExtract pipeline overview (a) and edge detection methodology (b), showing arrowhead orientation analysis and line tracing for straight, L-shaped, and multi-branch connections.

(a) the three-stage pipeline overview comprising node detection, text extraction, and edge detection; and (b) the edge detection methodology showing arrowhead orientation analysis and line tracing.

Node Detection. The first stage detects and classifies flowchart elements using YOLOv8 [11], chosen for its maturity, extensive documentation, and established track record in domain adaptation that facilitates the inclusion of custom symbol sets. We define six element classes based on the subset of ISO 5807 [3] symbols present in our diagrams, plus arrowheads which enable subsequent edge detection, as shown in Fig. 3: Process (rectangular boxes containing action descriptions), Decision (diamond shapes containing yes/no questions), Document (rectangles with wavy bottom edges referencing external procedures), Terminator (rounded rectangles marking start/end points), Connector (circular elements with identifiers for cross-page references), and Arrowhead (arrow tips indicating edge direction, essential for edge detection but not included as graph nodes). We initialize YOLOv8s (small variant) with weights pre-trained on the COCO dataset [21], a large-scale object detection benchmark containing 80 object categories across 330K images, providing general-purpose visual features, offering some transferability to our domain. Given the limited size of the training instances, we use the small variant to reduce overfit risk, as smaller models with fewer parameters are less prone to memorizing training examples when data is limited. However, our data set exhibits severe class imbalance, with 21 arrowheads (most common class; 357 samples) for every connector (rarest class, 24 samples), as seen in Table 1. We address this through a **Data Augmentation Strategy**, combining *Mosaic augmentation* [22], which combines four training images per sample, thereby increasing our effective dataset size, with *Brightness variation* (HSV, brightness metric, at ±30%) to simulate varying scan conditions. We intentionally avoid other types of augmentation (e.g., geometric, which rotates, translates, and flips the image) due to tight bounding box annotations, so as to prevent loss of spatial data characteristics.

Text Extraction. The second stage extracts textual content using EasyOCR [12], a deep learning-based OCR system that provides multilingual support and handles the text characteristics common in technical diagrams (different font sizes, orientations, and image quality of scanned documents). For each detected element (excluding arrowheads), we crop the corresponding image region and apply OCR to extract the contained text. Additionally, we perform a full-image scan to detect decision labels ("ja"/"nee" in Dutch, corresponding to yes/no) that appear along arrow paths rather than within bounded elements. These labels are stored separately for later assignment to the edges during edge detection.

Edge Detection. The third stage reconstructs the directed graph structure by determining which elements are connected by arrows. As pointed during the Background section, we derive connections from detected arrowheads and line segments. Detected arrowhead nodes from the first stage are used to derive edges, as shown in Fig. 2(b). For each detected arrowhead, we determine its orientation by identifying which end is closest to a node element: the "pointy" end (closest to a box) indicates the target node, while the "blunt" end indicates the direction toward the source. From the blunt end of each arrowhead, we trace connected line segments back toward potential source nodes by applying the Probabilistic Hough Transform [17] to detect line segments in a preprocessed binary image. Starting from the arrowhead position, we perform a graph-based traversal of detected segments, following connected paths until reaching proximity to a node element. This approach handles straight connections, L-shaped paths, and multi-branch configurations as illustrated in Fig. 2(b).

Once the source and target nodes are identified for an arrowhead, we create a directed edge. For decision nodes with multiple outgoing edges, we assign labels (ja/nee) based on the spatial relationship between detected label positions and arrow directions. Specifically, we score each label by its distance to the arrow midpoint and then run the text extractor to identify whether the label corresponds to ja or nee. Decision nodes may have multiple outgoing edges sharing a common source segment before branching; our traversal algorithm handles this

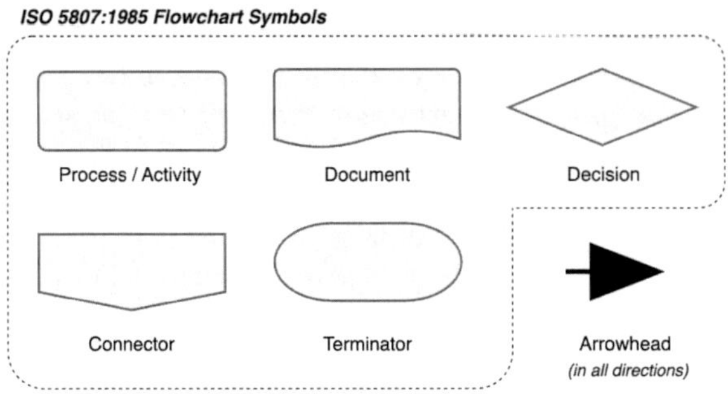

Fig. 3. Flowchart symbols taxonomy (based on ISO 5807:1985) and arrowheads.

by exploring all connected paths from each arrowhead independently, allowing reconstruction of complex branching structures. This arrowhead-anchored approach prioritizes precision over recall by proposing edges only where directional indicators have been explicitly detected, rather than inferring connections from line segments that may represent diagram borders, visual artifacts, or other non-connective structures.

3.3 Training Configuration

We train YOLOv8s for 250 epochs with image size 640×640, batch size 8, and cosine annealing learning rate scheduling with initial learning rate of 0.01, following YOLOv8 default recommendations [11]. The image size balances detection accuracy with computational efficiency given our hardware constraints (Apple M3 chip with 8 CPU cores and 10 GPU cores), completing training in approximately 40 min.

The pipeline outputs a JSON structure containing nodes (list of elements with unique ID, type, bounding box coordinates, and extracted text) and edges (list of directed connections with source ID, target ID, edge type, and optional label). This representation enables direct ingestion into knowledge constructs: nodes map to ontological concepts (e.g., process steps as procedural actions), edges represent causal or temporal relationships, and the JSON-LD format facilitates RDF conversion for semantic web integration [5].

3.4 Evaluation

We evaluate each pipeline component separately, structuring them as individual detection and classification tasks. For node detection, we measure precision, recall, and F1 for detecting the five node classes (excluding arrowheads), along with classification accuracy for assigning correct types to detected nodes. For edge detection, we measure precision, recall, and F1 for recovering directed edges between nodes, along with accuracy of assigning correct labels (ja/nee/none) to detected edges. OCR accuracy is measured as character-level match rate between

Table 2. Detection Performance on Test Set

Task	Precision	Recall	F1	Accuracy
Node Detection	98.4%	99.2%	98.8%	–
Node Classification	–	–	–	97.6%
Text Extraction	–	–	–	99.2%
Edge Detection	85.5%	54.6%	66.7%	–
Arrowhead Detection	–	–	–	73.1%
Edge Label Assignment		–	–	73.8%

Table 3. Results Comparison with VLM Baselines from [23]

Method	Node F1	Edge F1
Qwen2-VL-7B	0.340	0.107
Pixtral-12B	0.295	0.015
FlowExtract	**0.988**	**0.667**

extracted and ground truth text. For detection metrics, we match predicted and ground truth bounding boxes using intersection-over-union (IoU), the ratio of overlap area to union area. A detection is considered correct if IoU > 0.5, similar to comparable papers [16]. Higher thresholds would demand stricter localization, while lower values would risk accepting misaligned boxes.

To contextualize our results, we compare them against VLM baselines evaluated on the same set of documents in previous work [23]. Two state-of-the-art open models were tested: Pixtral-12B and Qwen2-VL-7B. Models were prompted to extract entities (nodes) and relations (edges) from flowchart images in an instruction-guided setting, as seen in the original work [23]. The prompt template requested structured JSON output containing node types, bounding boxes, text content, and directional connections. No token limit was imposed, and models received the full flowchart image with the extraction task description. Evaluation used the same ground truth annotations as our pipeline, with matching based on textual closeness of extracted results and category selection correctness.

4 Results

Table 2 presents the main evaluation results on the held-out test set. Our proposed pipeline achieves near-perfect node detection with 98.8% F1, compared to 34.0% for the best VLM baseline (Table 3). The different node classes achieve detection rates above 97%, with the exception of arrowheads, which only achieve 73.1% accuracy. This demonstrates that YOLOv8 with mosaic augmentation effectively handles the severe class imbalance, successfully detecting rare classes (terminator, connector), amid limited training examples. Node type classification accuracy reaches 97.6%, indicating that detection errors are primarily localization failures rather than misclassification.

For edge detection, our approach achieves 66.7% F1 versus 10.7% for the best VLM, representing a six-fold improvement. The results show high asymmetry between precision (85.5%) and recall (54.6%), indicating that when edges are detected, they are usually correct, but many ground truth edges are missed. This asymmetry reflects the arrowhead-anchored design, which proposes edges only where directional indicators have been explicitly detected rather than inferring connectivity from line structures alone. For detected edges, label assignment (ja/nee) achieves 73.8% accuracy. Analysis reveals that edge recall is directly limited by arrowhead detection performance: since edge detection requires detecting the arrowhead that indicates connection direction, missed arrowheads directly translate to missed edges. Individual analysis reveals that missed arrowheads tend to be either small at standard zoom levels or partially occluded by overlapping line segments. Text extraction achieves 99.2% character-level accuracy, indicating that OCR is not a significant error source; the high performance reflects the clean, printed nature of the source documents.

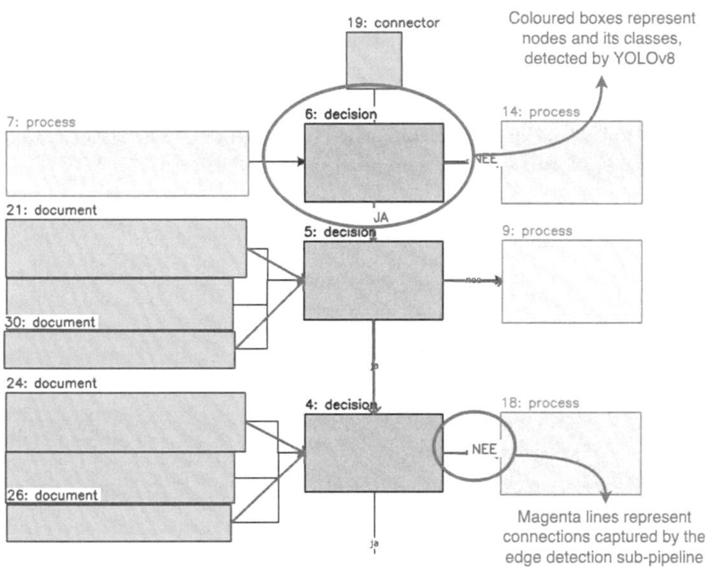

Fig. 4. Example of extraction results from one of the maintenance diagrams. Detected nodes are shown as bounding boxes and extracted edges as magenta lines overlaid on the original structure. The original textual content within the nodes has been computationally redacted (opaque fills) to anonymize proprietary procedural data, while preserving the structural morphology.

Figure 4 provides a qualitative visualization of the extraction pipeline applied to a sample maintenance diagram. The visual overlay confirms the node detection stage successfully isolates discrete elements within dense layouts. More critically, the extracted connections (magenta lines) demonstrate the system's high precision to trace procedural flow, even in long documents. It also seems to handle multi-branching logic, though capturing seems to be limited to a maximum of 2-3 connections into a single node when dealing with highly dense clusters of edges, thus affecting recall. Furthermore, the figure confirms that when connections are established, the spatial heuristics accurately anchor the path to the correct source and target elements without generating hallucinatory cross-links, as seen by the fact that no magenta lines seem to fall out of the connection paths. This confirms that, while arrowhead omissions restrict total recall (such as missing branches within dense graphical clusters), the successfully parsed connections draft a precise flowchart skeleton.

5 Discussion

The results provide empirical support for the architectural principle identified in Sect. 2.2, namely that standardized technical diagrams benefit from separating element detection from connectivity reconstruction. Node detection achieves very high performance at 98.8% F1, demonstrating that element recognition is effectively solved for this diagram class when approached with conventional object detection methods. The challenge lies entirely in reconstructing connectivity. This confirms the pattern documented across engineering diagram domains, where symbol detection and text recognition have advanced substantially through neural architectures while connection extraction remains the primary bottleneck [9]. Our contribution is therefore not only an ISO 5807-based diagram parser, but also targeted evidence that the separation principle transfers successfully to procedural flowcharts, with implications for how extraction systems should be architected when standardized visual conventions are present.

The 66.7% edge F1 could reflect either a failure of structural reasoning or a failure of perception. The precision and recall split reveals the answer. Edge detection achieves 85.5% precision but only 54.6% recall, indicating that when arrowheads are detected, the Hough-based line tracing reliably recovers the correct source node. The bottleneck is upstream: arrowheads are missed due to small apparent size or partial occlusion by overlapping line segments. This finding is sharper than the general observation that vision-language models struggle with spatial reasoning. We have isolated the performance ceiling to a specific perceptual task rather than to the graph reconstruction logic itself. The line tracing component functions correctly; improvements to arrowhead detection translate directly into system-level gains without requiring changes to the connectivity algorithm.

The arrowheads-first architecture reflects a deliberate design choice rather than the only viable option. An alternative strategy, exemplified in recent P&ID digitization work [10], detects the line network first and attaches directional information afterward. That approach would likely achieve higher recall, since a missed arrow does not eliminate the underlying line structure from consideration.

However, lines-first introduces ambiguity in dense diagram regions where multiple lines converge toward shared junction points, requiring additional heuristics to determine which line segments constitute which edges. Arrowheads-first guarantees that each detected arrowhead corresponds to exactly one directed edge, eliminating edge-count ambiguity at the cost of recall when arrowheads go undetected. For procedural flowcharts where directionality carries semantic weight and edge identity must be unambiguous, we argue this tradeoff is appropriate. The choice should be revisited for diagram types where the underlying network matters independently of connection direction, which may not present arrowheads.

The precision-oriented performance profile directly implements the conservative extraction philosophy established in Sect. 2.3. High precision ensures that detected edges are trustworthy, allowing human validators to extend the extracted graph rather than correct it. This aligns with the principle of positioning human and algorithmic components where each exhibits comparative cognitive advantage [6,13]. The system contributes a reliable structural skeleton; human reviewers contribute completeness and contextual judgment that automated methods cannot reliably provide. For asset lifecycle management applications where propagated errors carry operational and potential safety consequences, this division of labor supports the kind of human-AI collaboration that industrial knowledge management increasingly requires [5,13]. The directed graph output can be directly ingested into maintenance knowledge management systems, where process nodes populate a queryable procedure library and decision nodes with their ja/nee-labeled edges encode the branching logic of diagnostic workflows, enabling operator support systems to traverse the relevant path from a reported fault state to the indicated corrective action.

Notwithstanding the encouraging results, we also acknowledge some limitations. Firstly, arrowhead detection recall directly caps edge performance and cannot be circumvented through downstream improvements. Alternative architectures such as lines-first detection offer different tradeoffs but not unambiguous improvements; the appropriate choice depends on whether precision or recall matters more for the downstream application. A secondary limitation is scope. FlowExtract targets digitally-created flowcharts employing arrow-based directional conventions, covering ISO 5807 and similar technical diagram standards. Adaptation to substantially different diagram types, such as handwritten flowcharts, would require retraining the detection model with appropriate samples. Additionally, both YOLOv8 and the Hough transform are sensitive to image quality; degraded or poorly scanned documents would likely require preprocessing steps prior to extraction. Finally, the pipeline processes documents in isolation and does not resolve cross-document references encoded through connector symbols. Future work could extend the system to match connector labels across documents. Merging partial graphs would enable extraction of complete procedures stemming from different documents; a common pattern in industrial maintenance where troubleshooting guides often reference sub-procedures stored separately. Assessment and validation with human operators is also among the plans for further work.

6 Conclusion

We introduced *FlowExtract*, a pipeline for extracting directed graphs from standardized maintenance flowcharts. The system separates element detection from connectivity reconstruction, combining standard domain-adapted node detection with a novel arrowhead-anchored edge detection method that traces connecting lines backward from detected directional indicators. Evaluated on industrial troubleshooting diagrams, FlowExtract achieves near-perfect node detection and outperforms vision-language model baselines on edge extraction by a factor of six, with a precision-oriented profile where detected connections are typically correct.

These results validate the architectural principle that standardized technical diagrams benefit from treating element detection and connectivity reconstruction as distinct tasks, with neural methods suited to bounded symbols and geometric methods suited to continuous line structures. The precision-oriented extraction profile fits well within human-in-the-loop workflows, where conservative automated extraction reduces the cognitive burden of validation by positioning human reviewers to extend an incomplete but reliable skeleton rather than detecting commission errors. For organizations seeking to digitize legacy maintenance documentation, this hybrid pipeline offers a practical starting point for unlocking procedural knowledge and integrating it into asset lifecycle management systems.

Acknowledgments. This research was funded by the European Union's Horizon Europe research and innovation programme under the AIXPERT project (Grant Agreement No. 101214389), which aims to develop an agentic, multi-layered, GenAI-powered framework for creating explainable, accountable, and transparent AI systems. The authors wish to extend special thanks to Philips Lifestyle Consumer B.V. for the valuable collaboration and support in this work.

Disclosure of Interests. The authors have no competing interests to declare that are relevant to the content of this article.

References

1. Chen, Bet al.: SpatialVLM: endowing vision-language models with spatial reasoning capabilities. In: Proceedings of the IEEE/CVF Conference on Computer Vision and Pattern Recognition (CVPR), pp. 14455–14465 (2024)
2. Pan, H., Zhang, Q., Caragea, C., Dragut, E., Latecki, L.J.: FlowLearn: evaluating Large Vision-language models on flowchart understanding. In: Proceedings of the 27th European Conference on Artificial Intelligence (ECAI), pp. 73–80. IOS Press (2024)
3. ISO: ISO 5807:1985 Information Processing – Documentation Symbols and Conventions for Data, Program and System Flowcharts, Program Network Charts and System Resources Charts. International Organization for Standardization (1985)
4. Mentzas, G., Hribernik, K., Stahre, J., Romero, D., Soldatos, J.: Editorial: human-centered artificial intelligence in industry 5.0. Front. Artif. Intell. **7**, 1429186 (2024)

5. Celino, I., Carriero, V.A., Azzini, A., Baroni, I., Scrocca, M.: Procedural knowledge management in Industry 5.0: Challenges and opportunities for knowledge graphs. Web Seman. Sci. Serv. Agents World Wide Web **84**, 100850 (2025)
6. Emmanouilidis, C., et al.: Enabling the human in the loop: linked data and knowledge in industrial cyber-physical systems. Annu. Rev. Control. **47**, 249–265 (2019)
7. Huang, Y., Lv, T., Cui, L., Lu, Y., Wei, F.: LayoutLMv3: pre-training for Document AI with unified text and image masking. In: Proceedings of the ACM International Conference on Multimedia, pp. 4083–4091 (2022)
8. Arbaz, A.: GenFlowchart: parsing and understanding flowchart using generative AI. In: Proceedings of the International Conference on Knowledge Science, Engineering and Management (KSEM), pp. 95–107 (2024)
9. Jamieson, L., Moreno-García, C.F., Elyan, E.: A review of deep learning methods for digitisation of complex documents and engineering diagrams. Artif. Intell. Rev. **57**(136) (2024)
10. Park, S., Kim, H., Paik, S., Kim, K.: Deep learning-based method to recognize line objects and flow arrows from image-format piping and instrumentation diagrams for digitization. Appl. Sci. **11**(21), 10054 (2021)
11. Jocher, G., Chaurasia, A., Qiu, J.: Ultralytics YOLOv8 (2023). https://github.com/ultralytics/ultralytics
12. JaidedAI: EasyOCR: Ready-to-use OCR with 80+ Supported Languages (2020). https://github.com/JaidedAI/EasyOCR
13. Emmanouilidis, C., Waschull, S., Bokhorst, J.A.C., Wortmann, J.C.: Human in the AI loop in production environments. In: Dolgui, A., Bernard, A., Lemoine, D., von Cieminski, G., Romero, D. (eds.) APMS 2021. IAICT, vol. 633, pp. 331–342. Springer, Cham (2021). https://doi.org/10.1007/978-3-030-85910-7_35
14. Parasuraman, R., Manzey, D.H.: Complacency and bias in human use of automation: an attentional integration. Hum. Factors **52**(3), 381–410 (2010)
15. Hu, X., et al.: Enhancing Flowchart Understanding in Vision-Language Models through Arrow-Based Augmentation, arXiv preprint arXiv:2501.08829 (2025)
16. Stürmer, J.M., Graumann, M., Koch, T.: From engineering diagrams to graphs: digitizing P&IDs with transformers. In: Proceedings of the IEEE 12th International Conference on Data Science and Advanced Analytics (DSAA). IEEE (2025)
17. Duda, R.O., Hart, P.E.: Use of the hough transformation to detect lines and curves in pictures. Commun. ACM **15**(1), 11–15 (1972)
18. Schäfer, B., Keuper, M., Stuckenschmidt, H.: Arrow R-CNN for handwritten diagram recognition. Int. J. Doc. Anal. Recogn. **24**, 3–17 (2021)
19. Lyell, D., Coiera, E.: Automation bias and verification complexity: a systematic review. J. Am. Med. Inform. Assoc. **24**(2), 423–431 (2017)
20. Heartex: Label Studio: Data labeling software (2023). https://github.com/heartexlabs/label-studio
21. Lin, T.-Y., et al.: Microsoft COCO: common objects in context. In: Fleet, D., Pajdla, T., Schiele, B., Tuytelaars, T. (eds.) ECCV 2014. LNCS, vol. 8693, pp. 740–755. Springer, Cham (2014). https://doi.org/10.1007/978-3-319-10602-1_48
22. Bochkovskiy, A., Wang, C.Y., Liao, H.Y.M.: YOLOv4: Optimal Speed and Accuracy of Object Detection. arXiv preprint arXiv:2004.10934 (2020)
23. Gil de Avalle, G., Maruster, L., Emmanouilidis, C.: Procedural Knowledge Extraction from Industrial Troubleshooting Guides Using Vision Language Models. arXiv preprint arXiv:2601.22754 (2026)

Human-in-the-Loop Condition-Based Maintenance Framework for Collaborative Robots: Integrating Diagnostic Uncertainty, Human Feedback, and Economic Evaluation

Cristina Tonelli, Silvia Scarpa, Adalberto Polenghi(✉), and Andrea Mor

Department of Management, Economics and Industrial Engineering, Politecnico di Milano, P.za Leonardo da Vinci 32, Milan 20133, Italy
{cristina.tonelli,silvia1.scarpa,adalberto.polenghi,andrea.mor}@polimi.it

Abstract. Manufacturing environments increasingly rely on collaborative robots, whose variable motion conditions challenge traditional deterministic diagnostic models. This paper presents a Human-in-the-Loop Condition-Based Maintenance framework designed to manage diagnostic uncertainty and to adapt maintenance decisions through selective operator feedback. The approach combines a convolutional autoencoder for anomaly detection with an uncertainty-based decision logic and a feedback policy that updates the diagnostic model during operation. Experiments using trajectory and failure-induced data from a Franka Emika Panda cobot assess the framework under varying training-data availability, streaming conditions, adaptive learning dynamics, and cost considerations. Results show that uncertainty modelling enhances detection stability, while selective feedback improves learning efficiency and reduces operator workload. The framework maintains high accuracy across heterogeneous operating conditions and effectively balances automated diagnosis with human supervisory input.

Keywords: Maintenance · Condition-Based Maintenance · Collaborative Robots · Cobot · Artificial Intelligence · Smart Manufacturing

1 Introduction

The increasing adoption of collaborative robots in industrial environments has changed the conditions under which maintenance systems operate. Unlike traditional industrial robots, cobots perform tasks with variable motion profiles, changing interaction forces, and direct contact with human operators. While this variability enhances shop-floor flexibility [22], it generates behaviours that are irregular and challenging to diagnose using conventional methods; indeed, most

G. Pezzotta et al. (Eds.): APMS 2026, IFIP AICT 808, pp. 370–384, 2027.
https://doi.org/10.1007/978-3-032-38594-9_25

diagnostic methods rely on deterministic thresholds or supervised models that assume stable operating conditions and access to representative fault data [18]. These assumptions rarely hold for collaborative robots, where real degradation events are infrequent, heterogeneous, and difficult to acquire [2].

Currently, scientific literature about condition-based maintenance systems for collaborative robots shows room for improvement, driven by the above limitations. Existing approaches focus primarily on anomaly detection while providing limited mechanisms for uncertainty quantification, adaptation to changing regimes, or structured operator involvement. Most models enforce binary classifications without isolating ambiguous cases. At the same time, human expertise, particularly valuable in variable manufacturing contexts, is typically engaged informally rather than through targeted and economically justified interventions. This reactive approach leads to either excessive reliance on automated decisions under uncertainty or inefficient use of operator time for routine cases.

Given these premises, the goal of this research work is to propose a Human-in-the-Loop Condition-Based Maintenance (HIL-CBM) framework that explicitly models diagnostic uncertainty and involves human judgment as a constitutive element. Two main research questions were set:

- **RQ1**: How can diagnostic uncertainty be formally modelled and managed within a CBM architecture for collaborative robots operating under variable conditions?
- **RQ2**: To what extent does structured human feedback improve diagnostic reliability and economic sustainability compared to fully automated maintenance decisions?

The proposed framework integrates anomaly detection with an uncertainty gate that isolates ambiguous samples, enabling selective human feedback where it provides the greatest value; in this regard, training data availability and uncertainty calibration were analysed. An adaptive retraining mechanism incorporates operator corrections to improve model performance over time, while an economic model evaluates the operational costs associated with different intervention strategies. The objective is to maintain diagnostic reliability under variable operating conditions while ensuring sustainable operator workload and operational expenses.

Results demonstrate that uncertainty modelling improves diagnostic reliability, selective feedback enhances adaptability while limiting operator workload, and the proposed approach achieves high accuracy with sustainable operational costs. These findings advance research on cobots' maintenance by formalising diagnostic uncertainty, structuring human involvement, and connecting technical performance to economic viability.

The remainder of the paper is organised as follows. Section 2 reviews related work and identifies the main research gaps. Section 3 presents the proposed HIL-CBM framework. Section 4 describes the experimental setup and reports the main results. Section 5 presents the conclusions, limitations, and future developments.

2 State of the Art for Cobot Maintenance Applications

Research on maintenance for collaborative robots has expanded considerably in recent years, driven by the diffusion of data-driven approaches and increasing cobot deployment in flexible manufacturing environments [11]. To assess the current state of research systematically, a structured literature review following the PRISMA protocol was conducted across Scopus, Web of Science and IEEE Xplore, using the following query: *("collaborative robot*" OR "cobot*") AND (maintenance OR "condition based maintenance" OR cbm OR "predictive maintenance" OR diagnostics OR prognostics OR phm OR "anomaly detection" OR "fault detection" OR "fault diagnosis").* The search covered publications up to early 2025 and retrieved 684 documents, subsequently screened for cobot as unit of analysis, manufacturing context, maintenance focus and experimental validation. As shown in Fig. 1, this process yielded 24 relevant papers forming the eligible papers for the analysis.

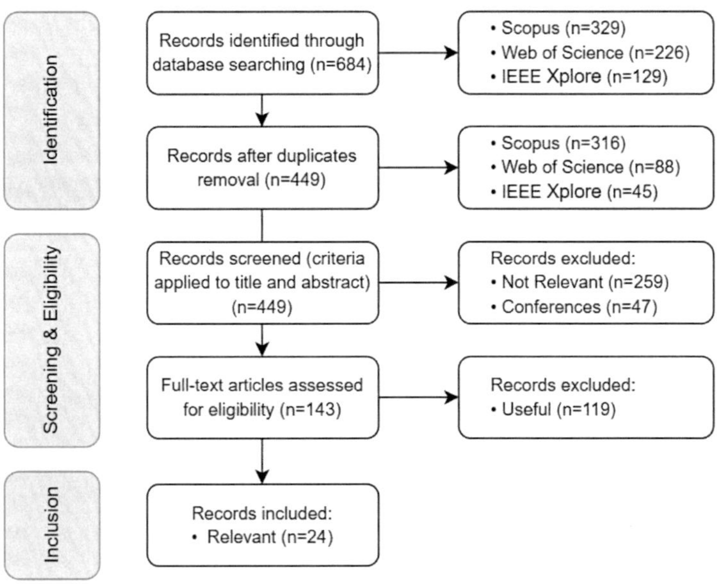

Fig. 1. Flow Diagram of PRISMA Protocol.

The temporal evolution of publications confirms a young yet rapidly expanding research field, with scientific output increasing sharply after 2019, following the industrial adoption of cobots and the diffusion of predictive-maintenance initiatives in Industry 4.0 environments [22].

The thematic analysis was carried out considering as ground theory, the Prognostics and Health Management (PHM), advocated as general ground theory for CBM solution development. The PHM levels, here reduced to data acquisition, fault detection and diagnostics, prognostics (RUL - Remaining Useful Life estimation) and advisory decision support, were used to map the eligible papers see Table 1, to help framing the scientific state of the art. Most studies focus on data acquisition and anomaly detection, demonstrating strong algorithmic maturity but limited progress toward integrated CBM workflows. Internal robot signals, such as joint torques, currents, and position errors, dominate data sources [8,16], while external sensing appears mainly in specialised validation studies [6,13]. Deep-learning methods, particularly autoencoders and convolutional networks, are widely adopted and achieve high detection accuracy but often lack interpretability and robustness across operational contexts [2].

Among the 24 relevant studies, only three formally quantify uncertainty [10, 18,26] and only one explicitly links uncertainty to human supervision [19]. Most contributions adopt decision mechanisms that presuppose a clear and stable boundary between normal and anomalous behaviour. This assumption overlooks the ambiguous and often overlapping patterns that arise in cobot operations, where task variability and human interaction introduce forms of uncertainty that current models do not explicitly represent. Similarly, human involvement is rarely embedded within CBM architectures beyond passive monitoring [4,12], and no study provides a structured mechanism for selective operator feedback or evaluates the economic implications of human intervention.

Table 1. PHM Levels Coverage of Relevant Studies

Research work(s)	Data Acquisition	Fault Det./Diagnostics	Prognostics (RUL estimation)	Advisory Dec. Support
Bruno et al. (2025), Quintián et al. (2025), Ayankoso, Gu et al. (2024), Polenghi & Macchi (2024), Minh et al. (2024), Bertoli et al. (2024), Polenghi et al. (2024), Graabæk et al. (2023), Choi et al. (2023), Nabissi et al. (2023), Wescoat et al. (2022), Mejìa et al. (2021), Park et al. (2021), Quintián et al. (2020)	X	X		
Guida et al. (2024)	X		X	
Ayankoso, Kaigom et al. (2024), Kolvig-Raun et al. (2024), Aliev & Antonelli (2021), Wescoat et al. (2021)	X	X	X	
Zhang et al. (2022), Xin et al. (2022), Marvel et al. (2020)	X	X		X
Zhou et al. (2025), Heddy et al. (2015)	X	X	X	X

From the analysis of the state of the art, three main gaps were identified:

Gap 1: Lack of integrated CBM frameworks for collaborative robots. Only few papers implement the full PHM levels for a comprehensive CBM solution for collaborative. Most of them focused on data acquisition and fault detection and diagnostics.

Gap 2: Methodological fragmentation and absence of uncertainty representation. The corpus shows heterogeneous data sources and deterministic models with limited consideration for ambiguity or probabilistic decision boundaries, undermining robustness in variable environments.

Gap 3: Minimal involvement of human expertise in maintenance decision-making. Human judgement remains peripheral even though operators play a central role in cobot-equipped work environments; structured feedback mechanisms and economic modelling of human intervention are rarely addressed.

These gaps motivate the development of the HIL-CBM framework capable of integrating uncertainty-aware decision logic and human expertise within a unified and experimentally validated architecture tailored to collaborative robots. Anyway, prognostics is considered out of the scope of this research work.

3 Proposed HIL-CBM Framework for Collaborative Robots

Building on the three gaps identified in the literature, this work develops a HIL-CBM framework that combines data-driven diagnostics, uncertainty-aware decision logic, and selective human feedback.

Figure 2 provides a high-level overview of the proposed HIL-CBM framework, adapted from the conceptual structure introduced by Polenghi and Macchi (2024) [19]. Two interdependent loops can be distinguished: a forward loop, in which monitored signals from the cobot are processed and uncertain diagnostic outputs are routed to the human operator; and a backward loop, in which validated labels are fed back into the system to support adaptive retraining. The diagnostic information from the CBM algorithm enables the operator to stop cobot's operation if a failure is detected.

The framework builds on trajectory-specific one-dimensional convolutional autoencoders trained exclusively on healthy data as the core detection mechanism. The diagnostic layer is extended with an uncertainty gate to address the ambiguity inherent in collaborative robot operations: rather than forcing a binary healthy–unhealthy decision, borderline cases are assigned a dedicated class. These uncertain samples are forwarded to the operator, whose feedback is reintegrated into the model through incremental retraining strategies, is designed to improve boundary precision over time. Finally, the economic model has the purpose of assessing the balance between the system performance and the related costs.

Figure 3 details the flow diagram of experiments to realise the proposed HIL-CBM framework for cobot: (i) a data-driven diagnostic layer based on a one-dimensional convolutional autoencoder; (ii) an uncertainty classification layer

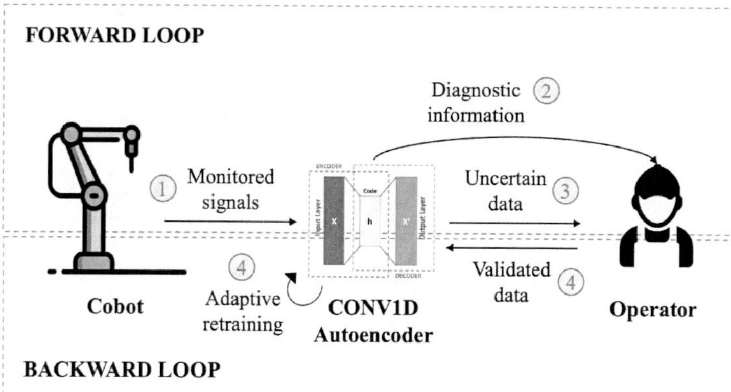

Fig. 2. Overview of the proposed HIL-CBM Framework, adapted from Polenghi and Macchi, 2024 [19].

that isolates borderline conditions; (iii) a human-feedback component that validates ambiguous cases and supports adaptive retraining; and (iv) an economic evaluation module that quantifies the operational implications of alternative maintenance policies.

3.1 Training-Data Scaling and Streaming Stability Experiment

The first experiment evaluates how the anomaly detection layer scales with training-data availability and how it behaves under streaming inference. Training sets per Pick-And-Place (PAP) trajectory are varied from 1 to 100 healthy cycles, and for each configuration 21 convolutional autoencoders are trained across three trajectories (63 models). All models are then tested on an identical evaluation stream of 1,000 cycles, delivered in 10 batches of 100, ensuring strict comparability.

Each autoencoder defines its own threshold as the maximum Mean Absolute Reconstruction Error (MARE) computed on its training data. The experimental design isolates the effect of training-data quantity by keeping all other parameters constant. The ultimate objective is to identify three operational training-data configurations representing low, medium, and high information regimes, which will be used as baseline conditions in subsequent experiments.

3.2 Threshold Optimisation and Uncertainty Management Experiment

The second experiment introduces the uncertainty layer and tests how explicit uncertainty regions improve decision reliability compared to binary thresholding. For each of the three training-data configurations, the pipeline performs a full sweep over 360 threshold settings, generated by combining three base multipliers

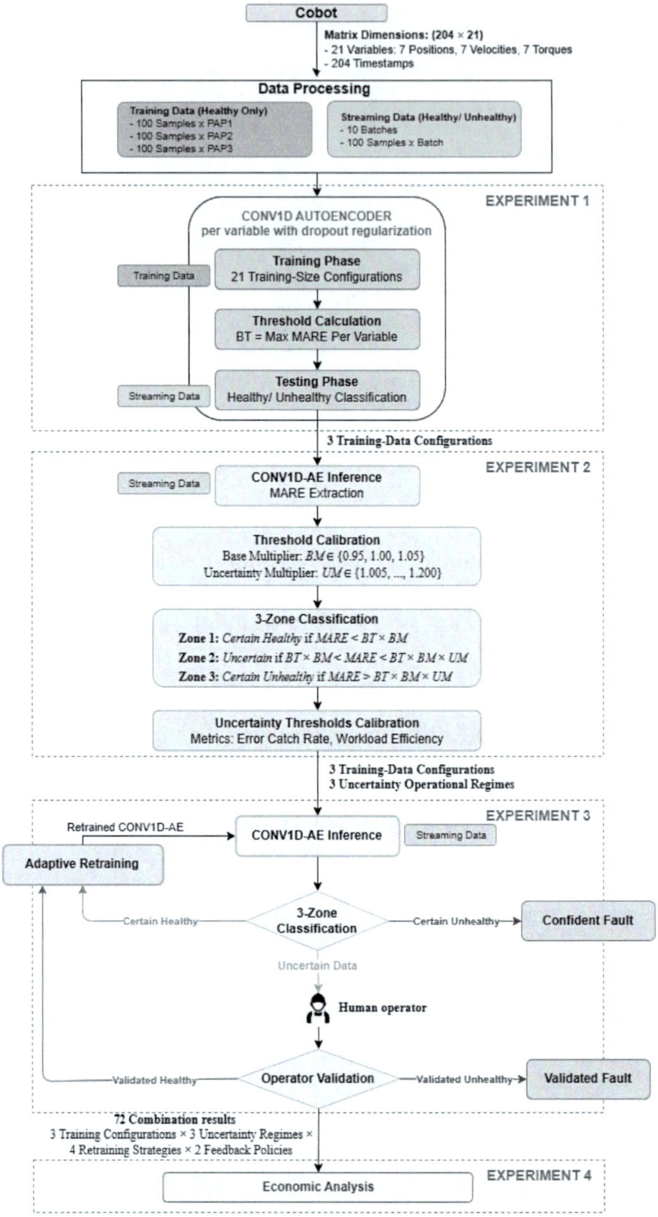

Fig. 3. Flow diagram of the proposed HIL-CBM Framework.

(0.95, 1.00, 1.05) with an uncertainty-multiplier grid ranging from 1.005 to 1.200 in 0.005 increments.

The base multiplier recalibrates the original training threshold, encoding different operational attitudes (sensitivity, balance, specificity). The uncertainty multiplier controls the width of the uncertainty band, dividing the reconstruction-error space into three zones: *Certain Healthy*, *Uncertain*, *Certain Unhealthy*. The outcomes across the 21 monitored variables are aggregated via ANY rule.

Two dedicated metrics quantify the behaviour of each threshold configuration: the *Error Catch Rate (ECR)*, which measures the capacity of the uncertainty layer to intercept potentially incorrect automatic decisions, and the *Workload Efficiency (WE)*, which evaluates how selectively operator involvement is requested. The aim is to identify a single optimal value of the base multiplier and three representative uncertainty operating regimes for each training-data configuration: workload-optimised, error-catch-optimised, and balanced.

3.3 Evaluation of Retraining Strategies and Feedback Timings Experiment

The third experiment evaluates the adaptive component by comparing how different retraining policies integrate human feedback and influence detection behaviour under streaming conditions. Four learning strategies are defined:

- *Static*: no retraining
- *Certain*: retraining only on samples in the *Certain Healthy* zone
- *Feedback*: retraining only on samples in the *Uncertain* zone, validated as healthy by the operator
- *Combined*: integration of both retraining sources

Each strategy is tested under two feedback-timing policies, resulting in eight total configurations. The *Batch* policy requests operator feedback at the end of every 100-cycle batch; the *Accumulated* policy postpones feedback until 30 uncertain samples have been collected across batches, potentially reducing interaction frequency.

All configurations are applied to the uncertainty settings selected from the previous experiment. Each setup is evaluated over ten consecutive batches, simulating temporal evolution in streaming scenarios. Operator labels are assumed perfectly accurate, isolating the effect of retraining mechanisms. The goal is to compare how different retraining strategies and feedback timings shape the adaptive behaviour of the detection layer.

3.4 Economic Analysis and Operational Optimisation Experiment

The fourth experiment extends the validation by incorporating an explicit economic dimension and quantifying how different scenarios translate into overall maintenance cost. Each configuration is evaluated through an integrated cost model that includes three components: the direct operator cost of feedback (Eq. 2), the opportunity cost of lost production during interaction (Eq. 3), and the cost of errors (Eq. 4).

All operational quantities required by the cost model are inherited from the previous experiments. Remaining parameters are fixed based on industrial and laboratory evidence: operator wage $C_w = 60$ €/h, product value $v = 20$ €, production time $(\tau) = 12\,\text{min/unit}$, walking time $t_{\text{walk}} = 3\,\text{min}$, baseline feedback time $t_{\text{feed}} = 0.5\,\text{min}$, and maintenance duration $t_{\text{maint}} = 60\,\text{min}$. Operator task demand during feedback is modelled through a non-linear time function (Eq. 1), where batch size acts as a proxy for accumulated operator workload.

$$T_{\text{req},j} = t_{\text{feed}} \cdot N_{\text{feed},j} \cdot \left(1 + \gamma \cdot \left(e^{\delta(N_{\text{feed},j}-1)} - 1\right)\right) \tag{1}$$

This choice is consistent with classical evidence that memory retention and processing efficiency follow exponential-type dynamics [7], with findings showing that working-memory load increases non-linearly with repeated task execution [23]. The exponential parameters $\gamma = 0.3$ and $\delta = 0.04$ are calibrated using a half-saturation criterion, a standard modelling approach in psychometrics [14].

It should be noted that cognitive load is not directly measured in this study; the time-based function serves as a tractable proxy for workload accumulation, and references to operator workload throughout the paper reflect this modelling assumption rather than empirical cognitive assessment. With these parameters defined, each scenario is processed through the three cost functions (Eqs. 2–4), and their sum defines the total cost (Eq. 5).

$$C_{\text{req}} = \left(\sum_{j=1}^{N_{\text{req}}} T_{\text{req},j} + N_{\text{req}} \cdot t_{\text{walk}}\right) \cdot C_w \tag{2}$$

$$C_{\text{opp}} = \left(\sum_{j=1}^{N_{\text{req}}} T_{\text{req},j} + N_{\text{req}} \cdot t_{\text{walk}}\right) \cdot \frac{v}{\tau} \tag{3}$$

$$C_{\text{err}} = N_{\text{FP}} \cdot t_{\text{maint}} \cdot (C_w + \tfrac{v}{\tau}) + N_{\text{FN}} \cdot v \cdot (1 + 0.2) \tag{4}$$

$$C_{\text{TOT}} = C_{\text{req}} + C_{\text{opp}} + C_{\text{err}} \tag{5}$$

4 Results and Key Findings

The experiments are carried out leveraging trajectory and failure-induced data collected from a Franka Emika Panda cobot. Trajectories and failures have been defined and induced to represent realistic scenarios. For more information, please refer to [18]. The four experiments collectively validated the HIL-CBM framework and illustrated how its components behave under realistic operating conditions. The results highlight how anomaly detection performance, uncertainty management, human-in-the-loop adaptation, and economic factors interact, offering a comprehensive view of the framework's technical robustness and practical feasibility.

4.1 Performance Under Training-Data Scaling

The first experiment revealed a characteristic three-phase learning behaviour: an initial regime of instability, a rapid growth zone, and a saturation region where additional data generate only marginal improvements. Within this structure, three different configurations were selected:

- **25 training-data per trajectory:** minimum-viable regime suitable for exploratory applications, with **mean accuracy** of **59.5%** and **coefficient of variation** of **0.825**.
- **50 training-data per trajectory:** recommended regime for standard industrial deployment, with **mean accuracy** of **77.5%** and **coefficient of variation** of **0.539**.
- **100 training-data per trajectory:** optimal regime for mission-critical scenarios, approaching peak reliability, with **mean accuracy** of **89.7%** and **coefficient of variation** of **0.339**.

The presence of local non-monotonicities indicated that self-supervised learning may undergo latent-space reorganisation as data complexity increases, demonstrating that increasing training set size does not guarantee strictly monotonic performance improvement.

4.2 Effects of Threshold and Uncertainty Optimisation

The second experiment revealed how the *Base Multiplier (BM)* and the *Uncertainty Multiplier (UM)* jointly reshape the balance between detection reliability and operator workload. Across all training-data regimes, **BM = 1.00** consistently appeared as the most stable and operationally meaningful setting: lowering the multiplier to 0.95 produced excessive operator interventions, while raising it to 1.05 caused the *Error Catch Rate* to collapse below 10%.

With BM fixed at 1.00, the UM became the primary driver of the efficiency–reliability frontier:

- **25 training-data per trajectory:** *UM* values of **1.04** (workload-optimised), **1.085** (balanced), and **1.17** (error-catch-optimised) emerged, with steep trade-off surfaces revealing structural sensitivity.
- **50 training-data per trajectory:** the system became substantially more robust, with *UM* values of **1.05**, **1.085**, and **1.15**, and trade-off curves flattening across wider parameter ranges.
- **100 training-data per trajectory:** diminishing returns became evident, with *UM* values of **1.04**, **1.07**, and **1.085**, confirming the plateau observed in the first experiment.

The experiment demonstrated that uncertainty calibration is a decisive mechanism for shaping detection behaviour. As training data grow, trade-offs shrink, with the efficiency-reliability frontier becoming progressively easier to satisfy.

4.3 Dynamics of Retraining Strategies and Feedback Timings

The third experiment evaluated how retraining strategies and feedback timings affect *Model Level Accuracy (MLA)*, computed per batch as the proportion of the model's correct autonomous classifications.

- **25 training-data per trajectory:** the model is in an early learning regime. ***Static*** **accuracy** remains around **91%**, while adaptive strategies generate large improvements. ***Combined–Batch*** reaches **97.4% accuracy**, and ***Feedback–Accumulated*** reaches **97.1%** with only 4 feedback requests (vs 10 for *Batch*). At the broadest uncertainty window (UM = 1.17), both strategies converge to **99.5% model accuracy**.
- **50 training-data per trajectory:** the model becomes more stable. ***Static*** **accuracy** rises to about **96%**, while **adaptive configurations** consistently exceed **98–99%**. Peak values remain close across policies: around **99.5% model accuracy** at UM = 1.15 for both ***Feedback–Batch*** and ***Combined–Accumulated***. *Accumulated* feedback achieves these results with roughly half the retraining sessions.
- **100 training-data per trajectory:** the model operates near its accuracy ceiling. ***Static*** **accuracy** reaches **98.4%**, while the best **adaptive strategies** achieve **99.5–99.6%** with minimal retraining (2–3 sessions). Differences in accuracy between *Batch* and *Accumulated* become negligible.

Overall, **model accuracy** progresses from **91%** to **99.6%**, with the strongest improvements obtained through ***Feedback*** and ***Combined*** strategies. As training-data availability increases, policy differences shrink and ***Accumulated*** feedback becomes the most cost-effective option, sustaining high accuracy with minimal operator involvement.

4.4 Economic and Operational Impacts

The fourth experiment evaluated the performance of the full HIL-CBM system by jointly analysing diagnostic reliability and the economic cost required to sustain it. Performance is measured through *Production Level Accuracy (PLA)*, which integrates both autonomous predictions and human-validated uncertain cases, while economic efficiency is captured by *Total Operational Cost (TOC)*.

Across all evaluated configurations, ***Production Level Accuracy*** remains consistently high, ranging from **94.2%** to **99.6%**, with the highest values observed for the ***Feedback*** and ***Combined*** retraining strategies. Systems based on **50 or 100 training-data** per trajectory achieve near-perfect reliability (**99.6%**) and require minimal human correction, whereas the **25 training-data** configurations remain slightly less stable (**97–99%**).

Cost analysis reveals a strong dependence on number of training data and type of feedback policy. The **highest costs** occur in the **25 training-data** ***Static*** configuration, while the **lowest** are obtained with ***Combined–Accumulated*** at moderate uncertainty levels. For models with **50 and 100**

training-data per trajectory, most effective configurations maintain **PLA** above **99.5%** with **low TOC** values, confirming that well-initialised systems drastically reduce both uncertainty and operator workload. ***Accumulated*** feedback modes present consistently lower costs compared to *Batch* ones.

Table 2 presents a summary of the most important results obtained by the application of the HIL-CBM framework.

Table 2. HIL-CBM Framework Performance Across Training-Data Regimes

Cond.	Metric	Low (N=25)	Med. (N=50)	High (N=100)
No HIL-CBM	Accuracy	59.5%	77.5%	89.7%
	Op. Cost	Extreme	High	Moderate
With HIL-CBM	Model Acc.	91–99.5%	96–99.5%	98–99.6%
	Prod. Acc.	97–99%	99.3–99.6%	99.6%
	Op. Cost	Med–Low	Very Low	Minimal

5 Conclusions

The results demonstrate that a Human-in-the-Loop Condition-Based Maintenance framework can turn diagnostic uncertainty into a functional interface between CBM algorithm and operator, enabling selective supervision rather than continuous monitoring. By combining a convolutional autoencoder with uncertainty bands and incremental retraining, the system achieves high production level accuracy while reducing redundant interventions and overall maintenance cost. The findings confirm that human judgment, when engaged only on uncertain cases, improves model reliability, stabilises learning under drift and supports economically sustainable maintenance practices in cobot-equipped work environments.

Regarding the research questions, the experiments show that formalising uncertainty as a third detection state (RQ1) improves diagnostic reliability compared to a binary threshold, while selective human feedback (RQ 2) achieves high accuracy with minimal involvement and favourable cost profiles.

The research contributes to theory by formalising uncertainty as a third detection state, extending CBM from deterministic thresholds to uncertainty-aware decision-making. It couples detection performance with economic modelling of human involvement, introduces a systematic evaluation of adaptive retraining policies under streaming conditions, and proposes dedicated metrics, such as *Error Catch Rate* and *Workload Efficiency*, that quantify the value of uncertainty management and human intervention. These contributions provide analytical foundations for studying hybrid diagnostic systems that combine machine reasoning and selective human oversight.

From a practical standpoint, the framework addresses a concrete challenge faced by manufacturers deploying collaborative robots: maintaining diagnostic reliability without requiring continuous operator involvement. By confining human intervention to genuinely uncertain cases, the approach makes condition-based maintenance feasible in operational contexts where operator time is limited and fault data are scarce. The framework offers a deployable methodology for CBM applied to cobots under different levels of data availability, enabling reliable anomaly detection from healthy-only datasets and selective operator validation that reduces false alarms and prevents excessive operator workload. The parametric cost model allows managers to identify economically optimal retraining and feedback strategies, while the modular per-variable architecture supports scalable integration across cobots and production settings.

The study is limited by its use of simulated feedback and laboratory data. Real human behaviour, interface effects, and naturally occurring degradation were not tested, and economic parameters were estimated rather than empirically calibrated. Sociotechnical dynamics such as trust, acceptance and automation bias also lie outside the experimental scope. The operator workload model adopts a time based-proxy rather than direct cognitive measurement, which limits the precision of workload-related claims.

Future developments include empirical validation with human operators, field trials under real production conditions, and extension to multi-class and hierarchical fault identification. Also, ablation studies are envisioned as a robust methodological approach to verify each element of the proposed solution in industrial settings. Advancements should incorporate reliability-weighted feedback, explainable interfaces and ergonomic visual analytics for a broader assessment of the HIL-CBM solutions for cobots.

Acknowledgments. This research is part of the HumanTech Project, which is financed by the Italian Ministry of University and Research (MUR) for the 2023–2027 period as part of the ministerial initiative "Departments of Excellence" (L. 232/2016). The initiative rewards departments that stand out for the quality of the research produced and funds specific development projects.

Disclosure of Interests. The authors have no competing interests to declare that are relevant to the content of this article.

References

1. Aliev, K., Antonelli, D.: Proposal of a monitoring system for collaborative robots to predict outages and to assess reliability factors exploiting machine learning. Appl. Sci. **11**(4) (2021). https://doi.org/10.3390/app11041621
2. Ayankoso, S., Gu, F., Louadah, H., Fahham, H., Ball, A.: Artificial-intelligence-based condition monitoring of industrial collaborative robots: Detecting anomalies and adapting to trajectory changes. Machines **12**(9), 630 (2024). https://doi.org/10.3390/machines12090630

3. Ayankoso, S., Kaigom, E., Louadah, H., Fahham, H., Gu, F., Ball, A.: A hybrid digital twin scheme for the condition monitoring of industrial collaborative robots. Procedia Comput. Sci. **232**, 1099–1108 (2024). https://doi.org/10.1016/j.procs.2024.01.108
4. Bertoli, A., Ferraguti, F., Fantuzzi, C.: An IoT-enabled software architecture for user-friendly fault diagnosis and identification: the welding COBOT use case. In: 2024 7th Iberian Robotics Conference (ROBOT), pp. 1–6 (2024). https://doi.org/10.1109/ROBOT61475.2024.10797369
5. Bruno, G., Aliev, K., Awouda, A., Chiabert, P.: A digital twin implementation framework for collaborative robots. In: IFIP Advances in Information and Communication Technology, vol. 740 (2024). https://doi.org/10.1007/978-3-031-93319-6_3
6. Choi, S.H., et al.: A comparative study on the failure detection methods using time-series data image generation and CNN for driving module of COBOTs. In: 2023 9th International Conference on Control, Decision and Information Technologies (CoDIT), pp. 241–244 (2023). https://doi.org/10.1109/CoDIT58514.2023.10284371
7. Ebbinghaus, H.: Über das Gedächtnis: Untersuchungen zur experimentellen Psychologie. Duncker & Humblot (1885)
8. Graabæk, S.G., Schou, C., Pedersen, M.A.A., Johansen, K.S.: An experimental comparison of anomaly detection methods for collaborative robot manipulators. IEEE Access **11**, 8021–8037 (2023). https://doi.org/10.1109/ACCESS.2023.3289068
9. Guida, R., Bertolino, A.C., De Martin, A., Sorli, M.: Comprehensive analysis of major fault-to-failure mechanisms in harmonic drives. Machines **12**(11) (2024). https://doi.org/10.3390/machines12110776
10. Heddy, G., et al.: Linear temporal logic (LTL) based monitoring of smart manufacturing systems. In: Annual Conference of the PHM Society, vol. 7 (2015). https://doi.org/10.36001/phmconf.2015.v7i1.2684
11. Kolvig-Raun, E.S., Kjærgaard, M.B., Brorsen, R.: Joint stress estimation and remaining useful life prediction for collaborative robots to support predictive maintenance. IEEE Rob. Autom. Lett. **9**(4), 3554–3561 (2024). https://doi.org/10.1109/LRA.2024.3368296
12. Marvel, J.A., Bagchi, S., Zimmerman, M., Antonishek, B.: Towards effective interface designs for collaborative HRI in manufacturing: metrics and measures. J. Hum.-Robot Interact. **9**(4) (2020). https://doi.org/10.1145/3385009
13. Mejía, J.R., Isaías, O.A.A., Paschapur, P.: Anomaly detection in motion timeseries using the bosch xdk and dynamic time warping. In: SKILL 2021 (2021)
14. Michaelis, L., Menten, M.L.: Die kinetik der invertinwirkung. Biochem. Z. **49**, 333–369 (1913)
15. Minh, T.B., Do, X.P., Nguyen, Q.H., Nguyen, K.H.V., Phan, T.T.T.: A digital twin implementation framework for a collaborative robot based on ISO 23247. In: Todor, D., Kumar, S., Choi, S.B., Nguyen-Xuan, H., Nguyen, Q.H., Trung Bui, T. (eds.) ICSET 2023. GET, pp. 747–755. Springer, Singapore (2024). https://doi.org/10.1007/978-981-97-1868-9_74
16. Nabissi, G., Longhi, S., Bonci, A.: Ros-based condition monitoring architecture enabling automatic faults detection in industrial collaborative robots. Appl. Sci. **13**(1) (2023). https://doi.org/10.3390/app13010143
17. Park, Y.S., Yoo, D.Y., Lee, J.W.: Programmable motion-fault detection for a collaborative robot. IEEE Access **9**, 133123–133142 (2021). https://doi.org/10.1109/ACCESS.2021.3114505

18. Polenghi, A., Cattaneo, L., Macchi, M.: A framework for fault detection and diagnostics of articulated collaborative robots based on hybrid series modelling of artificial intelligence algorithms. J. Intell. Manuf. **35**(5), 1929–1947 (2024). https://doi.org/10.1007/s10845-023-02076-6
19. Polenghi, A., Macchi, M.: Proposal of a human-in-the-loop-based framework for advancing maintenance applications for collaborative robots. In: IFAC-PapersOnLine, vol. 58, pp. 742–747 (2024). https://doi.org/10.1016/j.ifacol.2024.09.214
20. Quintián, H., et al.: Detecting performance anomalies in the multi-component software a collaborative robot. In: Analide, C., Novais, P., Camacho, D., Yin, H. (eds.) IDEAL 2020. LNCS, vol. 12490, pp. 533–540. Springer, Cham (2020). https://doi.org/10.1007/978-3-030-62365-4_51
21. Quintián, H., Jove, E., Zayas-Gato, F., Basurto, N., Cambra, C., Herrero, Á.: Detecting software anomalies in robots by means of one-class classifiers. Appl. Artif. Intell. **39**(1), 2538459 (2025)
22. Stefanini, R., Tancredi, G.P.C., Vignali, G., Monica, L.: Industry 4.0 and intelligent predictive maintenance: a survey about the advantages and constraints in the Italian context. J. Qual. Maint. Eng. **29**(5), 37–49 (2022). https://doi.org/10.1108/JQME-12-2021-0096
23. Sweller, J.: Cognitive load during problem solving: effects on learning. Cogn. Sci. **12**(2), 257–285 (1988). https://doi.org/10.1016/0364-0213(88)90023-7
24. Wescoat, E., Kerner, S., Mears, L.: A comparative study of different algorithms using contrived failure data to detect robot anomalies. Procedia Comput. Sci. **200**, 669–678 (2022)
25. Wescoat, E., Krugh, M., Mears, L.: Random forest regression for predicting an anomalous condition on a UR10 COBOT end-effector from purposeful failure data. Procedia Manuf. **53**, 644–655 (2021). https://doi.org/10.1016/j.promfg.2021.06.064
26. Xin, X., Keoh, S.L., Sevegnani, M., Saerbeck, M., Khoo, T.P.: Adaptive model verification for modularized industry 4.0 applications. IEEE Access **10**, 125353–125364 (2022). https://doi.org/10.1109/ACCESS.2022.3225399
27. Zhang, S., Li, S., Li, X., Xiong, Y., Xie, Z.: A human-robot dynamic fusion safety algorithm for collaborative operations of COBOTs. J. Intell. Rob. Syst. **104**(1), 1–14 (2021). https://doi.org/10.1007/s10846-021-01534-8
28. Zhou, J., Zheng, L., Wang, Y.: Collaborative optimization for multirobot manufacturing system reliability through integration of SysML simulation and maintenance knowledge graph. J. Manuf. Syst. **80**, 749–775 (2025). https://doi.org/10.1016/j.jmsy.2025.04.010

Industrial Metaverse: A Platform for Human Engagement in Production System Design

Adalberto Polenghi(✉), Marco Pasquandrea, Mahmoud Samy Rezk Elashry, Edoardo Palmitessa, Tesfalem Mekonen Mengestu, Tidaru Dessie Alamnie, Umair Ahmed, and Marco Taisch

Department of Management, Economics and Industrial Engineering, Politecnico di Milano, P.za Leonardo da Vinci 32, 20133 Milan, Italy
adalberto.polenghi@polimi.it

Abstract. Product volatility and market uncertainty are driving manufacturing companies toward highly customized products and increasingly flexible, reconfigurable production systems. To address these challenges, advanced technologies such as Digital Twins (DT), Artificial Intelligence (AI), and eXtended Reality (XR) are being adopted to enhance engineering design processes and reduce time-to-market. While Concurrent Engineering has historically improved product development efficiency, limited attention has been given to production system design, which remains critical to introduce new products rapidly. This research investigates how the Industrial Metaverse (IM), a comprehensive environment integrating DT, AI, and XR, can support production system design while aligning with Industry 5.0 principles of human centricity. The study focuses on the detailed design phase, where both hardware and software components are verified and tested. In this context, the IM is explored as a platform to actively engage human stakeholders through immersive and collaborative environments, enhancing the interaction in the virtual worlds for design reviews and training. The findings are based on lessons learned from the METABRAKE project, a collaborative academia-industry project aimed at developing and testing IM applications for product-production system concurrent engineering. Through a laboratory demonstration, the study highlights the capability of immersive technologies to improve design review and virtual training, while also identifying key challenges and lessons learned on technical integration and organizational processes.

Keywords: Industrial Metaverse · Digital Twin · Extended Reality · Production System Design · Virtual Commissioning · Operator Training

1 Introduction

Product volatility and market uncertainty are reshaping the way in which manufacturing companies design and manage their products and production systems.

G. Pezzotta et al. (Eds.): APMS 2026, IFIP AICT 808, pp. 385–399, 2027.
https://doi.org/10.1007/978-3-032-38594-9_26

Products are becoming more and more customized whilst production systems are required to be flexible and reconfigurable to accommodate new product variants that are requested by the market in an efficient way [12]. In this regard, technologies such as Digital Twin (DT), Artificial Intelligence (AI) and eXtended Reality (XR) are leveraged to improve engineering design processes [5] with the final goal of reducing the time-to-market of newly-developed or newly-commissioned products [4]. On the methodological side, Concurrent Engineering has long been considered as an approach to make new product development effective and efficient, by reducing design reviews and speed up the overall design processes [12]. However, most of the effort was put on product rather than production system design, leaving room for improvements for companies willing to propose new products on the market [8]. Hence, there is a need to study how it is possible to improve production system design, leveraging advanced technologies like DT, AI and XR in a comprehensive environment, named recently Industrial Metaverse (IM), while being compliant with a core Industry 5.0 pillar, that is human centricity; indeed, the IM can create a safe and collaborative working environment enhancing human collaboration and support human-technology interaction.

1.1 Research Objective and Scope

It is therefore the objective of this research work to shed light on how the IM can serve as a platform during production system design to engage human stakeholders in the manufacturing context. The research question this work aims to answer is *How to realize an IM solution to improve production system design via human engagement?* Within the design processes, theis research focuses on the detailed design, where hardware and software should be verified and tested, also thanks to human-machine interaction. Indeed, the results here described must be intended as lessons learned from a collaborative project named METABRAKE. The remainder of the manuscript is organized as follows: Section 2 provides the background about the METABRAKE project; Section 3 describes the derived framework about human stakeholder engagement in production system design via Industrial Metaverse; Section 4 describes the achievements in regard to i) detailed design review and ii) virtual training); Sections 5 and 6 deal into the lessons learned for the development, drawing on considerations related to technical barriers, people skills and competences and company processes.

2 Background on METABRAKE Project

The METABRAKE project is a three-year collaborative project between academia and industry whose objective is to explore and test the feasibility of leveraging the IM for co-designing and co-engineering innovative products together with their production processes and systems. This is supported by extant scientific literature as, despite the recognized potential, there is not enough evidence on IM impact over concurrent engineering and human engagement [1]; this study aims to explore this gap though. The overarching research question the project was aiming to answer was indeed *How can the Industrial Metaverse enhance concurrent engineering of products and production system design?* To achieve this, the project focuses on the virtualization of products, their production processes and systems, looking for a collaborative environment where multiple stakeholders can test and verify design choices. Within this wide goal and research question of the METABRAKE project, the specific research question addressed in this work is about IM for production system design, engaging humans in verification and testing activities (see Subsect. 1.1).

3 Industrial Metaverse as Digital Platform for Human Engagement Across Production System Design Phases

The IM can be conceived as a persistent, immersive, and multi-user collaborative virtual space that leverages and expands standard virtual commissioning solutions, that are built on physics-based simulation and high-fidelity 3D models [10]. For this reason, the IM has been selected and realized in a proof-of-concept (PoC) for production system design, with the goal of realizing an architecture for human engagement. Via iterative design and tests, the project allowed multiple IM architecture reviews, allowing to depict an overall framework (Fig. 1) able to conceptualize and synthesize IM as a platform for human engagement along multiple stages of the production system design process.

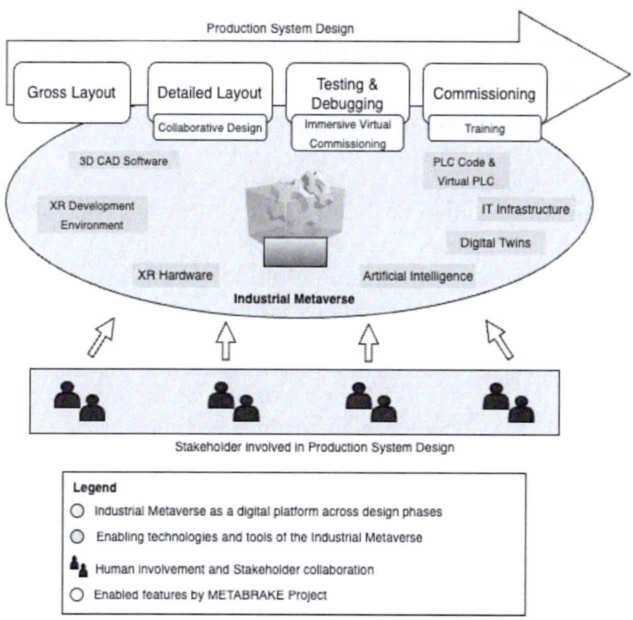

Fig. 1. Industrial Metaverse as digital platform for multiple human stakeholder engagement across production system design phases.

As visible from Fig. 1, the project demonstrated that IM can be seen as a digital platform supporting production system design along two dimensions:

- **Across production system design phases**, by supporting different applications for the various phases, including:
  - *Detailed Layout:* the IM enables cross-functional and cross-organizational collaboration within immersive and unified virtual environments, allowing stakeholders from different departments and companies to interact in real time. Collaborative design sessions can be held in which teams discuss and review layout proposals simultaneously; design changes can be visualized instantly in 3D, enhancing understanding of spatial and process impacts.
  - *Testing & Debugging:* the IM allows immersive virtual commissioning [7] to test production machine control logic before physical installation. Human–machine interfaces (HMIs) can be evaluated in an interactive and realistic environment, and operators and engineers can take active roles in the virtual factory, performing tests, detecting errors, and validating system behavior.
  - *Commissioning:* during physical installation of production systems, the IM can support operator training to reduce ramp-up time. Training on activating and operating the production equipment, as well as on maintenance procedures, can be anticipated before the production system is physically installed, avoiding time waste for effective production.
- **Empowering the virtual world through active human engagement**:
  - *Active roles for humans in simulations:* humans can actively participate in virtual simulations, performing tasks, making decisions, and interacting with Digital Twins (DTs) of machines and processes. This involvement allows realistic evaluation of workflows, design decisions, and safety aspects; operator insights can be integrated in real time, enhancing system validation and reducing design errors.
  - *Stakeholder collaboration via immersive and interactive experiences:* stakeholders from different functions and locations can collaborate seamlessly in shared virtual spaces, exploring layouts, testing scenarios or technical solutions, and discussing modifications interactively in photo-realistic and industry-like virtual worlds.

Being immersed in a virtual environment reproducing the real conditions fosters collaboration and promotes the involvement of people often out of the design process, such as operators, maintenance technicians or plant supervisor. Such condition is unique to IM, which extends traditional simulation or virtual commissioning approaches [3].

The enabling technologies of the IM that make this digital platform concept possible include:

- **3D CAD Software:** modeling tool for realistic product and production system representation in the IM;
- **XR Development Environment:** game engine software in which the immersive virtual environment is developed;

- **XR Hardware:** XR headset and hardware (e.g., haptic gloves) required for immersive and interactive experiences;
- **PLC Code & Virtual PLC:** control logic of production machines, enabling simulation-driven rather than animation-based representation within the XR development environment;
- **IT Infrastructure:** server, firewall, and Internet connectivity required to effectively run simulations in the IM;
- **Digital Twins:** digital representations of processes and production systems whose behavior is managed by control logic systems;
- **Artificial Intelligence:** as a recognized useful technology of the IM [5], AI can foster visually enhanced virtual worlds and improve data-driven decision-making by making structured and unstructured data available.

The features enabled by the METABRAKE project through these technologies (see Fig. 1) have been developed and tested within the laboratory environment, as presented in Sect. 4.

4 Development and Testing in Laboratory Setting

The realized PoCs pave the way for the understanding of the technical process development, also driven by the objective of integrating humans inside the production system design process. In this regard, the research work envisions the interaction with the virtual worlds as the way in which human stakeholders are engaged, regardless of their functional area of work and expertise. Therefore, within the production system design, Subsect. 4.1 describes the detailed design review step via immersive environment of the IM; Subsection 4.2 also explores a preliminary integration AI into the production system design itself, made available by the high-fidelity and reality-like scene in IM; finally, Sect. 4.3 proposes a virtual immersive training to be used as well during production system design either for internal operators or for customers whose operators can be trained and provide feedback even before prototyping of the production system. All the development and testing were realized within the Marco Garetti Lab on a seven-station assembly line that is composed by both manual and automatic operation, including a robotic cell. The line realizes fuzzy mobile phones in a realistic way, including traditional automation of production system as well as a MES (Manufacturing Execution System) for production control.

4.1 Detailed Design Review via Industrial Metaverse

The detailed design review is the final step within the production system design that allows to make specific and detailed reviews to avoid and solve errors prior to the prototyping and realization phase, such as collision or misbehavior due to errors in the control logic. In the laboratory the assembly line was already available, but lacking detailed 3D CAD; therefore the CAD models were created while the PLC code was retrieved and simplified as we discarded almost all safety functions given the focus on the main assembly process. The assembly line was then recreated in an immersive virtual environment to produce its Digital Twin; in this work, given the production system design as scope of work, Digital Twin is intended as a high-fidelity model from a 3D perspective and able to replicate the behavior as it will be in the operational phase [2]. The Digital Twin is the core part of the Industrial Metaverse that, combined with XR technologies, allows for user immersivity and interaction.

The IM architecture is shown in Fig. 2 (refer to [7] for more details).

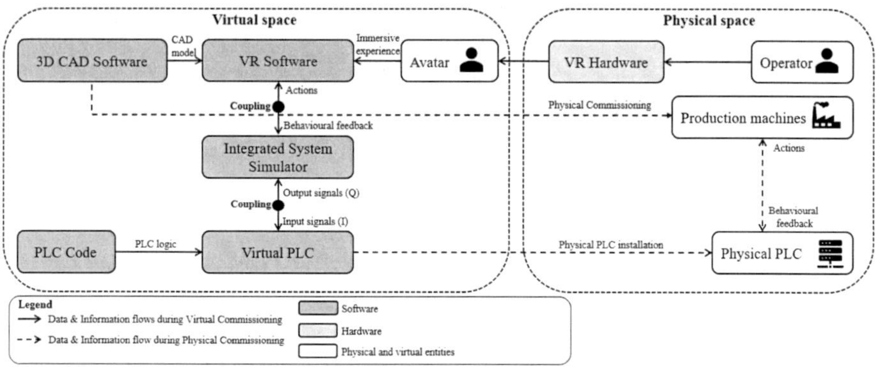

Fig. 2. Architecture of the Industrial Metaverse from Palmitessa et al., 2025 [7].

As anticipated, 3D CAD models were realized using Siemens NX, including all kinematics; Siemens NX with the MCD (Mechatronic Concept Designer) version was selected for the ease of studying kinematic constraints and of connecting the CAD model with the PLC code. In this way, during the project a more common virtual commissioning method was trialled and compared to IM. The PLC software managing all stations was simplified and partially re-written using Siemens TIA Portal, chosen because the stations are equipped with Siemens PLCs. In order to run the PLC code virtually, Siemens PLCSIM Advanced was used as it can host multiple virtual PLC instances simultaneously with full instruction-set compatibility with Siemens PLCs, so that TIA Portal programs can be downloaded into the virtual controller and executed.

To fully exploit the potential of XR, and specifically VR in this project, Unity was chosen as game engine for creating the immersive reality environment and was selected because of its real-time physics engine, photorealistic rendering capabilities, flexible scripting environment (C#). The CAD models were exported from Siemens NX as STEP files, converted to FBX format, and imported into Unity; FBX format demonstrated greater exploitability inside Unity, although STEP files can also be used.

The last step was to connect the PLC software and the virtualized assembly line in Unity. This was done via SIMIT, Siemens' dedicated simulation platform for industrial plant behavior modelling. This behavioral simulation layer makes the PLC believe it is communicating with real hardware; to the authors' knowledge, there is currently no industrially viable alternative to SIMIT for this step in the creation of the IM if not hard coding.

Finally, significant effort was devoted to improve the visual realism of the assembly line inside Unity through material tuning and color baking. To do so Unity's Universal Render Pipeline (URP) shader was used; Physically Based Rendering (PBR) materials were implemented through shader maps for roughness, metallic, and normal details, along with lighting optimization managed by a dedicated script.

Dedicated scripts were created to assign physical properties to products and equipment, and to animate them based on interactions with SIMIT and controls from an XR headset (Meta Quest 3 with hand recognition enabled). The final results can be seen in Fig. 3 where in the top part on the left is Unity, on the right PLCSIM Advanced, while in the bottom part on the right is SIMIT and on the left one of the possible interaction of the user in free-hand mode.

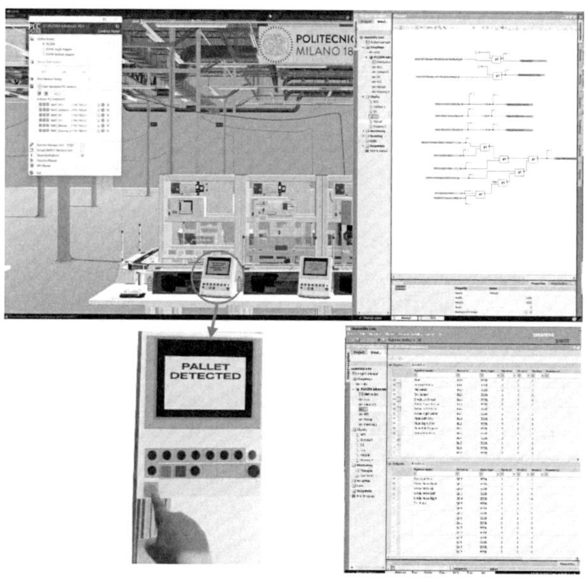

Fig. 3. Architecture of S7-PLCSIM Advanced, SIMIT, and Unity.

In summary, the ecosystem leverages PLCSIM Advanced to execute the PLC control logic, SIMIT to emulate plant behavior in a closed-loop configuration, and Unity to deliver the 3D visualization of the manufacturing equipment and provide the user interaction layer.

The final result is an immersive experience for multiple concurrent users who can move alongside the assembly line, observe it in operation, and interact with it by pressing buttons on the HMI (Human Machine Interface) of each station, reading HMI displays, and placing and removing parts and line pallets.

Design Reviews. Leveraging the IM, it is possible to ease the design review process as the production system correct functioning and behavior can be tested in a safe but immersive reality in which humans are engaged and interact with the line. The way in which design reviews are then carried out evolved over the project development. At the very first stage, it was planned to consider the IM platform also as a sort-of design review tool in which users can freely move parts, modify shapes and dimensions, and interact with production system features. However, this has been limited due to:

- **Programming effort.** Making the IM a design tool would have required to introduce degrees of freedom within the virtual environment that are non-trivial to program and must be carefully planned beforehand, thus making the IM as a design review tool less effective as the users will be allowed to modify only those features made available by the programmer.
- **Accountability of changes.** Leveraging feedback from industrial partner, it was evident that a multi-stakeholder tool, i.e. IM, in which humans can freely modify the design of the production system might undermine the control over such modifications. This is combined with the need in industry to have a clear accountability and responsibility of the final design.

Therefore, the way in which design reviews are carried out is less formal and, at the moment of writing, based on feedback provided by the human, that could be a production or maintenance operator, technician, engineer or designer, to the design team via the IM itself thanks to the multi-user possibility but with no possibility to directly modify the production system feature in the IM platform.

Besides the feedback to the design team is not straightforward via the IM, some groups, typically the production operators and related, do not usually take part in design reviews, leaving them out of the design processes; however, their participation in the immersive experience enriched the discussion and highlighted potential issues in machine layout and human-machine interactions that are difficult to spot in other ways. Providing an engaging common ground for product and process engineers helps the mutual understanding and constructive discussion.

4.2 Preliminary Insights from Integration of AI in the Industrial Metaverse

The assembly line includes a quality control station based on a vision system. Therefore, an AI/ML system was developed and embedded into the Industrial Metaverse to learn how to distinguish compliant from non-compliant part and to run the quality inspection without the need for any physical prototype, leveraging synthetic data generated from baseline ones obtained via the IM itself (Fig. 4).

To achieve this, a series of images of good and defective parts was generated in the virtual world under different lighting conditions and properly labeled; these images were used to train a machine learning model via YOLO11, compatible with Unity. The resulting model was exported as an ONNX file and imported into Unity, as ONNX is the file format supported by Unity Sentis – the library within Unity that enables the execution of AI models directly inside the engine.

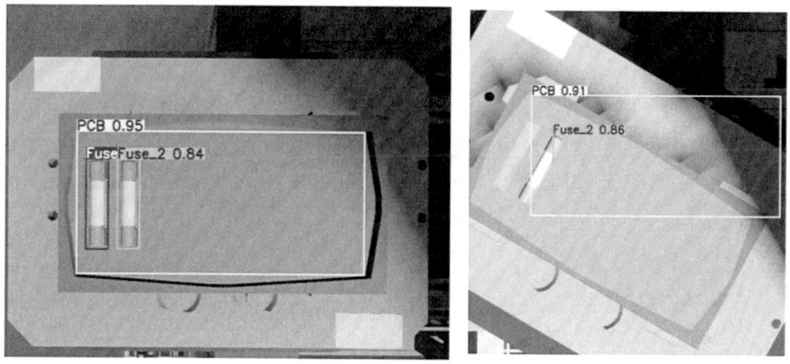

Fig. 4. Example of ML model output.

A virtual camera was created inside the Unity model; the camera captures an image of the sub-assembly passing beneath it, invokes the AI/ML model to analyze the image and determine compliance, and sends the decision to SIMIT, which triggers the appropriate actions according to the PLC code (e.g., labeling the part as rejected and skipping subsequent assembling steps).

Through this integration, it was assessed that AI can be embedded into the IM and that a quality control system can be fully developed and virtually tested without producing a single physical part, thus opening potential to embed and test AI during the production system design stage and not only afterwards.

4.3 Virtual Immersive Training

The virtual immersive training is an established practice to train low-skilled operators in order to be able to operate on new manufacturing equipment in a safe environment and with no risk for operational continuity of the production system. Given all the available models and software from the detailed design, the team investigated the realization of an immersive training experience for production lines still in the design phase, or in the manufacturing phase, for the future operators to be ready.

Therefore, a comprehensive set of immersive training modules has been conceptualized and developed considering two architectural options:

- with advanced systems integrating PLCs, SIMIT, and Unity, similarly to what described in Sect. 4.1;
- via animation-based modules with UI panels, and different aids such as flashing indicators, highlighted components, or contextual overlays that support cognitive retention and procedural understanding beyond what is typically possible in live environments, including haptic gloves for more immersive experience.

At the current stage of the project, the second option was selected in order to decouple detailed design and training as their needs and goals are different. Nonetheless, it was possible to reuse all 3D CAD models. By providing a realistic, immersive, interactive and self-guided training, operators can develop procedural knowledge, situational awareness, and operational confidence prior to interacting with the actual physical assembly line – even before commissioning, that is during the detailed design of the line itself. The immersive training modules are developed using the Unity engine by importing the NX CAD models, designing the scene and layouts, creating interaction points, and applying interactive scripting for user-guided training. The virtual environment includes instruction panels, indicators, and interactive and highlighted buttons to navigate through each specific step and module. To make the virtual immersive training more realistic for operators, haptic gloves are incorporated to provide a more reality-like experience and better human-machine interaction. The selected gloves are the TouchDIVER Pro gloves by WEART as they can deliver tactile feedback such as vibration, force, texture, and simulated temperature variations so the system allows more effective learning by engaging multiple senses simultaneously, which has been shown to improve retention and task performance [9].

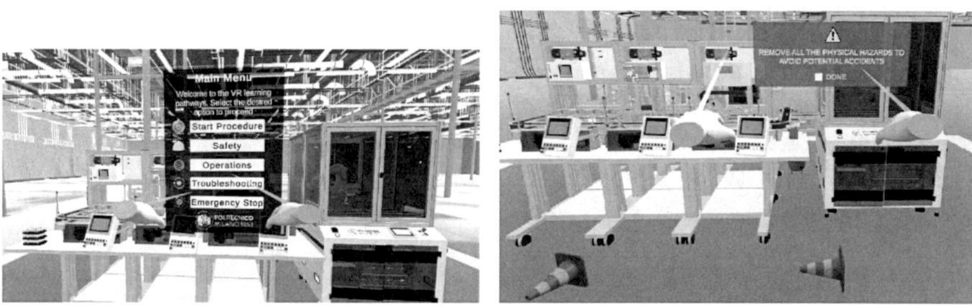

(a) Main menu of the virtual immersive training environment.

(b) Safety module, focus on checking hazardous situations.

Fig. 5. Virtual immersive training, main menu and safety module.

The developed virtual training is systematically divided into five essential modules (Fig. 5), providing step-by-step interactive guidelines to the operator for machine operation, initialization, safety, and emergency stop:

1. **Start-up procedure.** The operator is guided through step-by-step machine startup, checking power connections and verifying that each station is in the correct operating condition, initializing the machine by turning on the compressor, switching on each station, and operating the T-cell and robot cell. At each step, operators are directed by instructions, arrows, highlighted buttons, and a checklist.
2. **Safety module.** This module simulates guiding the operator on safety considerations at all aspects of the procedure. It starts by providing information

about basic PPEs, then guides the operator to check and remove any potential hazard, asking for confirmation before proceeding (Fig. 5b). The module also ensures that the emergency stop button is accessible.
3. **Operations.** This is the most comprehensive and interactive module, developed around the main functions of the assembly line and providing operators with a deep understanding of manufacturing steps and equipment. Operators can perform the same operations virtually in an immersive environment by interacting with products, HMIs, highlighted buttons, and arrow indications. At the start, a welcome panel provides an overview of the module, followed by a flowchart of the line representing each station; thereafter, each station is operated individually by following instructions, indications, graphics, animations, and HMI interactions.
4. **Troubleshooting.** The operator is guided to identify potential problems by checking power connections, verifying that machine parts are correctly assembled with no looseness, vibration, or smoke, and verifying variables such as machine pressure, temperature, and lubrication. Effects such as vibration sounds and smoke are added to increase operator awareness.
5. **Emergency stop.** This module trains operators to observe unusual machine behavior (vibration, smoke, noise), to maintain a safe distance from the machine, to press the emergency stop button on the HMI panel to stop the machine immediately, and to contact the relevant technical or maintenance department for assistance.

5 Lessons Learned and Managerial Implications

5.1 Lessons Learned

Lessons learned are grouped in three categories, namely technical barriers, people skills and competences and company processes.

Technical Barriers

- **Software tools integration and interoperability.** The implementation of the IM is possible today with existing software tools; however, there is no integrated environment for its deployment from production system design to live virtual reality representation. Multiple software tools must be connected; alternative are present but connectors must be hard coded.
- **Photorealism of virtual world.** A photorealistic and interactive scene in the IM is computationally demanding and tightly linked to high-quality HMI. Hence, IM for production system design cannot run standalone on a headset, but must be always connected to high-performance workstations; also, XR headset technology is advancing fast but at the current state it still poses challenges for long session, due to users' fatigue and discomfort.
- **Full scene modeling.** The completeness of the environment surrounding the manufacturing process requires careful decision-making to avoid adding computational burden that does not meaningfully contribute to the user experience and the final goal of the IM.

- **Physics-driven behavior.** It is not yet computationally viable to integrate complete process physics into the IM (e.g., calculating real-time press-fitting forces), although actual control logic and geometry can be included.

People Skills and Competences

- **PLC programming.** The capability to program a virtual PLC, connect to a behavior model and link to a virtual reality engine are not typical competences in industry, especially in regards to the use of SIMIT, or whatever connector, between the PLC simulation and the game engine.
- **UI/UX designer for manufacturing.** Programming the VR engine and setting up 3D rendering is more typical of dedicated professionals common in the game industry but practically absent in the manufacturing environment, thus requiring up-skilling of 3D CAD designer or looking for additional professionals. CAD models created by the process design team need to be simplified before import into the VR engine, as fully detailed models tend to contain features useful for design analysis that are redundant in VR, creating unnecessary additional programming workload and computational overhead.

Company Processes Considerations

- **New methodological approach to design.** Technology development is one part of the story; review of engineering design processes is necessary to make technologies effective and reach the goal of improved performance. Virtual commissioning is already established practice in industry for production system design, but still it lacks proper industrial scaling as a de facto practice as well as immersivity and multi-stakeholder collaboration are not considered, leaving human outside of the design process [11].
- **Required resources.** Proper hardware, software and time are needed to improve production system design practice via IM; high-performance workstations, additional software for connecting CAD and PLC as well as game engine for virtualization are not common in industry and must be considered within the budget, alongside the time for new processes.

5.2 Managerial Implications

Besides lessons learned, some managerial implications can be drawn also considering informal feedback from consortium partners during the project development.

- **Vendor lock-in effect.** To the best of our knowledge, there is currently no commercial software or bundle capable of moving from the concept design of a production system all the way to a deployed Industrial Metaverse. Available tools can address only single tasks or subsets of them, not the complete journey. Multiple CAD software, PLC coding platforms, and virtual reality platforms exist, but their integration remains a challenge that limits the number of viable combinations. Nonetheless, some software providers, like Siemens that was used in the project, are able to cover most of the architecture, possibly creating a vendor lock-in effect if manufacturing companies want to scale up the solution.

- **Early stakeholders engagement.** The Industrial Metaverse applied to production system design allows early involvement of all stakeholders in the production system design. This virtual environment enables realistic human-in-the-loop evaluation of machines long before any physical prototype is available. The actual design, including the real PLC control logic, can be observed and interacted with in real time. The 3D representation in Unity allows not only process engineers, but also production and logistics operators and managers at all levels – in short, all major stakeholders – to observe machine behavior, interact with parts and controls, and assess usability under realistic operating conditions, including line feeding.
- **Intellectual property concerns.** The development and use of IM as a platform for early stakeholder engagement imply that DT, AI models, and control logic are shared in a common environment. This may be a concern in critical sectors where intellectual property is an added value. Therefore, substantial effort must be made to prevent knowledge leaks, such as creating mock-up units or adequate privacy-preserved architectural design of the IM.
- **Reduce time to operation.** Leveraging the possibility to anticipate design reviews in a fully virtual environment reduces the time needed to redo or revise physical prototypes of machines or lines. If combined with immersive training potential, the expected benefit is the overall reduction of the engineering design process, shortening the time from conceptualization to physical commissioning and ramp-up in customer premises.

6 Conclusions

In manufacturing contexts characterized by product volatility and demand uncertainty, companies rely on a mix of enabling technologies to exploit the potential of physical and virtual/cyber worlds for design and management processes optimization [6]. Particular emphasis is placed on production system design; in this context, the METABRAKE project aims to enable effective concurrent engineering of product and production systems through the Industrial Metaverse, conceived as a persistent and immersive environment integrating DT, AI, and XR technologies into a unified platform.

This work sheds light on current advancements in developing the IM for an assembly line in a laboratory environment, focusing on i) detailed production system design reviews and ii) virtual immersive training. Both solutions require integrating multiple software tools not originally designed for seamless interoperability. PLC logic, 3D CAD models, and game engines must be properly combined within an architecture that preserves engineering design processes while enhancing them through human engagement. The IM enables immersive interaction with production systems driven by real PLC logic, allowing operators and technicians to test and validate system behavior before physical prototyping.

The present research shows the IM as a digital platform enabling human engagement and stakeholder collaboration to support production system design across phases from concept to commissioning, giving active roles to humans in simulations through immersive and interactive experiences, even remotely.

A main limitation of this research work is that only qualitative analysis was performed, without any quantitative metrics related to design process improvements, user experience, or architectural alternatives. Connected to this, the lessons learned and implications should be further assessed as they come from a single use case application. The current results open to further research addressing both technological advancements and managerial considerations regarding the effectiveness and adoption of IM in manufacturing companies. On the technological side, research on digital continuity to conceptualize and model semantic relationships between products, processes, and production systems is needed to define their mutual influence via ontologies or information models; development of open-source or software connectors (especially CAD–game engine) remains necessary to foster integration of IM with current industrial tools while avoiding lock-in effects; improvement in user experience via haptic devices such as gloves and suits is required to enhance realism toward more natural interaction with production systems. On the managerial side, research should focus on how engineering design processes should be revised to accommodate IM, reducing non-value-added activities. Additionally, theories such as UTAUT (Unified Theory of Acceptance and Use of Technology) should be used as lens to assess the effectiveness of these technologies in complex socio-technical contexts.

Acknowledgements. This work was supported by the Italian Government (Fondo per la Crescita Sostenibile (F.C.S.), Accordi di Innovazione nella filiera del settore automotive, D.M. 31 December 2021, D.D. 18 March 2022, and D.D. 10 October 2022, Project METABRAKE, Prog. No. F/340038/04/X59).

Disclosure of Interests. The authors have no competing interests to declare that are relevant to the content of this article.

References

1. Design thinking and modeling methods: Review of manufacturing system design in the interplay of industry 4.0 and industry 5.0 (part i). J. Manuf. Syst. **76**, 158–187 (2024). https://doi.org/10.1016/j.jmsy.2024.07.012
2. Digital twins in manufacturing: A unified conceptual framework. Annu. Rev. Control. **60**, 101031 (2025). https://doi.org/10.1016/j.arcontrol.2025.101031
3. Barbieri, G., et al.: A virtual commissioning based methodology to integrate digital twins into manufacturing systems. Prod. Eng. **15**(3), 397–412 (2021). https://doi.org/10.1007/s11740-021-01037-3

4. Düser, T., et al.: Application of the metaverse in product engineering - a workshop for identification of potential field of action. In: He, S., Lai, J., Zhang, L.J. (eds.) METAVERSE 2023. LNCS, vol. 14210, pp. 39–52. Springer, Cham (2023). https://doi.org/10.1007/978-3-031-44754-9_4
5. Guo, J., et al.: Industrial metaverse towards Industry 5.0: connotation, architecture, enablers, and challenges. J. Manuf. Syst. **76**, 25–42 (2024). https://doi.org/10.1016/j.jmsy.2024.07.007
6. Lee, J., et al.: 2026 roadmap on artificial intelligence and machine learning for smart manufacturing. Mach. Learn.: Eng. (2026). https://doi.org/10.1088/3049-4761/ae5967, http://iopscience.iop.org/article/10.1088/3049-4761/ae5967
7. Palmitessa, E., Pasquandrea, M., Cattaneo, L., Polenghi, A.: Towards the industrial metaverse: a proposal and preliminary validation of its architecture for immersive virtual commissioning of production systems. IFAC-PapersOnLine **59**(24), 90–95 (2025). https://doi.org/10.1016/j.ifacol.2025.11.846, 15th IFAC Workshop on Intelligent Manufacturing Systems IMS 2025
8. Putnik, G.D., Putnik, Z.: Defining sequential engineering (SeqE), simultaneous engineering (SE), concurrent engineering (CE) and collaborative engineering (ColE): on similarities and differences. Procedia CIRP **84**, 68–75 (2019). https://doi.org/10.1016/j.procir.2019.07.005, 29th CIRP Design Conference 2019, 08–10 May 2019, Póvoa de Varzim, Portugal
9. Shanmugam, M., Venusamy, K., Subin, S., Srivatsan, S., Kumar, N.: A comprehensive review of haptic gloves: advances, challenges, and future directions. In: 2023 Second International Conference on Electronics and Renewable Systems (ICEARS). pp. 227–233 (2023). https://doi.org/10.1109/ICEARS56392.2023.10085607
10. Striffler, N., Voigt, T.: A 3d approach for the virtual commissioning of processing plants. IEEE Access **13**, 21190–21209 (2025). https://doi.org/10.1109/ACCESS.2025.3536088
11. Ullrich, M., Thalappully, R., Heieck, F., Lüdemann-Ravit, B.: Virtual commissioning of linked cells using digital models in an industrial metaverse. Automation **5**(1), 1–12 (2024). https://doi.org/10.3390/automation5010001
12. Yildiz, E., Møller, C., Bilberg, A.: Demonstration and evaluation of a digital twin-based virtual factory. Int. J. Adv. Manuf. Technol. **114**(1), 185–203 (2021). https://doi.org/10.1007/s00170-021-06825-w

Towards an Integrated Production Scheduling and Maintenance Planning Using Reinforcement Learning

Ricardo Caballero[1(✉)], Eike Broda[1], Nicollas Luiz Schweitzer de Souza[2], Enzo M. Frazzon[2], and Michael Freitag[1,3]

[1] BIBA - Bremer Institut für Produktion und Logistik GmbH at the University of Bremen, Hochschulring 20, 28359 Bremen, Germany
{cab,brd,fre}@biba.uni-bremen.de

[2] Graduate Program in Production Engineering, Federal University of Santa Catarina, R. Eng. Agronômico Andrei Cristian Ferreira, Florianópolis 88040-900, Brazil
{nicollas.schweitzer,enzo.frazzon}@ufsc.br

[3] University of Bremen, Faculty of Production Engineering, Badgasteiner Straße 1, 28359 Bremen, Germany

Abstract. Production scheduling and maintenance planning are closely interdependent functions in manufacturing systems, since maintenance actions affect machine availability, production capacity, backlog, and service performance. This paper proposes a reinforcement learning (RL) approach for coordinating production control and preventive maintenance in a simulated two-stage manufacturing system with parallel machines, stochastic processing times, finite work-in-progress buffers, stochastic demand, and age-dependent machine failures. The decision problem is formulated as a Markov Decision Process (MDP). A proximal policy optimization (PPO) agent is trained to select dispatching rules, such as First-Come-First-Served (FCFS), Shortest Processing Time (SPT), and Earliest Due Date (EDD), either with or without a preventive maintenance request. The learned policy is compared with heuristic baseline combinations of dispatching rules and corrective, time-based, and condition-based maintenance strategies. The results show that the PPO agent achieved the lowest mean total cost among the evaluated policies and reduced corrective maintenance events. However, the agent did not achieve the highest service level, indicating a cost-service trade-off. The study contributes a simulation-based proof of concept for RL-supported integrated production and maintenance planning and identifies requirements for further validation, including extended training, statistical testing, and application to more realistic industrial scenarios.

Keywords: Reinforcement learning · Production scheduling · Maintenance planning · Production planning and control

Published by Springer Nature Switzerland AG 2027
G. Pezzotta et al. (Eds.): APMS 2026, IFIP AICT 808, pp. 400–415, 2027.
https://doi.org/10.1007/978-3-032-38594-9_27

1 Introduction

Modern manufacturing systems operate under increasing complexity and uncertainty, driven by shorter product life cycles, higher product variety, and dynamic market conditions [1]. As a result, production planning and control (PPC) systems must respond to disturbances such as fluctuating demand, machine failures, and varying processing times [2,3]. Digitalization and artificial intelligence (AI) can support more adaptive production systems, although their industrial adoption still depends on digital integration and organizational readiness [4,5]. Within PPC, production scheduling and maintenance planning are particularly relevant because they directly affect throughput, service performance, and operational reliability [6–8]. Production scheduling is commonly addressed through optimization models, heuristics, and dispatching rules [9]. These approaches are efficient and widely used, but often rely on predefined decision logic and simplified assumptions, which can limit adaptability in dynamic environments [8,9]. Maintenance planning is often treated separately through time-based or condition-based policies [10]. This separation is problematic because maintenance affects machine availability and system capacity, while scheduling decisions influence utilization, degradation, and maintenance opportunities [6,7].

The integration of production scheduling and maintenance planning is already an established research stream. Early models coordinated preventive maintenance with single-machine scheduling [11,12], while later studies considered deterioration, cumulative damage, predictive-maintenance information, and multi-state production systems [13,14]. Recent work has also applied reinforcement learning (RL) and multi-agent RL to joint maintenance and production scheduling under machine degradation and condition-based maintenance [13,15]. Thus, this paper does not claim that integration itself is new. Instead, it investigates RL as a mechanism for learning state-dependent coordination policies under stochastic production and failure dynamics.

RL is relevant for this setting because it learns control policies through repeated interaction with an environment and can adapt decisions to the observed system state. In production scheduling and control, RL has shown potential for handling stochastic and dynamic shop-floor conditions [2,3,16–18]. However, existing approaches often focus on specific system configurations, predefined maintenance structures, or problem-specific optimization settings. The research gap addressed here is therefore the simulation-based learning of coordinated dispatching and preventive-maintenance decisions in a stochastic production system with finite buffers, machine degradation, corrective maintenance, and service-level effects.

The study addresses the following research question: How can RL coordinate dispatching-rule selection and preventive-maintenance decisions in a stochastic production system, and how does the resulting policy perform against fixed heuristics regarding cost, service level (SL), and maintenance-related indicators? The contribution is threefold: (i) the formulation of integrated production scheduling and maintenance planning as a simulation-based sequential decision problem, (ii) the implementation of a proximal policy optimization (PPO) agent that selects dispatching-only or dispatching-plus-maintenance actions based on production and machine-health states, and (iii) the comparison of the learned policy with classical dispatching and maintenance strategies to analyze cost, service, and maintenance trade-offs. The remainder of the paper is structured as follows: Sect. 2 reviews related work, Sect. 3 describes the simulation model and baselines, Sect. 4 presents the MDP and PPO implementation, Sect. 5 discusses the results, and Sect. 6 concludes the paper.

2 Related Work

This section reviews research at the intersection of production scheduling, maintenance planning, and RL. The aim is to position the present study within existing work and to clarify the specific contribution of the proposed approach. The section first discusses integrated production scheduling and maintenance planning. It then reviews RL-based approaches for production scheduling, maintenance planning, and coordinated PPC decisions.

2.1 Integrated Production Scheduling and Maintenance Planning

Production scheduling and maintenance planning have traditionally been studied as separate decision problems. Production scheduling focuses on assigning jobs to resources over time, while maintenance planning aims to preserve or restore machine availability. However, both decisions are strongly interdependent. Maintenance activities reduce available production capacity during their execution, while production schedules influence machine utilization, degradation exposure, and the timing of maintenance opportunities.

Several studies have therefore investigated integrated production scheduling and maintenance planning. Cassady and Kutanoglu [11] proposed an early integrated model for coordinating preventive maintenance planning and single-machine production scheduling. Their results showed that joint decision-making can improve performance compared with treating scheduling and maintenance independently. Kuo and Chang [12] extended this perspective by considering a cumulative damage failure process and by analyzing how preventive maintenance decisions interact with production schedules. Further contributions have addressed integrated production and maintenance planning in flow shop and multi-machine contexts [6], while recent reviews confirm that production, maintenance, and resource scheduling are strongly related planning problems [7].

More recent work has extended integrated planning toward degradation processes, predictive maintenance, and condition-based maintenance. Zhai et al. [14] proposed a predictive-maintenance-integrated production scheduling approach that connects prognostics and health management information with integrated production scheduling and maintenance planning. Zhang et al. [10] investigated the integrated decision of production scheduling and condition-based maintenance planning for multi-unit systems with variable replacement thresholds. Yan et al. [19] considered distributed flow shop scheduling with flexible maintenance and applied deep reinforcement learning to account for maintenance-related decisions in the scheduling process.

These studies demonstrate that integrated production-maintenance planning is an established research field. Classical optimization, dynamic programming, genetic algorithms, and heuristic or metaheuristic methods have already provided important contributions. However, these approaches often require problem-specific formulations, predefined maintenance structures, or repeated re-optimization when the production environment changes. This can limit their responsiveness in stochastic and event-driven production systems. Therefore, RL is not positioned in this paper as a replacement for established optimization and heuristic methods, but as a complementary approach for learning adaptive control policies under dynamic system conditions.

2.2 Reinforcement Learning for Production Scheduling

RL has gained increasing attention in production scheduling because it can model scheduling as a sequential decision-making problem. Instead of computing a complete schedule once, an RL agent learns a policy through repeated interaction with an environment. This is especially relevant for stochastic production systems in which jobs, machine states, buffers, and disturbances evolve over time [16].

A central methodological stream concerns the design of simulation-based RL environments for scheduling. Lang et al. [20] formalized production scheduling problems as RL environments based on discrete-event simulation and OpenAI Gym. Their work showed how simulation models can be connected with reusable RL algorithms. Steinbacher et al. [21] proposed a modelling framework for RL-based scheduling applications and emphasized the importance of state representation, action abstraction, reward design, and simulation fidelity. In later work, Steinbacher et al. [22] studied production control with RL for a matrix-structured production system and showed how RL can support dispatching and routing decisions in flexible production settings.

Other studies have focused on RL for dispatching-rule selection and dynamic scheduling. Tassel et al. [23] introduced an RL environment for job-shop scheduling, while Tassel et al. [17] showed that RL can learn dispatching strategies for large-scale industrial scheduling instances. Kardos et al. [24] applied Q-learning to dynamic job-shop scheduling and compared the learned policy with standard dispatching rules. Zhou et al. [18] proposed an RL approach with composite rewards for smart-factory scheduling, allowing several production objectives to be considered simultaneously. Wang et al. [25] developed a data-driven simulation-optimization framework for generating priority dispatching rules in dynamic job shops with uncertainties.

Recent deep reinforcement learning (DRL) studies have further extended this line of research. Yuan et al. [26] applied proximal policy optimization to dynamic job shop scheduling. Yan et al. [27] investigated dynamic flexible job shop scheduling with sequence-dependent setup times, while Lu et al. [28] considered dynamic scheduling in distributed heterogeneous flexible job shops with integrated inventory allocation and product delivery. These studies show that RL and DRL can handle increasingly complex scheduling environments. Nevertheless, most of them focus mainly on production-oriented objectives such as makespan, tardiness, throughput, workload balance, or setup efficiency.

Systematic reviews confirm this tendency. Esteso et al. [2] showed that production scheduling is one of the most frequent application areas of RL in PPC. Panzer and Bender [3] identified the growing role of deep RL in production systems, but also highlighted challenges related to modelling assumptions, transferability, and industrial validation. Ngwu et al. [29] similarly emphasized that RL-based scheduling methods still face open issues regarding robustness, interpretability, benchmarking, and deployment in real manufacturing environments.

2.3 Reinforcement Learning for Maintenance Planning and Coordinated PPC Decisions

RL has also been applied to maintenance planning. In this context, maintenance is formulated as a sequential decision problem in which an agent decides when to perform maintenance based on machine condition, degradation state, or system performance. Feng and Li [30] proposed an RL-based predictive maintenance decision model for multistage production systems. Their study showed that maintenance decisions affect not only the machine itself, but also upstream and downstream production dynamics such as blocking and starvation. Yang et al. [13] formulated the joint optimization of preventive maintenance and production scheduling for multi-state production systems as a Markov decision process and used RL to derive production and maintenance policies.

More recent work has moved toward joint production and maintenance control. Zhang et al. [15] proposed a counterfactual-attention multi-agent reinforcement learning framework for joint condition-based maintenance and production scheduling in a multi-stage hybrid flow shop. Their work is particularly relevant because it treats production scheduling and maintenance as interconnected decisions in a learning-based framework. However, the use of multi-agent architectures and condition-based maintenance also introduces complexity regarding state representation, coordination, and scalability.

Beyond maintenance, RL is increasingly used as a coordination mechanism across several PPC functions. Göppert et al. [31] investigated RL-controlled lineless assembly systems and emphasized the role of automated scenario analysis for evaluating learning-based production control. Park et al. [32] applied RL to robust scheduling in semiconductor manufacturing, showing that learned policies can improve responsiveness under variability in production requirements and machine availability. Kaven et al. [33] used multi-agent RL for online layout planning and scheduling in flexible assembly systems, demonstrating that RL can coordinate interdependent planning tasks. Hoss et al. [34] further emphasized the need for RL scheduling frameworks that consider real-world constraints such as buffers, transport, setup times, and machine breakdowns. In addition, Caballero et al. [35] proposed a conceptual framework for AI-driven integrated planning of production and predictive maintenance, highlighting the need to connect predictive insights with RL-based planning decisions.

Overall, the reviewed literature confirms that integrated production-maintenance planning is an established field, but also shows remaining gaps regarding the joint treatment of dispatching, finite-buffer dynamics, maintenance decisions, and service-level effects. Table 1 summarizes the main research streams, contributions, limitations, and relevance to the present study.

Table 1. Summary of related work and research positioning

Research stream	Main contribution, limitation, and relevance
Integrated production and maintenance planning [6, 7, 11, 12]	These studies establish the need to consider production scheduling and maintenance planning jointly. However, many approaches rely on analytical models, optimization formulations, or predefined planning structures, which can limit their use in dynamic online control.
Predictive/condition-based integrated approaches [10, 13, 14, 19]	These works extend integrated planning toward degradation, predictive maintenance, and condition-based decisions. Many models remain tailored to specific system settings or require repeated re-optimization when operating conditions change.
RL for production scheduling [17, 18, 20–23, 26]	These studies show that RL can support adaptive scheduling under dynamic conditions. Nevertheless, most approaches focus on production key performance indicators, while maintenance is often ignored or treated as an external disturbance.
RL/MARL for coordinated PPC decisions [2, 3, 15, 30, 31, 33, 34]	These contributions demonstrate the potential of RL for maintenance and coordinated PPC decisions. But, the integrated treatment of dispatching, finite-buffer dynamics, and preventive maintenance triggering remains insufficiently explored.

3 Problem Description and System Model

3.1 Manufacturing System Overview

The experimental study considers an event-discrete simulation model of a serial two-stage production system with parallel machines per stage (see Fig. 1). The system consists of two production stages arranged in series ($S_1 \rightarrow S_2$), each comprising two identical parallel machines, resulting in a total of four machines. Between the stages, a finite Work-In-Progress (WIP) buffer is installed, while the source buffer is assumed to be sufficiently large. If the WIP buffer is full, the machine before is blocked until one of the machines at stage 2 consumes the next job from the buffer.

Jobs are released into the source buffer and must be processed sequentially at Stage 1 and Stage 2 before entering the finished jobs buffer. Each job is characterized by a release time, a due date, and stochastic processing times at both stages. Processing times are sampled from stage-specific distributions to represent operational variability.

Demand arrives stochastically at the finished jobs level according to a Poisson process. If the finished jobs inventory is insufficient to satisfy demand, unmet demand accumulates as backlog and is penalized economically.

Machine degradation is modeled via an age-dependent hazard function, a common representation in maintenance-aware production systems where the probability of failure increases with accumulated machine usage [6,30]. Machine age increases during processing, and the likelihood of failure increases with operating time. When a failure occurs, corrective maintenance (CM) is triggered automatically. Preventive maintenance (PM) can be initiated proactively and restores the machine to an as-good-as-new condition [10,19,30]. At each stage, only one maintenance operation can be executed at a time. So if both machines on the stage fail, the second failing machine needs to wait until the first machine is repaired.

If PM should be applied to the machine, a PM flag is set for this machine. Before the next job starts, the machine will check whether the stage's maintenance operator is available. If this is the case, and the other machine is not currently under PM or CM, the PM will be started. Otherwise, the machine first selects another job and re-checks its availability after this job finishes. Machines that break and require CM remain in the broken state until a maintenance operator becomes available.

The modeled system therefore captures the fundamental trade-off between production efficiency, service performance, and operational reliability under uncertainty [6,7].

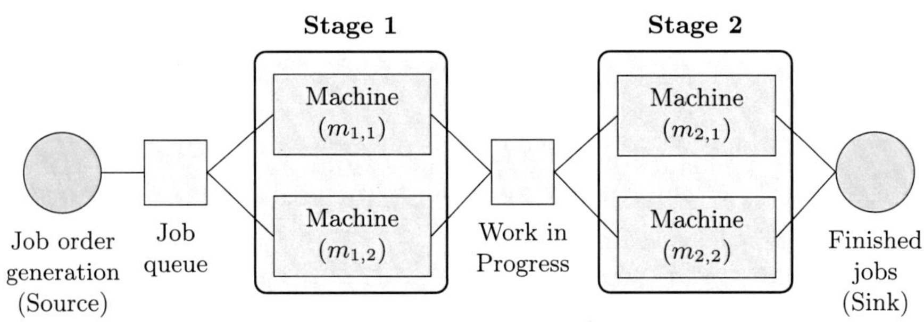

Fig. 1. Overview of the two-stage manufacturing system with parallel machines and intermediate work in progress buffer.

3.2 Baselines: Dispatching Rules and Maintenance Strategies

In the model, the following dispatching rules are considered. A dispatching rule is applied whenever one of the machines has the capacity to execute a job. The dispatching rule then decides which job from the previous buffer is selected next. Because each rule has a different optimization aim, their performance varies. Dispatching rules represent widely used heuristic approaches for production scheduling due to their simplicity and low computational requirements [3, 17].

- **First-Come-First-Served (FCFS/FIFO):** Jobs are processed in the order they arrived in the queue.
- **Shortest Processing Time (SPT):** The job with the shortest processing time is prioritized and selected first.
- **Earliest Due Date (EDD):** The jobs with the earliest due date is processed first.

Additionally, three maintenance strategies are defined which are to be combined with the dispatching rules.

- **Corrective Maintenance (CM):** This strategy applies reactive maintenance. Machines work until a breakdown occurs and are repaired afterwards using corrective maintenance.
- **Time-Based Maintenance (TBM):** The machines are maintained in a predefined interval.
- **Condition-Based Maintenance (CBM):** The machines are maintained based on their current condition which is described by the Remaining Useful Life (RUL). If this RUL is below the specified threshold, a maintenance is started.

The dispatching rules and maintenance strategies are combined into a set of nine baseline policies, as shown in Table 2. These baseline strategies are heuristics that represent static decision rules that do not adapt to the current system state. In contrast, the RL agent uses a state-dependent policy, as described in the next subsection.

Table 2. Overview of the defined baseline policies

	FCFS	SPT	EDD
CM	FCFS_CM	SPT_CM	EDD_CM
TBM	FCFS_TBM	SPT_TBM	EDD_TBM
CBM	FCFS_CBM	SPT_CBM	EDD_CBM

4 Reinforcement Learning-Based Planning Approach

4.1 Decision Scope

The decision problem considered in this study consists of selecting system-level production and maintenance control actions at predefined decision epochs. The RL agent does not directly assign a specific job to a specific machine. Instead, it selects a dispatching logic to be applied to all eligible machines during the next decision interval. In addition, the selected action can include a preventive-maintenance request. At each decision epoch, RL agents choose one action from the following set of actions: (i) apply FCFS, (ii) apply SPT, (iii) apply EDD, or (iv - vi) apply one of these three dispatching rules while requesting preventive maintenance. This action is not an independent action for each of the four machines. Rather, it defines the system-level control logic used by the production system during the next decision interval.

A decision epoch occurs in a predefined time interval ΔT, which is fixed for the simulation time. Until time ΔT has passed since the last decision, the individual rule per machine, derived from the action, is kept for all machines and afterward a new set of actions is applied to the machines.

Machine failures are not under the agent's direct control. Instead, failures are generated probabilistically according to an age-dependent hazard function, and CM is automatically triggered upon failure. This creates delayed and stochastic consequences of the agent's decisions: preventive maintenance can reduce future failure risk but temporarily decreases production capacity, whereas delaying maintenance can increase failure probability, backlog, and service level deterioration. The interdependence between dispatching and maintenance decisions is the central source of complexity in the problem.

4.2 Markov Decision Process Formulation

The integrated scheduling and maintenance decision problem is formulated as MDP. An MDP is defined by the tuple (S, A, P, R, γ), where S represents the set of system states, A the set of actions, P the transition probabilities between states, R the reward function, and γ the discount factor [16].

State Space. The system state $s \in S$ captures the relevant information required to make dispatching and maintenance decisions. The state representation includes machine status, job queue information, and maintenance-related variables. In particular, the state vector contains: machine status (idle, processing, failed, under maintenance), number of jobs waiting in the queues, total size of the backlog, demand rate of the system, machine age and remaining useful life. This information allows the agent to evaluate both short-term production performance and long-term machine reliability when selecting actions.

Action Space. The set of available actions $a \in A$ consists of selecting a dispatching rule, with or without the initiation of preventive maintenance. The action set is defined as follows, where PM indicates the initiation of preventive maintenance:

$$A = \{FCFS, SPT, EDD, FCFS\_PM, SPT\_PM, EDD\_PM\} \quad (1)$$

State Transitions. The transition function $P(s'|s,a)$ describes the probabilistic evolution of the production system after applying action a in state s. System dynamics are governed by job arrivals, processing completion events, and stochastic machine failures. Machine failures follow an age-dependent hazard model, which increases the probability of failure as machine age increases. Preventive maintenance reduces the failure risk but temporarily removes the machine from production.

Reward Function. The reward function $R(s,a)$ evaluates the immediate system performance after executing an action. The reward reflects production efficiency and reliability objectives and includes penalties for tardiness, machine downtime, and excessive backlog. This structure encourages the agent to balance production throughput with preventive maintenance decisions.

The reward function $R(s,a)$ is defined as the sum of the inventory costs in the last time step, the penalty cost for the current backlog, the cost for all maintenance operations in the last time step and penalty cost for all PM in the time step.

$$\begin{aligned} R(s,a) = -(&|\text{inventory units}| \times \text{inventory cost} + |\text{backlog}| \times \text{backlog penalty} \\ &+ \text{cost of maintenance} + |\text{nPM}| \times \text{PM penalty}) \end{aligned} \quad (2)$$

Discount Factor. The discount factor $\gamma \in [0,1]$ determines the importance of future rewards relative to immediate rewards. In the context of production control, the discount factor allows the agent to account for long-term effects of maintenance decisions, such as future failures or improved system availability.

4.3 Implementation

The approach is implemented as a Python script. In the script a discrete-event simulation is implemented which simulates the model described in the previous section. As RL agent the PPO algorithm was selected and used from the library Stable-baselines 3 [36]. PPO is suitable because the action space is discrete but policy-based, the environment is stochastic and the objective is not a one shot schedule but repeated control over horizon with delayed maintenance effects [23, 26].

4.4 Parameters

The length of a time step ΔT is set to 50 time units, and the horizon of the simulation is 80. Therefore, the simulation runs for a total of 4.000 time units.

The simulation parameters are an infinite-capacity job queue and a very small work-in-progress buffer with 20 jobs. The processing times are Gaussian functions with an expected value of 4 time units and a variance of 1.0 on stage 1 and 5 time units and a variance of 1.5 on stage 2. The job's due date also follows a Gaussian distribution with a mean of 20 time units after the job's release time and a variance of 4.0. The demand rate is derived from a Poisson distribution with the expectation of 0.3 new jobs per time unit. As this is executed only every ΔT, the value is multiplied accordingly to $0.3 \times \Delta T$.

The duration of a PM is 6 time units with a cost of 10. A CM takes 20 time units and has costs of 30. For the time-based maintenance, an interval of 80 time units is assumed, and the condition-based maintenance is triggered if the RUL is below the threshold of 15 time units.

The RL agent is defined to use 200 episodes of learning, so the data basis for the agent policy are 8000 decisions. It receives an observation array containing a set of integers and floats. It contains the sizes of all queues and the jobs ready to be shipped. Additionally, it includes the number of jobs in the backlog that have not yet been produced and the overall demand rate. Also, for each machine, the current age, RUL, current remaining processing time, and the information about the machine state (working, broken, under maintenance, blocked, idle). The learning rate was set to 0.001, and all other parameters were left at the default values of the Stable Baselines 3 library.

5 Simulation Model and Results

The environment for these results was implemented as a discrete-event simulation representing the simplified production system described above. The verification and validation of the simulation model was conducted by comparing baseline heuristic performance with expected scheduling behavior, checking the Gantt charts of the runs and by ensuring consistent system dynamics under repeated simulation runs.

In the simulation, the baseline policies are fixed, determining job dispatching whenever a machine becomes idle and executing preventive maintenance according to the maintenance strategy. In contrast, the reinforcement learning agent learns a control policy through interaction with the simulation environment. At each decision epoch, the agent observes the current system state and selects an action from the action set defined in the MDP formulation (see Sect. 4.2). The objective of the learning process is to identify policies that achieve better system performance compared to the baseline heuristics. After the learning process, the agent has learned a policy that is then applied in the exact same simulation as the baseline policies.

For the following results, all simulations were run in 50 replications to reduce statistical effects of random numbers. The learning took 50.2 s on an Intel i7-8550U and the run of the 50 replications took 67.5 s.

Table 3 shows the mean values. The key performance indicators (KPIs) are the total costs and the service level (SL). The costs are calculated as described in the RL agent's reward function. The SL describes the number of jobs that have been shipped compared to the number requested. A SL of 100% would indicate that all jobs have been produced in time. Additionally, the table lists the amount of applied corrective maintenance (nCM) and preventive maintenance (nPM) during the runtime and their quotient. The last group of results are the mean time to repair (MTTR) and mean time between two failures (MTBF).

Table 3. Mean results of 50 simulation runs with **bold highlight** of the best result. nCM is the amount of executed corrective maintenance, nPM of preventive maintenance.

Rule	Total cost	SL [%]	nCM	nPM	$\frac{CM}{PM}$	MTBF	MTTR
SPT_CM	84510	98.78	91.5	0.0	-	43.5	20.0
SPT_CBM	77812	98.90	81.5	36.2	2.2	49.1	15.7
SPT_TBM	67160	**99.07**	66.0	85.7	0.8	60.6	12.1
EDD_CM	85447	98.13	92.0	0.0	-	43.1	20.0
EDD_CBM	78180	98.21	81.1	36.4	2.2	49.1	15.6
EDD_TBM	69129	98.45	67.2	85.5	0.8	59.5	12.2
FCFS_CM	85237	98.13	91.7	0.0	-	43.3	20.0
FCFS_CBM	77628	98.29	80.5	36.5	2.2	49.5	15.6
FCFS_TBM	68842	98.24	66.6	85.9	0.8	60.0	12.1
PPO_Agent	**65694**	98.21	**56.6**	158.1	0.4	**70.2**	**9.7**

Table 3 shows that the PPO_Agent performs best in regard to costs, with costs of 65694, SPT_TBM has the next highest costs at 67160. This is what was expected, as the optimization aim of the RL agent was costs. In regard to the SL, the agent is only ranked 7th, but near all other rules and only 0.23% below the average of all benchmark SLs. Regarding the amount of maintenance operations, the agent has the lowest amount of corrective maintenance, but triggers the most preventive maintenance operations of all rules compared. Still this leads

Table 4. Confidence intervals (confidence level 95%) of the PPO Agent and the best baseline *SPT_TBM*

	PPO_Agent		SPT_TBM	
KPI	Value	Conf. int.	Conf. int.	Value
Total cost	65694	[64483; 66905]	[65717; 68605]	67160
SL [%]	98.21	[97.91; 98.51]	[98.86; 99.28]	99.07
nCM	56.6	[55.44; 57.75]	[64.58; 67.52]	66.1
MTBF	70.2	[68.64; 71.73]	[59.16; 61.95]	60.56
MTTR	9.7	[9.61; 9.76]	[11.98; 12.20]	12.1

to the lowest MTTR and the highest MTBF. The results numbers also allow a crosscheck of the logic as all scenarios only with corrective maintenance ($*\_CM$) have a MTTR of 20, which is exactly the duration set for each CM operation.

Table 4 shows the confidence intervals for 95% confidence for the PPO Agent and the best baseline SPT_TBM. It shows, that for total cost the PPO_Agent is better, but not significantly. For the SL, the SPT_TBM baseline is significantly better, but still slightly and the agent was not trained in that regard. For the last three KPIs the PPO_Agent performs significantly better.

6 Conclusion and Outlook

This paper presented a simulation-based reinforcement learning approach for coordinating dispatching-rule selection and preventive-maintenance decisions in a two-stage production system. The problem was formulated as an MDP and solved using a PPO agent that selects between dispatching-only and dispatching-plus-maintenance actions. The results show that the PPO agent achieved the lowest mean total cost and reduced corrective maintenance compared with the heuristic baselines. It also improved maintenance-related indicators, especially MTBF and MTTR. At the same time, the agent did not achieve the highest service level, which indicates a trade-off between cost-oriented maintenance behavior and service performance. Overall, the study provides a proof of concept for RL-supported integrated production and maintenance planning. Future work will focus on larger production systems, additional production KPIs, longer training, and validation in more realistic industrial scenarios.

Acknowledgments. This research was funded by the Deutsche Forschungsgemeinschaft (DFG, German Research Foundation) – Projektnummer(547349768) and the Coordination for the Improvement of Higher Education Personnel (CAPES – Brazil, Project no. 88881.964228/2024-01).

Disclosure of Interests. The authors have no competing interests to declare that are relevant to the content of this article.

References

1. Brecher, C. (ed.): Advances in Production Technology. LNPE, Springer, Cham (2015). https://doi.org/10.1007/978-3-319-12304-2
2. Esteso, A., Peidro, D., Mula, J., Díaz-Madroñero, M.: Reinforcement learning applied to production planning and control. Int. J. Prod. Res. **61**(16), 5772–5789 (2023). https://doi.org/10.1080/00207543.2022.2104180
3. Panzer, M., Bender, B.: Deep reinforcement learning in production systems: a systematic literature review. Int. J. Prod. Res. **60**(13), 4316–4341 (2022). https://doi.org/10.1080/00207543.2021.1973138
4. Heimberger, H., Jäger, A., Maloca, S.: Künstliche Intelligenz in der Produktion. Technical report, Fraunhofer-Institut für System- und Innovationsforschung ISI (2024). https://doi.org/10.24406/publica-4047

5. Lerch, C., Jäger, A., Maloca, S.: Ai-readiness and production resilience: empirical evidence from German manufacturing in times of the COVID-19 pandemic. Technol. Forecast. Soc. Chang. **181**, 121755 (2022). https://doi.org/10.1016/j.techfore.2022.121755
6. Al-Shayea, A., Fararah, E., Abouel Nasr, E., Mahmoud, H.A.: Model for integrating production scheduling and maintenance planning of flow shop production system. IEEE Access **8**, 208826–208836 (2020). https://doi.org/10.1109/ACCESS.2020.3038719
7. Geurtsen, M., Didden, J.B.H.C., Adan, J., Atan, Z., Adan, I.: Production, maintenance and resource scheduling: a review. Eur. J. Oper. Res. **305**(2), 501–529 (2023). https://doi.org/10.1016/j.ejor.2022.03.045
8. Quadras, D., Frazzon, E.M., Mendes, L.G., Pires, M.C., Rodriguez, C.M.T.: Adaptive simulation-based optimization for production scheduling: a comparative study. IFAC PapersOnLine **55**(10), 424–429 (2022). https://doi.org/10.1016/j.ifacol.2022.09.430
9. Urgo, M., Lanza, G., Vrabič, R., Gyulai, D.: Future-proof production scheduling and control. CIRP Ann. Manuf. Technol. **74**, 971–991 (2025). https://doi.org/10.1016/j.cirp.2025.04.095
10. Zhang, Z., Li, J., Wang, Z., Liu, Y.: Integrated decision of production scheduling and condition-based maintenance planning for multi-unit systems with variable replacement thresholds. J. Manuf. Syst. **72**, 263–276 (2024). https://doi.org/10.1016/j.jmsy.2024.04.026
11. Cassady, C.R., Kutanoglu, E.: Integrating preventive maintenance planning and production scheduling for a single machine. IEEE Trans. Reliab. **54**(2), 304–309 (2005). https://doi.org/10.1109/TR.2005.845967
12. Kuo, Y., Chang, Z.A.: Integrated production scheduling and preventive maintenance planning for a single machine under a cumulative damage failure process. Nav. Res. Logist. **54**(6), 602–614 (2007). https://doi.org/10.1002/nav.20232
13. Yang, H., Li, W., Wang, B.: Joint optimization of preventive maintenance and production scheduling for multi-state production systems based on reinforcement learning. Reliab. Eng. Syst. Saf. **214**, 107713 (2021). https://doi.org/10.1016/j.ress.2021.107713
14. Zhai, S., Kandemir, M.G., Reinhart, G.: Predictive maintenance integrated production scheduling by applying deep generative prognostics models: approach, formulation and solution. Prod. Eng. Res. Devel. **16**(1), 65–88 (2021). https://doi.org/10.1007/s11740-021-01064-0
15. Zhang, N., Shen, Y., Du, Y., Chen, L., Zhang, X.: Counterfactual-attention multi-agent reinforcement learning for joint condition-based maintenance and production scheduling. J. Manuf. Syst. **71**, 70–81 (2023). https://doi.org/10.1016/j.jmsy.2023.08.011
16. Sutton, R.S., Barto, A.G.: Reinforcement Learning: An Introduction, 2nd edn. MIT Press, Cambridge, MA (2018)
17. Tassel, P., Kovacs, B., Gebser, M., Schekotihin, K., Kohlenbrein, W., Schrott-Kostwein, P.: Reinforcement learning of dispatching strategies for large-scale industrial scheduling. In: Proceedings of the International Conference on Automated Planning and Scheduling, vol. 32, no. 1, pp. 638–646 (2022). https://doi.org/10.1609/icaps.v32i1.19852
18. Zhou, T., Tang, D., Zhu, H., Wang, L.: Reinforcement learning with composite rewards for production scheduling in a smart factory. IEEE Access **9**, 752–766 (2021). https://doi.org/10.1109/ACCESS.2020.3046784

19. Yan, Q., Wu, W., Wang, H.: Deep reinforcement learning for distributed flow shop scheduling with flexible maintenance. Machines **10**(3) (2022). https://doi.org/10.3390/machines10030210
20. Lang, S., Kuetgens, M., Reichardt, P., Reggelin, T.: Modeling production scheduling problems as reinforcement learning environments based on discrete-event simulation and openAI gym. IFAC-PapersOnLine **54**(1), 793–798 (2021). https://doi.org/10.1016/j.ifacol.2021.08.093
21. Steinbacher, L.M., Ait-Alla, A., Rippel, D., Düe, T., Freitag, M.: Modelling framework for reinforcement learning based scheduling applications. IFAC-PapersOnLine **55**(10), 67–72 (2022). https://doi.org/10.1016/j.ifacol.2022.09.369, 10th IFAC Conference on Manufacturing Modelling, Management and Control MIM 2022
22. Steinbacher, L.M., Wegmann, T., Freitag, M.: Production control with reinforcement learning for a matrix-structured production system. Int. J. Prod. Res. **63**(11), 4114–4136 (2025). https://doi.org/10.1080/00207543.2024.2436126
23. Tassel, P., Gebser, M., Schekotihin, K.: A reinforcement learning environment for job-shop scheduling. In: Proceedings of Bridging the Gap Between AI Planning and Reinforcement Learning (PRL) – Workshop at ICAPS 2021 (2021). https://doi.org/10.48550/arXiv.2104.03760
24. Kardos, C., Laflamme, C., Gallina, V., Sihn, W.: Dynamic scheduling in a job-shop production system with reinforcement learning. Procedia CIRP **97**, 104–109 (2021). https://doi.org/10.1016/j.procir.2020.05.210, 8th CIRP Conference of Assembly Technology and Systems
25. Wang, H., Peng, T., Nassehi, A., Tang, R.: A data-driven simulation-optimization framework for generating priority dispatching rules in dynamic job shop scheduling with uncertainties. J. Manuf. Syst. **70**, 288–308 (2023). https://doi.org/10.1016/j.jmsy.2023.08.001
26. Yuan, M., Yu, Q., Zhang, L., Lu, S., Li, Z., Pei, F.: Deep reinforcement learning based proximal policy optimization algorithm for dynamic job shop scheduling. Comput. Oper. Res. **183**, 107149 (2025). https://doi.org/10.1016/j.cor.2025.107149
27. Yan, B., Liu, X., Lu, S., Hu, C., Wang, X., Zhou, Z.: Deep reinforcement learning approach for a dynamic flexible job shop problem with sequence dependent setup times. Comput. Ind. Eng. **207**, 111310 (2025). https://doi.org/10.1016/j.cie.2025.111310
28. Lu, L., Deng, Q., Hu, Y., Luo, Q., Gao, S., Zhang, J.: Deep reinforcement learning for dynamic scheduling in distributed heterogeneous flexible job shop with integrated inventory allocation and product delivery. Eng. Appl. Artif. Intell. **162**, 112681 (2025). https://doi.org/10.1016/j.engappai.2025.112681
29. Ngwu, C., Liu, Y., Wu, R.: Reinforcement learning in dynamic job shop scheduling: a comprehensive review of AI-driven approaches in modern manufacturing. J. Intell. Manuf. **37**(3), 1093–1108 (2025). https://doi.org/10.1007/s10845-025-02585-6
30. Feng, M., Li, Y.: Predictive maintenance decision making based on reinforcement learning in multistage production systems. IEEE Access **10**, 18910–18921 (2022)
31. Göppert, A., Rachner, J., Schmitt, R.H.: Automated scenario analysis of reinforcement learning controlled line-less assembly systems. Procedia CIRP **93**, 1091–1096 (2020). https://doi.org/10.1016/j.procir.2020.04.116
32. Park, I.B., Huh, J., Kim, J., Park, J.: A reinforcement learning approach to robust scheduling of semiconductor manufacturing facilities. IEEE Trans. Autom. Sci. Eng. **17**(3), 1420–1431 (2020). https://doi.org/10.1109/TASE.2019.2956762

33. Kaven, L., Huke, P., Göppert, A., Schmitt, R.H.: Multi agent reinforcement learning for online layout planning and scheduling in flexible assembly systems. J. Intell. Manuf. **35**(8), 3917–3936 (2024). https://doi.org/10.1007/s10845-023-02309-8
34. Hoss, J., Schelling, F., Klarmann, N.: A production scheduling framework for reinforcement learning under real-world constraints (2025). https://arxiv.org/abs/2506.13566
35. Caballero, R., et al.: A conceptual framework for AI-driven, integrated planning of production and predictive maintenance. Procedia Comput. Sci. **276**, 215–222 (2026). https://doi.org/10.1016/j.procs.2026.02.027
36. Raffin, A., Hill, A., Gleave, A., Kanervisto, A., Ernestus, M., Dormann, N.: Stable-baselines3: reliable reinforcement learning implementations. J. Mach. Learn. Res. **22**(268), 1–8 (2021). http://jmlr.org/papers/v22/20-1364.html

Decision Support Systems for Sustainable Maintenance Enabled by I4.0 Technologies: A Bibliometric Analysis

Simone Arena[1](✉), Mattia Braggio[1,2], Alexandre Voisin[2], and Chiara Franciosi[2]

[1] Department of Mechanical, Chemical, Material Engineering, University of Cagliari, Via Marengo 2, Cagliari 09123, Italy
simone.arena@unica.it
[2] Université de Lorraine, CNRS, CRAN, F-54000 Nancy, France

Abstract. The rapid digital transformation spurred by Industry 4.0 has redefined the manufacturing landscape, transitioning traditional facilities into smart factories. Key enabling technologies, including the Internet of Things (IoT) and Artificial Intelligence (AI), have facilitated a shift toward data-driven decision-making. Within this context, maintenance has emerged as a critical lever for sustainable manufacturing, directly impacting asset lifecycle, resource efficiency and social welfare. This paper performs a bibliometric analysis to map the evolving research landscape at the intersection of Decision Support Systems (DSS) in manufacturing, Industry 4.0 (I4.0) technologies, maintenance processes and sustainable production performance. Given the limited number of studies addressing all these dimensions simultaneously, the analysis is extended to adjacent research domains to provide a broader and more structured understanding of the field. The results highlight a clear imbalance in the current literature. While the integration between DSS, maintenance and I4.0 technologies represents a well-established and rapidly growing research stream, the incorporation of sustainability within these frameworks remains limited and often restricted to economic performance aspects. The keyword co-occurrence analysis further reveals a fragmented knowledge structure, where technological, operational and sustainability-related domains are only partially interconnected.

Keywords: DSS · Sustainability · Maintenance · Industry 4.0

1 Introduction

Over the past fifty years, the manufacturing sector has undergone a profound transformation driven by rapid technological advancements and increasingly complex market and environmental demands [1]. Maintenance processes have progressively assumed a strategic role in manufacturing systems, contributing not only to reduced downtime and operational costs but also to improved equipment reliability and overall system

Published by Springer Nature Switzerland AG 2027
G. Pezzotta et al. (Eds.): APMS 2026, IFIP AICT 808, pp. 416–431, 2027.
https://doi.org/10.1007/978-3-032-38594-9_28

productivity [2]. In modern industrial environments, maintenance can no longer be considered a localized or isolated activity. Instead, it has become part of a complex socio-technical ecosystem involving multiple data sources, interconnected production assets and advanced analytical systems [3]. As manufacturing systems become increasingly automated, interconnected and data-driven, maintenance has evolved from a reactive, cost-oriented function into a strategic and proactive capability aimed at ensuring operational continuity and long-term asset performance [4]. Consequently, the integration of maintenance processes with I4.0 technologies, such as, the IoT and Machine Learning (ML), has become essential to ensure timely and agile responses to production failures [5]. Beyond operational improvements, maintenance also plays a critical role in supporting corporate sustainability objectives. Effective maintenance strategies can reduce the occurrence of defective products, minimize material waste, optimize energy consumption and extend the lifespan of industrial assets, thereby contributing to the economic, environmental and social dimensions of sustainable manufacturing [6–8]. Therefore, the integration of Industry 4.0 technologies and maintenance processes represents a promising avenue toward sustainable manufacturing [9]. In this scenario, DSS have emerged as key tools to support maintenance-related decision-making. DSS enable organizations to transform large volumes of operational data into actionable insights with the purpose of assisting decision-makers in selecting and implementing the most appropriate maintenance strategies [10, 11]. The literature reports several successful applications of DSS in improving maintenance management. Rosati et al. [5] proposed a DSS that integrates IoT sensors and Random Forest regression to monitor machining quality and automate wear annotation in real time. Similarly, Lolli et al. [12] developed a cloud-based framework that transforms heterogeneous data into intuitive risk indicators via a Graphical User Interface, optimizing both production planning and equipment reliability. Expanding this perspective, Schmidt and Wang [13] demonstrated a DSS that integrates multi-source data from CMMS and SCADA systems. By employing Monte-Carlo simulations, they proved that condition-based approaches can reduce costs by up to 40% and unplanned stops by up to eight times compared to reactive methods. From a sustainability perspective, Yang et al. [14] propose an AI-driven DSS, specifically leveraging Reinforcement Learning (RL), to optimize maintenance scheduling and lifecycle management using operational data. By integrating heterogeneous datasets, their approach contributes to improved sustainability by minimizing failures, extending product longevity and reducing both financial and environmental costs in industrial settings. By analyzing the literature, it emerges that, while several studies investigate DSS for maintenance optimization, others explore the role of I4.0 technologies in enabling predictive maintenance and a growing body of research addresses sustainability in manufacturing systems. However, the integration of DSS for maintenance, I4.0 technologies and sustainability goals remains fragmented across the literature [15], making it difficult to understand how these research streams interact and evolve within the broader context of data-driven manufacturing systems, highlighting the need for a structured mapping of the scientific landscape surrounding this emerging research domain. To address this gap, this study performs a bibliometric analysis aimed at systematically exploring the literature at the intersection of DSSs, maintenance processes, I4.0 technologies and sustainability in manufacturing systems. Given the limited number of studies simultaneously addressing all these dimensions, the analysis also explores adjacent research domains (i.e., the partial combinations of the four domains) to identify the technological drivers, dominant research themes and emerging scientific directions shaping the evolution of DSS for sustainable maintenance. The remainder of the paper is organized as follows: Sect. 2 presents the research methodology adopted for the identification and selection of relevant scientific contributions. Section 3 reports the results of the bibliometric analysis and examines the main research clusters emerging from the literature. Finally, Sect. 4 discusses the implications of the findings and outlines future research directions.

2 Research Methodology

A structured search strategy was developed using the Scopus database to systematically investigate the intersection of DSS, maintenance processes, I4.0 technologies and sustainability in manufacturing. Scopus was chosen for its broad coverage of peer-reviewed literature in engineering, manufacturing, and management. The search was conducted within titles, abstracts, and keywords to capture contributions explicitly addressing the topics, without applying initial filters to include the widest possible set of relevant studies. Keywords were then organized into four thematic groups representing the main research domains (keywords within the groups are connected with OR), as shown in Table 1. Group A includes keywords related to DSSs and the industrial context, thus defining the core focus of the analysis, while Groups B (maintenance), Group C (sustainability) and Group D (I4.0 technologies) represent the three thematic domains investigated. The selection for Group D is based on the nine key technologies discussed by Franciosi et al. [9], as these perfectly match the nine enabling technologies defined by the Italian Ministry of Economic Development in the National Industry 4.0 Plan.

Table 1. Keywords groups

Group A	Group B	Group C	Group D
"DSS", "Manufacturing", "Industry", "Industrial"	"Maintenance"	"Sustainability", "Sustainable", "Economic", "Social", "Environmental", "Triple bottom line"	"Big Data", "IoT", "Horizontal and vertical system integration", "Simulation", "Cloud computing", "Augmented reality", "Autonomous robots", "Additive manufacturing", "Cybersecurity"

The search process was designed to first identify studies covering the full intersection of the four research domains by combining keywords from all groups, thus capturing contributions addressing DSS, maintenance, I4.0 technologies and sustainability simultaneously. To achieve a broader understanding of the scientific landscape, additional searches were then performed by combining DSS-related terms (Group A) with pairs of the remaining keyword groups. This approach allowed the exploration of adjacent research domains while maintaining a consistent focus on DSS applications in industrial environments. The following search configurations were implemented, connecting the group with AND: Search 1 considers all groups, Search 2 does not consider Group C, Search 3 does not consider Group D and Search 4 does not consider Group B. This multi-query strategy enables a structured exploration of both the core intersections and partial overlaps among the research domains. By examining these configurations, the study offers a comprehensive view of how literature on DSS for maintenance evolves in relation to I4.0 technologies and sustainability. Figure 1 conceptually illustrates the four searches, highlighting the relationships between maintenance, sustainability and I4.0 within the broader context of DSS applications in manufacturing systems.

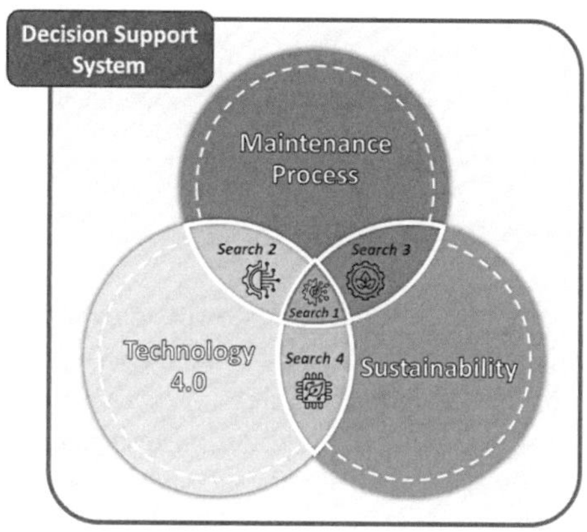

Fig. 1. Conceptual representation of the research domains

Table 2. Inclusion and exclusion criteria

Inclusion criteria	Exclusion criteria
1. The study focuses on DSSs applied within industrial or manufacturing contexts. 2. The document is a journal article, including both theoretical and empirical contributions. 3. The paper was published between 2011 (when industry 4.0 concept was introduced) and 2026. 4. The full text of the article is available for analysis.	1. The document is not an academic journal article. 2. The publication is written in languages other than English. 3. The full text is not available.

To ensure the relevance and quality of the selected literature, a set of inclusion and exclusion criteria was applied during the screening phase, as reported in Table 2.

After applying these criteria and removing internal duplicates within each search, the remaining unique contributions were included in the final dataset. A screening phase was then conducted by all authors for each search to ensure the actual relevance of the selected papers. Figure 2 reports the initial number of contributions retrieved from Scopus and the final number of papers obtained after screening and duplicate removal.

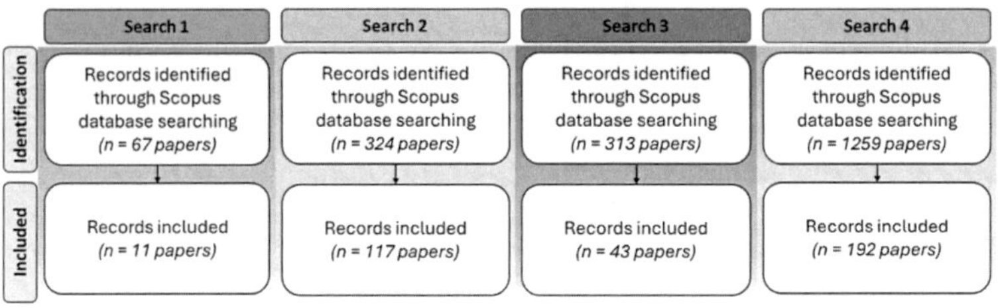

Fig. 2. Records identified and included in the bibliometric analysis

3 Bibliometric Analysis Results

This section presents the results of the bibliometric analysis based on the four search configurations described in the methodology. The analysis is structured to provide a comprehensive view of the research field from three complementary perspectives: first, the core intersection (Fig. 1) is examined to highlight its key characteristics and limitations; second, the temporal evolution of scientific production is analyzed to assess the maturity and development of the research domains; and third, a keyword co-occurrence analysis is performed to explore relationships among the main topics, identifying dominant themes and emerging research directions.

3.1 Core Intersection Analysis: Mapping an Emerging Research Area

Table 3 provides a structured overview of the contributions identified within the core intersection (Search 1), examining the maintenance processes according to the standard EN17007 [16], which classifies maintenance into management (planning and decision-making activities), realization (execution of maintenance tasks) and support processes (monitoring and information management), together with the I4.0 technologies employed and the sustainability dimensions addressed. The table shows a research domain characterized by a fragmented and only partial integration of its core components. On one hand, the individual connection between these domains appears to be relatively well established; on the other hand, their simultaneous integration within comprehensive DSSs remains limited. In this scenario, most contributions focus on management and support process, such as maintenance scheduling, monitoring and strategy selection [4, 6, 12–14, 17–21], while fewer studies address the realization phase, including repair execution and on-field maintenance activities [12, 17, 19–22], highlighting a still limited integration of operational maintenance tasks within current DSS frameworks.

Table 3. Overview of the studies identified in the core intersection (Search 1)

	Maintenance Process			**I4.0 Technology**									**Sustainability**		
Reference	Management	Realization	Support	IoT	Big Data	H&V Integration	Simulation (DT)	Cloud computing	AR-VR	Autonomous Robot	Additive Manufacturing	Cyber Security	Environment	Social	Economic
Razzaq et al. [6]	x		x	x	x								x		x
Almeida et al. [18]	x		x	x									x	x	x
Cardeal et al. [17]	x	x	x								x		x		x
Liu et al. [14]	x		x	x	x			x					x		x
Lolli et al. [12]	x	x	x								x				x
Wakiru et al. [22]	x	x				x									x
Linnéusson et al. [4]	x		x				x						x		x
Schmidt & Wang [13]	x		x	x	x			x							x
Cho et al. [19]	x	x	x	x	x	x							x		x
Li & Parlikad [20]	x	x	x	x										x	
Deppe et al. [21]	x	x	x								x				x

From a technological perspective, the results show a clear predominance of data-centric solutions, particularly IoT and Big Data, which represent the key enablers for data acquisition and advanced analytics in condition monitoring and predictive maintenance [6, 13, 14, 18–20]. Conversely, more implementation-oriented technologies, such as augmented and virtual reality, autonomous robots and cybersecurity, are not represented. Concerning system integration solutions, including horizontal and vertical integration [19, 22] and simulations [4], are addressed only in a small number of studies. This indicates that the transition from isolated DSS applications towards fully interconnected, system-level decision environments is still at an early stage. This gap is significant since integrated architectures are essential to enable real-time, adaptive and cross-functional decision-making within I4.0 contexts. Concerning sustainability, the economic dimension is the most commonly addressed, particularly in terms of cost reduction and efficiency improvements [4, 6, 12–14, 17–19, 21, 22], followed by environmental aspects [4, 6, 14, 17–19], while the social dimension remains largely overlooked [18, 20]. Thus, currently adopted DSSs only partially capture the broader implications of sustainable maintenance, which is often considered from a performance optimization perspective, while it should be considered as a holistic concept that encompasses human and organizational factors as well. Finally, the limited number of contributions identified within this core intersection confirms that this research area is still in an early stage of development, despite the growing maturity of each individual domain. For this reason, the analysis is extended to adjacent research domains (Search 2, Search 3 and Search 4). This broader perspective allows the identification of more consolidated research streams aiming at highlighting emerging patterns and research gaps that are not yet fully visible within the core intersection alone.

3.2 Temporal Evolution of Scientific Production across Research Domains

Figure 3 presents the temporal distribution of publications collected through the four search configurations over the period 2011–2026. The results show not only a general increase in scientific output, but also significant differences in the development and maturity of the research domains investigated. The first observation concerns the early stage of the field (before 2016), where all search configurations show a very limited number of publications. This may be seen in the context of the still-developing nature of I4.0 concepts during that period, when enabling technologies such as IoT and advanced analytics were not yet extensively adopted in industrial environments. Consequently, both the availability of data and the technological infrastructure required to develop advanced DSS for maintenance were still limited. Starting from 2017–2018, the number of contributions starts to increase, particularly for Search 2 and Search 4. This trend can be associated with the consolidation of I4.0 technologies and the growing industrial interest in data-driven maintenance strategies. The widespread adoption of IoT sensors and advanced analytics significantly improved the availability of real-time operational data, enabling the development of robust decision-support tools.

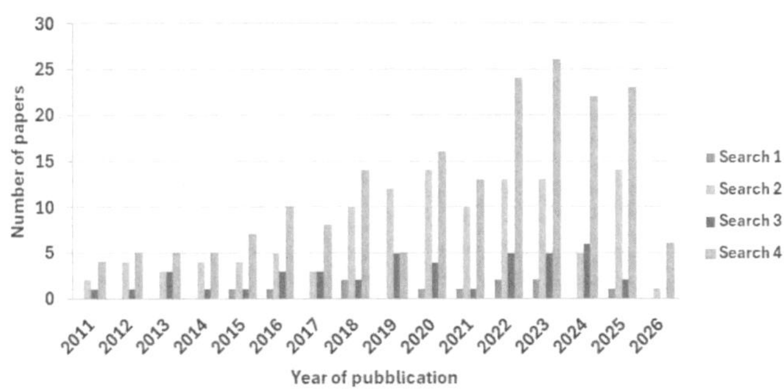

Fig. 3. Temporal evolution of the collected paper for the different research domains

Predictive maintenance has emerged as one of the most prominent applications of I4.0, due to its ability to predict potential failures before they occur, reduce downtime and optimize operational efficiency. During this phase, as also shown by the trend of search 4, sustainability-related concepts, especially those concerned with economic performance, also begin to appear as decision-making objectives, reflecting an increasing awareness of the benefits associated with effective maintenance strategies. Then, the growth becomes more structured. Search 2 exhibits a strong and continuous increase, confirming that the integration of DSS, maintenance and digital technologies represents the most mature and consolidated research stream. This trend reflects a broader industrial shift toward data-driven maintenance, supported by increasing investments in digital transformation and the progressive adoption of smart manufacturing paradigms. Search

3 exhibits a more gradual and delayed growth. This suggests that sustainability aspects have been incorporated into maintenance decision-making only in a later phase, once the technological foundations of digital maintenance were already established. Hence, the literature appears to follow a sequential evolution: first focusing on technological feasibility and performance optimization and only subsequently integrating environmental and social dimensions. Trends after 2022–2023 indicate a potential shift toward a new research phase. The technology-driven research growth begins to stabilize, contributions integrating sustainability and system-level perspectives become more prominent; indeed, there is a substantial increase in results associated with search 4. This may signal a transition from I4.0 toward more human and sustainability-oriented paradigms, where digital technologies support broader performance objectives. Despite some growth in Search 1 contributions, they remain limited, highlighting that the simultaneous integration of DSS, maintenance, I4.0 technologies and sustainability is both recent and inherently complex. Combining data-driven decision-making, system integration and multi-dimensional sustainability goals continues to pose significant technological and organizational challenges.

3.3 Keywords Co-occurrence Analysis

A keyword co-occurrence analysis was performed using a combination of author-assigned and indexed keywords extracted from the Scopus database, applying the full counting method in VOSviewer to map relationships among terms based on their joint occurrence in the selected publications. This method identifies the most relevant keywords and their interconnections, offering insights into the structure and relationships of research topics. The resulting network highlights thematic clusters, revealing the main research streams and the field's underlying structure. The visualization uses a distance-based mapping technique, where node positions reflect co-occurrence patterns [23]. To improve clarity and robustness, only keywords with at least five co-occurrence links were included.

Search 2. Figure 4 shows the keyword co-occurrence network for Search 2. This is characterized by a relatively mature and internally structured research domain, where the interaction between data-driven technologies and maintenance decision-making is clearly established, although not yet fully integrated. The yellow cluster is centered around decision making, predictive analytics and information management, outlining the core analytical layer of DSS. This does not simply represent data processing activities, but it reflects the progressive shift toward decision-centric maintenance paradigms, where value is generated through the transformation of data into valuable knowledge. The presence of the keyword asset management within this cluster is particularly relevant, as it indicates a transition that has occurred in recent years from equipment-level optimization toward more systemic and lifecycle-oriented decision frameworks [14]. In this scenario, DSS are evolving into valuable tools that can aid maintenance optimization strategies, balance trade-offs between cost, performance and risk and support long-term planning decisions [24]. The blue cluster, which combines important I4.0 technologies, such as the IoT and CPS, with more general concepts like smart manufacturing, captures the technological core of the investigated domain [25]. These elements play a key role in enabling real-time monitoring and improving data availability across industrial systems since they are closely related to fault detection and data acquisition [26]. Thus, they represent the foundational layer upon which data-driven maintenance strategies are built, facilitating the continuous collection and transmission of operational information. However, keywords' position within the network, in terms of their proximity and connections to other ones, suggests that these technologies are predominantly associated with sensing and data generation, rather than being fully embedded within advanced decision-making processes. Thus, this highlights a structural gap between data infrastructures and decision-support capabilities, where the main challenge is the ability to effectively transform data into actionable and context-aware decisions. The green cluster deals with the operational and algorithmic dimensions of maintenance, combining preventive maintenance, maintenance scheduling and advanced techniques such as RL, deep learning and optimization [27]. The coexistence of traditional maintenance practices and advanced AI methods depicts the scenario where these established approaches are being progressively adopted in combination with data-driven and adaptive models. Finally, the red cluster, includes keywords such as costs, forecasting and life cycle [28], highlighting the presence of economic and lifecycle-related considerations within the research domain. However, compared to the main technology- and decision-oriented clusters, these keywords show fewer co-occurrence links with the dominant I4.0 and predictive maintenance concepts. This suggests that lifecycle and cost-related aspects are acknowledged in the literature but are not yet systematically integrated into the core development of data-driven DSS for maintenance. As a result, current research streams still tend to prioritize technological development and predictive capabilities, while broader sustainability and long-term system perspectives remain less explored.

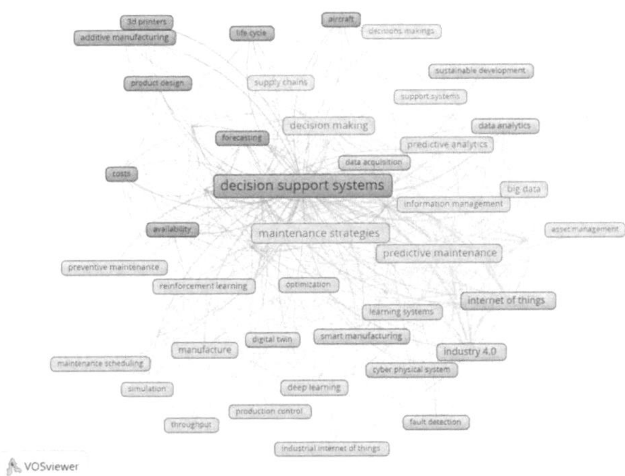

Fig. 4. Keyword co-occurrence analysis for Search 2

Search 3. The keyword co-occurrence map for Search 3 is characterized by a relatively small number of nodes and a compact structure (a direct consequence of the limited number of contributions identified in this domain), as reported in Fig. 5. Nonetheless, this aspect provides an important insight: the research area at the intersection between DSS and sustainable maintenance is still in an early stage of development, with a narrow and not yet fully diversified conceptual base. Within this structure, DSSs clearly act as the central element, linking maintenance-related concepts such as predictive maintenance and condition monitoring with economic-oriented terms, like costs [1]. It is worth mentioning that sustainability is interpreted through an efficiency-driven perspective, where improvements in maintenance performance are implicitly associated with sustainability outcomes. Therefore, sustainability does not emerge as an explicit and structured objective to strive for, but as a secondary effect of cost reduction and operational optimization. By analysing Fig. 5, it can also be noted that decision making, maintenance and condition-based maintenance form a connected group, complemented by cost-benefit analysis. This can indicate that DSS are mainly used to evaluate or compare maintenance strategies from an economic standpoint [29], but not to explicitly manage trade-offs across multiple sustainability dimensions. The role of lifecycle-related thinking further confirms this pattern. Indeed, although life cycle appears in the network, its connections remain peripheral and weakly integrated with the core decision-making structure. Therefore, it is still at a conceptual level and is not yet operationalized within DSS in a systematic way. Another aspect that emerged concerns the role of advanced analytics within this domain [30]. Unlike technology-driven research streams, AI appears only weakly connected to the core of the network, indicating that sustainability-oriented DSS are not yet fully leveraging data-driven or adaptive capabilities. In this context, they seem to rely on more static evaluation approaches focusing on assessing performance outcomes rather than supporting and continuously improving decision-making processes.

Fig. 5. Keyword co-occurrence analysis for Search 3

Search 4. Figure 6 reports the keyword co-occurrence map for Search 4. It can be noticed that the integration between I4.0 technologies and sustainability leads to a broad and highly interconnected set of concepts, outlining a complex and multi-layered knowledge structure. The red cluster represents the technological and digital core of the field. It includes key I4.0 technologies such as AI, ML, big data, the IoT and CPS, together with enabling concepts like data analytics, automation and embedded systems [31]. These are closely connected to application domains such as predictive maintenance [5] and digital twin, where they play a central role in enabling data-driven decision-support capabilities. Also, this cluster incorporates system-level concepts, such as supply chain, industrial management and smart manufacturing, as well as sustainability-related terms such as sustainable development and green manufacturing [32]. This suggests that the technological-oriented research streams are expanding toward broader systems and the sustainability domain. However, these are not yet fully integrated into a unified framework, but they currently coexist: the technological development is still leading, while sustainability remains only partially integrated. The green cluster includes keywords such as simulation, optimization, risk assessment, uncertainty and sensitivity analysis, together with economic and lifecycle-related concepts, such as cost-benefit analysis, industrial economics, life cycle and circular economy [33]. It highlights the role of modeling and evaluation approaches in supporting DSS, especially for managing system complexity and uncertainty [34]. Interestingly, keywords related to sustainability, such as environmental technologies and circular economy, indicate ongoing efforts to integrate sustainable and circular objectives into analytical frameworks, although this integration is primarily within evaluation and modeling rather than directly in decision-support processes. The blue cluster is characterized by keywords such as production planning, supply chain management, efficiency and industrial research [35]. It also includes emerging production technologies such as 3D printing and additives [36]. Keywords such as life cycle assessment and economic and social effects are particularly relevant, as they can be considered an effort to incorporate sustainability aspects through structured evaluation frameworks. In this way, DSS are increasingly enhanced by including a wider set of performance indicators, capturing not only economic outcomes but also environmental and social impacts across the lifecycle of industrial systems. Finally, yellow cluster highlights a performance- and evaluation-oriented perspective, focusing on optimizing energy use and reducing environmental impact [37].

It includes keywords such as discrete event simulation, energy utilization, environmental impact, key performance indicators and benchmarking, reflecting the use of quantitative methods to analyze production processes [38] and assess system performance under varying conditions [39]. In this context, sustainability aspects are mainly focused on understanding how resources are consumed and how process configurations may influence overall system performance.

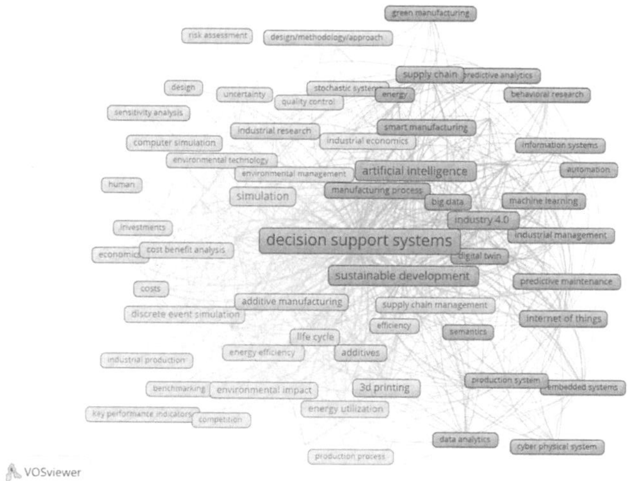

Fig. 6. Keyword co-occurrence analysis for Search 4

4 Conclusion and Managerial Implications

The results of this study provide a structured overview of how DSS for maintenance are evolving at the intersection of I4.0 technologies and sustainability within manufacturing systems. By combining bibliometric analysis with keyword co-occurrence mapping, the study identifies not only the dominant research streams but also the gaps that still limit the development of a cohesive research domain. The first important outcome concerns the different maturity levels across the investigated areas. The analysis of publication trends and keyword networks shows that research on DSS for maintenance enabled by I4.0 technologies represents the most mature and consolidated stream. In this field, the integration of data acquisition, advanced analytics and maintenance strategies is now well established, reflecting strong industrial interest in predictive and data-driven maintenance approaches. Technologies such as IoT and ML are no longer emerging concepts, but rather core components of modern maintenance frameworks. Conversely, the domain of DSS for sustainable maintenance remains less developed. The findings indicate that sustainability is still interpreted from an efficiency-oriented perspective, mainly associated with cost reduction and performance improvement. Environmental and social dimensions continue to play a marginal role and, although lifecycle approaches are present in the literature, they are not yet systematically embedded in decision-making processes. Consequently, sustainability is rarely treated as an explicit decision objective and is more often considered as an implicit outcome of optimized maintenance strategies. The analysis of the core (Search 1) and the adjacent domains (Search 2, e 3 and 4) further reinforces these considerations. The keyword network shows a high level of complexity and connectivity, where it is evident that there is an increasing convergence between technological and sustainability perspectives. However, this convergence remains only partial. Technological clusters are still dominant and internally cohesive, while sustainability-related concepts are more dispersed and often connected through intermediate nodes such as modelling, simulation or performance evaluation. Overall, the results show that a unified framework capable of jointly addressing data-driven decision-making and sustainability objectives is still lacking. These findings provide several implications for both research and industrial practice. From a conceptual perspective, the literature has progressively evolved from a primary focus on enabling technologies and data-driven capabilities toward the inclusion of sustainability considerations. However, the integration between these dimensions remains limited, with technological innovation advancing more rapidly than its alignment with broader system-level and sustainability goals. Thus, there is a need to move beyond technology-centric approaches and to develop DSS frameworks that explicitly incorporate sustainability as a core decision variable. From a methodological and practical perspective, future DSS frameworks should combine lifecycle assessment methods, multi-criteria decision-making techniques and socio-technical considerations within data-driven architectures. Although advanced maintenance technologies are widely available, their potential to support sustainable decision-making remains underutilized. From a managerial perspective, current DSS solutions still focus mainly on operational and economic optimization, with limited integration of environmental and social dimensions. These findings may help industrial managers identify gaps and guide investments toward more sustainability-oriented DSS architectures enabled by I4.0 technologies. Despite its contributions, this study presents some limitations. First, the analysis is based exclusively on the Scopus database, which, although comprehensive, may not capture all relevant publications. Second, the keyword-based search strategy, while systematic, may be affected by variations in terminology, potentially overlooking relevant studies using different expressions. Future research should address these limitations by extending the analysis to additional databases and including other types of scientific contributions. Further studies will include a systematic content analysis of the collected papers, aiming at providing a comprehensive picture of the investigated topic.

Disclosure of Interests. The authors have no competing interests.

References

1. Jasiulewicz-Kaczmarek, M., Żywica, P., Gola, A.: Fuzzy set theory driven maintenance sustainability performance assessment model: a multiple criteria approach. J. Intell. Manuf. **32**, 1497–1515 (2021). https://doi.org/10.1007/s10845-020-01734-3
2. Mallioris, P., Aivazidou, E., Bechtsis, D.: Predictive maintenance in industry 4.0: a systematic multi-sector mapping. CIRP J. Mfg. Sci. Technol. **50**, 80–103 (2024). https://doi.org/10.1016/j.cirpj.2024.02.003
3. Metso, L., Baglee, D., Marttonen-Arola, S.: Maintenance as a combination of intelligent it systems and strategies: a literature review. 9 (2018)
4. Linnéusson, G., Ng, A.H.C., Aslam, T.: A hybrid simulation-based optimization framework supporting strategic maintenance development to improve production performance. Eur. J. Oper. Res. **281**, 402–414 (2020). https://doi.org/10.1016/j.ejor.2019.08.036
5. Rosati, R. et al.: From knowledge-based to big data analytic model: a novel IoT and machine learning based decision support system for predictive maintenance in industry 4.0. J. Intell. Manuf. **34**, 107–121 (2023). https://doi.org/10.1007/s10845-022-01960-x

6. Razzaq, A., Khan, Z.A., Riaz, M., Pamucar, D.: Sustainable decision support system in industry 4.0 under uncertainties with m-polar picture fuzzy information aggregation. Alex. Eng. J. **116**, 271–295 (2025). https://doi.org/10.1016/j.aej.2024.11.104
7. Franciosi, C., Voisin, A., Miranda, S., Riemma, S., Iung, B.: Measuring maintenance impacts on sustainability of manufacturing industries: from a systematic literature review to a framework proposal. J. Clean. Prod. **260**, 121065 (2020). https://doi.org/10.1016/j.jclepro.2020.121065
8. Franciosi, C., Iung, B., Miranda, S., Riemma, S.: Maintenance for sustainability in the industry 4.0 context: a scoping literature review. IFAC-PapersOnLine. **51**, 903–908 (2018). https://doi.org/10.1016/j.ifacol.2018.08.459
9. Franciosi, C., Voisin, A., Miranda, S., Iung, B.: Integration of I4.0 technologies with maintenance processes: what are the effects on sustainable manufacturing? IFAC-PapersOnLine. **53**, 1–6 (2020). https://doi.org/10.1016/j.ifacol.2020.11.001
10. Alzoubi, S., Amayreh, K.T., Farea, M.M., Baker El-Ebiary, Y.A., Ahmad Saany, S.I., Bisht, N.: A review of effectiveness and efficiency methodology of decision support system for selecting suppliers. In: 2023 International Conference on Computer Science and Emerging Technologies (CSET), pp. 1–7. IEEE, Bangalore (2023). https://doi.org/10.1109/CSET58993.2023.10346850
11. Arena, S., Florian, E., Zennaro, I., Orrù, P.F., Sgarbossa, F.: A novel decision support system for managing predictive maintenance strategies based on machine learning approaches. Saf. Sci. **146**, 105529 (2022). https://doi.org/10.1016/j.ssci.2021.105529
12. Lolli, F., Coruzzolo, A.M., Peron, M., Sgarbossa, F.: Age-based preventive maintenance with multiple printing options. Int. J. Prod. Econ. **243**, 108339 (2022). https://doi.org/10.1016/j.ijpe.2021.108339
13. Schmidt, B., Wang, L.: Predictive maintenance of machine tool linear axes: a case from manufacturing industry. Procedia Mfg. **17**, 118–125 (2018). https://doi.org/10.1016/j.promfg.2018.10.022
14. Liu, Y., Yang, M., Guo, Z.: Reinforcement learning based optimal decision making towards product lifecycle sustainability. Int. J. Comput. Integr. Mfg. **35**, 1269–1296 (2022). https://doi.org/10.1080/0951192X.2022.2025623
15. Orošnjak, M., Saretzky, F., Kedziora, S.: Prescriptive maintenance: a systematic literature review and exploratory meta-synthesis. Appl. Sci. **15**, 8507 (2025). https://doi.org/10.3390/app15158507
16. European Committee for Standardization: EN-17007-2017
17. Cardeal, G., Leite, M., Ribeiro, I.: Decision-support model to select spare parts suitable for additive manufacturing. Comput. Ind. **144**, 103798 (2023). https://doi.org/10.1016/j.compind.2022.103798
18. Almeida, J.C., Ribeiro, B., Cardoso, A.: A human-centric approach to aid in assessing maintenance from the sustainable manufacturing perspective. Procedia Comput. Sci. **220**, 600–607 (2023). https://doi.org/10.1016/j.procs.2023.03.076
19. Cho, S., May, G., Perez, R., Lazaro, O., De La Maza, B., Kiritsis, D.: A hybrid machine learning approach for predictive maintenance in smart factories of the future. In: Advances in Production Management Systems. Smart Manufacturing for Industry 4.0, pp. 311–317. Springer International Publishing, Cham (2018). https://doi.org/10.1007/978-3-319-99707-0_39
20. Li, H., Parlikad, A.K.: Social internet of industrial things for industrial and manufacturing assets. IFAC-PapersOnLine. **49**, 208–213 (2016). https://doi.org/10.1016/j.ifacol.2016.11.036

21. Deppe, G., Lindemann, C., Koch, R.: Development of an economic decision support for the application of additive manufacturing in aerospace. In: Proceedings of the Annual International Solid Freeform Fabrication Symposium - Additive Manufacturing Conference (SFF), pp. 1560–1569 (2020)
22. Wakiru, J.M., Pintelon, L., Muchiri, P., Chemweno, P.: Integrated maintenance policies for performance improvement of a multi-unit repairable, one product manufacturing system. Prod. Plan. Control. **32**, 347–367 (2021). https://doi.org/10.1080/09537287.2020.1736684
23. Van Eck, N.J., Waltman, L.: Visualizing bibliometric networks. In: Measuring Scholarly Impact, pp. 285–320. Springer International Publishing, Cham (2014). https://doi.org/10.1007/978-3-319-10377-8_13
24. Aruvali, T., Marchi, M.D., Rauch, E.: Monitoring system architecture for long-term resilience in manufacturing. In: ITechCET 2022, Kerala, India, p. 030007 (2024). https://doi.org/10.1063/5.0189301
25. Thoppil, N.M., Vasu, V.: An industrial IoT framework for predictive maintenance of CNC lathe spindles: integrating deep learning and cloud-based analytics. J. Vib. Eng. Technol. **13**, 590 (2025). https://doi.org/10.1007/s42417-025-02144-6
26. Cattaneo, L., Macchi, M.: A digital twin proof of concept to support machine prognostics with low availability of run-to-failure data. IFAC-PapersOnLine. **52**, 37–42 (2019). https://doi.org/10.1016/j.ifacol.2019.10.016
27. Sai, V.C., Shcherbakov, M.V., Tran, V.P.: Data-driven framework for predictive maintenance in industry 4.0 concept. In: Creativity in Intelligent Technologies and Data Science, pp. 344–358. Springer International Publishing, Cham (2019). https://doi.org/10.1007/978-3-030-29743-5_28
28. Choi, S.-W., Lee, E.-B., Kim, J.-H.: The engineering machine-learning automation platform (Emap): a big-data-driven ai tool for contractors' sustainable management solutions for plant projects. Sustainability. **13** (2021). https://doi.org/10.3390/su131810384
29. Caicedo Solano, N.E., García Llinás, G.A., Montoya-Torres, J.R., Ramirez Polo, L.E.: A planning model of crop maintenance operations inspired in lean manufacturing. Comput. Electron. Agric. **179**, 105852 (2020). https://doi.org/10.1016/j.compag.2020.105852
30. Kotsilitis, S., Chairetakis, K., Katsari, A., Marcoulaki, E.: The SUPREEMO experiment for smart monitoring for energy efficiency and predictive maintenance of electric motor systems. In: Proceedings of the 30th ESREL and 15th PSAM, pp. 3415–3422. Research Publishing Services (2020). https://doi.org/10.3850/978-981-14-8593-0_4047-cd
31. Liu, Y., Hou, J.: Digital industry transformation strategy analysis and decision-based on intelligent decision technology. IDT. **18**, 2389–2406 (2024). https://doi.org/10.3233/IDT-230636
32. Manco, P., Caterino, M., Rinaldi, M., Fera, M.: Additive manufacturing in green supply chains: a parametric model for life cycle assessment and cost. Sustain. Prod. Consump. **36**, 463–478 (2023). https://doi.org/10.1016/j.spc.2023.01.015
33. Panagou, S., La Cava, G., Fruggiero, F., Mancusi, F.: Selective complexity determination at cost based alternatives to re-manufacture. In: Advances in Production Management Systems. Production Management Systems for Responsible Manufacturing, Service, and Logistics Futures, pp. 215–228. Springer Nature, Cham (2023). https://doi.org/10.1007/978-3-031-43688-8_16
34. Dong, Q., Zhang, Y., Wang, N.: Reliability of two-stage competing failure systems with dynamic load adjustment. Appl. Math. Model. **149**, 116303 (2026). https://doi.org/10.1016/j.apm.2025.116303
35. Dev, N.K., Shankar, R., Swami, S.: Diffusion of green products in industry 4.0: reverse logistics issues during design of inventory and production planning system. Int. J. Prod. Econ. **223**, 107519 (2020). https://doi.org/10.1016/j.ijpe.2019.107519

36. Jayapal, J., Varadarajan, S.: Development of interactive decision support system for part selection in additive manufacturing. In: APMS2025, pp. 16–29. Springer Nature Switzerland, Cham (2026). https://doi.org/10.1007/978-3-032-03550-9_2
37. Ouyang, T., Liu, Q., Tao, J., Xu, C.: Big data-based risk assessment and decision-support model for sustainable development. In: MVDL 2025, p. 25. SPIE, Hong Kong (2025). https://doi.org/10.1117/12.3071988
38. Jing, L. et al.: A quantitative simulation-based conceptual design evaluation approach integrating bond graph and rough VIKOR under uncertainty. J. Clean. Prod. **380**, 134928 (2022). https://doi.org/10.1016/j.jclepro.2022.134928
39. Zappa, S., Roda, I., Macchi, M.: Lifecycle extension of industrial assets: a framework for feasibility assessment and strategy selection. In: APMS 2025, pp. 443–458. Springer Nature Switzerland, Cham (2026). https://doi.org/10.1007/978-3-032-03534-9_30

Mapping Criteria for Designing Machine Learning–Driven Integrated Quality-Maintenance Engineering Frameworks

Elisa Gonzalez Santacruz[1(✉)], Mohan Rajashekarappa[1], David Romero[2], Zeynab Allahkarami[1], Jon Bokrantz[1], and Anders Skoogh[1]

[1] Chalmers University of Technology, Gothenburg, Sweden
{elisamar,rmohan,zeynaba,jon.bokrantz,anders.skoogh}@chalmers.se
[2] Tecnológico de Monterrey, Mexico City, Mexico

Abstract. Increasing global competition and the growing complexity of modern manufacturing systems demand operations that are quality-driven, resilient, and sustainable. Quality Engineering (QE) directly determines product reliability, customer satisfaction, and organisational financial viability, while Maintenance Engineering (ME) ensures equipment availability, prevents unplanned downtime, and sustains the conditions under which quality targets are met. However, both functions have traditionally operated in silos, managing separate data streams, KPIs, and decisions, despite defects and failures often sharing common root causes. Machine Learning (ML) has been identified as the bridging technology to achieve meaningful integration, enabling real-time analysis of heterogeneous data sources across both domains and creating conditions for a QE-ME unified approach to defect prevention, failure prognosis, and continuous improvement. Yet, no consolidated reference exists in the scientific literature that maps which components are necessary for such QE-ME integration. This paper addresses this gap through a literature review and structured comparative analysis of data-driven QE and ME frameworks, using comparison matrices. The objective is to identify and compare their key components to determine commonalities and differences towards their convergence in an "ML-driven Integrated Quality-Maintenance Engineering Reference Framework". For industry practitioners, the findings offer actionable guidelines on which components to prioritise when designing such kind of frameworks. For researchers, they provide a structured evidence-based map of the field that surfaces the existing research gap and points to the most critical open challenges at the ML-driven QE-ME intersection.

Keywords: Quality Engineering Maintenance Engineering · Machine Learning · Data-Driven Decision-making · Smart Factory

1 Introduction

Due to market globalisation and an increasingly competitive environment, manufacturing companies must innovate and optimise their production systems to meet customer expectations. Achieving competitiveness today demands near-perfect quality, although

Published by Springer Nature Switzerland AG 2027
G. Pezzotta et al. (Eds.): APMS 2026, IFIP AICT 808, pp. 432–446, 2027.
https://doi.org/10.1007/978-3-032-38594-9_29

mature organisations operate with very low defect rates, customers expect completely defect-free products [1]. *Product quality* has consequently become a cornerstone of competitive strategy in manufacturing [2].

Equally critical is *maintenance,* which ensures the resource efficiency and reliability of industrial equipment necessary to sustain high levels of effectiveness, quality, and financial performance [3]. Both functions share a fundamental interdependence – production equipment degrades progressively, and the quality of the final product is directly correlated with the degradation state of the machines that produce it [4].

Strengthening the interaction between *Quality Engineering (QE)* and *Maintenance Engineering (ME)* can reduce production costs, enhance productivity, and improve customer satisfaction [5], with integrated approaches shown to increase industrial profit by up to 40% [6]. Furthermore, growing pressure for quality-driven, resilient, and sustainable production adds urgency to this integration, as high-quality output cannot be sustained without efficient maintenance [6, 7].

The emergence of Industry 4.0 has created technological conditions to make this *QE-ME integration* feasible. Through the convergence of Internet of Things sensors, cloud computing, big data analytics, and artificial intelligence, manufacturing systems can now monitor physical processes, communicate in real time across machines and domains, and support autonomous decision-making [8, 9].

Within this ecosystem, *Machine Learning (ML)* has emerged as the critical bridging technology. It enables the simultaneous analysis of heterogeneous data from "quality" and "maintenance" sources, extracting hidden relationships in high-dimensional and dynamic industrial environments [10], and supports both predictive quality monitoring, classifying products as defective or non-defective based on process data [11], and predictive maintenance, detecting early failure signatures and estimating time to failure [12]. ML thus provides the analytical infrastructure needed to move both domains from reactive, siloed operations towards a *unified, data-driven approach to defect prevention and equipment reliability* [13].

Despite this potential, QE and ME have traditionally been studied and managed in isolation, with each domain developing its own ML methodologies, data requirements, and evaluation frameworks independently [6, 14]. Although recent years have seen growing recognition of their interdependence [9], no consolidated reference exists in the scientific literature that maps which components are necessary for such QE-ME integration, particularly with an "ML-driven" approach, or to the extent to which researchers agree on what those components are.

Industry practitioners implementing *ML-driven Integrated Quality-Maintenance Engineering Frameworks* (and their respective systems) lack actionable guidance on where to start, while researchers lack a structured basis for identifying where consensus has been reached and where critical gaps remain. This paper addresses that gap.

This paper aims to identify and compare the key components to determine commonalities and differences between existing frameworks towards the design of "ML-driven Integrated Quality-Maintenance Engineering (ML-IQME) Reference Framework". One research question guides this research process: *Which criteria are identified as core for integrating Machine Learning-driven Quality Engineering and Maintenance Engineering frameworks into a unified reference framework?*

The paper is organised as follows. The introduction establishes the research context, motivation, and research question. Section 2 presents related works. Section 3 describes the methodology used to construct the comparison matrices. Section 4 offers the findings through a comprehensive comparison analysis of the reviewed QE and ME frameworks, assessing the extent to which they collectively address the components required for designing an "ML-IQME" Reference Framework, and highlighting where agreement across frameworks points to established practice versus where limited coverage reveals the components that remain underexplored or unresolved in the fields. Section 5 discusses the implications of the findings for industry practitioners and researchers and acknowledges the limitations of the study. The paper closes with the conclusions and directions for future research.

2 Related Works and Research Gap

To contextualise the *research question* and validate the *research gap* motivating the current work, a *scoping review* was conducted before the comparative analysis. The review followed a search in Scopus and Google Scholar using the search string ('quality engineering' AND 'maintenance engineering' AND 'machine learning' AND 'framework'). From 139 papers retrieved, titles and abstracts were screened to select only those explicitly addressing these terms, following the multi-source approach described by Arksey and O'Malley (2005) [15] for scoping reviews. Papers were selected only when their title or abstract explicitly approached the integration of QE and ME functions through ML, rather than addressing them as independent. The following works were identified as a few that explicitly address the integration of QE and ME. Even among these, existing studies treat them as parallel, with unidirectional links or frame their relationship within broader objectives. No prior study has been conducted as a *structured comparison* to identify their core components, assess convergence across the literature, and establish the foundations for the design of ML-IQME frameworks. The most relevant works identified include:

Frankó & Varga's (2021) [16] survey on ML solutions for smart maintenance and quality control, which categorises tasks from both domains and maps their corresponding ML techniques to each. Although QE and ME are addressed within the same conceptual scope, they are treated as parallel, independent functions. *No analytical links between quality and maintenance data streams are established, and no shared integration components are proposed.*

Jourdan et al. (2021) [17] reviewed 47 publicly available datasets, classifying them by descriptive attributes and associating them with independent quality control and maintenance use cases. *The study does not develop the synergistic potential between both data domains and identify shared components.*

Riccio et al. (2024) [18] proposed a predictive maintenance framework in which product quality parameters serve as ML inputs for anticipating equipment failures, establishing one of the most explicit functional bridges between QE and ME in recent literature. *However, the integration remains unidirectional; quality operates as a predictor of maintenance rather than as a coequal domain, and critical QE structural components, such as target quality policies or quality data management mechanisms, are not systematically considered.*

Koulinas et al. (2024) [19] addressed production, maintenance, and quality control simultaneously as a set of variables within a reinforcement learning optimisation problem, extracting interpretable decision rules via decision trees. *Yet the relationship between QE and ME is never explicitly modelled as an integration problem, but rather as a consequence of the optimisation objective.*

3 Study Research Methodology

The research methodology followed for this study included four main steps: (i) the pre-selection of thematic categories, (ii) the search for ML-driven QE and ME frameworks in the Scopus meta-database, (iii) the application of a binary assessment, and (iv) the derivation of criteria from the studied frameworks.

This study identifies and compares ML-driven QE and ME frameworks to recognise their key components and determine their commonalities and differences towards their convergence for the design of ML-IQME Frameworks.

Step 1 – A set of *thematic categories* was defined based on the findings of the scoping review, which led to the identifying the key dimensions commonly found in smart manufacturing systems, and that were considered relevant for mapping the key components for integrating "smart" quality and maintenance systems. The *thematic categories* pre-selected were the following: (i) Data Quality, (ii) Data Maintenance, (iii) ML Technique, (iv) Target Maintenance Policy, (v) Target Quality Policy, and (vi) Target Output. These categories served as the analytical lens through which each framework was later assessed.

Step 2 – A *literature review* was conducted in Scopus meta-database, targeting recent studies on ML techniques applied to QE and ME to answer the research question. The literature search used targeted keywords that met the defined inclusion criteria (see Table 1). Each framework was reviewed in full to extract relevant information aligned with the predefined thematic categories.

Step 3 – A *binary assessment* was applied across all studied frameworks and thematic categories. Each criterion was scored as either *fully addressed,* explicitly proposed, implemented, or validated, or *not addressed.*

Step 4 – For each thematic category, *the criteria were extracted* directly from the content of the studied frameworks rather than from predefined criteria, allowing the *binary assessment* to reflect what is actually discussed in the literature. To ensure transparency and traceability in this process, two examples are provided: Under *ML Technique,* a framework was marked as fully addressed if it explicitly described and validated a specific ML algorithm (e.g., XGBoost or CNN) within the manufacturing context; and under *Target Maintenance Policy,* full coverage required the framework to not only mention a maintenance strategy but also demonstrate how it is operationalised through the system. If a criterion was not mentioned at all, it was marked as not addressed.

4 Literature Review Method

The literature search was conducted in the *Scopus meta-database* and covered journal articles and conference papers published in English without date restriction in the fields of "Engineering" and "Computer Science", applying the following *search string* across title, abstract, and keywords:

(«quality engineering» OR «quality management» OR «quality control») AND («maintenance» OR «maintenance engineering» OR «predictive maintenance» OR «quality and reliability» OR «condition monitoring») AND («framework» OR «model» OR «approach») AND («artificial intelligence» OR «machine learning») AND («Industry 4.0» OR «smart manufacturing» OR «digital transformation»)

The search returned 161 records. Titles and abstracts were screened against three *inclusion criteria* presented in Table 1. Studies that addressed only one domain in isolation, used an ML technique as a peripheral tool, or lacked sufficient methodological detail for comparison were excluded. Following title and abstract screening, 16 records were assessed in full-text, of which 10 met all inclusion criteria and were retained for analysis. The screening process is illustrated in Fig. 1.

Table 1. Inclusion criteria applied during the literature screening process

#	Inclusion Criterion	Description
1	Quality Engineering and Maintenance Engineering are Addressed Jointly	The paper must explicitly address both quality engineering and maintenance engineering as connected or integrated functions, not each in isolation.
2	Machine Learning Technique(s) Applied	The paper must apply at least one ML technique as a core component of the proposed approach.
3	Framework, Architecture, or Conceptual Diagram for Comparison	The paper must present a structured framework, architecture, or conceptual diagram that allows systematic comparison of its components with other studies.

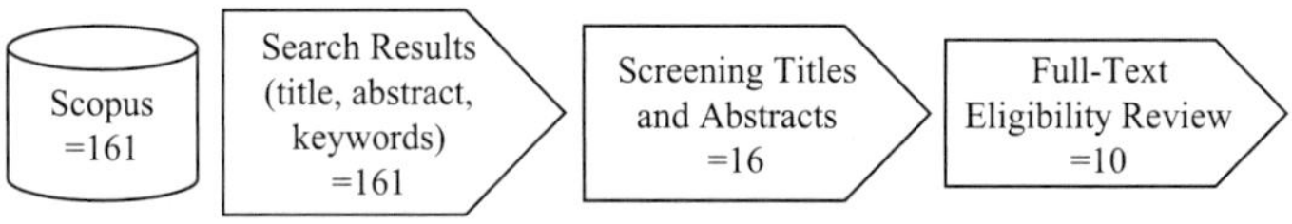

Fig. 1. Literature screening and selection process

The search aimed to identify guidelines, frameworks, and structured approaches at the intersection of QE and ME that incorporate ML as a key enabling technology, rather than isolated algorithm applications. Following the screening, 10 frameworks were selected for analysis and are discussed in Sect. 5.

5 Study Results

This section presents the results of the *comparative analysis* conducted on the 10 frameworks identified through a literature review. The 10 frameworks were examined across *six selected thematic categories,* each represented by *six comparison matrices,* as detailed in Tables 2 to 7, which collectively cover the key components required for pursuing an *ML-driven QE-ME unified approach.* For each *thematic category,* its respective *comparison matrix* captures whether each framework is "fully addressed" or "not addressed" in the corresponding criteria, enabling a systematic comparison across studies.

5.1 Studied ML-Driven Quality and/or Maintenance Engineering Frameworks

A total of 10 *ML-driven QE or ME frameworks* were studied, based on the literature review conducted:

Framework 1 (F1): Lee & Kim (2019) [20] – The framework argues conceptually that predictive maintenance and quality management converge under Industry 4.0, but does not present an ML architecture that integrates them. Quality and maintenance are treated as expressions of the same underlying data-driven system; however, no joint model, shared data pipeline, or integrated output is specified. Evidence is drawn from secondary industrial cases, not original implementation.

Framework 2 (F2): Hanzelik, Kummer & Abonyi (2022) [21] – ML is applied to quality assurance through software sensors that continuously predict difficult-to-measure product parameters in chemical manufacturing. The term "maintenance" in this framework refers exclusively to ML model maintenance, preventing model deterioration through CRISP-ML, MLOps, and PMML lifecycle management, not to physical equipment maintenance. Quality and asset maintenance are not integrated; the framework addresses model sustainability as a prerequisite for reliable quality monitoring.

Framework 3 (F3): Rydzi et al. (2024) [22] – ML is applied exclusively to quality prediction: CatBoost and XGBoost classify end-of-line products as OK or NOK using process parameter data from automotive assembly. Maintenance is listed as a related domain in the broader framing, but is not part of the framework's data pipeline or decision logic; no maintenance signal or maintenance outcome is modelled.

Framework 4 (F4): Okuyelu & Adaji (2024) [23] – The review presents quality monitoring and fault prognosis as two separate application areas where ML and IoT can deliver improvements, without proposing a framework that technically connects them. Quality and maintenance are discussed in parallel as co-beneficiaries of real-time ML monitoring, but no shared data model, joint output, or integrated decision mechanism is described.

Framework 5 (F5): Ejjami & Boussalham (2024) [24] – ML-driven quality control and predictive maintenance are presented as two of three independent pillars of an Industry 5.0 manufacturing system, alongside supply chain optimisation. Each pillar is discussed separately with its own AI applications; no technical mechanism is proposed to connect quality and maintenance under a shared model or data architecture. The framework's contribution is governance-oriented rather than integrative at the ML level.

Framework 6 (F6): Kaftan et al. (2025) [25] – ML (NLP, BERT, and knowledge graphs) is applied jointly to quality and maintenance records, analysing unstructured logs from both domains within the same root cause analysis pipeline. This is the only framework in the sample where quality and maintenance data are technically processed together, though integration remains at the analytical layer; no shared predictive model or unified operational output is produced. The framework explicitly identifies the absence of any approach linking AI-based Root Cause Analysis (RCA) to ISO 9001 or IATF 16949 compliance requirements.

Framework 7 (F7): Mielgo et al. (2025) [26] **–** The only framework in the sample that explicitly designs ML to serve both quality control and predictive maintenance simultaneously from a shared sensor data pipeline. CNN/ViT and contrastive learning process the same input signals to produce both defect classification and equipment degradation outputs under one architecture. Full integration is not yet validated; the framework is under active development, and only preliminary results are reported.

Framework 8 (F8): Ouled Laghzal & El Ouadi (2025) [27] – ML is applied to quality-oriented continuous improvement methodologies (Lean, Six Sigma, TQM), augmenting existing frameworks such as DMAIC with AI-driven dynamic control. Maintenance is referenced as a domain that similarly benefits from AI, but it is not technically integrated into the framework's architecture; quality and maintenance remain separate areas of application with no shared ML pipeline or combined output.

Framework 9 (F9): Alkhatib et al. (2025) [28] – ML is applied to quality classification: GBM and Random Forest detect defective engine valves from dimensional measurement data within the PMQ framework. Predictive maintenance appears as a keyword and is referenced in the framework's stated scope, but the case study implementation and all reported results are limited to quality defect prediction; no maintenance model, equipment signal, or maintenance output is included in the deployed system.

Framework 10 (F10): Nguyen et al. (2026) [29] – presented a review of AI-driven Digital Twins (DTs) in manufacturing, organised under a four-level manufacturing hierarchy: machine, cell, shop floor, and enterprise. Covering ML techniques as reinforcement learning. Maintenance is an extensive domain in this paper, since it addresses predictive maintenance, Remaining Useful Life (RUL) estimation, and fault diagnosis at every level. While quality appears at the cell and shop floor through defect prediction and quality prediction. The bridge between both domains is indirect: quality deviation signal equipment degradation to trigger maintenance actions.

5.2 Comparison Matrix for the Data Quality Thematic Category

The *Data Quality thematic category* captures the types of quality-related signals each framework uses as ML model inputs. Structured process signals such as binary pass/fail labels and process parameter deviations are the most widely represented, appearing in F3, F7, F8, F9, and F10, reflecting a strong reliance on sensor-based and dimensional data. Unstructured inputs such as fault descriptions and warranty records appear only in F6, highlighting a gap in the exploitation of text-based operational data across the reviewed frameworks (see Table 2).

Table 2. Comparison matrix for the data quality thematic category

DATA QUALITY: Types of quality-related signals used as ML model inputs to detect defects or classify product outcomes.

Criterion	F1	F2	F3	F4	F5	F6	F7	F8	F9	F10
Visual/Surface Quality							●	●		●
Functional/Acoustic (Sound, Vibration)			●							
Binary Pass/Fail Label (OK/NOK)			●				●	●	●	●
Fault/Defect Description (Text, Fault Codes)						●				
Process Parameter Deviation (Torque, Pressure)		●	●							●

5.3 Comparison Matrix for the Data Maintenance Thematic Category

The *Data Maintenance thematic category* covers the equipment-side sensor modalities used to monitor asset conditions. Temperature and pressure/flow readings are the most common, present in four frameworks each, consistent with their low cost and broad applicability. Maintenance logs and work orders appear only in F6, which is notable since these records carry rich diagnostic history; their absence in other frameworks reflects the field's preference for structured sensor signals over unstructured operational records (see Table 3).

Table 3. Comparison matrix for the data maintenance thematic category

DATA MAINTENANCE: Equipment-side sensor modalities and operational records used to monitor asset condition and anticipate failures.

Criterion	F1	F2	F3	F4	F5	F6	F7	F8	F9	F10
Vibration Signals	●									●
Temperature/Thermal Readings	●	●					●			●
Pressure/Flow/RPM/Current	●	●	●							●
Maintenance Logs						●				
Mould/Tooling Wear & Degradation							●			●
Equipment Failure History	●			●				●		●

5.4 Comparison Matrix for the Machine Learning Thematic Category

The *Machine Learning thematic category* shows the lowest average coverage across the matrix and the greatest divergence among frameworks. Classical ML methods and neural networks appear most frequently, but no algorithmic family is universal. Deep learning and computer vision appear in only three frameworks (F7, F8, and F10), AutoML in three (F2, F3, and F8), and NLP approaches in only one (F6). This spread indicates that the field has not converged on a preferred technique for integrated quality-maintenance applications; algorithm selection remains highly context-dependent (see Table 4).

Table 4. Comparison matrix for the Machine Learning thematic category

MACHINE LEARNING TECHNIQUE: Computational methods applied to learn from data and generate predictions or classifications.										
Criterion	**F1**	**F2**	**F3**	**F4**	**F5**	**F6**	**F7**	**F8**	**F9**	**F10**
Gradient Boosting (XGBoost/CatBoost)		●	●						●	
Classical ML (SVM, KNN, Decision Tree, RF)		●	●					●	●	●
Deep Learning							●	●		●
Neural Networks	●						●	●	●	●
NLP						●				
AutoML		●	●					●		
Computer Vision							●	●		●

5.5 Comparison Matrix for the Target Maintenance Policy Thematic Category

The *Target Maintenance Policy thematic category* considers different maintenance strategies. Predictive maintenance and intelligent/smart maintenance each appear in the majority of frameworks, establishing them as the dominant paradigm in the reviewed literature. Condition-based maintenance appears in three frameworks (F1, F5, and F10), and prognostics and health management in one (F7). Self-maintenance and AutoML recalibration, which represent a higher level of autonomy, appear only in F2 and F3, suggesting that fully automated maintenance decision-making remains an open challenge (see Table 5).

Table 5. Comparison matrix for the Target Maintenance Policy thematic category

TARGET MAINTENANCE POLICY: The strategic maintenance paradigm is the framework that supports the type of maintenance decision it is designed to produce.										
Criterion	**F1**	**F2**	**F3**	**F4**	**F5**	**F6**	**F7**	**F8**	**F9**	**F10**
Predictive Maintenance (PdM)	●	●		●	●			●		●
Condition-Based Maintenance (CBM)	●				●					●
Intelligent/Smart Maintenance	●	●	●	●						●
Prognostics and Health Management (PHM)							●			
Self-Maintenance/AutoML Recalibration		●	●							

5.6 Comparison Matrix for the Target Quality Policy Thematic Category

The *Target Quality Policy thematic category* accounts for different QE approaches. Quality control (defect detection) is the most universally addressed criterion, present in nine of all 10 frameworks, followed closely by Quality Assurance (process and system level) in seven. Sensor-based quality monitoring appears in seven frameworks, reflecting the central role of real-time measurement in quality-maintenance ML integration. Notably, formal QMS standards alignment (e.g., ISO 9001 and IATF 16949) appears in only one framework (F6), revealing a significant gap between technical ML capability and the compliance requirements of regulated manufacturing sectors (see Table 6).

Table 6. Comparison matrix for the target quality policy thematic category

TARGET QUALITY POLICY: Quality management strategy within which ML outputs must operate, including compliance context and formal standards alignment.										
Criterion	**F1**	**F2**	**F3**	**F4**	**F5**	**F6**	**F7**	**F8**	**F9**	**F10**
Quality Control (QC)	●	●	●	●	●		●	●	●	●
Quality Assurance (QA)	●	●			●	●		●	●	●
Six Sigma/Lean		●						●	●	
Sensors-based Quality Monitoring	●	●	●	●			●		●	●
QMS Standards (ISO9001/IATF16949)						●				

5.7 Comparison Matrix for the Target Output Thematic Category

The *Target Output thematic category* includes diverse kinds of system delivers. All 10 frameworks address real-time diagnosis and monitoring, making it the only universally covered criterion in the entire matrix. Forecasting and maintenance/quality decision-making are present in nine frameworks each, confirming the functional core of the field. More advanced output types, such as prognosis and Remaining Useful Life (RUL) estimation (three frameworks), root cause identification (three frameworks), and governance/audit trail (three frameworks), show lower coverage, pointing to the dimensions where the field still lacks consolidated approaches. Self-corrective output, where the system automatically applies corrections without human approval, appears only in F3, reflecting the field's prevailing preference for semi-autonomous operation (see Table 7).

Table 7. Comparison matrix for the target output thematic category

TARGET OUTPUT: Decisions, signals, and artefacts that the system delivers to practitioners.										
Criterion	**F1**	**F2**	**F3**	**F4**	**F5**	**F6**	**F7**	**F8**	**F9**	**F10**
Forecasting (Future Quality/Failure)	●	●	●	●	●		●	●	●	●
Maintenance/Quality Decision-Making	●	●	●	●	●	●		●	●	●
Diagnosis/Monitoring (Real-Time)	●	●	●	●	●	●	●	●	●	●
Prognosis/RUL Estimation	●						●			●
Root Cause Identification						●		●	●	

(*continued*)

Table 7. (*continued*)

TARGET OUTPUT: Decisions, signals, and artefacts that the system delivers to practitioners.										
Feedback (Output Feedback to Process)	●	●	●						●	●
Self-Corrective (Auto Error Correction)			●							
Governance/Audit Trail/Explainability					●	●			●	

6 Discussion

The *six comparison matrices* reveal two complementary patterns: a robust consensus on the "functional outputs" and "operational infrastructure" required for ML-driven QE-ME integration, and significant divergence on the algorithmic, data, and governance dimensions. At the output level, all 10 frameworks address real-time diagnosis and monitoring (F1–F10). Within the *Target Quality Policy,* quality control is widely applied since almost all the 10 frameworks address it, except F6, and sensor-based monitoring appears in seven frameworks (see Table 6). Within the *Target Maintenance Policy,* predictive maintenance appears in six frameworks and intelligent/smart maintenance in five, together forming the dominant paradigm in the reviewed literature (see Table 5). These patterns are consistent with prior reviews on ML in (smart) manufacturing [10, 12] and confirm the functional core of the field. A further point of consensus concerns human oversight: nine frameworks position semi-autonomous operation, where practitioners validate and act upon ML outputs, as the dominant interaction model, while full automation appears in only one framework in a partial capacity. This indicates the field has converged not towards replacing human judgment, but towards structuring the interface (co-piloting) between domain expertise and ML outputs more effectively to keep the human-in-the-loop.

The most significant divergence appears in the *ML Technique thematic category,* which shows the lowest average coverage in the comparison matrix (see Table 4). Classical ML algorithms appear in five frameworks and Gradient Boosting in three frameworks (F3, F8, and F9), while Deep Learning is addressed by three frameworks (F7, F8, and 10), AutoML by three frameworks (F2, F3, and F8), and NLP-based approaches by only one framework (F6) (see Table 4). There is no consensus on which ML techniques are most appropriate for the development of ML-driven Integrated Quality and Maintenance Engineering applications. This divergence is compounded by evidence that algorithm performance is "context-dependent". Gradient boosting achieves high classification accuracy in structured automotive quality tasks (F3: 94% accuracy; F9: F1-score = 0.98) but exhibits severe overfitting under production conditions in spectroscopic chemical processing tasks (F2: training $R^2 = 0.999$ vs. production $R^2 = 0.747$). The frameworks rely predominantly on structured sensor data, such as binary pass/fail labels (F3, F7, F8, F9, and F10), temperature readings (F1, F2, F7, and F10), while unstructured operational data such as maintenance logs and fault descriptions is addressed by only one framework (F6), and Quality Management Systems (QMS) standards integration (ISO 9001 and IATF 16949) by one framework (F6). This reveals a persistent gap between technical ML capability and the compliance and auditability requirements that govern regulated manufacturing sectors.

A comparative reading of all the frameworks surfaces four distinct orientations. The first, represented by F3 and F9, treats quality and maintenance as *a concrete ML implementation challenge* requiring specific algorithms validated on real manufacturing data. F7 extends the scope by designing a shared sensor pipeline for both domains using deep learning. The second, represented by F6, argues that the *most actionable signals reside in unstructured text, maintenance logs, corrective action reports, and relies on NLP and knowledge graphs;* it is the only framework addressing tacit operational knowledge. The third, common to F1, F4, F5, and F10 frameworks, frames ML as enabling a *systemic paradigm* to shift rather than a tool-level improvement, asserting that the combination of IoT, big data, and ML produces emergent properties, resilience, transparency, and adaptability beyond individual algorithm performance. The fourth, shared by F2 and F8 frameworks, *foregrounds institutional and methodological readiness:* F8 identifies the structural incompatibility between DMAIC (Define, Measure, Analyse, Improve, Control) and the ML lifecycle; F2 demonstrates that without lifecycle management (i.e., CRISP-ML, MLOps, and PMML) models deteriorate silently after deployment; and F9 shows that without an embedded interpretability step, practitioner trust remains insufficient for adoption. These orientations explain the difference observed in the six comparison matrices and indicate that the field approaches *ML-Quality-Maintenance Engineering integration* from different entry points.

Synthesising across the six comparison matrices and the cross-framework analysis, five key criteria emerge as necessary conditions for *sustained ML-driven QE-ME integration:* (i) a unified data architecture connecting IoT sensors, edge devices, ERP, and inspection systems into a shared pipeline; (ii) a structured ML lifecycle framework covering continuous model monitoring and triggered retraining, not only initial deployment CRISP-ML (F2) and the PMQ Relearn phase (F9) satisfy this; CRISP-DM as applied in F1 does not; (iii) embedded interpretability mechanisms integrated into the quality decision workflow, as demonstrated by the Validate phase in F9; (iv) iterative retraining capability to sustain accuracy as production conditions evolve; and (v) formal governance protocols determining how model outputs influence decisions.

No reviewed framework fully satisfies all five criteria simultaneously. The most critical unresolved gap is the absence of a production-validated system that jointly addresses quality and maintenance under a single ML architecture within a compliance framework compatible with ISO 9001 and/or IATF 16949. The reported Quality 4.0 adoption rate of 13–20% (F9) confirms that the binding constraint is not algorithmic capability but institutional readiness: (i) infrastructure cost, (ii) practitioner trust, and (iii) standards integration must be addressed in parallel with model performance for integration to succeed at scale.

7 Conclusions and Future Work

This paper distinguishes itself from previous related research works [15–18] by being the first one to map the key criteria at the intersection of QE and ME with an ML-driven approach to support the design of "ML-IQME" Reference Frameworks.

The study presented a *comparative analysis* of *10 ML-driven QE or ME frameworks,* using *structured comparison matrices* across *six analytical thematic categories:* (i) Data Quality, (ii) Data Maintenance, (iii) Machine Learning Technique, (iv) Target Maintenance Policy, (v) Target Quality Policy, and (vi) Target Output. The findings main confirm that ML can be considered as the "bridging technology" for QE and ME integration, due to its capacity for real-time data analysis of multi-stream data from different production systems (i.e., quality and maintenance), identification of hidden patterns in data, and real-time feedback simultaneously from different data streams to have a proactive approach to prevent defects and improve equipment reliability. Other findings show strong consensus around real-time diagnosis and monitoring, predictive maintenance, quality control and assurance alignment, and semi-autonomous human oversight (i.e., human-in-the-loop) as foundational components.

Significant *research gaps* persist in algorithmic specificity, multi-modal data exploitation, governance, and compliance with standards such as ISO 9001 and IATF 16949, confirming that the binding constraint is not an algorithmic capability but institutional readiness. The *comparison matrices* provide a replicable, evidence-based map of the QE and ME fields for both practitioners prioritising integration investments and researchers identifying open research challenges.

For researchers, the findings provide an integrated, structured evidence-based map of both fields that surfaces the existing research gap and points out the most critical open challenges and promising directions at the *QE-ME intersection* with *ML as their unified approach.* For industry practitioners, the findings offer actionable guidelines on how to leverage QE and ME data management systems through an "ML-driven" approach.

Future work will focus on the design, testing, and validation of an "ML-driven Integrated Quality-Maintenance Engineering Reference Framework" that will aim to support manufacturing companies to reduce production costs, enhance productivity, and improve customer satisfaction in the face of the growing pressure for quality-driven, resilient, and sustainable production systems.

Acknowledgements. This work has been performed within the Sustainable Production Initiative and the Production Area of Advance at Chalmers University of Technology; their support is greatly appreciated. Furthermore, the study was supported by the Vinnova - Sweden's Innovation Agency under Grant Number 2025-01110: "Advanced AI Architectures for Integrated and Enhanced Manufacturing Operations (AIMOps) Project".

Disclosure of Interests. The authors have no competing interests relevant to this paper's content.

References

1. Escobar, C.A., Morales-Menendez, R.: Machine learning techniques for quality control in high conformance manufacturing environment. Adv. Mech. Eng. **10**(2), 1687814018755519 (2018)
2. Talha, M.: Total quality management (TQM): an overview. Bottom Line. **17**(1), 15–19 (2004)
3. Kayode, J.F., Afolalu, S.A., Monye, S.I., Adaramola, B.A.: Overview of maintenance scope and reliability in the manufacturing sector. In: 2024 International Conference on Science, Engineering and Business for Driving Sustainable Development Goals, pp. 1–7 (2024)

4. Nazabadi, M.R., Najafi, S.E., Mohaghar, A., Sobhani, F.M.: The joint policy of production, maintenance, and product quality in a multi-machine production system by reinforcement learning and agent-based Modeling. Int. J. Res. Ind. Eng. **13**(1), 71–87 (2024)
5. Bengtsson, M., Fundin, A., Deleryd, M., et al.: Integrating quality and maintenance development: opportunities and implications. In: 23rd International Congress on Condition Monitoring and Diagnostic Engineering Management: Advances in Maintenance and Condition Diagnosis Technologies towards Sustainable Society, pp. 821–828 (2010)
6. Colledani, M., Tolio, T.: Integrated quality, production logistics and maintenance analysis of multi-stage asynchronous manufacturing systems with degrading machines. CIRP Ann. **61**(1), 455–458 (2012)
7. Psarommatis, F., May, G., Azamfirei, V.: Envisioning maintenance 5.0: insights from a systematic literature review of industry 4.0 and a proposed framework. J. Mfg. Syst. **68**, 376–399 (2023)
8. Rüßmann, M., Lorenz, M., Gerbert, P., et al.: Industry 4.0: the future of productivity and growth in manufacturing (2015). https://www.bcg.com/publications/2015/engineered_products_project_business_industry_4_future_productivity_growth_manufacturing_industries
9. Rosin, F., Forget, P., Lamouri, S., Pellerin, R.: Impact of industry 4.0 on decision-making in an operational context. Adv. Prod. Eng. Mgmt. **16**(4), 500–514 (2021)
10. Wuest, T., Irgens, C., Thoben, K.-D.: An approach to monitoring quality in manufacturing using supervised machine learning on product state data. J. Intell. Manuf. **25**(5), 1167–1180 (2014)
11. Yorulmuş, M.H., Bolat, H.B., Bahadır, Ç.: Predictive quality defect detection using machine learning algorithms: a case study from automobile industry. In: Intelligent and Fuzzy Techniques for Emerging Conditions and Digital Transformation. Lecture Notes in Networks and Systems, vol. 308. Springer, Cham (2022)
12. Carvalho, T.P., Soares, F.A.A.M.N., Vita, R., Francisco, R.D.P., Basto, J.P., Alcalá, S.G.S.: A systematic literature review of machine learning methods applied to predictive maintenance. Comput. Ind. Eng. **137**, 106024 (2019)
13. Traini, E., Bruno, G., D'Antonio, G., Lombardi, F.: Machine learning framework for predictive maintenance in milling. IFAC-PapersOnLine. **52**(13), 177–182 (2019)
14. BouAbid, H., Dhoubi, K., Gharbi, A.: Integrated production and maintenance policy for manufacturing systems prone to products' quality degradation. Adv. Prod. Eng. Mgmt. **19**(4), 512–526 (2024)
15. Arksey, H., O'Malley, L.: Scoping studies: towards a methodological framework. Int. J. Soc. Res. Methodol. **8**(1), 19–32 (2005). https://doi.org/10.1080/1364557032000119616
16. Frankó, A., Pál, V.: A survey on machine learning-based smart maintenance and quality control solutions. Infocommunications J. **13**(4), 28–35 (2021)
17. Jourdan, N., Longard, L., Biegel, T., Metternich, J.: Machine learning for intelligent maintenance and quality control: a review of existing datasets and corresponding use cases. In: Conference on Production Systems and Logistics (2021)
18. Riccio, C., Menanno, M., Zennaro, I., Savino, M.M.: A new methodological framework for optimizing predictive maintenance using machine learning combined with product quality parameters. Machines. **12**(7), 443 (2024)
19. Koulinas, G.K., Paraschos, P.D., Koulouriotis, D.E.: A machine learning framework for explainable knowledge mining and production, maintenance, and quality control optimization in flexible circular manufacturing systems. Flex. Serv. Mfg. J. **36**(3), 737–759 (2024)
20. Lee, S.M., Lee, D., Kim, Y.S.: The quality management ecosystem for predictive maintenance in the industry 4.0 era. Int. J. Qual. Innov. **5**(1), 4 (2019)
21. Hanzelik, P.P., Kummer, A., Abonyi, J.: Edge-computing and machine-learning-based framework for software sensor development. Sensors. **22**(11), 4268 (2022)

22. Rydzi, S., Zahradnikova, B., Sutova, Z., Ravas, M., Hornacek, D., Tanuska, P.: A predictive quality inspection framework for the manufacturing process in the context of industry 4.0. Sensors. **24**(17), 5644 (2024)
23. Okuyelu, O., Adaji, O.: AI-driven real-time quality monitoring and process optimization for enhanced manufacturing performance. J. Adv. Math. Comput. Sci. **39**(4), 81–89 (2024)
24. Ejjami, R., Boussalham, K.: Industry 5.0 in manufacturing: enhancing resilience and responsibility through AI-driven predictive maintenance, quality control, and supply chain optimization. Int. J. Multidiscip. Res. **6**(4), 1–31 (2024)
25. Kaftan, P., Lanquillon, C., Stache, N.C.: AI-supported root cause analysis in automotive quality problem solving: a cross-domain literature review. In: Artificial Intelligence in HCI Lecture Notes in Computer Science, vol. 15820, pp. 177–197. Springer Nature Switzerland (2025)
26. Mielgo, P., Bregon, A., Martınez-Prieto, M.A.: Deep learning for robust manufacturing: from quality control to predictive maintenance. Ann. Conf. PHM Soc. **7**(1) (2025)
27. Laghzal, S.O.: Integrating artificial intelligence into continuous improvement for automotive manufacturing. Int. J. Adv. Comput. Sci. Appl. **16**(11), 906–914 (2025)
28. Alkhatib, F., Allam, M., Swarnakar, V., et al.: Implementing and evaluating the quality 4.0 PMQ framework for process monitoring in automotive manufacturing. Sci. Rep. **15**(1), 24742 (2025)
29. Nguyen, P., Kim, M., Nichols, E., Yoon, H.-S.: AI-driven digital twins for manufacturing: a review across hierarchical manufacturing system levels. Sensors. **26**(1), 124 (2026)

Developing a Data-Driven Maintenance Service: A Digital Platform Enabled Asset Management Approach Based on TBO Optimization

Lorenzo Ghedini[1(✉)], Irene Roda[1], Marco Macchi[1], Alejandro Andres Martinez Ortega[2], and Alessandro Pozzetti[1]

[1] Department of Management, Economics and Industrial Engineering, Politecnico di Milano, Piazza Leonardo da Vinci, 20133 Milan, Italy
{lorenzo.ghedini,irene.roda,marco.macchi, alessandro.pozzetti}@polimi.it

[2] RMES Analytics, Cerro El Plomo 5420 of. 5420, Santiago, Chile
alejandro.martinez@polimi.it

Abstract. The increasing digitalization of industrial operations is enabling the widespread availability of asset-related data. However, organisations still face challenges in transforming such data into Asset Management practices. In this context, digital platforms offer the potential to support the development of data-driven services that integrate data, analytical models and decision-support functionalities. This paper presents the development of a data-driven maintenance management service enabled by a digital platform for industrial Asset Management. Moreover, the study formalises how platform-based data infrastructures and analytical capabilities can be leveraged to construct reliability-based representation of assets. It also shows how these models can be integrated into a decision-support mechanism for maintenance planning. In particular, the proposed approach leverages platform-based data infrastructures to enable a more integrated and dynamic estimation of Time Between Overhaul (TBO). This is archieved by combining operational data and reliability modelling within a unified environment that directly supports maintenance decision-making. The service is illustrated through a laboratory-scale application to a fleet of Komatsu 930E haul trucks. In this context, operational and failure data are used to estimate Weibull reliability models, determine optimal overhaul intervals and generate a maintenance plan under operational constraints. The results show how digital platforms can support the systematic integration of data, reliability-based digital models and optimisation-based decision-support mechanisms. This enables the development of data-driven maintenance services that operationalise Asset Management principles.

Keywords: Industrial Asset Management · Digital Service · Time Between Overhauls · Industry 4.0 · Digital Platforms

Published by Springer Nature Switzerland AG 2027
G. Pezzotta et al. (Eds.): APMS 2026, IFIP AICT 808, pp. 447–461, 2027.
https://doi.org/10.1007/978-3-032-38594-9_30

1 Introduction

The industrial sector is undergoing a profound transformation driven by digitalization. Recent analyses highlight how the global economy has increased the need for more advanced levels of industrialisation, informatization and digitisation to enhance efficiency, competence and competitiveness [1]. To cope with these challenges, companies have widely adopted Industry 4.0 technologies, such as advanced data analytics and IoT, to collect and process operational information, thus supporting more accurate engineering decision-making [2]. These developments not only affect industrial operations but also reshape business models, fostering a shift from traditional product-based logic toward performance-oriented and service-based value propositions [3]. Thus, as machines increasingly interact and exchange information in real time, industrial systems become more flexible, intelligent and collaborative, pushing firms to operate within broader digital ecosystems involving both suppliers and customers [4].

Within this digital evolution, Asset Management (AM) has gained renewed strategic relevance. On one side, AM has progressively evolved from a maintenance-oriented function into a holistic, lifecycle-oriented approach aimed at maximizing asset value creation [5, 6]. On the other side, Industry 4.0 technologies are enabling the generation of unprecedented volumes of information on asset behavior, conditions and usage. Such data allow companies to characterize degradation mechanisms, understand the influence of operational or human factors on failures, and enable the delivery of asset-related processes, such as condition monitoring, health assessment, risk management and process optimization, as structured digital services [7–9]. For these reasons, AM is increasingly viewed as a strategic lever for improving competitiveness in industry [10]. This role becomes particularly critical in asset-intensive industries such as mining. In this sector large-scale equipment operates under harsh and variable conditions, leading to high maintenance costs and significant operational risks. Thus, unplanned downtime and suboptimal maintenance decisions can have substantial economic and safety implications, making data-driven Asset Management approaches especially valuable.

Nevertheless, the effective adoption of AM remains challenging. AM practices are still often applied intuitively rather than systematically, due to the lack of clear operational guidelines and decision-support mechanisms capable of transforming data into structured and repeatable actions [10]. This misalignment highlights a persistent gap between the availability of data and the ability to exploit them for robust, data-driven AM decisions. It is within this context that digital platforms can be recognized as key enablers for structuring, integrating and exploiting operational data in Asset Management. By providing shared data environments and embedded analytical capabilities, platforms allow organisations to develop data-driven services that support industrial asset management and maintenance decision-making processes [11]. These services rely on the ability to transform heterogeneous operational data, such as usage information, perfor-mance indicators and failure records, into models that can be used to analyse asset be-haviour and support planning activities [12].

Thus, this paper presents the development of a data-driven maintenance management service enabled by a digital platform for industrial AM. In this study, the platform considered acts as an infrastructure for integrating data, analytical models, and decision-support functionalities. Moreover, the study formalises how platform-based data infrastructures and analytical functionalities can support the construction of asset-level digital twin models grounded in reliability analysis, by leveraging approaches that combine reliability models with operational condition-monitoring data [13, 14]. It also shows how these models can be systematically integrated into a decision-support mechanism for maintenance planning based on TBO estimation.

In doing so, the paper contributes by structuring a service-oriented framework that links operational data, reliability modelling and maintenance decision-making within a digital platform environment. The proposed service is illustrated through a laboratory-scale application to a fleet of Komatsu 930E haul trucks, available within the industrial context under investigation. These trucks can be viewed as asset systems composed of multiple subsystems, such as engine, alternator and other components, which are treated as individual assets. Their complex subsystem structure, high operational variability and significant maintenance costs make them suitable for testing data-driven mainte-nance approaches. The implementation is carried out within a specific digital platform environment (RMES Suite), already adopted within the client existing portfolio. In particular, the use of this platform is driven by its capabilities for data integration, storage and analyt-ics on industrial asset data. In this study, these data are used to estimate overhaul inter-vals and generate a maintenance plan under operational constraints. However, although the study is conducted in a mining context, the proposed ap-proach is not tied to the specific application domain. Rather, the contribution lies in the generalizability of the service structure, which integrates operational data, reliability modelling, and decision-support mechanisms. Thus, such a structure can be transferred to other asset-intensive industries where similar types of data (e.g., failure records, us-age information, and cost parameters) are available.

The remainder of this paper is structured as follows. Section 2 reviews the foundations of digital platform for industrial Asset Management. Section 3 introduces the reliability modelling adopted for the TBO estimation. Section 4 discusses the results obtained. Finally, Sect. 5 presents the conclusions, contributions and opportunities for future research.

2 Digital Platforms for Industrial Asset Management

Digital platforms have become central components in the evolution of industrial value creation architectures [15]. Beyond their role as technological infrastructures that support coordination, information exchange and the development of new service offerings, recent literature conceptualises them as meta-organisational architectures that structure interactions across organisational boundaries [16]. In this sense, platforms act as coordination mechanisms enabling dis-tributed innovation and shaping how value is created and exchanged among multiple actors, including customers, suppliers, technology partners and service providers [17, 18].

In the context of AM, digital platforms enable the integration of data from distributed assets and support the transformation of operational data into analytical insights.

Existing applications primarily focus on data integration, condition monitoring, and analytics-driven services such as predictive maintenance and performance monitoring, some examples are reported in [19–21]. This data integration capability is particularly relevant for AM, which relies on decision-making processes based on heterogeneous and often fragmented information sources [10]. In this context, digital platforms provide the infrastructure to transform operational data into digital models of asset behaviour, enabling users to formalize degradation patterns and evaluate operating conditions while supporting maintenance decision-making processes [22].

While these capabilities highlight the potential of digital platforms to support Asset Management applications, their effective use in industrial contexts is still limited [23]. In fact, industrial B2B platforms are characterised by high operational complexity, heterogeneous asset structures, lack of standardisation, and the need to coordinate multiple actors within complex environments making their implementation difficult [22–24]. Thus, there is a need to better understand how industrial digital platforms can be effectively used to support Asset Management processes. Given the complexity of B2B environments and the characteristics of industrial assets, it becomes relevant to investigate how platform-based systems can be used to combine operational data and analytical models within concrete service implementations aimed at supporting AM decision-making.

To address this gap, the present study develops a data-driven maintenance service in which reliability-based digital models are directly integrated into a decision-support mechanism for maintenance planning. The proposed approach operationalises TBO estimation within a platform-enabled environment, showing how operational data from multiple sources can be transformed into maintenance decisions through a unified data infrastructure that connects reliability modelling, optimisation and operational processes. The selected application context is particularly suitable due to the high operational impact and complexity of maintenance decisions in asset-intensive environments, where reliability, cost and operational constraints must be jointly managed.

To provide an integrated view of the proposed approach, Fig. 1 illustrates the architecture of the platform-enabled maintenance service, while implementation details are described in Sect. 3. The service is structured as a layered process in which operational data are first collected and integrated through platform-based storage and data management mechanisms, enabling the handling of heterogeneous operational and failure data. These data are organised through structures such as subsystem decomposition, failure modes, event classifications and cost parameters, ensuring consistent integration across asset and planning data.

Building on this data environment, asset-level digital models based on reliability analysis are developed to characterise degradation behaviour. In particular, Weibull-based modelling techniques implemented within the platform environment are used to represent failure dynamics and support further analysis. Finally, the decision-support layer implements the TBO optimisation procedure. This layer is realised through analytical models and optimisation logic executed via dedicated scripts (e.g., Python-based implementations) that directly access platform data, remaining fully integrated within the platform environment. The optimisation links reliability information with cost parameters to determine maintenance intervals, which are then translated into a maintenance plan accounting for operational constraints.

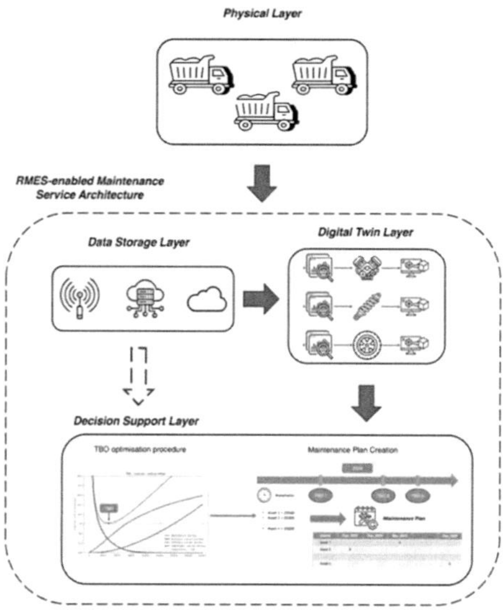

Fig. 1. Architecture of the platform-enabled maintenance service

3 Laboratory Scale Service Deployment

Building on the service architecture illustrated in Fig. 1, this section describes the laboratory-scale deployment of the proposed maintenance service. The proposed solution has been developed in a laboratory setting based on operational and failure data collected from a real industrial use case. The development was carried out in collaboration with the platform provider and informed by the requirements and data made available by the industrial partner. Therefore, while the implementation is performed at laboratory scale, it is grounded in a real application context and reflects actual maintenance planning needs.

The implementation focuses on how operational data, reliability-based modelling, and TBO-driven optimisation can be combined within a unified platform-enabled service to support maintenance planning decisions. In particular, the proposed approach lies in the integration of reliability modelling, cost-based optimisation and maintenance planning within a unified platform-enabled service. Specifically, the service is tested with reference to an industrial use case involving a client managing a fleet of Komatsu 930E haul trucks.

In particular, these vehicles represent a suitable industrial asset system for this study, as their operation relies on multiple subsystems (e.g., engine, alternator and other components), each treated as an individual asset and subject to scheduled overhauls characterised by a known or estimated TBO. Thus, at the fleet level, the Komatsu 930E can be used as a representative asset system to evaluate how a reliability-informed optimisation service can support maintenance planning.

Finally, the generated outputs were reviewed by the industrial partner, who provided an initial assessment of their consistency with operational expectations and existing maintenance practices. This interaction ensured that the proposed solution reflects real industrial constraints and supports its applicability in practice

The rest of this section is structured as follows. Section 3.1 presents a description of the Komatsu 930E and the associated maintenance context. Section 3.2 outlines the optimisation model adopted to determine the maintenance intervals and plan. Lastly, Sect. 3.3 describes the implementation of the model and discusses its laboratory-scale assessment.

3.1 Komatsu 930

The Komatsu 930E-5, represented in Fig. 2, is a large-capacity haul truck commonly used in open-pit mining operations. Designed to transport heavy loads under demanding working conditions, it represents a key production asset whose continuous availability is essential for overall site performance. The machine combines a high-power diesel engine with an AC electric drive system and is capable of carrying payloads up to 290 metric tons, making it a representative example of complex industrial equipment requiring structured maintenance planning.

Fig. 2. Representation of a Komatsu 930-E

The truck is composed of several major components, including the diesel engine, the traction alternator, the electric wheel motors, and the hydraulic and braking systems, each with its own operational role and maintenance requirements. These components work under different load profiles and operating conditions. Their utilisation is typically monitored through working-hour counters such as engine hours and cycle counts. These measurements represent the primary data source for assessing component usage and anticipating when overhaul activities may be required. The 930E provides an appropriate context for this study because its maintenance is operationally critical. Unplanned downtime on trucks of this scale can significantly affect production continuity, while high component replacement costs, inventory constraints, and their impact on maintenance budgets and cost-per-ton metrics make maintenance decisions particularly critical. These challenges are further compounded by limited data availability, the high cost of overhauls, and operational pressures to keep the fleet running, turning maintenance planning into a complex decision process that requires balancing component lifetime extension against the risk of catastrophic failures. This combination of operational relevance and structural complexity makes the 930E a suitable asset system for examining how an optimisation service can support the coordination of maintenance activities. In this work, maintenance planning is approached through TBO values associated with key assets. These values, combined with operating-hour data, provide a framework for constructing a feasible maintenance plan on a laboratory scale.

3.2 TBO Computation

The optimisation model adopted in this work is based on the concept of TBO, which specifies the operating interval after which a component is preventively overhauled or replaced. Time-based policies are widely discussed in maintenance engineering, as they explicitly balance the cost of scheduled interventions against the risk and impact of unexpected failures [25]. However, they are not necessarily always optimal. Maintenance intervals are often defined by machine manufacturers based not only on cost and reliability considerations, but also on service-related business models. This may lead to conservative or extended maintenance thresholds. This is particularly relevant for complex industrial assets such as the Komatsu 930E haul trucks, where multiple assets accumulate working hours over time and require periodic overhaul.

The use of TBO as a decision variable is consistent with established literature [26]. shows that overhaul decisions can be framed as a cost minimisation problem. In this formulation the optimal interval is obtained by trading off preventive maintenance costs against the increasing probability and consequences of failure as time elapses [27]. extend this logic to locomotive equipment by combining failure probabilities (both gradual and sudden) with economic indicators and different repair types. Although their formulations differ in detail, both contributions share the same underlying principle: the TBO is chosen by minimising an expected-cost function driven by the reliability behaviour of the component.

In this study, the TBO of each asset is determined through a cost model that explicitly uses the reliability at the candidate overhaul interval. In line with the asset hierarchy defined in the previous section, reliability is modelled through a Weibull distribution fitted to historical failure data for each component. Given observed failure times and operating hours, the shape and scale parameters of the Weibull model are estimated. This allows the reliability function $R(t)$ and derived indicators such as the Mean Time Between Failures (MTBF) to be computed.

Based on these elements, the average cost associated with a given overhaul interval TBO is expressed as:

$$\text{C\_avg} = (\text{Failure cost} + \text{Maintenance cost}) / \text{int\_0\^{}t}\ (\text{R}(\tau) * \text{dt}) \tag{1}$$

$$\text{Failure cost} = \left(\text{C\_a(t)}^{*}(1 - \text{prob}) + \text{C\_ca(t)} * \text{prob}\right)^{*}(1 - \text{R(t)}) \tag{2}$$

$$\text{Maintenance cost} = \text{C\_p(t)} * \text{R(t)} \tag{3}$$

This formulation is consistent with the general structure of expected cost models used in maintenance optimization. It is adapted to the specific characteristics of the industrial case under study. In particular, the cost structure and parameter definitions reflect both the available data and the modelling assumptions agreed upon with the industrial partner.

Where:

- R(t) is the reliability of the component at the candidate overhaul interval;
- C_p(t) is the cost of performing scheduled preventive maintenance;
- C_a(t) is the cost of accidental (corrective) maintenance following a non-catastrophic failure;
- C_ca is the cost associated with a catastrophic failure;
- "Prob" is the probability that a failure, if it occurs, is catastrophic rather than accidental;
- The denominator $\int_0^{\tau} R(t) * dt$ represents the expected uptime over the cycle and allows expressing the result as a cost per unit of effective operating time

This formulation reflects the fact that two mutually exclusive outcomes can occur within an operating cycle of length TBO. With probability R(t), the component survives up to the planned overhaul, leading to a preventive cost Cp. With probability 1 − R(t), it fails before the scheduled intervention, resulting in either an accidental maintenance cost Ca or a catastrophic failure cost Cca, weighted by the probability "Prob".

The optimal overhaul interval is therefore obtained by solving

$$\text{TBO} = \arg\ \min\ \text{C\_avg(TBO)} \tag{4}$$

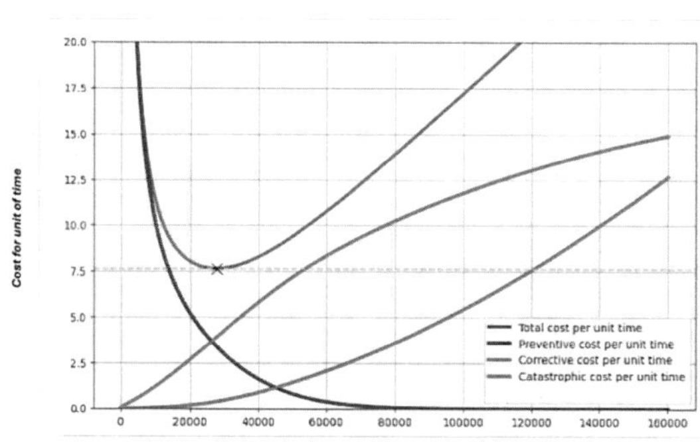

Fig. 3. Costs expressed as a function of operating hours

The structure of this cost function is fully consistent with the approaches discussed by [26, 27]. In all cases, the TBO is selected by minimising an expected cost that combines preventive and failure-related terms, weighted by reliability, as showed in Fig. 3. The model adopted here preserves this conceptual foundation while using a simplified and tractable expression suited to laboratory-scale deployment and to the data available for this study.

In practical terms, computing the TBO requires three main categories of input data:

- Operating-hour records for each component, used to determine exposure times.
- Historical failures, used to estimate the Weibull parameters and derive the reliability function $R(t)$ and the MTBF. In addition, the same dataset was used to identify the probability of catastrophic failures ("prob" in the model). Based on a discussion with the industrial partner, a classification criterion was defined to distinguish between catastrophic and accidental failures. This classification considers both the timing of occurrence (early-life failures) and the associated cost. On this basis, the proportion of catastrophic failures was estimated and assumed constant over time.
- Cost parameters Cp(t), Ca(t) and Cca, representing preventive maintenance cost, accidental maintenance cost, and catastrophic failure cost, respectively. Cp(t) and Ca(t) were modelled as time-dependent functions, estimated through linear regression based on historical intervention data, thus capturing their variation over the component lifecycle. In contrast, due to the limited number of observed catastrophic failures, the corresponding cost C_{ca} was assumed constant over time and, where available, estimated as the average cost of the observed catastrophic events.

The resulting component-specific TBO values provide the basis for constructing the maintenance plan described in the next section, where these intervals are combined and coordinated at fleet level under operational and resource constraints. Building on this representation, the TBO model acts as a decision-support mechanism by directly exploiting the reliability function to evaluate the trade-off between preventive interventions and the economic consequences of failures, thereby determining the most appropriate maintenance interval for each component.

3.3 Implementation and Validation

The implementation of the proposed service begins by applying the component-specific TBO values to the historical operating data of the Komatsu 930E fleet. Once the reliability behaviour of each component had been modelled through the Weibull analysis, the TBO optimisation model was applied to determine the most appropriate overhaul interval. These intervals were then used to identify the expected month in which each component of each truck would reach its overhaul threshold. This step produces an initial maintenance plan in which interventions are directly derived from the accumulated operating hours of the components.

However, this preliminary plan does not automatically satisfy the operational constraints of the maintenance facility, such as the maximum number of interventions executable in a single month or the maximum budget available. For this reason, an optimisation procedure was introduced to adjust the plan while ensuring that reliability remains within acceptable limits.

The optimisation relies on two criteria:

- First, residual reliability is used to assess whether an intervention can be postponed or advanced. Components with lower reliability at the planned intervention month are given priority and are not rescheduled, while components with higher reliability can be shifted with a lower associated risk.
- Second, the proximity to the end of life is evaluated. Interventions for components that are close to their TBO threshold are kept in the planned month, whereas components

still far from the threshold can be moved more flexibly. By combining these two criteria, the algorithm redistributes interventions across months to satisfy capacity or budget constraints while maintaining an acceptable risk profile.

Although this implementation does not include a full-scale industrial validation, two forms of laboratory-scale validation were performed:

- First, the results were reviewed by the industrial partner, who confirmed that the estimated TBO values and the resulting prioritisation logic were coherent with operational experience and consistent with the expected behaviour of the components.
- Second, the scheduling algorithm was tested under different capacity and budget constraints to verify that interventions were shifted in a consistent manner: components with low residual reliability or near end-of-life were retained in the scheduled month, while components with higher reliability or greater distance from the TBO threshold were shifted appropriately.

These checks confirm that the implemented logic behaves as expected and provides a consistent basis for the construction of a feasible fleet-level maintenance plan.

As a result, the proposed decision-support model enables the construction of a reliability-informed and resource-feasible maintenance plan for the entire fleet, allowing maintenance activities to be prioritised, coordinated and redistributed across months according to the estimated component behaviour and the operational constraints of the facility. The maintenance plan is directly derived from the component-specific TBO values obtained through the reliability-based modelling and cost optimisation process, ensuring coherence between component-level decisions and fleet-level scheduling.

4 Results and Discussion

The procedure presented in the previous chapter allows examining how digital platforms support the development of data-driven maintenance services within Asset Management contexts. The results of the proposed approach are summarised in Tables 1, 2 and 3. Table 1 reports the cost parameters for each asset, including preventive, corrective and catastrophic costs. Table 2 presents the estimated Weibull parameters and the probability of catastrophic failures. Based on these inputs, Table 3 reports the resulting TBO values obtained from the optimisation model.

Table 1. Cost parameters for each asset [dollars/event]

Asset	Preventive Cost	Corrective Cost	Catastrophic Cost
Diesel Motor	708241	570744	750000
Traction Motor	240081	208049	533000
Wheel	45759	44387	72000
Alternator	82412	60598	170000
Suspension	8266	8106	112000

Table 2. Reliability parameters for each asset

Asset	Shape	Scale [hours]	Probability
Diesel Motor	1.65	28336	0.08
Traction Motor	2.32	62713	0.04
Wheel	1.18	42897	0.09
Alternator	3.13	13216	0.08
Suspension	2.17	45338	0.04

Table 3. TBO results for each assets [hours]

Asset	Time Between Overhauls
Diesel Motor	67595
Traction Motor	78639
Wheel	98859
Alternator	19419
Suspension	29876

Beyond the analytical results, the findings highlight significant variability in the optimal overhaul intervals across different assets. For instance, the alternator exhibits a shorter TBO, reflecting higher degradation rates and a cost structure more sensitive to failure events. Conversely, components such as wheels and traction motors show longer intervals, indicating a lower relative impact of failures compared to preventive interventions. The magnitude of both costs and TBO values reflects the characteristics of large-scale mining equipment, where maintenance interventions involve high operational and logistical costs and operating cycles extend over long periods. As a result, optimal overhaul intervals may span several thousands of operating hours, corresponding to multi-year planning horizons. These results confirm that the optimisation model captures the heterogeneity of asset behaviour and supports differentiated maintenance strategies at the asset level, rather than relying on uniform scheduling policies.

In this study, the proposed approach can be interpreted as a reliability-based digital model supporting maintenance decision-making. The model is structured as a two-level analytical process.

At the first level, the model operates at the asset level, where each subsystem (e.g., engine, alternator and other major elements) is represented as an individual asset. For each asset, historical operational and failure data are used to estimate Weibull-based reliability models. These models enable the computation of performance indicators such as reliability functions and failure probabilities over time, describing the degradation behaviour of each asset. At the second level, these asset-specific models are integrated into a decision-support layer, where reliability information is combined with cost parameters. Here, the TBO optimisation model evaluates the trade-off between preventive maintenance and failure-related costs, determining the most appropriate maintenance interval for each asset and supporting the construction of a maintenance plan as illustrated in Fig. 4.

Moved events: 269 / 269

	Ubicación técnica	Componente	Natural	Assigned	Δ months
0	A-01-01-04-A19-HT0093	SUSPENSION	Oct_2026	None	0
1	A-01-01-04-A19-HT0142	SUSPENSION	Jul_2026	None	0
2	A-01-01-04-A19-HT0105	SUSPENSION	Sep_2026	None	0
3	A-01-01-04-A19-HT0152	SUSPENSION	Dic_2025	Feb_2026	2
4	A-01-01-04-A19-HT0127	SUSPENSION	Ago_2026	None	0
5	A-01-01-04-A19-HT0123	SUSPENSION	Abr_2026	Jun_2026	2
6	A-01-01-04-A19-HT0106	SUSPENSION	Dic_2026	None	0
7	A-01-01-04-A19-HT0158	SUSPENSION	Feb_2026	None	0
8	A-01-01-04-A19-HT0153	SUSPENSION	Ene_2026	Feb_2026	1
9	A-01-01-04-A19-HT0129	SUSPENSION	Jun_2026	None	0

Fig. 4. Maintenance schedule representation

In this sense, the proposed implementation corresponds to a digital shadow, as it does not include real-time bidirectional interaction with the physical system but focuses on integrating data, modelling and decision-support functionalities within a unified analytical workflow.

The implementation also highlights how the scheduling logic behaves under operational constraints. When capacity or budget limits are introduced, the optimisation redistributes interventions over time. Interventions associated with low residual reliability are prioritised and maintained in the planned month, while less critical components are shifted to subsequent periods. This results in a more balanced distribution of maintenance activities, reducing peak intervention loads while preserving system reliability.

Beyond the analytical results, the application highlights a set of benefits and challenges associated with platform-enabled Asset Management services. From the asset user perspective, the integration of data, modelling and optimisation supports more timely and informed maintenance decisions by linking asset behaviour representation with operational planning. From the platform provider perspective, the implementation shows how the platform enables the development and testing of advanced data-driven services, supporting their refinement and potential reuse across contexts.

At the same time, some challenges emerge. From the asset user perspective, the adoption of data-driven decision-support mechanisms increases coordination complexity and requires alignment across different roles. From the platform provider perspective, developing such services requires significant capabilities in data integration, modelling and system design to ensure robustness.

Although the application refers to a fleet managed within a single organisational context, the underlying mechanism is not limited to this configuration. The same logic can be extended to multi-organisational settings, provided that operational data can be accessed consistently. In such cases, the platform enables the integration of heterogeneous data sources and supports shared modelling and decision-support capabilities across distributed assets.

Overall, the results show how data, reliability models and optimisation can be integrated into a coherent service supporting maintenance decision-making. Through this integration, operational data are transformed into structured representations of asset behaviour and directly exploited within decision processes. The study therefore highlights how digital platforms can support the operationalisation of Asset Management principles by embedding model-based reasoning into maintenance planning activities.

At the same time, some limitations should be acknowledged. The robustness of the proposed approach depends on the quality and availability of input data, as reliability parameters and cost variables represents a critical aspect that is often difficult to define consistently in industrial practice. For example, maintenance costs may vary depending on whether indirect costs, such as production losses, are included, highlighting the need for more standardised approaches to data collection and cost modelling within maintenance organisations. Future research should investigate the sensitivity of TBO results to variations in failure behaviour and cost assumptions, including the use of confidence intervals and scenario-based analyses. Finally, extending the approach to multi-organisational settings remains exploratory and would requires dedicated empirical validation involving heterogeneous data sources and shared modelling capabilities across distributed assets.

5 Conclusion

With the increasing digitalisation of industrial operations, digital platforms are emerging as key infrastructures for enabling data-driven AM practices. This paper presented the development of a data-driven maintenance management service enabled by a digital platform, integrating operational data, reliability modelling and optimization to support maintenance decision-making. The study operationalises TBO estimation by linking asset behaviour modelling with maintenance decision logic, enabling the generation of overhaul intervals and the construction of a resource-feasible maintenance plan. From a practical perspective, the main contribution lies in the development and implementation of a platform-enabled service that integrates data, reliability modelling and optimisation into a coherent workflow supporting maintenance planning decisions and providing a structured approach to support AM practices in industrial contexts. From a theoretical perspective, the paper contributes to ongoing discussions on the operationalisation of Asset Management within digital environments. It shows how data, analytical models and decision-support logic can be concretely integrated into platform-enabled services, shifting the focus from conceptual descriptions of digital platforms to their practical configuration as infrastructures supporting AM decision-making. The study was conducted as a laboratory-scale proof of concept based on a single industrial fleet. The results were assessed in collaboration with an industrial partner and were considered consistent with operational expectations. However, the findings remain limited by the scope of the dataset and by the absence of a full-scale industrial deployment. Future research should therefore focus on the development of structured validation in real industrial settings. This includes defining performance evaluation procedures and comparing maintenance outcomes against existing planning strategies to further consolidate the practical applicability of the proposed approach.

Acknowledgments. This study was carried out within the MICS (Made in Italy – Circular and Sustainable) Extended Partnership and received funding from the European Union Next-GenerationEU (PIANO NAZIONALE DI RIPRESA E RESILIENZA (PNRR) – MISSIONE 4 COMPONENTE 2, INVESTIMENTO 1.3 – D.D. 1551.11-10-2022, PE00000004). This manuscript reflects only the authors' views and opinions, neither the European Union nor the European Commission can be considered responsible for them.

Disclosure of Interests The authors report that there are no competing interests to declare.

References

1. Xu, L.D., Xu, E.L., Li, L.: Industry 4.0: state of the art and future trends. Int. J. Prod. Res. **56**(8), 2941–2962 (2018). https://doi.org/10.1080/00207543.2018.1444806
2. Cimini, C., Adrodegari, F., Paschou, T., Rondini, A., Pezzotta, G.: Digital servitization and competence development: a case-study research. CIRP J. Mfg. Sci. Technol. **32**, 447–460 (2021). https://doi.org/10.1016/j.cirpj.2020.12.005
3. Gaiardelli, P., Pezzotta, G., Rondini, A., et al.: Product-service systems evolution in the era of industry 4.0. Serv. Bus. **15**, 177–207 (2021). https://doi.org/10.1007/s11628-021-00438-9
4. Rantala, T., Ukko, J., Nasiri, M., Saunila, M.: Shifting focus of value creation through industrial digital twins—from internal application to ecosystem-level utilization. Technovation. **125** (2023). https://doi.org/10.1016/j.technovation.2023.102795
5. Roda, I., Macchi, M.: A framework to embed asset management in production companies. In: Crespo Márquez, A., Macchi, M., Parlikad, A. (eds.) Value Based and Intelligent Asset Management, pp. 103–122. Springer, Cham (2020). https://doi.org/10.1177/1748006X17753501
6. ISO 55000: Asset Management— Overview, Principles and Terminology. https://www.iso.org/standard/55088.html (2024). Accessed 27 May 2026
7. Alcayaga, A., Wiener, M., Hansen, E.G.: Towards a framework of smart-circular systems: an integrative literature review. J. Clean. Prod. **221**, 622–634 (2019). https://doi.org/10.1016/j.jclepro.2019.02.085
8. Zambetti, M., Pinto, R., Pezzotta, G.: Industry 4.0 data-related technologies and Servitization: a systematic literature review. In: IFIP International Conference on Advances in Production Management Systems (APMS), pp. 347–360. Springer, Cham (2020). https://doi.org/10.1007/978-3-030-57997-5_41
9. Kamp, B., Zabala, K., Zubiaurre, A.: How can machine tool builders capture value from smart services? Avoiding the service and digitalization paradox. J. Bus. Ind. Mark. **38**, 303–316 (2023). https://doi.org/10.1108/JBIM-12-2021-0588
10. Polenghi, A., Roda, I., Macchi, M., Pozzetti, A.: Information as a key dimension to develop industrial asset management in manufacturing. J. Qual. Maintenance Eng. **28**, 567–583 (2022). https://doi.org/10.1108/JQME-09-2020-0095
11. Fraile, F., Sanchis, R., Poler, R., Ortiz, A.: Reference models for digital manufacturing platforms. Appl. Sci. **9** (2019). https://doi.org/10.3390/app9204433
12. Marquez, A.C., Fernandez, J.F.G., Fernández, P.M.G., Lopez, A.G.: Maintenance management through intelligent asset management platforms (IAMP). Emerging factors, key impact areas and data models. Energies. **13** (2020). https://doi.org/10.3390/en13153762

13. Zare, A., Lazarova-Molnar, S.: Modular validation within digital twins: a case study in reliability analysis of manufacturing systems. In: 2024 Winter Simulation Conference (WSC), pp. 2903–2914. IEEE, Piscataway (2024). https://doi.org/10.1109/WSC63780.2024.10838952
14. Kaul, T., Bender, A., Sextro, W.: Digital twin for reliability analysis during design and operation of mechatronic systems. In: Beer, M., Zio, E. (eds.) Proceedings of the 29th European Safety and Reliability Conference (ESREL2019), pp. 2340–2347. Research Publishing, Singapore (2019). https://doi.org/10.3850/978-981-11-2724-3_0876-cd
15. Reim, W., Andersson, E., Eckerwall, K.: Enabling collaboration on digital platforms: a study of digital twins. Int. J. Prod. Res. **61**, 3926–3942 (2022). https://doi.org/10.1080/00207543.2022.2116499
16. Hein, A., Schreieck, M., Riasanow, T., et al.: Digital platform ecosystems. Electron. Markets. **30**, 87–99 (2020). https://doi.org/10.1007/s12525-019-00377-4
17. Gawer, A.: Bridging differing perspectives on technological platforms: toward an integrative framework. Res. Policy. **43**, 1239–1249 (2014). https://doi.org/10.1016/j.respol.2014.03.006
18. Müller, J.M.: Antecedents to digital platform usage in industry 4.0 by established manufacturers. Sustainability. **11** (2019). https://doi.org/10.3390/su11041121
19. Jovanovic, M., Sjödin, D., Parida, V.: Co-evolution of platform architecture, platform services, and platform governance: expanding the platform value of industrial digital platforms. Technovation. **118** (2022). https://doi.org/10.1016/j.technovation.2020.102218
20. Martins, M., Rijo, R., Grilo, C., Ferreira, L., Silva, S., Martinho, R.: Smartool - a digital platform for condition-based maintenance in industry 4.0 environments. In: Proceedings of the 2023 8th International Conference on Cloud Computing and Internet of Things (CCIOT 2023), pp. 53–58. ACM, New York (2023). https://doi.org/10.1145/3627345.3627368
21. Turkin, I., Leznovskyi, V., Zelenkov, A., et al.: The use of IoT for determination of time and frequency vibration characteristics of industrial equipment for condition-based maintenance. Computation. **11** (2023). https://doi.org/10.3390/computation11090177
22. Pauli, T., Fielt, E., Matzner, M.: Digital industrial platforms. Bus. Inf. Syst. Eng. **63**, 181–190 (2021). https://doi.org/10.1007/s12599-020-00681-w
23. Patrucco, A.S., Trabucchi, D., Buganza, T., et al.: Technology-enabled multi-sided platforms in B2B relationships: a critical analysis and directions for future research. Ind. Mark. Mgmt. **122**, A2–A11 (2024). https://doi.org/10.1016/j.indmarman.2024.08.012
24. den Hartigh, E., Stolwijk, C.C.M., Ortt, J.R., Punter, L.M.: Configurations of digital platforms for manufacturing: an analysis of seven cases according to platform functions and types. Electron. Markets. **33** (2023). https://doi.org/10.1007/s12525-023-00653-4
25. Zheng, Z., Zhou, W., Zheng, Y., Wu, Y.: Optimal maintenance policy for a system with preventive repair and two types of failures. Comput. Ind. Eng. **98**, 102–112 (2016). https://doi.org/10.1016/j.cie.2016.05.007
26. Pascual, R., Ortega, J.H.: Optimal replacement and overhaul decisions with imperfect maintenance and warranty contracts. In: Reliability Engineering and System Safety, pp. 241–248 (2006). https://doi.org/10.1016/j.ress.2005.01.018
27. Osyaev, A., Rauba, A., Kosarev, A.: Algorithm of the target function of time between overhauls taking into account gradual and sudden failure of the locomotive equipment. In: MATEC Web of Conferences. EDP Sciences (2018). https://doi.org/10.1051/matecconf/201823901029

How Service Can Improve Environmental Impact of Heat Pump: Life Cycle Assessment as a Design Decision Tool

Claire Fabrer[1,2](✉), Thècle Alix[1,2], Laurent Mora[1,2], and Nicolas Perry[1,2]

[1] University of Bordeaux, CNRS, Bordeaux INP, I2M, UMR 5295, 33400 Talence, France
claire.fabrer@u-bordeaux.fr

[2] Arts et Metiers Institute of Technology, CNRS, Bordeaux INP I2M, UMR 5295, 33400 Talence, France

Abstract. Though servitisation is a competitive and ecological opportunity, designing a product-service system offer remains challenging, particularly when evaluating the environmental of the offer by considering both product specificities and service quality. This work aims to present Life Cycle Assessment (LCA) as a decision-support tool for PSS design. Several market scenarios are proposed, including service quality-focused, IoT-enabled, and circular strategy oriented approaches. The use case focuses on a French residential air-to-water heat pump and is partly based on field data characterising reference and degraded condition. The results show that fossil and mineral resources depletion are the most critical indicators, and that the use phase is not the dominant phase for all impact categories. Reinforcing human involvement in service provision should be prioritized when designing the offering. The proposed IoT services can improve environmental impacts, provided that digitalisation remains efficient and appropriately scaled. Retrofit is relevant, depending on the indicator considered. The proposed method offers several advantages for designers, and further work should focus on sensitivity analysis as a fine-tuning tool.

Keywords: Design · Decision-making · Life Cycle Analysis · Heat Pump · Servitisation

1 Introduction

1.1 Life Cycle Analysis for Product-Service System

Delivering value in use instead of selling pure products has many strategic and environmental benefits [1]. However this shift called servitisation, is complex. It refers to the innovation of an organisation's capabilities and processes to move from selling products to selling integrated products and services that deliver value in use [2]. The latter is defined as a Product-Service System, or PSS [3].

Designing a PSS offer that delivers a sustainable value proposition is a condition for a long-term viability, but it is challenging. In a user-centric value system, the challenges

Published by Springer Nature Switzerland AG 2027
G. Pezzotta et al. (Eds.): APMS 2026, IFIP AICT 808, pp. 462–476, 2027.
https://doi.org/10.1007/978-3-032-38594-9_31

include, among others, optimizing the operation phase by reducing the risk of failure, adapting to usage in a personalized way, and collecting data real-time [4].

These challenges increase the interest in Life Cycle Assessment (LCA), a method used to evaluate environmental impacts (taking into consideration all the phases of a product, system or service) across several criteria, making it more robust and more informative for decision making than a single-criterion carbon analysis. It is widely accepted by the scientific community and regulated by ISO 14040 and 14044. LCA has become the reference tool for the environmental assessment component in PSS integrated design frameworks, as promoted by [5–7].

However, the methodology is challenging to apply in these cases, especially for the definition of i) the functional unit, ii) the system boundaries and iii) the reference system [8]. A review on LCA application for PSS cases shows that these difficulties are not always adequately addressed. Moreover, models have generally poor data quality and quality assessment, and should rely more on empirical data [9]. In particular, use phase inputs often rely on assumptions (e.g.: [10]) whereas it is possible to collect field data with survey (e.g.: [11]) or measurements.

Regarding the use of LCA results as a decision tool, there are still some gaps. Even if LCA is a multi-indicator methodology, only half of the PSS-LCA studies do not only integrate GWP (Global Warming Potential) [7]. When several indicators are used, the support for interpreting the results is limited. Some authors develop parameter contribution analysis [12], convert environmental burden into monetary terms [7] or compare the scenarios based on relative difference [10]. However, identifying and prioritising the most impactful indicators is rarely addressed.

This study aims to show how LCA can help design a PSS offer by analysing synergies between products and services. This will contribute to the PSS domain by proposing an exemplary PSS LCA, fed with empirical data for the use phase, and illustrate how to take into account its results for design decisions. The use case is a residential air-to-water heat pump (HP) for an application in a renovated house in France.

1.2 Environmental Impact of HP Processes

Regarding LCA of HP, studies show that the operational phase invariably has the greatest impact. Existing analysis mainly focus on technology choice, the impact of climate or, more rarely, house insulation [13]. Heat pump performance is described by the Seasonal Coefficient Of Performance (SCOP). This indicator, defined as the heat energy produced during one winter divided by the energy consumed during the same period, is a reference for describing HP performance. Thermal engineering studies have investigated the impact of different processes on performance. A well-designed maintenance strategy can prevent up to 25% of SCOP degradation. Two complementary strategies address this issue: increasing maintenance frequency to every one or two years, and using intelligent fault detection method [14]. The latter could reduce SCOP penalization by up to 10% [15]. Sizing also influences energy consumption, as the use of an auxiliary system can reduce consumption by up to 6% [16]; however this effect is highly climate dependent [17]. In the B2B market, performance-based contracts are flourishing. These offers are supported by a range of services and processes, including monitoring and needs optimisation, flexibility provision, and predictive maintenance [18]. In France, service-focused Energy Performance Contracts (CPE) lead on average to energy savings of 16% [19].

In the residential sector, such services are beginning to emerge. However, the potential benefits of the optimisation measures often remain out of reach, as basic services are sometimes unreliable. In France, recurring faults and frequent overconsumption are reported by consumer protection associations for one third of respondents [20]. As a result, the return on investment for end-users is not always shorter than the actual lifespan of the HP, and avoidable environmental impacts arise from excess electricity consumption and premature equipment replacement. These issues may be linked to the specificities of French value chain, at least in comparison with Germany; [21] emphasise the strong influence of installation quality on performance and report significant flaws in 100 HP installations in France. They estimate a 20% energy-savings potential relative to the average performance of their sample. Studies focusing on in-situ performance report similar findings [22]. observe a 40% performance reduction attributable to inadequate installation practices, while [23] identifies improvement potential in sizing, water temperature, and performance monitoring.

Finally, the environmental impact results of different process. As such, LCA results affect views on product change, organisation, and actor that implement them. The following analysis first provides insights on the LCA (choice of scenarios, functional unit, data used in Sect. 2). The results in Sect. 3 and their discussion in Sect. 4 shed light on how they support the prioritisation of design strategy, for the product and the associated services and processes.

2 Methodology

2.1 Conceptual Model

The conceptual model follows the four standardized steps of LCA according to ISO 14040 and is represented in Fig. 1. First, the goal and scope are critical for PSS system definition, functional unit declaration and, perimeter of the study. Compared scenarios are described in this section, including a baseline scenario for a transactional offer, i.e. product-based offer where the consumer has ownership of the product. Scenarios are characterized by the quality of the use phase, or performance configurations (Reference/Degraded) and the type of market offer. Secondly, the life cycle inventory lists data sources; empirical data is recommended in particular for the use phase because PSS aims to modify consumer behaviour. Thirdly, the life cycle impact assessment method is selected by favouring methods that include normalization, for instance EF 3.1. Finally, result analysis includes four steps. Normalization is performed relative to the impacts of an average individual in the world [24]. Other methods exist, for instance absolute sustainability by comparing with planetary boundaries, but are still hard to deploy. The chosen normalisation factors are adapted to the duration of the functional unit. The normalisation step makes it possible to identify the most impactful indicators, on a single scale and within the same scope of analysis. For the chosen indicators, scenarios are compared in detail, and major contributors are identified to help industrial stakeholders in their design process.

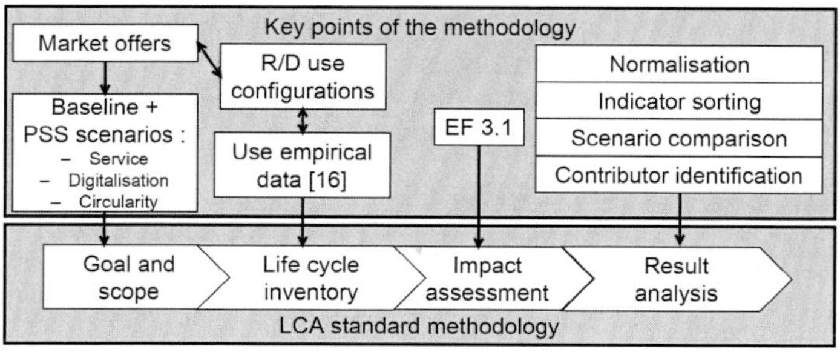

Fig. 1. Conceptual model of the proposed methodology

2.2 Goal and Scope

Scenarios. A comparative LCA is performed to assess differences between several heat pump installation conditions, as well as different performance-based offers. To obtain brand - and company - agnostic results, modelling assumptions are defined based on the average French value chain. The scope encompasses residential housing equipped with air-to-water heat pumps undergoing thermal renovation. This LCA is attributional, static, cut-off, and cradle-to-grave.

As installation quality has been proven to be a major factor influencing on performance [16], two performance configurations are studied to model the impact of the general quality of service:

- Reference performance (R): the HP is sized and installed in accordance with best practices, as described in the EN 15316 standard. This is a situation where great care is given to installation quality. This has greater chances to happen in a PSS offer because installers have incentives to do so, and is also normal in a transactional offer.
- Degraded performance (D): the HP installation process lacks human control, resulting in one or several defects that degrade the performance of the equipment. This situation is too common in transactional offers because economic viability of installer enterprises is mainly based on a high number of installations, less on their performance or their compliance. The risk of this kind of flaws in PSS offers is assumed to be largely reduced, although non-zero.

To define a scenario, performance configurations are combined with market offers, which contains the services delivered to customer. These offers illustrate the difference between product-based and performance-based business models and are modelled by the different processes needed to implement them:

- Transactional offer (TO): the HP is sold following the conventional business model, with transfer of ownership to the user and an optional maintenance contract.
- Functional offer (FO): the HP is sold through a performance-based contract, and the seller retains ownership of the product: it is a PSS offer. To ensure business profitability, the provider increases control over installation and maintenance through

human resources. This offer aims to highlight the role of human services including sizing, installation, advice, and maintenance.

Two additional offers, going further in PSS design by adding respectively enhanced digitalisation and circularity, are studied under the reference performance hypothesis:

- Functional offer with predictive maintenance (FO+): FO conditions apply and IoT devices supporting predictive maintenance are added to optimise monitoring and intervention planning.
- Functional offer with circular strategy (FOC): FO conditions apply and, when the HP reaches 15 years of age, it is retrofitted and gains an additional 10 years of operation. It should be noted that this process is not currently implemented as a standard practice for residential HP.

Functional Unit. Following the guidelines proposed by [25], the functional unit reflects the service delivered by the product, i.e. the thermal energy required to provide indoor thermal comfort during winter. This energy demand is quantified using the thermal heat loss of the dwelling, combined with climate zones defined in French regulation RT2012.

The empirical data available, detailed below, influence the numerical values selected for these parameters. The functional unit is therefore defined as the thermal energy required to heat a residential house located in the H2d climate zone, with a thermal heat loss of 12 kW, over a period of 20 years.

2.3 Scenario Parameters

Reference and Degraded Configurations. The ADEME dataset [21] contains information on residential houses, climate conditions, and HP technologies. Cases in which air-to-water heat pumps are used exclusively for space heating are extracted ($n = 35$). To avoid mixing the effects of installation quality with those of climate or house characteristics, only cases compliant with the functional unit, located in the same climate zone and presenting the same energy demand ($\pm$ 500 kWh) are selected.

HP1 is used for the reference configuration. It has a SCOP of 3.12 and is equipped with a radiant floor, which allows a lower supply water temperature and results in better performance. During the 2023–2024 winter season, heat production reached 9121 kWh.

By contrast, HP4 is used as the degraded configuration. The emitters are cast-iron radiators, which require a higher water temperature to operate. In addition, several flaws have been identified: poor connection and positioning of the external unit, as well as user misconfiguration leading to inappropriate thermostat settings. This overall setup results in a SCOP of 2.91 for a heat production of 10071 kWh.

The differences between HP1 and HP4 are an example of the gap happening when an installation lacks control. Other flaws are possible (e.g. sizing, refrigerant leaks, hydraulic misconnection), but are outside the scope of this study.

Tested Offers. The offers tested for the R and D configurations are theoretical market offers that could be implemented as Product-Service System offers. These offers are designed to place different levels of emphasis on the three key PSS pillars: service (FO), digitalisation (FO+), and circular strategy (FOC). Data sources vary depending on the parameter considered. Energy consumption is based on R and D configurations; moreover, for FO+ scenario, the assumption is that the digital monitoring allows controlling the quality of installation. Product lifespan is very difficult to estimate because no quantitative study has been found to this day; qualitative feedback from various manufacturers have been integrated for this matter. For maintenance frequency, manufacturer recommendations (one year) is the reference for FO and FOC, while the French legal frequency (two years) is the reference for FO+ and TO. In the first case, remote monitoring allows a just-in-time intervention, in accordance with law. In the second case, half of French users do not respect the mandatory frequency [21] so the duration is extended to four years. Repair diagnostic is performed on-site, requiring a technician visit, except for FO+, for which it is remote. Finally, end-of-life scenarios are based on standard recycling, except for FOC where a retrofit step is introduced extending the product lifespan by 10 years.

Table 1 lists the different parameters used for modelling the different scenarios.

Table 1. Parameters for the tested offer scenarios

Parameter	TO	FO	FO+	FOC
Type of offer	Product selling	Location with human services supporting performance contract	Location with digital and human services supporting performance contract	Location with human services supporting performance contract, and retrofit of product
Product lifespan	12 years (production of 1.6 HP in 20 years)	15 years (production of 1.3 HP in 20 years)	15 years (production of 1.3 HP in 20 years)	25 years (production of 0.8 HP in 20 years)
Phases	Production Installation Operation Maintenance Recycling	HP production Sizing Installation Monitoring Operation Maintenance Recycling	HP and digital devices production Sizing Installation Monitoring Operation Predictive maintenance Recycling	HP production Sizing Installation Monitoring Operation Maintenance Retrofitting Recycling
Energy consumption	R or D scenario	R or D scenario	R scenario, −5% accounting for IoT benefits	R scenario
Maintenance frequency	Once every 4 years	Yearly	Once every 2 years	Yearly
Repair diagnostic	In-situ	In-situ	Remote	In-situ

(*continued*)

Table 1. (*continued*)

Parameter	TO	FO	FO+	FOC
End-of-life scenario	Recycling	Recycling	Recycling	Retrofit and recycling

2.4 Life Cycle Inventory

Regarding the data linked to the HP specification under study, data from the default Ecoinvent HP dataset are used. The characteristics of the value chain are derived from the Product System Representation (PSR) framework, covering production, distribution, installation, and disposal. In addition, several Environmental Product Declarations (EPDs) are used for specific elements, including the thermostat, packaging, and transport distances. The operation phase, which represents the most impactful life-cycle phase, is modelled using ADEME data. As explained in Sect. 2.2, two main installations (HP1 and HP4) are selected, and their consumption is used for the calculation as they represent an installation without defects and one with several performance-degrading flaws, respectively.

Additional modelling steps are implemented to cover activities associated with the different offers proposed. The FO+ offer requires digital monitoring, which implies additional material and energy consumption during operation; data on these aspects are taken from ADEME monitoring device datasets. The FO+ offer also involves the development of a predictive algorithm, modelled using AI computing infrastructure. The computer vision model chosen likely overestimates the impacts: this is justified by a conservative approach regarding the additional processes associated with digitalisation infrastructure. Finally, the FOC offer includes a retrofitting step, which is modelled following a methodology similar to that used in an ADEME study on smartphone retrofitting in France [26].

Table 2 summarizes the life cycle inventory. Unless otherwise stated, all processes and subprocesses are modelled using the Ecoinvent v3.11 cut-off database.

Table 2. Life cycle inventory

Phase	Item and quantity	Source
Production	Air-to-water heat pump of 10 kW (emptied: 128 kg), R134a (3.09 kg), mineral oil (1.7 kg) Additional electronic accessories: LCD screen (0.5 kg), PWB (1.2 kg), thermostat (0.3 kg, PEP n°43984) Packaging: wood (11.3 kg), cardboard (6.3 kg), PE (4.4 kg) Exterior unit, electronics (65,8 kg) from Asia: boat, 20 700 km + truck, 150 km Interior unit, refrigerant, oil (68.8 kg) from Europe: truck, 1500 km	Ecoinvent v3.11 PEP n°46455

(*continued*)

Table 2. (*continued*)

Phase	Item and quantity	Source
Distribution	1000 km	PSR
Sizing, installation	For each: 100 km	PSR
Operation	Electricity consumption (French electricity mix, low voltage): HP 001: 2891 kWh/year (SCOP = 3.12); HP 004: 3417 kWh/year (SCOP = 2.91) Both case: 26 g/year of fugitive emission (split HP)	[21] PSR 3.1
Maintenance	Once every two years, 100 km Refill of refrigerant, oil change (1.7 kg) Repair included: 1/10 HP, change of refrigerant and oil. HP has 1/3 chances to meet a failure.	PSR 3.1 Own assumptions
Disposal	Recycling, transport of waste	PSR 3.1
Monitoring devices	10 sensors (PEP n°42409), internet access, switch, 2.4 SSD disks for 1104 Go, storage energy: 12072 kWh	[21] Negaoctet
Predictive maintenance	10 000 HP in the infrastructure 26.28 TB of data for training and 3650000 inferences per year: using the computer vision model, 5607 kWh/year in total, so 11 kWh/HP/20 years 0.002 GPU based on electricity consumption	[27] [28]
Retrofit	Logistics: utility vehicle (100 km), truck (500 km), packaging Retrofitted materials: half of the (emptied) HP, packaging (x3.5), truck 1000 km for 64 kg. Refrigerant and oil change New materials: additional electronics, half of the (emptied) HP, sea freight 20700 km for 71 kg.	[26]

3 Results

3.1 Normalised Results

The normalised results of the LCA analysis are presented in Fig. 2. They are expressed in dimensionless units, representing the share of each indicator's impact relative to 20 years of average global consumption (2010 baseline). The normalisation factors, with more details about assessed indicators, are described in [24].

Among the 16 indicators assessed, the six most relevant are abiotic depletion of fossil resources (ADPf), with values ranging from 0.51 to 0.64; abiotic depletion of minerals and metals (ADPe), ranging from 0.52 to 0.65; ionising radiation (IR) from 0.040 to 0.047; non-carcinogenic human toxicity (HTnc), ranging from 0.16 to 0.21; freshwater eutrophication (Ef) from 0.14 to 0.18 and global warming potential (GWP) from 0.067 to 0.078. The contribution analysis of these three indicators is detailed in the following section: GWP, due to its widespread use in environmental assessment, and ADPf and ADPe due to their high normalised scores.

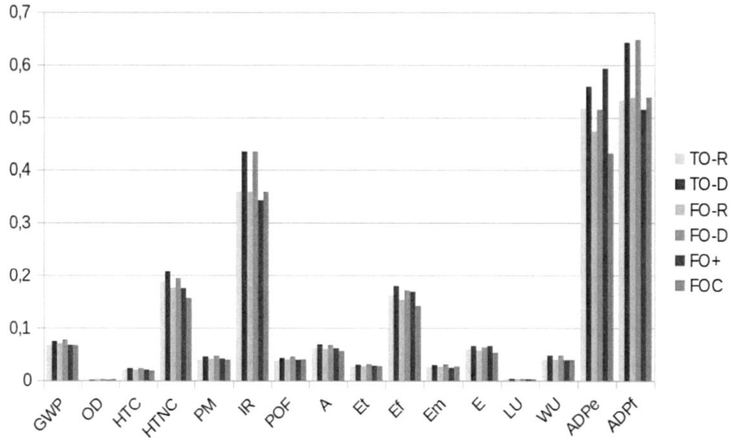

Fig. 2. Normalised result of LCA for 16 EF 3.1 method indicators: global warming potential (GWP), ozone depletion (OD), human toxicity: carcinogenic (HTc) and non-carcinogenic (HTnc), particule matter (PM), ionization radiations (IR), photochemical oxidant formation (POF), acidification (A), eutrophication: terrestrial (Et), freshwater (Ef) and marine (Em), ecotoxicity (E), land use (LU), water use (WU), abiotic depletion: minerals (ADPe) and fossil fuels (ADPf).

3.2 Focus on 3 Indicators

Overall Scores. Relative variation against scenario reference, TO-R, are calculated for each scenario and summarized in Table 3.

Table 3. Comparison between TO-R and the other scenario for the three selected indicators

Indicator	TO-D	FO-R	FO-D	FO+	FOC
GWP	10.73%	−0.94%	9.79%	−0.41%	4.01%
ADPe	7.99%	−11.26%	−3.27%	14.19%	−6.32%
ADPf	20.65%	−0.76%	21.41%	−3.18%	1.30%

Global Warming Potential. GWP is a contribution of several greenhouse gases referred as kg CO2 equivalent. The most impactful life-cycle phase is the operation phase, accounting on average for 58% of total impacts. This contribution is relatively stable across the six scenarios, ranging from 55 to 62%. The production phase is the second most impactful phase, contributing from 20 to 30% of the total impact depending on the scenario. For the FOC scenario, the combined contribution of production and retrofitting represents approximately 25% of total impacts.

The most impactful scenarios are FO-D and TO-D, while the least impactful are FO+, FOC and TO-R. The standard deviation across scenarios is 6% (Fig. 3).

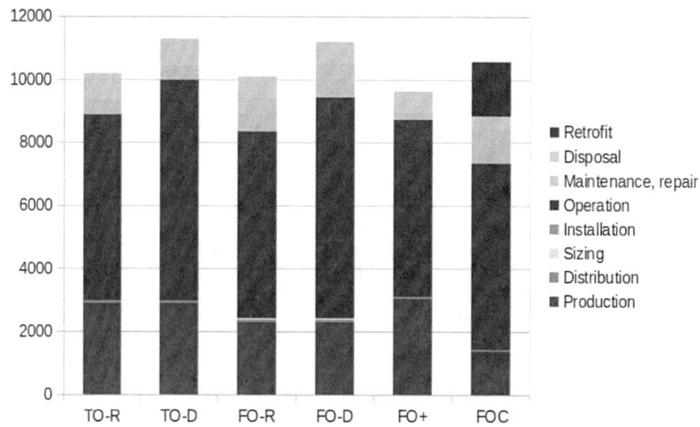

Fig. 3. Decomposition of impact by life cycle phase for global warming potential indicator

Fossil Fuels Depletion. This indicator relates to fossil fuels depletion, e.g. oil and gas, and its unit is MJ. The operation phase is the dominant contributor, accounting for at least 95% of total impacts across all scenarios. The most impactful scenarios are the degraded configurations, whether under Transactional Offers (TO) or Functional Offers (OF). The standard deviation across scenarios is 11% (Fig. 4).

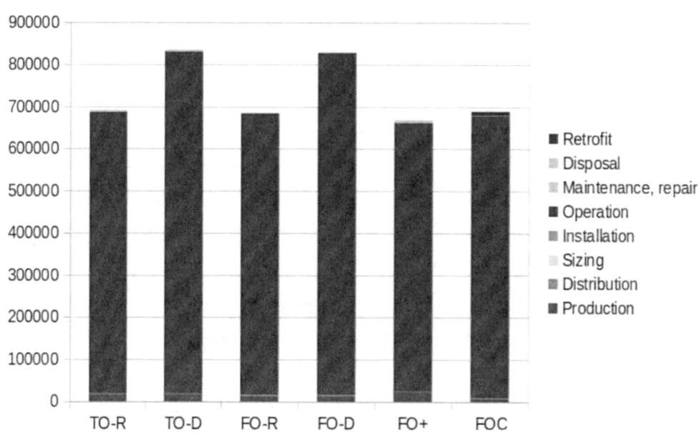

Fig. 4. Decomposition of impact by life cycle phase for fossil fuels depletion indicator

Mineral Depletion. This indicator assesses the depletion of metals and minerals compared to antimony depletion, which is considered to be the fastest element to be depleted under current extraction conditions. Its unit is kg Sb (antimony) eq. This is the only indicator for which the operation phase is not dominant, contributing between 31.2% and 45.8% of the total impact. The production phase is the most impactful phase accounting for 45.6% of the impact for the FO-D scenario and 64.1% in the FO+ scenario. For the FOC scenario, the combined contribution of production and retrofitting represents approximately 48% of the total impact.

The FO+ scenario is the most impactful for this indicator, followed by TO-D, while the FOC scenario exhibits the lowest mineral depletion impact. The standard deviation across scenarios is 10% (Fig. 5).

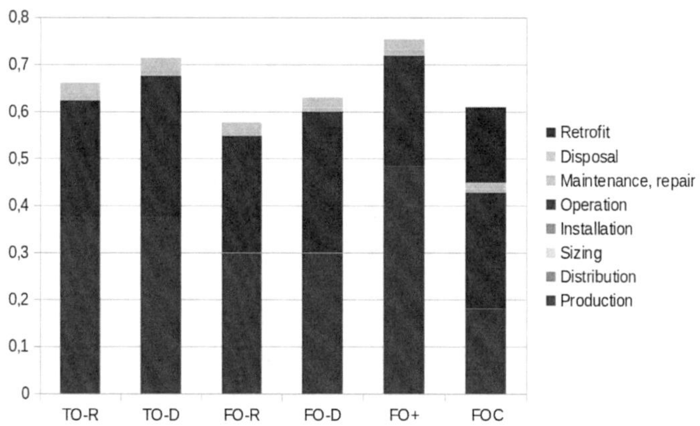

Fig. 5. Decomposition of impact by life cycle phase for mineral depletion indicator

4 Discussion and Conclusion

4.1 Interpretation of the Score

The LCA results show that, in some cases, services can help improve environmental performance. For HP, the priority indicators visible in Fig. 2 are mainly linked to electricity consumption, namely ionising radiation (IR), abiotic depletion of fossil fuels (ADPf), and global warming potential (GWP), as well as to copper demand, which significantly affects non-carcinogenic human toxicity (HTnc) and freshwater eutrophication (Ef).

The operation phase is the dominant life-cycle phase for most indicators. As the French electricity mix is largely nuclear-based and low carbon, the GWP indicator does not dominate the normalised results instead ionising radiation shows a higher relative importance. This underlines the relevance of having multiple criteria to characterise the environmental impacts of heat pumps.

Poor installation quality (setting, connections, ...) can lead to significant additional impacts: over-consumption may result in an increase of up to 20% in the ADPf indicator. The comparison between the reference R and degraded D configurations exhibits the largest relative differences, indicating that installation quality is an effective lever for improving both HP performance and environmental outcomes.

Circular strategies allow significant resource savings, especially for the ADPe indicator, however, reverse-logistics processes are not impact-neutral and must be carefully assessed.

4.2 LCA as Decision Tool

The predominance of the operation phase highlights the need to reduce consumption during use and justifies eco-design approaches that prioritise this objective. Increasing the IoT capabilities of HP yields improvements for GWP, ADPf and other indicators, but these gains remain less significant than those obtained by improving installation quality when required (maximum variation of 3% compared to the TO-R score for FO+, versus 10% between the R and D configurations). This finding suggests that human control and expertise should be prioritised before increasing the use of additional resources for IoT devices.

Using multiple indicators within the LCA methodology allows designers to broaden their perspective and design objectives. In this study, ADPe emerges as the most sensitive indicator when IoT devices are introduced. A local sensitivity analysis shows that, to mitigate the additional impacts induced by IoT integration, such systems should achieve greater energy savings, as well as implement complementary strategies including sensor optimisation and data flow streamlining.

The development of a PSS offer must account for these parameters. Such offers may increase the likelihood of installations being carried out under optimal conditions; however, this outcome is not guaranteed, as traditional transactional offers can also deliver high-quality services. Under these conditions, the environmental impacts associated with increased technician travel frequency may result in higher scores for FO than for TO.

5 Conclusion and Further Work

The work lies at the intersection of:

- Product-Service Systems (PSS) design literature, particularly regarding the environmental assessment of functional vs. transactional offers.
- Life Cycle Assessment (LCA) as a sustainable design decision-support tool.
- Eco-design and circular economy strategies, especially regarding the integration of digital technologies (IoT) and retrofitting.

The paper contributes to the literature by:

- Proposing a scenario-based LCA framework adapted to PSS design, combining product performance and service configurations.
- Demonstrating the importance of multi-criteria assessment to avoid burden shifting, particularly in digitalised PSS.
- Providing empirical insights into the trade-offs between human-based services and digital solutions.

There are four key points of the presented methodology: (i) the combination of performance configuration and market offer to produce scenario; (ii) the gathering of empirical use data and (iii) normalisation step to identify the most critical indicators.

LCA is used not only as an assessment tool but as a decision-support framework enabling the comparison of alternative configurations combining product performance and service offerings. More specifically, the proposed methodology supports decision-making at three levels:

- Scenario comparison: by combining technical configurations (e.g., performance levels) with business models (e.g., transactional vs. functional offers), LCA enables a systematic comparison of PSS alternatives.
- Identification of environmental hotspots: the contribution analysis highlights the most impactful life-cycle phases and processes, guiding designers toward priority improvement actions (e.g., installation quality vs. IoT deployment).
- Multi-criteria trade-off analysis: the use of multiple impact indicators (e.g., GWP, ADPf, ADPe) allows decision-makers to avoid burden shifting, the normalisation helps to arbitrate between conflicting objectives (e.g., energy savings vs. resource depletion linked to digitalisation).

Focusing on HP enables a comparison between human-centred services and digitally augmented services. In the analysed case, ensuring a high-quality operational environment for HP proves to be more critical than implementing IoT-dependent services, even though digitalisation remains a valuable means of reducing energy-related impacts.

The importance of the multi-criteria character of LCA is highlighted. Environmental analysis should be extended to several criteria, to identify the risks of pollution being transferred: diminishing GWP scores may increase ADPe scores. While GWP is often the primary focus in similar studies, in this case it is not the most critical, as suggested by normalised scores. Selecting ADPe as a decision-making criterion highlights the importance of reasonable and targeted digitalisation.

The results of this study are partially transferable with two levels of generalisation:

1. Methodological generalisability (high): The proposed framework is broadly applicable beyond the heat pump case study, as it relies on: the coupling between technical configurations and service offers a scenario-based LCA approach, and the use of normalisation to prioritise indicators. Therefore, the methodology can be applied to other PSS contexts involving energy-using products (e.g., HVAC systems, mobility services, appliances).
2. Quantitative results (context-dependent): The numerical results are strongly dependent on contextual parameters, such as: the electricity mix (e.g., nuclear-based vs. fossil-based systems), the user behaviour and installation practices, and the product-specific characteristics. For instance, the relative importance of ionising radiation observed in this study is directly linked to the French electricity mix and may differ significantly in other contexts.

Further work is required to strengthen these conclusions. First, empirical data collection should explicitly include maintenance practices and IoT systems as variables to improve the robustness of service-impact assessments. Evaluating differences between market offers also remains challenging, as such offers are not yet widely implemented; nevertheless, this constitutes a valuable research direction for PSS, and other customer-centred business models.

In the context of this study, where use-phase impacts dominate and the assessment covers a long-term horizon, dynamic LCA would be more appropriate than a static approach. Finally, no global sensitivity analysis was conducted. Such an analysis could represent a key lever to help designers achieve sustainable design goals by fine-tuning model parameters.

Acknowledgments. This study was funded by the Nouvelle Aquitaine regional council under grant number 13907920 - 16226920.

Disclosure of Interests. The authors have no competing interests to declare that are relevant to the content of this article.

References

1. Goedkoop, M.J., van Halen, C.J.G., te Riele, H.R.M., Rommens, P.J.M.: Product service systems, ecological and economic basics. In: Report for Dutch Ministry of Housing, Spatial Planning and the Environment (VROM), The Hague (1999)
2. Baines, T.S., Lightfoot, H.W., Benedettini, O., Kay, J.M.: The servitization of manufacturing: a review of literature and reflection on future challenges. J. Mfg. Technol. Mgmt. **20**, 547–567 (2009)
3. Tukker, A.: Eight types of product–service system: eight ways to sustainability? Experiences from SusProNet. Bus. Strat. Env. **13**, 246–260 (2004)
4. Brissaud, D., Sakao, T., Riel, A., Erkoyuncu, J.A.: Designing value-driven solutions: the evolution of industrial product-service systems. CIRP Ann. **71**, 553–575 (2022)
5. Maliqi, M., Boucher, X., Villot, J., Lamy, D.: Collaborative multi-criteria decision-making: evaluation of design scenarios for PSS heating systems. In: Camarinha-Matos, L.M., Ortiz, A., Boucher, X., Barthe-Delanoë, A.-M. (eds.) Navigating Unpredictability: Collaborative Networks in Non-linear Worlds, pp. 316–330. Springer Nature Switzerland, Cham (2024)
6. Werrel, M., Yi, L., Glatt, M., Aurich, J.C.: Technical product-service systems: a methodology to reduce the carbon footprint in PSS design. Procedia CIRP. **116**, 77–82 (2023)
7. Guan, H.: A Design Framework for Customer-Oriented PSS Based on Three Dimensional Concurrent Engineering Approach. Ph.D. thesis,. Université de Bordeaux (2019)
8. Kjaer, L.L., Pagoropoulos, A., Schmidt, J.H., McAloone, T.C.: Challenges when evaluating product/service-systems through life cycle assessment. J. Clean. Prod. **120**, 95–104 (2016)
9. Koide, R., Murakami, S., Nansai, K.: Prioritising low-risk and high-potential circular economy strategies for decarbonisation: a meta-analysis on consumer-oriented product-service systems. Renew. Sust. Energ. Rev. **155**, 111858 (2022)
10. Maliqi, M., Boucher, X., Villot, J., Vuillaume, F.: Adaptation of environmental assessment to PSS specificities: heating appliance case study. Int. J. Environ. Res. **18**, 25 (2024)
11. Johnson, E., Plepys, A.: Product-service systems and sustainability: analysing the environmental impacts of rental clothing. Sustainability. **13**, 2118 (2021)
12. Guyon, O., Millet, D., Garcia, J., et al.: Prioritisation of modelling parameters of a free-floating car sharing system according to their sensitivity to the environmental impacts. J. Clean. Prod. **296**, 126081 (2021)

13. Aridi, M., Pannier, M.-L., Aridi, R., Lemenand, T.: A comprehensive review of life cycle assessments for domestic heat pumps: environmental footprint and future directions. Energ. Buildings. **336**, 115605 (2025)
14. Mauro, A.W., Pelella, F., Viscito, L.: Performance degradation of air source heat pumps under faulty conditions. Case Studies Thermal Eng. **45**, 103010 (2023)
15. Pelella, F., Viscito, L., Mauro, A.W.: Soft faults in residential heat pumps: possibility of evaluation via on-field measurements and related degradation of performance. Energy Convers. Mgmt. **260**, 115646 (2022)
16. Dongellini, M., Naldi, C., Morini, G.L.: Influence of sizing strategy and control rules on the energy saving potential of heat pump hybrid systems in a residential building. Energy Convers. Mgmt. **235**, 114022 (2021)
17. Shen, B., Abdelaziz, O., Rice, C.K.: Compressor selection and equipment sizing for cold climate heat pumps. In: Proceedings of the 11th IEA Heat Pump Conference, Montréal (2014)
18. Barz, T., Hemm, R., Jentsch, R., et al.: Annex 56 Digitalization and IoT for Heat Pumps Final Report. IEA Heat Pumping Technologies TCP, Paris (2024)
19. Rosenstein, F., Bibet-Chevalier, A., Huet, C., et al.: Chiffres clés — novembre 2022. Observatoire National des Contrats de Performance Énergétique (ONCPE), Paris (2022)
20. UFC-Que Choisir: Pompes à chaleur air-eau — une satisfaction entachée de problèmes. In: Quechoisir.org. https://www.quechoisir.org/actualite-pompes-a-chaleur-a (2024). Accessed 1 Aug 2025
21. Dupret, M., Bramkamp, U.: Performance pompes à chaleur: réalisation d'une campagne de mesure sur des pompes à chaleur en résidentiel individuel. ADEME, Angers (2025)
22. O'Hegarty, R., Kinnane, O., Lennon, D., Colclough, S.: Air-to-water heat pumps: review and analysis of the performance gap between in-use and product rated performance. Renew. Sust. Energ. Rev. **155**, 111887 (2022)
23. Deng, J., Wei, Q., Liang, M., et al.: Does heat pumps perform energy efficiently as we expected: field tests and evaluations on various kinds of heat pump systems for space heating. Energ. Buildings. **182**, 172–186 (2019)
24. European Commission, Joint Research Centre: Updated characterisation and normalisation factors for the environmental footprint 3.1 method. Publications Office, Luxembourg (2023)
25. Kjaer, L.L., Pigosso, D.C.A., McAloone, T.C., Birkved, M.: Guidelines for evaluating the environmental performance of product/service-systems through life cycle assessment. J. Clean. Prod. **190**, 666–678 (2018)
26. Fangeat, E., Eskenazi, L., Fourboul, E., et al.: Evaluation de l'impact environnemental d'un ensemble de produits reconditionnés. ADEME, Angers (2022)
27. Desroches, C., Chauvin, M., Ladan, L., Vateau, C., Gosset, S., Cordier, P.: Exploring the sustainable scaling of AI dilemma: A projective study of corporations' AI environmental impacts. arXiv preprint https://arxiv.org/abs/2501.14334 (2025)
28. Falk, S., Ekchajzer, D., Pirson, T., et al.: More than carbon: cradle-to-grave environmental impacts of GenAI training on the Nvidia A100 GPU. Environ. Impact Assess. Rev. **121**, 108525 (2026)

Mapping Rebound Mechanisms in Circular Manufacturing: A Causal Loop Diagram Approach

Mariantonietta Ferrante[1], Veronica Arioli[2(✉)], Roberto Sala[2,3], and Claudio Sassanelli[1]

[1] Department of Mechanics, Mathematics, and Management, Polytechnic University of Bari, Via Orabona, 4, 70126 Bari, Italy
m.ferrante6@phd.poliba.it, claudio.sassanelli@poliba.it

[2] Department of Management, Information and Production Engineering, University of Bergamo, Dalmine, Italy
{veronica.arioli,roberto.sala}@unibg.it

[3] Research Center on Innovation and Service Management in Industrial Firms (ASAP), Dalmine, Italy

Abstract. The manufacturing industry is undergoing a strategic transition toward a circular economy to mitigate its substantial environmental footprint. Although circular strategies such as remanufacturing, recycling, and servitization aim to decouple value creation from resource consumption, their implementation often triggers unintended rebound effects. These effects arise when efficiency gains stimulate systemic responses that partially or fully offset the expected environmental benefits. Although these offsets are well documented, research on rebound mechanisms (RMs) in business-to-business (B2B) contexts remains fragmented and largely exploratory. This paper addresses this gap by adopting a system dynamics perspective to map the RMs activated by circular strategies in B2B settings through a Causal Loop Diagram (CLD). The analysis identifies the key variables and feedback structures that shape these mechanisms, providing a qualitative framework for understanding how sustainability gains can be eroded across core business processes (i.e., business model, production, product design, and procurement). The resulting CLD provides a clear and comprehensive view of how circular strategies, despite being designed for environmental improvement, can inadvertently trigger systemic rebound effects. This work contributes to advancing a more nuanced and system-oriented understanding of circular economy implementation in manufacturing.

Keywords: Rebound Effects · Circular Manufacturing Systems · Product-Service Systems · System Thinking · Causal Loop Diagram

G. Pezzotta et al. (Eds.): APMS 2026, IFIP AICT 808, pp. 477–492, 2027.
https://doi.org/10.1007/978-3-032-38594-9_32

1 Introduction

The manufacturing industry is transitioning toward a circular economy (CE), driven by the European Commission Circular Economy Action Plan [1]. This shift addresses the significant environmental impact of the sector; manufacturing accounts for nearly 57% of global greenhouse gas emissions [2]. In Europe, the industry is responsible for over half of total emissions, primarily due to energy-intensive processes [3]. As a result, an increasing number of manufacturers are abandoning the "take-make-use-dispose" linear model, widely recognized as environmentally unsustainable [4], in favour of the CE paradigm.

This new approach to production and consumption is explicitly designed to operate within ecological limits [5]. By decoupling value creation from resource consumption, the CE has become a focal point in both academic research and industrial strategy [6]. Manufacturers are adopting circular strategies to minimize natural resource use and close material and energy loops [7].

This study focuses specifically on business-to-business (B2B) manufacturing systems, where circular value creation and circular resource flows are reconfigured through key strategies including remanufacturing, recycling, and servitization [8]. For instance, servitization strategy operationalized in Product-Service System (PSS) business models have high circular potential. When integrated, these approaches enhance resource productivity, extend product lifecycles, and minimize both waste and environmental degradation [9], ultimately delivering a triad of environmental, economic, and social benefits. While these strategies are typically operationalized at the business model level, their implementation necessarily interacts with broader system elements, including production processes, product design decisions, and procurement mechanisms, which are considered here as interdependent components of the same industrial system rather than standalone analytical dimensions.

However, despite these potential advantages, the implementation of circular strategies can trigger unintended consequences known as the rebound effect. Rebound effects occur when sustainability-oriented actions—such as resource efficiency gains—stimulate systemic responses (e.g., increased consumption or lower prices) that partially or fully offset the intended environmental benefits [10, 11].

In literature, rebound mechanisms (RMs) are defined as the qualitative causal connections between interdependent elements that lead to a specific systematic effect [12]. In essence, these mechanisms provide the underlying causal explanations for why and how rebound effects emerge.

Recent studies highlight both the magnitude and the variability of these effects. For example, an analysis of 530 documented rebound cases reports a median rebound of around 47%, meaning that nearly half of the intended environmental gains are often lost to systemic offsets [13]. These estimations vary drastically, spanning from negative to extreme backfire scenarios, where impacts exceed 200%, illustrating how rebound effects can entirely counteract sustainability efforts [13, 14]. Notwithstanding the impact of these undesired effects, research remains fragmented and largely exploratory [15–17]. Furthermore, there is a pronounced lack of tools, methods, and frameworks to assess the potential occurrence of rebound effects when implementing circular strategies in manufacturing [18]. Because these effects stem from complex, non-linear interactions within industrial environment, they require an analytical lens suited to capturing dynamic feedback relationships.

System dynamics (SD) offers such a lens. SD is explicitly designed to model how changes propagate across interconnected variables and accumulate over time. This makes it particularly suitable for understanding rebound effects, which result not from isolated actions but from the recursive feedback loops embedded in industrial environments. Among SD tools, the Causal Loop Diagram (CLD) is especially appropriate at this stage of inquiry: it provides a qualitative yet rigorous representation of feedback structures, enabling researchers to identify reinforcing and balancing loops that may amplify or dampen sustainability outcomes. To address these gaps, this paper aims to map the RMs triggered by circular strategies within a business-to-business (B2B) context using a CLD. As a core qualitative pillar of SD, the CLD allows for the visualization of "closed loops", revealing how a change in one variable propagates through the system and ultimately influence itself [19]. Through this approach, the study identifies the key variables that drive such mechanisms, offering deeper insight into how rebound effects emerge within industrial systems. This study is guided by the following Research Questions (RQ):

- *(RQ1) Which key variables are essential for defining and characterizing rebound effects in circular manufacturing?*
- *(RQ2) How can RMs be systematically mapped within circular manufacturing systems?*

The remainder of this paper is structured as follows. Section 2 establishes the research context and theoretical foundation. Section 3 details the methodology employed to develop the CLD, integrating the identified RMs and their associated variables. Section 4 presents the proposed CLD, providing a systemic map of how these mechanisms manifest within circular strategies. This is followed by Sect. 5, which discusses the findings and highlights the contributions to the field. In both sections particular emphasis was placed on RMs most directly connected to PSS configurations and their systemic implications. Finally, Sect. 6 concludes the paper by summarizing key findings, addressing research limitations, and offering directions for future study.

2 Research Context

Rebound effects occur when sustainable actions, whether intentional or unintentional, trigger systemic responses that reduce the potential environmental benefits. This creates a significant discrepancy between expected and actual improvements, often resulting in higher resource consumption than the initial baseline [10, 12]. These effects emerge not from isolated decisions but from interactions across interconnected economic, technological, and behavioural structures, which amplify or counteract the initial intention of sustainability-oriented interventions.

While the B2B context remains under-researched, existing literature suggests that rebound effects in this context are typically driven by technological or efficiency gains that produce unintended consequences [20, 21]. In particular, the circular strategies introduced in manufacturing, such as remanufacturing, reuse, servitization, may trigger different RMs [22].

These strategies are particularly relevant because they simultaneously modify production processes, cost structures, and user behaviour, thereby creating multiple pathways through which rebound effects can emerge across the value chain. These mechanisms provide the underlying causal explanations for the potential occurrence of rebound effects [12].

Recent studies [23, 24] identify mechanisms affecting both the production and consumption sides of the value chain. By definition, these mechanisms often share a common input (e.g., increased efficiency) and result in a similar outcome (e.g., expanded production or resource use), yet each captures a distinct causal dynamic. Importantly, these mechanisms should not be interpreted in isolation, as they are structurally interconnected through shared variables such as cost, price, demand, and investment decisions. For instance, the price mechanism implies that lower operational costs reduce the service price for the industrial user, which may inadvertently incentivize the user to increase the intensity of equipment use or expand their own production capacity.

This dynamic can offset the resource savings achieved through the manufacturer's initial optimization. Similarly, the re-spending or reinvestment mechanism occurs when savings achieved by the producer through optimized circular processes generate additional capital. If this capital is reinvested in scaling up production or entering new markets, the absolute environmental impact may increase despite the relative efficiency gains. These examples illustrate that rebound effects arise through reinforcing feedback structures in which efficiency gains are progressively translated into higher system-wide activity levels.

In essence, a RM describes how efficiency gains resulting from the implementation of a circular strategy within a specific business process may stimulate increased output, ultimately leading to higher overall resource consumption. More broadly, RMs represent the causal pathways through which localized efficiency improvements propagate across interconnected business processes, producing unintended systemic consequences that undermine initial sustainability objectives.

The RMs considered in this study, synthesized from the literature [23, 24], are presented in Table 1. Table 1 details how these mechanisms trigger rebound effects across different business processes (i.e., business model, product design, production, and procurement), illustrating the pathways through which efficiency improvements can paradoxically lead to increased resource use.

Table 1. Rebound mechanisms considered

ID	Rebound mechanisms	Definition	Business process	Ref.
RM1	Price	Efficiency improvements reduce production costs and product prices, stimulating demand for the same or other products and increasing overall resource use.	Business model	[23]

(*continued*)

Table 1. (*continued*)

ID	Rebound mechanisms	Definition	Business process	Ref.
RM2	Output	Efficiency improvements reduce production costs or constraints, enabling firms to increase the supply of the same product and thus total resource use.	Procurement	[23]
RM3	Time	Efficiency gains in manufacturing increase output per unit time, leading to higher overall production volumes.	Production	[23]
RM4	Sufficiency	When one producer adopts sufficiency (less consumption), other producers compensate by increasing supply, offsetting potential resource savings.	Business model	[23]
RM5	Re-investing	Firms use savings generated by efficiency improvements into expanding production, developing new products, or entering new markets, increasing overall resource use.	Business model	[23]
RM6	Substitution	Efficiency in one product triggers demand shift toward other, potentially more resource-intensive goods.	Product design	[23]
RM7	Imperfect substitution	Secondary or recycled inputs do not fully replace primary materials (in quality), leading to increased total resource demand.	Product design	[23]
RM8	Consumption efficiency	Improved efficiency in product consumption encourages higher utilization, increasing demand for resources.	Production Product design	[23]

(*continued*)

Table 1. (*continued*)

ID	Rebound mechanisms	Definition	Business process	Ref.
RM9	Resource market	Efficiency improvement reduces resource use at the market level, but lower price increases resource use.	Production	[23]
RM10	Composition	Efficiency improvements reduce production costs and prices, increasing demand across sectors.	Product design	[23]
RM11	Structural change	Efficiency improvement shifts production patterns toward solutions with higher overall resource use.	Production	[23]
RM12	New market	Efficiency improvements enable changes in the structure of the economy, converting existing production and creating new markets.	Procurement	[23]
RM13	Market price	Efficiency increases producer re-spending and re-investment, increasing total consumption.	Business model	[23]
RM14	Cross-factor/ Cost-dependent output	Efficiency gains in one production factor (e.g., energy) increase utilization of other factors (e.g., capital, materials), resulting in higher overall output.	Production	[23]
RM15	Frontier	Efficiency improvements expand the production frontier with the creation of new products, leading to higher resource demand.	Procurement	[23]
RM16	International	Efficiency improvements are transferred internationally without adequate incentives, raising global resource use.	Procurement	[23]

(*continued*)

Table 1. (*continued*)

ID	Rebound mechanisms	Definition	Business process	Ref.
RM17	Demand adjustment with investment adjustment	Reduced demand lowers prices, encouraging consumption and increasing resource use.	Business model	[23]
RM18	Re-design	Efficiency in design leads to the addition of new features in products that increase total resource use.	Product design	[23]
RM19	Producer-induced demand adjustment	Efficiency improvements reduce production costs or create excess capacity, prompting producers to stimulate downstream demand and general resource consumption.	Production	[23]
RM20	Economies of scale	Lower per-unit costs from higher production volumes stimulate increased output and resource use.	Procurement	[23]

3 Research Methodology

This study employs System Thinking, which posits that all elements within a system are interconnected, as the overarching analytical perspective to capture the interdependencies and feedback mechanisms characterizing circular manufacturing systems. Methodologically, the research relies on a qualitative SD modelling approach, operationalized through the development of a CLD that illustrates the variables pertinent to circular manufacturing systems, their causal relationships, and feedback mechanisms, thereby elucidating the RMs under study, following the main phases delineated by Sterman [19].

The first phase consists in the *RMs identification*, i.e., the characterization of the rebound effects inside the system under study (the circular strategies in a B2B context), with the identification of the different variables involved, their causal relationships and their polarities (+ and –). This process allows depicting if the variation (increase or decrease) of a variable, causes the same (+) or the opposite (−) variation in the following one. Variables and causal relationships are identified through an iterative qualitative coding process based on the literature review presented in Sect. 2, especially the definition of each RM explained in Table 1, that already displays fundamental features that enable mapping CLD structures (i.e., intention, trigger, driver, causal relationship, and causal relationship polarity) [23]. For instance, considering the RM1, we have: "Efficiency improvements <intention> reduce <causal relation and polarity> production costs and product prices <trigger>, stimulating demand for the same or other products <causal relationship> and increasing <polarity> overall resource use."

The following step deals with *CLD development*, i.e., the translation of the collected variables and relationships into the map. Variables referring to similar concepts across different rebound mechanisms are harmonized and merged to avoid redundancy and ensure consistency within the overall CLD structure. Once developed, the CLD is analysed for *feedback loops identification*, i.e., the explanation of the rebound effects thanks to the identification of the reinforcing feedback loops within the system and their interpretation on the basis of the system thinking archetypes [19]. It is important to highlight that the consistency of the model structure and feedback logic is continuously checked during the development process through iterative revisions of the CLD.

To develop the CLD the software VENSIM (https://vensim.com/software/) has been used, which is particularly useful for identifying the feedback loops within the model.

4 Results

The developed CLD represents the dynamics of circular strategies in manufacturing systems affecting resource consumption. In general, manufacturers will adopt circular strategies to reduce overall resource consumption and therefore enhance the sustainability impacts of their production systems (visible in the balancing loop named as B-circular strategy). By analysing the RMs found in the literature and presented in Table 1, to define the fundamental features for developing the CLD, it is possible to observe that many RMs share variables between each other. Therefore, all twenty RMs are acting in successions of cause-effect relations that begin with the adoption of circular strategies but result in an exponential growth of overall resource consumption. The developed CLD integrates in a single systemic representation the RMs, showing their strong interconnections and revealing that several mechanisms have shared variables, creating overlapping feedback structures and generating cascading rebound effects. This resulting CLD containing all the RMs coloured differently on the basis of the categorization in production (in orange), business model (in blue), product-design (in red), and procurement (in green) related, is shown in Fig. 1. For space constraints, only business model-related RMs are detailed in this section.

The price mechanism (RM1 in Fig. 2a and c) occurs when improvements in production efficiency reduce production costs for manufacturers. In B2B context, these costs reductions may lead firms to increase production volume or utilize previously idle production capacity. As a result, product prices for downstream industrial customers may decrease, stimulating demand from other firms of the same or other products and ultimately increasing overall resource consumption. Similarly, the increase in production volume can also be explained as excess capacity of the producer; therefore, the same mechanism can also account for RM19. These RMs, shown in Fig. 2a fall into the "fixes that fail" SD archetype, which represents that the problem (availability of resource) is solved by some fix (circular strategy action) with immediate positive effect, but then the "side effects" of this solution (increase of overall resource consumption) turn out in the future.

The sufficiency mechanism (RM4) occurs when a producer reduces resource use in response to decreased resource availability (i.e., by adopting sufficiency strategy and reducing material inputs in production). In B2B context, this reduction can create a gap in the supply of resource, which in turn may incentivize other firms to increase their demand for the same resource. This market response can ultimately lead to a rise in overall resource consumption (see Fig. 2b).

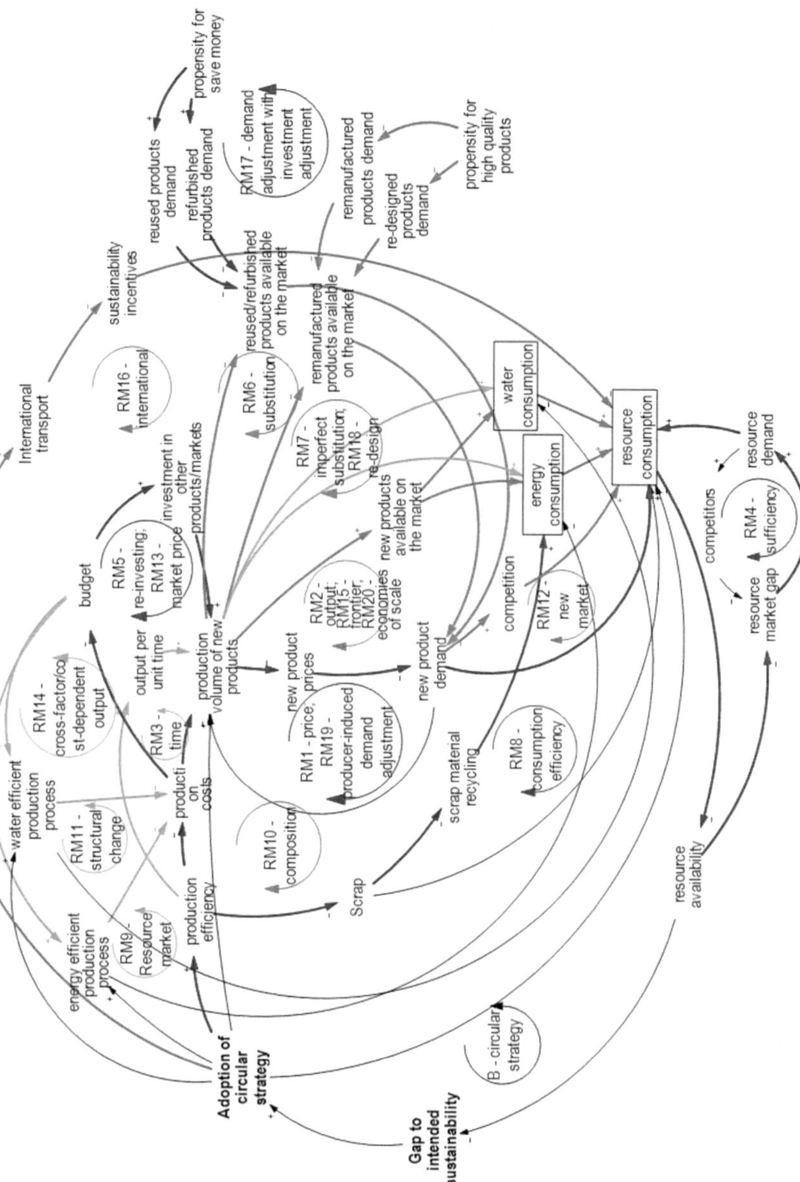

Fig. 1. Causal Loop Diagram of circular manufacturing systems. Blue arrows identify business model-related connections. Red arrows identify product design-related connections. Orange arrows identify production-related connections. Green arrows identify procurement-based connections. Brown arrows identify the double production & product design-related connections.

The re-investing mechanism (RM5) happens when manufacturers use savings generated by the reduction of production costs induced by efficiency improvements into expanding production capacity, developing new product lines, or entering new industrial markets (RM13), increasing the production volume. In B2B contexts, such reinvestments are often directed toward scaling production or strengthening competitive positioning within supply chains. Knowing that the increase in production volume results in decrease of product prices stimulating new products demand (RM1, RM19), ultimately the overall resource consumption increases. These RMs, shown in Fig. 2c, correspond to a combination of "fixes the fail" archetypes.

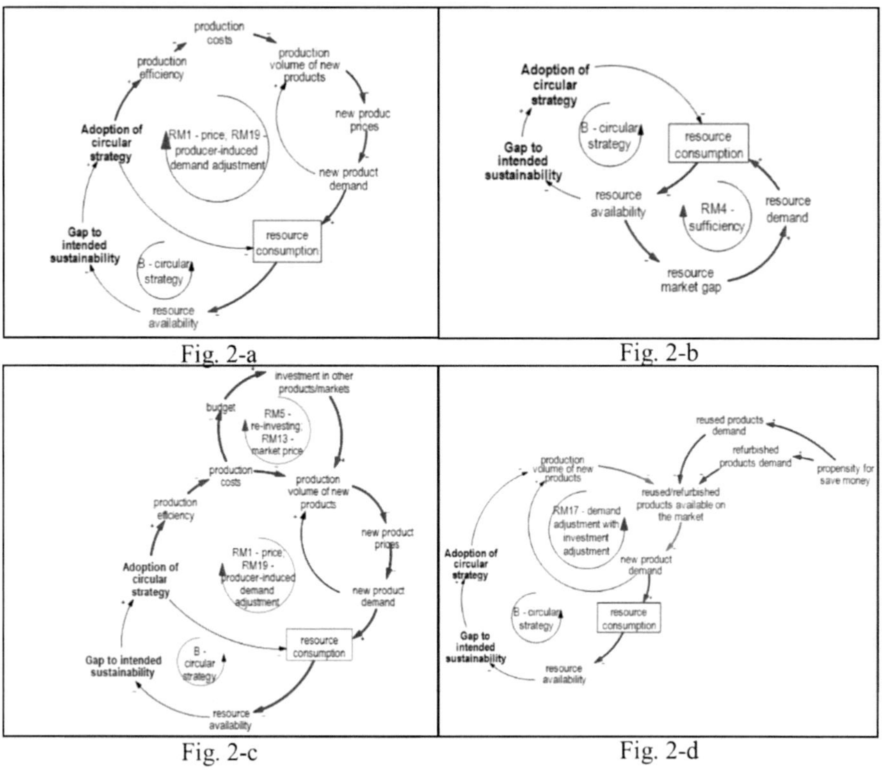

Fig. 2. Business model-related Rebound Mechanisms mapped in the developed Causal Loop Diagram. Details of Fig. 1.

The demand adjustment with investment adjustment mechanism (RM17), reported in Fig. 2d, occurs when lower prices of reused or refurbished products influence purchasing decisions of industrial customers. While lower prices may initially stimulate demand for reused/refurbished products, increase consumption can lead to unintended decreased availability of them over time. This scarcity may initiate demand for newly manufactured products, therefore increasing overall resource consumption. Here, the propensity of saving money drives the RM, therefore influencing/moderating its strengths.

The analysis of the business model-related RMs reveals the individual mechanisms can interact and amplify each other, strongly influencing the side effects of circular manufacturing strategies. Specifically, these RMs, are connected through variables such as production efficiency, production volumes, product prices, and demand levels, which act across different feedback structures.

These interdependencies generate cascading effects across the system, where efficiency gains in production or resource use trigger subsequent behavioural and market adjustments that extend beyond the initial intentions. Here, the economic dimension plays a central role in shaping system dynamics.

Production costs, product prices, budget re-investments, propensity of saving money, are all variables included in the analysed RMs and therefore operating as counteracting drivers of unintended environmental consequences.

5 Discussions

Within the business model process, five distinct RMs were identified (RM1, RM4, RM5, RM13, and RM17). This process represents a critical focal point for sustainability research due to its unique capacity to be triggered by both producers and users through the implementation of circular business models and PSS. Building on the systemic relationships already visualised in the CLD, these mechanisms should not be interpreted as isolated effects but as interconnected pathways that collectively structure rebound dynamics across the system.

The findings highlight a significant overlap between the price mechanism (RM1) and the producer-induced demand adjustment (RM19). Although these mechanisms originate in two different business processes, business model and production, respectively, they share identical causal configurations. Both are triggered by improvements in production efficiency and culminate in increased output. This convergence underscores that diverse systemic pathways can lead to the same unintended outcome: a net increase in resource consumption.

In PSS models, this is particularly evident as providers optimise asset utilisation to improve operational efficiency, only to find that the resulting cost reductions stimulate higher aggregate demand. In this case, a producer-driven action elicits an unexpected response from the consumer side; this highlights the need to identify and analyse the underlying behavioural mechanisms that give rise to such effects [25].

The sufficiency mechanism (RM4) presents a particularly challenging paradox. While sufficiency strategies aim to reduce resource use at the source, this study shows that a producer's reduced consumption can inadvertently signal greater resource availability or diminished market pressure to other firms.

In a B2B supply chain, this may incentivise competitors or downstream partners to increase their own demand for those resources. As a result, dematerialisation efforts in PSS models, designed to deliver functions with fewer physical assets, may be counterbalanced by broader increases in market demand for the same resources, as the absence of ownership on the user side can weaken incentives for long-term handling and ultimately shorten resource lifespans [26].

Furthermore, the reinvestment mechanism (RM5) is intrinsically linked to the market price mechanism (RM13). The efficiency gains that characterise circular transitions generate capital savings which, in a competitive B2B environment, are often reinvested into scaling production or developing new product lines. This dynamic involves both PSS providers, who seek to strengthen their competitive positioning, and PSS customers, who may redirect their operational savings toward other resource-intensive products. Indeed, consumer choices represent an additional and significant pathway through which RMs can be triggered [27]. The reinforcement between efficiency improvements and increased production rate also highlights the importance of considering time explicitly.

Many circular strategies reduce downtime, shorten process cycles, or improve asset availability, thereby increasing the rate of output per unit of time. While this accelerates productivity, it can simultaneously elevate total resource use if production volumes rise proportionally. In such cases, resource efficiency per unit decreases more slowly than output increases, generating a rebound driven by throughput expansion.

Finally, the demand adjustment with investment adjustment (RM17) highlights the role of economic incentives in the circular transition. In this mechanism, the industrial drive for cost savings promotes the adoption of reused or refurbished products. In PSS models, this dynamic is further intensified, as firms often integrate refurbished components or remanufactured assets into their service offerings to maintain competitive pricing and extend asset lifetimes. However, as lower prices stimulate demand, the resulting scarcity of secondary materials can inadvertently push the market back toward newly manufactured products. This suggests that the strength of this RM is heavily moderated by the price elasticity of the B2B market, the stability of secondary material supply, and the perceived value of refurbished assets within PSS models.

In particular, the additional activities embedded in PSS models, such as maintenance, refurbishment, and remanufacturing, may themselves unintentionally activate the previously identified mechanisms, thereby giving rise to further rebound effects [28].

A deeper reflection on RM2 and RM3 reveals that, although both mechanisms address how efficiency-oriented circular strategies create unintended systemic outcomes, they operate at distinct conceptual levels. RM2 captures rebound effects as qualitative causal pathways, describing how improved efficiency or reduced material intensity triggers behavioural, market, or operational responses that increase total resource use. RM3, in contrast, translates these causal structures into quantifiable dynamics, using index-based variables to detect how changes in efficiency influence system behaviour over time. RM2 highlights where mechanisms are activated within business processes, whereas RM3 reveals how strongly these mechanisms propagate through the system. Together, the two mechanisms provide a coherent conceptual bridge between structural understanding and measurable system response.

Ultimately, the analysis suggests that the introduction of circular strategies, such as circular business models and PSS, that are designed to decouple value creation from resource use may paradoxically accelerate systemic resource depletion, thereby generating rebound effects [27].

This work offers several significant contributions to both theoretical knowledge and industrial practice by providing a comprehensive and schematic mapping of RMs through a CLD. By demonstrating how circular strategies, traditionally designed to deliver environmental benefits, can instead trigger systemic rebound effects, this study moves beyond fragmented analyses and advances a more integrated and systemic understanding of the circularity paradox.

A primary theoretical contribution lies in the identification of key variables, such as production efficiency, asset utilization, and market price elasticity, that act as fundamental drivers of rebound effects in B2B contexts. In such scenarios, a localized gain in one business process, for instance within the business model, can provoke a larger environmental loss in another, such as an expansion in production volume. This allows the identification of cross-process interactions, such as how efficiency gains in the business model domain can translate into increased production volumes in operational processes, thereby amplifying environmental impacts. By aligning these mechanisms with SD archetypes, the study also provides a standardised framework for identifying and discussing sustainability failures in manufacturing.

From a managerial perspective, understanding these causal pathways offers a concrete diagnostic tool for risk assessment. Rather than treating circularity as inherently beneficial, managers are encouraged to actively monitor the system-wide consequences of efficiency improvements. The CLD can function as a diagnostic mapping tool to identify critical leverage points—such as pricing policies, capacity utilization decisions, and reinvestment strategies—where small operational changes may generate disproportionate rebound effects. This perspective enables managers to move from reactive sustainability assessment toward anticipatory management of rebound risk. For example, firms can redesign incentive structures to decouple efficiency gains from production expansion, limiting the tendency to reinvest cost savings into additional output. Similarly, monitoring price transmission effects in B2B markets can help anticipate demand-driven rebounds before they materialize at the system level.

Finally, the research carries important policy implications by highlighting the need for regulatory approaches that extend beyond the promotion of resource efficiency alone. To meet the absolute environmental targets advanced by the European Commission, policymakers must increase awareness of B2B rebound effects. Potential frameworks could include resource-productivity standards or instruments aimed at governing the reinvestment of efficiency gains, ensuring that the transition to a CE yields a genuine reduction in aggregate resource consumption rather than a systemic redistribution of environmental burdens.

6 Conclusions

This paper aims to map the RMs triggered by circular strategies within a B2B context to understand how rebound effects are activated and the specific variables through which they propagate. To trace this propagation, a CLD was employed.

The CLD enables the illustration of variables pertinent to circular manufacturing systems, their causal relationships, and the associated feedback mechanisms, thereby elucidating the RMs under study. Moreover, it integrates these RMs into a single systemic representation, highlighting their dense interconnections. This holistic approach reveals that several mechanisms share common variables, creating overlapping feedback structures that can generate cascading rebound effects across the system.

A key contribution of this study lies in consolidating previously separate RMs into a unified system perspective. While each mechanism can be understood individually, the

CLD demonstrates that they are strongly interdependent and often share core variables. This systemic view exposes reinforcing dynamics that remain hidden when RMs are analysed in isolation.

The analysis of four core business processes—business model, production, product design, and procurement—shows that the business model is a critical trigger point for rebound effects, particularly through mechanisms such as price (RM1), sufficiency (RM4), reinvestment (RM5), market price (RM13), and demand adjustment (RM19). These mechanisms illustrate how efficiency gains can be offset by behavioural and market responses that increase overall resource consumption. In particular, PSS business models amplify these dynamics by strengthening linkages between efficiency, pricing, and demand.

Business model-related RMs are highly interconnected and do not operate independently. Instead, they reinforce one another through shared system variables—such as production efficiency, output levels, and demand—which act as transmission nodes for rebound propagation across the industrial system.

Despite its contributions, the study has three main limitations.

First, it focuses on internal manufacturing system dynamics and excludes broader consumer-side behaviours.

Second, the detailed analysis is concentrated on the business model, limiting full exploration of cross-process interactions.

Third, the model is specific to circular manufacturing and does not directly capture cross-sector rebound dynamics.

Future research should first move from qualitative mapping to quantitative validation by applying the CLD to empirical PSS cases and real-world data. Second, the analysis should be extended across all business processes to capture full cross-functional propagation of RMs.

Finally, converting the CLD into a simulation model would enable quantitative testing of policy and managerial interventions, allowing identification of key leverage points to effectively decouple value creation from resource consumption.

Disclosure of Interests. The authors have no competing interests.

References

1. European Commission: Circular economy action plan. https://environment.ec.europa.eu/strategy/circular-economy-action-plan_en (2015). Accessed 10 Apr 2025
2. Zacharia, M.: Over 50% of global emissions from construction & manufacturing. In: One Click LCA. https://oneclicklca.com/en/resources/articles/global-emissions-from-construction-and-manufacturing (2025). Accessed 15 May 2025
3. Karakosta, C.: The role of industrial emissions within the EU: trends and policy. In: Climate Policy Info Hub. https://climatepolicyinfohub.eu/role-industrial-emissions-within-eu-trends-and-policy.html (2016). Accessed 15 May 2025
4. Kara, S., Hauschild, M., Sutherland, J., McAloone, T.: Closed-loop systems to circular economy: a pathway to environmental sustainability? CIRP Ann. **71**, 505–528 (2022). https://doi.org/10.1016/J.CIRP.2022.05.008

5. Blomsma, F., Bauwens, T., Weissbrod, I., Kirchherr, J.: The 'need for speed': towards circular disruption—what it is, how to make it happen and how to know it's happening. Bus. Strategy Environ. **32**, 1010–1031 (2023). https://doi.org/10.1002/BSE.3106
6. Despeisse, M., Acerbi, F.: Toward eco-efficient and circular industrial systems: ten years of advances in production management systems and a thematic framework. Prod. Manuf. Res. **10**, 354–382 (2022). https://doi.org/10.1080/21693277.2022.2088634
7. Gregson, N., Crang, M., Fuller, S., Holmes, H.: Interrogating the circular economy: the moral economy of resource recovery in the EU. Econ. Soc. **44**, 218–243 (2015). https://doi.org/10.1080/03085147.2015.1013353
8. Acerbi, F., Sassanelli, C., Taisch, M.: A conceptual data model promoting data-driven circular manufacturing. Oper. Manag. Res. **15**, 838–857 (2022). https://doi.org/10.1007/s12063-022-00271-x
9. Gusmerotti, N.M., Testa, F., Corsini, F., et al.: Drivers and approaches to the circular economy in manufacturing firms. J. Clean. Prod. **230**, 314–327 (2019). https://doi.org/10.1016/J.JCLEPRO.2019.05.044
10. Zink, T., Geyer, R.: Circular economy rebound. J. Ind. Ecol. **21**, 593–602 (2017). https://doi.org/10.1111/JIEC.12545
11. Castro, C.G., Trevisan, A.H., Pigosso, D.C.A., Mascarenhas, J.: The rebound effect of circular economy: definitions, mechanisms and a research agenda. J. Clean. Prod. **345**, 131136 (2022). https://doi.org/10.1016/J.JCLEPRO.2022.131136
12. Lange, S., Kern, F., Peuckert, J., Santarius, T.: The Jevons paradox unravelled: a multi-level typology of rebound effects and mechanisms. Energy Res. Soc. Sci. **74**, 101982 (2021). https://doi.org/10.1016/J.ERSS.2021.101982
13. Andrew, E., Pigosso, D.C.A.: Multidisciplinary perspectives on rebound effects in sustainability: a systematic review. J. Clean. Prod. **470**, 143366 (2024). https://doi.org/10.1016/J.JCLEPRO.2024.143366
14. Guzzo, D., Andrew, E., Van der Loo, I., et al.: Towards the Prevention of Rebound Effects in Europe and beyond: Insights for Policymaking: Science for Policy Brief. European Commission (2025)
15. Madlener, R., Turner, K.: After 35 years of rebound research in economics: where do we stand? In: Rethinking Climate and Energy Policies: New Perspectives on the Rebound Phenomenon, pp. 17–36 (2016). https://doi.org/10.1007/978-3-319-38807-6_2
16. Ruzzenenti, F., Font Vivanco, D., Galvin, R., et al.: Editorial: the rebound effect and the Jevons' paradox: beyond the conventional wisdom. Front. Energy Res. **7**, 489512 (2019). https://doi.org/10.3389/FENRG.2019.00090/BIBTEX
17. Siderius, T., Poldner, K.: Reconsidering the circular economy rebound effect: propositions from a case study of the Dutch Circular Textile Valley. J. Clean. Prod. **293** (2021). https://doi.org/10.1016/j.jclepro.2021.125996
18. Lowe, B.H., Bimpizas-Pinis, M., Zerbino, P., Genovese, A.: Methods to estimate the circular economy rebound effect: a review. J. Clean. Prod. **443** (2024)
19. Sterman, J.D.: System Dynamics: Systems Thinking and Modeling for a Complex World. MacGraw-Hill Company (2000)
20. Skiba, J., Saini, A., Friend, S.B.: The effect of managerial cost prioritization on sales force turnover. J. Bus. Res. **69**, 5917–5924 (2016). https://doi.org/10.1016/j.jbusres.2016.05.004
21. Papagiannidis, E., Mikalef, P., Conboy, K., Van de Wetering, R.: Uncovering the dark side of AI-based decision-making: a case study in a B2B context. Ind. Mark. Manag. **115**, 253–265 (2023). https://doi.org/10.1016/j.indmarman.2023.10.003
22. Ferrante, M., Sassanelli, C., Pigosso, D.C.A.: Rebound effects in circular manufacturing: overview of potential rebound mechanisms activated by circular strategies across key business processes. Bus. Strategy Environ. (2026). https://doi.org/10.1002/bse.70562

23. Guzzo, D., Walrave, B., Videira, N., et al.: Towards a systemic view on rebound effects: modelling the feedback loops of rebound mechanisms. Ecol. Econ. **217** (2024). https://doi.org/10.1016/j.ecolecon.2023.108050
24. Metic, J., Pigosso, D.C.A.: Research avenues for uncovering the rebound effects of the circular economy: a systematic literature review. J. Clean. Prod. **368** (2022). https://doi.org/10.1016/J.JCLEPRO.2022.133133
25. Van der Loo, I.G.H., Pigosso, D.C.A.: Explaining the rebound effects of sustainable design: a behavioural perspective. In: Proceedings of the Design Society. Cambridge University Press, pp. 1497–1506 (2024)
26. Ackermann, L., Tunn, V.S.C.: Careless product use in access-based services: a rebound effect and how to address it. J. Bus. Res. **177** (2024). https://doi.org/10.1016/j.jbusres.2024.114643
27. Guzzo, D., Pigosso, D.C.A.: Identifying rebound effects in product-service systems: actors, mechanisms, triggers and drivers. In: Proceedings of the Design Society. Cambridge University Press, pp. 1279–1288 (2024)
28. Chun, Y.Y., Lee, K.M.: Environmental impacts of the rental business model compared to the conventional business model: a Korean case of water purifier for home use. Int. J. Life Cycle Assess. **22**, 1096–1108 (2017). https://doi.org/10.1007/s11367-016-1227-1

How Servitization Enables—And Constrains—Sustainable Value Creation: An Empirical Analysis Among Manufacturing Firms

Veronica Arioli[1(✉)], Fabiana Pirola[1,2], Luca Lussignoli[2,3], Federico Adrodegari[2,3], and Nicola Saccani[2,3]

[1] University of Bergamo, Bergamo, Italy
{veronica.arioli,fabiana.pirola}@unibg.it
[2] ASAP Interuniversity Research Center on Servitization, Florence, Italy
{luca.lussignoli,federico.adrodegari,nicola.saccani}@unibs.it
[3] University of Brescia, Brescia, Italy

Abstract. In recent years, manufacturing companies have been operating in an increasingly complex environment shaped by two concurrent drivers: the evolution of business models and the ecological transition. The diffusion of servitization and Product–Service Systems (PSS), has been accompanied by growing pressure to reduce environmental impacts throughout the entire product life cycle. The relationship between servitization and sustainability has attracted increasing attention in the literature, leading to the emergence of concepts such as sustainable servitization and sustainable PSS. While prior studies highlight the potential sustainability benefits of servitized business models, they also reveal ambiguities and inconsistent evidence, suggesting that servitization cannot be considered inherently sustainable. Building on this literature, this study explores how the barriers hindering the practical implementation of sustainable servitization manifest in practice through qualitative evidence from nine manufacturing companies characterized by different levels of servitization maturity. The findings identify key challenges faced by firms when integrating sustainability into PSS and highlight practices that can help address them. The study contributes to the literature by providing empirical insights into sustainable value creation in manufacturing and by identifying best practices that can support companies in advancing their sustainable servitization strategies.

Keywords: Servitization · Product-Service Systems · Environmental Sustainability · Empirical analysis · Barriers

1 Introduction

In recent years, manufacturing companies have found themselves operating in an increasingly complex environment, where the evolution of business models and the ecological transition represent two concurrent and now structural drivers. The strategic shift toward

Published by Springer Nature Switzerland AG 2027
G. Pezzotta et al. (Eds.): APMS 2026, IFIP AICT 808, pp. 493–508, 2027.
https://doi.org/10.1007/978-3-032-38594-9_33

service-oriented business models, such as Product-Service Systems (PSS) [1], is accompanied by a drive to reduce environmental impacts throughout the entire life cycle of products and systems [2–4]. In this scenario, sustainability is no longer an external or ancillary objective but acquiring a strategic value that must be integrated into the processes of designing, offering, and delivering solutions.

Servitization has been studied in combination with sustainability, sustainable development, and sustainable practices. Concept of "sustainable servitization" and "sustainable PSS" [5] rose in the literature. The literature has suggested the potential benefits the servitization and the adoption of PSS model can generate for sustainability achievement, but also ambiguity and unclear positions have been taken [6], leading to the authors to go beyond the "a priori" sustainability of servitization and PSS, and go further in the investigation of the factors influencing this relationship [7]. However, it remains limited in its understanding of the multidimensional and interconnected challenges that hinder the effective integration of sustainability into service offerings [8, 9]. In practice, companies face significant challenges in leveraging servitization for sustainable value creation.

Building on the existing literature on barriers and challenges associated with sustainable servitization, this study aims to explore how such challenges manifest in practice in different manufacturing realities. This led to the formulation of the following research question (RQ): *To what extent does the implementation of servitized business models in manufacturing companies lead to the creation of sustainable value, and what dimensions influence this relationship?*

To address this RQ, qualitative evidence from nine manufacturing companies characterized by different levels of servitization maturity have been collected in this study. In addition to identifying the difficulties encountered by companies when integrating sustainability within their service-oriented business models, the study also highlights several best practices adopted by firms.

The article is structured as follows. A literature background and pre-analytical vision that guided the research is described in Sect. 2. Section 3 presents the methodology adopted for the study and related method for data collection and data analysis. The results of this latter data analysis are described and presented in Sect. 4, as a set of themes that affects the sustainable value creation in servitized companies. Section 5 discusses the results. Finally, Sect. 6 concludes the study summarizing results while presenting limitations and future developments.

2 Literature Background

The literature on servitization describes the transformation of manufacturing companies from product sellers to providers of integrated product-service solutions [10]. In this transformation, scientific literature also converges in highlighting how, as the degree of integration of the service component in the offer increases, PSSs can express a higher potential for reducing environmental impact [1, 11, 12]. This potential derives mainly from greater asset intensity of use, the extension of their useful life, and an optimization logic focused on overall performance rather than on the product itself [9]. In this perspective, with reference to the taxonomy proposed by Tukker (2004) [1], PSSs oriented towards use (i.e., use-oriented, such as renting, leasing and sharing) and, above all, towards results (i.e., result-oriented, such as pay-per-results, pay-per-X models, and outsourcing) are frequently indicated as the configurations with the greatest potential for improving environmental performance rather than the solely transactional provision of services after the selling of the product (i.e., product-oriented). From this standpoint, servitization is not merely an evolution of the business model, but a potential driver of environmental sustainability.

However, following research has further emphasized the need to integrate explicit environmental objectives from the design stages of servitized business models [13], as servitized solutions may also drive to unexpected sustainability consequences. This discussion has recently culminated in the identification of rebound effects that hinder the real potentials of servitized models [14]. Therefore, despite the theoretical premises, environmental sustainability in industrial practice is often considered an implicit benefit of servitized models rather than an explicitly governed and measured objective. This highlights the persistent gap between theoretical expectations and empirical reality.

A growing body of literature highlights the role of digitalization as an enabler of sustainability in servitized models. Digital technologies, monitoring systems, and data platforms make it possible to track product usage, measure environmental performance, and optimize life cycles. This trend is often referred to as digital servitization [15], which integrates digital transformation and servitization. However, there is limited understanding of how these three dimensions (servitization, digitalization, and sustainability) intersect and how their combined application can be effectively implemented within the manufacturing context [16].

The challenge is not merely the introduction of digital solutions, or integration of sustainability since the phase of design of servitized solutions. Rather, the entire servitization process should be accompanied by a strong environmental commitment which is often difficult to operationalize in practice. In this context, Ozturkoglu et al. (2025) [8], identify in their work different barriers that companies can encounter in their sustainable servitization process related to different dimensions – business, human, economic, market and environment – among which it is possible to mention lack of understanding of customer needs, lack of skilled worker, problems for adapting new technology and other organizational problems, cultural problems, lack of strategic orientation, high market risk, high investment cost, financial vulnerability and constraints, lack of environmental awareness, lack of green management and lack of environmental regulations. Additional recent studies further emphasize barriers such as lack of understanding of customer needs, high market risk, lack of a shared vocabulary, financial constraints, trust [17], resource requirements, and customers' strong focus on economic benefits [18]. However, studies that specifically examine the barriers to servitization from a sustainability perspective are lacking in the literature [8], and these challenges need to be further detailed and investigated directly from the voice of manufacturing firms to understand their interconnection and how to address them.

3 Methodology

This research employed an exploratory multiple case study [19] to ensure covering multiple aspects that could enhance (or hinder) the potential of servitized business models in sustainable value creation and therefore increasing the generalizability of the results.

The study adopted a qualitative approach for data collection and analysis through the use of Gioia method [20]. Gioia method is suitable for inductive, qualitative-interpretivist research [20]. It gave the authors the possibility of properly building a good data structure showing how the informant-based (1st-order) codes relate to researcher-based (2nd-order) themes and dimensions. NVivo software was employed to assist with the coding of interview transcripts and Excel was used for mapping the codes, themes, and aggregate dimensions in line with the Gioia methodology.

Semi-structured interviews were conducted with 9 manufacturing companies between May 2025 and July 2025. The sample was selected because it represented manufacturing companies with a strong commitment to services and a servitization culture thanks to their belonging to the research center on innovation and service management in industrial firms (ASAP) interuniversity center that involved the authors of this work. Therefore, these companies were accessible to the authors. Participants were selected using a purposive sampling approach based on their direct involvement in service strategy, service operations, digital transformation, business development, and sustainability-related activities: senior manager, service business development managers and service operations managers, service sales managers, and sustainability managers. This multi-role perspective contributed to understanding different viewpoints, enhancing thematic analysis, as well as the comprehensiveness and reliability of the analysis. The following Fig. 1 shows the adopted methodology and Table 1 gives a summary of the interviews.

The authors were able to map the business offers of all the companies and classify them into the Tukker (2004) PSS categorization (see Table 1). Most of the firms have a predominant product-oriented business, they provide a wide range of services to their customers in addition to product sales. Only two companies (A and D) have use-oriented models, i.e., rentals, as predominant business models, while result-oriented models are only proposed in sporadic forms (I). This is however in line with the current landscape, where the adoption of use-oriented and result-oriented solutions appears to be less frequent than more traditional product-oriented PSS [21]. Deeply investigating the service offers, recurrent are repairs and maintenance programs, after-sale assistance, training and consultancy services, and remote monitoring. However, consultancy of energy saving is offered as intentionally sustainable service by Company C, and refurbishment and second life by Companies A, B, F, and G.

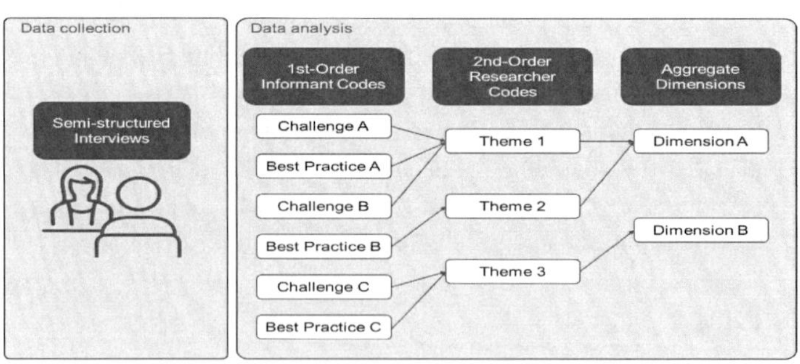

Fig. 1. Data collection and data analysis methods.

Table 1. Data collection and summary case information.

Company	Industrial Sector	PSS model	Interviewed roles	Duration
A	Machinery & Material Handling	Use-oriented	Operations Director, Sustainability Manager	1 h 14 min
B	Energy Management & Electronics	Product-oriented	IoT Program Marketing Manager, Service Marketing & Business Development	53 min
C	Heating, Ventilation, Air Conditioning, and Refrigeration (HVAC/R)	Product-oriented	Service Market Analyst	33 min
D	Office Automation & IT Services	Use-oriented	Head of Service Planning, PMO & HSEQ (Health, Safety, Environmental and Quality)	1 h 01 min
E	Textile Machinery	Product-oriented	Chief Sales	52 min
F	Foodservice Equipment	Product-oriented	Servitization Manager	39 min
G	Machine Tools	Product-oriented	Service & Sales Innovation Manager	37 min
H	Electrical Engineering & Home Automation	Product-oriented	Global service and after sales manager, Digital business innovation partner	45 min
I	Renewable Energy & Clean Technologies	Product-oriented	General Manager Business Unit Service & Aftersales	51 min

4 Results

The application of the previously described methodology resulted in the identification of 92 informant-based (1st-order) codes, 20 research-based (2nd-order) codes, and 6 aggregate dimensions. For example, the challenge 'lack of service-specific sustainability metrics' (I52: 'We measure the sustainability impacts of our service offerings') clusters within 'Environmental data measurement and impact assessment for service business development', ultimately contributing to the 'Data, digitalization and measurement' dimension'. Different challenges and best practices resulted from the interviewer responses. It is important to state for clarity of purposes, that both challenges and best practices resulted from the analysis are not exclusively related to services, but often reflect broader sustainability issues that extend beyond the service domain. Moreover, the best practices do not always directly address the challenges highlighted. Instead, they often represent partial or emerging responses to broader sustainability issues (e.g., electrification initiatives or the adoption of renewable energy sources, sustainability reports redaction). However, they have been reported for highlighting the complexity of this topic. The following Table 2 gives a summary of the results, organized based on the first-order concepts, second-order themes, and aggregate dimensions in line with the Gioia data structure.

Table 2. Overview on aggregate dimensions, themes derived from research-based (2nd-order) codes, best practices (●) and challenges (○) for each of the interviewed companies

Best practices and challenges from informant-based (1st-order) codes									Research-based (2nd-order) codes	Aggr. Dim.
A	B	C	D	E	F	G	H	I		
●									Lifecycle and resources efficiency operations	Sustainable strategy and vision
●			●					●	Technology and digitalization as sustainability enabler	
●					●				Sustainability operational targets and initiatives	
	●○	●			○		●	●	Strategic integration of sustainability in the business model (also considering services)	
			○				○		Economic viability of sustainability	
●			●						Cross-functional collaboration for sustainability	Resources and organizational structure
	○		○	○					Specialized sustainability and service competences	
	○							●	Economic resources enabling service and sustainability development	
●		●	○			●	●	●	Product usage monitoring through digital technologies	Data, digitalization and measurement

(*continued*)

Table 2. (*continued*)

Best practices and challenges from informant-based (1st-order) codes									Research-based (2nd-order) codes	Aggr. Dim.
A	B	C	D	E	F	G	H	I		
	●	●				●		●	Data-driven maintenance and performance optimization	
●								●	Digital optimization of service operations	
●○	○	○	○			○	○		Environmental data measurement and impact assessment for service business development	
		●	○	○	○	○			Sensitivity and maturity of the external context	Awareness
			○		○		○	●	Cognitive and cultural mindset	
			●	○				●	Sustainability as a source of corporate value and positioning	Value capture and communication
	●		●						Economic interpretation of sustainability value	
	○		○	○	○		○		Communication of sustainability benefits of services	
	○	●							Usage behavior and operational adoption	Customer engagement
	○	○		○	○	○			Sustainability interest mediated by economic rationales	
	●					○		●	Motivation for engagement (proactive or reactive)	

4.1 Sustainable Strategy and Vision

The thematic analysis of the interviews' transcripts highlights how sustainability is increasingly embedded within firms' strategic vision, although its integration across organizational functions and service business activities remains uneven.

Sustainability is interpreted as the ability to reduce resource consumption across the entire lifecycle of products and services. This perspective is reflected in best practices aimed at *producing only what is necessary* and *optimizing the use of resources during service operations* (A). For instance, Company A highlights that providing technicians only with the spare parts strictly required for an intervention contributes to reducing waste and unnecessary logistics.

The findings show that technology and digitalization are widely perceived as key strategic enablers of sustainability (A, D, and I). Several firms, as best practice, report a deliberate *strategic effort to leverage digital technologies not only to improve productivity but also to reduce environmental impact* (A). Examples include the adoption of digital tools that increase product efficiency, reduce intervention times, and enable better monitoring of system performance (I). In addition, companies are pursuing technological transitions, such as *electrification initiatives or the adoption of renewable energy sources*, that are framed as strategic pathways toward reducing emissions and improving environmental performance (A).

Third, firms report the presence of specific sustainability operational targets and initiatives at company level, which translate the strategic vision into concrete actions. These best practices aim at *reducing the emissions generated by service fleets, selecting environmentally friendly chemicals and materials used in service activities* (A), and implementing renewable energy solutions such as the *installation of photovoltaic panels* (F). They demonstrate that sustainability is not only a conceptual objective but can be operationalized through measurable environmental goals. In addition, these *sustainability initiatives can strengthen employer attractiveness* by appealing to employees who value environmental responsibility (I).

The findings also show that sustainability can become strategically integrated within the broader business model. In some organizations, sustainability is not perceived as a separate objective but rather as an *outcome of delivering efficient and high-performing solutions to customers* (H). In these cases, sustainability becomes embedded within the firm's broader strategic identity, where business success and environmental responsibility are perceived as mutually reinforcing rather than conflicting objectives (B, H, and I). However, only maintenance is perceived as strategy leveraging the sustainability of the businesses, i.e., *maintaining high equipment performance through preventive maintenance is seen as a way to reduce energy consumption and emissions* (C and I). Best practices such as *remanufacturing* or reduction of the use of primary resource are also considered in this term. On the other hand, challenges still remain when considering the service business. For instance, sustainability efforts *remain limited without being fully integrated into broader service strategies* (F).

A clear challenge inside this dimension concerns the economic viability of sustainability initiatives. *Sustainability initiatives must also be economically sustainable*, otherwise they are unlikely to be adopted or maintained over time (D). This highlights the importance of aligning environmental objectives with business performance and financial feasibility.

4.2 Resources and Organizational Structure

Organizational resources and structures are important in enabling the integration of sustainability within businesses and, in particular, service activities.

Some companies highlight the role of cross-functional collaboration for sustainability. Sustainability initiatives often require the involvement of multiple departments and the coordination of different competences within the organization. Regarding best practices, in Company A they have established *cross-functional teams that work on sustainability-related activities such as environmental management and energy efficiency*. In other cases, like Company D, these *cross-functional teams have been created voluntary thanks to the interest of employees* in working on themes such as climate, sustainability, and social responsibility. Specialized sustainability and service competences is another recurrent theme, mostly associated with challenges. Several companies emphasize the *need for specialized sustainability and service competences* (B, D and E), *for transferring to the customer the sustainability implications of the service offerings* (D and E) or even building new specific services, such as *consultancy in optimizing the use of their machines while considering sustainability aspects* (B). Integrating sustainability into service offerings requires specific expertise that is not always available within existing organizational structures. Lastly, the findings also point to the importance of economic resources enabling service and sustainability development. The implementation of digital solutions and advanced service models often requires significant investments, which can represent a challenge for organizations (B and I). While digital technologies are recognized as a key enabler of both servitization and sustainability, their adoption may face internal resistance due to associated costs. However, best practice in this direction could be the presence of *investment funds that consider service offerings as a form of asset protection that can facilitate the development of service activities and strengthen their strategic role* (I).

4.3 Data, Digitalization and Measurement

The thematic analysis also highlights the critical role of digital technologies, data collection, and measurement of environmental impacts in enabling sustainability within service. Firms increasingly rely on digital tools to monitor product usage, measure environmental impacts, and optimize service operations. However, the adoption and implementation of these technologies also present several challenges, particularly in terms of data availability and system integration.

Digital technologies enable product usage monitoring, providing companies with detailed information on how products are used and behave in real operating conditions. Regarding best practices, through connected devices, monitoring platforms, and cloud-based portals, firms can collect and analyze large volumes of operational data. These tools *allow both companies and customers to access information about product usage, operating hours, and system performance* (A, C, H). However, these solutions often *require connected products and integrated digital infrastructures*, which can represent a challenge in certain contexts (D).

Another recurrent theme is identified in the fact that data collected from the products and components are often used for data-driven maintenance and performance optimization (B, C, G, I). Best practices highlight that by leveraging digital data and analytical tools (e.g., Artificial Intelligence), companies are increasingly *shifting from traditional time-based maintenance approaches toward condition-based maintenance strategies* (B). And this strongly relates to sustainability benefits: through sensors, counters, and data analytics, firms can monitor component conditions and *replace parts only when necessary*, reducing both unnecessary resource consumption, material waste and operational costs (B). Remote diagnostics and predictive maintenance solutions also allow companies to *improve product performance while reducing the need for on-site interventions*, therefore reducing emissions (C).

Digital technologies are also used to support the digital optimization of service operations (A and I). Best practices are associated with several companies using *geolocation systems, route optimization tools, and internal digital platforms to improve the efficiency of service activities*. These tools help optimize technicians' routes, reduce travel distances, and minimize fuel consumption and emissions associated with service operations. In some cases, *internally developed digital tools allow companies to calculate travel distances and convert them into* CO_2 *equivalents*, enabling both internal monitoring and communication of environmental impacts to customers.

The above theme strongly influences another recurrent theme: environmental data measurement and impact assessment. Even though some companies quantify environmental data thanks to the above mentioned best practices, mainly CO_2 emissions and energy consumption, the impacts are mainly used to manage the companies' own environmental footprint (that includes the one of the service fleets) rather than to demonstrate the sustainability of their business models, including their services. Therefore, in this they found challenges. As for best practices at company level, they mentioned conducting a Life Cycle Assessment (LCA) of their products (A, B, C, D, G, H), placing *greater emphasis on the product itself than on the services provided throughout the product lifecycle*. While at service business unit, only the *energy consumption monitored through digital services become source of business development*, i.e., the shared contracts based on energy saving (C).

4.4 Awareness (Internal and External)

The main obstacles to integrating servitization and sustainability do not lie exclusively in available technologies, organizational resources and structures, but also in the level of awareness of sustainability. Thanks to the analysis' results, the awareness of sustainability can be divided into two dimensions: sensitivity and maturity of the external context and internal cognitive-cultural mindset.

From the external perspective, it is clear that sustainability is becoming increasingly important to customers (C, D). Respondents emphasize that *interest is growing* and that sustainability is becoming an increasingly relevant criterion in the evaluation of suppliers, particularly through *greater attention to the entire supply chain* (C). However, this interest is not equally distributed. Challenges arise when the interest in sustainability is mediated by the company size. In fact, *large customers are significantly more sensitive to the issue*, often because they *are bound by certifications, internal policies, or structured organizational requirements* (D). In contrast, *small and medium-sized enterprises show very limited or no interest*, especially when sustainability is not perceived as a direct economic lever (G). Geography also emerges as a critical factor: sensitivity to the issue varies significantly between countries, with marked differences between European and American markets (F). Furthermore, although the company perceives itself as ready for more advanced business models (e.g., use and result-oriented services), *the market does not yet appear mature enough to fully embrace them* (G).

A second theme emerges: internal awareness. Several respondents as main challenge report *low awareness of sustainability issues, particularly within the sales force* (D, F, and H). Salespeople do not have concrete data, metrics, or adequate argumentative tools to support a sustainability-oriented value proposition (F). In Company H sustainability is perceived as a rhetorical lever ("*I talk about it, but there is little substance behind it*"), particularly when it comes to digital services, which run the risk of being presented as sustainable more for narrative purposes than for actual content. However, alongside these critical issues, there is also a best practice: a *growing internal awareness among workers of green issues*, which could form a favorable cultural basis for future strategic developments (I).

4.5 Value Capture and Communication

The ability to effectively articulate and communicate the sustainable value of their business remains uneven across organizations. The analysis reveals different ways through which companies interpret, communicate, and leverage sustainability within their value propositions.

An emergent theme is related to the leverage of sustainability as a source of corporate value and positioning. Best practices sees sustainability becoming an important element of corporate communication and reputation (D, I). For instance, *some firms have implemented digital tools that display environmental indicators*, such as emissions reductions or equivalent environmental benefits, to raise awareness among customers and users (D). Similarly, *sustainability reporting is increasingly perceived as a strategic communication tool that strengthens the company's positioning and legitimacy in the market* (I). These best practices suggest that sustainability can become a relevant component of corporate identity and external communication, contributing to the overall value proposition offered by the firm. At the same time, the analysis highlights challenges creating a limited valorization of sustainability benefits in several organizations. In some cases, firms *focus mainly on regulatory compliance rather than actively leveraging sustainability initiatives as a source of competitive advantage* (E). Although certain activities, such as improving the durability of consumable parts, can generate environmental benefits, these *initiatives are not always managed in a structured way nor communicated effectively to stakeholders* (E). As a result, the potential value associated with these sustainability efforts often remains underexploited.

Another theme emerges from the fact that several firms frame sustainability primarily through an economic interpretation of sustainability value. In these cases, sustainability is understood and communicated mainly in terms of economic benefits, such as cost efficiency, durability, and improved return on investment. For example, some companies emphasize the *growing relevance of total cost of ownership considerations during the purchasing phase* (B), highlighting how the combination of products and services can generate economic benefits over time. Similarly, *product durability is often interpreted by customers not primarily as an environmental benefit but as an economic advantage* (B), since longer product lifetimes translate into better investment returns. These best practices suggest that economic arguments often represent the most effective way to make sustainability relevant for customers.

Another key theme concerns the communication of sustainability value, representing a Challenge, particularly due to the intangible nature of both services and sustainability outcomes. Several respondents report *difficulties in transferring the value of services during the sales process*, especially when sustainability benefits are not immediately visible or quantifiable. In these cases, the *lack of clear communication and tangible indicators* makes it difficult for customers to fully recognize the environmental and economic benefits associated with service offerings (B, D, F, H). This communication gap can limit the ability of firms to effectively differentiate their value propositions based on sustainability, also in well-established servitized models, like rental models (D).

4.6 Customer Engagement

The thematic analysis highlights how customer engagement is one of the main critical areas. It is neither automatic nor linear but emerges as a phenomenon that is influenced by three main dimensions.

The first emergent theme is product usage behavior. In this sense, best practice involves directly the service business. For instance, offering *consulting services emerges as a best practice, as they reduce uncertainty in product usage, support operational adoption* (C), and *favor energy efficiency*. However, challenges are associated with the *diversity of the customers' context and needs and the risks associated to this diversity* (B).

The second recurring theme is the centrality of economic rationality in decision-making (B, C, E, F, G), which creates structural challenges. *Sustainability is only relevant to the customer when there is a direct economic return that can be demonstrated*, for instance, a reduction in costs or investment. In several cases, even environmentally virtuous practices (such as the complete refurbishment of a machine) are evaluated exclusively in terms of economic savings, without the environmental dimension representing an independent motivation (G). Interest in sustainability therefore appears to be almost systematically mediated by economic considerations. Even when interest is declared to be high, it remains subordinate to the costs necessary to achieve it. Furthermore, the very possibility of "being sustainable" is perceived as a function of available resources: large customers can afford it, while others cannot (E). This introduces a structural dimension of inequality into engagement.

The third theme concerns the nature of motivation for engagement. In many cases, *interest in sustainable initiatives is reactive: regulatory obligations, legal constraints, external pressures* (G, I). Sustainability therefore does not arise from an intrinsic value-driven impulse, but from compliance requirements, representing a Challenge. However, there are also signs of more proactive engagement, even if still sporadic: when *customers access financing or incentives linked to sustainability objectives* (e.g., decarbonization projects), sustainability becomes a key issue and actively guides choices (I), creating best practice. In these cases, the engagement mechanism is activated by a combination of economic incentive and environmental objective, creating a hybrid form of motivation that, however, still is mediated by economic consideration rather than a real commitment to sustainability practices.

5 Discussion

This study addresses the research question of the extent to which the implementation of servitized business models in manufacturing companies leads to the creation of sustainable value, and which dimensions influence this relationship. The findings suggest that, although servitized business models are theoretically positioned as enablers of sustainability, the actual sustainable value creation is influenced by multiple interrelated dimensions. Specifically, sustainable value creation is shaped by the incorporation of sustainability within their strategic vision, the resource and organization, digitalization and data management, the awareness on sustainability, the value capture and its communication to the external, and the customers engagement. These dimensions together determine whether servitization can effectively translate into sustainability outcomes or remain primarily economically driven. Moreover, firms identify challenges that often reflect broader sustainability issues extending beyond the service domain. This highlights a limited understanding, in practice, of the connection between servitization and sustainability. This section aims to synthesize the evidence in order to better understand the challenges specifically related to the service domain.

Challenges may remain in aligning sustainability with service activities, ensuring economic viability, and fully leveraging service-based business models as strategic drivers of sustainability. Additionally, firms can struggle to develop appropriate organizational structures, specific sustainable competences, and financial resource allocation mechanisms to effectively support the transition toward more sustainable servitized models. While digitalization and data management play a key enabling role in supporting sustainability within service activities, as widely suggested by existing literature [16], companies still face challenges related to data integration, system connectivity, and effective measurement of environmental impacts. This suggests that the full potential of digital technologies for the definition of a sustainable value proposition for servitized models remains underdeveloped. Both the presence of sustainability experts and environmental data measurement could significantly enhance internal and external awareness. However, awareness does not automatically translate into sustainability valorization. Indeed, environmental valorization is mainly related to the development of sustainability reports—which may strengthen a company's image—rather than the value proposition of its offerings. Significant challenges persist in terms of effectively articulating, measuring, and communicating this value to customers and other stakeholders. Furthermore, when valorizing service offers, the economic dimension tends to prevail. This aligns with customer interest in sustainability, which is often mediated by economic rationales, thereby hindering the potential of servitization in creating genuine sustainable value. The results, specifically the recurrent economic and financial challenges across various areas (e.g., sustainable strategy and vision, resources and organizational structure, value capture and communication, and customer engagement) are closely aligned with existing literature [8, 18]. Similarly, the cultural barriers as seen in the awareness area, and customer-related challenges, mainly detailed in customer engagement area, are aligned with previous studies [8, 17]. Therefore, confirming the importance of these aspects.

However, this panorama is not equally present in all interviewed companies, therefore delineating a wide range of possible tensions. It is possible to learn about best practices like: (i) strengthening lifecycle performance of the products in the mission and strategic vision of the company; (ii) strengthening digitalization in the mission and strategic vision of the company, increasing both internal awareness and customers one; (iii) adopting data, digitalization, and measurement as the main orchestrator for enhancing economic interpretation of environmental value; and (iv) adopting a proactive approach in engaging customers not only at the moment of the sale but also in the use and operational phase of the product.

Finally, the results do not delineate a "best-case scenario". Although the sample includes companies offering use-oriented PSSs, that are theoretically seen as best cases for sustainability value creation, significant challenges that fully hinder their potential for sustainability remain. For instance, companies A and D are unable to fully leverage their rental models as strategic means to achieve sustainability due to a lack of clear environmental impacts of the business models. This further reinforces the critical enabling power of data, digitalization, and measurement and the need to further explore this aspect at empirical level.

6 Conclusion

The qualitative analysis identified 6 macro-themes that influence the adoption of servitization as a lever for environmental sustainability: (i) sustainable strategy and vision, (ii) resources and organizational structure, (iii) data, digitalization, and measurement (iv) value capture and communication, (v) awareness, and (vi) customer engagement. These dimensions represent an integrated system of barriers and drivers that act together throughout the transition process towards sustainable servitized models. The empirical findings confirm several challenges previously identified in the literature, particularly those related to financial constraints, cultural barriers, and customer-related challenges. In addition, the findings extend and operationalize the existing dimensions highlight the critical role of digital data infrastructures for monitoring product usage and measuring environmental impacts. Limitation of the study relies on the literature analysis on the challenges that is not done systematically. While this allowed for understanding the phenomena and delineating the interviews, future research could benefit from a Systematic Literature Review to integrate the fragmented body of knowledge on sustainable servitization and provide a more exhaustive and replicable mapping of the field. Another limitation is related to the sample under analysis; the majority of participating firms do not yet exhibit advanced PSS models, with ownership loss (except two firms). As a result, the analysis lacks additional significant challenges and best practices. This would allow for a deeper exploration in following studies. Finally, although some differences emerged among companies, the exploratory nature of the study and the limited sample size do not allow robust conclusions on industry-specific patterns. Future research could investigate how sectoral characteristics influence sustainable servitization challenges and enabling mechanisms.

Acknowledgments. This research is inspired by the research center on innovation and service management in industrial firms (ASAP) (www.asapsmf.org).

Disclosure of Interests. The authors have no competing interests to declare.

References

1. Tukker, A.: Eight types of product-service system: eight ways to sustainability? experiences from suspronet. Bus. Strategy Environ. **13**, 246–260 (2004)
2. Vezzoli, C., Ceschin, F., Diehl, J.C., Kohtala, C.: New design challenges to widely implement sustainable product–service systems. J. Clean. Prod. **97**, 1–12 (2015)
3. Annarelli, A., Battistella, C., Nonino, F.: Product service system: a conceptual framework from a systematic review. J. Clean. Prod. **139**, 1011–1032 (2016)
4. Reim, W., Lenka, S., Frishammar, J., Parida, V.: Implementing sustainable product-service systems utilizing business model activities. In: Procedia CIRP, pp. 61–66 (2017)
5. Vezzoli, C., Ceschin, F., Diehl, J.C., Kohtala, C.: Why have "sustainable product-service systems" not been widely implemented? Meeting new design challenges to achieve societal sustainability. J. Clean. Prod. **35**, 288–290 (2012)
6. Blüher, T., Riedelsheimer, T., Gogineni, S., Klemichen, A., Stark, R.: Systematic literature review—effects of PSS on sustainability based on use case assessments. Sustainability. **12**, 6989 (2020)
7. Roman, P., Thiry, G., Muylaert, C., Ruwet, C., Maréchal, K.: Defining and identifying strongly sustainable product-service systems (SSPSS). J. Clean. Prod. **391**, 136295 (2023)
8. Ozturkoglu, Y., Ozturkoglu, O., Danisman, E.: New business model proposal in the digital age: sustainability-focused servitization. J. Enterp. Inf. Manag. **38**, 1776–1802 (2025)
9. Saccani, N., Adrodegari, F., Scalvini, L.: Aligning product-service systems with environmental sustainability: investigating the key role of revenue and pricing mechanisms. Resour. Conserv. Recycl. **209**, 107792 (2024)
10. Vandermerwe, S., Erixon, D.: Servitization of business updated: now, new, next. Eur. Manag. J. **41**, 479–487 (2023)
11. Bocken, N., Strupeit, L., Whalen, K., Nußholz, J.: A review and evaluation of circular business model innovation tools. Sustain. Switz. **11** (2019)
12. Baines, T.S., Lightfoot, H.W., Kay, J.M.: Servitized manufacture: practical challenges of delivering integrated products and services. Proc. Inst. Mech. Eng. Part B-J. Eng. Manuf. **223**, 1207–1215 (2009)
13. Tukker, A.: Product services for a resource-efficient and circular economy - a review. J. Clean. Prod. **97**, 76–91 (2015)
14. Guzzo, D., Pigosso, D.C.A.: Identifying rebound effects in product-service systems: actors, mechanisms, triggers and drivers. Proc. Des. Soc. **4**, 1279–1288 (2024)
15. Frank, A., Mendes, G., Ayala, N., Ghezzi, A.: Servitization and industry 4.0 convergence in the digital transformation of product firms: a business model innovation perspective. Technol. Forecast. Soc. Change. **141**, 341–351 (2019)
16. Beducci, E., Acerbi, F., De Carolis, A., Taisch, M.: Exploring the role of digital servitization for sustainability: a framework for environmental and social impact. Clean. Environ. Syst. **17**, 100269 (2025)

17. Dethier, F. et al.: A cross-sector analysis of consumer intention towards sustainable product-service systems: evidence from mobility, clothing and tooling. J. Clean. Prod. **486**, 144369 (2025)
18. Benedettini, O., Adrodegari, F.: Moving to sustainable servitization: categorisation and analysis of underlying approaches. J. Clean. Prod. **545**, 147716 (2026)
19. Yin, R.K.: Applications of Case Study Research. SAGE Publications, Washington DC (2012)
20. Magnani, G., Gioia, D.: Using the Gioia methodology in international business and entrepreneurship research. Int. Bus. Rev. **32**, 102097 (2023)
21. Pezzotta, G., et al.: The Digital Servitization of Manufacturing Sector: Evidence from a Worldwide Digital Servitization Survey. (2023)

Decision-Making Within a Leasing Business Model: Enabling Refurbishment of Products at the End-of-Lease Under Stochastics Condition

Sepideh Kordestani(✉), Jenny Bäckstrand, and Vanajah Siva

Department of Supply Chain and Operations Management, School of Engineering, Jönköping University, Jönköping, Sweden
Sepideh.Kordestani@ju.se

Abstract. Leasing is one approach towards a circular business strategy to enable the transition to CE. At the end of a lease, products are either purchased by the customer or returned to an OEM to be refurbished and resold to a new customer. Leasing contracts outline the rights, conditions, and responsibilities of both the customers and the OEM, including return or purchase conditions and penalties. However, defining these terms poses a challenge to OEMs especially under stochastic conditions. These challenges arise because the customers' decisions influence the decision of an OEM and vice versa. Furthermore, different decision paths lead the OEM to adopt different refurbishment strategies. To enhance circularity, the life cycle of returned products can be extended through R-strategies such as refurbishment.

This study develops a stochastic Stackelberg game-theoretic model in which an OEM acts as the leader and customers as followers. The game evaluates the interplay between initial pricing, leasing revenue, customer segmentation, and residual value. The findings demonstrate that customers' decisions to return products are driven by the OEM's upfront pricing decisions. Additionally, the study identifies a parabolic relationship between leasing revenue and NPV. Finally, results reveal that the optimal refurbishment strategy is dynamic: in-house operations are economically justified for high-value products that can amortize fixed costs. These insights provide actionable guidelines to balance secondary market supply, ensuring the long-term profitability of leasing and refurbishment in support of circularity.

Keywords: Product as Service · Refurbishment · Optimization · Game Theory

1 Introduction

The traditional supply chain with a linear pattern of take-make-use-dispose leads to Earth's dramatic resource depletion and waste generation [1]. Circular economy (CE) is gaining increasing attention as an alternative to this linear pattern to maintain prosperity while reducing dependence on primary materials and energy [2]. In practice, CE is operationalized through a wide range of strategies and business models, including but not

Published by Springer Nature Switzerland AG 2027
G. Pezzotta et al. (Eds.): APMS 2026, IFIP AICT 808, pp. 509–524, 2027.
https://doi.org/10.1007/978-3-032-38594-9_34

limited to R-strategies and circular business models. R-strategies encompass practices such as refuse, reduce, reuse, repair, refurbishment, remanufacturing, recycling, and energy recovery [3].

Circular business models represent the rationale of how an organization creates, delivers, and captures value by slowing, closing, or narrowing resource loops [4]. Retaining ownership of a product through the circular business model of leasing is a common circular business model [5–7], which is an effective way to facilitate retaining the product's maximum possible value [8]. Leasing arrangements are governed by contracts that establish key parameters, such as the lease price, minimum acceptable quality standards, and the end-of-lease purchase price. These parameters directly affect the customer's decision to either purchase or return the product. Such decisions commonly involve strategic interactions between the provider and the customer, where the use of game theory for analysis is deemed appropriate [9]. Game theory is applied in competitive or cooperative scenarios, such as business pricing and negotiations, to predict behavior and determine the optimal strategy when one participant's outcome depends on the actions of another [9, 10].

When products are returned at the end of a lease, their condition is often restored through "R-strategies," which is refurbishment, in this study, to be resold to new customers. This study is motivated by a real-world case of an original equipment manufacturer (OEM) faced with challenges in developing a leasing model for its robotic lawnmowers; however, the model is generalized for broader applications by analyzing a wider range of parameters.

Beyond the lease contract itself, the OEM must also determine its optimal refurbishment strategy. An OEM can adopt either an in-house or an outsourced approach. Under the in-house refurbishment strategy, products are refurbished by the OEM that initiated the lease. Under the outsourced refurbishment strategy, the refurbishment is handled by a third party [11, 12]. Existing studies largely treat product returns as exogenous or deterministic outcomes, offering limited insight into how OEMs' leasing contract design endogenously shapes customer return behavior and refurbishment decisions under stochastic conditions.

The purpose of this study is to investigate how an OEM's decision in leasing business strategy in terms of leasing contract influences the customer's end-of-lease decision (i.e., whether to return or purchase the product) and customers' decision influence OEM refurbishment strategy. Specifically, this study explores how factors such as initial new product price, return volume, customer heterogeneity, leasing revenue ratios, and minimum quality thresholds collectively impact the strategic decisions of both the OEM and the customer.

The remainder of the paper is structured as follows: the next section provides an overview of the theoretical background, followed by the model definition, which details the parameters, variables, and underlying assumptions. The paper then presents the analysis and discussion using game theory model, followed by presentation of theoretical and practical implications and suggestions for future research.

2 Theoretical Background

Circular business models are claimed to be one of the main enabling factors for the transition to a CE [13], which aligns economic and ecological goals by reducing waste and conserving resources [6]. To develop a circular business models OEMs usually adopt one of the three circular strategies of retaining product ownership, product life extension [14, 15].

Retaining product ownership refers to a business strategy in which products are no longer sold outright; instead, services are sold to end customers for example through leasing [13, 16].

Product life extension focuses on designing products to last longer to preserve value, enable reuse or secondary markets, strengthen customer loyalty, and create competitive advantage through durability and premium positioning [14].

Design for end-of-life management involves deliberately designing products and manufacturing processes to maximize product, component or material recoverability at the end of life, enabling recovered product, component or material to be reused in new products through efficient R-strategy and collaboration with specialized partners [14, 15]. The 10R-strategy framework, distinguishes short loops (R0 Refuse, R1 Reduce, R2 Resell/reuse), middle-length loops (R3 Repair, R4 Refurbishment, R5 Remanufacture, R6 Repurpose), and long loops (R7 Recycle materials, R8 Recover energy, R9 Remine) [3, 6].

. The circular business strategy in this study is a synthesis of different circular business strategies, retaining product ownership through a leasing business model and enhancing product life extension via refurbishment (R4). Refurbishment involves the process of restoring used products to a condition that is close to new, but not necessarily to their original specifications [17]. Extending the product life cycle through refurbishment produces substantial benefits, such as mitigating carbon emissions, conserving natural resources, diverting materials from waste streams, and creating skilled job opportunities in local economies [18]. Furthermore, the leasing business model offers OEMs comprehensive insights into the condition of their products, deterring informal sectors and illegal markets from participating in reverse logistics and R-strategies [13, 19].

In the case of refurbishment of returned products, the responsible actor shall be decided. While the OEM acts as the focal actor, three strategies may be applied [11, 12] (Abbey et al., 2024; Meade & Sarkis, 2002), namely:

- Vertical or in-house strategy, where an OEM facilitates refurbishment internally.
- Hybrid or outsourcing strategy, where an OEM collaborates with one or several partners to facilitate refurbishment.
- Market-led governance, where external actors independently facilitate refurbishment.

Atasu, Guide Jr. and Van Wassenhove [20], Guide Jr. and Van Wassenhove [21], and Govindan, Soleimani and Kannan [22], examine market-led refurbishment, in which the OEM concentrates on new product production while independent third parties undertake refurbishment, and consistently report this structure as detrimental to OEMs leading to creating direct competition against the OEM's own products,, loss of market share, brand damage and loss of control over OEM's intellectual capital. Ferguson and Toktay [23] argue that an OEM should use vertical integration or preemptive collection to deter the third-party remanufacturer and cannibalization of their products. Agrawal, Atasu and Van Ittersum [24] demonstrate that OEMs can benefit from the entry of third-party remanufacturers (TPRs) because behavioral experiments indicate that consumers are likely to pay more for a new product in the presence of third-party refurbishment.

There is no universally optimal refurbishment strategy; rather, effective decision-making requires a comprehensive assessment of multiple contextual factors and cannot rely solely on cost-based considerations [25]. Product characteristics relate to attributes such as production volume, product lifecycle, product value, weight, perishability and the level of customization and complexity can influence decision making about circular practices [11, 26, 27].

The lease contract outlines the rights, condition and responsibilities of both the customers and leasing provider during the lease term, including the leasing payments, duration of lease and penalties for both sides [28]. The term and condition in leasing contracts would affect the incentives of customers to lease the product, purchase it at the end of lease or return it back.

2.1 Game Theory

Game theory is appropriate to analyze strategic interactions where the outcome for a participant depends on the actions of others. Non-cooperative game theory models typically rely on the Nash equilibrium for simultaneous strategies, or the Stackelberg model for sequential, leader-follower interactions [29]. In a Stackelberg game, the power dynamic is defined by this sequential structure: the leader maximizes their payoff by anticipating the follower's rational reaction, while the follower subsequently determines their optimal response based on the leader's initial decision [30].

Taken together, prior research highlights the strategic importance of refurbishment governance and leasing contracts [20, 21, 24, 28]. However, it provides limited analytical guidance on how contract parameters and heterogeneous customer return behaviors dynamically interact under uncertainty, particularly when the refurbishment strategy is an endogenous OEM decision. As decisions making in our study for the OEM and the customers exhibit obvious sequential order, thereby Stackelberg game is a good constitute [29]. Hence Stackelberg game theory is appropriate to fulfill the purpose of this study.

3 Model Definition

This study is motivated by a real-world case of an OEM developing leasing business strategy for its robotic lawnmowers; however, the model is generalized for broader applications by analyzing a wider range of parameters. This study employs an analytical, game-theoretic model to explore forward-looking strategies for informing future decision-making [31]. A stochastic Stackelberg Game is developed, comprising an OEM as the Leader and a heterogeneous population of customers as the Followers. In this study, the OEM makes decisions regarding residual price, resale price and refurbishment strategy to maximize its NPV, while its decision regarding the residual price influences the customers' decision to purchase the product or return it at the end of lease rationally based on their individual economic calculations.

Sets and Indicators

- t = 1,2,...,T: Time periods in year
- $\tau \in \{3, 5\}$: Lease duration in years
- $\theta \in \{P, R\}$: customer types where P = Professional, R = Residential

Parameters

- α_θ: Population share of professional and residential users
- L_τ: Total lease revenue from a product leased for τ years
- P_n: New product price
- ${C_{in}}^\tau$: Refurbishment cost per unit (in-house)
- ${C_{out}}^\tau$: Refurbishment cost per unit (outsourced)
- F_{in}: Fixed cost of in-house refurbishment facility
- ${v_{min}}^\tau$: The minimum quality threshold for lease duration of τ (lower for longer leasing time to natural depreciation)
- $c_{transport}$: Transportation cost per unit distance
- C_{OpEx}: the annual fixed cost for in-house
- $\gamma_{{P_s}^\tau}$: Resale loss coefficient (where $0 \leq \gamma_{{P_s}^\tau} \leq 1$), dependent on the resale price

Decision Variables

- ${P_r}^{\tau,\theta}$: Residual price (price a customer pays to buy the product at the end of lease) for duration τ, customer θ $S \in \{0, 1\}$: One-time choice of refurbishment strategy (**1** for In-house, **0** for Outsourced)
- ${P_s}^\tau$: Second-hand market resale price for duration τ
- ${R_\theta}^\tau$: Number of products return from leasing duration τ by customer θ

Stochastic Elements

- $D(t)$:Number of products leased in period t (Modeled as:$D(t)$~N ($\mu_{D,t}$, $\sigma_{D,t}$)
- $q(v, \tau)$: remaining value of product at the end-of-lease, following a segment-specific distribution V ~N ($\mu_{\theta,\tau}$, $\sigma_{\theta,\tau}$)
- D_s: Realized transportation distance for returned units, where D_s~$N(\mu_{d,s}, \sigma_{d,s})$

Decision Logic and Equilibrium Solution

OEM as a 'leader' defines the leasing terms and conditions including leasing price, minimum quality threshold, and residual price. Customers as 'followers' decide to return the product at the end of lease or purchase it.

A customer of type θ will return the product only if the cost of returning (including the expected fine and the remaining value of the product) is less than the residual price ${P_r}^{\tau,\theta}$:

$$\text{Return condition}: V + f(V) < P_r^{\tau,\theta} \tag{1}$$

Where $f(V)$ is defined as below:

$$f(V) = \max\left(0, v^{\tau}_{min} - V\right) \tag{2}$$

If a customer returns the product, and the remaining value (V) is below the minimum quality threshold for each leasing duration $\left(v^{\tau}_{min}\right)$, customer must pay the difference as fine. The minimum quality threshold is defined in the contract by the OEM at the start of lease.

The fine is paid if the customer returns the product, the value of which is lower than the minimum quality threshold. There are two scenarios for return

- Case 1 ($V \geq v_{min}$): there is no fine and customer return if $V < P_r^{\tau,\theta}$
- Case 2 ($V < v_{min}$): there is fine, and customer return if $V + (v_{min} - V) < P_r^{\tau,\theta} \rightarrow v_{min} < P_r^{\tau,\theta}$

The expected fine in case 2, collected from the returned units of the customer θ:

$$E\left[f_\theta\right] = \int_0^{v_{min}{}^{\tau}} \left(v_{min}{}^{\tau} - V\right) \cdot q_\theta(v, \tau).dv \tag{3}$$

Based on the return condition, the probability of return corresponds to the cumulative distribution function (CDF) of the remaining value up to the indifference threshold Assuming $P_r^{\tau,\theta} \geq v_{min}{}^{\tau}$ this is expressed as:

$$P(R_\theta) = \int_0^{P_r^{\tau,\theta}} q_\theta(v, \tau)dv \tag{4}$$

Otherwise, if $P_r^{\tau,\theta} < v_{min}{}^{\tau}$, the return condition is never met, and the probability of return is zero.

3.1 The OEM Optimization Model (Leader)

The OEM maximizes the total expected profit over the years. However, this profit depends on the customer's behavior.

Variable Cost per Unit

The variable cost per unit is the sum of the transportation and refurbishment costs. expected cost depends on the chosen strategy S:

$$C_r(S) = S\cdot \left(C_{in}{}^{\tau} + c_{transport}\cdot \mu_{d,1}\right) + (1 - S)\left(C_{out}{}^{\tau} + c_{transport}\cdot \mu_{d,0}\right) \tag{5}$$

Expected Profit

The periodic profit for OEM incorporate revenue from current leases, buying products by customers at the end-of-lease, and the income from selling refurbishment minus variable cost per unit and operational costs:

$$E(\pi_t) = \sum\nolimits_{\mathrm{i}=0}^{\tau-1} \mu_{D,t-i} \cdot (\mathrm{L}_\tau/\tau) + \sum\nolimits_{\theta\epsilon\{P,R\}} \alpha_\theta \cdot \mu_{D,t-\tau}$$

$$\cdot \left[(1 - P(R_\theta))P_r^{\tau,\theta} + P(R_\theta)\left(\gamma_{P_s^\tau} \cdot P_s^\tau - C_r(S)\right)\right] - S \cdot C_{OpEx} \quad (6)$$

Global Objective Function

The OEM maximizes the NPV in the simiulated time period:

$$\max(NPV) = \sum_{t=1}^{T} \frac{E(\pi_t)}{(1+r)^t} - S \cdot F_{in} \quad (7)$$

3.2 Simulation Assumptions

1. The resale price ($P_s{}^\tau$) is assumed to be uniform within each age cohort (τ). This reflects the OEM's policy of standardized refurbishment, ensuring that all secondary-market products meet a determined quality regardless of their initial return condition.
2. While product quality at the end-of-lease is stochastic, the refurbishment cost ($C_{in}{}^\tau$, $C_{\text{out}}{}^\tau$) is assumed to be constant. It is assumed that the received fine from customers can cover the difference in product quality.
3. In accordance with the discussion with experts from an OEM, empirical evidence indicates that customer interest in buying refurbished products remains viable up to a resale price point of 70% of the new product price for three-year lease durations and 50% for five-year durations. Consequently, the simulation incorporates a resale loss coefficient to account for the 'lost sales portion'; as the resale price exceeds these established thresholds, the model reflects a corresponding loss in sales volume to mirror realistic market demand.
4. The parameters are defined using a modular, ratio-based framework. This approach ensures greater generalizability, allowing a model derived from a specific case study to be applied to diverse operational scenarios. On the other hand, decision variables for the residual price is defined as a coefficient y_τ of the depreciated product value (see Table 1)

Table 1. The modular definitions of parameters

Parameter	logic	
Initial price	P_n	
Leasing Revenue (L_τ)	$L_\tau = \rho_\tau \times P_n$	($\rho_\tau \leq 1$)
Residual Price	$P_{r,\,\tau} = y_\tau \times (P_n - L_\tau)$	$P_n \geq L$
Minimum quality threshold	$v_{min} = \delta_\tau \times P_n$	$\delta_\tau \leq 1$
Second-hand market resale price	$P_s{}^\tau = \beta_\tau \times P_n$	$\beta_\tau \leq 1$

3.3 Computational Methodology and Model Architecture

The proposed model was developed based on the case study, specific assumptions, and the decision logic identified in the previous sections. Figure 1 provides a conceptual overview of the model architecture. Programmed in Python, the model evaluates how various parameters influence the decision-making of both customers and the OEM. To capture long-term dynamics, the model simulates each scenario over a 20-year horizon (T = 20).

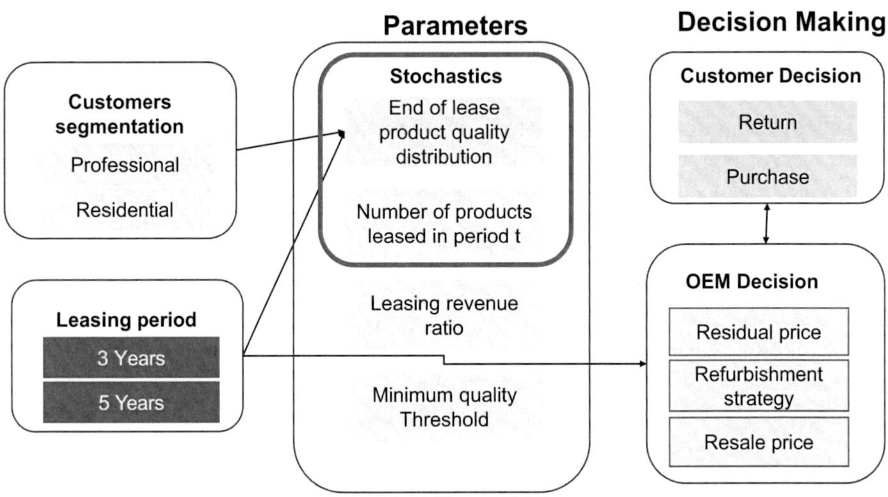

Fig. 1. Model Overview

4 Results and Discussion

The below section discusses how the change in different parameters influences the decisions variable outcomes. Parameters including Minimum quality threshold, leasing revenue ratios.

4.1 Minimum Quality Threshold Analyses

The simulation results (Fig. 2) for various minimum quality thresholds ($v_{min}{}^{\tau}$) illustrate that the optimal residual price (P_r^{τ}) remains threshold-invariant across a wide range. Specifically, the return volume remains constant at 31,794 units for $v_{min}{}^{3}$ values ranging from 6,700 to 9,750. This stability occurs because the optimal residual price ($P_r^3 = 10{,}400$ and $P_r^3 = 5200$) remains constant and sufficiently high to satisfy the return condition, effectively absorbing stricter quality requirements without deterring customers.

However, as the minimum quality threshold reaches the critical quality limit at the optimal peak ($v_{min}{}^{3} = 10{,}400$), the customers no longer return the products at the end of lease.. At this point, the cost of returning the unit eventually exceeds the residual price, making buybacks the rational choice. Across the observed $v_{min}{}^{\tau}$ ranges, the optimal strategy for refurbishment remains outsourcing. In addition, the resale prices remain constant across all scenarios $\left(P_s^3 = 10400 \text{ and } P_s^5 = 5200\right)$. The resale price-to-new-product price ratio remains within the preferred price range for customers, ensuring no loss of demand for refurbished products.

Fig. 2. The analysis of the minimum quality threshold on number of returns ($L_3 = 6500$, $L_5 = 8645$, $P_n = 13000$)

4.2 The Analysis of Leasing Revenue Ratios per Product

As illustrated in Fig. 3, varying the leasing revenue per product significantly impacts the return volume, the residual price, and ultimately, the OEM's refurbishment strategy. When the leasing revenue increases from the baseline tier (L_3=6500, L_5=8645) to (L_3=7410, L_5=9855), the total number of products returned by customers at the end of the lease initially peaks. However, beyond this point, a continuous increase in leasing revenue leads to a steady decline in return volumes (Fig. 3).

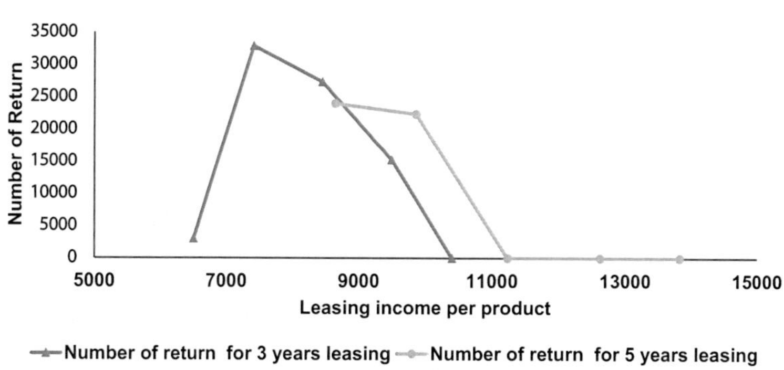

Fig. 3. The analysis of the effect of leasing revenue per period on Number of Return, (v_{min}^3, v_{min}^5) = (6700,5360), (P_n=13000)

The reason for this behavior can be attributed to optimal residual price. By increasing revenue initially residual price increases then decrease (Fig. 4). The lower residual price makes purchasing the product at the end of the term more economically attractive for the customer than returning it, which inherently increases the likelihood of customers buying products at the end-of-lease.

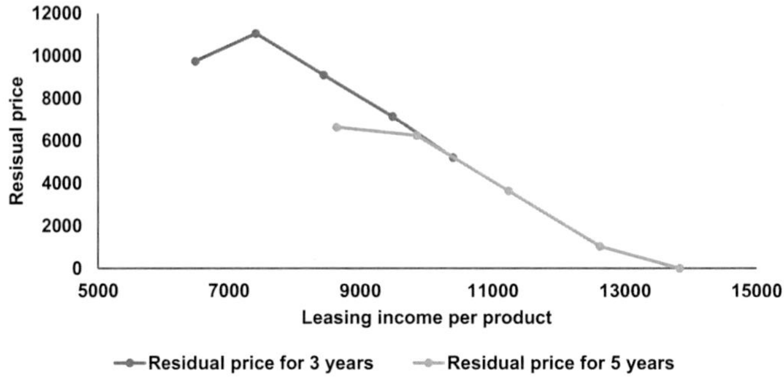

Fig. 4. The analysis of the effect of leasing revenue per period on residual price, $(v^3_{min}, v^5_{min}) =$ (6700,5360), (P_n=13000)

The shift in product returns directly dictates the economic viability of the refurbishment strategy, triggering the optimal transition from in-house (S = 1) operations to outsourced (S = 0) by decreasing the number of returns (Fig. 5).

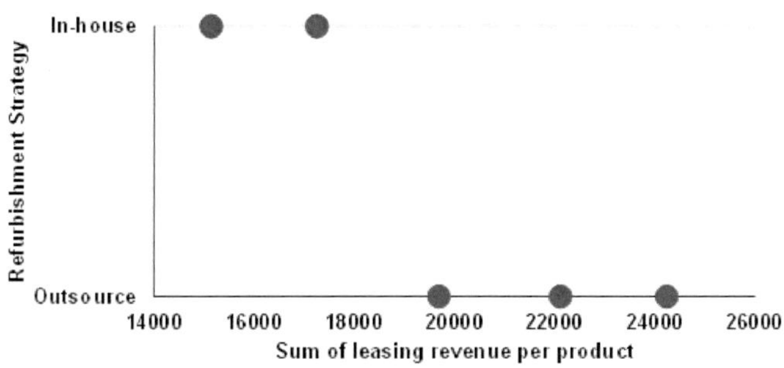

Fig. 5. Analyses of leasing revenue on refurbishment strategy

Regarding the overall NPV, the simulation reveals a distinct parabolic trend. Increasing the leasing rate per product initially raises the NPV until a specific optimal threshold is reached. Once the leasing revenue exceeds this optimum, the NPV begins to decline sharply. This downturn occurs because the combination of high leasing rates and low residual prices incentivizes customers to buy their products; consequently, the OEM experiences a shortage of returned cores and forfeits a significant portion of its revenue derived from the profitable resale of refurbished products (See Fig. 6).

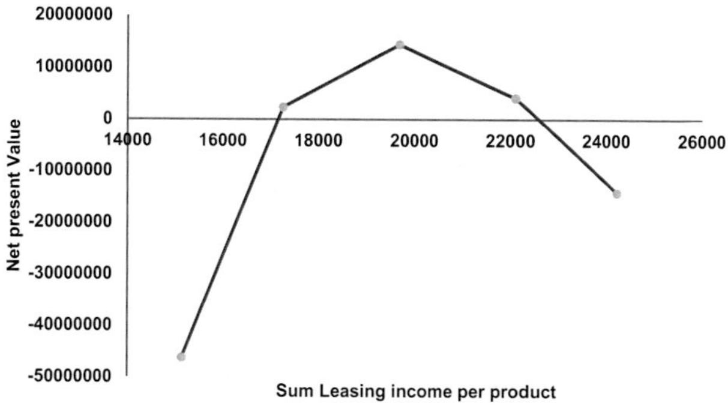

Fig. 6. Analyses of Leasing revenue on NPV and Refurbishment strategy

4.3 New Product Price Analysis

The sensitivity analysis of the initial new product price (P_n) reveals that, across all scenarios, the absolute resale values scale proportionally with the initial price. Consequently, the ratio of the resale price to the new product price remains strictly constant. Specifically, for the 3-year lease duration, this ratio is maintained at the maximum threshold that prevents a loss in resale volume (70%). For the 5-year lease duration, the ratio stabilizes just below its respective maximum threshold (at 49%).

In the proposed model, the fixed cost (F_{in}) for developing the in-house refurbishment is considered constant regardless of the asset's value. Consequently, as the initial new product price rises, the fixed cost investment required for in-house operations becomes more economically viable, justifying the transition from an outsourced model to an integrated, in-house refurbishment facility (see Fig. 3).

Furthermore, the simulation shows that return volumes remain constant regardless of the new product price. Finally, regarding the residual price: while an increase in the new product price naturally drives up the absolute monetary value of the residual price, the underlying optimization coefficient y_τ (see Table 1) remains completely stable across all scenarios.

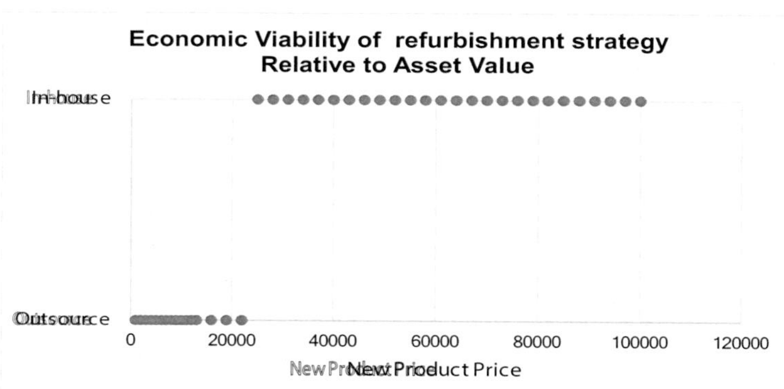

Fig. 7. The analyze of influence of new product price on refurbishment strategy

4.4 Customer Segment Proportions Analysis

In the preceding simulations, it was assumed that the proportion of customer categories for each lease duration was equally distributed at a 50/50 ratio. This section analyzes how variations in the ratio of customer segments influence return volumes, residual values, and the NPV.

The simulation results indicate that shifting the ratio of customer segments does not alter the OEM's optimal residual price. In addition, the resale price of refurbished products for all ratio of customer segments remains constant, to the maximum point that doesn't lead to resale loss. In contrast, as the ratio of Professional customers, increases, the total number of product returns for the 3-year lease duration decreases. Notably, for the 5-year lease duration, the determined minimum quality threshold parameter ($v_{min}^5 = 5,330$) is higher than the optimal value of variable of residual price for this duration 5 ($P_r{}^5 = 5200$). So, based on our model (see Eq. 4) the number of returns remains at zero across all scenarios for 5-years leasing duration.

Furthermore, the results demonstrate that an increase in the Professional customer ratio leads to a corresponding increase in the OEM's NPV (Fig. 4). The model yields a remarkably high optimal residual price for a 3-year duration ($P_r{}^3$=10,400). At this price point, it is more economically advantageous for the OEM when customers buy the products at the end of the lease, rather than returning them for refurbishment and resale (Fig. 8)

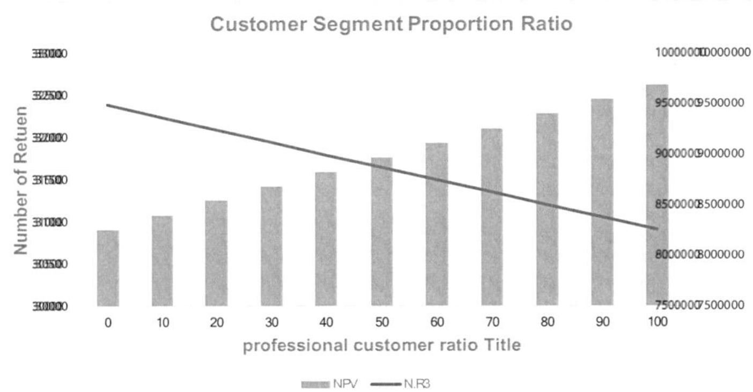

Fig. 8. Customer segment analysis and its effect on NPV and number of return

4.5 Decisions Interactions

Synthesizing the analyses from the previous sections to fulfill the study's aim, Fig. 7 illustrates how different parameters affect the decision variables. Specifically, it demonstrates that the OEM's decision regarding the residual price affects the customer's behavior (the number of returns), which subsequently shapes the refurbishment strategy (Fig. 9).

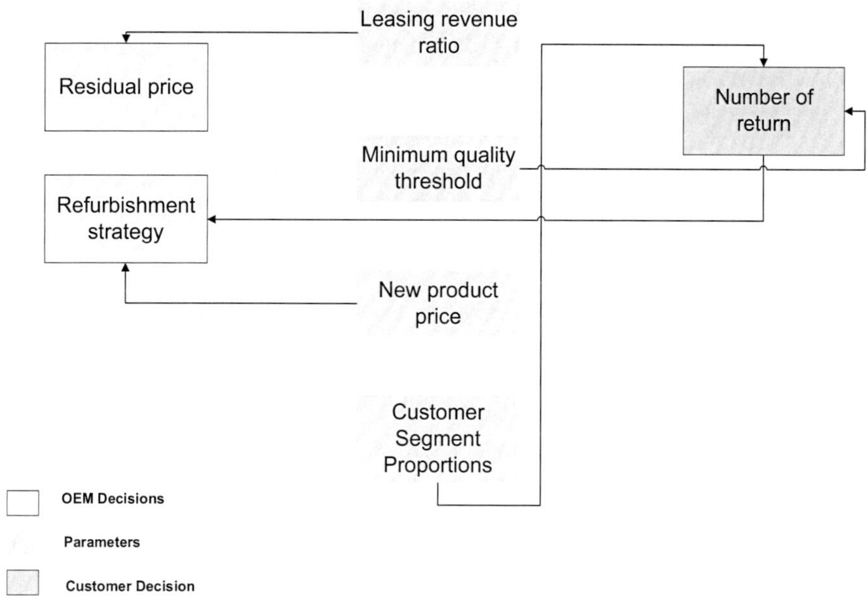

Fig. 9. Parameters and decision variables interactions

5 Discussion and Conclusion

This study investigates the strategic decision-making dynamics of an OEM to establish end-of-lease contract terms within a stochastic condition. By synthesizing leasing and refurbishment, this paper presents an analytical, game-theoretic foundation for navigating decision making in circular strategies.

Specifically, the study evaluates how an OEM's decision in determining the terms of leasing contract including initial product pricing, customer segment proportions, and minimum quality thresholds influences the customer return behaviors and subsequent OEM governance decisions. Consequently, the primary insights presented yield distinct theoretical and managerial contributions.

5.1 Theoretical Contributions

This study advances circular economy literature in three ways. First, it proves that product returns are not independent, external variables; rather, return volumes are strictly driven by the OEM's upfront leasing and residual pricing strategies. Second, it identifies a parabolic relationship between leasing revenue and NPV. increasing the primary lease rate initially boosts NPV, it eventually forces a sharp decline. This occurs because the model compensates for high lease rates by lowering the residual price, which in turn financially incentivizes customers to buy the product at the end of the lease rather than returning it. This starves the return core for refurbishment stream, proving that limiting secondary market supply is just as detrimental to profitability as secondary market cannibalization.

Finally, it demonstrates that the optimal refurbishment strategy is dynamic. In-house operations are viable when a initial product price and return volume can safely amortize fixed investment costs. Conversely, when aggressive leasing rates suppress return volumes, those fixed costs cannot be justified, making outsourcing the only rational strategy.

5.2 Managerial Implications

The result of this paper provides operation managers with an actionable, forward-looking roadmap for balancing contract terms and refurbishment strategy governance:

- Optimize Pricing to Prevent Secondary Market Starvation: OEMs must carefully calibrate the relationship between leasing rates and residual prices. Maximizing upfront leasing rates in isolation suppresses the optimal residual price, financially incentivizing customer purchasing. To secure the steady stream of returned products essential for feeding the refurbished market, managers must maintain a pricing equilibrium that preserves the economic attractiveness of returning the product.
- Leverage the Invariant "Safe Zone" for Quality Control: Return volumes remain entirely stable across a wide range of minimum quality thresholds. Managers can utilize this invariant phase to enforce stricter quality standards without deterring returns.
- Align Infrastructure Capacity with Product Asset Value: Decision-makers must evaluate product value and anticipated return volumes when selecting a refurbishment strategy. Developing an integrated, in-house facility involves substantial fixed costs. For example, in-house refurbishment strategy is justified for premium, high-priced products where the asset margins can effectively amortize the fixed infrastructure investment.

5.3 Conclusion and Future Research

In conclusion, this study provides a quantitative framework for OEMs to maximize the economic viability of circular business models through strategic decisions. While this model provides robust strategic guidelines, it assumes perfectly rational economic behaviour from customers, which may vary in real-world applications due to behavioural biases. Additionally, the finding that high proportions of Professional customers drastically increase NPV through buybacks is sensitive to the initial parameters that generate very high optimal residual prices. Future research should evaluate the model across a wider spectrum of boundary conditions, including varying depreciation rates and alternative minimum quality thresholds.

Finally, while the model analyses the impact of the minimum quality threshold on return behaviour, future studies should investigate how exceptionally strict thresholds might negatively impact initial market demand and the overall attractiveness of the leasing contract to prospective customers.

Acknowledgment. This study was supported by funding from the European Union's Horizon Europe program under the Marie Skłodowska-Curie Actions (MSCA), grant agreement number 101073508.

Disclosure of Interests. The authors have no competing interests to declare that are relevant to the content of this article.

References

1. Voukkali, I. et al.: Factors affecting social attitude and behavior for the transition towards a circular economy. Sustain. Chem. Pharm. **36**, 101276 (2023)
2. Ellen MacArthur Foundation: Growth within: a circular economy vision for a competitive europe (2015)
3. Vermeulen, W.J., Campbell-Johnston, K.: Extended producer responsibility. In: Handbook of Recycling, pp. 587–600 (2024)
4. Oghazi, P., Mostaghel, R.: Circular business model challenges and lessons learned—an industrial perspective. Sustainability. **10**, 739 (2018)
5. Geissdoerfer, M., Pieroni, M.P., Pigosso, D.C., Soufani, K.: Circular business models: a review. J. Clean. Prod. **277**, 123741 (2020)
6. Stahel, W.R.: The Circular Economy: A User's Guide. Routledge Taylor & Francis Group (2019)
7. Kristensen, H.S., Mosgaard, M.A.: A review of micro level indicators for a circular economy–moving away from the three dimensions of sustainability? J. Clean. Prod. **243**, 118531 (2020)
8. https://www.ellenmacarthurfoundation.org/circulate-products-and-materials
9. Rapoport, A.: Game Theory as a Theory of Conflict Resolution. Springer Science & Business Media (2012)
10. Von Neumann, J., Morgenstern, O.: Theory of Games and Economic Behavior, 2nd Rev. (1947)
11. Abbey, J.D., Guide Jr, V.D.R., Sun, X.: Closed-loop supply chains: a strategic overview. In: Tang, C.S. (ed.) Sustainable Supply Chains: a Research-Based Textbook on Operations and Strategy, pp. 355–378. Springer, University of California (2024)
12. Meade, L., Sarkis, J.: A conceptual model for selecting and evaluating third-party reverse logistics providers. Supply Chain Manag. Int. J. **7**, 283–295 (2002)
13. Gnoni, M.G., Mossa, G., Mummolo, G., Tornese, F., Verriello, R.: Circular econimy strategies for electronic equipment: a fuzzy cognitive map. Environ. Eng. Manag. J. (EEMJ). **16** (2017)
14. Atasu, A., Dumas, C., Van Wassenhove, L.N.: The circular business model. Harv. Bus. Rev. **99**, 72–81 (2021)
15. Sabaghi, M., Mascle, C., Baptiste, P.: Evaluation of products at design phase for an efficient disassembly at end-of-life. J. Clean. Prod. **116**, 177–186 (2016)
16. Tukker, A., Tischner, U.: Product-services as a research field: past, present and future. Reflections from a decade of research. J. Clean. Prod. **14**, 1552–1556 (2006)
17. Van Weelden, E., Mugge, R., Bakker, C.: Paving the way towards circular consumption: exploring consumer acceptance of refurbished mobile phones in the Dutch market. J. Clean. Prod. **113**, 743–754 (2016)
18. Wu, X., Zhou, Y.: Buyer-specific versus uniform pricing in a closed-loop supply chain with third-party remanufacturing. Eur. J. Oper. Res. **273**, 548–560 (2019)
19. Östlin, J., Sundin, E., Björkman, M.: Importance of closed-loop supply chain relationships for product remanufacturing. Int. J. Prod. Econ. **115**, 336–348 (2008)

20. Atasu, A., Guide Jr, V.D.R., Van Wassenhove, L.N.: So what if remanufacturing cannibalizes my new product sales? Calif. Manag. Rev. **52**, 56–76 (2010)
21. Guide Jr, V.D.R., Van Wassenhove, L.N.: OR FORUM—the evolution of closed-loop supply chain research. Oper. Res. **57**, 10–18 (2009)
22. Govindan, K., Soleimani, H., Kannan, D.: Reverse logistics and closed-loop supply chain: a comprehensive review to explore the future. Eur. J. Oper. Res. **240**, 603–626 (2015)
23. Ferguson, M.E., Toktay, L.B.: The effect of competition on recovery strategies. Prod. Oper. Manag. **15**, 351–368 (2006)
24. Agrawal, V.V., Atasu, A., Van Ittersum, K.: Remanufacturing, third-party competition, and consumers' perceived value of new products. Manag. Sci. **61**, 60–72 (2015)
25. Chopra, S., Meindl, P.: Supply Chain Management. Strategy, Planning & Operation. Springer (2007)
26. Mallick, P.K., Salling, K.B., Pigosso, D.C., McAloone, T.C.: Closing the loop: establishing reverse logistics for a circular economy, a systematic review. J. Environ. Manag. **328**, 117017 (2023)
27. Fleischmann, M., Krikke, H.R., Dekker, R., Flapper, S.D.P.: A characterisation of logistics networks for product recovery. Omega. **28**, 653–666 (2000)
28. Harish, M.A., Cakravastia, A., Iskandar, B.P.: Nash game theory leasing contract model of new and recondition complex equipment. In: Proceedings of the International Manufacturing Engineering Conference & the Asia Pacific Conference on Manufacturing Systems, pp. 355–361. Springer (2020)
29. Leng, M., Parlar, M.: Game theoretic applications in supply chain management: a review. INFOR Inf. Syst. Oper. Res. **43**, 187–220 (2005)
30. Agi, M.A., Faramarzi-Oghani, S., Hazır, Ö.: Game theory-based models in green supply chain management: a review of the literature. Int. J. Prod. Res. **59**, 4736–4755 (2021)
31. Shevchenko, A., Montabon, F., Pagell, M., Wu, Z.: Sustainability in supply chain management. In: Handbook of Research Methods for Supply Chain Management, pp. 352–367. Edward Elgar Publishing (2022)

Waste Management in the Cosmetics Industry: A Life Cycle-Based Analysis

Laila El Warraqi(✉), Roberto Rocca, and Luca Fumagalli

Department of Management, Economics and Industrial Engineering, Politecnico di Milano, Piazza Leonardo da Vinci, 32, 20133 Milan, Italy
{laila.elwarraqi,roberto.rocca,luca1.fumagalli}@polimi.it

Abstract. Growing concerns over climate change, biodiversity loss and resource depletion are accelerating the transition toward more sustainable and more circular production models across industrial sectors. Concerning the cosmetics industry, these pressures are intensified by the extensive use of plastics, water, energies, solvents, and chemically complex formulations, as well as by rising consumer expectations and increasingly stringent European regulations on waste management. The cosmetics sector still faces major challenges in understanding, quantifying, and managing the environmental impacts of its production processes and associated waste streams. This paper presents a life cycle-based waste impact analysis across four representative cosmetic manufacturing companies located in Italy. Data were collected through systematic examination of official environmental declarations, plant documentation, interviews with environmental and technical managers and site visits. The resulting database includes detailed information for different waste categories, covering European Waste Code (EWC) classification, annual quantities, and current treatment pathways. The paper aims to compare different treatment strategies together with their impacts, through environmental impacts selected from the Ecoinvent dataset. The analysis reveals consistent patterns across companies - such as the dominance of aqueous cleaning wastes, mixed packaging, and organic residues – together with variabilities linked to specific production technologies. Results demonstrate how life cycle analyses can function as a decision-support tool to evaluate circular strategies and identify environmental risk exposure. These could inform sustainable manufacturing configurations aligned with the European waste hierarchy.

Keywords: Cosmetics · Sustainability · Circular Economy · Waste Management · Life Cycle Analysis · LCA · Ecoinvent

1 Introduction

Environmental challenges such as climate change, biodiversity loss, and pollution are accelerating the transition toward Circular Economy (CE) models. At the European level, the European Green Deal [1] establishes the objective of climate neutrality by 2050, promoting economic growth decoupled from resource use. Complementary initiatives,

Published by Springer Nature Switzerland AG 2027
G. Pezzotta et al. (Eds.): APMS 2026, IFIP AICT 808, pp. 525–540, 2027.
https://doi.org/10.1007/978-3-032-38594-9_35

including the Circular Economy Action Plan and the EU Packaging and Packaging Waste Regulation, aim to ensure that packaging is reusable or recyclable by 2030 and to foster circular business models [2].

Within this policy framework, the cosmetics industry is increasingly required to align with sustainability principles. The sector represents a major economic player in Europe, with retail sales of approximately €104 billion in 2024 and over 3,5 million jobs supported across the value chain [3]. Given its scale and reliance on petrochemical-based inputs, packaging materials, and energy-intensive processes, the environmental footprint of cosmetics manufacturing is significant [4]. Concerns related to plastic pollution, microplastics, and resource depletion have intensified regulatory and consumer pressure toward more sustainable production systems [5].

In response to the waste it produces and its effects on the environment [6], different studies have shown the relevance of Life Cycle Assessment (LCA). Examples are given by Torkayesh et al. [7] who provided a study on the integration of LCA and multi-criteria decision making for sustainable waste management; Mulya et al. [8] who provided an overall study on LCA of solid waste management; Batool et al. [9] who presented a review on LCA studies for food waste management; Barbhuiya et al. [10] who focused on LCA of construction materials. Furthermore, Rocca et al. [11] demonstrated the growing relevance of LCA as a key methodology for evaluating environmental sustainability in the cosmetics sector. However, the sector still faces structural gaps in integrating LCA results into operational decision-making and supplier management. In parallel, sustainable supplier selection models tailored to cosmetics manufacturing have been proposed to strengthen sustainability performance across the value chain [12]. Moreover, improvements in industrial energy efficiency are increasingly recognized as a strategic lever for reducing both environmental impacts and operational costs within cosmetics production processes [13]. While the presented studies provide important analytical tools, to the best of the authors knowledge, limited research has explored how life cycle-based waste assessment can support circular transition pathways within the cosmetics industry. In particular, the integration of environmental impact assessment related to waste generation into operational planning remains fragmented, especially in production-oriented sectors such as cosmetics manufacturing.

In Europe, Italy, together with other European countries (e.g., France, Germany, Spain), plays a central role in cosmetics manufacturing [3]. This regional concentration of expertise provides favourable conditions for implementing circular and sustainability-oriented innovations along the value chain. In this context, the present study contributes by positioning life cycle-based waste assessment as a structured decision-support mechanism for sustainable manufacturing, aligned with CE principles. The study presents the preliminary results from four Italian cosmetic companies within the National COSMEND project [14], analysing end-of-waste opportunities and alternative treatment configurations. To this aim, the remainder of the paper is structured as follows: Sect. 2 reviews the background literature on sustainability and circular economy practices in the cosmetics sector; Sect. 3 describes the methodology; Sect. 4 provides the results of the waste impacts analysis; Sect. 5 presents the discussions; finally, Sect. 6 provides the conclusions of this work.

2 Theoretical Background

2.1 Sustainability in the Cosmetics Industry

Sustainability in the cosmetics industry encompasses strategies across the product life cycle, from raw material sourcing to End-of-Life (EoL) management. Waste management remains a critical challenge, as the sector generates multiple waste streams, including packaging materials, expired ingredients, and manufacturing by-products. The heavy reliance on single-use plastic packaging results in significant waste generation, with packaging representing up to 70% of the sector's waste footprint and over 120 billion cosmetic packaging units produced annually [15, 16]. Additional streams include unused or expired ingredients and off-spec production batches, which often require disposal and represent lost resource value [16].

Within this context, the European waste hierarchy provides a guiding framework, prioritizing prevention, reuse, recycling, recovery, and disposal. Transitioning from disposal-oriented practices toward higher-value recovery options is therefore central to aligning cosmetics manufacturing with CE principles [17].

Circular strategies in cosmetics focus primarily on upcycling, recycling, and reuse. Upcycling involves transforming by-products into higher-value inputs, for example by extracting bioactive compounds from agri-food residues for cosmetic formulations [15]. This approach promotes industrial symbiosis, whereby one sector's waste becomes another's resource. Practical examples include the valorisation of coffee grounds or olive oil by-products into cosmetic ingredients [15].

Packaging redesign is another key strategy. Refillable systems, mono-material designs, and post-consumer recycled plastics aim to reduce waste generation and improve recyclability [18]. LCA studies indicate that reusable packaging systems can significantly reduce environmental impacts compared to single-use designs [18, 19]. In parallel, regulatory drivers such as the EU Packaging and Packaging Waste Regulation reinforce the shift toward recyclable or reusable packaging by 2030 [20]. Since packaging can account for a substantial share of product-related emissions [21], its circular optimisation is particularly relevant.

Beyond packaging and ingredients, cleaner production and waste prevention measures support the upper levels of the waste hierarchy. Process optimisation, improved cleaning systems, and closed-loop water or solvent reuse reduce waste generation at source [15]. When waste cannot be prevented, valorisation pathways – including biological treatments or material recovery – aim to retain resource value rather than resorting to disposal [15].

Despite growing attention to circular practices, literature and industry efforts remain limited. Research has predominantly focused on sustainable inputs and packaging innovation, while less attention has been given to output-side waste management and end-of-waste strategies [22]. Similarly, industry surveys show that circular initiatives are often limited to packaging improvements, with fewer structured actions targeting production waste valorisation [22].

Addressing this gap requires a systematic assessment of waste streams generated within cosmetics manufacturing and the evaluation of recovery pathways consistent with the waste hierarchy. In this context, the present study investigates waste generation and end-of-waste opportunities in selected cosmetics companies, assessing alternative treatment scenarios and their environmental implications. The following sections describe the methodology and present the results of this analysis.

3 Methodology

This section explains the approach followed to collect waste data and estimate the impacts generated by each type of waste. The methodology used is summarised in Fig. 1.

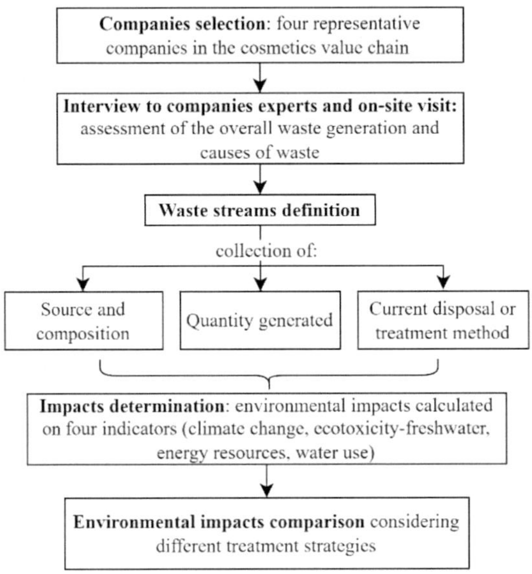

Fig. 1 Research methodology.

3.1 Case Study Overview and Data Collection

To conduct this study, four Italian companies in the cosmetics supply chain have been considered to investigate their waste generation and management practices. These partner companies were selected as representatives of different stages in the value chain (formulation, production, and EoL treatment) and because of their willingness to engage in sustainability initiatives.

Data were collected through on-site visits, semi-structured interviews, and the examination of internal reports over six months between 2025 and the beginning of 2026. Key experts were interviewed to identify waste streams resulting from the companies' operations. The focus has been devoted to production-related wastes rather than post-consumer waste, including any materials that become waste during manufacturing, packaging, and distribution processes. For each waste stream, the following information has been gathered: i) source and composition (i.e., what process or material generates the waste); ii) quantity generated (measured in kg per year); iii) current disposal or treatment method (e.g., landfill, incineration, recycling, etc.). Table 1 provides an overview of the companies and the most impactful type of waste identified by each, together with their annual profit, to compare waste quantities generated.

Table 1. Companies overview.

Company ID	Role in the value chain	Annual profits [€]
A	Brand owner and retailer in the mid-to-downstream segment of the cosmetics value chain, focusing on product development, branding, marketing, and direct sales.	18.000.000
B	Upstream contract manufacturer in the cosmetics value chain, specializing in product formulation, research and development (R&D), and large-scale production for beauty brands.	45.000.000
C	Upstream OEM contract manufacturer in the cosmetics value chain, providing R&D, formulation, and large-scale production services for global beauty brands rather than selling directly to end consumers.	150.000.000
D	Brand owner and retailer in the mid-to-downstream segment of the cosmetics value chain, focusing on product development, branding, marketing, and direct sales.	30.000.000

3.2 Waste Stream Mapping and Analysis

Using the data collected from the four companies, a systematic waste stream mapping to visualize and quantify the flow of wastes generated by the four companies has been performed. In particular, the mapping activity was based on the information extracted from the Italian *Modello Unico di Dichiarazione Ambientale (MUD)* (i.e., the national Single Environmental Declaration Form), internal registers, technical documentation, interviews, and site visits. For each company, all identified waste streams were traced from the phase of generation within the production process to their declared management operation (i.e., namely R13 – storage before recovery, D15 – storage before disposal, R1 – energy recovery, D8 – biological treatment, D9 – physico-chemical treatment) and destination facilities. This enabled the reconstruction of the pathway of each waste which have been classified according to the European Waste Catalogue (EWC) (i.e., a standardised EU system used to classify and identify waste materials), linking: i) the process phase of origin (e.g., production, filling and packaging, washing operations, maintenance, R&D activities); ii) the annual quantities generated (measured in kg/year); iii) the hazardous or non-hazardous classification; iv) the declared treatment operation and final destination.

On this basis, waste flows have been structured into macro-categories recurring across the four companies, including: packaging waste (e.g., EWC 150101, 150102, 150106), aqueous liquid waste from washing operations (EWC 161002), organic cosmetic waste

(EWC 160305* - indicated with "*" to specify it includes hazardous substances, 160306), chemical and solvent waste (e.g., EWC 140603, 120301), and process sludges (e.g., EWC 070612).

The mapping allowed the identification of the most significant flows in quantitative terms, such as washing waters (EWC 161002), mixed-material packaging (EWC 150106), and organic cosmetic waste (EWC 160306). Furthermore, the analysis revealed the prevalence of packaging-related waste across all four companies, as well as the presence of hazardous streams requiring specific management and traceability. Overall, the waste stream mapping provided a comparable baseline of waste generation and management practices across the four case-study companies, forming the methodological foundation for the subsequent environmental impact assessment and feasibility analyses, as presented in Sect. 4.

3.3 Environmental Impact Assessment

To quantitatively assess the environmental implications of current waste management versus possible circular scenarios, an environmental impact analysis has been conducted using Ecoinvent database [23], a global resource for environmental data, which provides representative life cycle inventories for waste treatment processes and material production. In this work, the LCA is employed as a comparative decision-support instrument to evaluate alternative waste treatment configuration, to support the evaluation of circular options under different environmental performance objectives. A functional unit was defined as the management of 1 kg of waste for each identified waste stream (with separate analyses per waste type), as well as an aggregated analysis for the total annual waste from the case companies. System boundaries have been identified from the point where a material becomes waste (at the factory level) to its final processing or disposal. In the "baseline" scenario, each waste stream was modelled according to its current treatment process given by the company (e.g., incineration with energy recovery for hazardous organic waste, landfilling for certain wastes, recycling for cardboard, etc.). In the "circular" scenario, alternative treatments were modelled based on possible treatment alternatives available on Ecoinvent (e.g., recycling plastic waste into new plastic, digesting organic waste, etc.). This approach allows a comparison of environmental impacts between the current state and a hypothetical improved practice where circular strategies are implemented. As examples, the incineration of municipal solid waste, the recycling process for polypropylene plastic, and anaerobic digestion of organic waste were all modelled using Ecoinvent processes adapted to the Italian context (using the appropriate electricity mix and transport distances where applicable).

For the impact assessment, the focus has been devoted to four key indicators related to the objectives of the analysis, namely: "Climate change" (i.e., greenhouse gas emissions), "Energy resources: non-renewable", "Ecotoxicity: freshwater" and "Water use".

4 Results

4.1 Overview of the Waste Generation Across the Four Companies

The analysis of the MUD declarations and companies' data reveals a heterogeneous but structurally comparable waste profile across the four companies. Figure 2 presents the aggregated annual waste quantities (kg/year) by company, providing an overview of the relative contribution of each site. Waste is generated across different life cycle stages of the manufacturing process. Production-related activities primarily generate sludges from on-site treatment processes, solvent waste, and aqueous liquid waste originating from washing and cleaning operations. In parallel, packaging-related waste constitutes a significant part of the waste fractions, including paper and cardboard packaging, plastic packaging, and mixed-material packaging, highlighting the structural relevance of packaging within the cosmetics value chain and its significant contribution to the overall waste profile of the sector.

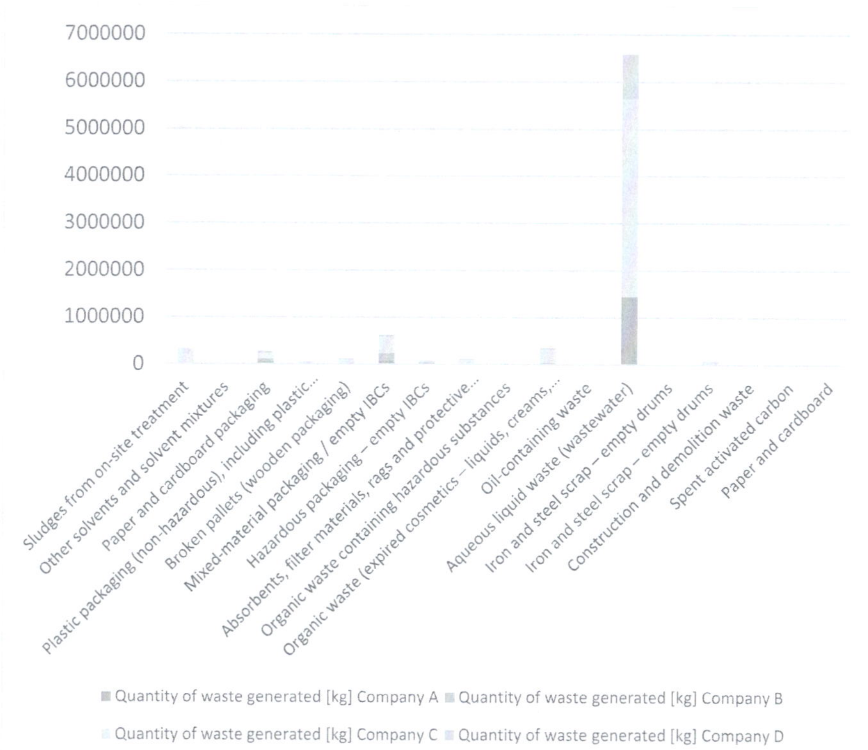

Fig. 2 Overview of the main waste generated and quantities [kg] by the companies considered.

4.2 Analysis of Selected Key Waste Streams

Based on three operational criteria – (i) annual quantity generated, (ii) recurrence across companies, and (iii) environmental relevance and potential for improvement along the European waste hierarchy – four waste streams were selected for detailed analysis: paper and cardboard packaging (EWC 150101), mixed-material packaging (EWC 150106), aqueous liquid waste/washing waters (EWC 161002), and organic cosmetic waste (EWC 160306). EWC codes are reported according to the European List of Waste (LoW).

For each stream, the analysis integrates: i) waste management practices declared by the companies (research and development operations); ii) impact factors derived from the Ecoinvent database and converted according to the Environmental Footprint (EF) methodology; and iii) total annual impacts, calculated through linear scaling of unit impacts (impact per kg $\times$ considered environmental impact indicator).

4.2.1 Paper and Cardboard Packaging

This waste stream is generated by all four companies and mainly arises from raw material reception, logistics, and secondary packaging activities. The total annual quantity amounts to 275.668 kg (Table 2), with a significant contribution from Company C.

The declared treatment operation is R13 (storage pending recovery), consistent with a recycling-oriented management approach within the national collection and recycling system for cellulosic packaging.

To represent available management options within Ecoinvent, four scenarios were modelled (Table 3): two "market" scenarios associated with recovery/recycling pathways (i.e., Scenario 1: global market; Scenario 2: Italian market), and two alternative incineration scenarios with energy recovery (Scenario 3: heat recovery; Scenario 4: electricity recovery). Unit results (Table 3) indicate that Scenario 2 (Italian market) provides the most balanced environmental performance. Compared to Scenario 1 (global market), it significantly reduces Climate change (from 0,0918 to 0,0113 kg CO_2-eq/kg) and shows particularly low Water use values. Scenario 3 exhibits the lowest Climate change impact (Table 3), a result attributable to energy credits embedded in incineration datasets. However, this option does not enable material recovery and, compared to Scenario 2, presents higher Water use (Table 3), making it less consistent with circularity objectives within the European waste hierarchy. Scenario 4 shows the least favourable environmental performance overall, particularly for Water use and Freshwater ecotoxicity. Overall, the evidence supports the preference for material recovery through dedicated paper recycling supply chains, with incineration considered an alternative benchmark scenario rather than a priority circular option.

Table 2. Quantity of mixed-material packaging waste generated by the companies.

Company ID	A	B	C	D	Total
Quantity [kg/year]	48.440	60.230	122.400	44.598	275.668

Table 3. Environmental impacts per 1 kg of mixed-material packaging (EWC 150101).

Scenario	Ecoinvent Data-set	Climate Change [kg CO_2-eq]	Ecotoxicity freshwater [CTUe]	Energy resources (non-renewable) [MJ]	Water use [m^3]
Scenario 1	Market for waste paper, sorted (Global Market)	0,0918	4,85	0,708	0,00614
Scenario 2	Market for waste packaging paper (Italian Market)	0,0113	0,135	0,158	0,000876
Scenario 3	Municipal incineration (heat recovery, Global)	0,0042	0,142	0,0336	0,00359
Scenario 4	Municipal incineration (electricity recovery, Global)	0,0821	2,77	0,658	0,0702

4.2.2 Mixed-Material Packaging

The mixed-material packaging stream (including composite packaging and, where applicable, emptied containers/Intermediate Bulk Containers (IBCs)) is generated by all four companies and represents one of the major mass flows (Table 4), with a total annual quantity of 620.760 kg. Regarding declared operations, Companies A, B, and D report R13 (storage pending recovery), while Company C reports R1 (energy recovery). R1 and R13 operations are defined under EU waste legislation.

Within the Ecoinvent framework, the stream was modelled through three scenarios (Table 5): i) scenario 1 - material recovery (dataset "market for waste polyethylene", used as a proxy for the dominant plastic fraction); ii) scenarios 2–3 - municipal incineration (PET and PE datasets), representing energy recovery options with different process parameterisations. The results highlight consistent trade-offs across indicators (Table 5). In terms of Climate change, incineration scenarios (Scenarios 2–3) generate substantially higher impacts compared to material recovery. This outcome supports material recovery as the preferred option when decarbonisation of EoL packaging is prioritised. For Energy resources (non-renewable) and Freshwater ecotoxicity, incineration scenarios show lower impacts than Scenario 1 (Table 5). This pattern is consistent with typical LCA modelling characteristics: (i) the presence of energy credits in incineration with recovery, and (ii) upstream burdens associated with recovery processes (sorting, handling, and reprocessing), which may influence indicators beyond the global warming potential. For Water use indicator, incineration (Scenarios 2–3) increases impacts compared to recovery (Scenario 1) (Table 5), therefore treatment choice may introduce additional pressures on water resources, similarly to the impact associated with climate change, even when freshwater ecotoxicity and non-renewable energy resources indicators appear more favourable. Overall, results support a strategy aligned with the waste hierarchy: priority to material recovery where technically and economically feasible, with incineration considered a secondary, less circular alternative.

Table 4. Quantity of mixed-material packaging waste generated by the companies.

Company ID	A	B	C	D	Total
Quantity [kg/year]	81.460	153.300	350.000	36.000	620.760

Table 5. Environmental impacts per 1 kg of mixed-material packaging (EWC 150106).

Scenario	Ecoinvent Dataset	Climate Change [kg CO_2-eq]	Ecotoxicity freshwater [CTUe]	Energy resources (non-renewable) [MJ]	Water use [m^3]
Material recovery (Scenario 1)	Market for waste polyethylene	1,48	1,61	0,423	0,039
Incineration (Scenario 2)	Treatment of waste PET, municipal incineration	3,19	0,75	0,342	0,0497
Incineration (Scenario 3)	Treatment of waste polyethylene (PE), municipal incineration	3,10	1,26	0,296	0,0723

4.2.3 Aqueous Liquid Waste

Aqueous liquid waste (or wastewater) constitutes a dominant flow in terms of mass, with a total annual quantity of 6.583.930 kg/year (Table 6). The stream is particularly relevant for Companies A, C, and D, while it is marginal for Company B.

Declared management operations include D8 (biological treatment), D8/D9 (biological and physico-chemical treatment), and D15 (preliminary storage prior to disposal). Operations D8, D9, and D15 are defined within the EU classification of disposal operations.

Within Ecoinvent, three wastewater treatment options were evaluated (Table 7): two wastewater treatment datasets (Scenario 1 "average"; Scenario 2 "unpolluted") and one residual landfill dataset (Scenario 3), used as a proxy for alternative residual management pathways available in the database.

Results (Table 7) show that, although Climate change per kg is lower than for plastic packaging, the very high volume makes total annual impacts non-negligible (Scenario 1: 2.363.573 kg CO_2-eq by multiplying annual quantity per unitary indicator). The Water use indicator is structurally relevant for this stream (Scenario 1: 1.106.100 m^3), consistent with both the intrinsic nature of the waste and the EF water deprivation modelling approach. Freshwater ecotoxicity varies significantly between scenarios (Table 7), indicating high sensitivity both to wastewater composition assumptions and to dataset parameterisation (Scenario 1 vs. Scenario 2). Consequently, for this stream, the main leverage for improvement lies not only in downstream treatment choice but mainly in reduction at source (lower volumes and pollutant load), as volume largely determines total annual impacts.

Table 6. Quantity of wastewater generated by the companies.

Company ID	A	B	C	D	Total
Quantity [kg/year]	1.439.350	1.000	4.211.200	932.380	6.583.930

Table 7. Environmental impacts per 1 kg of aqueous liquid waste (EWC 161002).

Scenario	Ecoinvent Data-set	Climate Change [kg CO_2-eq]	Ecotoxicity freshwater [CTUe]	Energy resources (non-renewable) [MJ]	Water use [m^3]
Wastewater treatment (Scenario 1)	Treatment of wastewater, average	0.359	41.4	3.85	0.168
Wastewater treatment (Scenario 2)	Treatment of wastewater, unpolluted	0.123	7.89	1.16	0.0288
Residual landfill (Scenario 3)	Treatment of incineration residue	0.344	36.3	1.92	0.0373

4.2.4 Organic Cosmetic Waste

This stream includes expired cosmetic products (liquids, creams, oils) and mixed solid materials generated during production, packaging, and quality control activities. The total annual quantity amounts to 350.406 kg/year (Table 8), strongly influenced by Company C.

From a management perspective, Company C declares R1 for the solid fraction and D15 for liquid/powder fractions; the other companies declare combinations of disposal and recovery depending on composition.

Since Ecoinvent does not always provide a specific dataset for off-spec cosmetic waste, three treatment options were explored for an organic waste assimilable to "biowaste" (Table 9): open dump (Scenario 1, used as a non-circular reference scenario), anaerobic digestion (Scenario 2), and industrial composting (Scenario 3).

Unit results (Table 9) show that shifting from Scenario 1 to biological treatment options substantially reduces Climate change impacts: annually from 185.014 kg CO_2-eq (Scenario 1) to 41.000 (Scenario 2) and 21.515 (Scenario 3) – if multiplying annual volumes per unitary indicators.

However, important trade-offs emerge. Scenario 3 (composting) shows the highest Freshwater ecotoxicity (Table 9), whereas anaerobic digestion provides a more balanced profile between GWP reduction and containment of ecotoxicity and Water use.

Overall, results support anaerobic digestion as the most balanced circular option among the three tested scenarios, while the open dump scenario is the least consistent with the European waste hierarchy and with circularity and decarbonisation objectives.

Table 8. Quantity [kg] of organic waste generated.

Company ID	A	B	C	D	Total
Quantity [kg/year]	5.428	33.816	285.300	25.862	350.406

Table 9. Environmental impacts per 1 kg of aqueous liquid waste (EWC 160306).

Scenario	Ecoinvent dataset	Climate Change [kg CO_2-eq]	Ecotoxicity freshwater [CTUe]	Energy resources (non-renewable) [MJ]	Water use [m^3]
Scenario 1	Biowaste, open dump (RoW)	0,528	4,35	0	0
Scenario 2	Biowaste, anaerobic digestion (RoW)	0,117	1,52	0,415	0,00277
Scenario 3	Biowaste, industrial composting (RoW)	0,0614	8,34	0,4	0,0127

5 Discussion

5.1 Multi-indicator Trade-Offs

Across all waste categories analysed, climate change emerges as the most sensitive indicator to treatment type selection. For plastic-based mixed-material packaging, material recovery significantly reduces greenhouse gas emissions compared to incineration scenarios, even when energy recovery benefits are included. This confirms the importance of material circularity under decarbonisation objectives and aligns with current European policy priorities. However, the results also demonstrate that conclusions change when other indicators are considered. For instance, certain incineration scenarios show lower impacts for non-renewable energy use due to embedded energy recovery advantages in the Ecoinvent datasets. Similarly, composting of organic cosmetic waste achieves the lowest climate impact but demonstrates higher freshwater ecotoxicity compared to anaerobic digestion. These findings underline the importance of multi-indicator LCA approaches instead of relying only on carbon footprint metrics to guide waste management decisions, since options that may appear circular may introduce burden shifting across impact categories. The presence of these trade-offs implies that the preferred option depends on the environmental objective prioritised. If climate mitigation is the primary objective, material recovery and anaerobic digestion represent the most favourable pathways. If toxicity-related impacts are emphasised, alternative conclusions may emerge. Furthermore, from this study, it emerges the distinction between impact intensity and volume relevance. Indeed, mixed-material packaging demonstrates relatively high impact intensity per kilogram, entailing that treatment choice significantly influences total environmental burden. In contrast, aqueous liquid waste shows comparatively lower per-unit climate impacts; however, it generates large annual volumes. As a result, wastewater management becomes environmentally relevant primarily due to scale rather than treatment intensity. This distinction has strategic implications. For high-impact, lower-volume streams (e.g., packaging), optimising treatment strategies brings substantial environmental benefits. For high-volume, lower-intensity streams (e.g., wastewater), upstream process optimisation and volume reduction strategies could bring higher improvements than evaluating different treatment technologies.

5.2 Impact of Modelling Assumptions and CE Implications

The results are also influenced by the structure of the Ecoinvent datasets. Energy recovery credits embedded in incineration processes can reduce apparent fossil energy demand, occasionally making incineration appear favourable under certain indicators. Similarly, the difference between global, European, and country-specific (e.g., Italy) datasets affects results due to variations in background energy systems and process efficiencies. These findings highlight the importance of transparent modelling assumptions in LCAs-based decision support. Therefore, on one side, absolute values should be interpreted with caution; on the other side, comparative trends between scenarios are more robust in order to guide strategic choices.

More broadly, this study illustrates why LCA is particularly relevant for waste management and EoL decision-making. Waste treatment options often generate both direct impacts (e.g., emissions from incineration or treatment energy use) and indirect effects (e.g., substitution credits from recovered energy or avoided virgin material production). LCA explicitly accounts for these mechanisms, enabling consistent comparison between recovery, recycling, and disposal pathways under a defined functional unit (1 kg of waste) and system boundary. Therefore, applying environmental impact assessment to waste streams supports CE implementation in three ways: i) it helps identify when circular options deliver environmental benefits and when they risk burden shifting (e.g., reduced GWP but increased ecotoxicity); ii) it enables scenario-based evaluation aligned with the waste hierarchy by quantifying the relative performance of prevention-oriented versus treatment-oriented strategies; iii) it provides a transparent basis for prioritising EoL strategies across different waste types, especially when companies rely on generic treatment codes (e.g., R13, D15) that do not specify actual downstream processes. In particular, this last point is also relevant for servitized circular models (e.g., take-back, recovery), since contractual allocation of responsibilities requires traceable EoL performance rather than generic intermediate codes. Indeed, from a CE perspective, the results confirm that material recovery strategies generally outperform disposal-oriented treatments when climate and resource objectives are considered. In particular: i) recycling of paper and plastic packaging supports material circularity and reduces reliance on virgin raw materials; ii) anaerobic digestion of organic cosmetic waste represents a promising valorisation strategy; iii) wastewater management can offer potential for reduction through internal recirculation systems (e.g., water reuse after decontamination). Furthermore, some waste streams (e.g., hazardous organic waste) are constrained by regulatory frameworks that limit recovery options. This suggests that eco-design and substitution of hazardous substances may represent more effective long-term strategies than downstream treatment optimisation. Furthermore, the limited visibility on downstream treatment strategies highlights the relevance of digitalised traceability systems as enabling conditions to improve data granularity and strengthen life cycle-based decision support for circular transitions.

6 Conclusions

This study evaluated four key waste streams generated in the cosmetics supply chain, focusing on four companies – i.e., paper and cardboard packaging (EWC 150101), mixed-material packaging (EWC 150106), aqueous liquid waste (EWC 161002), and organic cosmetic waste (EWC 160306) – using an Environmental Footprint (EF 3.0) based LCA approach. Environmental impacts were quantified for climate change, freshwater ecotoxicity, non-renewable energy resource use, and water use, combining company-reported practices with Ecoinvent datasets and annual waste quantities. Results show that environmental performance varies significantly across waste streams and treatment pathways. For packaging waste, material recovery generally outperforms incineration in terms of climate change and circularity objectives, despite trade-offs in other indicators due to modelling credits in energy recovery scenarios. For aqueous liquid waste, environmental relevance is primarily volume-driven: although per-kg impacts are lower, the large quantities generated make total annual impacts substantial, highlighting the importance of reduction at source. For organic cosmetic waste, biological treatments – particularly anaerobic digestion – significantly reduce climate impacts compared to non-circular scenarios, although trade-offs emerge for ecotoxicity. Overall, the findings confirm that optimal waste management strategies depend on waste characteristics, scale, and the environmental objective prioritised. Multi-indicator assessment is therefore essential to avoid carbon-only decision-making.

From a strategic perspective, implementation of circular options may be constrained by regulatory limitations (e.g., wastewater reuse), logistical challenges in waste storage, economic feasibility of biological treatments, and variability in waste composition. Advancing circular waste management in the cosmetics sector, therefore, requires not only technological solutions but also regulatory alignment and supply chain coordination. In this sense, life cycle-based waste assessment can act as an enabling assessment tool to support servitization-oriented circular strategies (i.e., by providing support in prioritising waste streams, evaluating alternative EoL configurations, and defining measurable performance targets for service-based strategies, such as recovery or waste valorisation services). Finally, it is worth mentioning that the results are based on secondary Ecoinvent datasets and should be interpreted as comparative rather than absolute values. Future research should integrate primary treatment data and economic assessment to strengthen decision support for circular transition pathways.

Acknowledgments. This work was carried out within the COSMEND project, funded by Fondazione LGH (Gruppo A2A). This work has received funding from the European Union's HORIZON-EIE-2022 programme under grant agreement No 101112710. In any case, the present work cannot be considered as an official position of the supporting organization, but it reports just the point of view of the authors.

Disclosure of Interests. The authors have no competing interests to declare that are relevant to the content of this article.

References

1. European Commission: The European Green Deal (2019)
2. European Commission: Circular Economy Action Plan (2020)
3. Cosmetics Europe Cosmetics Europe
4. Vital, X.: Environmental impacts of cosmetic products: part 1: the growing importance of metrics. In: Sustainability: How the Cosmetics Industry Is Greening Up, pp. 17–46. Wiley (2013)
5. Cubas, A.L.V., Bianchet, R.T., dos Reis, I.M.A.S., Gouveia, I.C.: Plastics and microplastic in the cosmetic industry: aggregating sustainable actions aimed at alignment and interaction with UN sustainable development goals. Polymers (Basel). **14**(21), 4576 (2022)
6. Chadha, G.D., Singh, R.: Circular beauty: sustainable resource recovery and waste management in the cosmetic industry. In: Technological Advancements in Waste Management: Challenges and Opportunities. TAWMCO 2023 (2025)
7. Torkayesh, A.E. et al.: Integrating life cycle assessment and multi criteria decision making for sustainable waste management: key issues and recommendations for future studies. Renew. Sust. Energ. Rev. **168**, 112819 (2022)
8. Mulya, K.S., Zhou, J., Phuang, Z.X., Laner, D., Woon, K.S.: A systematic review of life cycle assessment of solid waste management: methodological trends and prospects. Sci. Total Environ. **831**, 154903 (2022)

9. Batool, F. et al.: Environmental impacts of food waste management technologies: a critical review of life cycle assessment (LCA) studies. Trends Food Sci. Technol. **143**, 104287 (2024)
10. Barbhuiya, S., Das, B.B.: Life cycle assessment of construction materials: methodologies, applications and future directions for sustainable decision-making. Case Stud. Constr. Mater. **19**, e02326 (2023)
11. Rocca, R., Acerbi, F., Fumagalli, L., Taisch, M.: Development of an LCA-based tool to assess the environmental sustainability level of cosmetics products. Int. J. Life Cycle Assess. **28**(10), 1261–1285 (2023)
12. Acerbi, F., Rocca, R., Fumagalli, L., Taisch, M.: Enhancing the cosmetics industry sustainability through a renewed sustainable supplier selection model. Prod. Manuf. Res. **11**(1) (2023)
13. Rocca, R., Perossa, D., Fumagalli, L.: Analysis and modelling for industrial energy efficiency in the cosmetics industry: a real industrial case in an Italian manufacturing company. Cosmetics. **11**(5), 161 (2024)
14. Fondazione LGH: Gruppo a2a COSMEND – end of waste nella filiera cosmetica (2024)
15. Martins, A.M., Silva, A.T., Marto, J.M.: Advancing cosmetic sustainability: upcycling for a circular product life cycle. Sustainability (Switzerland). **17**(13), 5738 (2025)
16. Waste Management in the Cosmetics Industry: Building a circular economy for beauty
17. European commission waste framework directive
18. Gatt, I.J., Paul, R.: Reusability and recyclability of plastic cosmetic packaging: a life cycle assessment. Resour. Conserv. Recycl. Adv. **15**, 200098 (2022)
19. Tua, C., Biganzoli, L., Grosso, M., Rigamonti, L.: Life cycle assessment of reusable plastic crates (RPCs). Resources. **8**(2), 110 (2019)
20. European Commission Packaging and Packaging Waste Regulation 2025/40 (PPWR)
21. How circular supply chains are transforming the cosmetics industry
22. Mondello, A., Salomone, R., Mondello, G.: Exploring circular economy in the cosmetic industry: insights from a literature review. Environ. Impact Assess. Rev. **105**, 107443 (2024)
23. Ecoinvent Dataset

Designing Sustainable BMs for Testbeds in Industry 4.0: An Empirical 5G Testbed Study

Pedro Gonçalves[1,2], Ana Simões[1(✉)], Pedro Senna[1], and Bruno Parreira[3]

[1] INESC TEC, Porto, Portugal
ana.c.simoes@inesctec.pt
[2] Faculty of Economics of the University of Porto, Porto, Portugal
[3] NOS Communications, Porto, Portugal

Abstract. Testbeds play a critical role in supporting the experimentation, validation, and diffusion of emerging technologies within Industry 4.0. Despite their growing importance, existing research remains predominantly technical and offers limited insight into how sustainable testbed business models can be designed. This study addresses this gap by analysing how testbed characteristics, service offerings, value creation and capture mechanisms can be integrated into a coherent BM, with a particular focus on 5G-enabled environments. Supported by a mixed interpretivist–pragmatic philosophy, the study adopts a qualitative exploratory approach, combining a systematic literature review with semi-structured interviews involving 16 stakeholders from Portuguese and international testbed initiatives. Reflexive thematic analysis was used to identify key patterns, supported by triangulation with literature and secondary sources. Findings show that sustainable testbed BMs rely on three interconnected dimensions: (1) the role of testbeds as controlled experimentation environments that reduce uncertainty and enable technology validation; (2) an extended service portfolio including consulting, training, networking, and matchmaking; and (3) hybrid BM configurations based on strong partnerships, diversified revenue streams, and flexible pricing mechanisms. Trust, transparency, and long-term collaboration emerge as critical enablers across these dimensions. The study proposes a BM framework that integrates these elements, offering theoretical insights and practical guidance for the design and positioning of testbeds in Industry 4.0 contexts.

Keywords: Testbeds · Business Model · Industry 4.0 · 5G · Sustainability · Innovation Ecosystems · Technology Adoption

1 Introduction

Industry 4.0 represents a transformation of industrial systems based on cyber-physical systems and IoT technologies, creating new challenges for organisations in adopting emerging technologies [1, 2]. Alongside these transformations, manufacturing organisations have increasingly collaborated with academics to develop new technologies [3].

Published by Springer Nature Switzerland AG 2027
G. Pezzotta et al. (Eds.): APMS 2026, IFIP AICT 808, pp. 541–555, 2027.
https://doi.org/10.1007/978-3-032-38594-9_36

However, as knowledge of new technologies remains limited, access to testing environments such as testbeds and living labs is necessary before market entry [4]. These testing environments provide a range of tools to evaluate and refine the technology, thereby reducing risks and failure rates, and improving its readiness for industrial application [5, 6]. In addition to providing access to technological hardware, a testbed promotes knowledge dissemination through training and standardisation efforts [7].

In recent years, one of the most frequently discussed emerging technologies with the potential to drive the Industry 4.0 ecosystem forward is 5G, the fifth-generation network [8]. This new generation is not merely an incremental improvement over its predecessor but signifies a major innovation, bringing new regulatory paradigms. 5G could help tackle future challenges in communications, maintenance, and manufacturing by providing greater connectivity between devices, lower energy usage, potentially reduced latency, and faster data transfer rates [8, 9].

The focus on 5G is a deliberate scope choice rather than an assumption that all testbeds are 5G-based. 5G is relevant because it is a general-purpose enabling technology for Industry 4.0, requires costly and specialised infrastructure, raises data-governance and integration challenges, and remains difficult for many SMEs to test internally. Although the empirical focus is 5G, the resulting design principles may inform testbeds for other Industry 4.0 technologies with similar uncertainty and infrastructure requirements.

Despite growing interest in testbeds and related experimentation environments [5–7, 10, 11], existing research remains fragmented and predominantly technical, while business models (BM) studies remain largely generic and provide limited guidance on how testbed-specific value creation, delivery and capture mechanisms can support long-term sustainability and diffusion impact in Industry 4.0 contexts [12–17]. This study is therefore directed at improving understanding of testbed BMs for future development and strategic positioning in new contexts, proposing sustainable pricing mechanisms tailored for testbeds, and analysing the roles of partners and funding agents to ensure long-term sustainability.

Accordingly, this study is guided by the following research question: How can a sustainable BM for a 5G testbed be developed by integrating its key characteristics, service portfolio, and value creation and capture mechanisms? To address this question, the study pursues three research objectives: RO1: To identify and characterise the key features and differentiating factors of testbeds as testing and experimentation environments; RO2: To analyse the service portfolio of testbeds and its role in supporting technology adoption and stakeholder value; RO3: To define the key components of a sustainable BM for testbeds, including partnerships, revenue mechanisms, and pricing strategies.

This paper contributes by translating 5G testbeds from a predominantly technical infrastructure into a business-model problem centred on value creation, delivery and capture. It identifies how extended services support the perceived value of testbeds and proposes a compact BM Canvas-based framework linking testbed characteristics, ecosystem partnerships, hybrid revenue streams and flexible pricing mechanisms.

The remainder of the paper is organised as follows. Section 2 reviews the literature on testbeds, technological infrastructures and BMs. Section 3 presents the methodology. Section 4 reports the empirical findings. Section 5 discusses the contribution of the proposed framework, and Sect. 6 presents the conclusions, limitations and future research directions.

2 Literature Review

Testbeds have emerged as critical infrastructure for experimenting with and validating Industry 4.0 technologies such as IoT, cyber-physical systems, and 5G [5–7]. They provide controlled environments that reduce uncertainty, support technology adoption, and facilitate collaboration among industrial firms, technology providers, and research institutions. By providing access to advanced infrastructure and expertise, testbeds are particularly valuable for SMEs, enabling experimentation under realistic conditions and accelerating technology diffusion [10, 11, 18].

Technological infrastructures such as testbeds share structural and functional characteristics with other complex, multi-actor systems that require coordinated value creation and long-term sustainability. Although BMs have been widely discussed in the context of innovation and technology adoption, there remains a limited understanding of how they apply to specific technological infrastructures, such as testbeds.

From a theoretical perspective, a BM can be understood as the architecture through which value is created, delivered, and captured [12]. In the context of technological infrastructures, this perspective becomes particularly relevant, as these systems involve multiple stakeholders, diverse value propositions, and complex resource configurations. Furthermore, the increasing need for BM innovation in response to technological change reinforces the importance of aligning technological capabilities with new forms of value creation [13, 14].

Technological infrastructures typically operate within collaborative ecosystems, where value is co-created through interactions between industry actors, research institutions, and public entities. In the case of testbeds, this role extends beyond providing access to technical resources to encompass additional services such as consulting, mentoring, and training that support organisations in adopting new technologies [19–21]. These complementary services are particularly relevant for SMEs, which often face limited resources, a lack of expertise, and difficulties integrating new technologies.

Technological infrastructures operate through service-oriented BMs that extend value beyond physical assets, combining digital solutions, expertise, and collaborative services [15–17]. These models illustrate how technological infrastructures can extend their value proposition beyond physical assets, offering integrated digital and service-based solutions.

The empirical examples in Table 1 are comparable technological infrastructures, including testbeds, applied research centres, innovation networks and competence centres, selected because they illustrate alternative ways of organising value propositions and revenue mechanisms around shared technological resources. They serve as benchmarks for interpreting testbed-specific BM elements.

Across these models, a common pattern is the reliance on hybrid revenue structures that combine public funding with private income from services and partnerships, supported by governance mechanisms such as trust and stakeholder alignment [27].

The reviewed literature shows that existing BM frameworks clarify generic dimensions such as value proposition, resources, partners, customer segments and revenue

Table 1. Synthesis of technological infrastructure BM types

Example	Infrastructure type	Interpreted BM type	Core Value Proposition	Revenue Logic
POSTECH [22]	Research university/laboratory	Academic & Research	Knowledge creation, education, R&D	Public funding, grants, IP licensing
TNO [23], ISQ [23]	Applied technological infrastructure	Technological Development	Testing, prototyping, certification	Projects, consultancy, services
EIT [24]	Innovation network	Knowledge Transfer	Networking, training, ecosystem building	Memberships, events, programs
INESC TEC iiLab [25], SiiLab [26]	Testbed/demonstration hub	Hybrid Models	Combined services + ecosystem orchestration	Mixed public-private revenue

logic [12–14] while the BM Canvas provides a practical framework for systematising key components such as partners, activities, resources, value propositions and revenue streams [28].

However, these frameworks do not explain how such dimensions should be configured for testbeds as shared technological infrastructures. In particular, prior work provides limited guidance on how to combine controlled experimentation, neutrality between partners, access to scarce technical resources, intellectual property governance, training and consulting services, and public-private funding into a coherent and sustainable model [7, 13, 27]. This gap is especially relevant for 5G-enabled testbeds, where infrastructure costs, technical uncertainty, data governance and ecosystem coordination are central to adoption [8, 11]. Therefore, this study advances the literature by adapting business-model logic to the testbed context and by empirically deriving a framework that integrates value proposition, value delivery and value capture mechanisms.

3 Methodology

3.1 Research Strategy

A qualitative exploratory approach was adopted, combining interpretivist and pragmatic perspectives to analyse testbed BMs through literature review and semi-structured interviews [29, 30].

Following this mixed philosophy, an exploratory study was conducted, employing interpretivism to understand the business structures of existing testbeds through the analysis of publicly available information and pragmatism to obtain practical knowledge through interviews with field experts and stakeholders. This combination was particularly suitable for capturing the complexity of testbeds within their organisational and social contexts and for developing a sustainable BM with practical relevance for the design and positioning of 5G testbeds in Industry 4.0 contexts. To ensure ethical data collection, all participants received a consent form in advance, outlining the research purpose and the procedures for maintaining anonymity.

3.2 Data Collection and Data Analysis

Table 2. Interviewee profile

ID	Role	Country	Sector	Size
I1	Consulting Team Manager	Portugal	R&D	Large
I2	Researcher / Professor	Portugal	R&D	Large
I3	Project Manager	Portugal	R&D	Large
I4	Researcher	Portugal	R&D	Large
I5	Research Centre Manager	Portugal	R&D	Large
I6	Research Centre Manager	Portugal	R&D	Large
I7	Team Leader	Portugal	Machine Vision and Intelligent Systems	SME
I8	Head of Digital Transformation	Portugal	Computer Systems Design	SME
I9	CTO	Portugal	Robotics & Automation	SME
I10	CEO	Portugal	Wearable IoT Sensing Solutions	SME
I11	CEO	Portugal	3D Digital Twin & Industrial Simulation	SME
I12	Researcher	Sweden	Testbed and Digital Manufacturing innovation	Large
I13	Research Centre Manager	Portugal	R&D	Large
I14	Researcher / Professor	Spain	R&D	Large
I15	Manufacturing Director / Professor	South Korea	R&D	Large
I16	Researcher	Italy	Technology Transfer & Innovation Support	Large

Semi-structured interviews with open-ended questions were conducted with researchers and organisations involved in national pilots and projects, as well as researchers from international laboratories. This method ensured the collection of data on the study's main topics while allowing further clarification and development of the issues discussed until theoretical saturation was reached [31]. In line with the study's objectives, the interview guide was organised into three sections: testbed characteristics, service offerings, and BM design, along with how these elements influence stakeholders' perceived value and the testbed's usability.

Of the 16 interviewees selected for this research (Table 2), 7 were researchers and coordinators from Portuguese institutions, 5 were members of technological organisations in different positions, and 4 were researchers and developers from international institutions. To maintain anonymity, each interviewee was assigned a unique identification code. The interviews were conducted between March and July 2025 through Microsoft Teams. Interviews ranged from 35 to 99 min, with an average of 52 min. With the interviewees' knowledge and consent, all interviews were recorded digitally to ensure data accuracy and later transcribed into written text.

Data were analysed using reflexive thematic analysis supported by NVivo, combining deductive coding based on the literature with inductive identification of emerging themes [31, 32]. The codes were then organised into broader themes through repeated comparison, reducing the initial categories to key themes aligned with the three main objectives of the study. Relationships between themes were critically analysed by considering alternative explanations, thereby strengthening the validity of the results [31].

Coding consistency was strengthened through an iterative codebook process. The initial codebook was derived from the research objectives and literature review and refined during transcript analysis as new in vivo codes emerged. Coding decisions and code definitions were documented in NVivo to preserve an audit trail. Emerging themes and ambiguous excerpts were discussed among the research team until interpretive agreement was reached, emphasising transparency, reflexive comparison and triangulation rather than statistical inter-coder reliability.

4 Findings

The findings are structured around the three research objectives and interpreted through three interrelated BM dimensions: value proposition, value delivery and value capture. The value proposition dimension concerns the role of testbeds in reducing uncertainty and enabling realistic technology validation. The value delivery dimension concerns the extended service portfolio through which testbeds support experimentation, training, consulting, networking and post-testing activities. The value capture dimension concerns the mechanisms that sustain the testbed over time, including partnerships, hybrid revenue streams and flexible pricing models.

4.1 Innovative and Differentiating Characteristics of a Testbed as a Testing and Experimentation Environment

Answering the first objective, this section outlines the innovative and differentiating characteristics of a testbed as a testing and experimentation environment. As stated by I12 and I15, there are different types of testbeds, some more focused on research and education, while others are more commercially oriented. Throughout this section, stakeholders are grouped into the testbed itself, technology providers, and industrial clients. Technology providers, industrial clients, academic institutions, and the public and private entities that play a role in the testbed's activities are also treated as partners in the broader ecosystem.

Partner Expectations. Several concerns and interests were expressed during the interviews about partnerships with a testbed. When working with a testbed for new technologies, industrial clients often worry about the technology's maturity and readiness. As I9 states, "Many times these technologies are not mature enough. Before introducing a product into the market, or testing solutions in an environment closer to reality, these tests must ensure that the technology works as promised by the vendors." I2, I4, I8, and I13 confirm that a testbed's role in a research & development project is to address the uncertainty of introducing a new technology into an existing solution, identify weaknesses, and validate the final solution.

More than simply testing whether the technology functions, I5, I7 and I8 emphasise the importance of verifying whether it works under realistic factory-floor conditions and whether it adapts not only to the product but also to the existing process. This reinforces the role of testbeds in validating technologies under near-real conditions before industrial deployment.

Technology readiness is closely linked to cost risk. I2, I3, I12 and I16 emphasise the losses associated with stopping production lines to test prototypes, while I7 and I11 highlight that testbeds reduce costs by enabling early validation and providing access to equipment, such as 5G infrastructure, that would otherwise be costly to acquire and maintain.

I11 highlights this economic value directly: "We are using equipment we did not have. To test with 5G, we would have to buy an antenna and maintain a private 5G network, which is an unbearable cost. By participating in a testbed, we have access to all this equipment without paying for it." I7 and I13 add that testing is usually completed much more quickly than if industrial clients worked directly with technology providers in their own industrial environments.

Before testing, partners must address confidentiality, legal arrangements, data protection and intellectual property. These concerns are especially relevant when multiple actors from the same industry use the same testbed, as noted by I10, I12 and I16. On the provider side, I10, I11, I15 and I16 emphasise the need for clear contractual rules and protection of intellectual property. To address these risks, interviewees recommend transparent communication channels, legal support where necessary, clear project roadmaps and coordination mechanisms such as shared digital platforms, as suggested by I6, I8, I10 and I16.

The industrial client may also worry about supplier or technology lock-in, becoming dependent on a single provider or solution once the project concludes. For that reason, I16 recommends involving legal expertise within the testbed framework to assess both the partnership terms and the technology's legal and ethical aspects. To address these challenges more broadly, I8 and I10 argue that partners must be offered transparency, visibility, and trust through clear communication channels. I6 adds that there should be a clear roadmap and an entity responsible for coordinating the project, updating all partners on unexpected changes, and analysing their impact. I10 suggests a digital platform where partners can share information, documents, reports, and contacts.

Testbed Restrictions and Advantages. Just as industrial clients may worry about the reliability of a technology in their own environment, interviewees also emphasise the importance of the infrastructure already available to the client. I3, I9, I10, I13, and I14 underscore that industrial infrastructure is often outdated and poorly compatible with new technologies. In other cases, clients already possess the basic technological foundation needed for integration, allowing the testbed to build on existing resources and deliver a more complete solution. Access to a broader range of technologies in the testbed enables more realistic experimentation, reduces variables, and improves the overall process, according to I2, I3, I10, and I13.

This infrastructural variability significantly influences project scope and testing costs. I1 notes that outdated infrastructure may expand the project's scope and therefore increase its cost, whereas successful adoption can later simplify scaling and reduce maintenance costs. The value of the testbed is especially visible for SMEs, which usually lack the expertise and the budget to build internal innovation departments. In that context, a partnership with a testbed gives access to expert personnel and a wider set of testing technologies, as highlighted by I1, I3, I4, I9, and I11.

In the specific case of 5G, I3 compares it with Wi-Fi to highlight its advantages. Although Wi-Fi may approach similar speeds, it remains a localised network and can become unreliable in remote industrial areas. By contrast, 5G can support high-speed connectivity, decentralised data storage, and real-time updates across broader spaces. According to I3 and I5, the testbed allows industrial clients to test both Wi-Fi and 5G configurations and determine which one best meets their objectives. I3 and I10 also point out that 5G infrastructure enables processing raw data at the antenna level and either storing it in the cloud or feeding it back into the system, thereby reducing the need for local hardware and enabling more scalable experimentation.

The findings also show that the value of a testbed extends beyond technological infrastructure. Although 5G and other Industry 4.0 technologies are versatile and promising, they require experienced personnel, who are difficult to recruit and retain because of strong market demand. I1, I4, and I9 identify this as a major constraint. As a response, I9, I12, I15, and I16 propose collaborative partnerships with universities, which can provide a renewable pool of human resources while also giving students practical exposure to real projects. Finally, I7 notes that the testbed stands out because, unlike direct collaboration with a single provider, it enables industrial clients to evaluate not only a single technology but also the integration of several technologies within the same solution.

These findings reinforce the role of governance mechanisms, particularly trust, transparency, and coordination, in multi-stakeholder infrastructures, as highlighted in prior literature [27].

4.2 Services Available in a Testbed

Building on the characterization of testbeds, the interviews show that their service portfolio should extend well beyond experimentation. Testbeds may offer a broad spectrum of services, from technical validation and demonstration to education, consulting, networking, and matchmaking. In this sense, the testbed is not merely an infrastructure provider; it also acts as mediator, capability builder, and orchestrator across the project lifecycle.

Services and Experience Customisation. To outline the services discussed by participants, it is first necessary to understand the context in which each service should be delivered. I1, I3, I10, and I12 believe that before a project roadmap is even constructed, an analysis of the industrial client's ecosystem should be conducted. This includes identifying the client's pains and their origins, performing a digital maturity assessment to understand which technologies and capabilities are already available, and conducting a market analysis to assess the potential demand for the technology provider's solution or to identify alternative solutions that could also be considered.

Interviewees also emphasise that the likely impact of the proposed solution on the industrial client should be assessed in advance. I2 and I11 note that the benefits of adoption must be explained clearly, particularly in terms of profitability, efficiency, and differentiation. At the same time, challenges must also be made explicit. Because projects are often highly tailored, technology providers need to show flexibility during the testing phase, ensuring that the technology adapts to the client's needs. On the industrial side, I12 and I16 warn that introducing a solution too early to the workforce may generate resistance if employees fear replacement before the technology has even proven its value.

After this initial assessment, respondents describe a planning phase in which the project stages, activities, resource requirements, testbed design, responsibilities of each partner, and implementation processes are defined. I2, I3, I5, I7, I10, I11, and I15 stress that the solution must be adaptable not only to the client's technology and processes but also to the end user. Otherwise, greater effort will be demanded from the user, producing a negative experience and weakening adoption.

The core of the service portfolio remains testing and validation. I2, I5, I7, I8, I10, I12, I14, and I16 agree that expert support is essential throughout this phase, because specialists are needed to monitor, collect, analyse, and communicate test data, as well as to design the roadmap for additional tests, adjustments, or implementation. The presence of experienced personnel shortens project duration, reduces risks, increases the probability of success, and improves reproducibility. Once the solution has been validated in the laboratory and in near-real conditions, it is ready for deployment and integration into existing industrial infrastructures, with only minor adjustments in some cases.

Beyond project-specific services, the testbed can also facilitate the broader diffusion of technology. I8, I10, I12, I15, and I16 identify networking and matchmaking services as particularly valuable, whether through events, demonstrations, or project brokerage. I12 describes a possible ecosystem-orchestrator role that would "try to extract from each of the projects they work with what the main value proposition is and who the responsible actors are, and to connect them to other projects." Likewise, demonstrations and guided visits can help potential industrial clients understand the available technologies, how they function, and why they may be relevant to their own environment. In these cases, the testbed becomes a neutral and safe space for open discussion of a technology's potential, rather than a purely commercial setting.

Educational initiatives also emerged as an important service category. Partnerships with academic institutions can help students gain exposure to new technologies before entering the labour market, while simultaneously supplying the testbed with new human resources and fresh ideas. I7 makes this diffusion role explicit when noting that "these students will go to the market, they will probably be responsible for the digital transformation of their organisations." For this reason, interviewees suggest internships, open days, and other training-oriented activities as mechanisms for strengthening both technology dissemination and workforce development.

Post-testing Services. Post-testing services are considered essential for maintaining the value created during the project. Industrial clients need support not only before and during testing, but also after deployment. Interviewees identify two main forms of post-project assistance: technological support and training. According to I12, long-term ownership of maintenance should not remain with the testbed if it wishes to stay focused on innovation and cutting-edge technologies. Instead, technological support after deployment should gradually be transferred to the technology provider, who developed and owns the solution.

At the same time, respondents emphasise the value of a short-term period of extended support after implementation. I8 notes that many problems only emerge after several weeks of in-house use, especially when new users are introduced. This extended involvement can therefore help identify additional flaws and improve the interface for future projects. Some interviewees also suggest a re-evaluation of the industrial client's digital maturity at the beginning of this support period, so that new training priorities and future project opportunities can be identified.

Training is particularly important once the technology has been fully deployed and integrated. I1, I3, I4, I5, I7, I11, I13, and I16 stress that clients should be enabled to understand the technology and gain independence. Otherwise, they may feel trapped in the relationship or exposed to ongoing maintenance fees. I12 frames this point clearly: "Companies that want maintenance support might be afraid of being left alone with a new technology, but I do not think they are ready to pay testbed fees forever." He suggests that maintenance managers should be involved during the development process so that internal maintenance strategies can be co-developed and refined later through focused innovation sprints.

The diversity of services identified reflects a service-oriented BM logic, consistent with prior research on servitization and technological infrastructures [19–21].

4.3 Sustainable BM for a Testbed

Developing a sustainable BM is central to a testbed's long-term viability. In line with the literature on technological infrastructure BMs [12–14], testbeds must articulate a clear value proposition, enable value co-creation among stakeholders, and establish effective mechanisms for value capture. The empirical findings, based on interviews with stakeholders across research institutions, technology providers, and industrial organisations (I1–I16), provide insight into how these elements are operationalised in practice.

The results highlight the importance of diverse and complementary partnerships. Interviewees (e.g., I9, I11, I13, I14) emphasise the role of government entities in reducing financial and regulatory barriers, while others (I1, I2, I7, I10, I12, I13) stress the contribution of technology providers in expanding the testbed's technological capabilities. Academic institutions and training organisations (I4, I9, I12, I15, I16) are also identified as key partners, supporting knowledge creation and access to skilled human resources. These findings reinforce the role of testbeds as ecosystem orchestrators rather than standalone infrastructures.

Table 3. BM canvas synthesis for a sustainable 5G testbed

BM Canvas	Configuration for a sustainable 5G testbed
Key partners	Research institutions; academic institutions; technology providers; industrial clients; public funding entities; training organisations; industrial and innovation networks (I1, I2, I4, I7, I9, I10, I12–I16)
Key activities	Testing and validation; solution development; demonstrations; consulting; mentoring; training; matchmaking; digital maturity assessment; project coordination; post-testing support (I1–I8, I10–I16)
Key resources	Physical testbed infrastructure; 5G and digital infrastructure; data-analysis and network-control tools; researchers, engineers and technical experts; project-management and coordination capabilities (I1, I3, I4, I9–I13, I16)
Value proposition	Controlled near-real experimentation; reduced uncertainty, risk and implementation cost; access to scarce 5G capabilities; faster technology validation; support for technology adoption by SMEs; training and knowledge diffusion (I1–I5, I7–I13, I16)
Customer relationships	Project-based collaboration; co-development agreements; long-term partnerships; membership-based engagement; transparent communication; roadmap coordination and post-project follow-up (I2, I4–I12, I14, I16)
Channels	Technology providers; publicly funded projects; demonstrations and visits; events, fairs, conferences and workshops; academic networks; client referrals (I1–I5, I7, I9, I12–I16)
Customer segments	Manufacturing SMEs and start-ups; technology providers; industrial clients seeking to test Industry 4.0 solutions; large industrial firms; training organisations (I1, I3, I4, I7–I16)
Cost structure	Equipment maintenance and updating; specialised human resources; infrastructure and connectivity costs; training, coordination and project-management costs; marketing and ecosystem engagement (I1, I3, I4, I9–I12, I15, I16)
Revenue streams	Public funding; private collaborative projects; project-based services; consulting and training fees; memberships or subscriptions; sponsorships; royalties or licensing where appropriate (I1, I3–I6, I9–I15)

Customer acquisition is a multi-channel process that combines indirect and direct strategies. Several interviewees (I1, I4, I7, I9, I14, I16) note that industrial clients often engage with testbeds through technology providers or publicly funded projects, while others highlight the importance of proactive strategies such as events, demonstrations, and participation in innovation networks. The findings suggest that effective acquisition requires deliberate ecosystem engagement rather than passive participation.

Retention is consistently identified as more valuable than continuous acquisition. Interviewees (I2, I4, I5, I9, I10, I11, I14, I16) emphasise that long-term relationships depend on trust, transparency, and the consistent delivery of value. Additional factors such as certification (I10, I13, I15) and the uniqueness of the testbed's infrastructure, particularly in the case of 5G, also contribute to partner return. However, as several participants noted (e.g., I7, I12), clients may gradually develop internal capabilities, requiring testbeds to continuously innovate and update their offerings to remain relevant.

Financial sustainability is primarily based on hybrid revenue models. Interviewees (I1, I3, I4, I5, I9, I11, I12, I13, I14, I15) identify public funding as the primary financial foundation, complemented by private revenue streams from project-based services, consulting, training, and infrastructure access. Additional mechanisms, including sponsorships, royalties, and data-related services (I3, I10, I11, I15), are considered potential complements, although their implementation requires careful balancing to avoid limiting accessibility.

Three main pricing approaches emerge from the data. Per-project pricing is the most widely supported model (I1, I3, I5, I7, I8, I9, I10, I12, I13, I14, I16), as it allows clear structuring of services and costs. Membership models (I4, I6, I9, I12, I13, I14, I15) provide recurring access to services and networks, while credit-based systems (I6, I7, I8, I13) offer flexibility but require careful management to avoid inefficiencies. Across all models, interviewees stress the importance of adaptability to different stakeholder needs.

To systematise the findings, Table 3 presents a BM Canvas synthesis for a sustainable 5G testbed. The table organises the findings reported in the previous sections into a structured BM logic, making explicit the relationships between value proposition, value delivery and value capture.

Overall, the findings indicate that sustainable testbed BMs depend on integrating ecosystem partnerships, diversified revenue mechanisms, and flexible service and pricing strategies, supported by continuous innovation and strong stakeholder alignment.

5 Discussion

The findings show that the novelty of the proposed framework lies in adapting generic business-model logic to the specific operating conditions of 5G-enabled testbeds. While the study builds on established business-model and technology-adoption concepts, its contribution is to configure these concepts around three testbed-specific dimensions: controlled experimentation as the core value proposition, an extended service portfolio as the main value-delivery mechanism, and hybrid public-private funding with flexible pricing as the main value-capture mechanism. This configuration treats trust, neutrality, IP and data governance, and ecosystem orchestration as central design requirements rather than peripheral contextual factors.

Reducing uncertainty and enabling technology validation are therefore interpreted as core value propositions of the testbed BM. For SMEs, the value of the testbed is not limited to access to infrastructure; it also lies in generating validated evidence about compatibility, performance under near-real conditions and implementation feasibility. For technology providers, the value proposition lies in credible demonstration, certification and accelerated market access.

Consistent with Rogers [18], the findings confirm that compatibility, observability, and trialability are key determinants of technology adoption, particularly in industrial environments characterised by operational risk and legacy infrastructure. The scarcity of 5G testbeds identified by I2, I4, and I16, together with the lack of resources and knowledge, particularly among SMEs, positions testbeds as key environments for experimentation and validation of general-purpose technologies [10] while also helping to alleviate data-management and regulatory concerns [27].

However, introducing new technologies into existing systems requires technical expertise to assess, design, and test new solutions, as well as an ecosystem that enables the sharing of knowledge, expertise, and ideas among partners. Such integrations may be disruptive to an existing BM [13], requiring complementary services beyond technology testing [19]. To overcome this hindrance, hybrid models of public-private collaboration, complete with training, consulting, and certification services, emerge as the most sustainable strategy for testbeds.

Trust and transparency are identified as key factors influencing partner return (I2; I10; I11), aligning with [27] and Teece's [12] notion that a BM outlines an idea's feasibility and profitability through value creation, delivery, and capture. In this sense, the results support the view that testbeds enhance compatibility, observability, and trialability, simplify the integration and evaluation of new solutions within Industry 4.0 contexts, and sustain themselves through diversified revenue streams and service-oriented value propositions.

6 Conclusions

This study addressed the research question by analysing how testbed characteristics, service offerings, and BM mechanisms contribute to the development of sustainable testbeds in Industry 4.0 contexts. By combining insights from the literature with empirical evidence from stakeholders, the study identified the key factors that underpin value creation, delivery, and capture in testbed environments.

The limited availability of fully functioning 5G testbeds increases their value, particularly for organisations that otherwise lack access to expensive infrastructures and specialised expertise. At the same time, financial sustainability depends on hybrid models that integrate public funding with private revenue from project-based services, training, consulting, certification, memberships, sponsorships, and other complementary streams. Testbeds, therefore, act not only as experimentation platforms but also as innovation intermediaries that simplify the integration and evaluation of new solutions within Industry 4.0 contexts, while building long-term organisational sustainability. While the study provides insights into how BM design can support the use of testbeds, it does not directly measure technology adoption outcomes, which represents an avenue for future research.

While the study provides valuable insights, its findings are exploratory and based on a limited sample of stakeholders. Therefore, the results should be interpreted as context-dependent. Future research could expand the analysis to additional geographical contexts, testbed types, and quantitative validation of the proposed BM framework.

Acknowledgments. This work is co-financed by Component 5—Capitalization and Business Innovation, integrated in the Resilience Dimension of the Recovery and Resilience Plan within the scope of the Recovery and Resilience Mechanism (MRR) of the European Union (EU), framed in the Next Generation EU, for the period 2021–2026, within project Produtech_R3, with reference 60.

Disclosure of Interests The authors have no competing interests to declare that are relevant to the content of this article.

References

1. Almada-Lobo, F.: The Industry 4.0 revolution and the future of Manufacturing Execution Systems (MES). jim. **3**, 16–21 (2016). https://doi.org/10.24840/2183-0606_003.004_0003
2. Liao, Y., Deschamps, F., Loures, E.D.F.R., Ramos, L.F.P.: Past, present and future of Industry 4.0—a systematic literature review and research agenda proposal. Int. J. Prod. Res. **55**, 3609–3629 (2017). https://doi.org/10.1080/00207543.2017.1308576
3. Schlechtendahl, J., Keinert, M., Kretschmer, F., Lechler, A., Verl, A.: Making existing production systems Industry 4.0-ready: holistic approach to the integration of existing production systems in Industry 4.0 environments. Prod. Eng. Res. Devel. **9**, 143–148 (2015). https://doi.org/10.1007/s11740-014-0586-3
4. Dutta, G., Kumar, R., Sindhwani, R., Singh, R.K.: Digital transformation priorities of India's discrete manufacturing SMEs – a conceptual study in perspective of Industry 4.0. CR. **30**, 289–314 (2020). https://doi.org/10.1108/CR-03-2019-0031
5. Abulibdeh, A., Zaidan, E., Abulibdeh, R.: Navigating the confluence of artificial intelligence and education for sustainable development in the era of Industry 4.0: challenges, opportunities, and ethical dimensions. J. Clean. Prod. **437**, 140527 (2024). https://doi.org/10.1016/j.jclepro.2023.140527
6. Tagliazucchi, G., Della Santa, S., Gherardini, F.: Design of a living lab for autonomous driving: an investigation under the lens of the triple helix model. J. Technol. Transf. **49**, 876–899 (2024). https://doi.org/10.1007/s10961-023-10009-x
7. Koch, C., Blind, K.: Towards agile standardization: testbeds in support of standardization for the IIoT. IEEE Trans. Eng. Manag. **68**, 59–74 (2021). https://doi.org/10.1109/TEM.2020.2979697
8. Park, A., Jabagi, N., Kietzmann, J.: The truth about 5G: It's not (only) about downloading movies faster! Bus. Horiz. **64**, 19–28 (2021). https://doi.org/10.1016/j.bushor.2020.09.009
9. Taboada, I., Shee, H.: Understanding 5G technology for future supply chain management. Int J Log Res Appl. **24**, 392–406 (2021). https://doi.org/10.1080/13675567.2020.1762850
10. Jabagi, N., Park, A., Kietzmann, J.: The 5G revolution: expectations versus reality. IT Prof. **22**, 8–15 (2020). https://doi.org/10.1109/MITP.2020.2972139
11. Singh, A., Payal, A., Bharti, S.: A walkthrough of the emerging IoT paradigm: visualizing inside functionalities, key features, and open issues. J. Netw. Comput. Appl. **143**, 111–151 (2019). https://doi.org/10.1016/j.jnca.2019.06.013
12. Teece, D.J.: Business models, business strategy and innovation. Long Range Plan. **43**, 172–194 (2010). https://doi.org/10.1016/j.lrp.2009.07.003
13. Zott, C., Amit, R., Massa, L.: The business model: recent developments and future research. J. Manag. **37**, 1019–1042 (2011). https://doi.org/10.1177/0149206311406265
14. Foss, N.J., Saebi, T.: Fifteen years of research on business model innovation: how far have we come, and where should we go? J. Manag. **43**, 200–227 (2017). https://doi.org/10.1177/0149206316675927
15. Marston, S., Li, Z., Bandyopadhyay, S., Zhang, J., Ghalsasi, A.: Cloud computing — the business perspective. Decis. Support. Syst. **51**, 176–189 (2011). https://doi.org/10.1016/j.dss.2010.12.006

16. Sharma, S., Sharma, B.: Optimal selection of application loading on cloud services. Int. J. Prod. Res. **54**, 6512–6531 (2016). https://doi.org/10.1080/00207543.2016.1173256
17. Attaran, M., Woods, J.: Cloud computing technology: improving small business performance using the internet. J. Small Bus. Entrep. **31**, 495–519 (2019). https://doi.org/10.1080/08276331.2018.1466850
18. Rogers, E.M.: Diffusion of Innovations. Free Press [u.a.], New York, NY (1983)
19. Witell, L., Löfgren, M.: From service for free to service for fee: business model innovation in manufacturing firms. J. Serv. Manag. **24**, 520–533 (2013). https://doi.org/10.1108/JOSM-04-2013-0103
20. Sewpersadh, N.S.: Disruptive business value models in the digital era. J. Innov. Entrep. **12**, 2 (2023). https://doi.org/10.1186/s13731-022-00252-1
21. Frank, A.G., Mendes, G.H.S., Ayala, N.F., Ghezzi, A.: Servitization and Industry 4.0 convergence in the digital transformation of product firms: a business model innovation perspective. Technol. Forecast. Soc. Chang. **141**, 341–351 (2019). https://doi.org/10.1016/j.techfore.2019.01.014
22. Pohang University of Science and Technology: Pohang University of Science and Technology (POSTECH). https://www.postech.ac.kr/eng/index.do
23. ISQ – Engenharia, Inovação e Sustentabilidade: ISQ – Engenharia, Inovação e Sustentabilidade, https://www.isq.pt/, (2025)
24. European Institute of Innovation & Technology: European institute of innovation & technology. https://www.eit.europa.eu/ (2025)
25. Laboratório de Indústria e Inovação do INESC TEC: iiLab INESC TEC. https://www.inesctec.pt/pt/laboratorios/iilab-laboratorio-de-industria-e-inovacao (2025)
26. SII-Lab—Stena Industry Innovation Lab: SII-Lab—stena industry innovation lab. https://www.sii-lab.se/?lang=en
27. Santoso, J., Wibowo, M., Raharjo, B.: Trustworthiness in supply chains: leveraging private blockchain solutions. IJSOM. **12**(2), 123–148 (2024). https://doi.org/10.22034/ijsom.2024.110372.3087
28. Osterwalder, A., Pigneur, Y., Clark, T.: Business Model Generation: A Handbook for Visionaries, Game Changers, and Challengers. Wiley, Hoboken, NJ (2010)
29. Raftery, J., McGeorge, D., Walters, M.: Breaking up methodological monopolies: a multi-paradigm approach to construction management research. Constr. Manag. Econ. **15**, 291–297 (1997). https://doi.org/10.1080/014461997373024
30. Goldkuhl, G.: Pragmatism *vs* interpretivism in qualitative information systems research. Eur. J. Inf. Syst. **21**, 135–146 (2012). https://doi.org/10.1057/ejis.2011.54
31. Saunders, M., Lewis, P., Thornhill, A.: Research Methods for Business Students. Pearson, Harlow Munich (2016)
32. Saldaña, J.: The Coding Manual for Qualitative Researchers. SAGE, Los Angeles, Calif. London New Delhi Singapore Washington DC (2016)

The IFIP WG5.7 Service Systems Special Interest Group Research Agenda Evolution on Service and Product-Service Systems Design, Engineering and Management

Shaun West[1](✉), David Romero[2], Paolo Gaiardelli[3], Veronica Arioli[3], Claudio Sassanelli[4], and Giuditta Pezzotta[3]

[1] Lucerne University of Applied Sciences and Arts, Lucerne, Switzerland
shaun.west@hslu.ch
[2] Tecnológico de Monterrey, Mexico City, Mexico
[3] University of Bergamo, Bergamo, Italy
{paolo.gaiardelli,veronica.arioli,giuditta.pezzotta}@unibg.it
[4] Politecnico di Bari, Bari, Italy
claudio.sassanelli@poliba.it

Abstract. Over the past decade, Service Systems and Product-Service Systems (PSSs) have become important research areas within the IFIP WG5.7 on Advances in Production Management Systems (APMS). In particular, the Special Interest Group (SIG) on Service Systems Design, Engineering & Management (SSDE&M) has provided an interdisciplinary forum for advancing research on service-oriented solutions in manufacturing and industrial service contexts. Despite the growing number of contributions within this SIG, a systematic synthesis of its research streams remains limited. This paper investigates the evolution of the IFIP WG5.7 SSDE&M SIG research agenda over the past decade of APMS conferences. Drawing on a structured literature review and thematic analysis, the study adopts a backcasting perspective to examine how research themes have evolved and how the SIG's focus has shifted in response to servitization, digitalization, and sustainability. The analysis identifies four distinct phases in the evolution of this research area and four dominant research streams shaping the field. Building on this retrospective reflection, the paper adopts a forecasting approach to identify key research gaps and propose future investigations for Service Systems and PSSs research. The main contribution is a conceptual research framework that links research streams, persistent gaps, and future directions to support the renewal of the SSDE&M SIG research agenda.

Keywords: Service Systems · Product-Service Systems · Servitization · Services Lifecycle Management · Research Agenda

Published by Springer Nature Switzerland AG 2027
G. Pezzotta et al. (Eds.): APMS 2026, IFIP AICT 808, pp. 556–571, 2027.
https://doi.org/10.1007/978-3-032-38594-9_37

1 Introduction

Over the past 20 years, manufacturing companies have increasingly adopted service-oriented strategies to boost competitiveness and generate new sources of value [1]. Vandermerwe & Rada [2] described this change as "servitization", which involves integrating products and services to deliver value throughout the lifecycle of industrial assets and consumer products. Simultaneously, *Product-Service Systems (PSSs)* emerged as a framework explaining the shift from product-centric models to integrated product-service solutions [3], with Tukker [4] later developing typologies for such systems. Subsequently, scientific research has further enhanced the *servitization perspective* by investigating combined product-service value propositions and their implications for manufacturing firms [5]. Accordingly, research on *PSSs* and *servitization* has expanded across the fields of operations management, industrial engineering, and service science.

Recent advances in *digital technologies* have accelerated this (digital) transformation. *Digitalization* enables novel forms of *(digital) servitization* through connected products, industrial data platforms, and advanced service offerings [6, 7]. As a result, research on *service systems* has increasingly concentrated on issues such as lifecycle service engineering, service ecosystem collaboration, and sustainability within service-driven business models [8, 9].

Within this context, the International Conference on Advances in Production Management Systems (APMS) has constituted a prominent forum for research on manufacturing systems and industrial innovation. Specifically, the IFIP WG5.7 Special Interest Group (SIG) on *Service Systems Design, Engineering and Management* is dedicated to advancing research on the design, engineering, and management of service systems in industrial settings: https://www.ifipwg57.org/special-interest-groups/

Over the past decade, a growing body of contributions within this SIG has addressed topics such as PSS design, digital servitization, service operations, and sustainability in service systems. This increasing relevance is also reflected in the evolution of dedicated special sessions and tracks at APMS conferences in recent years, as summarized in Table 1. Notwithstanding this expansion, the research within the community has not yet been systematically synthesized. Accordingly, this paper aims to analyze the development of the *service systems research agenda* within the IFIP WG5.7 SSDE&M SIG and identify future research directions. To address this *relevant gap,* this paper develops a *conceptual framework* linking *research streams, cross-cutting gaps, and future research directions.* The framework synthesizes the evolution of service systems research and supports the definition of future APMS research priorities. By reviewing contributions from the past decade of APMS conferences, the paper consolidates the evolution of this research stream, delineates dominant research themes, and highlights research gaps that may guide future research. This SIG evolution reflects the broader development of PSS and servitization research, which has moved from product-service design towards digital servitization, ecosystems, and sustainability. Its main distinction lies in its manufacturing systems focus, with a stronger emphasis on engineering methods, lifecycle management, industrial operations, and digital technologies in production and production systems.

The rest of this paper is organised as follows. Section 2 details the method used to select the literature for the review of relevant contributions. Section 3 examines the development of service systems research in APMS conferences, outlining key phases in

Table 1. Development of APMS conference special sessions/tracks related to service systems and product-service systems between 2021 and 2025

Year	Relevant APMS Special Sessions/Tracks
2021	• Integrated Manufacturing & Service Operations Management for PSSs. • Engineering of Smart Product-Service Systems of the Future.
2022	• Service & Operations Management in the Context of Digitally-Enabled PSSs. • Sustainable & Digital Servitization.
2023	• Exploring Digital Servitization in Manufacturing. • Digitally Enabled and Sustainable Service & Operations Management in PSS Lifecycle.
2024	• Barriers and Challenges for Transition towards Circular and Sustainable Production Processes and Servitized Business Models. • Methods and Tools to Achieve the Digital & Sustainable Servitization of Manufacturing Companies.
2025	• Enhancing the Value Creation Mechanism of Manufacturing Value Chains through Digital Platforms, Circular Strategies, and Servitization Principles. • Methods and Tools for Assessing the Value of Digital, Sustainable, and Servitized Offerings of Manufacturing Companies.

its evolution. Section 4 identifies the main research streams emerging from the literature. Section 5 presents a conceptual framework linking these research streams to the identified research gaps and proposes a future research agenda. Finally, Section 6 presents the conclusions and outlines future work for the IFIP WG5.7 SSDE&M SIG and the broader APMS community.

2 Literature Identification Method

This study employs a *structured literature review* coupled with *interpretive thematic analysis* to investigate the development of *service systems research* within the APMS community. *Structured literature reviews* are commonly used in business and management research to consolidate diverse contributions and detect patterns within a research area [10]. When examining the development of a research domain, *thematic analysis* provides a systematic approach for identifying recurring concepts, research themes, and methodological trends within qualitative datasets and bodies of literature [11]. The reviewed papers were analyzed using a *hybrid inductive-deductive thematic coding approach.* Initial categories were informed by Service Systems and PSS literature and refined inductively from the APMS conference papers. Codes were iteratively compared across papers, discussed in the workshop, and consolidated into four research phases and four research streams. Such methods are widely employed in research synthesis and theory development to assess the evolution of scholarly fields and highlight opportunities for future investigation [12].

This literature review focuses on papers presented at and published in the APMS proceedings from 2018 to 2025. Restricting the review to this conference context enables a targeted examination of the evolution of *service systems research* within the APMS community. A *staged screening process* was adopted to identify relevant contributions. First, papers were retrieved from the APMS proceedings based on their association with the SIG thematic domain. The selected papers were subsequently analyzed and grouped by research focus, thereby enabling the identification of recurring themes and dominant research streams. This initial search resulted in approximately 40 papers.

Second, these papers were subsequently screened for relevance based on their focus on *service system design, PSSs, digital servitization, service operations management, or sustainability in service-oriented manufacturing contexts.* Following this relevance screening, approximately 20 papers were retained for *detailed thematic analysis.* The selection was *purposive* rather than exhaustive, focusing on contributions that were most representative of the evolution of *service systems research* within the community. Papers were selected for their *thematic relevance* and ability to illustrate *key shifts in research focus* over time, as described in Table 1. These papers constitute the core dataset used to identify recurring research themes, methodological approaches, and shifts in research focus over the analyzed period. The selected contributions were then grouped by research theme and examined to identify phases in the *evolution of service systems research* within the APMS community. The analysis integrates both *retrospective* and *prospective perspectives.* The initial stage employs a *backcasting approach* to explore how research topics have developed over time. Through *thematic analysis,* the study captures shifts in research focus, emerging themes, and methodological advancements, thereby enabling the identification of phases in the evolution of service systems research and key research streams within the APMS community. The second stage employs a *forecasting perspective* to identify *future research opportunities.* In addition to examining the *future research directions* outlined in the reviewed papers, the authors conducted a *forward-looking analysis* through an online workshop. These sessions critically reflected on findings of the literature review and discussed *emerging research challenges* in service systems research. The workshop was held with three of the authors; the workshop was transcribed, and additional insights were captured in meeting notes. The resulting material was analyzed alongside future research recommendations from the reviewed papers to inform the conceptual framework and research agenda presented in this paper.

3 IFIP WG5.7 SSDE&M SIG Research Agenda Evolution

The *thematic analysis* of the reviewed papers reveals a progression in the focus of research presented within the IFIP WG5.7 SSDE&M SIG over the past years. While individual studies address a variety of topics related to *service systems,* several recurring themes and shifts in research emphasis emerge over time. These developments reflect both the maturation of PSS research and the influence of broader changes in manufacturing systems, such as digital technologies and sustainability considerations. Based on this analysis, four phases in the evolution can be identified: (i) foundations, (ii) digital enablement, (iii) ecosystems and sustainability, and (iv) performance. The following subsections describe these four phases and outline the dominant research themes characterizing each stage of development.

3.1 Phase 1 – Foundations of Product-Service Systems

The first phase represents the *foundations stage* of PSS research within the APMS community, roughly covering 2015–2019 in the APMS proceedings. During this time, research concentrated on developing conceptual bases and engineering methods for integrated product-service solutions in manufacturing firms. As outlined in Table 2, key themes included (i) servitization and PSSs, (ii) service engineering techniques, (iii) PSS design methods, and (iv) lifecycle-focused views.

Table 2. Phase 1: Foundations of Product-Service Systems

Author(s) / Year	Key Research Themes
Marjanovic et al. (2018) [13]	Service Engineering Foundations for PSSs.
Freitag & Wiesner (2018) [14]	Methods for Designing Industrial (Smart) Service Systems.
Medini et al. (2018) [15]	Engineering Approaches for Integrated Product-Service Offerings.
Larsen et al. (2018) [16]	Lifecycle Perspectives in PSS Development.
Senderek et al. (2019) [17]	Integration of Product and Service Development Processes.
Orellano et al. (2020) [18]	Frameworks for PSS Implementation in Manufacturing Firms.

Phase 1 reflects a *shift* from broad servitization concepts towards the engineering of PSS as structured design objects. The *dominant unit of analysis* is the firm or product-service offering, with *methods primarily grounded* in conceptual frameworks, design methodologies, and case studies. *Remaining gaps concern* the limited integration of lifecycle value, economic assessment, and sustainability outcomes into early PSS design.

A *central focus* concerned the development of *service engineering* and *PSS design methodologies*. Researchers examined how services could be systematically co-created with physical products, as well as how engineering principles from product development may be adapted to service system design. Several studies have proposed conceptual frameworks, modelling approaches, and design methodologies to support integrated offerings and to address organizational and engineering challenges associated with combining product and service domains. Research further explored service architectures, modular service concepts, and lifecycle-oriented approaches aimed at supporting maintenance, operational support, and performance enhancement across industrial asset lifecycles. From a *methodological standpoint,* scientific research predominantly relied on *conceptual frameworks, design-oriented approaches, literature reviews, and case studies.* While these studies established the foundations of PSS research within the APMS community, notable gaps persisted, particularly with regards to economic evaluation, lifecycle value models, and the sustainability implications of PSSs.

Overall, Phase 1 laid the "conceptual" and "methodological" groundwork for future research. By advancing service engineering techniques, product-service integration methods, and lifecycle thinking, this phase established the basis for later developments in digital servitization, service ecosystems, and sustainability-focused service systems.

3.2 Phase 2 – Digitally-Enabled Service Systems

The second phase marks the period when *digital technologies* began to exert a significant influence on the development of service systems and PSSs within the APMS community. Covering approximately 2018–2022 in the APMS proceedings, this phase illustrates the growing impact of *Industry 4.0 technologies* on *service-oriented business models* in manufacturing firms, as well as their increasing use in *service development and delivery*. Scientific research has increasingly explored how *digital infrastructures* and *connected technologies* can support the creation, delivery, and value capture of integrated "product-service" offerings. As summarized in Table 3, this phase was characterized by the emergence of (i) digitally enabled services, (ii) smart connected products, and (iii) data-driven service models.

Table 3. Phase 2: Digitally-enabled service systems

Author(s) / Year	Key Research Themes
Medini et al. (2018) [15]	Digital Technologies Supporting Product-Service System Development.
Romero et al. (2019) [19]	The Impact of Digital Technologies on Services Characteristics.
Moser et al. (2019) [20]	Digitalization as a Driver of Service-Oriented Business Models.
Stoll et al. (2020) [21]	Data-Driven Services and Digital Service Platforms.
Sala et al. (2020) [22]	Smart Product-Service Systems and Digital Service Delivery.
Zambetti et al. (2020) [23]	Integration of Digital Technologies in Industrial Service Systems.

Phase 2 marks a *shift* in problem framing from PSS design to digitally enabled service delivery. The *unit of analysis expands* from the individual offering to connected assets, data infrastructures, and service platforms. *Methods* are becoming more empirical and technology-oriented, though *gaps remain* in data governance, business-case development, and lifecycle value assessment for digital services.

A *key theme* during this phase was the rise of *IoT-enabled services* and *smart connected products*. Researchers investigated how *connected industrial assets* enable continuous monitoring and advanced services such as predictive maintenance, remote diagnostics, and performance optimization. Studies also underscore the increasing relevance of data in *service delivery*, exploring how data from connected products supports outcome-based services, performance-focused contracts, and new service models. In addition, *digital platforms* and information infrastructures were examined as mechanisms for coordinating service activities and collaboration among manufacturers, service providers, and customers. *Methodologically*, research increasingly drew on *empirical case studies, exploratory studies, and technology-enabled service models,* including early applications of "digital twins" and "digital service infrastructures". Notwithstanding these advances, several gaps remained, particularly concerning the business case for digital servitization, the governance of data sharing, and lifecycle value assessment.

In summary, Phase 2 marks the shift from foundational PSS research towards digitally enabled service systems, establishing the foundation for future research on service ecosystems and sustainability-oriented service systems.

3.3 Phase 3 – Service Ecosystems and Sustainability

The third phase marks the stage where *service systems research* expanded from *firm-level service development* to *broader service ecosystems and sustainability outcomes.* This *transition* was driven by digital infrastructures that increasingly connected manufacturers, service providers, technology partners, and customers beyond the boundaries of individual firms. As a result, research attention shifted towards multi-actor coordination, data sharing, lifecycle performance, resource efficiency, and circular economy concerns. This period, roughly from 2021 onwards in the APMS proceedings, reflects an increasing emphasis on collaboration among multiple actors to deliver integrated service solutions. Research increasingly examines how PSSs operate within networks of organizations and how service-oriented business models can foster more sustainable industrial practices. As summarized in Table 4, this phase is characterized by growing emphasis on (i) circular PSSs, (ii) service ecosystems, (iii) lifecycle sustainability, and (iv) collaborative value creation.

Table 4. Phase 3: Service ecosystems and sustainability

Author(s) / Year	Key Research Themes
Kvadsheim et al. (2021) [24]	Circular PSSs and Sustainability in Service Models.
Nujen et al. (2021) [25]	Service Ecosystems and Collaborative Value Creation.
Bertoni & Machchhar (2022) [26]	Lifecycle Sustainability Perspectives in Product-Service Systems.
Colombo et al. (2022) [27]	Ecosystem Coordination in Digitally-Enabled Service Systems.
Schneider et al. (2022) [28]	Governance and Collaboration in Industrial Service Ecosystems.

Phase 3 broadens the problem framing from firm-level service provision to multi-actor ecosystems and sustainability outcomes. The *transition* to this phase occurs as research expands its *unit of analysis* to networks of manufacturers, service providers, technology partners, and customers. This *shift* is enabled by an increased adoption of ecosystem analysis, sustainability frameworks, and cross-industry cases. *Persistent gaps* in measuring impacts and distributing value, risk, and responsibility drive further evolution.

A *central research focus* during this phase concerns the *integration of sustainability within PSSs*. Researchers explored how service-oriented business models support *circular economy strategies* (including R-strategies) by extending asset lifetimes, improving resource efficiency, and enabling practices such as reuse, refurbishment, and remanufacturing. These studies highlight how service-based offerings shift value creation from product ownership towards lifecycle performance and long-term asset utilization. Another key theme is the increasing prominence of *multi-actor service ecosystems*. Contributions examined how manufacturers, service providers, technology partners, and customers collaborate in the design and delivery of integrated service solutions, emphasizing coordination mechanisms, governance structures, and shared data infrastructures. *Methodologically,* studies increasingly adopt *ecosystem-level analyses, sustainability assessment frameworks, and cross-industry case studies*. However, several research gaps persist, particularly with regards to robust methods for assessing sustainability impacts and understanding how value and risk are distributed across service ecosystems.

As outlined, Phase 3 broadens the research scope by linking service systems to ecosystem collaboration and sustainability challenges, thereby laying the groundwork for later research on integrated service system performance and lifecycle value assessment.

3.4 Phase 4 – Integrated Service System Performance

The fourth phase, currently emerging, marks a shift in research towards *evaluating the overall performance of service systems across their lifecycle*. Beginning to appear in recent APMS contributions, this phase builds upon earlier work on digital servitization and service ecosystems by placing greater emphasis on the *outcomes and impacts of PSSs*. Research increasingly investigates how service-oriented business models influence economic performance, sustainability outcomes, and risk distribution across service ecosystems. As summarized in Table 5, this phase is characterized by a growing emphasis on (i) lifecycle value assessment, (ii) ecosystem governance, and (iii) integrated economic and environmental performance.

Table 5. Phase 4: Integrated service system performance

Author(s) / Year	Key Research Themes
Schneider et al. (2022) [28]	Governance Structures in Industrial Service Ecosystems.
Colombo et al. (2022) [27]	Ecosystem Coordination in Digitally-Enabled Service Systems.
Franke et al. (2024) [29]	Lifecycle Value Assessment in Product-Service Systems.
Ardolino et al. (2024) [30]	Integration of Economic & Sustainability Performance in Service Systems.

This emerging phase reframes service systems research around integrated performance across the lifecycle. The *transition* to this phase is marked by a *shift of the unit of analysis* to the service system, including economic, operational, environmental, and governance dimensions. This evolution highlights the need for *integrated methods* that connect lifecycle value assessment, operational data, ecosystem governance, and sustainability measurement, distinguishing this phase from previous ones.

A *central research focus* during this phase concerns the development of *methods for lifecycle value assessment*. Researchers explore how PSSs can be evaluated using concepts such as *Total Cost of Ownership (TCO), Total Value of Ownership (TVO), and broader lifecycle performance indicators* to capture financial, operational, and environmental impacts across the lifecycle of industrial assets. Another key theme relates to the governance of service ecosystems. Contributions examine how manufacturers, service providers, technology partners, and customers coordinate through governance structures, contractual arrangements, and data-sharing mechanisms to support viable service-oriented business models. *Methodologically,* emerging studies increasingly adopt *integrated lifecycle models, data-driven analytics, and cross-disciplinary approaches*. However, several research gaps remain, particularly regarding robust methods for linking economic, operational, and environmental performance across service ecosystems.

In general, this emerging phase advances service systems research towards evaluating lifecycle performance, economic viability, and sustainability outcomes.

4 Key Research Streams Identified

The analysis of the papers over the past decade uncovers several recurring themes that underpin the development of *service systems research* within the APMS community. While individual studies explore diverse aspects of PSSs and servitization, certain dominant research streams stand out across the reviewed contributions. Four main research streams emerge from the *thematic analysis*. These streams highlight the key topics studied by the APMS community and show how research has shifted from *service engineering* and *system design* to broader issues related to *digital technologies, service operations, and sustainability in service systems*. The four research phases in this study are "analytical periods", not strictly chronological stages. Table 6 summarizes the identified research streams and presents illustrative evidence from the reviewed papers. From the workshop, there were concerns that the research was, to some degree, influenced by targeted research calls (e.g., Horizon Europe) rather than by a genuine research need.

The *thematic analysis* of the reviewed papers identifies four dominant research streams shaping service systems research within the APMS community (see Table 6). These streams reflect the main directions of research over the past decade and illustrate how the field has evolved from *service system design* towards broader issues involving *digital technologies, service operations, and sustainability*. While each stream focuses on different aspects of PSS development, they are closely interconnected. Together, they demonstrate the progression of research from *engineering-oriented design approaches* to *digitally enabled service systems, ecosystem collaboration, and sustainability-oriented service models*.

Table 6. Cross-cutting research streams identified

Research Stream	Main Focus	Key Contributions	Examples Studies
Service System Design and Engineering	Methods and Frameworks for Designing PSS and Service Architectures	• Service Engineering Methods • Modular Service Design • Lifecycle-Oriented Design • Integration of Product and Service Development	Marjanovic et al. (2018) [13] Freitag & Wiesner (2018) [14] Medini et al. (2018) [15] Larsen et al. (2018) [16] Senderek et al. (2019) [17]
Digital Servitization	Role of Digital Technologies in Enabling Service Systems	• IoT-Enabled Services • Connected Products • Digital Platforms • Predictive Maintenance • Data-Driven Service Models	Marjanovic et al. (2019) [33] Moser et al. (2019) [20] Stoll et al. (2020) [21] Sala et al. (2020) [22] Zambetti et al. (2020) [23]
Service Operations and Management	Organizational and Operational Capabilities Supporting PSS	• Servitization Capabilities • Service Delivery Networks • Ecosystem Coordination • Collaborative Service Provision	Moser et al. (2019) [20] Orellano et al. (2020) [18] Holst et al. (2020) [31] Rakic et al. (2020) [32]
Sustainability and Circular Service Systems	Sustainability and Circular Economy in Service Systems	• Circular PSS Models • Lifecycle Sustainability • Resource Efficiency • Ecosystem Governance	Kvadsheim et al. (2021) [24] Bertoni & Machchhar (2022) [26] Colombo et al. (2022) [27] Schneider et al. (2022) [28]

5 Towards a Future Research Framework and Agenda

The previous analysis delineates *distinct research stages, thematic areas, and overarching research gaps* within service systems research. To synthesize these insights, this study develops a *conceptual research framework* that connects the identified *research streams* to *key research gaps* and *emerging directions for future research.* The *conceptual research framework* combines four main *research domains* identified in the reviewed studies, which collectively capture the *key themes* shaping the *service systems research agenda* within the APMS community over the last decade.

Figure 1 depicts the *conceptual research framework* connecting research streams, overarching research gaps, and future research directions. The upper section shows the main *research streams* identified in the literature. At the same time, the middle part highlights *cross-cutting research gaps* that impact multiple streams, including economic viability, lifecycle value assessment, ecosystem governance, and sustainability measurement. The bottom section outlines *future research directions* to address these research gaps. Although research on PSSs has progressed in areas such as service system design, digital (and smart) technologies, and organizational transformation, several challenges remain. Specifically, further investigation is required to better understand how service systems generate lifecycle value, how complex service ecosystems can be effectively managed, how sustainability impacts can be measured, and how operational data can be leveraged to enhance service system performance.

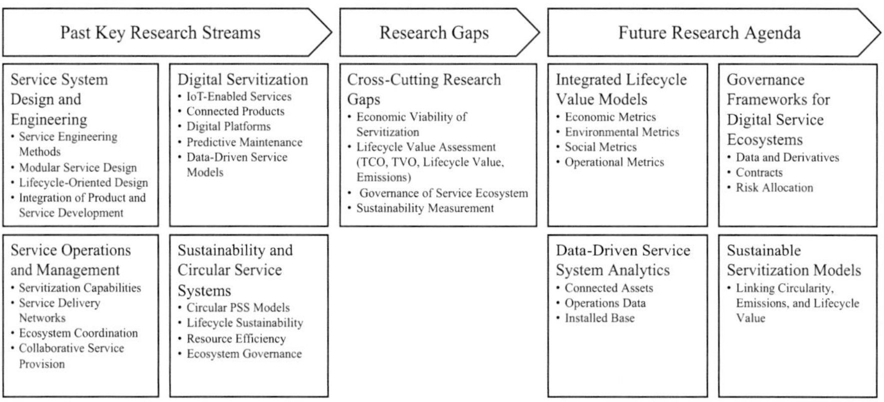

Fig. 1. Conceptual Research Framework Linking Research Streams, Cross-Cutting Research Gaps, and Future Research Directions

Building on this synthesis, several directions for future research emerge (see Table 7), including (i) integrated lifecycle value models, (ii) data-driven service system analytics, (iii) governance frameworks for digital service ecosystems, and (iv) sustainable servitization models. Together, these directions highlight the need for a more integrated understanding of service systems that links lifecycle value creation, ecosystem coordination, and sustainability outcomes.

Integrated Lifecycle Value Models: A key priority for future research is developing *integrated lifecycle value models for PSSs.* Although concepts such as "TCO" and "TVO" are widely discussed in the academic literature, few *analytical approaches* integrate economic, environmental, social, and operational performance across the lifecycle of industrial assets. Future research should therefore investigate *modelling methods* that incorporate financial indicators, operational performance data, and lifecycle sustainability metrics (i.e., Scope 3 emissions) to provide a comprehensive assessment of the total value created by PSSs. Such models would facilitate more informed decision-making regarding service pricing, asset lifecycle management, and performance-based service contracts.

Table 7. Towards a future research agenda for the IFIP WG5.7 SSDE&M SIG

Research Direction	Focus of Future Research
Integrated Lifecycle Value Models	Development of models that integrate economic, environmental, social, and operational metrics to assess the lifecycle value of PSSs, including approaches such as TCO, TVO, and lifecycle sustainability assessment. • RQ1: How can integrated lifecycle value models be developed to assess economic, environmental, social, and operational performance in PSSs? • RQ2: How can lifecycle value models incorporate operational data from industrial assets to improve service pricing and lifecycle decision-making? • RQ3: How can lifecycle sustainability metrics, including Scope 3 emissions, be integrated into lifecycle value assessment frameworks?
Data-Driven Service System Analytics	Use of operational data from connected assets to analyze and optimize service system performance through predictive analytics, digital twins, and industrial data platforms. • RQ4: How can operational data from connected assets be used to improve the monitoring and optimization of service system performance? • RQ5: What role can predictive analytics, digital twins, and industrial data platforms play in supporting lifecycle decision-making in PSS environments? • RQ6: How can data-driven analytics be integrated with lifecycle value models to improve decision support for service-based business models?
Governance Frameworks for Digital Service Ecosystems	Investigation of governance structures supporting multi-actor PSS ecosystems, including data ownership, contractual arrangements, and allocation of operational and financial risks. • RQ7: What governance structures are most effective for coordinating multi-actor service ecosystems in PSSs? • RQ8: How should responsibilities, risks, and value be distributed among actors participating in digital service ecosystems? • RQ9: How can data ownership, access rights, and contractual arrangements be structured to support collaboration in digitally enabled service systems?
Sustainable Servitization Models	Development of service-oriented business models linking circular economy strategies, lifecycle resource use, and emissions, including Scope 3 impacts, with lifecycle value creation. • RQ10: How do service-oriented business models influence lifecycle resource use, asset utilization, and environmental performance in manufacturing systems? • RQ11: How can circular economy strategies such as reuse, refurbishment, and remanufacturing be integrated into PSS business models? • RQ12: How can sustainability performance, including Scope 3 emissions, be measured and managed within service ecosystems?

Data-Driven Service System Analytics: Another important research direction involves utilizing *operational data* to analyze service system performance. The growing availability of data from connected products, sensors, and industrial data platforms offers new opportunities for analyzing asset behavior and service operations. Future research should examine how *predictive analytics, digital twins, and advanced data processing techniques* can assist in monitoring and optimizing service systems. Combining operational data with lifecycle models may enable a more accurate evaluation of service system performance and facilitate better decision-making within PSS environments.

Governance Frameworks for Digital Service Ecosystems: As PSSs increasingly operate within multi-actor service ecosystems, developing *governance frameworks* to coordinate these collaborative networks remains a key research priority. *Service delivery* often entails strong "collaboration" among manufacturers, service providers, technology partners, and customers. These interactions raise crucial questions about data ownership, contractual agreements, and the distribution of financial and operational risks. Future research should therefore investigate *governance models* that foster "collaboration" and "coordination" within digital service ecosystems, while supporting effective management of inter-organizational service relationships.

Sustainable Servitization Models: A final research direction involves developing *sustainable servitization models* that incorporate *circular economy principles* into *lifecycle value creation.* Although PSSs are often associated with improved resource efficiency, there is limited empirical evidence linking *servitization* to *measurable environmental outcomes.* Future research should therefore explore how service-oriented business models influence *lifecycle resource consumption, asset utilization, and emissions* within service ecosystems. Attention should be paid to lifecycle environmental impacts, including Scope 3 emissions from supply chains, service operations, and asset-use phases. Integrating lifecycle sustainability assessment with economic and operational performance metrics will be vital for evaluating the overall sustainability of PSSs.

6 Conclusions and Future Work

This paper reviewed the past decade of the IFIP WG5.7 SSDE&M SIG research work, published in the APMS conference proceedings, to study the evolution of its *research themes,* identify its current *research streams,* and propose *future investigations* in Service Systems and PSSs research. The analysis identified *four research phases* and *four dominant research streams:* (i) Service System Design and Engineering, (ii) Digital Servitization, (iii) Service Operations and Management, and (iv) Sustainability and Circular Service Systems. The paper's main contribution is a *conceptual framework* that links these research streams, identifies cross-cutting research gaps, and outlines future research directions.

Methodologically, the study combines a structured review of APMS contributions with *thematic analysis.* This approach identified recurring research themes, shifts in emphasis, and unresolved challenges across a body of work spanning conference editions and sessions.

The findings suggest that service systems research has evolved from early work on PSS design towards digitally enabled services, multi-actor ecosystems, and sustainability-oriented service systems. The proposed research agenda highlights the need for further work on lifecycle value models, data-driven service analytics, ecosystem governance, and sustainable servitization and provides a basis for future collaborative research within the APMS service systems community.

This study is limited by its focus on APMS contributions. It does not review the wider PSS and servitization literature. Future work will also involve the renewal of the IFIP WG5.7 SSDE&M SIG *research framework and agenda* through a *collaborative research process* to identify *new research priorities, emerging themes, and analytical dimensions* in the Service Systems domain [see 34].

Acknowledgements. The authors would like to acknowledge the contributions of the IFIP WG5.7 SSDE&M SIG members to the past, present, and future of the research agenda on service systems.

Disclosure of Interests. The authors have no competing interests relevant to this paper's content.

References

1. Baines, T., Bigdeli, A.Z., Bustinza, O.F., Shi, V.G., Baldwin, J., Ridgway, K.: Servitization: revisiting the state-of-the-art and research priorities. Int. J. Oper. Prod. Manag. **37**(2), 256–278 (2017)
2. Vandermerwe, S., Rada, J.: Servitization of business: adding value by adding services. Eur. Manag. J. **6**(4), 314–324 (1988)
3. Mont, O.: Clarifying the concept of product–service system. J. Clean. Prod. **10**(3), 237–245 (2002)
4. Tukker, A.: Eight types of product–service system: eight ways to sustainability? Bus. Strategy Environ. **13**(4), 246–260 (2004)
5. Baines, T.S., Lightfoot, H.W., Benedettini, O., Kay, J.M.: The Servitization of manufacturing: a review of literature and reflection on future challenges. J. Manuf. Technol. Manag. **20**(5), 547–567 (2009)
6. Coreynen, W., Matthyssens, P., Van Bockhaven, W.: Boosting Servitization through digitalization: pathways and dynamic resource configurations for manufacturers. Ind. Mark. Manage. **60**, 42–53 (2017)
7. Kohtamäki, M., Parida, V., Oghazi, P., Gebauer, H., Baines, T.: Digital Servitization business models in ecosystems: a theory of the firm. J. Bus. Res. **104**, 380–392 (2019)
8. Tronvoll, B., Sklyar, A., Sörhammar, D., Kowalkowski, C.: Transformational shifts through digital Servitization. Ind. Mark. Manage. **89**, 293–305 (2020)
9. Kharlamov, A.A., Parry, G.: The impact of Servitization and digitization on productivity and profitability of the firm: a systematic approach. Prod. Plann. Control. **32**(3), 185–197 (2021)
10. Saunders, M., Lewis, P., Thornhill, A.: Research Methods for Business Students, 8th edn. Pearson (2019)
11. Bryman, A., Bell, E.: Business Research Methods, 4th edn. Oxford University Press (2015)
12. Homburg, C., Klarmann, M., Vomberg, A.: Handbook of Market Research. Springer, Cham (2024)
13. Marjanovic, U., Lalic, B., Majstorovic, V., Medic, N., Prester, J., Palcic, I.: How to increase share of product-related Services in Revenue? Strategy towards Servitization. In: IFIP International Conference on Advances in Production Management Systems, vol. 536, pp. 57–64. Springer, Cham (2018)

14. Freitag, M., Wiesner, S.: Smart service lifecycle management: a framework and use case. In: IFIP International Conference on Advances in Production Management Systems, vol. 536, pp. 97–104. Springer, Cham (2018)
15. Medini, K., Boucher, X., Peillon, S., Vaillant, H.: Economic assessment of PSS value networks–an algorithmic approach. In: IFIP International Conference on Advances in Production Management Systems, vol. 535, pp. 141–149. Springer, Cham (2018)
16. Larsen, M.S.S., Andersen, A.L., Nielsen, K., Brunoe, T.D.: Modularity in product-service systems: literature review and future research directions. In: IFIP International Conference on Advances in Production Management Systems, vol. 535, pp. 150–158. Springer, Cham (2018)
17. Senderek, R., Kuntz, J., Stich, V., Frank, J.: Smart service engineering: promising approaches for a digitalized economy. In: IFIP International Conference on Advances in Production Management Systems, vol. 566, pp. 674–681. Springer, Cham (2019)
18. Orellano, M., Boucher, X., Neubert, G., Coulon, A.: A framework to support value co-creation in PSS development. In: IFIP International Conference on Advances in Production Management Systems, vol. 592, pp. 361–368. Springer, Cham (2020)
19. Romero, D., Gaiardelli, P., Pezzotta, G., Cavalieri, S.: The impact of digital technologies on services characteristics: towards digital Servitization. In: IFIP International Conference on Advances in Production Management Systems, vol. 566, pp. 493–501. Springer, Cham (2019)
20. Moser, B., Kampker, A., Jussen, P., Frank, J.: Organization of Sales for smart product service systems. In: IFIP International Conference on Advances in Production Management Systems, vol. 566, pp. 518–526. Springer, Cham (2019)
21. Stoll, O., West, S., Gaiardelli, P., Harrison, D., Corcoran, F.J.: The successful commercialization of a digital twin in an industrial product service system. In: IFIP International Conference on Advances in Production Management Systems, vol. 593, pp. 275–282. Springer, Cham (2020)
22. Sala, R., Bertoni, A., Pirola, F., Pezzotta, G.: The data-driven product-service systems design and delivery (4DPSS) methodology. In: IFIP International Conference on Advances in Production Management Systems, vol. 592, pp. 314–321. Springer, Cham (2020)
23. Zambetti, M., Pinto, R., Pezzotta, G.: Industry 4.0 data-related technologies and Servitization: a systematic literature review. In: IFIP International Conference on Advances in Production Management Systems, vol. 592, pp. 347–360. Springer, Cham (2020)
24. Kvadsheim, N.P., Nujen, B.B., Powell, D., Reke, E.: Realizing value opportunities for a circular economy: integrating extended value stream mapping and value uncaptured framework. In: IFIP International Conference on Advances in Production Management Systems, vol. 630, pp. 739–747. Springer, Cham (2021)
25. Nujen, B.B., Kvadsheim, N.P., Mwesiumo, D., Reke, E., Powell, D.: Transition towards circular economy: an intraorganizational perspective identifying knowledge wastes. In: IFIP International Conference on Advances in Production Management Systems, vol. 630, pp. 758–766. Springer, Cham (2021)
26. Bertoni, A., Machchhar, R.J.: A framework to address complexity and changeability in the design of circular product-service systems. In: IFIP International Conference on Advances in Production Management Systems, vol. 664, pp. 19–25. Springer, Cham (2022)
27. Colombo, B., Boffelli, A., Gaiardelli, P., Kalchschmidt, M., Madonna, A., Sangalli, T.: A multiple case study on collaboration for a circular economy: a focus on the Italian textile supply chain. In: IFIP International Conference on Advances in Production Management Systems, vol. 663, pp. 408–415. Springer, Cham (2022)
28. Schneider, D., Vernim, S., Enck, T., Reinhart, G.: Approach towards sustainability modelling and sustainability risk assessment in manufacturing systems. In: IFIP International Conference on Advances in Production Management Systems, vol. 663, pp. 440–447. Springer, Cham (2022)

29. Franke, M., Deng, Q., Hribernik, K.A., Thoben, K.D., Ciaccio, G.: Towards a service marketplace to empower circular economy transition: an example application in the supply chain of textile industry. In: IFIP International Conference on Advances in Production Management Systems, vol. 728, pp. 235–249. Springer, Cham (2024)
30. Ardolino, M., Sala, R., Scalvini, L., Sajjad, S.K., Adrodegari, F., Pezzotta, G.: Barriers and challenges toward the Servitization of the machinery sector: evidence from theory and practice. In: IFIP International Conference on Advances in Production Management Systems, vol. 728, pp. 275–289. Springer, Cham (2024)
31. Holst, L., Stich, V., Schuh, G., Frank, J.: Towards a comparative data value assessment framework for smart product service systems. In: IFIP International Conference on Advances in Production Management Systems, vol. 592, pp. 330–337. Springer, Cham (2020)
32. Rakic, S., Simeunovic, N., Medic, N., Pavlovic, M., Marjanovic, U.: The role of service business models in the manufacturing of transition economies. In: IFIP International Conference on Advances in Production Management Systems, vol. 592, pp. 299–306. Springer, Cham (2020)
33. Marjanovic, U., Rakic, S., Lalic, B.: Digital servitization: the next "Big Thing" in manufacturing industries. In: IFIP International Conference on Advances in Production Management Systems, vol. 566, pp. 510–517. Springer, Cham (2019)
34. Sassanelli, S., Arioli, V., West, S., Romero, D., Gaiardelli, P., Pezzotta, G.: The IFIP WG5.7 service systems special interest group renewed research framework and agenda on product-service systems and digital Servitization. In: To Appear in IFIP International Conference on Advances in Production Management Systems. Springer, Cham (2026)

The IFIP WG5.7 Service Systems Special Interest Group Renewed Research Framework and Agenda on Product-Service Systems and Digital Servitization

Claudio Sassanelli[1(✉)], Veronica Arioli[2], Shaun West[3], David Romero[4], Paolo Gaiardelli[2], and Giuditta Pezzotta[2]

[1] Politecnico di Bari, Bari, Italy
claudio.sassanelli@poliba.it
[2] University of Bergamo, Bergamo, Italy
{veronica.arioli,paolo.gaiardelli,giuditta.pezzotta}@unibg.it
[3] Lucerne University of Applied Sciences and Arts, Lucerne, Switzerland
shaun.west@hslu.ch
[4] Tecnológico de Monterrey, Mexico City, Mexico

Abstract. Product-Service Systems (PSSs) and Digital Servitization are increasingly recognized as key enablers for sustainable and data-driven industrial transformation. However, the rapid evolution of digital technologies, circular economy principles, and service ecosystems is reshaping the PSS research landscape, calling for updated and integrated research frameworks. This paper proposes a Research Framework and Agenda developed within the IFIP WG5.7 Special Interest Group (SIG) on Service Systems Design, Engineering and Management (SSDE&M). The Research Framework and Agenda are grounded in a two-step methodology combining an online brainstorming workshop and a structured survey involving the SIG members. The results identify and structure current research priorities across five core research areas, while also revealing emerging research themes related to ecosystem integration, data-driven value creation, and lifecycle management. Building on these insights, the proposed Research Framework and Agenda organise PSS research into three interconnected levels: (i) Design and Methods, (ii) Business and Organizational Transformation, and (iii) Ecosystem and Governance Context, complemented by four cross-cutting analytical dimensions: (i) Circular Economy and Rebound Effects, (ii) Digital Technologies and Artificial Intelligence, (iii) Service Ecosystems and Governance, and (iv) Responsible and Socially Sustainable Service Systems. The proposed Research Framework and Agenda contribute to consolidating fragmented research streams and provide a structured basis for future research work within the IFIP WG5.7 SSDE&M SIG and broader PSS research community, supporting both academic research and industrial practice.

Keywords: Product-Service Systems (PSSs) · Digital Servitization · Research Framework · Research Agenda · International Survey

G. Pezzotta et al. (Eds.): APMS 2026, IFIP AICT 808, pp. 572–587, 2027.
https://doi.org/10.1007/978-3-032-38594-9_38

1 Introduction

Product-Service Systems (PSSs) and *Digital Servitization* have become central paradigms in the evolution of manufacturing and industrial systems, enabling firms to transition from "product-centric offerings" towards "integrated solutions" that combine "product-service bundles and digital technologies" [1]. This transition is increasingly recognized as a key driver for value creation, competitiveness, and sustainability [2–5], particularly in the context of ongoing *Digital Transformation* and *Circular Economy transitions,* also known as the "Digital and Green Twin Transition" [6].

The International Federation for Information Processing (IFIP) Working Group (WG) 5.7 has played a pivotal role in advancing research on production management systems, including "service systems" and "product-service systems". In particular, the Special Interest Group (SIG) on *Service Systems Design, Engineering and Management (SSDE&M)* focuses on the design, engineering, and management of service systems in industrial contexts, fostering interdisciplinary dialogue on emerging challenges and opportunities in PSS research: https://www.ifipwg57.org/special-interest-groups/

Previous contributions within this domain have identified a set of core research areas that structure the PSS research field [7], including: (i) Digital Servitization Strategies and Business Models, (ii) Technology-enhanced Sustainable PSS Business Models, (iii) Tools for Assessing PSS Designs and Performances, (iv) PSS Knowledge Management along the Lifecycle, and (v) Innovative PSS Design Methods and Tools. These themes have provided a solid foundation for understanding the development and implementation of *PSSs* and *Digital Servitization.* However, recent developments highlight the need to revisit and extend this structure. The increasing integration of *Circular Economy principles,* the rapid advancement of *Digital Technologies* such as Artificial Intelligence (AI) and the industrial Internet of Things (IoT), and the growing importance of *service ecosystems and governance mechanisms* are reshaping the PSS research landscape. At the same time, *emerging concerns* related to *ethics, regulation, and social and environmental sustainability* are further expanding the scope of PSS research. As a result, existing classifications risk remaining fragmented and insufficient to capture the systemic and multi-level nature of current PSS research challenges.

To address this gap, this paper proposes a *Research Framework and Agenda* for the PSS domain, developed within the IFIP WG5.7 SSDE&M SIG. Both build upon the previously established research areas [7] while integrating emerging research themes identified through a *collaborative research process,* involving the majority of the IFIP WG5.7 SSDE&M SIG members. Specifically, the *Research Framework and Agenda* are grounded in a two-step methodological approach consisting of an initial online brainstorming workshop followed by a structured survey administered to the SIG members and interested participants. The workshop, organized in conjunction with the renewal of the SIG leadership, aimed to introduce participants to each other, present ongoing research activities, and stimulate discussion on current challenges and future research directions in the PSS domain. The subsequent survey enabled the systematic collection and evaluation of research priorities and challenges, and emerging research topics, combining both quantitative assessments and qualitative inputs. Building on the analysis of these contributions, this paper proposes a structured *Research Framework* that organises PSS research across *three interconnected levels of analysis:* (i) Design and

Methods, (ii) Business and Organizational Transformation, and (iii) Ecosystem and Governance Context and *a set of four cross-cutting analytical dimensions:* (i) Circular Economy and Rebound Effects, (ii) Digital Technologies and Artificial Intelligence, (iii) Service Ecosystems and Governance, and (iv) Responsible and Socially Sustainable Service Systems that cross over the three interconnected levels aforementioned. These four dimensions reflect key emerging priorities within the IFIP WG5.7 SSDE&M SIG and provide a complementary lens for analysing how different research areas intersect and evolve.

The proposed *Research Framework and Agenda* contribute to the PSS literature by (i) expanding and consolidating existing research areas from previous PSS and digital servitization research agenda(s) into a coherent multi-level structure, (ii) integrating emerging cross-cutting research themes, and (iii) providing a structured basis for future research within the IFIP WG5.7 SSDE&M SIG and the broader PSS research community.

The remainder of the paper is structured as follows. Section 2 reviews the relevant literature. Section 3 describes the research methodology employed. Section 4 presents the identified research areas, challenges, and opportunities emerging from the IFIP WG5.7 SSDE&M SIG activities. Section 5 discusses the implications of the findings, and Sect. 6 concludes the paper.

2 Research Context

Over the past decade, an increasing number of contributions within the IFIP WG5.7 SSDE&M SIG have addressed topics such as *PSS design, digital servitization, service operations, and sustainability in service systems* [8]. Several studies have offered conceptual frameworks, modelling methods, and methodologies to support product-service bundles design and integration, helping businesses navigate organizational and engineering complexities. With the growing impact of Industry 4.0 and 5.0, these frameworks and methodologies have increasingly embedded *digital technologies* [9], acting as key enablers for real-time monitoring and advanced capabilities, such as remote diagnostics and predictive maintenance.

The scientific literature also has underlined the crucial role that data plays today: *insights from connected products actively power new outcome-based and performance-driven service models.* To support this transition, digital platforms and IT infrastructures have proven fundamental for aligning service activities and improving teamwork among manufacturers, service providers, and customers. Notwithstanding these technological advancements, studies shed light on the main challenges and opportunities of *(digital) servitization* in manufacturing companies [10, 11], delineating a diverse spectrum of realities and consequently highlighting specific areas for improvement [12]. Beyond *digitalization,* another major focus of IFIP WG5.7 SSDE&M SIG is the integration of *sustainability* within PSS [13]. In this context, contributions have proposed quantitative metrics and evaluation frameworks for *sustainability assessment,* aiming to measure the environmental and social impacts of these offerings throughout their lifecycle [14]. This is strongly connected to the development and support of PSS ecosystems. Research in this area analyzes the collaborative efforts among manufacturers, service providers, tech partners, and consumers to co-create integrated solutions, with a strong emphasis on governance frameworks, coordination strategies, and shared data infrastructures [15, 16].

3 Research Methodology

The proposed *Research Framework and Agenda* are grounded in a two-step approach consisting of a preliminary online brainstorming workshop (kick-off) and a subsequent survey administered to the SIG members and interested participants. This diversity reflects the interdisciplinary nature of the research topic. This *research methodology* enabled the integration of qualitative insights with structured evaluations of relevant research areas and emerging topics (see Table 1).

Table 1. Research Methodology Steps

Steps	Date	No. of Participants
Brainstorming Workshop	January 30, 2026	19 participants from Academia
Survey Evaluation	From January 30, 2026 To February 20, 2026	19 responses from Academia

The *brainstorming workshop* was conducted as an initial kick-off activity to present the past and current research work of the IFIP WG5.7 SSDE&M SIG members in order to stimulate discussion and capture a broad range of perspectives on current research challenges, opportunities, and directions in the PSS domain. This first phase provided qualitative insights and helped surface diverse viewpoints from the online workshop participants due to their different backgrounds.

Then, a *structured survey* was distributed to collect systematic feedback on predefined research areas, defined based on [1], as well as additional inputs on emerging and current research topics. Recurrent research challenges and opportunities of *servitization* were also addressed in the survey, as defined by previous work of the IFIP WG5.7 SSDE&M SIG [10]. The survey combined *closed-ended* and *open-ended questions. Closed-ended questions* were designed to evaluate predefined items in research areas, challenges, and opportunities using a Likert scale (ranging from 1 = strongly disagree to 5 = strongly agree), enabling a quantitative evaluation of respondents' perceptions. *Open-ended questions* were included in the survey to capture novel insights and alternative perspectives. The resulting responses, reported in Sect. 4.1, were analyzed through qualitative content analysis to identify recurring themes and patterns. This mixed structure enabled a combination of quantitative assessment and qualitative contributions.

Then, *content analysis* allowed the integration of *exploratory insights* with semi-structured evaluations. This approach supported the identification of *research priorities* and the development of *thematic clusters and research levels* presented in this paper. These findings were progressively clustered into *high-order conceptual categories,* leading to the identification of the *three interconnected levels of analysis* (micro, meso, and macro) and the *four transversal analytical dimensions* spanning the entire PSS research landscape, that characterize the renewed research framework.

4 Results: Brainstorming Workshop and Survey

4.1 Descriptive Results

The study involved 19 participants with expertise in service systems, servitization, and PSS, including senior academics, postdoctoral researchers, and Ph.D. candidates from interdisciplinary backgrounds such as management engineering, operations management, manufacturing engineering, business, lifecycle management, and service engineering. Participants rated the *five core research areas* as defined by [7] according to their relevance to current research and the objectives of IFIP WG5.7 SSDE&M SIG's (from 1-low importance to 5-highest importance). The results of this evaluation are shown in Fig. 1 and provide a basis for establishing a rating of *research interests,* which reveals a clear pattern of prioritization and highlights differences in both intensity of interest and level of consensus among participants. Furthermore, the results provide a basis for establishing a ranking of *research priorities.*

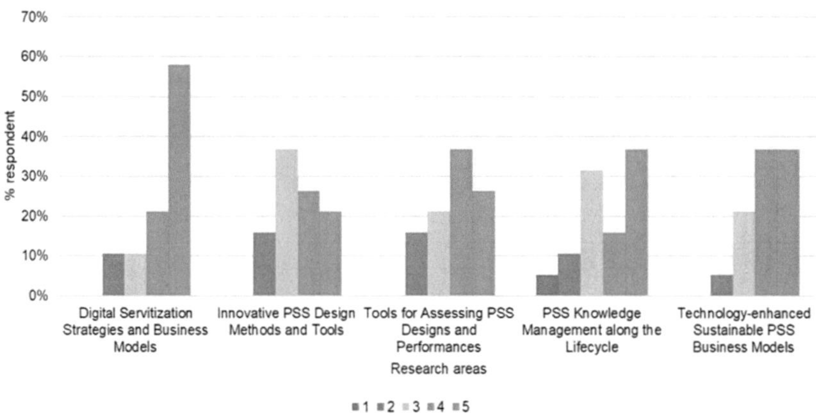

Fig. 1. IFIP WG5.7 SSDE&M SIG Research Interests and Priorities Identified

At the top, *Digital Servitization Strategies and Business Models* emerge as the dominant research priority, with 78% of respondents assigning high ratings (4–5), and more than half (56%) selecting the maximum score. This strong concentration at the upper end of the scale indicates not only high interest but also broad consensus on its central role within the field. Second, it is possible to identify the *Technology-enhanced Sustainable PSS Business Models* area, which confirms the importance of integrating sustainability and digitalization, with 72% high ratings and a very strong alignment among respondents, reinforcing the idea that the future of PSS lies at the intersection of these two dimensions. *Tools for Assessing PSS Designs and Performances* occupy a solid interest with predominantly medium-to-high scores (67% high ratings). The distribution suggests a consistent and widespread interest, particularly from researchers focused on quantitative methods, evaluation, and decision-support tools. This area appears to play a crucial enabling role within the broader research landscape.

In contrast, *PSS Knowledge Management along the Lifecycle* shows a more heterogeneous and polarized distribution, with 56% high ratings but also a noticeable spread across lower values. This suggests that, although the topic is recognized as relevant, there is less agreement on its priority, possibly due to differences in research focus or varying levels of maturity across subfields.

Finally, *Innovative PSS Design Methods and Tools* ranks lowest, with responses concentrated around mid-range values (3–4) and fewer maximum scores. This indicates that the area is perceived as interesting but not central, functioning more as a supporting domain rather than a primary driver of current research efforts.

Figure 2 highlights the main *research challenges* associated with the "Digital Servitization" trend in the service systems design, engineering, and management, based on the number of respondents identifying each issue. Overall, the results point to a strong concentration of challenges related to (i) ecosystem integration, (ii) data utilization, and (iii) value creation from data. The most critical research challenge is *(service) ecosystem network development (including competitors and IT providers),* identified by the highest number of respondents. This underscores the complexity of building and managing *multi-actor service ecosystems,* which are essential for delivering *digital service offerings* but require new forms of collaboration and coordination. Closely following, several *data-related research challenges* emerge, such as (i) the difficulty in designing services from product usage data, (ii) the difficulty in extracting knowledge from PSS, and (iii) the difficulty in value communication. These results indicate that organizations are still struggling to transform data into actionable insights and meaningful (digital) service offerings, as well as to effectively communicate the value generated.

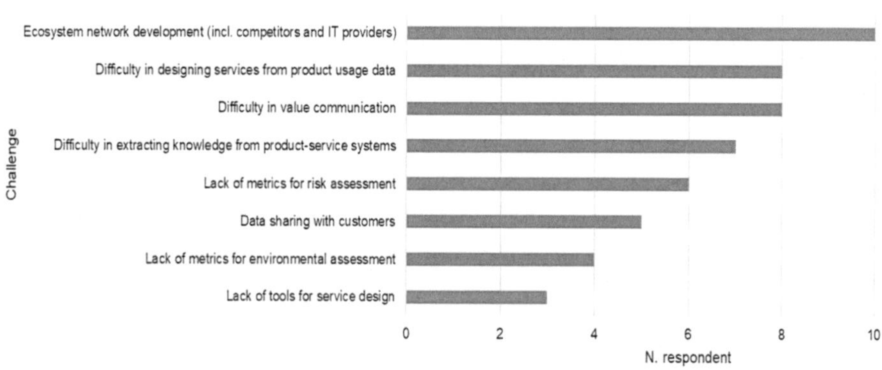

Fig. 2. SSDE&M Main Research Challenges Identified

Another relevant issue is the *lack of metrics for risk assessment,* suggesting that companies face uncertainty when evaluating and managing risks associated with "servitized" and "data-driven" business models. Similarly, *data sharing with customers* is identified as a significant challenge, highlighting concerns related to data governance, trust, and transparency. Mid-level research challenges include the lack of metrics for environmental assessment and the lack of tools for service design, pointing to gaps in both sustainability evaluation and practical design support.

Other research challenges suggested directly by the respondents and therefore more specific research concerns, emerging topics, and areas that are highly relevant within particular contexts are: (i) methodological development at the process level, (ii) intra- and inter-organizational changes, including service ecosystem transformation, (iii) cost engineering for PSS, and (iv) difficulty in value assessment. This suggests that the focus shifts away from internal optimization towards external integration and data-driven value (co-)creation.

Figure 3 illustrates the main *research opportunities* associated with the SSDE&M trend based on the number of respondents mentioning each aspect. The greatest potential is in *economic and service performance evaluation,* indicating a strong interest in the ability of "Digital Servitization" to improve measurement, monitoring, and optimization of performance. This suggests that *data-driven approaches* are seen as a key enabler for enhancing both operational and strategic decision-making. Closely following, *competitive differentiation* emerges as a major opportunity. This highlights how *servitization,* particularly when combined with *digital technologies,* is perceived as a way to create unique value propositions and strengthen market positioning.

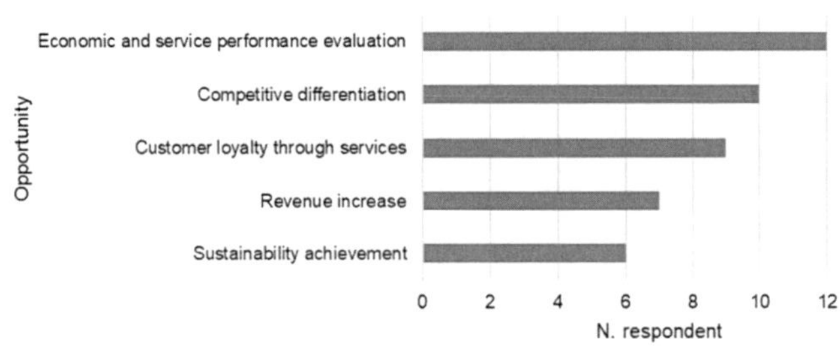

Fig. 3. SSDE&M Main Research Opportunities Identified

Another prominent theme is *customer loyalty through services,* confirming that *servitization* enables firms to build long-term relationships with customers by offering continuous value rather than one-off transactions. *Revenue increase* is also frequently mentioned, reflecting the expectation that "service-based" and "data-driven" business models can generate new and more stable revenue streams. *Sustainability achievement* appears as a relevant opportunity, though with slightly fewer mentions. This suggests that while "sustainability" is recognized as important, it may be perceived more as a complementary benefit rather than the primary driver in all contexts. Further research opportunities suggested directly by the respondents point to more specific research concerns, emerging topics, and areas of high relevance within particular contexts, including: (i) assessment of circularity performance, and (ii) industrial resilience.

4.2 Content Analysis

The analysis of the survey responses was enriched by the discussion during the kick-off meeting, providing the definition of the *Research Framework and Agenda* (see Table 2). The point of discussion does not represent entirely new research areas, challenges, and opportunities, but rather reflects a *systemic evolution of PSS research* towards implementation, ecosystem integration, and digitally enabled, lifecycle-oriented service systems. However, organizations are still constrained by limited capabilities in data exploitation, ecosystem governance, and value articulation, highlighting a critical gap between potential and implementation. *Content analysis* revealed the presence of important research areas enriching the driving ones:

- *Organizational Transformation and Change Management* – This research area extends the domain of *Digital Servitization Strategies and Business Models*, encompassing the organizational and strategic shift required to transition from "product-centric" to "service-oriented" business models. It represents a high-priority and highly conceptually coherent cluster, underscoring that the principal research challenge is no longer defining servitization, but rather understanding how to implement it effectively within organizations.
- *End-to-End Lifecycle Management* – This research area complements the *PSS Knowledge Management along the Lifecycle* one, by focusing on holistic lifecycle thinking and data integration.
- *Vertical Technological Applications* – This research area focuses on technological enablers that support the development and scaling of *Servitized and Data-driven Business Models*, and point towards the emergence of sector-specific applications.
- *Integration with Supply Chain and Circular Economy* – This research area goes beyond the Technology-enhanced Sustainable PSS Business Models one, by reflecting a strong shift towards system-level integration beyond firm boundaries, linking servitization with circular economy and supply chain dynamics.
- *Ethics and Regulation in Digital PSS* – This research area reflects a new emerging area that addresses the ethical, legal, and societal implications of digital servitization, highlighting the growing importance of governance and responsible innovation.

Building on the survey findings, brainstorming workshop discussions, and subsequent content analysis, the identified *research priorities* and *emerging themes* were progressively clustered into higher-level conceptual categories. This process led to the definition of *three interconnected levels of analysis* and *a set of four cross-cutting analytical dimensions* spanning the PSS research landscape. Table 2 synthesizes the resulting Research Framework and Agenda, linking the identified research areas with their research focus, illustrative research topics, and associated transversal dimensions.

The results are conceptually consistent with *PSS and (Digital) Servitization literature,* where research can therefore be organized across three different layers:

- *Design and Methods (micro-level)* – Focusing on how PSS are designed, engineered, and evaluated, including the use of digital technologies (e.g., IoT, AI, digital twins) and methodological frameworks for PSS development and performance assessment.
- *Business and Organizational Transformation (meso-level)* – Addressing how firms transform their business models, capabilities, and internal processes to adopt PSS and digital servitization, including lifecycle integration, and knowledge flows across PSSs.
- *Ecosystem and Governance Context (macro-level)* – Examining how PSS operate within broader ecosystems, including supply chain collaboration, circular economy integration, regulatory frameworks, and ethical considerations related to digital technologies and data.

In addition to the *three-level structure,* the *content analysis* revealed a *set of four cross-cutting research areas* that span across the entire PSS research landscape. These areas do not represent standalone research domains; rather, they function as "transversal dimensions" that shape how research problems are framed and addressed across micro, meso, and macro levels. Specifically, four *cross-cutting emerging research areas* can be identified: (i) Circular Economy and Rebound Effects – in PSSs and Service Systems, (ii) Digital Technologies and Artificial Intelligence – for (Digital) Service Systems, (iii) Service Ecosystems and Governance – for Organizational Transformation, and (iv) Responsible and Socially Sustainable Service Systems – to meet ESG (Environmental, Social, and Governance) criteria. These dimensions intersect multiple research domains and levels, highlighting key thematic research priorities that cut across PSS design methods, organizational transformation, and ecosystem-level dynamics. For instance, digital technologies influence PSS design methods (micro-level), enabling new "servitized" and "data-driven" business models (meso-level), and reshaping data governance in ecosystems (macro-level). Similarly, circular economy principles affect product design, organizational strategies, and supply chain configurations.

All these findings led to the development of a *Research Framework and Agenda* conceptualizing the main research priorities in the PSS domain – see Fig. 4. This representation illustrates how the identified research areas are structured across *three interconnected levels of analysis,* while also highlighting *a set of four cross-cutting analytical dimensions emerging from the content analysis,* thereby emphasizing *a unified nature of methodological, organizational, and ecosystem perspectives in PSS research.*

5 Discussion

The results of the workshop and survey provide a structured and community-driven perspective on current research priorities in the PSS domain. Building on these findings, this section discusses the implications of the proposed *Research Framework and Agenda,* highlighting its contribution to structuring the research landscape, identifying emerging directions, and outlining future research opportunities for the IFIP WG5.7 SSDE&M SIG and the broader PSS research community.

Table 2. Research Framework and Agenda for the PSS Domain

PSS Research Level	Research Area	Research Focus	Illustrative Research Topics	Cross-Cutting Analytical Dimensions
1. Design and Methods (micro-level)	Innovative PSS Design Methods and Tools	Development of design approaches, methods, and frameworks supporting the creation of PSSs.	Socially responsible service system design.	Responsible and Socially Sustainable Service Systems
	Tools for Assessing PSS Designs and Performances	Development of methods and metrics for evaluating the economic, environmental, and customer value performance of PSSs.	PSS assessment methods such as Total Cost of Ownership (TCO) and Total Value of Ownership (TVO).	Circular Economy and Rebound Effects
	Vertical Technological Applications	Application of enabling technologies (e.g., IoT, AI, digital platforms) to support sector-specific PSS solutions.	IoT-based assurance services for catastrophic risks in the agrifood industry.	Digital Technologies and Artificial Intelligence
2. Business and Organizational Transformation (meso-level)	Digital Servitization Strategies and Business Models	Strategic and organizational transformation towards digitally enabled service-oriented business models.	Culture and change management in digital servitization; Contextual value creation and capture in digital service ecosystems.	Service Ecosystems and Governance

(*continued*)

Table 2. (*continued*)

PSS Research Level	Research Area	Research Focus	Illustrative Research Topics	Cross-Cutting Analytical Dimensions
	Technology-enhanced Sustainable PSS Business Models	Development of sustainable and circular PSS business models enabled by digital technologies.	Circular business models and digital transformation for sustainable value networks; Simulation-based analysis of collaborative consumption.	Circular Economy and Rebound Effects; Digital Technologies and Artificial Intelligence
	PSS Knowledge Management along the Lifecycle	Management of knowledge and information flows across the lifecycle of PSSs.	AI-enabled document flow for cross-border logistics and customs compliance.	Digital Technologies and Artificial Intelligence
	End-to-End Lifecycle Management	Integration and coordination of PSS across lifecycle stages, from design and production to operation and end-of-life.	Integration of servitization and circular economy in spare parts management through digital spares and virtual warehouses.	Circular Economy and Rebound Effects
3. Ecosystem & Governance Context (macro-level)	Integration with Supply Chain and Circular Economy	Coordination of actors, resources, and value flows across supply chains and circular ecosystems.	Implementation of circular economy strategies and potential rebound effects in manufacturing.	Circular Economy and Rebound Effects; Service Ecosystems and Governance
	Ethics and Regulation in Digital PSS	Ethical, social, and regulatory implications of digitalized PSSs.	Social and ethical considerations in responsible service systems.	Responsible and Socially Sustainable Service Systems

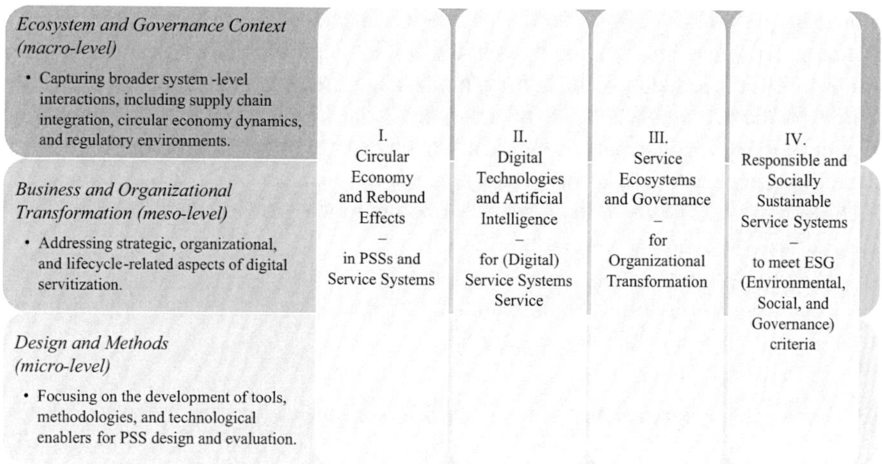

Fig. 4. Research Framework and Agenda for the PSS Domain

5.1 Consolidation of PSS Research into a Multi-Level Structure

The first key contribution of this study lies in the consolidation of existing and emerging research areas into a coherent three-level structure of analysis, encompassing (i) Design and Methods, (ii) Business and Organizational Transformation, and (iii) Ecosystem and Governance Context. This structuring is consistent with prior scientific literature while offering a clearer articulation of how different research streams relate to each other.

The results confirm that research in PSS is no longer confined to methodological development or business model innovation in isolation but increasingly spans multiple levels of analysis. In particular, while traditional research has focused on *PSS design methods and performance assessment tools,* the survey highlights a strong shift towards *organizational transformation and ecosystem-level challenges.* This is evident in the high prioritization of *digital servitization strategies and business models,* as well as in the identification of ecosystem-related challenges such as *network development and data sharing.* This evolution suggests that *PSS research* is moving from a predominantly "method- and technology-orientation" towards a more "systemic- and implementation-orientation" where organizational and ecosystem dynamics play a central role.

5.2 Cross-Cutting Analytical Dimensions in PSS Research

A second important insight emerging from the study is the relevance of *a set of four cross-cutting analytical dimensions* that span across the three interconnected levels of analysis. These dimensions, (i) Circular Economy and Rebound Effects, (ii) Digital Technologies and Artificial Intelligence, (iii) Service Ecosystems and Governance, and (iv) Responsible and Socially Sustainable Service Systems, reflect key drivers shaping the current and future PSS research agenda.

The results clearly indicate that *digital technologies and data-related challenges* are central across multiple research areas, particularly in relation to value (co-)creation, knowledge extraction, and (data-driven) service design. At the same time, *circular economy considerations,* including rebound effects and circularity performance, are increasingly embedded in both business models and lifecycle management approaches. Moreover, the prominence of *ecosystem-related challenges* highlights the importance of understanding PSS as part of broader service ecosystems involving multiple actors, including competitors, customers, and technology providers. Finally, the emergence of *ethical, social, and regulatory concerns* points to the growing need for responsible innovation and governance in digital PSSs.

These four dimensions provide a valuable analytical lens for interpreting research developments and highlight the interconnected nature of technological, organizational, societal, and environmental aspects in PSSs.

5.3 Emerging Priorities and Gaps in PSS Research

The *content analysis* reveals several emerging research priorities and gaps that warrant further investigation. First, there is a clear need to *advance methods and tools for data-driven service design and value assessment.* Despite the increasing availability of product usage data, respondents highlighted significant challenges in transforming data into actionable insights and meaningful service offerings. This indicates a persistent gap between technological capabilities and their effective application in PSS contexts, particularly in relation to (big) data analytics, decision-support systems, and value communication. In addition, *ecosystem integration and governance* emerge as critical areas for future research. The difficulty in developing and managing service ecosystems suggests that existing governance models and frameworks are insufficient to address the complexity of multi-actor collaboration, especially in digital and platform-based environments. This calls for new or renewed approaches that consider data sharing, trust, coordination mechanisms, and value co-creation across heterogeneous actors.

Furthermore, *lifecycle integration and circularity* represent another relevant research direction. While circular economy principles are increasingly embedded in PSS business models, their implementation raises new challenges, including the management of rebound effects, the integration of lifecycle data across different phases, and the development of robust performance and circularity metrics. These challenges highlight the need for more holistic and data-driven PSS lifecycle management approaches.

Lastly, the results emphasize the importance of *organizational transformation and capability building,* including culture, skills, and change management. The transition towards "servitized" and "data-driven" business models requires not only technological innovation but also significant changes in organizational structures, processes, and mindsets. In this context, future research should further investigate how organizations can effectively align technological, organizational, and ecosystem dimensions to enable the successful PSS implementations.

5.4 Implications for the SIG and the Broader Research Community

The proposed *Research Framework and Agenda* provide a structured basis for guiding future activities within the IFIP WG5.7 SSDE&M SIG and the broader PSS research community. By integrating research areas across multiple levels and linking them with cross-cutting dimensions, the proposed *Research Framework and Agenda* can support the definition of research efforts, the organization of workshops and conference tracks, and the identification of collaborative research opportunities.

Furthermore, the proposed *Research Framework and Agenda* facilitate the positioning of individual research contributions within a broader context, enabling researchers to better understand how their work relates to ongoing developments in the field. It also encourages interdisciplinary collaboration by highlighting the need to address PSS challenges from multiple perspectives, including engineering, management, data science, and sustainability.

More generally, the proposed *Research Framework and Agenda* contribute to advancing the PSS research field by providing a comprehensive and flexible structure that captures its increasing complexity and dynamism. It supports the transition towards a more integrated understanding of service systems, where design, organizational transformation, and ecosystem interactions are considered jointly.

From a *theoretical perspective,* the proposed *Research Framework and Agenda* contribute to the PSS literature by integrating previously fragmented research streams into a unified and multi-level structure, while explicitly incorporating emerging cross-cutting dimensions that shape current research developments, while from a *practical perspective,* the proposed *Research Framework and Agenda* provide a useful reference for researchers and practitioners to position their research work, identify research gaps, and support the definition of future research within the IFIP WG5.7 SSDE&M SIG and the broader PSS research community.

6 Conclusions

This paper presented a *Research Framework and Agenda* for the PSS domain, developed within the IFIP WG5.7 SSDE&M SIG. Building on a two-step methodology combining an online brainstorming workshop and a structured survey, the study identified and structured current research priorities emerging from the SIG community.

The proposed *Research Framework and Agenda* consolidate existing research areas into *a coherent three-level structure of analysis:* (i) Design and Methods, (ii) Business and Organizational Transformation, and (iii) Ecosystem and Governance Context, while integrating *a set of four cross-cutting analytical dimensions,* namely: (i) Circular Economy and Rebound Effects, (ii) Digital Technologies and Artificial Intelligence, (iii) Service Ecosystems and Governance, and (iv) Responsible and Socially Sustainable Service Systems. This *dual perspective* enables a comprehensive representation of the PSS research landscape, capturing both "structural" and "thematic" field developments.

The *findings* highlight a clear shift in *research priorities* towards: (i) Digital Servitization Strategies, (ii) Sustainable and Technology-enabled Business Models, and (iii) Ecosystem-Level Challenges, while also confirming the continued relevance of research on (iv) PSS Design Methods and Performance Assessment Tools as enabling foundations. In particular, the increasing importance of *data-driven value creation, lifecycle integration, and multi-actor ecosystem coordination* reflects the growing complexity of PSS implementation in industrial contexts.

However, this study presents some limitations. The proposed *Research Framework and Agenda* are based on a relatively small sample of participants, primarily from academia, and reflect the perspectives of the IFIP WG5.7 SSDE&M SIG members at a specific point in time. Furthermore, it should be acknowledged that a significant share of current research trends in the PSS domain is influenced by the strategic priorities and funding programmes of the European Commission. While this alignment contributes to coherence and impact, it may also lead to a concentration of research efforts around policy-driven themes, potentially limiting the visibility of emerging or niche research topics. In this regard, the proposed *Research Framework and Agenda* can also serve as a tool to support the identification and valorization of underexplored research areas that are not yet fully reflected in current funding agendas.

Future research should aim to further validate and refine the proposed *Research Framework and Agenda* by involving a broader range of stakeholders, including industry practitioners, and by expanding the empirical basis through additional workshops, surveys, or bibliometric analyzes. Moreover, deeper investigations into the interactions between the different research levels and cross-cutting dimensions could provide further insights into the evolution of PSS research and its role in supporting the ongoing "Digital and Green Twin Transition".

Acknowledgments. The authors would like to acknowledge the contributions of the IFIP WG5.7 SSDE&M SIG members to this PSS research landscaping effort.

Disclosure of Interests The authors have no competing interests to declare.

References

1. Romero, D., Gaiardelli, P., Pezzotta, G., Cavalieri, S.: The impact of digital technologies on services characteristics: towards digital Servitization. In: IFIP International Conference on Advances in Production Management Systems, vol. 566, pp. 493–501. Springer, Cham (2019)
2. Baines, T., Bigdeli, A.Z., Bustinza, O.F., Shi, V.G., Baldwin, J., Ridgway, K.: Servitization: revisiting the state-of-the-art and research priorities. Int. J. Oper. Prod. Manag. **37**(2), 256–278 (2017)
3. Ozturkoglu, Y., Ozturkoglu, O., Danisman, E.: New business model proposal in the digital age: sustainability-focused Servitisation. J. Enterp. Inf. Manag. **38**, 1776–1802 (2025)
4. Kohtamäki, M., Parida, V., Oghazi, P., Gebauer, H., Baines, T.: Digital Servitization business models in ecosystems: a theory of the firm. J. Bus. Res. **104**, 380–392 (2019)
5. Saccani, N., Adrodegari, F., Scalvini, L.: Aligning product-service systems with environmental sustainability: investigating the key role of revenue and pricing mechanisms. Resour. Conserv. Recycl. **209**, 107792 (2024)
6. Kilinc, T., Sjödin, D., Parida, V.: Navigating digital Servitization for the twin transition: how manufacturers can support customers with digitalization and sustainability. Bus. Strateg. Environ. **34**, 5370–5385 (2025)
7. Pirola, F., Boucher, X., Wiesner, S., Pezzotta, G.: Digital Technologies in Product-Service Systems: a literature review and a research agenda. Comput. Ind. **123**, 103301 (2020)
8. West, S., Romero, D., Gaiardelli, P., Arioli, V., Sassanelli, S., Pezzotta, G.: The IFIP WG5.7 service systems SIG research agenda evolution on service and product-service systems design, engineering and management. In: To Appear in IFIP International Conference on Advances in Production Management Systems. Springer, Cham (2026)

9. Pirola, F., Pezzotta, G., Arioli, V., Sala, R.: Design and engineer data-driven product service system: a methodology update. In: IFIP International Conference on Advances in Production Management Systems, vol. 664, pp. 367–375. Springer, Cham (2022)
10. Pezzotta, G., Arioli, V., Adrodegari, F., et al.: The digital Servitization of manufacturing sector: evidence from a worldwide digital Servitization survey. In: IFIP International Conference on Advances in Production Management Systems, vol. 690, pp. 165–180. Springer, Cham (2023)
11. Ardolino, M., Sala, R., Scalvini, L., Sajjad, S.K., Adrodegari, F., Pezzotta, G.: Barriers and challenges toward the Servitisation of the machinery sector: evidence from theory and practice. In: IFIP International Conference on Advances in Production Management Systems, vol. 728, pp. 275–289. Springer, Cham (2024)
12. Arioli, V., Pezzotta, G., Romero, D., et al.: Digital Servitisation business typologies in the manufacturing sector. Int. J. Ind. Eng. Manag. **16**, 1–23 (2025)
13. Kvadsheim, N.P., Nujen, B.B., Powell, D., Reke, E.: Realizing value opportunities for a circular economy: integrating extended value stream mapping and value uncaptured framework. In: IFIP International Conference on Advances in Production Management Systems, vol. 630, pp. 739–747. Springer, Cham (2021)
14. Arioli, V., Sala, R., Pirola, F., Pezzotta, G.: Quantitative assessment of product-service system sustainability: a literature review. In: IFIP International Conference on Advances in Production Management Systems, vol. 630, pp. 198–214. Springer, Cham (2024)
15. Colombo, B., Boffelli, A., Gaiardelli, P., Kalchschmidt, M., Madonna, A., Sangalli, T.: A multiple case study on collaboration for a circular economy: a focus on the Italian textile supply chain. In: IFIP International Conference on Advances in Production Management Systems, vol. 732, pp. 408–415. Springer, Cham (2022)
16. Carminati, L., Arioli, V., Sala, R., Pirola, F., Pezzotta, G.: Towards effective implementation of digital product passports: stakeholders involved and data requirements. In: IFIP International Conference on Advances in Production Management Systems, vol. 766, pp. 537–553. Springer, Cham (2025)

Integrating Artificial Intelligence and Human Resource Management Practices to Support Knowledge Management Processes

Mariavittoria Marinucci(✉), Roberto Sala, Fabiana Pirola, and Sergio Cavalieri

Dipartimento di Ingegneria Gestionale, dell'Informazione e della Produzione, University of Bergamo, Viale Marconi, 5, 24044 Dalmine, BG, Italy
{mariavittoria.marinucci,roberto.sala,fabiana.pirola, sergio.cavalieri}@unibg.it

Abstract. In contemporary industrial and service contexts, organizations are increasingly required to leverage knowledge as a strategic resource while, at the same time, adopting advanced Artificial Intelligence (AI) technologies to support decision-making and operational activities. Although the relevance of these domains has significantly increased in recent years, the existing literature tends to examine Human Resource Management (HRM) practices, AI technologies, and Knowledge Management (KM) processes separately. As a result, there is still limited understanding of how these elements interact and jointly contribute to the development of organizational knowledge capabilities. To address this limitation, this study develops a conceptual framework that integrates HRM practices, AI technologies, and KM processes within a unified perspective. The framework is grounded in a structured review of the literature and is aimed at identifying the main relationships among these dimensions. In particular, the study focuses on how HRM practices can support the adoption and effective use of AI technologies, and how these technologies, in turn, can enhance key KM processes. The main contribution of this work lies in providing an integrated view of these three domains and in highlighting the role of AI as an enabling mechanism linking HRM practices and KM processes, offering a more comprehensive understanding of knowledge dynamics in contemporary organizations.

Keywords: Knowledge Management · Human Resource Management Practices · Artificial Intelligence

1 Introduction

The evolution of industrial systems towards the Industry 5.0 paradigm marks a new technological milestone characterised by a high degree of collaboration between humans and machines [1]. Unlike Industry 4.0, which focuses primarily on automation and production efficiency, Industry 5.0 places the emphasis on human creativity, sustainability and

Published by Springer Nature Switzerland AG 2027
G. Pezzotta et al. (Eds.): APMS 2026, IFIP AICT 808, pp. 588–600, 2027.
https://doi.org/10.1007/978-3-032-38594-9_39

the well-being of workers [1]. In this context, manufacturing companies are undergoing a critical transition towards Servitisation 5.0, implementing human-centred service models geared towards creating long-term value through Product-Service Systems (PSS) [2, 3]. However, this transformation is hampered by data management that is often inefficient: whereas in the past organizations suffered from a lack of data, today they struggle to manage the sheer volume of it [4]. It is estimated, in fact, that around 55% of the data collected by businesses falls into the category of 'dark data' – that is, unknown information that remains unused, preventing truly informed and transparent decision-making [4, 5]. Traditional models of Knowledge Management (KM) – understood as the processes of identifying, organising, storing and disseminating knowledge [6] – are now showing structural limitations when it comes to processing massive volumes of data to enable effective decision-making [4]. To address these challenges, organizations are called upon to review their KM strategies to ensure they have a positive impact on competitiveness and financial performance. In this context, Artificial Intelligence (AI) is emerging as a key technological catalyst, capable of capturing, processing and distributing knowledge in real time [7]. The advent of generative AI has further revolutionised the sector, offering new ways of synthesising and generating content that reduce the cognitive load on knowledge workers [8]. However, despite its recognised potential, many organizations face significant barriers to integrating AI into their knowledge management processes, ranging from cultural barriers and technological limitations to ethical concerns regarding privacy and security [9] [10]. In this context, Human Resource Management (HRM) practices emerge as a critical enabling mechanism, as they shape employees' skills, motivation and behaviours through practices such as training, performance management and incentive systems, thereby influencing the adoption and effective use of digital and knowledge-based technologies [11].

Nevertheless, the existing literature has not yet fully explored how HRM practices can support the integration of AI into KM processes, particularly in knowledge-intensive and service-oriented organizations, where value creation increasingly depends on knowledge-intensive activities and the integration of products and services. To address this gap, this study seeks to answer the following research question: How can HRM practices support the adoption and effective use of AI technologies to enhance KM processes in knowledge-intensive organizations and service-based organizations?

The integration of these technologies not only accelerates the dissemination of knowledge but also enables a shift from human-supported decisions to augmented or automated decisions, depending on the complexity of the problem to be solved [4]. The original contribution of the study lies in the proposal of an integrated framework and a systematic procedure designed to guide managers in the orchestration of human and technological resources, with particular attention to service-oriented contexts.

The remainder of the paper is structured as follows: sect. 2 provides the theoretical background, discussing the role of Human Resource Management practices in relation to Knowledge Management processes and Artificial Intelligence. Section 3 then highlights the main gaps emerging from the literature. Section 4 describes the research methodology adopted in this study. Section 5 presents the results and introduces the proposed conceptual framework. Finally, Sect. 6 discusses the main conclusions, outlines the limitations of the study, and suggests directions for future research.

2 Theoretical Background

The following section outlines the theoretical framework underlying this study, focusing on the interrelationship between KM, HRM practices, and AI, with particular attention to service-oriented and servitized contexts.

KM refers to the systematic set of processes designed to identify, organise, store and disseminate data, information and knowledge within an organization [6]. In recent years, KM has become increasingly critical due to the exponential growth of data, which has intensified the challenge of transforming information into actionable knowledge. In this context, a significant proportion of organizational data remains unused, often referred to as 'dark data', which on average accounts for more than half of the available information [5]. As a result, traditional KM approaches are showing structural limitations in handling large volumes of data and supporting effective decision-making processes [4].

In service-oriented and servitized environments, the role of KM becomes even more central. In these contexts, value creation increasingly depends on the integration of products and services and on continuous interaction with customers. Knowledge is not only generated internally, but also co-created through service delivery processes and customer interactions, making the effective management of knowledge flows a key driver of service performance, innovation and competitiveness. This is particularly relevant in Product-Service Systems (PSS), where knowledge integration across organizational boundaries becomes essential.

From a theoretical perspective, knowledge is typically distinguished into explicit and tacit forms. Explicit knowledge can be codified and easily transferred, whereas tacit knowledge is deeply embedded in individuals' experiences and is difficult to formalise [1]. The dynamic interaction between these two forms is described by the SECI model (Socialisation, Externalisation, Combination and Internalisation), which explains how knowledge is created and shared through continuous social interaction within organizations [1]. However, despite the extensive development of KM literature, limited attention has been devoted to understanding how KM processes are jointly shaped by HRM practices and emerging digital technologies. Within this context, HRM plays a fundamental role as an enabler of KM processes. In knowledge-intensive organizations, individuals represent the primary source and carrier of knowledge, making HRM practices crucial for fostering knowledge creation, sharing and application [12]. HRM contributes to KM by shaping employees' skills, motivation and behaviours through practices such as recruitment, training and development, performance management and reward systems [11, 13]. In particular, high-commitment HRM practices are essential to promote a knowledge-oriented culture, facilitate collaboration and overcome barriers such as knowledge hoarding, which can limit the effectiveness of KM initiatives [11, 13]. Without alignment between HRM practices and KM strategies, organizations risk failing to fully exploit their knowledge assets [13]. Alongside the human dimension, technological advancements are profoundly transforming KM. AI is emerging as a key enabler capable of capturing, processing and analysing large volumes of structured and unstructured data, thereby enhancing knowledge creation and supporting more informed decision-making processes [4]. AI technologies, including Machine Learning, Knowledge-Based System, Computer Vision, Robotics, Natural Language Processing, Optimization, Generative AI

[14], enable organizations to extract insights, automate knowledge-intensive activities and improve both the speed and accuracy of decisions.

The integration of AI into KM processes introduces a dynamic and recursive logic. Rather than following a linear sequence, KM processes become part of a continuous feedback loop in which the outcomes of decisions generate new knowledge that feeds back into the system [4]. This evolution also reshapes the role of knowledge workers. Less experienced employees can leverage AI tools to rapidly acquire explicit knowledge and perform routine tasks, while more experienced workers focus on higher-level cognitive activities such as interpretation, validation and synthesis of knowledge [8]. However, despite its potential, AI adoption also presents significant challenges, including issues related to data quality, ethical concerns, trust, and the risk of over-reliance on automated systems [9, 10].

These considerations highlight that KM processes should be interpreted through a socio-technical perspective, where human and technological elements are deeply interconnected. HRM practices and AI technologies act as complementary enablers: while HRM shapes the behavioural and cultural conditions necessary for knowledge creation and sharing, AI enhances the organization's ability to process, analyse and exploit knowledge at scale.

Despite the growing relevance of KM, HRM and AI in both academic and managerial contexts, existing literature has predominantly analysed these dimensions in isolation or through partial relationships [4]. While HRM studies have focused on behavioural and organizational mechanisms supporting KM processes, and AI research has emphasised technological capabilities and data-driven decision-making, limited attention has been devoted to understanding how these elements jointly contribute to enabling KM processes. This lack of integration is particularly critical in knowledge-intensive and service-oriented environments, where value creation increasingly depends on the interaction between human and technological resources.

3 Research Gap

Despite the growing relevance of Human Resource Management, Artificial Intelligence, and Knowledge Management in contemporary organizations, existing studies have largely investigated these domains separately or through partial relationships [4]. Previous research has extensively explored how HRM practices influence knowledge sharing and organizational learning, highlighting the role of practices such as training, performance management, and leadership in fostering knowledge-based activities within organizations [11]. On the other hand, another stream of literature has focused on the adoption of Artificial Intelligence technologies to support knowledge management systems and decision-making processes, demonstrating how AI can facilitate knowledge acquisition, processing, and dissemination [4]. However, despite these advances, limited attention has been devoted to understanding how HRM practices and AI technologies jointly contribute to enabling and strengthening KM processes within organizations. This gap becomes even more critical in service-oriented and servitized contexts, where value creation increasingly relies on knowledge-intensive activities, continuous customer interaction, and the integration of products and services. In such environments, knowledge is not only managed internally but also co-created across organizational boundaries, requiring a tighter alignment between human capabilities and technological infrastructures.

As a result, there is still limited understanding of how HRM practices and AI technologies can be effectively integrated to support KM processes in service-based and knowledge-intensive organizations. To address this gap, this study adopts a socio-technical perspective and proposes a conceptual framework that integrates HRM practices, AI technologies, and KM processes.

4 Methodology

This study adopts a structured literature-based approach to develop the proposed conceptual framework. The methodological process consisted of three main stages aimed at identifying the core processes of Knowledge Management, the most important practices of Human Resource Management and the relationships between KM processes and HRM practices. To ensure a systematic identification of relevant contributions, two separate search queries were conducted using the Scopus database following the Preferred Reporting Items for Systematic Reviews and Meta-Analysis (PRISMA) methodology.

4.1 Identification and Clustering of Knowledge Management Processes in the Service Context

The first step of the research aimed to identify and classify the main processes related to Knowledge Management. For this purpose, a search was conducted in the Scopus database, using the following query:

(TITLE-ABS-KEY ("knowledge management") AND TITLE-ABS-KEY ("technology") AND TITLE-ABS-KEY ("service" OR "servitization" OR "maintenance" OR "Product Installation" OR "Spare parts" OR "Remanufacturing" OR "Refurbishing" OR "Recycling" OR "Take Back" OR "Inspection" OR "Diagnosis" OR "Extended Warranty" OR "repair") AND TITLE-ABS-KEY (framework)) AND (LIMIT-TO (DOCTYPE, "re")) AND (LIMIT-TO (SUBJAREA, "COMP") OR LIMIT-TO (SUBJAREA, "BUSI") OR LIMIT-TO (SUBJAREA, "ENGI") OR LIMIT-TO (SUBJAREA, "DECI")) AND (LIMIT-TO (LANGUAGE, "English"))*

As illustrated in Fig. 1, an initial pool of 1316 documents was identified. After applying filters on document type, subject areas, and language, the number of documents was reduced to 31. A further screening based on title and abstract, also considering the type of technologies addressed and retaining only studies referring to Artificial Intelligence-related technologies, led to 20 papers, while full-text analysis resulted in a final sample of 11 studies.

The objective of the query was to obtain a comprehensive overview of the Knowledge Management processes discussed in the literature, particularly in technology-enabled service contexts. The search was restricted to review papers in order to capture consolidated knowledge structures and existing conceptual frameworks related to KM. Following the identification of relevant papers, a qualitative content analysis was performed

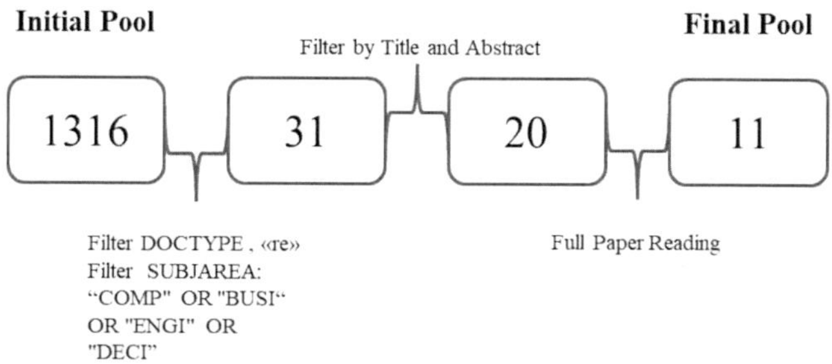

Fig. 1. Papers selection process KM

to extract the terminology used to describe KM processes. This was deemed necessary as different authors often refer to similar KM activities using different terms, such as acquisition, capture, discovery, or identification.

4.2 Identification and Clustering of Human Resource Management Practices

The second step of the research focused on identifying the Human Resource Management practices that influence the previously defined KM processes. A second query was therefore run using the Scopus database:

TITLE-ABS-KEY (("knowledge management" OR "Knowledge Acquisition" OR "Knowledge Storage" OR "Knowledge Sharing" OR "Knowledge Application" OR "Knowledge Reuse") AND "framework" AND "Human Resource Management" AND "impact") AND (LIMIT-TO (DOCTYPE, "ar")) AND (LIMIT-TO (SUBJAREA, "ENGI") OR LIMIT-TO (SUBJAREA, "BUSI"))

The PRISMA protocol was also applied in this phase. As shown in Fig. 2, the initial search resulted in 160 documents. After applying filters on document type and subject areas, the dataset was reduced to 64 papers. The screening based on title and abstract further reduced the sample to 29 studies, while full-text analysis led to a final selection of 16 relevant articles.

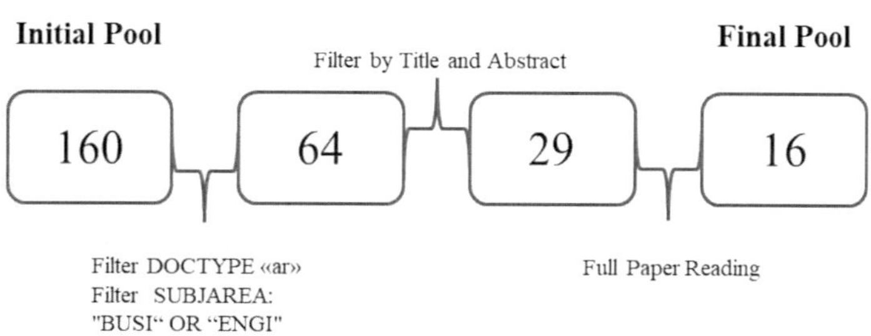

Fig. 2. Papers selection process KM - HRM

This search was limited to research articles in order to capture empirical and conceptual studies analyzing the relationship between HRM practices and knowledge management processes. The analysis of the selected articles allowed the identification of the main HRM practices that influence the effectiveness of KM processes within organizations.

5 Results and Conceptual Framework

In this section, the results of the analysis are presented, providing a structured synthesis of the relationships between KM, HRM, and AI. Through a systematic examination of the literature, this section identifies the key KM processes, the HRM practices that enable them, and the role of AI as a technological enabler. By integrating these elements, the study develops a conceptual framework that captures the dynamic and interdependent nature of knowledge creation, management, and utilization in digitally driven environments.

5.1 Clustering of Knowledge Management Process

The analysis of the literature identified a wide variety of terms used to describe Knowledge Management activities. These terms often refer to similar underlying processes but differ in terminology across studies. To address this heterogeneity, a clustering process was conducted to group related activities into a coherent set of KM phases. The results of this clustering process led to the identification of five core KM processes (Table 1):

More specifically, the analysis showed that several terms converge into each of these phases. For instance, Knowledge Acquisition includes activities such as acquisition, identification, discovery, sensing, creation, capture and socialization. Knowledge Storage encompasses processes such as codification, classification, processing, conversion, visualization and standardization. Knowledge Sharing includes activities such as transfer, communication, combination, externalization and internalization. Knowledge Application refers to processes such as use, exploitation, matching, optimization and response. Finally, Knowledge Reuse includes activities such as reuse, update, learning and exploration.

This clustering process allowed the consolidation of fragmented terminology into a structured KM process model, providing a clear foundation for further analysis. The identified KM phases are consistent with established knowledge management literature and represent the key mechanisms through which organizations create, manage and exploit knowledge.

5.2 Identification of HRM Practices Influencing KM Process

The second stage of the analysis is the clusterisation of the HRM practices since the literature highlights that HRM plays a fundamental role in enabling knowledge creation, facilitating knowledge sharing and supporting organizational learning. Through this process, different HRM practices were categorized and linked to their potential impact on knowledge acquisition, storage, sharing, application and reuse. This mapping process enabled the identification of the HRM dimensions that support knowledge creation, facilitate knowledge sharing and enable the effective use of knowledge within organizations.

Table 1. KM Clustering process

Macro-phase	Definition	Activity	Ref
Knowledge Acquisition	It is the process of extracting relevant information from various sources to facilitate data-driven decision-making. It is defined as the creation of a catalogue of knowledge services from information or knowledge sources. In more complex contexts, it involves acquiring and integrating external knowledge with existing knowledge to meet new requirements.	Acquisition	[4, 15–17]
		Socialization	[1]
		Sensing	[18]
		Creation	[4, 16, 17, 19]
		Capture	[20–23]
		Discovery	[16]
		Identification	[4, 24]
Knowledge Storage	It refers to the identification, organization and preservation of data and information within an organization. This process aims to preserve knowledge in a repository (archive) so that it can be retrieved in the future by other employees, making it independent of the individual who originally produced it. Efficient archiving is crucial in determining how easily knowledge can be retrieved later on.	Codification	[17]
		Storage	[4, 19–23]
		Standardization	[17]
		Classification	[22]
		Processing	[20]
		Conversion	[15]
		Visualization	[22]
		Representation	[22]
		Assimilation	[24]
Knowledge Sharing	It is the process through which knowledge is disseminated, exchanged and communicated between individuals or groups, both within and outside the organization. It enables the rapid dissemination of insights and best practices, accelerating the pace of innovation and improving the quality of collective decision-making.	Transfer	[19]
		Sharing	[4, 20–23]
		Combination	[1]
		Externalization	[1]
		Internalization	[1]
		Retrieval	[21, 23]
Knowledge Application	It involves using knowledge to solve challenges, promote innovation and develop new skills within an organization. It focuses on meeting the needs of end users by delivering specific services or carrying out specific tasks. It includes incorporating data-driven insights into decision-making frameworks to make decisions more accurate, efficient and effective.	Use	[20]
		Application	[4, 15, 19, 21, 23, 24]
		Match	[16]
		Optimization	[16]
		Exploitation	[23]
		Respond	[18]

(*continued*)

Table 1. (*continued*)

Macro-phase	Definition	Activity	Ref
Knowledge Reuse	It involves retrieving and applying solutions to past problems or answers to questions of 'know-how' in order to tackle similar problems in the present or future. Organizations aim to reuse codified knowledge (either unchanged or by recombining existing elements) to achieve economies of scale and cost savings associated with the replication of knowledge.	Update	[22]
		Reuse	[16, 22]
		Learning	[18]
		Exploration	[17]

The analysis allowed the identification of several key HRM practices, including:

- *Recruitment, selection and workforce entry*: The selection process should not be limited to current skills, but should focus on learning potential, networking skills and cultural alignment with the company's shared values [13].
- *Training and development*: Training is essential for updating skills, facilitating the internalisation of knowledge and creating a common language that breaks down barriers to internal communication [1, 4, 11, 12].
- *Performance management*: Performance appraisal must explicitly incorporate criteria relating to contributions to knowledge-building processes, rewarding those who not only achieve operational objectives but also actively participate in the creation and dissemination of knowledge [25].
- *Compensation and rewards*: Reward systems, whether tangible (bonuses, financial incentives) or intangible (recognition, status), are essential for motivating individuals to overcome the natural tendency to hoard knowledge [11, 13, 25, 26].
- *Career development and talent management*: A career management approach based on sharing experience reduces the risk of organizational memory loss during staff turnover and increases employees' emotional commitment [11, 13].
- *Knowledge-based HR practices*: These practices are specifically designed to enhance the ability to acquire, assimilate and transform knowledge [25].
- *Leadership and work organization*: Support from senior management and employee empowerment are critical drivers; a decentralised structure facilitates the flow of information and mutual trust [27].
- *Sustainable and wellbeing-oriented HRM*: In line with Industry 5.0, employee well-being and a pro-social working environment are seen as cornerstones of sustainable competitiveness [1].

5.3 Identification of AI technologies

The identification and classification of AI technologies within the proposed framework is grounded in the need to provide a structured and operational understanding of how different technological solutions contribute to KM processes and HRM practices. In particular, the framework adopts a categorization that includes Machine Learning,

Knowledge-Based Systems, Computer Vision, Natural Language Processing, Robotics, Optimization algorithms, and Generative AI [14].

5.4 Development of the Integrated HRM-AI-KM Framework

Building on the clustering of Knowledge Management processes and the identification of relevant Human Resource Management practices, this study proposes an integrated conceptual framework that combines HRM, Artificial Intelligence, and KM within a dynamic and interdependent system.

The framework presented in Fig. 3 is rooted in a socio-technical perspective, where organizations are interpreted as complex systems shaped by the continuous interaction between human capabilities, technological infrastructures, and knowledge processes. Rather than following a linear structure, the framework is built on a circular logic, emphasizing the presence of ongoing feedback loops connecting HRM, AI, and KM.

The aim of this framework is to explain how different organizational dimensions jointly contribute to the development and management of knowledge in highly digitalized environments. Instead of depicting a sequential process, it highlights a set of interdependent components that evolve over time and mutually influence one another.

Within this configuration, Human Resource Management emerges as a key enabling factor. Practices such as recruitment, training, performance evaluation, reward systems, and leadership are crucial in shaping both employees' skills and their attitudes toward knowledge. Beyond supporting traditional organizational goals, these practices foster an environment that promotes learning, facilitates knowledge sharing, and encourages experimentation. In particular, the development of digital skills and the ability to work with data become increasingly relevant, especially in environments where advanced technologies are introduced.

Artificial Intelligence represents a second, distinct layer within the framework. Rather than being considered as an isolated technological component, AI is interpreted here as a set of tools that can support and extend organizational knowledge processes. Technologies such as machine learning, natural language processing, computer vision, generative AI, and optimization techniques allow organizations to handle large volumes of information and to extract insights that would otherwise remain difficult to identify. In this sense, AI does not replace human knowledge but complements it by enhancing analytical and decision-making capabilities.

The contribution of AI becomes particularly evident when looking at specific knowledge management activities. For instance, data-driven solutions can be used to uncover new knowledge patterns, while language-based technologies enable a more effective circulation of information across individuals and organizational units. In parallel, decision-support systems contribute to the practical use of knowledge in day-to-day operations, whereas automation tools allow knowledge to be embedded into routines and processes.

Within this framework, Knowledge Management processes constitute the space where these interactions take shape. Activities such as knowledge acquisition, storage, sharing, application, and reuse make it possible to convert fragmented information into actionable insights. These processes are inherently connected to both human and technological components, as they rely on employees' behaviors as well as on the digital tools adopted by the organization. A further relevant element of the model is the presence of feedback dynamics. The outcomes generated through knowledge-related activities tend to propagate throughout the system, influencing its other components. For example, insights derived from the application and reuse of knowledge may prompt revisions in training initiatives or lead to adjustments in performance management practices. At the same time, the use of AI technologies continuously produces new data, which can be leveraged to enhance algorithms and progressively improve technological solutions. These elements do not operate independently, but co-develop over time, influencing each other in multiple ways. From this viewpoint, knowledge management emerges not as a static set of activities, but as a dynamic capability that depends on the alignment between people, technologies, and organizational practices.

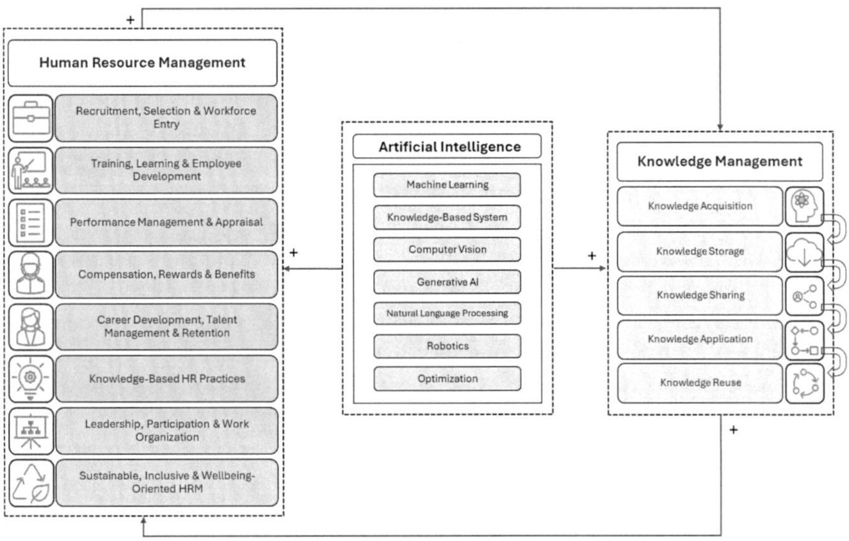

Fig. 3. Framework HRM - AI - KM

6 Conclusions, Limitations and Future Research

This study proposes an integrated conceptual framework that combines Human Resource Management practices, Artificial Intelligence technologies and Knowledge Management processes, providing a holistic perspective on how organizations can enhance their knowledge capabilities in digitally enabled environments. By adopting a socio-technical approach, the framework highlights the dynamic and reciprocal relationships among human, technological and knowledge dimensions, emphasizing the role of HRM in enabling AI adoption and the contribution of AI in supporting KM processes. Despite its theoretical contributions, this study presents some limitations. First, the framework is conceptual in nature and has not been empirically validated. Second, the literature-based clustering process may be influenced by the selection of sources and interpretation of terminology. Future research should therefore focus on empirically testing the proposed relationships through quantitative or qualitative methods, such as surveys or case studies. Additionally, further studies could explore the application of the framework in specific industrial contexts, such as manufacturing or service systems, and investigate the role of emerging AI technologies in shaping next-generation knowledge management practices.

Disclosure of Interests. The authors have no competing interests to declare.

References

1. Bonamigo, A., Barbosa, A.D.S., Rocha, E.D.A.S., Werner, S.M.: Facilitators and inhibitors of lean service 5.0: an assessment from the knowledge waste management perspective. VINE J. Inf. Knowl. Manag. Syst. **55**, 1501–1526 (2025). https://doi.org/10.1108/VJIKMS-02-2024-0050
2. Nicoletti, B., Appolloni, A.: Artificial intelligence for the Management of Servitization 5.0. Sustainability. **15**, 11113 (2023). https://doi.org/10.3390/su151411113
3. Vinuesa, R., Azizpour, H., Leite, I., et al.: The role of artificial intelligence in achieving the sustainable development goals. Nat. Commun. **11**, 233 (2020). https://doi.org/10.1038/s41467-019-14108-y
4. Leoni, L., Gueli, G., Ardolino, M., et al.: AI-empowered KM processes for decision-making: empirical evidence from worldwide organisations. J. Knowl. Manag. **28**, 320–347 (2024). https://doi.org/10.1108/JKM-03-2024-0262
5. Splunk: The State of Dark Data. White paper, Splunk (2019)
6. Beesley, L.G.A., Cooper, C.: Defining knowledge management (KM) activities: towards consensus. J. Knowl. Manag. **12**, 48–62 (2008). https://doi.org/10.1108/13673270810875859
7. Korzynski, P., Mazurek, G., Altmann, A., et al.: Generative artificial intelligence as a new context for management theories: analysis of ChatGPT. Cent Eur Manag J. **31**, 3–13 (2023). https://doi.org/10.1108/CEMJ-02-2023-0091
8. Storey, V.C.: Knowledge Management in a World of generative AI: impact and implications. ACM Trans. Manag. Inf. Syst. **16**, 1–14 (2025). https://doi.org/10.1145/3719209
9. Davenport, T.H., Davenport, T., Glaser, J., Gardner, E.: Advanced Introduction to Artificial Intelligence in Healthcare. Edward Elgar Publishing (2022)
10. Malik, A., Kumar, S., Basu, S., Bebenroth, R.: Managing disruptive technologies for innovative healthcare solutions: the role of high-involvement work systems and technologically-mediated relational coordination. J. Bus. Res. **161**, 113828 (2023). https://doi.org/10.1016/j.jbusres.2023.113828
11. Matošková, J., Směšná, P.: Human resource management practices stimulating knowledge sharing. Manag Mark. **12**, 614–632 (2017). https://doi.org/10.1515/mmcks-2017-0036
12. Oltra, V.: Knowledge management effectiveness factors: the role of HRM. J. Knowl. Manag. **9**, 70–86 (2005). https://doi.org/10.1108/13673270510610341
13. Andreeva, T., Kianto, A.: Does knowledge management really matter? Linking knowledge management practices, competitiveness and economic performance. J. Knowl. Manag. **16**, 617–636 (2012). https://doi.org/10.1108/13673271211246185
14. Marinucci, M., Sala, R., Arioli, V., Pirola, F.: The adoption of artificial intelligence in manufacturing services: key insights and strategic directions (2025)
15. Lam, C.H., Tan, P.S.H., Fong, C.Y., et al.: The effectiveness of HRM and KM in innovation performance: a literature review and research agenda. Int J Innov Learn. **9**, 339 (2011). https://doi.org/10.1504/IJIL.2011.040534

16. Wu, Z., Liao, J., Song, W., et al.: Product lifecycle–oriented knowledge services: status review, framework, and technology trends. Concurr. Eng. **25**, 81–92 (2017). https://doi.org/10.1177/1063293X16680260
17. Walsh, J.N., O'Brien, J.: A knowledge-based framework for service management. J. Inf. Knowl. Manag. **16**, 1750039 (2017). https://doi.org/10.1142/S0219649217500393
18. Calabrese, F.A.: Knowledge-based organizations in context. VINE. **36**, 12–16 (2006). https://doi.org/10.1108/03055720610667318
19. Marjanovic, O.: Towards a web-based handbook of generic, process-oriented learning designs. J. Educ. Technol. Soc. **8**(2), 66–82 (2005)
20. Dotsika, F., Patrick, K.: Towards the new generation of web knowledge. Vine. **36**, 406–422 (2006). https://doi.org/10.1108/03055720610716665
21. Omar, W.M., Abbas, A.D.K., Taleb-Bendiab, A.: SOAW2 for managing the web 2.0 framework. IT Prof. **9**, 30–35 (2007). https://doi.org/10.1109/MITP.2007.56
22. Wang, H., Meng, X.: Transformation from IT-based knowledge management into BIM-supported knowledge management: a literature review. Expert Syst. Appl. **121**, 170–187 (2019). https://doi.org/10.1016/j.eswa.2018.12.017
23. Jiang, Y., Yang, G., Li, H., Zhang, T.: Knowledge driven approach for smart bridge maintenance using big data mining. Autom. Constr. **146**, 104673 (2023). https://doi.org/10.1016/j.autcon.2022.104673
24. Roberts, N., Galluch, P.S., Dinger, M., Grover, V.: Absorptive capacity and information systems research: review, synthesis, and directions for future Research1. MIS Q. **36**, 625–648 (2012). https://doi.org/10.2307/41703470
25. Enad Al-Qaralleh, R., Atan, T.: Impact of knowledge-based HRM, business analytics and agility on innovative performance: linear and FsQCA findings from the hotel industry. Kybernetes. **51**, 423–441 (2022). https://doi.org/10.1108/K-10-2020-0684
26. Saeed, K., Janjua, U.I., Alharthi, S.Z., et al.: An empirical study to investigate the impact of factors influencing knowledge sharing in virtual teams. IEEE Access. **11**, 92715–92734 (2023). https://doi.org/10.1109/ACCESS.2023.3309009
27. Barua, B.: Impact of total quality management factors on knowledge creation in the organizations of Bangladesh. TQM J. **33**, 1516–1543 (2021). https://doi.org/10.1108/TQM-06-2020-0145

Development and Validation of a Roadmapping Methodology for Servitization

Alessandra Chisari(✉), Elena Beducci, Anna de Carolis, and Marco Taisch

Department of Management, Economics and Industrial Engineering, Politecnico di Milano, via Lambruschini 4/b, 20156 Milan, Italy
{alessandra.chisari,elena.beducci,anna.decarolis, marco.taisch}@polimi.it

Abstract.. Servitization, the transition from product—towards service-centric offerings, offers manufacturers an opportunity to achieve relevant strategic advantage, sustainable impact and increased efficiency, while tackling encompassing challenges and global trends. This transition, enhanced by the combined adoption of digital technologies, requires a significant company transformation, which implies challenges related to the creation and deployment of new activities, resources mindset and partnerships. To manage the transformation and the related challenges, roadmapping can support companies in planning strategic and operational activities and effectively steer efforts. Nonetheless, current literature offers limited approaches for roadmapping in servitization. This paper proposes and validates, through the application in two manufacturing companies, a multi-step roadmapping methodology, leveraging the Business Model Canvas framework. This tool, intended for the application during the initial new business model definition phase, supports companies in building roadmaps to guide and structure strategic and operational activities for servitization, harmonizing efforts across extended timeframes. The paper complements the current research on Product Service System (PSS) design considering the extended transformational process required to sustain the new offerings, while proposing a structured tool to guide manufacturers' efforts in deploying servitization strategies.

Keywords: Servitization · Product Service System · Roadmap · Business Model Canvas

1 Introduction

Manufacturing companies are increasingly impacted by transformational phenomena and challenges, such as technological innovation, economic and social trends and climate change [1]. Servitization, defined by Kowalkowski et al. (2017) [2] as *"the transformational processes whereby a company shifts from a product-centric to a service-centric business model and logic"* (p. 8), is considered an opportunity to tackle these challenges while potentially achieving financial gains, operational efficiency, and sustainability. Connected to servitization is the concept of Product Service System (PSS) which is *"a*

Published by Springer Nature Switzerland AG 2027
G. Pezzotta et al. (Eds.): APMS 2026, IFIP AICT 808, pp. 601–615, 2027.
https://doi.org/10.1007/978-3-032-38594-9_40

marketable set of products and services capable of jointly fulfilling a user's need" [3] (p.18).

Through servitization, manufacturing companies can increase their revenue streams, extend and strengthen customer relationships and loyalty and improve operational performances of their offering through dedicated services leveraging their expertise [4–6]. Servitization also presents a promising complementary and enhancing relationship with digitalization and sustainability. Digital technologies facilitate the transition towards servitization, while business models focused on servitization concretize monetization opportunities of digital offerings [7]. Indeed, digital technologies enable services of customization and co-creation, operational improvement, maintenance, and end-of-life services [8]. Additionally, servitization, if appropriately designed and managed, particularly when enhanced by digital technologies, can potentially lead to improved environmental sustainability through increased product longevity, closed resource loops, intensified usage, and increased resource efficiency [9, 10]. While offering promising opportunities for optimization, sustainability, differentiation, and increased resilience to shocks, the transition towards servitization is complex. Companies can fail in the transition because of low commitment, need for dedicated capabilities development, and scalability and profitability issues [11]. The servitization transition requires an encompassing organizational transformation, involving challenges related to the creation and deployment of new business models, the creation of new and dedicated relationships with suppliers and customers, the adoption of technological infrastructure, and risk management [6, 12–14].

Manufacturing companies transitioning towards servitization struggle with the creation and consolidation of the appropriate culture and with the alignment of strategic priorities [15]. Roadmapping, defined by Kerr and Phaal (2022) as "*a structured visual chronology of strategic intent*" can help companies in this endeavour [16]. The role of roadmapping has been recognized to overcome these challenges and to support the servitization transition, particularly in the context of digital servitization and small and medium enterprises, in managing the required cultural and organizational transformation [17]. While methodologies for PSSs' design have been extensively explored [18–21], existing literature offers limited approaches and methodologies to develop servitization roadmaps [8] able to adapt to the specific context of manufacturing companies. Thus, an encompassing, integrated and structured methodology to support manufacturers in setting clear strategic and operational priorities to guide servitization efforts is still missing.

Overcoming this gap, the research objective leading this paper is to propose and test a roadmapping methodology dedicated to the servitization of manufacturing companies. The paper proposes a methodology to guide the definition of servitized business model and to elaborate the related roadmap, allowing to identify and harmonize efforts of servitization across extended timeframes.

The findings contribute to the literature by complementing current perspective on PSSs' design, considering the extended transformational process required by manufacturing companies to sustain PSS offerings. To practice, this paper offers a structured tool to guide manufacturers efforts in deploying servitization strategies.

The paper is structured as follows: in Sect. 2 the research design adopted for this study is presented, in Sect. 3 the roadmapping methodology is introduced, Sect. 4 presents the two application cases, comparison and discussion on the model, in Sect. 5 conclusions are reported.

2 Research Design

The research objective of the paper is to develop a roadmapping methodology to support companies prioritize activities in the development and the implementation of digital service-based offerings. Thus, the research design, inspired by the Design Science Research Methodology (DSRM), defined by Peffers et al. (2007) [22], has been deployed, Fig. 1. The research design has been selected as it is appropriate to develop and validate an artifact, in this case, the roadmapping methodology, able to support manufacturers into identifying and prioritizing strategic and operational effort towards servitization.

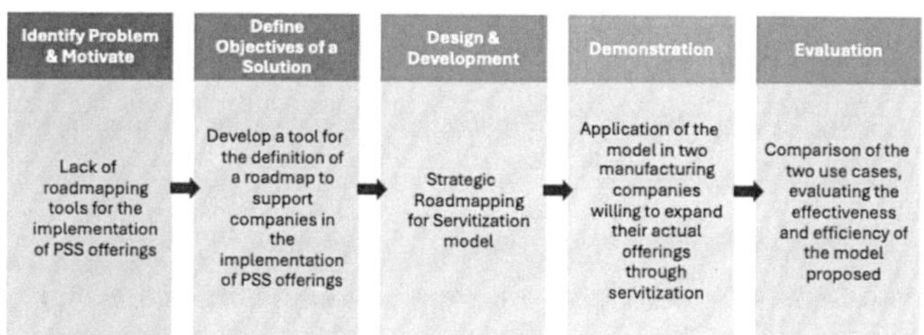

Fig. 1. Research design

Problem Identification and Motivation was executed by reviewing existing literature related to servitization, particularly focusing on tool supporting companies in managing the transition towards digital servitization. As stated in the previous section, while literature provide many tools related to the design of PSS, road mapping methodologies and tools supporting the subsequent transformation are missing.

In the second step, **"Define Objectives of a Solution"**, the artifact's objective was clarified. The roadmapping methodology (i.e., the artifact) objective is to support the definition of servitized business models and to elaborate the related roadmap, allowing to identify and harmonize efforts of servitization across extended timeframes.

The **"Design & Development"** phase focused on the artifact's conceptualization. To develop the model, instrumental tools for the definition of new servitized business models were selected. Roadmapping tools from adjacent research field and PSS design approaches have been revised to identify relevant trends and principles to adopt in the proposed methodology. Based on this research, the role of Business Model Canvas (BMC), Customer segmentation and Value Proposition Canvas (VPC) in the transition toward a PSS-focused business model was more thoroughly investigated, for their role in supporting the structured analysis and definition of business models. This structured approach supports the identification of key resources and capabilities for servitization, which are leveraged to populate the final roadmapping. Based on the insights collected in this phase, the roadmapping methodology was developed. The artifact leverages the BMC in a preliminary step to characterize the existing business model and to define the new business model centering the PSS offering. The definition of the new business model requires additional steps: the customer segmentation and the definition of the new PSS offerings according to the VPC. The new business model, defined according to the BMC framework, defines the key resources and key activities. These are leveraged to inform the operational and strategic activities that build the roadmap to support the transition. The roadmap is structured around the different developed service offerings, according to an extended temporal perspective, articulated in phases, highlighting possible synergies.

The **"Demonstration"** step consisted in the application of the developed methodology in two distinct manufacturing companies. These companies are both Original Equipment Manufacturers (OEM) and willing to expand their current offering through servitization, but they differ in terms of industry and size as shown in Table 1.

Table 1. Companies involved in the validation

Name	Location	N. Employees	Industry	Type of product
Company A	Milan, Italy	50–100	Industrial automation	Customized
Company B	Rome, Italy	11–50	Test equipment	Customized

In both cases, the tool was applied through on-site workshops characterized by a brainstorming and collaborative approach with the involvement of operations, technical and sales managers. In case of company A, the methodology was applied through a two-day workshop. While in company B the model has been applied over a period of four months, through multiple workshops, customer interviews and survey dedicated to each step of the tool. These two approaches have been selected to comply with both companies' availability and resources. Both the diversity in the companies' market and resource availability allowed to test the capacity to adapt to different context.

In company A, 4 company managers, the operations, technical and sales managers, have been involved in each step of the methodology, contributing with insights gained through the experience of each function. In company B, overall 6 company managers have been involved covering sales, design and operation, human resources and marketing areas. Each manager has been involved according to their availability and coherently to the specific activities' objective and discussion topic. Notably, the operations managers have always been involved, with the strong support from the sales and human resources managers, while the marketing manager has been involved sporadically, coherently with the activity scope.

Finally, **"Evaluation"** was used to assess the effectiveness and efficiency of the tool through the comparison of the two applicative cases.

3 Strategic Roadmapping for Servitization

Addressing the difficulties encountered by manufacturing companies in deploying servitization strategies, the proposed methodology aims to support companies in designing a roadmap to guide the transformation towards servitization. The methodology is composed of six sequential steps, Fig. 2. Recognizing that implementing digital servitization strategies means defining new value propositions, the steps have been designed to create new customer value and enable customers to achieve their desired outcomes more effectively [23].

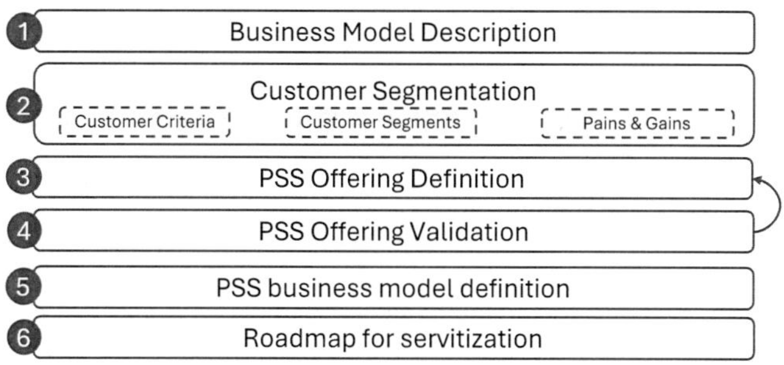

Fig. 2. Roadmapping methodology

The first step is the Description of the current business model. This step employs the BMC to clarify and frame the current state of the company: which is its value proposition and how it creates, delivers and captures value [24, 25]. The BMC has been recognized as a valuable tool to support manufacturers in the transition towards servitization, guiding companies in the analysis of their traditional approach and in the evolution towards PSS offerings [26–28]. The four pillars of the BMC are analysed:

- **Value Proposition**: it defines the value proposed to customers through the current product-service offerings. The company must describe the distinctive features of the proposal leading customers in choosing them and provide a list and description of the services currently provided, if any.
- **Value Creation**: to characterize this pillar, the company must describe the *key resources* – both tangible and intangible – (e.g., knowledge base), *key activities* (e.g., lead generation, offer creation, production, logistics) and *strategic partners*, required for the company's operations and to deliver the current offerings.
- **Value Capture**: here, revenue and cost streams are described.
- **Value Delivery**: the company must identify and characterize all customer segments served, along with the current channels used to reach and engage them and the methods of interaction with customers throughout the entire product lifecycle.

This final pillar, Value Delivery, forms the link to the next stage of the methodology, which involves the **Customer Segmentation**. The process of defining customer segments begins with identifying the *segmentation criteria* [29]. The identification of segmentation criteria involves the company to understand how their customers interact with their offerings, reflecting on their needs and characteristics what could affect how they behave when using the product (e.g. digital maturity, frequency of use). The criteria describe the current and potential customer base of the company's offering. Leveraging these key criteria, complementary and relevant *customer segments* are defined and named, they represent group of customers with different needs and requirements that can be served through distinct services. Following the VPC [30], based on this segmentation, the *'pains'*, factors that hinder customers in the execution of their activities, and the '*gains*', factors that support and enable customers in executing and improving their activities, are identified.

Relying on the idea that servitized business models should be based on the analysis and understanding of customer requirements, opportunities and pain points [31], the "pains" and the "gains" identified are taken as the foundation for subsequent step, which is the **PSS offering definition**. In this step, the new services are described in terms of their key features and potential challenges. The PSS defined are then validated across the needs and requirement of customers, coherently with Pezzotta et al. (2016) approach, in which the PSS prototype is then validate against customer requirements [18].

Subsequently, the new servitization strategies are defined through the deployment of the **BMC**. The same structure as the first step is used and every block is characterized for every proposal, highlighting elements in common to synergize efforts.

The final step, **definition of the roadmap**, leverages the new Value Creation pillar: activities, partnerships and resources to be built to support the new PSS offerings are identified and prioritized as activities composing the roadmap. These activities are organized into a structured roadmap template, where each activity is linked to different service offering, highlighting synergies, and graphically incorporated in the roadmap, divided into sequential stages. Prioritization of activities is based on their logical and operational interdependencies, ensuring that preparatory activities are implemented first to enable the successful implementation of the final service offering. The final objective of this structure is to allow the company to manage complexity incrementally (Fig. 3).

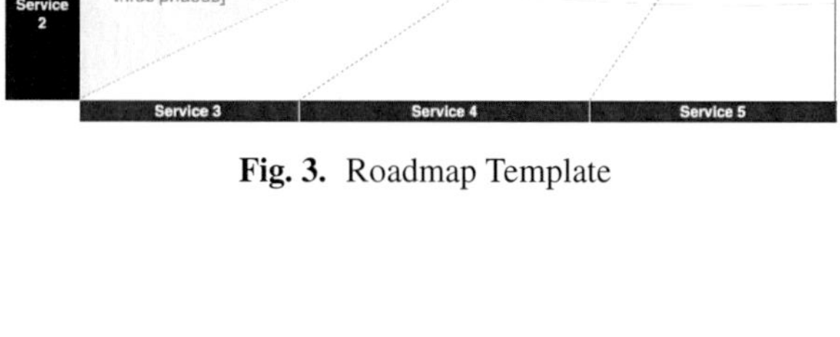

Fig. 3. Roadmap Template

4 Methodology Application and Discussion

The tool has been applied in two manufacturing companies, testing its adaptability and flexibility in different contexts and needs. Both companies involved are OEM, working in the Italian manufacturing context. The companies aimed at expanding their traditional product offerings with innovative services, facilitating the differentiation and the competitive advantage in saturated markets [32]. To do so, they needed support for designing the new service-oriented business model and defining the roadmap to implement it effectively.

4.1 Company A

Company A is an OEM specialized in industrial automation, operating in Northern Italy and employing 50–100 employees. The company is considered a world leader in this sector and more than 60 years of experience have contributed to the development of significant technological know-how, which fosters continuity in the innovation of the offerings. To maintain its competitive advantage, the company started the journey of servitization. Currently the offering is characterized by a diversified product portfolio with a high level of customization, designed to meet the various operational needs of end users.

The methodology in this case has been implemented through a two-day workshop at the company's headquarters. The technique deployed for each step is clarified in Fig. 4. The workshop was conducted in a collaborative and structured manner, using digital visualization tools for all participants to support structured decision-making. All participants contributed to the brainstorming sessions and validation activities.

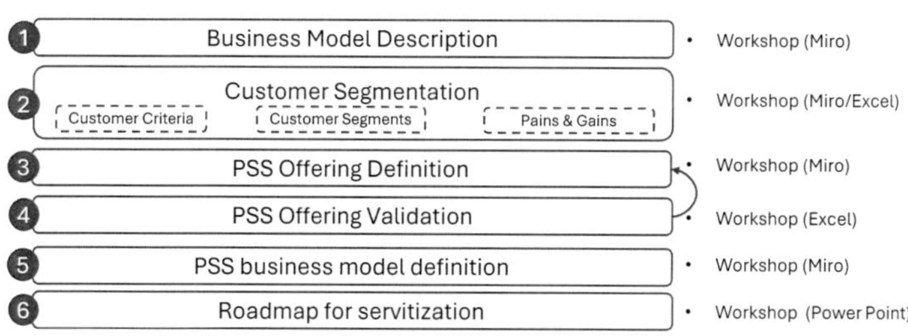

Fig. 4. Methodology applied in Company A

The results of the methodology application in company A are here summarized:

Business Model Description

During this step, a blank BMC was displayed on screen using Miro. The company team was guided through the process of filling in the blocks, starting with the value proposition. This has allowed the researchers and the team to obtain a clear picture of the company to identify new opportunities and enrich the value proposition through new services.

Definition of Customer Segments

After defining the customers in the Value Delivery section of the BMC, the team identified the key drivers characterizing the customer groups. Three sequential steps have been deployed. The first one, customer criteria, is instrumental to define and distinguish customer behaviors. In the second one, customer segments, customers with different behaviors are grouped in clusters. The third one, pain & gains, is needed to describe for each cluster, possible improvements derived from pain points and potential gains. Here after, the three steps are described in detail:

Customer Criteria At this stage, the definition of distinctive drivers related to the type of use and interaction with machines enabled the clustering of customers based on behavioral rather than technological needs. During the analysis of customer behaviors, eight different drivers emerged: the mix of materials and products processed, the level of machine automation, operators' experience, impact of machine downtime, available budget and participation of the engineering office in the machine design phase. A structured review led to the selection of three out of eight drivers (level of machine automation, impact of machine downtime and operators experience), identified as the most discriminative drivers for a servitized offering.

Customer Segments Based on these drivers, five customer clusters were identified. Four clusters were determined by the machine type and the impact of machine downtime. Additionally, the driver related to the operator's experience has been used to describe the fifth cluster, named "PLUS". Each cluster was described and named through both a full descriptive name and a short label (e.g., Cluster A). Finally, the resulting segmentation was visualized in Miro and validated by the team.

Pains & Gains After the identification of the customer segments targeted by the offering, the company identified the current pain points to overcome and the potential gain to achieve through a new service portfolio. The final output was also developed using Miro platform, which helped the team to visually organize the list of pains and gains using different colors to distinguish the clusters.

PSS Offering Definition

On the second day of the workshop, the new PSS offering was designed based on the findings of the previous steps: the definition of the new customer segments and their respective pain points and gains. The offering has been designed to be modular, enabling flexible configurations that can meet the specific needs of different customer profiles. Also in this case, the team adopted a brainstorming approach, and, being involved in the company's core processes, was able to define offerings consistent with end-users' needs, capable of evolving over time and aligned with the company's identity and market's expectations. Five new service offerings have been identified and outlined (e.g. Monitoring and Reporting).

Offering Validation

Following the definition of the service offering, a mapping exercise was carried out to assess its consistency and ability to effectively address the previously identified pain points and benefits. By applying the VPC framework, the respective pain relievers and gain generators associated with each service were defined. This analysis clearly highlighted how each service helps to mitigate the pain points and maximize the identified benefits.

New Service-Based Business Model

Having defined the new PSS offerings, the second part of the workshop was dedicated to the definition of the business model. Using the BMC displayed on a screen through Miro, the managers filled the blocks according to the new offerings together with the researchers. The final output consisted of a complete description, in terms of value proposition, creation, capture and delivery, for all the service offerings defined in the previous step.

Roadmap for Servitization

Following the formalization of the new business model, a roadmap was drawn up to prioritize the activities required for the development and implementation of the PSS offerings.

4.2 Company B

Company B is an OEM operating in Center Italy producing test equipment for multiple industrial contexts. The company's offering is recognized for its high degree of customization and continuous customer support. Coherently with the effort of digitalization of their product base, the company is interested in supporting their product offering with advanced digital services, coherent with the digital servitization strategy.

In Company B, the roadmapping methodology has been applied in a four-month long projects involving multiple workshops, customer interviews and a customer survey; the techniques deployed for each step are clarified in Fig. 5.

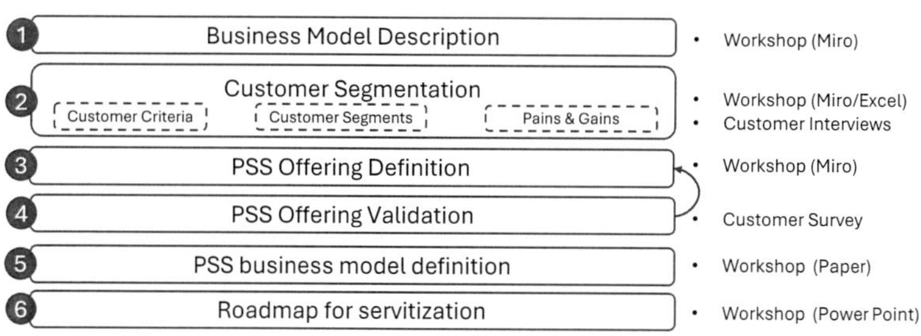

Fig. 5. Methodology applied in Company B

The results of the methodology application in company B are here summarized:

Business Model Description

The current Business Model description step was carried out through an 8-h workshop involving the research team and the company key figures, sales, design and operation and marketing. To guide the activity the tool Miro was selected, and the BMC was projected, visible to all the participants to incentivize discussion and brainstorming. In case of company B, this first step had been instrumental to identify the current offer characteristics representing a competitive advantage against competitors, which have then been leveraged as an opportunity to enhance or expand it in the PSS offerings.

The result of this step was a detailed description of the nine-dimension characterizing the current business model of the company.

Customer Segmentation

The result of the business model description, particularly those related to the value delivery pillar, were leveraged to define the new customer segmentation to guide the definition of the PSS offering.

Customer Criteria Leveraging the results of the business model description, a second 8-h workshop, involving researchers, and sales and design teams, was organized to identify critical customer criteria leading customer segmentation. This step deployed a brainstorming activity, guided through the projection of a MS Excel file summarizing the inputs, that identified 15 customer criteria that comprehensively describe the customer base, current and potential. These drivers mostly describe the behavioral dimension of the users base, with criteria such as "digital maturity" and "frequency of usage".

From these 15 criteria, 5 main and differential criteria have been identified to characterize customer segments to serve through PSS. These criteria are users typology (direct user or distributor); level of test criticality, test frequency, budget, and users' knowledge. Notably, while 5 criteria have been selected to identify a relevant and operational customer segmentation, all the criteria identified can be leveraged to guide more informed future activities, such as sales and marketing.

Customer Segments From the customer criteria seven customer segments have been described and named. Notably, 5 clusters refer to direct users of the equipment, characterized by different frequency and criticality of usage of the test equipment and different budgets. Two additional clusters identify distributors, thus separating them from the previous clusters, and non-expert users, which represents an additional characteristic which can be applied to the other clusters.

Pains & Gains To identify the pains and gains of each cluster, six customers interviews have been conducted in the span of two weeks. The customers have been selected to guarantee the representativeness of the sample in terms of application market and used product. The interviews followed a questionnaire designed to assign the customers to the correct cluster and to collect insights on the modality of usage and on pains and gains. The interviews have then been analyzed, and pains and gains identified and assigned in terms of magnitude to each customer segment. Particularly, two pain points were identified, lack of knowledge and operational failure/loss of performance, and three gain opportunities: new set-up definition, performance monitoring, system integration.

PSS Offering Definition

Based on the pains and gains, 6 service offerings to expand the current business model have been defined in an 8-h workshop. An initial proposal of service offerings, based on previous results, was presented by the researchers, and during the workshop the proposal was expanded. In this workshop, the main characteristics, critical resources, possible implementation barriers and initial pricing considerations were defined.

PSS Offering Validation

The PSS offering validation followed a two-stage procedure. First, the PSS offerings were mapped against the pain and gain to validate their ability to produce pain reliever and gain creator able to answer to customers' needs. Then, a customer survey was deployed to collect customers' feedback on the offering. The survey questionnaire was composed by two sections, the first related to the collection of information for customer segmentation, the second to collect customers' opinion on the service offering, both in terms of ability to answer users' need and deliver value, and in terms of monetization opportunity. The survey collected 23 answers, that validated the proposed offerings highlighting prioritization strategies according to customers' interest.

PSS Business Model Definition

After the definition of the PSS offerings, another 8-h workshop was organized to define the new business model structure and the strategic and operative roadmap. The Business model definition followed the BMC structure, a paper version of the BMC framework was printed and colored sticky notes (one color for each service offering) were used to characterize the new business model structure. This approach allowed to collect insights from key figures operating in different teams and to highlight synergies between service offerings.

Roadmap for Servitization

Finally, leveraging the results of the business model definition, particularly the dimensions related to key resources and key activities, the steps to deploy the new PSS offerings have been identified and prioritized. The roadmap was developed to guide the company approach to servitization. Notably, the roadmap also highlights those activities critical for multiple service offerings, thus providing companies a clear guide to deploy and guide the servitization strategies and to leverage synergies. Moreover, the roadmap includes both activities related to the company digital backbone and those related to process and organizational transformation.

4.3 Discussion and Comparisons

The roadmapping methodology was validated through the application in two companies operating in different contexts and with different available temporal and human resources, from the applications multiple considerations can be drawn.

In both cases, the initial stage of business model description and assessment was crucial for practitioners to reflect on elements of their business model that are often taken for granted. This step led the practitioners to reflect on their current value proposition and existing partnerships, which are central in the transition towards servitization. Both companies considered the step unexpectedly challenging, but crucial to reflect on the pillars supporting their business model and how they can be adapted and expanded to support servitization. Particularly, the reflection on the current value proposition led to the identification of the crucial elements to be complemented and strengthened with the service infusion. This enabled the servitization transition to support the companies' innovation coherently with their current competitive advantage and market positioning strategy.

Similarly, the subsequent steps, the identification of customer segmentation drivers and of clusters, was not immediate for the practitioners. The companies had to envision customers characteristics which are often intangible, related to the behavioural dimension. They were required to analyze the relationships they have with existing customers, and to reflect on submerged and tacit knowledge and considerations that currently implicitly drive the commercial phase and subsequent customer interactions. For these steps, the involvement of both the technical and commercial areas was instrumental to capture all these elements.

For the steps related to the new servitized offering configuration and business model structure definition, the methodology deploys a brainstorming approach supported by structured needs and desiderata of clients. This approach allowed to steer the definition of the service offering in a coherent manner, collecting complementary insights from different stakeholders. It also highlighted the technical and reputational knowledge required to successfully design and deploy the servitized offerings and the supporting business model structure. The phase of the roadmapping creation leverages the results of the new business model characterization, particularly the key resources and key activities section, proposing a rationalization of the steps, technological, organizational, and cultural, required to implement the servitization strategy.

The methodology has been applied in two companies operating in different market contexts, nonetheless no adjustment was required to implement it completely and with comparable and satisfactory results, proving the methodology's capability to adapt to different contexts. Moreover, it has been deployed on different timeframes and with different resources: in company A the methodology has been applied in a two-day workshop, while in Company B in a multi-month project. The longer application timeframe of Company B allowed to deepen the scope of the analysis, collect additional insights from clients, and validate the offering with customer insights, and in general, allow space for additional elaborations and reflections on the transition. Nonetheless, the results of the applications have been considered satisfactory by both companies, and the developed roadmaps are currently being used to guide their servitization efforts. The double approach tested the flexibility of the model, able to adapt to different resource availability, leading to satisfactory, while commensurate, results.

The methodology is developed in a modular perspective; thus, all the components can be expanded with more structured or dedicated tools, particularly in the design and customer needs identification phases.

Moreover, even if the literature provides several tools to support the transition towards servitization, most of them focus either on service design or on specific dimensions or steps (e.g., customer value), without providing an integrated tool to translate these concepts into a customised roadmap. In this respect, the proposed methodology links customer segmentation, value proposition design and prioritization of activities through a sequential process that leads to a servitization roadmap. The current approach, applied in two industrial cases, was validated and able to deliver results to a satisfactory level but could be further expanded to satisfy the needs of companies operating in more complex environments and markets, or with more complex internal structures.

5 Conclusions

This study developed and validated a methodology to support manufacturing companies in building roadmaps dedicated to guide and structure strategic and operational activities for servitization. The methodology meets current gaps in the literature and support manufacturers in steering servitization efforts, integrating digital and organizational perspective.

This work contributes to theory by complementing the literature on servitization. The methodology encompasses all steps leading to the development of a roadmap, complementing and expanding the current literature focus on methodologies for PSS design. From a practice perspective, the proposed methodology aids manufacturers into assessing current business model to identify opportunities for servitization, supporting the definition of relevant customer segments and needs, building the new servitized offering and business model, and roadmapping to guide its implementation.

The study also presents limitations offering avenues for future research. First, the methodology's validation involved the application in two industrial realities and could be expanded to further test the artifact generalizability and validity. Particularly, future research could further test the generalizability of the methodology through the application in other contexts. Moreover, the two application cases stopped after the roadmapping definition, the last stage of the methodology, and did not test the subsequent roadmap implementation, which is currently undergoing in both companies. Thus, future application should extend the temporal perspective, monitoring the whole roadmap implementation evaluating the effectiveness of the results and necessity for adjustments.

Furthermore, the servitization journey requires significant efforts not only from a strategic perspective, but also from a financial one, which may represent a risk, especially for SMEs. Moreover, another implementation risk could be related to the availability of personnel dedicated to service activities, which could slow down or hinder the transition towards servitization. Future research could therefore incorporate financial and human resource risk assessment, since these factors, together with strategy and business model definition, should be considered from the early stages of servitization. Additionally, future research opportunities also involve the expansion of the methodology's steps with dedicated tools. This approach would further strengthen the methodology and adapt it to specific contexts.

Acknowledgments. This study was carried out within the MICS (Made in Italy – Circular and Sustainable) Extended Partnership and received funding from the European Union Next-GenerationEU (PIANO NAZIONALE DI RIPRESA E RESILIENZA (PNRR) – MISSIONE 4 COMPONENTE 2, INVESTIMENTO 1.3 – D.D. 1551.11-10-2022, PE00000004). This manuscript reflects only the authors' views and opinions, neither the European Union nor the European Commission can be considered responsible for them.

Disclosure of Interests The authors have no competing interests to declare that are relevant to the content of this article.

References

1. World Manufacturing Foundation: The 2024 world manufacturing report—new perspectives for the future of manufacturing: Outlook 2030 (2024)
2. Kowalkowski, C., Gebauer, H., Kamp, B., Parry, G.: Servitization and deservitization: overview, concepts, and definitions. Ind. Mark. Manag. **60**, 4–10 (2017). https://doi.org/10.1016/j.indmarman.2016.12.007
3. Goedkoop, M.J., van Halen, C.J.G., te Riele, H.R.M., Rommens, P.J.M.: Product Service systems, Ecological and Economic Basics. Report for Dutch Ministries of Environment (VROM) and Economic Affairs (EZ) (1999)
4. Vandermerwe, S., Rada, J.: Servitization of business: adding value by adding services. Eur. Manag. J. **6**(4), 314–324 (1988)
5. Baines, T.S., Lightfoot, H.W., Benedettini, O., Kay, J.M.: The servitization of manufacturing. J. Manuf. Technol. Manag. **20**(5), 547–567 (2009). https://doi.org/10.1108/17410380910960984
6. Kamal, M.M., Sivarajah, U., Bigdeli, A.Z., Missi, F., Koliousis, Y.: Servitization implementation in the manufacturing organisations: classification of strategies, definitions, benefits and challenges. Int. J. Inf. Manag. **55**, 102206 (2020). https://doi.org/10.1016/j.ijinfomgt.2020.102206
7. Pirola, F., Boucher, X., Wiesner, S., Pezzotta, G.: Digital technologies in product-service systems: a literature review and a research agenda. Comput. Ind. **123**, 103301 (2020). https://doi.org/10.1016/j.compind.2020.103301
8. Beducci, E., Acerbi, F., De Carolis, A., Taisch, M.: Exploring the role of digital servitization for sustainability: a framework for environmental and social impact. Clean. Environ. Syst. **17**, 100269 (2025). https://doi.org/10.1016/j.cesys.2025.100269
9. Reim, W., Parida, V., Örtqvist, D.: Product–service systems (PSS) business models and tactics – a systematic literature review. J. Clean. Prod. **97**, 61–75 (2015). https://doi.org/10.1016/j.jclepro.2014.07.003
10. Kühl, C., Bourlakis, M., Aktas, E., Skipworth, H.: How does servitisation affect supply chain circularity? – a systematic literature review. J. Enterp. Inf. Manag. **33**(4), 703–728 (2019). https://doi.org/10.1108/JEIM-01-2019-0024
11. Sun, X., Oliva, R.: Failure modes in Servitization: a process theory. J. Oper. Manag. **72**(1), 42–63 (2026). https://doi.org/10.1002/joom.70009
12. Brax, S.: A manufacturer becoming service provider – challenges and a paradox. Manag. Serv. Qual. Int. J. **15**(2), 142–155 (2005). https://doi.org/10.1108/09604520510585334
13. Alghisi, A., Saccani, N.: Internal and external alignment in the servitization journey – overcoming the challenges. Prod. Plan. Control. **26**(14–15), 1219–1232 (2015). https://doi.org/10.1080/09537287.2015.1033496
14. Bigdeli, A.Z., Kapoor, K., Schroeder, A., Omidvar, O.: Exploring the root causes of servitization challenges: an organisational boundary perspective. Int. J. Oper. Prod. Manag. **41**(5), 547–573 (2021). https://doi.org/10.1108/IJOPM-08-2020-0507
15. Martinez, V., Bastl, M., Kingston, J., Evans, S.: Challenges in transforming manufacturing organisations into product-service providers. J. Manuf. Technol. Manag. **21**(4), 449–469 (2010). https://doi.org/10.1108/17410381011046571
16. Kerr, C., Phaal, R.: Roadmapping and roadmaps: definition and underpinning concepts. IEEE Trans. Eng. Manag. **69**(1), 6–16 (2022). https://doi.org/10.1109/TEM.2021.3096012
17. Rapaccini, M., Paiola, M., Cinquini, L., Giannetti, R.: Digital servitization journey in small- and medium-sized enterprises: the contribution of knowledge-intensive business firms. J. Bus. Ind. Mark. **38**(6), 1362–1375 (2023). https://doi.org/10.1108/JBIM-01-2022-0008

18. Pezzotta, G., Pirola, F., Rondini, A., Pinto, R., Ouertani, M.-Z.: Towards a methodology to engineer industrial product-service system – evidence from power and automation industry. CIRP J. Manuf. Sci. Technol. **15**, 19–32 (2016). https://doi.org/10.1016/j.cirpj.2016.04.006
19. Morelli, N.: Developing new product service systems (PSS): methodologies and operational tools. J. Clean. Prod. **14**(17), 1495–1501 (2006). https://doi.org/10.1016/j.jclepro.2006.01.023
20. Aurich, J.C., Wolf, N., Siener, M., Schweitzer, E.: Configuration of product-service systems. J. Manuf. Technol. Manag. **20**(5), 591–605 (2009). https://doi.org/10.1108/17410380910961000
21. Qu, M., Yu, S., Chen, D., Chu, J., Tian, B.: State-of-the-art of design, evaluation, and operation methodologies in product service systems. Comput. Ind. **77**, 1–14 (2016). https://doi.org/10.1016/j.compind.2015.12.004
22. Peffers, K., Tuunanen, T., Rothenberger, M., Chatterjee, S.: A design science research methodology for information systems research. J. Manag. Inf. Syst. **24**, 45–77 (2007)
23. Yang, M., Leposky, T.: An entrepreneurial framework for value co-creation in servitization. Ind. Mark. Manag. **107**, 484–497 (2022). https://doi.org/10.1016/j.indmarman.2022.11.002
24. Osterwalder, A., Pigneur, Y.: Business Model Generation: A Handbook for Visionaries, Game Changers, and Challengers. Wiley & Sons, New York (2013)
25. Brunner, M., Bachmann, N., Thienemann, A.-K., Tuezuen, A., Jodlbauer, H.: To the end of the line – including intermediaries and end customers in the business model CANVAS. J. Open Innov. Technol. Mark. Complex. **11**(3), 100623 (2025). https://doi.org/10.1016/j.joitmc.2025.100623
26. Adrodegari, F., Saccani, N.: A maturity model for the servitization of product-centric companies. J. Manuf. Technol. Manag. **31**(4), 775–797 (2020). https://doi.org/10.1108/JMTM-07-2019-0255
27. Adrodegari, F., Saccani, N., Kowalkowski, C.: A framework for PSS business models: formalization and application. Procedia CIRP. **47**, 519–524 (2016). https://doi.org/10.1016/j.procir.2016.03.073
28. García Lechuga, A., Cortés Robles, G., Arredondo Soto, K.C., Miranda Ackerman, M.A.: The integration of the business model canvas and the service blueprinting to assist the conceptual design of new product-service systems. J. Clean. Prod. **415**, 137801 (2023). https://doi.org/10.1016/j.jclepro.2023.137801
29. Cooil, B., Aksoy, L., Keiningham, T.: Approaches to customer segmentation. J. Relatsh. Mark. **6**, 9–39 (2007). https://doi.org/10.1300/J366v06n03_02
30. Osterwalder, A., Pigneur, Y., Bernarda, G., Smith, A.: Value Proposition Design: how to Create Products and Services Customers Want. John Wiley & Sons (2015)
31. Wirth, J., Neller, D., Bauernhansl, T.: The Servitization ecosystem canvas (SEC): towards a framework for developing service-oriented and data-driven business models in ecosystems. Procedia CIRP. **134**, 360–365 (2025). https://doi.org/10.1016/j.procir.2025.02.139

Mapping the Maturity of Servitization and PSS Research: Evidence from an International Scientific Panel

Luca Lussignoli[1], Nicola Saccani[1(✉)], Federico Adrodegari[1], Tim Baines[2], Donatella Corti[3], Heiko Gebauer[4], Christian Kowalkowski[5], Ugljesa Marjanovic[6], Jürg Meierhofer[7], Vinit Parida[8], Daniela Pigosso[9], Kentaro Watanabe[10], Shaun West[11], Marco Guillermo Opazo Basaez[12], Giuditta Pezzotta[13], and Mario Rapacini[14]

[1] University of Brescia, Piazza del Mercato, 15, 25121 Brescia, Italy
{luca.lussignoli,nicola.saccani,federico.adrodegari}@unibs.it
[2] Aston University, Birmingham B4 7ET, UK
t.baines@aston.ac.uk
[3] University of Applied Sciences and Arts of Southern Switzerland, Via Pobiette 11, 6928 Manno, Switzerland
donatella.corti@supsi.ch
[4] Fraunhofer Center for International Management and Knowledge Economy IMW, Martin-Luther-Ring 13, 04109 Leipzig, Germany
heiko.gebauer@unisg.ch
[5] Linköping University, 581 83 Linköping, Sweden
christian.kowalkowski@liu.se
[6] Faculty of Technical Sciences, University of Novi Sad, Trg Dositeja Obradovica 6, 21000 Novi Sad, Serbia
umarjano@uns.ac.rs
[7] ZHAW School of Engineering, Institut for Data Science (IDS), Technikumstrasse 81, CH-8401 Winterthur, Switzerland
juerg.meierhofer@zhaw.ch
[8] Entrepreneurship and Innovation, Luleå University of Technology, 97187 Luleå, Sweden
vinit.parida@ltu.se
[9] Technical University of Denmark (DTU), Koppels Allé, Building 404 DK, 2800 Kgs. Lyngby, Denmark
danpi@dtu.dk
[10] National Institute of Advanced Industrial Science and Technology (AIST), 6-2-3 Kashiwanoha, Kashiwa, Chiba 277-0882, Japan
kentaro.watanabe@aist.go.jp
[11] Hochschule Luzern – Technik & Architektur, Horw, Switzerland
shaun.west@hslu.ch
[12] Deusto Business School, Hermanos Aguirre, 2, 48014 Bilbao, Spain
marco.opazo@deusto.es
[13] Università degli studi di Bergamo, via Salvecchio 19, 24129 Bergamo, Italy
giuditta.pezzotta@unibg.itmario
[14] Università degli Studi di Firenze, P.zza S.Marco, 4, 50121 Florence, Italy
rapaccini@unifi.it

Published by Springer Nature Switzerland AG 2027
G. Pezzotta et al. (Eds.): APMS 2026, IFIP AICT 808, pp. 616–630, 2027.
https://doi.org/10.1007/978-3-032-38594-9_41

Abstract. Over the past three decades, research on servitization and Product-Service Systems (PSS) has evolved into a consolidated and multidisciplinary field. While numerous literature reviews have mapped dominant themes and theoretical foundations, limited attention has been devoted to assessing the maturity stage of different research streams and identifying their evolutionary trajectories. This study proposes a maturity assessment of servitization and PSS research based on a literature-informed expert panel involving the international Scientific Advisory Board of the ASAP Interuniversity Research Centre on Servitization. The study adopts a lifecycle positioning lens to assess five thematic areas. Through pre-meeting structured inputs, collective discussion, and post-meeting synthesis, the panel evaluated the research streams by positioning them across emergent, maturity, and relaunch stages. Findings reveal heterogeneous maturity levels within the field. Domains such as IoT-enabled service and subscription-based business models achieved conceptual maturity. In contrast, ecosystem governance, customer adoption dynamics, digital regulation remain in the emergent stage. Structural tensions, including organizational capability gaps, scalability challenges, and methodological limitations, suggest that theoretical consolidation has not yet translated into systemic implementation, acting instead as relaunch triggers for the field. By introducing a lifecycle-based perspective and integrating expert-based field evaluation, this study contributes a reflexive assessment of where servitization research currently stands and identifies the emergent challenges and relaunch dynamics.

Keywords: Servitization · Product-Service Systems (PSS) · Maturity Assessment

1 Introduction

Over the past three decades, servitization and Product–Service Systems (PSS) have evolved from marginal research topics into a consolidated and multidisciplinary field. This evolution is also reflected in the increasing number of publications retrieved from Scopus over time, as shown in Fig. 1. Since the early recognition that manufacturers increasingly compete through services rather than products alone [1], scholarly attention has progressively expanded toward advanced services, integrated solutions, lifecycle offerings, and outcome-based business models [2, 3].

As the interest in the field grew, research diversified across several scholarly communities. Bibliometric and co-citation analyses have identified at least three major servitization-related research communities: Product–Service Systems (PSS), solution business, and service science [4]. Within and across these communities, research has addressed strategic motivations, business model innovation, organizational capabilities, sustainability implications, and performance outcomes. More recently, the convergence between digitalization and servitization has reshaped the domain. Digital technologies, including IoT, big data analytics, cloud platforms, artificial intelligence, and cyber-physical systems, have enabled new forms of value creation and accelerated the transformation toward digital servitization [5–7]. Comprehensive reviews of digital servitization literature have identified dominant thematic areas such as transformation alignment, value co-creation, platform strategy, and business model innovation [8]. Similarly, the Smart PSS stream has emerged, combining PSS design, digital technologies, knowledge management, and sustainability-oriented business models [9].

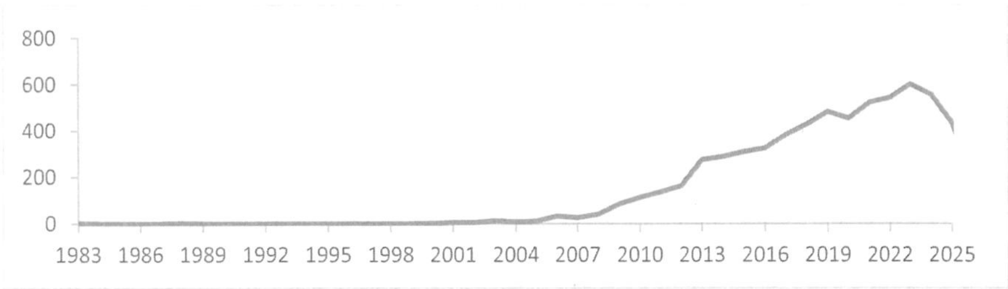

Fig. 1. Annual number of publications retrieved from Scopus. Query: TITLE-ABS-KEY (Servitization) OR TITLE-ABS-KEY("product-service-systems").

Taken together, these contributions demonstrate that servitization research has achieved considerable conceptual consolidation and thematic richness. However, this expansion also raises a fundamental question regarding the evolutionary stage of the field. Existing reviews have tended to map themes and clusters, identify theoretical lenses, and suggest future research directions, but have rarely positioned areas within an evolutionary lifecycle perspective [10, 11]. This absence is relevant as, without a structured assessment of maturity across areas, the field risks drifting toward incrementalism in consolidated domains while neglecting critical emerging challenges.

Against this backdrop, this study is therefore guided by two research questions:

- *RQ1. To what extent have the major areas of servitization and PSS research reached scientific maturity?*
- *RQ2. Which thematic streams remain underdeveloped or exhibit signals of emerging dynamics?*

To answer these questions, this study proposes a maturity assessment of servitization and PSS research based on a literature-informed expert panel involving the international Scientific Advisory Board (SAB) of the ASAP Interuniversity Research Center on Servitization (www.asapsmf.org). Rather than conducting a purely bibliometric or systematic review, the study adopts a reflexive field-level perspective grounded in expert elicitation. This approach enables a collective evaluation of the degree of consolidation, development, and emergence of major thematic areas.

The remainder of the paper is structured as follows. Section 2 presents the research methodology, including the dual analytical framework and the expert panel design. Section 3 reports the findings, providing a descriptive maturity mapping across five areas. Section 4 discusses what remains to be developed within each stream and highlights cross-cutting gaps. Section 5 concludes by outlining theoretical and managerial implications.

2 Methodology

2.1 Research Design

This study adopts a literature-based expert panel design, combining insights from prior servitization reviews with structured expert opinions. The approach draws inspiration from expert panel and Delphi logic, where domain experts collectively assess complex and evolving phenomena through structured discussion and iterative reflection [12, 13]. However, rather than implementing a multi-round statistical Delphi, the study relies on a structured Scientific Advisory Board (SAB) discussion format that integrates pre-meeting inputs, collective deliberation, and post-meeting synthesis.

The rationale for this design stems from the current state of servitization research. First, the field is characterized by fragmentation across scholarly communities and thematic streams [4]. While bibliometric reviews have successfully mapped clusters and topics (e.g. keyword-based analyses), they are less suited to capture signals of maturity or stagnation and emerging tensions. Second, recent consolidations of digital servitization research highlight the thematic diversification of the domain [8].

To structure the assessment, the study is grounded on a two-dimensional framework that combines a thematic area dimension with a lifecycle positioning dimension. As shown in Fig. 2, this combination results in a matrix that guides the empirical assessment.

Area	References	Maturity stage evolution
Digital technologies, AI and digitization	(Coreynen et al., 2017; Pirola et al., 2020; Shen et al., 2023)	
Business models and strategies	(Baines et al., 2009; Baines & Lightfoot, 2013; Wang et al., 2018)	
Supply chains, partnerships and ecosystems	(Oliva & Kallenberg, 2003; Rabetino et al., 2018; Shen et al., 2023)	
Environmental sustainability	(Tukker, 2004; Baines et al., 2017; Saccani et al., 2024)	
Customer perspective	(Baines et al., 2017; Valtakoski, 2017; Forkmann et al., 2017)	

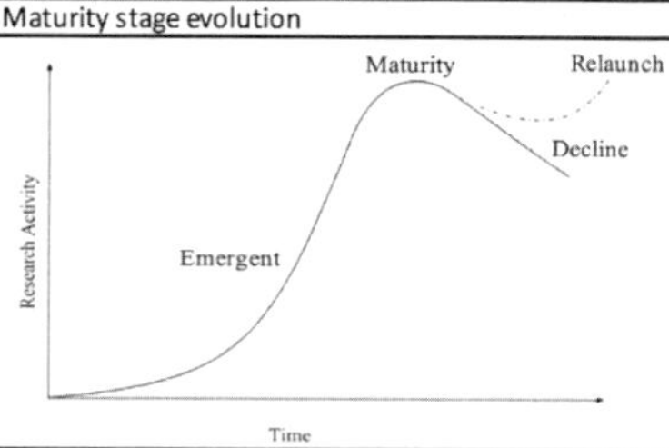

Fig. 2. The combination of thematic areas and lifecycle positioning results in a matrix guiding the empirical assessment.

The first dimension organizes the field into five areas that synthesize dominant and emerging streams identified in prior review efforts [4, 8–10]. These areas are digital technologies, AI and digitization; business models and strategies; supply chains, partnerships and ecosystems; environmental sustainability; customer perspective. Rather than redefining these streams, the present study aggregates them into structured analytical categories that enable a holistic yet differentiated evaluation of the field.

The second dimension consists of a lifecycle classification of research maturity. Building on prior servitization reviews that distinguish between developed and underdeveloped themes [10], the stages were selected to distinguish between streams that are still forming, consolidated, losing relevance, or being renewed by new pressures. Accordingly, each area is evaluated according to four stages: emergent, maturity, decline, and relaunch. Emergent streams refer to topics characterized by exploratory theorization, limited empirical validation, and unstable constructs. Maturity refers to consolidated knowledge and mainly incremental contributions. Decline indicates waning research interest or reduced relevance. Relaunch, instead, refers to previously established streams that are reopened by new technological, institutional, regulatory, or environmental pressures. Thus, emergence indicates the early development of a research stream, while relaunch captures the renewal of consolidated assumptions requiring revision. The lifecycle perspective is adopted as a pragmatic evaluative lens aimed at classifying knowledge consolidation and identifying signals of renewal or stagnation.

2.2 Expert Panel

The empirical basis of the study is a structured discussion involving the international SAB of the ASAP Interuniversity Research Center composed of senior scholars with recognized expertise in servitization and PSS research.

To improve transparency regarding the empirical basis of the study, Table 1 summarizes the composition of the expert panel. The panel was not intended to statistically represent the entire servitization and PSS research community, but to provide a theoretically informed and internationally diversified assessment based on senior scholarly expertise. The experts covered multiple disciplinary and thematic areas, thereby supporting a broad evaluation of the maturity and future evolution of servitization and PSS research.

Table 1. Expert panel composition

Dimension	Description
Invited experts	12 members of the ASAP Scientific Advisory Board
Academic profile	Senior academics, including full professors, associate professors, visiting professors, research professors, group leaders, and heads of research units
Disciplinary coverage	Industrial engineering; operations management; service engineering; industrial marketing; business administration; innovation and entrepreneurship; data science; decision science; engineering design; sustainability-oriented design
Thematic expertise	Servitization; advanced services; Product-Service Systems; service strategy; service design; smart services; digitalization; Industry 4.0; AI-enabled innovation; business model innovation; industrial ecosystems; circular economy; rebound effects; supply chain and logistics
Geographic coverage	United Kingdom; Switzerland; Germany; Sweden; Serbia; Spain; Denmark; Japan; Brazil
Institutional coverage	Universities, business schools, engineering schools, and applied research institutions
Industry engagement	Experts with experience in industry-oriented research, collaborative projects with manufacturing firms, technology transfer, applied service innovation, and servitization/PSS implementation

Panel selection followed purposive sampling criteria typical of expert panel studies [12, 13], ensuring seniority, international diversity, complementary expertise across research streams, and experience in industry-oriented projects. The panel followed a structured procedure based on pre-meeting inputs, an approximately two-hour moderated collective discussion, post-meeting synthesis, and collection of additional comments.

2.3 Data Collection

The data collection process combined individual reflection and collective discussion. Prior to the meeting, 12 SAB members received a structured discussion protocol that was literature-informed and organized according to the five areas. For each area, participants were asked to reflect on the degree of maturity of the research stream, to distinguish between consolidated and emerging topics, to identify underinvestigated issues, and to tentatively position the area within the lifecycle stages. This pre-meeting phase encouraged independent assessment before collective discussion, in line with best practices in expert elicitation [13].

During the meeting, which was actively attended by 10 of the initial 12 experts, each area was discussed sequentially with explicit reference to lifecycle positioning. Participants collectively evaluated the degree of conceptual consolidation, the robustness and diversity of empirical evidence, the prevalence of incremental versus exploratory contributions, and the existence of new drivers potentially triggering relaunch dynamics. Classification emerged through structured qualitative discussion and argumentation.

The discussion format ensured that both thematic content and maturity positioning were systematically addressed. Participants shared examples of mature contributions, identified emerging subtopics, highlighted blind spots and contradictions, and reflected on methodological evolution and interdisciplinarity where relevant. Following the meeting, a detailed meeting report was produced, synthesizing insights for each area, and experts were asked to provide additional comments and observations. The synthesis systematically mapped the findings onto the lifecycle stages defined in Sect. 2.1, thus forming the primary dataset for subsequent analysis.

2.4 Data Analysis

Data analysis followed a structured qualitative coding and synthesis logic aligned with the research framework, consistent with established principles of qualitative data analysis [14]. First, insights from the meeting report were aggregated within each thematic area and categorized according to the predefined lifecycle stages. This step allowed an internal mapping of the degree of consolidation within each stream. Second, each area was positioned along the lifecycle stages by considering the level of conceptual stabilization, the presence of standardized models and measurement approaches, and evidence of incrementalism versus paradigm shifts. The final lifecycle positioning did not rely on formal voting or numerical majority rule, but on an author-mediated interpretive synthesis of the collective expert assessment. When inputs converged, the corresponding stage was assigned directly; when mixed signals emerged, a composite positioning was adopted. Finally, transversal issues were identified to highlight systemic dynamics shaping the field.

3 Findings

This section presents the results of the structured maturity assessment across the five areas identified in the research framework. The findings are organized by thematic area, explicitly positioning the research streams along the established lifecycle stages: emergent, maturity, decline, and relaunch. Rather than offering prescriptive interpretation at this stage, the section reports the evolutionary dynamics of each area as evaluated during the expert discussion.

3.1 Digital Technologies, AI and Digitization

The discussion revealed that research on digital technologies in servitization has reached a partial stage of maturity. Foundational contributions on digital servitization have clarified how digital technologies enable the transition from product-centric to service-centric logics [5, 6]. Reviews have consolidated streams around transformation alignment, platform strategies, and business model innovation [8], while Smart PSS research has mapped digital technologies across design, lifecycle management, and sustainability [9].

Within this area, certain topics were clearly recognized as mature. IoT-enabled predictive maintenance, remote monitoring, and smart connected products were considered consolidated both conceptually and empirically. These domains exhibit common models, repeated empirical validation, and managerial transferability.

However, several subtopics remain in an emergent phase. Human-AI collaboration in service contexts was identified as a promising but still under-theorized area. While AI-enabled decision support and automation are increasingly discussed, the integration of human expertise and algorithmic intelligence in value co-creation processes remains insufficiently explored. Similarly, the role of digital technologies in enabling full lifecycle integration, beyond early design and monitoring phases, was considered a developing research stream.

Beyond technological capabilities, the panel also highlighted emerging ethical considerations related to digital services, including issues of data ownership, transparency, and customer autonomy. These concerns are increasingly relevant as digital infrastructures become central to servitized offerings and may shape future research on governance and accountability in digital servitization.

Finally, the panel identified specific triggers indicating a transition toward a relaunch phase. The impact of new regulatory frameworks (e.g., AI governance and data protection), the long-term consequences of software augmentation of physical products, and the evolving organizational capabilities required for digital servitization represent new institutional and technological pressures. Rather than simply being unresolved gaps, these dynamics are actively forcing scholars to revisit and update previously consolidated digital servitization models.

3.2 Business Models and Strategies

Business model innovation has been central to servitization research since its early stages [2]. The panel discussion confirmed that pay-per-use and subscription-based models are well established and conceptually mature [11]. The logic of advanced services and outcome-based contracts is extensively documented, and financial performance implications have been widely studied [15].

Nevertheless, maturity in this area appears uneven. While descriptive classifications of business models are abundant, the discourse about the scalability of servitized models remains underdeveloped. Many empirical studies document pilot implementations but provide limited longitudinal evidence on large-scale diffusion. This echoes prior calls for more robust empirical validation in servitization research [10].

Several research streams remain in the emergent stage. These include servitization-as-a-platform, regenerative and adaptive business models, and AI-supported dynamic pricing mechanisms. These streams connect business model innovation to ecosystem governance and digital platform strategies [8]. The co-evolution of technologies and business models was also identified as insufficiently theorized, particularly regarding alignment failures and organizational resistance.

Finally, the panel indicated that while the core conceptual foundations of service business models are mature, gaps are now triggering a relaunch phase. Specifically, the necessity to navigate legal and liability frameworks in service-based models, to gather evidence of servitization's macro-economic impact, and to understand the internal political dynamics shaping transformation requires revisiting established models through new institutional and macro-systemic lenses. This need for a relaunch is further evidenced by the fact that many current implementations still reflect a product-centric mindset. In practice, manufacturers often replicate traditional product logics within service models, underestimating the operational and relational complexities of true service delivery. This tension between product heritage and service logic confirms that conceptual maturity must now be relaunched into profound organizational and systemic transformation.

3.3 Supply Chains, Partnerships, and Ecosystems

Research on supply chains and ecosystem configurations in servitization reflects a transition from mature paradigms to emergent ecosystem dynamics. While traditional intra-firm transformation and dyadic customer relationships [3] display conceptual maturity, systematic models of multi-actor alignment and platform governance [8] remain in the emergent stage. Furthermore, the panel highlighted that the specific roles of intermediaries, distributors, and sales channels remain underexplored in empirical research, despite their continued industrial relevance.

However, the most significant finding in this area is the clear trajectory toward a relaunch driven by new structural and institutional pressures. Shifts in power dynamic, such as OEMs contracting directly with end-users, generate unprecedented tensions regarding loyalty, control, and competition. The need for a relaunch is particularly evident in the growing intersection of servitization with broader regulatory and geopolitical environments. The panel introduced the notion of "*service sovereignty*," linking servitization strategies to national industrial policies and digital infrastructure control. Although currently underdeveloped, these macro-level institutional conditions act as definitive catalysts for a relaunch, forcing the field to revisit established ecosystem governance models through entirely new geopolitical and regulatory perspectives.

3.4 Environmental Sustainability

The link between Product-Service Systems (PSS) and sustainability is widely acknowledged in the literature, particularly within the PSS community [10, 16]. Conceptually, the relationship between servitization and environmental performance is mature. However, practical measurement and empirical frameworks are still emergent. The panel discussion emphasized that although metrics for environmental impact exist, their application across complex lifecycle configurations is limited. In particular, measuring the concrete impact of service adoption on environmental performance remains methodologically challenging.

Furthermore, these methodological challenges, combined with new regulatory and climate-related pressures point to emergent investigation areas. Dynamics such as rebound effect prevention and mitigation, digital product passports, governance mechanisms supporting sustainable PSS, and decarbonization as a strategic driver act as institutional triggers forcing scholars to revisit established assumptions [17–19].

Finally, the necessity to integrate pricing and revenue models with sustainability outcomes and to align product and service innovation under a coherent environmental lens confirms this evolutionary shift. These specific gaps indicate that while the conceptual foundations of PSS and sustainability are mature, the operational and measurement frameworks remain emergent, driving the need for a systemic relaunch of the field.

3.5 Customer Perspective

The customer perspective was consistently identified as remaining in an emergent stage relative to other streams, although it has long been addressed in the literature. While the value of servitization for customers is conceptually recognized, empirical insights into customer adoption dynamics remain limited. In particular, procurement processes and buying center dynamics in B2B contexts are insufficiently explored; this misalignment between service offerings and purchasing logic may explain the scaling difficulties observed in practice.

Furthermore, behavioral dimensions of adoption and resistance, customer journey mapping in PSS contexts, make-or-buy strategic decisions, and the role of indirect customers represent critical, yet still emergent, research trajectories. The panel also highlighted cultural and institutional contexts as highly influential factors in servitization adoption. Differences in industrial culture and national institutional settings shape how customers perceive risk, value, and responsibility in PSS arrangements, suggesting a strong need for comparative research across regions and industries.

Overall, the lack of consolidated empirical validation confirms that this entire area remains firmly in the emergent phase, offering significant room for theoretical deepening and exploratory expansion before reaching maturity.

4 Discussion

4.1 Summary of Findings

Table 2 summarizes the maturity positioning of the five thematic areas analysed in the study. The first column reports the thematic area, while the second column provides an overall lifecycle positioning derived from the expert panel discussion. The following columns distinguish between consolidated topics, classified as mature, exploratory or still insufficiently validated topics, classified as emergent, and the main relaunch or evolution triggers identified by the panel. The table should therefore be read as a qualitative synthesis of the maturity assessment rather than as a quantitative scoring exercise. The assessment reveals heterogeneous levels of consolidation within the field. While certain domains, such as IoT-enabled services, subscription-based models, and the conceptual link between PSS and sustainability, display features of maturity, others remain in the emergent stage. Moreover, cross-cutting tensions related to scalability, organizational capabilities, and customer adoption indicate that theoretical consolidation does not automatically translate into systemic implementation. These findings set the stage for a deeper discussion of the structural constraints and relaunch or evolution dynamics shaping each stream.

Furthermore, across several areas, particularly digital technologies, business models, and ecosystems, the need for new organizational capabilities was repeatedly highlighted. Digital servitization requires data analytics competencies, cross-functional integration, ecosystem orchestration skills, and new managerial roles. Yet, research has only partially addressed how such capabilities are built, scaled, and embedded over time. This capability gap appears as a structural constraint limiting the evolution from the emergent stage to full maturity across multiple research streams.

In addition, the panel repeatedly emphasized methodological limitations across servitization research. The field remains largely dominated by descriptive and case-based studies, a pattern already highlighted in previous reviews [4, 10]. While such studies have been instrumental during the early emergent phases, participants stressed the urgent need for longitudinal designs, quantitative modeling, and configurational approaches such as qualitative comparative analysis (QCA). Establishing shared research protocols and data infrastructures was also suggested as a critical step to support cumulative knowledge consolidation and validate future paradigm relaunches.

4.2 Structural Implications for the Evolution of Servitization Research

The maturity assessment presented in Sect. 3 reveals that servitization and PSS research has not evolved uniformly across thematic streams. Rather than a field that has collectively reached maturity, the evidence suggests a heterogeneous configuration, where consolidated domains coexist with emergent and potentially relaunching areas. The following paragraphs discuss the main topics identified for advancing the scientific domain.

#1 Ecosystem Governance

The findings suggest that servitization research may be entering an institutional turn.

Table 2. Maturity positioning of servitization research streams based on expert panel discussion

Area	Overall Lifecycle Position	Maturity (Consolidated Topics)	Emergent (Exploratory & Empirical Topics)	Relaunch or evolution Triggers
Digital technologies, AI, and digitization	Emergent to Maturity, triggering Relaunch	IoT-enabled predictive maintenance; smart connected products; remote monitoring	Human–AI collaboration; lifecycle data integration; AI-enabled adaptive services; organizational capabilities	Regulatory impact (e.g., AI Act); software-dominant architectures
Business models and strategies	Conceptual Maturity, triggering Relaunch	Pay-per-use; subscription models; outcome-based contracts	Servitization-as-a-platform; regenerative models; AI-driven dynamic pricing; scalability	Liability frameworks; macro-level economic impact; internal political dynamics
Supply chains, partnerships, ecosystems	Emergent, with mature topics shifting toward Relaunch	Traditional dyadic relationships; value chain perspectives	Ecosystem governance; ecosystem orchestration models; intermediary roles	Shifts in power dynamics; regulatory influence; geopolitical factors ("services and sovereignty")
Environmental sustainability	Conceptual Maturity / Empirical Emergent	PSS–sustainability link; circular economy alignment	Measurement of sustainability performance; empirical frameworks	Rebound effect prevention and mitigation; digital product passports; decarbonization drivers; integration with pricing models
Customer perspective	Firmly Emergent	Conceptual customer value in PSS	Procurement processes; customer journeys; behavioral adoption and resistance; make-or-buy logic; indirect customers	Cultural and institutional context variations (need for comparative macro-lenses)

Regulatory frameworks (e.g., AI governance, environmental regulation), geopolitical considerations related to technological sovereignty, and ecosystem power shifts are increasingly shaping servitization trajectories. While earlier research primarily focused on intra-firm transformation and dyadic relationships, contemporary dynamics require broader ecosystem governance models [8]. This shift represents a definitive relaunch dynamic in the field. As digital regulation, decarbonization mandates, and geopolitical tensions intensify, servitization research must expand its theoretical toolkit to incorporate institutional theory, political economy perspectives, and governance frameworks. Failure to do so may result in theoretical misalignment with real-world transformations.

Addressing these challenges requires stronger interdisciplinary engagement. Perspectives from sociology, political science, cultural studies, and behavioral sciences could help explain institutional differences, governance mechanisms, and adoption dynamics that remain insufficiently explored in current servitization research.

#2 Customer Adoption as a Persistent Blind Spot
Among all streams, the customer perspective remains structurally emergent. While conceptualizations of customer value are well established, empirical investigation of procurement processes, behavioral resistance, and buying center dynamics is limited. This blind spot is particularly consequential because adoption dynamics act as a bottleneck for scaling servitized models. Without a deeper understanding of how customers evaluate risk, allocate responsibility, and engage in make-or-buy decisions, business model innovation may remain confined to pilot initiatives. Addressing this gap requires interdisciplinary engagement with behavioral economics, organizational decision-making, and purchasing theory. In lifecycle terms, this stream remains firmly in the emergent stage, yet its maturation is critical for the overall consolidation of the field.

#3 Environmental Sustainability Operationalization
Environmental Sustainability research in servitization displays conceptual maturity but empirical fragmentation. The PSS–sustainability link is widely acknowledged, yet measurement frameworks, pricing integration, and rebound effect prevention and mitigation remain emergent. The growing relevance of digital product passports, decarbonization commitments, and regulatory sustainability frameworks suggests open topics for research. However, this relaunch depends on integrating environmental performance metrics with business model logic and ecosystem governance, for instance by shifting towards innovative "pay-per-emission" revenue models to resolve the contradictions between business and sustainability logics [20].

#4 Methodological Gaps
Perhaps the most structural implication concerns methodology. The dominance of descriptive and case-based studies, while instrumental during early emergent phases, now limits cumulative theory building [4, 10]. The panel's emphasis on longitudinal designs, quantitative modeling, and configurational approaches signals a potential methodological inflection point. As the field matures, methodological innovation becomes a prerequisite for theoretical advancement. Without diversified research designs and standardized protocols, even emergent streams may struggle to progress beyond exploratory contributions. In lifecycle terms, methodological evolution will determine whether several areas successfully transition from the emergent stage to full maturity or remain perpetually exploratory.

5 Conclusions and Implications

This study set out to assess the maturity and emerging dynamics of servitization and PSS research through a structured expert-based evaluation grounded in a structured framework. By moving beyond thematic clustering toward lifecycle-based maturity positioning, this study offers a structured reflection on the evolutionary stage of servitization research and its future trajectory.

The findings reveal a field characterized by heterogeneous maturity. Certain domains, such as advanced service logics, subscription-based models, and the conceptual alignment between PSS and sustainability, display features of consolidation and incremental refinement. However, this maturity also introduces the structural risk of prolonged incrementalism, where research increasingly refines existing models rather than challenging underlying assumptions, potentially leading to stagnation. Other streams, including ecosystem governance, customer adoption dynamics, and digital regulation, remain firmly in the emergent stage. In addition, digital transformation pressures, sustainability regulation, and geopolitical concerns around technological sovereignty may act as evolution triggers, reshaping previously stabilized assumptions. Taken together, the results suggest that servitization research is not entering decline but rather transitioning toward a structurally more complex phase. The challenge is no longer the absence of conceptual models; instead, it concerns the integration of mature knowledge with emergent institutional, technological, and organizational dynamics.

The study contributes to servitization research in three main ways. First, it introduces a lifecycle-based perspective to assess the maturity of research streams. While prior reviews have mapped themes and clusters [4, 8, 10], they have rarely positioned streams along evolutionary stages. This study therefore integrates prior structuring efforts into a coherent analytical framework combining thematic areas and lifecycle positioning, offering a structured view of the field's progression. Second, the framework provides a granular picture of the degree of maturity of the specific research topics within each thematic area. This approach highlights that conceptual maturity in one stream does not guarantee systemic knowledge consolidation. For instance, business model frameworks may be theoretically mature, yet remain operationally constrained by capability bottlenecks and adoption dynamics. Third, it identifies the evolutionary trajectories across streams, organizing emergent challenges and relaunch triggers. In particular, the study identifies cross-cutting structural tensions, particularly organizational capability gaps, customer adoption blind spots, and methodological limitations, that shape the future trajectory of the field. These tensions suggest that further advancement will depend less on expanding thematic scope and more on deepening integration and methodological rigor.

From a managerial perspective, this study delineates where servitization knowledge is robust and where caution is required. In mature domains (e.g., predictive maintenance and subscription models), managers can rely on established foundations, though scaling and ecosystem integration remain practically demanding. Conversely, in emergent areas (e.g., AI-enabled services and sustainability measurement), the lack of consolidated frameworks entails higher uncertainty and experimentation costs but offers unique opportunities for strategic differentiation. Ultimately, bridging the gap between conceptual models and operational reality requires targeted investments in data analytics, cross-functional integration, and governance mechanisms.

This study also acknowledges several limitations that offer avenues for future research. First, our maturity assessment relies on expert evaluations and a pragmatically structured lifecycle framework rather than formalized quantitative metrics. Future studies could complement this by operationalizing lifecycle stages using large-scale bibliometric data. Second, the panel was primarily academic; incorporating direct industry perspectives and testing the framework across diverse scholarly communities would enrich future findings. Finally, given rapid technological and regulatory shifts, longitudinal reassessments are encouraged to capture the dynamic evolution of servitization research.

Disclosure of Interests. The authors have no competing interests to declare that are relevant to the content of this article.

References

1. Vandermerwe, S., Rada, J.: Servitization of business: adding value by adding services. Eur. Manag. J. **6**, 314–324 (1988). https://doi.org/10.1016/0263-2373(88)90033-3
2. Baines, T.S., Lightfoot, H.W., Benedettini, O., Kay, J.M.: The servitization of manufacturing: a review of literature and reflection on future challenges. J. Manuf. Technol. Manag. **20**, 547–567 (2009). https://doi.org/10.1108/17410380910960984
3. Oliva, R., Kallenberg, R.: Managing the transition from products to services. Int. J. Serv. Ind. Manag. **14**, 160–172 (2003). https://doi.org/10.1108/09564230310474138
4. Rabetino, R., Harmsen, W., Kohtamäki, M., Sihvonen, J.: Structuring servitization-related research. Int. J. Oper. Prod. Manag. **38**, 350–371 (2018). https://doi.org/10.1108/IJOPM-03-2017-0175
5. Coreynen, W., Matthyssens, P., Van Bockhaven, W.: Boosting servitization through digitization: pathways and dynamic resource configurations for manufacturers. Ind. Mark. Manag. **60**, 42–53 (2017). https://doi.org/10.1016/j.indmarman.2016.04.012
6. Kohtamäki, M., Parida, V., Oghazi, P., Gebauer, H., Baines, T.: Digital servitization business models in ecosystems: a theory of the firm. J. Bus. Res. **104**, 380–392 (2019). https://doi.org/10.1016/j.jbusres.2019.06.027
7. Paschou, T., Rapaccini, M., Adrodegari, F., Saccani, N.: Digital servitization in manufacturing: a systematic literature review and research agenda. Ind. Mark. Manag. **89**, 278–292 (2020). https://doi.org/10.1016/j.indmarman.2020.02.012
8. Shen, L., Sun, W., Parida, V.: Consolidating digital servitization research: a systematic review, integrative framework, and future research directions. Technol. Forecast. Soc. Chang. **191**, 122478 (2023). https://doi.org/10.1016/j.techfore.2023.122478
9. Pirola, F., Boucher, X., Wiesner, S., Pezzotta, G.: Digital technologies in product-service systems: a literature review and a research agenda. Comput. Ind. **123**, 103301 (2020). https://doi.org/10.1016/j.compind.2020.103301
10. Baines, T., Ziaee Bigdeli, A., Bustinza, O.F., Shi, V.G., Baldwin, J., Ridgway, K.: Servitization: revisiting the state-of-the-art and research priorities. Int. J. Oper. Prod. Manag. **37**, 256–278 (2017). https://doi.org/10.1108/IJOPM-06-2015-0312
11. Lightfoot, H., Baines, T., Smart, P.: The servitization of manufacturing: a systematic literature review of interdependent trends. Int. J. Oper. Prod. Manag. **33**, 1408–1434 (2013). https://doi.org/10.1108/IJOPM-07-2010-0196
12. Rapaccini, M., Adrodegari, F., Pezzotta, G., Saccani, N.: Overcoming the knowledge gaps in early-stage servitization journey: a guide for small and medium enterprises. IET Collab. Intell. Manuf. **6**, e12106 (2024). https://doi.org/10.1049/cim2.12106
13. Rowe, G., Wright, G.: Expert opinions in forecasting: the role of the Delphi technique. In: Armstrong, J.S. (ed.) Principles of Forecasting, pp. 125–144. Springer US, Boston (2001). https://doi.org/10.1007/978-0-306-47630-3_7

14. Miles, M.B., Huberman, A.M., Saldaña, J.: Qualitative Data Analysis: A Methods Sourcebook. Sage, Los Angeles (2014)
15. Wang, W., Lai, K.-H., Shou, Y.: The impact of servitization on firm performance: a meta-analysis. Int. J. Oper. Prod. Manag. **38**, 1562–1588 (2018). https://doi.org/10.1108/IJOPM-04-2017-0204
16. Tukker, A.: Eight types of product–service system: eight ways to sustainability? Experiences from sus pro net. Bus. Strateg. Environ. **13**, 246–260 (2004). https://doi.org/10.1002/bse.414
17. Kjaer, L.L., Pigosso, D.C.A., Niero, M., Bech, N.M., McAloone, T.C.: Product/Service-Systems for a Circular Economy: the route to decoupling economic growth from resource consumption? J. Ind. Ecol. **23**, 22–35 (2019). https://doi.org/10.1111/jiec.12747
18. Adisorn, T., Tholen, L., Götz, T.: Towards a digital product passport fit for contributing to a circular economy. Energies. **14**, 2289 (2021). https://doi.org/10.3390/en14082289
19. Bressanelli, G., Adrodegari, F., Perona, M., Saccani, N.: Exploring how usage-focused business models enable circular economy through digital technologies. Sustainability. **10**, 639 (2018). https://doi.org/10.3390/su10030639
20. Saccani, N., Adrodegari, F., Scalvini, L.: Aligning product-service systems with environmental sustainability: investigating the key role of revenue and pricing mechanisms. Resour. Conserv. Recycl. **209**, 107792 (2024). https://doi.org/10.1016/j.resconrec.2024.107792

Artificial Intelligence for After-Sales Services: A Case of Luxury Fashion Industry

Nataliia Roskladka(✉) and Giovanni Miragliotta

Politecnico di Milano, 20156 Milan, Italy
nataliia.roskladka@polimi.it

Abstract. The paper explores how AI can handle the main challenges in managing after-sales of luxury fashion products. Two most prominent AI solutions were identified: automated image analysis for defect detection and text elaboration for sentiment analysis. Their significance lies in their ability to streamline customer interactions and product evaluations, particularly using computer vision for defect identification and categorization for returned items and leveraging LLMs to assess repair feasibility, estimate service times, and improve communication between in-store assistants and customers. These technologies offer tangible improvements in service efficiency and quality control, reinforcing their strategic importance in after-sales processes in the luxury fashion industry.

Keywords: Artificial Intelligence · After-sales · Luxury and Fashion

1 Introduction

This paper explores how recent advancements in artificial intelligence (AI) can optimize after-sales services in the luxury fashion industry, enhancing efficiency, customer satisfaction, and key performance metrics. Despite AI's widespread adoption across various business functions, its application in after-sales remains weakly covered. A comprehensive review of the literature reveals numerous studies on AI implementation in the supply chain [1–3], but without a specific focus on its role in after-sales management. Some research discusses potential implementations that could indirectly impact after-sales services, such as predictive maintenance systems [4, 5], or chatbots for customer support [3], which contribute to performance improvements in its operations. However, there is a lack of vision on AI solutions across the entire after-sales workflow and their impact on customer satisfaction.

Given the recent advancements in AI, which have made it more accessible to businesses through pre-trained and open-source models [6, 7], companies now have ample room for improvement [8, 9]. Additionally, AI models have significantly improved in performance [10], driven by breakthroughs in computer vision [11, 12] and Large Language Models (LLMs) [6]. Beyond operational efficiency, the integration of AI into after-sales processes represents a step toward servitization, as it supports the transition from product-centric to service-oriented business models. This shift enables fashion and

Published by Springer Nature Switzerland AG 2027
G. Pezzotta et al. (Eds.): APMS 2026, IFIP AICT 808, pp. 631–646, 2027.
https://doi.org/10.1007/978-3-032-38594-9_42

luxury brands to increasingly generate value through personalized service offerings, data-driven product repair, and extending the customer experience, rather than solely through product sales. Moreover, AI-enabled after-sales support contributes to sustainable manufacturing by fostering repairability, extending product lifespans, and reducing waste. Through intelligent diagnostics and predictive repair planning, these technologies help optimize material consumption and minimize time for product delivery, aligning luxury companies with the broader goals of circularity and environmental responsibility.

This study examines how AI can enhance after-sales services, focusing on two key solutions: defect detection using computer vision and sentiment analysis through LLMs. The research adopts a qualitative approach, combining a literature review and expert interviews to provide empirical evidence that addresses the challenges identified in the literature and refines the proposals. The focus on the luxury industry is justified by the strategic importance of after-sales services in this sector [13]. Additionally, customer experience plays a critical role in the success of luxury brands [14], making after-sales a key differentiator [15].

The objective of this study is to identify inefficiencies in after-sales processes and evaluate the feasibility of AI-driven solutions by addressing the following two research questions: (1) What are the challenges in after-sales services that have the highest impact on customer satisfaction in the luxury fashion industry? and (2) How can applications in artificial intelligence handle after-sales service challenges in the luxury industry to improve its performance?

The findings highlight AI's ability to enhance service quality and improve operational efficiency, thereby impacting after-sales service lead times and net promoter score in the luxury fashion industry.

2 Literature Review

According to the research questions, the literature review consists of two main areas: (1) the luxury fashion industry and the business relevance of after-sales services underlying its challenges and customer satisfaction drivers; (2) the potential impact of AI-driven solutions on business and the most prominent AI applications for after-sales services.

2.1 Luxury Fashion Industry and After-Sales

The luxury fashion sector is characterized by elevated consumer expectations, in which brand perception and customer experience are paramount to long-term success [14]. In contrast to mass-market brands, luxury companies differentiate themselves through exclusivity, craftsmanship, and superior service quality, aligning their supply chain and customer engagement strategies to reinforce brand equity [16]. Customer loyalty is strongly influenced by post-purchase experiences, making after-sales services a strategic asset rather than a cost centre [13].

After-sales services are essential for maintaining a competitive edge in luxury retail, serving a dual purpose in customer retention and brand protection. The process includes handling post-purchase product management, such as repair services, returns, warranties, and customer care, and it is directly linked with customer retention. It interacts with the retail to address in-store experience issues and collaborates with production by reporting recurring defects and identifying ways to improve repair quality and the customer experience [17]. Thus, one of the primary challenges in after-sales operations is effectively detecting and analysing product defects to determine whether the product can be repaired or should be replaced if under warranty.

Companies investing in high-quality after-sales programs benefit from greater customer loyalty, stronger brand advocacy, and the ability to justify premium pricing [15]. Research highlights that structured after-sales strategies contribute significantly to profitability, with some industries generating up to 25% of their revenue from post-purchase services [18]. Thus, another key area of after-sales operations is effectively managing communication with the customers to keep them engaged and loyal to the brand they have chosen.

2.2 Artificial Intelligence Applications

AI as a Lever for Business Transformation. Artificial Intelligence has emerged as a transformative force across industries, enabling machines to analyse data, recognize patterns, and make autonomous decisions. Its integration into business operations has become a key driver of cost reduction, revenue growth, and process improvements [19]. According to an MIT Sloan Management Review article, over 80% of companies consider AI a strategic opportunity, with 85% viewing it as essential for maintaining a competitive advantage [20]. Despite its benefits, AI adoption presents technical, financial, regulatory, and social challenges that often complicate its integration into business models. Moreover, many organizations lack a structured AI roadmap, leading to difficulties in budgeting, resource allocation, and prioritization [19, 20]. According to Hendriksen (2023), integrating AI into supply chain management is not merely a technical advancement but a social transformation, shaped by human perception, trust, and cognitive adaptation [1].

Given the recent advancements and increased availability of highly performant pre-trained models, businesses can now leverage AI models with shorter implementation lead times. This has led to a growing number of companies integrating AI into their operations [8, 9].

AI for Text Analysis. Text analysis is one of the most widely used AI solutions, involving the processing, interpretation, and extraction of insights from large volumes of unstructured textual data. Large Language Models (LLMs) represent the edge of technological potential in text analysis. Advances in Natural Language Processing (NLP), particularly through LLMs, have significantly improved AI's ability to understand the context, semantics, and sentiment of a text [10]. These models, being pre-trained neural networks capable of understanding and generating human-like text, play a crucial role in automated customer service, sentiment analysis, and decision-making systems [10]. LLMs process vast textual corpora, refining natural language comprehension and enabling real-time AI-driven communication. Several studies in the literature demonstrate that AI-powered NLP models offer real-time sentiment classification, accurately detecting polarity shifts, sarcasm, and emotional intent, surpassing traditional sentiment analysis methods [6]. For implementing a sentiment analysis model, the structured pipeline consists of several key stages: data collection, text preparation (including text cleaning, spelling correction, and normalization), sentiment detection, sentiment classification, and output presentation. Studies indicate that businesses can now leverage pre-trained AI models like ChatGPT to perform sentiment analysis, significantly reducing the need for extensive in-house development while having access to more powerful models [10].

AI for Image Analysis. Image analysis leverages Computer Vision (CV) models to extract meaningful insights from visual data. Deep learning-based CV models have significantly improved defect detection, automated visual inspection processes, and reduced human errors. CV allows machines to interpret and process images and videos, with applications ranging from facial recognition and diagnostics to industrial quality control [10]. In supply chains, image analysis has been instrumental in automating defect detection, significantly enhancing quality control, accuracy, and efficiency [3, 15]. Traditional manual inspections are prone to inconsistencies, whereas deep learning-based CV models, such as YOLO and R-CNN, achieve over 95% accuracy, enabling real-time monitoring and process optimization [12, 21].

The complexity of defect detection implementation depends on the type of product material and the level of detail required to detect and recognize specific types of damage. The image analysis model implementation described by Chen et al. (2022) focused on defect detection in leather, which is often required in the luxury fashion industry [22]. The process begins with an image acquisition of the material to be inspected, followed by an image analysis phase, where the system processes the image, segments the defects from the surface, and identifies them based on their features. The extracted data are then used to assess leather quality and optimize the cutting process, ensuring that only leather that meets specific quality standards is allocated to the specified parts of the final product. These systems have been successfully used to inspect raw leather before the production phase, reducing manufacturing waste and ensuring compliance with the highest quality standards. This results in higher-quality products with fewer defects, ultimately lowering the number of after-sales requests related to production issues. The most challenging aspect of developing such models is training the computer vision system on a sufficiently large image dataset to enable accurate defect identification [15].

When integrated with LLMs, defect detection solutions can provide additional insights beyond defect identification [22]. For example, to assess repair feasibility and estimate service times, thereby enhancing operational efficiency and supporting in-store assistants to provide immediate feedback to the customers.

3 Research Methodology

This section outlines the research methodology adopted to assess AI implementation in after-sales services. A qualitative approach was employed to enable an in-depth exploration of the strategic, organizational, and technical factors influencing AI adoption [23]. The primary research objective is to assess the feasibility of AI-driven solutions for after-sales services and to identify the benefits and challenges associated with their implementation. To assess AI's impact on after-sales services, a structured performance measurement framework is applied to integrate financial, operational, and customer satisfaction metrics. This study uses the After Sales Performance Measurement Framework by Saccani et al. (2006) to evaluate AI's contribution [17]. This analysis is structured according to three key levels: (1) Activity (Task)-Level perspective: to enhance task efficiency and reduce manual intervention in specific operational activities; (2) Process-Level perspective: to improve and streamline overall process flow; (3) Business-Level perspective: to analyse the impact on the strategic level. The research also considers the fourth, transversal technological level, as suggested by the framework [17].

3.1 Literature Review and Product Focus

The literature analysis was conducted using snowball sampling to identify the main challenges of after-sales management that affect customer satisfaction in the luxury fashion industry and to explore potential AI applications to address them. The search process started with exploring the academic papers through Google scholar, using the keywords related to "Artificial Intelligence" and ("servitization" or "after-sales") and ("luxury" or "fashion"). Further research was more specific on certain arguments, like LLMs application, computer vision solutions, or AI impact for business. In this paper, we aim to analyse how AI implementations, extensively studied in the literature for manufacturing or supply chain management, can also be applied to after-sales services. To conduct the literature review, 86 selected scientific publications were categorized into three primary research (Luxury fashion industry, After Sales and Artificial Intelligence) areas described in Table 1 below.

This study focuses on leather goods, like handbags, belts, pouches, footwear, etc., due to their prevalence in the portfolio of the biggest luxury fashion houses. For example, it accounts for 71% of Kering's total sales; 71% at Saint Laurent; 92% at Bottega Veneta; 75% at Louis Vuitton [24–26].

3.2 Interviews with Experts in Fashion and Luxury

The first round of interviews was conducted to complete and validate the results from the literature review on after-sales challenges and AI solutions' relevance. Eleven interviews were carried out with 10 stakeholders in the luxury fashion industry of the above-mentioned companies: After-Sales Managers (2), Retail Operation Managers (2), Retail Operation Director (1), Client Service Specialists (3), and in-store After-Sales Care Experts (2). Each interview lasted approximately one hour and was conducted via Microsoft Teams.

For this study, semi-structured interviews were identified as the most appropriate method for collecting data to validate and get feedback on the relevance of proposed solutions. This approach allows participants to share their viewpoints while introducing new perspectives and challenges that may not have been anticipated by the authors, without losing the lead of the interview.

3.3 Interviews with AI Experts

The second category of interviews was conducted with AI companies specializing in AI consulting and the implementation of tailored AI solutions. The objective of these

Table 1. Literature review overview

Research area	Key Points	# of Papers	References
Fashion Luxury industry	Supply chain in fashion industry	3	Christopher et al., 2004, Brun et al., 2008; Caniato et al., 2011
	Customer centric approach, customer management and brand value	11	Bridson and Evans, 2004; Aaker, 2009; Burt and Sparks, 2002; Nueno, 1998; Morris et al., 2001; Abdullah, 2023; Töllner et al., 2011; Ascarza et al., 2017; Blattberg et al., 2001; Srivastava and Rai, 2018; Dyche, 2002
	Quality control	2	Czimmermann et al., 2020; Shen and Chan, 2019
After-sales	Process overview in Supply chain	6	Lamming et al., 2000; Saccani et al., 2006; Gaiardelli et al., 2007; Brun and Castelli, 2008; Durugbo, 2020
	Impact on customer satisfaction	4	Koskela et al., 2002; Rigopoulou et al.,2008; Peterson and Wilson, 1992; Choudhary et al., 2011
Artificial Intelligence	General overview in business	15	Alsheibani et al., 2020; Bellman, 1978; Research and ltd; J and J, 2024; Baj-Rogowska, 2017 Wamba Taguimdje et al., 2020; Coombs et al.,2020; Ransbotham et al., 2017; Ramasesh and Browning, 2014; Bąk, 2024; PWC, 2019; Wang et al., 2023a; Minaee et al., 2024; Shahab et al., 2024
	LLM and sentiment analysis	7	Brown, 2020; Witteveen and Andrews, 2019; Zhang et al., 2023; Liu et al., 2020; Wang et al., 2023b; Gao et al., 2023; Salmony and Faridi, 2021

(continued)

Table 1. *(continued)*

Research area	Key Points	# of Papers	References
	Sentiment analysis studies	14	Liu, 2020; Zhang et al., 2018; Yadav and Vishwakarma, 2020; Xia et al., 2016; Luo et al., 2022; Balahur and Perea-Ortega, 2015; Wang and Zhai, 2017; Axhiu et al., 2014; Bose et al., 2020; Kheiri and Karimi, 2023; Sudhir and Suresh, 2021; Yanwei et al., 2014; Wassan et al., 2021; Haque et al., 2018
	Computer vision, defect detection and quality control	9	Abdullah et al., 2024; Zhang and Chen, 2022; Ayub Khan et al., 2021; Abd Jelil, 2018; Banduka et al., 2024; Dalenogare et al., 2018; Chen et al., 2022; Keung WONG, 2019; in Textiles
	Cost models for AI project	5	Marbán et al., 2008; Turney, 2002; Majer and SoftKraft, 2024; Microsoft; Watton et al., 2023
	AI in supply chain	10	Wang et al., 2021; Jelonek and Kowalska, 2020; Kaur and Thomas, 2022; Toorajipour et al., 2021; Liu and Gonzalez, 2023; Schroeder and Yu, 2021; Wang and Rossi, 2023; Loch et al., 2011; Hendriksen, 2023; Min, 2010

interviews was to assess the feasibility of identified AI solutions and understand the key considerations, benefits, and challenges associated with deploying these technologies. In this case, four interviews were carried out with two product (solution) managers and two project managers responsible for AI solution implementation.

The structure of the interviews conducted with AI solution providers followed a format similar to that used with the luxury fashion experts. However, given that these companies operate in the same sector but specialize in different AI implementations, the questions were tailored to align with their specific projects and expertise. This customization enriched the research by incorporating real-world case studies, leveraging each company's experience and insights. Overall, the interviews provided a comprehensive understanding of the technological, operational, and financial considerations involved in implementing an AI-powered defect detection system and advanced sentiment analysis.

By combining industry-specific insights from the first round of interviews with luxury fashion experts and the second round with AI solutions experts, the study reflects both perspectives: the business one and the technical one required for AI adoption.

4 Results and Discussion

This section comprises two subsections that report the results of the literature review and the empirical study, aligned with two research questions that follow the primary objective of assessing AI implementation in after-sales services. The results present identified inefficiencies in after-sales operations and evaluation of the feasibility of AI-driven solutions, with a particular focus on defect detection and sentiment analysis.

4.1 After-Sales Challenges

After-sales services play a critical role in luxury fashion by bridging retail, production and supply chain management. The after-sales department operates across multiple functional areas, interacting with production for repair services, with retail for in-store service management, with warehouses for spare parts management, and with customer service to ensure customer satisfaction. The following Table 2 gives a summary of operational challenges in managing after-sales that impact customer satisfaction, identified in the literature and interviews with industry experts.

4.2 After-Sales Performance Measurement Model and the Impact of AI Implementation

Based on AI applications already implemented in supply chains [1, 27], this study proposes two AI-driven solutions. One of the key proposals is to automate the quality control process in stores by using CV integrated with LLMs for defect detection. Currently, CV is primarily used in pre-production phases to inspect raw materials before they are assembled into leather products [12].

Strategic Impact of Applying AI for After-Sales.

Table 2. After-sales operational challenges and KPIs affected

Challenge categories	Challenge	Evidence from the interviews	KPI impacted
Time and communication	Interaction between stores, front office, and back office [17]	Long information flow between the store, the front office, and a customer: an average of 27 interactions are registered between actors before kicking off the repair activity "*We conducted an analysis, and if we could eliminate all the exchanges of information between the customer and other involved parties, we could reduce repair lead time by 10%.*", shares one of the business experts	Lead time (overall process duration before handing out the repaired/new product to the customer)
Time, store assistants' expertise	High and constantly rising expectations about service level [18]	Lack of knowledge / competence in store to provide customers with complete visibility on the repair or replacement process and lead times "*The problem is the high turnover, now the knowledge is gone.*", states one of the retail operation managers	Lead time Net Promoter Score (NPS) – customer satisfaction and loyalty

(*continued*)

Table 2. (*continued*)

Challenge categories	Challenge	Evidence from the interviews	KPI impacted
Communication, attitude, in-store assistants' competence	Human factor in maintaining a customer-centric approach [2]	First manual product inspection may be subject to human errors, leading to longer lead times or complicated communication with customers Difficulty in dealing with customer requests, as customers are usually impatient and irritated when they need after-sales services "*Customers keep telling us that a lead time of 1-2 months for a product with such a high initial price is unacceptable.*" "*We prefer not to directly inform customers about repair costs because if I quote a price and then, upon verification with production, additional repairs are needed—leading to a higher cost—the customer becomes unmanageable and refuses to pay the increased amount. Unfortunately, we lack the technical knowledge necessary to provide an accurate repair estimate.*", confirm in-store assistants and after-sales care experts	NPS

By analysing AI's impact at each level of the framework presented by Saccani et al (2006), this research has demonstrated that AI implementation goes beyond immediate efficiency gains. It enhances individual tasks, leading to broader business improvements by optimizing resource utilization, increasing customer satisfaction, and ultimately driving revenue growth.

Defect Detection. Table 3 summarises the impact of an AI-driven defect detection solution on after-sales operations.

Table 3. Impact of AI defect detection application on After-sales

Level	Computer Vision application	LLMs application
Activity level	Quality check of damaged products	Repair feasibility assessment based on previous repair activities registered
	Defect identification and classification	Repair proposals generation based on product defects identified
		Cost assessment based on product price and previous repair activities
		Repair lead time estimation based on previous repair lead times
Process level	More streamlined process: less interaction exchange between the store and the front office to perform product evaluation and give feedback to the customer. More complete feedback to customers, enhanced in-store assistant knowledge, clearer identification of the reason to reject customer after-sales requests, reducing the lead time and workload of repairers in case of repair impossibility.	
Business level	Reduced workload for stores and front office staff, leading to fewer personnel involved in this process. Improved customer satisfaction due to clearer and more complete feedback, higher transparency, and shorter lead time in dealing with the request.	

At the activity level, AI solutions improve Lead Time, Rejection Rate, and Net Promoter Score, the key performance indicators highlighted by both literature and interviews. By shifting from a manual inspection process to an AI-driven approach, the study highlights that an AI-driven defect detection solution can streamline internal workflows (quality check and defect detection of customers' products) and share real-time repair information.

At the process level, the solution automates repetitive tasks, reducing lead times and optimizing resource allocation by centralizing repair knowledge. AI reduces the reliance on store employees for technical expertise due to possible gaps in technical knowledge, and provides customers with indications of repair feasibility.

At the business level, AI influences financial performance and brand positioning, leading to cost optimization, customer retention, and, consequently, revenue growth.

Sentiment Analysis. The second AI application complements the proposal to refine customer engagement by analysing customer feedback to improve the entire process. Table 4 summarises the AI application impact on the after-sales operations.

Table 4. Impact of AI sentiment analysis application on After-sales

Level	LLMs application
Activity level	Feedback categorization according to customer sentiment A corrective action proposal once the problem is identified
Process level	Personalized approach to each customer, specific marketing and after-sales proposals generation
Business level	Improved customer satisfaction due to a personal approach and caring sentiments.

These two applications have a significant impact on the service offered to the customer, enhancing brand perception, fostering long-term customer loyalty, and improving sales.

Operational Feasibility of Applying AI for After-Sales. The deepening of AI implementations at the business level requires structured cost estimation to evaluate financial viability, as these projects differ from traditional software projects in their high computational demands, specialized expertise, and ongoing maintenance costs [28].

The study compared three main AI development scenarios for the cost evaluation: (1) "Make": developing a solution in-house; (2) "Hybrid": using open-source libraries and pre-trained models; (3) "Buy": fine-tuning existing models. The costs associated with each scenario were split into one-time costs and ongoing operational costs (Table 5).

For the pre-trained and fine-tuned models, the operational expenses are typically much higher than initial upfront expenses due to pay-per-use pricing models. Often, these are more economically appealing options, as they allow for scalable cost management without unnecessary infrastructure expenses. Instead, the "Make" scenario assumes a significant portion of expenses to be allocated at the initial stage of the project to equip a team of data scientists, set up IT infrastructure and data management, and develop a solution. Table 5 summarises one-time costs and ongoing operational costs associated with an AI application.

Table 5. Costs associated with an AI application.

Costs category	Cost voice	Description
One-time costs	Project Set-up	Project management; change management team
	Data management	Data (collection and) preparation and cleaning, labelling, formatting
	Solution design and engineering	Development of a target model, objectives, and requirements Model development in the case of "make" scenario

(continued)

Table 5. (*continued*)

Costs category	Cost voice	Description
	Front-end development	API development
	Model training	Model fine-tuning, testing and validation
	Personnel training	Employees training on new applications
	IT infrastructure	Investments for cloud/servers to accommodate data elaboration, applicable for "make" scenario
Operations on-going costs	Licences	Costs for the right to use the solution, applicable in "buy" (or "Hybrid") scenario
	Maintenance and technical support	Continuous solution support, bug fixing, data management, updates, etc

Challenges Related to AI Applications for After-Sales
One of the primary technical challenges identified in the literature and confirmed by AI solution providers is the availability of high-quality data. Many AI implementations fail to deliver optimal results due to insufficient or poorly structured datasets, significantly limiting their effectiveness. Another key challenge is integrating AI into existing IT infrastructure, including databases and service platforms, to ensure seamless connectivity and accessibility. Additionally, AI solutions for after-sales services rely on customer-generated data, such as product images and sentiment analysis, raising concerns about data privacy and security. The use of cloud-based AI models further introduces risks, as customer data is stored externally, making it essential to implement robust data protection measures.

Focusing on the luxury sector, given its global presence, interviews revealed significant challenges in scaling AI-driven innovations across different countries, an issue highlighted by the Retail Manager of one luxury company. Moreover, there is potential resistance to AI-driven transformation, particularly among store employees who may perceive automation as disruptive to their workflows. This concern is also documented in the literature, which recommends a gradual AI implementation approach [2].

From an operational perspective, a major challenge in implementing AI in luxury After-Sales services stems from the diverse characteristics of different product categories. This study takes leather goods as a reference, thus more case studies are required to study the applicability of solutions for other product categories.

5 Conclusions

This research examines the integration of artificial intelligence into after-sales services in the luxury fashion industry, exploring its transformative potential and its impact on operational efficiency, customer satisfaction, and key performance metrics. By combining insights from academic literature and interviews, this study identifies the primary challenges in after-sales operations and proposes AI-driven solutions to address them effectively. A qualitative research approach was adopted to analyse AI's role in optimizing after-sales workflows. Using the Measurement Framework, this study evaluates AI implementation across four levels: activity, process, business, and technology. AI solutions, particularly defect detection and sentiment analysis, demonstrate improvements in service quality, communication efficiency, and process standardization. Defect detection emerges as a transformative solution, automating product assessments and reducing reliance on manual inspections in a store. By reducing store assistants' dependence on technical expertise, AI enables consistent repair evaluations and reduces rejection rates. AI-based classification algorithms for counterfeit detection and quality assurance through image processing are also recognized as complementary solutions for servitization and sustainability in the luxury context. The study reveals that AI eliminates redundant communication loops, minimizes human error for product inspection, and provides real-time repair cost estimates, streamlining operations. The presented solutions derive from the literature, and they were further completed and refined using the interview insights.

At the process level, AI enhances customer satisfaction, flexibility, and productivity. AI automates repetitive tasks, allowing employees to focus on complex interactions, thereby reducing lead times and improving resource allocation. Sentiment analysis further refines after-sales strategies by analysing customer feedback, overcoming limitations of traditional survey methods and improving service personalization, key factor for after-sales.

At the business level, AI-driven efficiency improvements translate into cost reduction, customer retention, and revenue growth. The study compares pre-trained, fine-tuned, and custom-built AI models, concluding that fine-tuned models provide more immediate gains.

The implementation of AI faces organizational and technical challenges. Store employees may resist the adoption of AI, fearing disruption of workflows. Additionally, data availability and privacy concerns pose significant obstacles, as AI models require large, high-quality datasets that are not always accessible.

Applying the after-sales Performance Measurement Framework, this study links AI-driven improvements to business objectives, demonstrating that AI adoption enhances not only operational efficiency but also financial performance and brand perception.

The study lacks the quantitative estimations of the impact of proposed solutions. Future research should further investigate the long-term impact of AI integration in after-sales services, particularly in terms of cost optimization, sustainability, and workforce adaptation. Expanding the analysis beyond luxury fashion to other product lines or industries (including multi-material compositions) could provide deeper insights into AI scalability and adaptability in different after-sales contexts.

Disclosure of Interests. The authors have no competing interests to declare that are relevant to the content of this article.

References

1. Hendriksen, C.: AI for supply chain management: Disruptive innovation or innovative disruption? J. Supply Chain Manag. **59**(3), 65–76 (2023)
2. Toorajipour, R., Sohrabpour, V., Nazarpour, A., Oghazi, P., Fischl, M.: Artificial intelligence in supply chain management: A systematic literature review. J. Bus. Res. **122**, 502–517 (2021)
3. Kaur, S., Thomas, R.: AI-driven supply chain transformation: Opportunities and challenges for luxury brands. Supply Chain Manag. Rev. **28**(4), 52–59 (2022)
4. Liu, M., Gonzalez, R.: Decision making in predictive maintenance: Literature review and research agenda for industry 4.0. Int. J. Prod. Res. **61**(5), 1457–1473 (2023)
5. Dalenogare, L.S., Benitez, G.B., Ayala, N.F., Frank, A.G.: The digital transformation of manufacturing: The role of technologies, business models, and operations. Int. J. Prod. Res. **56**(8), 2838–2856 (2018)
6. Wang, Z., Pang, Y., Lin, Y.: Large language models are zero-shot text classifiers. Preprint at arXiv:2312.01044 (2023)
7. Gao, K. et al.: Examining user-friendly and opensourced large GPT models: A survey on language, multimodal, and scientific GPT models. Preprint at arXiv:2308.14149 (2023)
8. Wamba-Taguimdje, S.-L., Wamba, S.F., Kamdjoug, J.R.K., Wanko, C.E.T.: Influence of artificial intelligence (AI) on firm performance: the business value of AI-based transformation projects. Bus. Process Manag. J. **26**(7), 1893–1924 (2020)
9. Tairov, I., Stefanova, N., Aleksandrova, A., Aleksandrov, M.: Review of AI-driven solutions in business value and operational efficiency. Econ. Ecol. Soc. **8**(3), 55–66 (2024)
10. Minaee, S. et al.: Large language models: A survey. Preprint at arXiv:2402.06196 (2024)
11. Thangakumar, J.: Revolutionizing leather quality assurance through deep learning powered precision in defect detection and segmentation by a comparative analysis of Mask RCNN and YOLO v8. In: 2024 International Conference on Advances in Data Engineering and Intelligent Computing Systems (ADICS), pp. 1–6 (2024)
12. Abdullah, A.B. et al.: Leather image quality classification and defect detection system using mask region-based convolution neural network model. Int. J. Adv. Comput. Sci. Appl. **15**(4) (2024)
13. Bridson, K., Evans, J.: The secret to a fashion advantage is brand orientation. Int. J. Retail Distrib. Manag. **32**(8), 403–411 (2004)
14. Caniato, F., Caridi, M., Castelli, C., Golini, R.: Supply chain management in the luxury industry: a first classification of companies and their strategies. Int. J. Prod. Econ. **133**(2), 622–633 (2011)
15. Abdullah, M.: Effect of after-sale services on customer satisfaction and loyalty in automation company case Cimcorp. (2023)
16. Moore, C.M., Birtwistle, G.: The burberry business model: creating an international luxury fashion brand. Int. J. Retail Distrib. Manag. **32**(8), 412–422 (2004)
17. Saccani, N., Songini, L., Gaiardelli, P.: The role and performance measurement of aftersales in the durable consumer goods industries: an empirical study. Int. J. Product. Perform. Manag. **55**(3/4), 259–283 (2006)
18. Kotler, P., Armstrong, G.: Principles of Marketing. Pearson Education, Upper Saddle River (2010)

19. Alsheibani, S.A., Cheung, Y., Messom, C.H., Alhosni, M.: Winning AI strategy: six-steps to create value from artificial intelligence. In: Proceedings of the Americas Conference on Information Systems (AMCIS), vol. 11 (2020)
20. Ransbotham, S., Kiron, D., Gerbert, P., Reeves, M.: Reshaping business with artificial intelligence: Closing the gap between ambition and action. MIT Sloan. Manag. Rev. **59**(1) (2017)
21. Abd Jelil, R.: Review of artificial intelligence applications in garment manufacturing. In: Artificial Intelligence for Fashion Industry in the Big Data Era, pp. 97–123. Springer, Singapore (2018)
22. Chen, Z., Deng, J., Zhu, Q., Wang, H., Chen, Y.: A systematic review of machinevision-based leather surface defect inspection. Electronics. **11**(15) (2022)
23. Bryman, A., Burgess, R.G., et al.: Analyzing Qualitative Data, vol. 11. Routledge, London (1994)
24. La Conceria: La pelletteria è il vero core business: Quanto pesano gli accessori nei bilanci delle griffe? (2018). https://www.laconceria.it/lusso/la-pelletteria-e-il-vero-core-business-quanto-pesano-gli-accessori-nei-bilanci-delle-griffe/. Accessed 8 Apr 2026
25. Le Monde: Luxury giant LVMH experiences unprecedented drop in sales (2024). https://www.lemonde.fr/en/economy/article/2024/10/16/luxury-giant-lvmh-experiences-unprecedented-drop-in-sales_6729586_19.html. Accessed 8 Apr 2026
26. The Fashion Law: LVMH Reports €84.7B in Sales for 2024 Despite Unfavorable Market (2024). https://www.thefashionlaw.com/lvmh-reports-e84-7b-in-sales-for-2024-despite-unfavorable-market/. Accessed 8 Apr 2026
27. Rahman, M.S., Bag, S., Hossain, M.A., Abdel-Fattah, F.A.M., Gani, M.O., Rana, N.P.: The new wave of AI-powered luxury brands online shopping experience: The role of digital multisensory cues and customers' engagement. Technol. Forecast. Soc. Change. **186**, 122086 (2023)
28. Zhang, W., Chen, H.: AIoT-enabled defect detection with minimal data: A few-shot learning approach combining prototypical and relational networks for smart manufacturing. Comput. Ind. Eng. **166**, 107973 (2022)
29. Turney, P.D.: Types of cost in inductive concept learning. arXiv preprint cs/0212034 (2002)

Author Index

Published by Springer Nature Switzerland AG 2027
G. Pezzotta et al. (Eds.): APMS 2026, IFIP AICT 808, pp. 647–649, 2027.
https://doi.org/10.1007/978-3-032-38594-9

FSC
www.fsc.org
MIX
Papier | Fördert gute Waldnutzung
FSC® C083411

Kolibri 360 GmbH
Ferdinand-Jühlke-Straße 7
99095 Erfurt, Deutschland
produktsicherheit@kolibri360.de